The New Testament Order
for Church and Missionary

Thanks Billy with more mahalo than words can say for building God's Kingdom together these 3 **ono** mos !!! One day I want to read this book and learn how to lead our LORD Jesus Christ's church in Christlike ways like you !!

Love and θ's aloha in Christ, Darin

The NEW TESTAMENT ORDER
for CHURCH and MISSIONARY

By
ALEXANDER RATTRAY HAY

General Superintendent
New Testament Missionary Union

Third Edition

WIPF & STOCK · Eugene, Oregon

Wipf and Stock Publishers
199 W 8th Ave, Suite 3
Eugene, OR 97401

The New Testament Order for Church and Missionary
By Hay, Alex Rattray
ISBN 13: 978-1-60899-934-7
Publication date 8/30/2010
Previously published by New Testament Missionary Union, 1947

To My Fellow-workers,
But for Whose
Loving Co-operation and Fellowship
This Book
Could Not Have Been Written.

FOREWORD TO THIRD EDITION

The first and second editions of this book have found their way into the hands of many Christian workers and missionaries throughout the world and not a few have written of help and blessing received. It has now been found necessary to publish a third edition.

We wish to give a word of warning. The methods described in this book have no power in themselves. It is the Spirit of God using them that brings the power. When man seeks to apply them in his own strength they are powerless.

Some have sought to apply New Testament principles and methods in congregations without fully understanding them. The results, naturally, have not been good. Others have endeavoured to apply a part of the Scriptural order, rejecting what they judged inadvisable. That also has brought disappointment. With some there has been a failure to realize the essential part the Holy Spirit must take and the need for the church member to face the claims of the Cross in his life that the Spirit may be able to give him understanding and guidance. While the method is important, let us not overlook the fact that the spiritual factors are most important. It is not a method that man can apply and use in his own strength and wisdom.

Another book, "Life in God, or The Power and Triumph of Perfect Love" has now been published. It is intended to be a companion volume to the present one. It deals with the principles governing the believer's life. If the Church is to be strong spiritually, the individual believer must know and experience the full provision for life and ministry that Christ, the Head of the Church, has given through His Spirit who dwells within.

We shall be glad to hear from readers to share with them in blessing and experience. All should seek together in faith and prayer that the Lord be given His true place in His Church so that it may be indeed "The fulness of Him that filleth all in all".

PREFACE TO FIRST EDITION

THE first draft of the manuscript of this book was written seventeen years ago, not with any thought of publication, but because we felt the need of setting down in order for our own benefit the principles and methods of church-planting that we were seeking to discover and put into practice. The years that have followed have brought increased understanding and knowledge. Using the manuscript in teaching these principles to churches, to new missionaries and to students has helped greatly to show what was needed to make it a sufficiently complete presentation of the subject.

The matter is of such importance and the Scriptural pattern has been so obscured by centuries of ecclesiasticism that we have found it necessary to deal thoroughly with the Scriptural evidence and its significance. Reference is made also to the historical evidence, which so fully supports the teaching of Scripture.

We do not offer this study as a text-book but simply as a statement of the experiences and guidance which the Lord has given. The only authoritative and complete text-book on church order and missionary procedure is God's Word. Our desire is to point to that Word.

An increasing number of fellow-workers have cooperated with us, labouring in several different countries, fellowshipping together in an endeavour to rediscover the secret of the power of the Early Church. The fact that the whole missionary group has been united in this endeavour has made it possible to seek to enter into a closer relation with our Lord. It has caused us to apply New Testament methods in all departments of the work. The result has been two-fold. First, there has been a deepening of the spiritual life of the worker himself. In the second place, there has been a much greater manifestation of the Holy Spirit's power in the work, particularly in the individual believers and in the churches.

When we began our ministry in the 'foreign field' thirty years ago, we had no thought of questioning the generally accepted methods of missionary work. It was only when face to face with the facts and problems of the work that there began to grow upon us a sense of disappointment and frustration as we saw the slowness of progress and the evident lack of power in the churches established.

This caused us to turn to God's Word to study the work of the first church-planters. There we could find no valid reason why we should not experience the same power of the Holy Spirit today as they did then. We do not mean the miraculous manifestations of the Spirit's power but the evidence of His presence in converts and churches. What we did discover was that the methods we were employing in our work were not those used by the New Testament Evangelists or by our Lord and that the pattern of our churches differed greatly from theirs.

At first we endeavoured to apply what seemed to be the most important of the New Testament methods. This we tried for several years. The New Testament way always brought increased blessing and spiritual power, but it became very evident that what still remained of the modern method was as clay mixed with the iron and a continual source of weakness and defeat.

It was no easy matter to discern what was really of the modern method and not in accord with the principles of the Scriptural pattern. We are so accustomed to certain practices and ways of doing things that it may take time to realize that they are based on principles contrary to the way in which the Spirit desires to work. Moreover, there is need for great caution. So often those who have sought to return to the New Testament way have stumbled into ruts and exaggerations and so strayed from the way.

Many of God's servants throughout the world are seeking to discover this way. There is, indeed, a wide-spread work of the Holy Spirit leading back to the divinely revealed order. This call of the Spirit is insistent and unmistakable. There has been a departing from the way of power and He would have us return, that the fulness of the Lord's power may be released again. Why should we be satisfied with only a very partial fulfilment of the promises of power and blessing? Why should we bow to the power of the forces of evil when we follow One to Whom has been given all power in Heaven and on earth?

Considerable attention is given in this study to the spiritual principles involved. We have found that it is imperative to do so. The New Testament method is as dead as any other method if it is applied without the guidance and power of the Spirit Who alone gives it life. It is really not a method but a spiritual order — the order in which Christ wishes to carry on His work through the Church by the power of His Spirit.

We have had in mind the young church-planter's need of suggestions and material for the instruction of the converts that they may be adequately prepared for taking their place in the New Testament congregation. Of course, it has not been possible, in such limited space, to do much more than outline the most important aspects of the teaching that should be given.

Surely it need not be said that we would not depreciate the work of faithful servants of the Lord who labour earnestly in the Gospel to the salvation of souls, following other methods. We followed those methods for many years and our sincerity and love for the Lord were no less then than they are now. But we have found that many missionaries and servants of God in the Homelands are just as conscious as we were of a great lack and just as anxious to discover the reason and find the way back to full power and blessing. It is with such that we desire to fellowship through this book as a fellow-servant in the work of the Gospel. No doubt the Lord has much more to say to us all and we shall be glad to have personal fellowship in these matters with any who may desire it.

We would acknowledge our indebtedness to a number of missionaries, members of other missionary fellowships as well as our own, who read the manuscript of this book and made suggestions and criticisms that have been helpful. We would also express our gratitude to those who shared the burden of the work of typing and proof-reading.

The cost of the publication of this book has been met by unsolicited gifts from missionaries.

Buenos Aires, 1947.

ALEX. R. HAY.

CONTENTS

CHARTS

PART I

THE NEW TESTAMENT EXAMPLE

"Oh, how unlike the complex works of men,
Heaven's easy, artless, unencumbered plan!
No meretricious graces to beguile,
No clustering ornaments to clog the pile;
From ostentation as from weakness free,
It stands like the cerulian arch we see,
Majestic in its own simplicity."

COWPER.

"TAKE HEED HOW YE BUILD"

He sent them forth to build a Temple fair
   And as they built, no matter where,
With them in Heavenly might 'twas He who built:
   The Master-Builder, He was there.

And to the Heavenly pattern true He built:
   The pattern wrought by God in Grace—
Ere man was made or Earth's foundations laid—
   To make man's heart His dwelling-place.

And He in place each living stone did set
   And fashioned it with passing skill,
And there in all His kingly glory dwelt
   And wrought in love His perfect will.

But then the builders sallied forth alone,
   They built not with the living stone;
A pattern new for building they devised;
   Within God's House no glory shone.

The Temple was no longer all of gold,
   And jewels lit with Heavenly light;
A house of gilded wood and straw man built:
   An earthly house of earthly might.

And then the wisdom of man's rebel heart,
   So full of doubt, of self so sure,
Strange fire did use to light the lamp of God,
   In worship vain, no longer pure.

Traditions loved beyond the Word of God,
   Heart's loyalty that's given first
To errant ways of man's own vaunting thought,
   Have marred His plan, betrayed His trust.

The Lord still knocks, although He stands without;
   The Church its strength may yet renew;
To all who open that He enter in
   He offers wealth, communion true.

But He would enter in as sovereign Lord;
   Not as a guest though honoured be,
But as the Master of the House to rule,
   For Builder, Light and Life is He.

All in obedience to the Lord must serve
   When He within His Church doth stand;
Man's wisdom must be yielded to His Word,
   Man's will give place to His command.

Then as He builds, the Church will mighty be —
   Hell's proudest gates shall not prevail —
Embattled strength of God no foe can break;
   O'er Him no might can e'er avail!

CHAPTER I

WHERE OUR WEAKNESS LIES

THE present world situation, both in so-called Christian lands and in what is termed the Mission Field, is profoundly influencing the thoughts of Christian men and women. The world is passing through a period of great crisis. Foundations have been shaken, old standards and values are being discarded as inadequate, moral standards have been lowered. Rationalism, materialism and unbelief are boldly aggressive, challenging the Church even from within. Forces are being discovered which God created for good but which Godless man is incapable of restraining. In the midst of it all, fear grips the hearts of men. A way of salvation — of material prosperity, security and peace — is sought, but man seeks it in his own way and turns still more resolutely from God. As one Tower of Babel collapses, he sets out to build another.

This situation has not developed suddenly. It is the result of great movements that have been manifesting themselves among men and nations and gathering momentum, particularly during the last three decades. Unmistakably, it is the development which prophecy· has caused us to expect as the preparation for the appearance of the Man of Sin.

As is to be expected, the rapidly changing conditions are seriously affecting the work of the Church. In most 'mission' lands there is a state of flux and ferment that is crystallizing into situations that present an entirely new set of problems, much more complex, much more difficult and fraught with great dangers. Modern civilization is advancing apace. Nationalism is steadily growing and manifesting an increasingly exclusive and militant spirit. In so-called Christian lands also the situation has changed — so much so that they must be recognized definitely now as mission fields urgently needing to be evangelized.

Under the stress and strain of these conditions the Church throughout the world is being tested and proved as perhaps it has not been since the days of fiery persecution in the Early Church. From the early trial it emerged triumphant. In spite of its weakness at that time, its material poverty, the fact that few of the learned and powerful were among its members, its defence-lessness and the blood that flowed, there was manifested a spiritual power that neither Satan nor man could conquer or restrain.

To what extent is the modern Church and modern methods of church planting standing the strain that is now bearing with ever increasing force upon them? Can we say, All's well with the Church: the gates of Hell are not prevailing against it?

It is instructive to take stock of the present progress of the Church's witness. Looking beyond local successes and leaving aside enthusiastic reports and optimistic prophecies, let us consider the facts as they are. Although, undoubtedly, there has been reason for encouragement at times and in some regions (for the Gospel is still the power of God unto salvation) on the whole the results have been far from satisfactory. They ought to have been much greater. We have a right, considering the teaching of God's Word and the recorded experiences of the Early Church, to expect much greater progress and the manifestation of much greater power. The history of modern missions shows nothing that can compare with the world-wide conquests of a very much smaller group of labourers during the first century of the Church.

No matter how full of faith and optimism our missionary vision may be, we face the fact that, at our present rate of progress, there is no hope of the world ever being evangelized. It is estimated that not two percent of the world's population today are believing Christians. Of the 2,000,000,000 persons in the world, 1,500,000,000 are without the Gospel. Not only so, but the proportion of heathenism, instead of showing any decrease, is steadily increasing against us. Whole nations are closed to the Gospel. In not a few others, increasingly powerful forces are determinedly seeking its exclusion. Vast regions in Asia, Africa and South America are, in great part, still unevangelized. Even in the older mission fields with the largest number of missionaries, the truth is that not much more than a beginning has been made. In all these fields the percentage of Christians is exceedingly small. The towns and villages in which churches are to be found are startlingly few compared with the vastly greater number in which there is no church.

Besides purely heathen lands, there are the Roman Catholic countries, where the great majority of the people are ignorant of the true Gospel. It is estimated that in Europe there are 400,000,000 unevangelized people. Nor does the situation in Protestant lands give any cause for satisfaction. The number of people who never attend a church of any kind is far greater than that of church-goers. In America it is estimated that 70,000,000 are not even nominally connected with any faith of any kind. And if we divide the church-goers into those who are true believers and those who are merely nominal Christians, we get a much smaller number still. A study of Protestant Church membership in America revealed that 30 per cent never attend church services, 90 per cent never engage in any soul winning activity, not 20 per cent attend prayer meeting — and the prayer meeting in most cases is a misnomer, for preaching has taken the place of prayer.

In addition to all this, we must face the facts regarding the lack of living faith and spiritual power, the unsoundness in doctrine and the dead formalism that have become widespread in the churches. The Protestant communions as a whole show little growth in membership. Startling evidence of the ineffectiveness of modern Protestantism is provided by the Protestant communities in France and Belgium. During the past hundred years their numbers have been steadily, even rapidly, decreasing.

To shut one's eyes to the real facts of the situation in either the 'Homelands' or the 'Mission Field', and to refuse to admit frankly the existence of weakness, failure and danger is not an evidence of faith; it only plays into the hands of the enemy. Resignation under such circumstances is not an evidence of true Christian patience and faithfulness. Pious wishful-thinking is not the fruit of true spiritual-mindedness. In God's dealings with men as seen in Scripture, He never told His Prophets to say all was well when all was not well. Those who did so were condemned as unfaithful prophets, prophesying smooth things. He always had the plain, unhappy truth declared and nothing hidden. The victory was to those who faced the facts, acknowledged unfaithfulness, obeyed God, believed His Word and challenged the enemy in unwavering faith.

2

In recent years, many of God's people have been seriously considering these matters and seeking to rediscover the secret of the power and success of the New Testament Church. The answer has not been hard to find. Rationalism (wrongly called Modernism today: it is modern only in its dress) has robbed many of simple faith. The Church has departed from the foundation laid by the Apostles. Organization and human ability take the place of the Spirit's power, of prayer, of faith and have given us man instead of God, man's work instead of God's work.

We are not working in the way the Apostles and those who followed them worked. We may preach the same Gospel, but our methods of work are not the methods they used. The structure of our Church differs greatly from the structure of theirs. Fundamental spiritual principles have been disregarded. Indeed, so radical has been the departure from the Apostolic model that their methods of working and the pattern of their churches appear to us today as something strange and entirely new.

This change is not a new thing. Its beginnings can be traced back to Apostolic times. In the Acts of the Apostles and the Epistles there is ample evidence of the tendency that very soon manifested itself to depart from the simplicity of the spiritual order. The church-planters of that time had to be ever watchful and faithful to resist this tendency. But their successors were not always so faithful and modifications of various kinds soon began to creep in. Only three hundred years later, in the time of the Emperor Constantine, we find the Church transformed with a complete human system of organization patterned after that of the State and of the great heathen religious systems.

The Reformation, when it came in the sixteenth century, accomplished great things and swept away by its purifying fire much of the mountain of rubbish under which the truth had been buried for centuries. Priestcraft and doctrinal error were largely eliminated. Much of the man-made ecclesiastical structure was abandoned. The right of all believers to partake of the symbols of the Lord's death at the Lord's Table was regained. However, the priesthood of all believers was not fully restored. Most of the reformed bodies carried over into Protestantism, in varying degrees, a part of the order and organization that they had been accustomed to and that seemed so essential to the functioning of the Church.

When, early in the nineteenth century, the missionary spirit of the Church revived, New Testament times were very far distant and modern Protestant Denominational systems firmly established. It was natural — well-nigh inevitable — that most of the missionaries, instead of returning to the Early Church model, should follow Denominational policy and practice without question, simply seeking to establish in the lands to which they had gone replicas of the churches to which they belonged.

The development which has taken place in missionary procedure since then has tended generally to depart further from the simplicity of Apostolic practice. Missions have gone in more and more for costly institutional, educational and social programmes, to the neglect, and, in some cases, almost to the exclusion, of direct evangelism. Increasing emphasis has been placed upon human wisdom, human plans and organization, and correspondingly less upon the wisdom, gifts and power of the Holy Spirit.

As we consider the results of modern evangelism, we find that the Gospel has not lost its power. Wherever it is faithfully preached, the seed sown bears fruit in repentance and true faith. This, we feel, is as evident today as it was in New Testament times. It is not there that the difficulty lies. It is in the individual converts and in the churches that we fail to see now the results obtained by the Early Church missionaries.

In the New Testament Church the evidence of the Holy Spirit's power did not end with the conversion of the individual; that was but the beginning. Generally there followed amongst those who were saved the manifestation of the gifts of the Spirit for the government, instruction and expansion of the Church. The power of the Holy Spirit continued to work mightily in and through the newly established churches: a power that could not be quenched from without, expanding, conquering. That is the outstanding feature of the Early Church.

It was the lack of this power in the churches established today that caused us to seek the reason for it and to study the New Testament principles and methods of church-planting. We saw in the converts won and in the churches formed a distinct lack of the Holy Spirit's power, resulting in weakness and dependence. Some believers lived consistent Christian lives and a few learned to give acceptable Gospel messages, but they seemed never to be able to get much beyond that point. They continued to be dependent upon the missionary or pastor; the spiritual gifts necessary for the government of the church and for teaching were lacking. Speaking generally, there was also a lack of an impelling evangelistic vision. A church would soon settle down to live to itself and become dulled to the sense of the need of the perishing multitudes around it. We were forced to admit that our churches were inferior at every point to those established in the Early Church days and to ask the question, Where is now that irresistible, dynamic power that overcame every obstacle, and that zeal which made every convert a witness and every congregation a centre for world evangelism? And where the gifts of the Spirit that equipped men to be preachers and Elders and Deacons and Teachers and Evangelists, so that the first church-planters were able to move on from place to place for the establishing of new congregations?

The power of the Holy Spirit to bring men to Christ is still with us. Revivals and even mass movements in the mission field, when thousands acknowledge Christ, continue to occur. But what follows such evidence of the Holy Spirit's presence and power? Unfortunately, it is then that our modern method departs from the New Testament order. Instead of expecting the manifestation of the gifts of the Spirit among those who are saved and allowing freedom for their exercise, and forming the congregations according to the simple, spiritual order of the New Testament Church, our cumbersome, modern ecclesiastical machinery is set up, too slow moving to cope with the situation, restricting the preaching of the Gospel to a chosen few (and thus effectively closing the mouths of a multitude of witnesses) moulding inexorably to its own pattern, reducing to its own speed, until the liberty, spontaneity and power of the Holy Spirit, the Originator of the movement, has been effectively stifled.

The history of evangelism in Great Britain and America provides examples as striking as any to be found in foreign fields. We have but to consider the relative simplicity of Methodism in its early days of revival and power, and of the Baptists when they first spread throughout the length and breadth of the United States. In both of these movements comparatively few limitations were placed upon the freedom of the Holy Spirit. At least He was permitted to use whom He would. Not many barriers of organization restricted His activity in the congregations. Anyone with the gift of the Spirit to preach, not only was permitted to preach, but was expected and urged to do so. The distinction between clergy and laity had not yet crystallized or was in abeyance.

In such movements we witness a break-away from the accepted order. The Holy Spirit had been bound and the Church lifeless and static, but He finds instruments He can use, the trammels of organization and formalism are thrown aside and there breaks forth again the true fire that burned in the New Testament Church when He manifested His gifts through all the members. Even what we may call the by-products of these movements — the consequent moral reformation in social and political spheres and the general quickening of the consciences of nations — have been tremendous in their significance, influencing generations and affecting the history of the world.

But the same reactionary influences soon reappeared. Man in his wisdom, fearing to continue to put confidence in the power of the Holy Spirit, felt he must take these movements in hand, organizing them to bring them into the realm of the humanly practicable and understandable and to give them, as he thought, efficiency, stability, permanency and respectability. Spiritual power was sought in eloquence, education, music and programmes. A superstructure of ecclesiastical organization was erected, largely silencing the 'laity' and quenching the Holy Spirit. The Church again became static, its power but a weak, struggling thing, its light but a glimmer.

Today we have highly organized, modern Denominations, with culture, wealth and beautiful buildings, striving year after year with all the human might they command to produce a little fruit. Faced with a world well-nigh in chaos, the power of the organized Church is inadequate and its message unconvincing. Men are turning away from the formal, respectable, comfortable but Cross-less and power-less religion it offers. They want strength and wisdom beyond their own; a sure word, a sure foundation, reality. They seek it elsewhere — in false cults, political ideologies, catch-words. They need Christ; but He is straitened in His people. They need the living God; but the Church gives them man.

A wave of materialism and Godlessness has swept over 'Christian' lands. A missionary on furlough writes, "One gets the impression that this is a land on the way back to heathenism." Bishop C. M. Chavasse says:

Today we confront a new phenomenon — a generation that has lost God and a whole dimension of life: the spiritual dimension. Half our countrymen are worse than heathen in that they believe in nothing — not even themselves.

Is it not high time that we turn to God's Word to see where we have erred, to return to the way of power, to withdraw the hand of man from the Spirit's work, to exercise faith again and permit the Builder of the Church to build with His power according to the pattern He has revealed, that His glory may once more fill His Church?

During world-war years when formal religion was valueless, the weakness of the organized Church became increasingly evident. It was not the Lord or the Word of God that failed in those days. In Him and in His Word alone men found strength and comfort. And many of those who passed through the fire say, 'Let us seek the way back to the simplicity of the New Testament Church that gave men Christ in the fulness of His life and power'.

God will yet speak and men shall hear. Against the Church which the Lord builds, the gates of hell shall not prevail. Today they are prevailing because there is much that is not of His building. But Christ did not give us the assurance of His Church's triumph as a pious hope that really could not be fulfilled. We are responsible to take His Word by faith and to walk in unwavering obedience that the mighty power of "the Son of the Living God" may be seen once more bringing healing, light and life to this needy world for which He died and to which He would speak in its darkness, suffering, Godlessness and despair.

CHAPTER II

THE APOSTOLIC MISSION FIELD

TO LAY a foundation for our study of the New Testament Church and missionary procedure we shall review first of all the general conditions that prevailed in the world in Paul's time. A comparison of these conditions with those existing today will be sufficient to show that they are fundamentally the same and that where any difference does exist, it is almost always decidedly in our favour. It is necessary to clear our vision of the mystic halo that would shroud the true story of the Early Church and the work of the first church-planters, obscuring the practical, everyday facts that ruled then just as they do now.

Spiritual Conditions

1. Among the Jews. Judaism was in a decadent state. It was not without a certain vitality due to the fact that it had been built upon a solid foundation of truth. But the foundations were obscured by a great accumulation of rubbish — tradition, formalism and priestcraft. Our Lord stated in plain language the prevailing conditions in Judaism at that time. He described the religious leaders as 'whited sepulchres'; and of the religion He said, "making the Word of God of none effect through your tradition". The truth was there, had anybody cared to dig for it. Yet, as in Romanism today, ignorance, deep-rooted prejudice and intolerance so completely held the field that there were few who cared or dared to seek the truth. Nevertheless, there were those in whose hearts there glowed the hope of the coming of the Messiah and the dawning of a brighter day of spiritual promise. God could still find a Mary and a Joseph, a John the Baptist, a Zacharias, an Elizabeth and an Anna.

The. situation amongst the Jews was a complicated one. Religion, nationality and race were well nigh synonymous. Patriotism was regarded as meaning faithfulness to all three. That, naturally, produced a most stubborn, unreasoning and fanatical form of religious prejudice.

2. Among the Heathen. Heathenism and the old religious systems were not less firmly entrenched, or more tolerant in their attitude, then than now. Heathen writers undertook to disprove and ridicule the faith of the Christians. Vested interests, represented by makers of idols, workers in witchcraft, and others, provided their full share of opposition. The grossest misrepresentations were circulated against the Christians to prejudice their cause. The populace was incited against them. Often they were forced under cover, and the privilege of public testimony denied them.

To those accustomed to the assertion, made in lands where Roman Catholicism dominates, that Protestants are atheists because of their refusal to worship Mary, the Saints and their images, it is interesting to note that in the Early Church,

The Christians incurred this charge by the rejection of the pagan gods, by their refusal to sacrifice, and by their disuse of images. Pagans could not understand how anyone could really believe in a god without these accessories.[1]

A remarkable similarity exists between the religious attitude of both the upper and lower classes in Apostolic times and that of the same classes today in many a mission field. Religion and society were interwoven in Greece and Rome, but although the common people had a real, though purely superstitious, belief in pagan deities and myths, the educated men, to a great extent, were practically agnostic. Although the educated people conformed to religious rites and observances, they did not believe in them. To them the gods, ritual and mythology, had become, to a great extent, merely symbols of ideals and aspirations.

Moral Conditions

It cannot be said that moral conditions were more favourable to the spread of the Gospel in Apostolic times than they are now.

---

[1] A. H. Newman, *Manual of Church History,* Vol. I, p. 238.

The sceptical philosophy of the Epicureans, with its blighting doctrine that pleasure is the only objective worth while in life, was the predominant influence, not only in Greece but also in Rome and, to a considerable extent, throughout the world. Consequently, morality was on an extremely low level — as low as in any heathen land today.

Jerusalem was dominated by formalism and priestcraft. Stalker describes the situation in Palestine thus:

> A nation enslaved; the upper classes devoting themselves to self-ishness, courtiership and scepticism; the teachers and chief professors of religion lost in mere shows of ceremonialism and boasting themselves the favourites of God, while their souls were honeycombed with self-deception and vice; the body of the people misled by false ideals; and seething at the bottom of society, a neglected mass of unblushing and unrestrained sin.[1]

Profligate, corrupt Rome, with her brutal sports, was hastening on the road to decay. She was at the zenith of her power and the world was enjoying a season of peace. But it was a false peace — a lull before the coming storm which was to break within a generation and which was already presaged by many unmistakable signs.

Peace and prosperity had brought luxury and ease. Rome and the provinces were already sunken in moral corruption. The people were generally given over to the pursuit of pleasure and sin, and officials, both high and low, indulged in bribery and extortion.

Corinth, with its wealth and its thousand priestess-prostitutes of Venus, was as corrupt morally as it could be, a condition that was reflected plainly in the difficulties that Paul had to face in the Corinthian church. Ephesus, with Diana worship, idolatry, and witchcraft, seemed almost to be the 'seat of Satan's Kingdom'.

Of the Cretans, Paul wrote, "One of their own number — a Prophet who is a countryman of theirs — has said, 'Cretans are always liars, dangerous animals, idle gluttons'. This testimony is true" (Titus 1:12. Weymouth). Crete at that time was evidently not a particularly attractive or promising field!

Political Conditions

Roman law was strict, but, to a great extent, it differentiated

---

[1] *The Life of Christ*, by James Stalker, p. 31.

against the foreigner and in favour of the Roman citizen. The administration of justice was often vitiated by bribery, influence, political wire-pulling, and personal ambition. Herod's court was, on the whole, corrupt.

The Jews were under the domination of a foreign power, and there was a strong under-current of heart-burning and resentment on that account. Politically, the situation was very far from being a happy one.

The political conditions and existing laws did not give any greater freedom of action or guarantee more efficient personal protection than is generally the rule throughout the modern mission field. There was a general toleration of all religions, but ways could always be found to persecute the Christians and these early missionaries were forced many a time to flee for their lives. And when the strength of the movement and the full implication of its exclusive claims began to be realized, the opposition became general and uncompromising until the fires of martyrdom were lit throughout the whole civilized world.

Social Conditions

Jewish society was dominated by the national religion. To break with that religion was to break with society. There were various religious and social groups: the priestly class; the orthodox and religiously-proud Pharisees; the materialistic Sadducees; Herodians under the influence of Hellenism and paganism; and the intellectual Scribes. Besides these, were various foreign groups — Romans, Greeks, Samaritans, and others. But the great majority of the people belonged to the despised lower stratum. These were generally ignorant and oppressed and there was much disease and suffering amongst them.

The attitude of society to the Gospel was not friendly. The religious leaders persecuted those who preached it. The intellectuals looked upon them and their message with contempt. The wealthy had no time for them, and the rulers regarded them as fanatics and adventurers. They faced fanaticism, ignorance, intolerance, vested interests, persecution, misrepresentation, injustice and hearts so hardened that they seemed to have lost all sense of need.

The poor "received Him gladly". They were, on the whole, glad to welcome the purer light which threw a ray of hope into their lives. But sometimes — yea, often — it was for the loaves and fishes that they followed. The number of those who became true followers of Christ was not great. The Apostle John bears testimony that when many professed to believe in Christ after they had seen His miracles, "Jesus did not commit himself unto them...... for He knew what was in man" (Jn. 2:23-25).

It was in the face of these difficulties that Christ ministered and the Apostles laid the foundations of the Church. The objective was the establishment of a virtually new and purely spiritual faith with distinct doctrines and a superior moral code. It entailed the complete eclipse of all other religions, including the Jewish, and the extinction of all existing religious organizations with their priests, ceremonies, laws and vested interests. Our Lord knew full well that the triumph of His Church would mean the complete revolutionizing of the whole social order and political system. The Early Church missionaries were called to precisely the same witness and faced the same situation. Is it surprising that the religious, social and political leaders of the day, inspired by the 'Prince of this world', sensed the danger and opposed Christ and the early missionaries of the Gospel with such bitter and relentless hate? The task to which we are called is not more difficult. Nor is it easier — unless we compromise.

The Converts

Our Lord's disciples were not men of culture, wealth or influence. On the contrary, they were humble men. It is in this class that the modern missionary generally finds the first Evangelists. Mostly it was the poor who were ready to accept our Lord's message. In the Early Church it was not otherwise. So far as intelligence, social position, wealth and influence are concerned, the converts of the first Evangelists were not superior to the average group of converts on the mission field today. Paul wrote of the Early Church members: "For ye see your calling, brethren, how that not many wise men after the flesh, not many mighty, not many noble, are called" (1 Cor. 1:26). James bears a similar testimony: "Hath not God chosen the poor of this world rich in faith, and heirs of the Kingdom which He hath promised to them that love Him?" (Jas. 2:5). The proportion of converts from the various classes seems to have been much the same as in our congregations on the 'mission field'.

Preparation of the Field

Much has been made of the fact that the Jews were scattered throughout the world and that the converts from among them, and also from among Gentiles influenced by Judaism, already had the theistic and moral background which enabled them to take the lead in the churches and give stability to the work so newly established. However, as Robert E. Speer remarks:

To be sure, these people had in the main already been schooled into the theistic faith of the Hebrews or had been brought up in it; but they could scarcely have been better subjects than some missionary converts of today; — the converts from the degraded Christian Churches of Asia for example.

In what respect these Jewish converts would be superior to converts from the Roman Catholic Church in Catholic lands, for instance, would be hard to determine. Of the Jews of that time Stalker writes:

It might have been expected that (Christ) would find a nation saturated with the ideas and inspired with the visions of His predecessors, the prophets, at whose head He might place Himself and from which He might receive an enthusiastic and effective cooperation. But it was not so. He appeared at a time when the nation had lapsed from its ideals and caricatured their sublimest features. Instead of meeting a nation mature in holiness and consecrated to the heaven-ordained task of blessing all other peoples, which He might easily lead up to its own final development, and then lead forth to the spiritual conquest of the world He found that the first work which lay before Him was to proclaim a reformation in His own country, and encounter the opposition of prejudices that had accumulated there through centuries of degradation.[1]

There is no doubt that some converts from Judaism became zealous and efficient members of the Church and helpers of Paul, but it is also evident that the presence of Jewish converts in the churches was not an unmixed blessing, for many of them were the cause of a great deal of trouble. It was they who denounced Paul's Gospel and sought to wreck his work by bringing the churches under the bondage of legalism. Wherever there was a considerable number of Jewish converts this problem was acute. On the other hand, it would appear that in many places they were few in number and it seems very probable that the membership of not a few very successful churches was purely Gentile.

---

[1] *Life of Christ*, p. 34.

The fact was that the Holy Spirit had to do — and still has to do — just as big a work in the heart and life of a Jew as in a Gentile. The average Jew had as many prejudices to overcome, as much to unlearn and as great a need of reformation and spiritual enlightenment as the Gentile, and certainly the Holy Spirit was as ready and able to manifest His power through Gentiles as through Jews.

If the presence of the Jewish converts in many of the Churches of that time was as important as some suggest, is there any reason why the same benefit should not be experienced in some parts of the mission field today? The Jews are still widely scattered throughout the world. It is to be presumed that they are not less instructed in their faith today than they were then, or less suitable to become the instruments of the Holy Spirit. Why do not Jewish converts, in mission fields where there are Colonies of Jews, become the Spirit-filled leaders in the churches? Among Jewish converts generally today the difficulty is just the same as among Gentile converts — the lack of the evidence of the power of the Holy Spirit following their conversion.

Both Jewish converts and Gentile converts were greatly used in the spreading of the Gospel in Early Church times. Their power, however, had nothing to do with race, nationality or religious background. It was due to the fact that they were filled with the Holy Spirit. Those who went from the Spirit-filled church in Jerusalem, in its first years, would certainly be mighty in faith and witness. But many who went from that same church a number of years later, when legalism had marred the purity of its faith and a great number were 'zealous for the law', wrought only harm and loss wherever they went.

Miracles

Our Lord wrought many different kinds of miracles, including the raising of the dead. These signs, as proofs of His authority, power and love, served a definite purpose in His ministry among men. However, while His miracles were an important proof of His Messiahship, how many of those who witnessed them were brought to a true faith in Him? It would be expected that the great number of miracles which He was continually working should have convinced at least the majority of the people of His divine nature and mission, but they did not. The religious leaders rejected the evidence, attributing the power to Satan. Many of those who gladly availed themselves of healing and partook of the food which He miraculously provided, sought only the material benefits and had no spiritual conviction. Also, with many who were convinced by His miracles, the conviction was of the mind, not of the heart — it was belief, not faith.

It is quite clear that our Lord did not seek to win men by His miracles. He refused to give a sign. The motive of His miracles was always His compassion. They were an evidence of God's love. All the miracles that He wrought did not prevent His rejection by the religious leaders and by the nation and His crucifixion.

The Apostles also wrought miracles, but the motive for which they wrought them and the results which followed were just the same as in our Lord's case. The Apostles never sought to evangelize through miracles. They relied entirely, in their ministry, upon the convicting and regenerating power of the Holy Spirit. The miracles that were wrought by them did not always bring conviction to those who witnessed them. The casting of the evil spirit out of the soothsayer was the direct cause of much trouble at Philippi. The restoration of the lame Lystrian by Paul had a great effect upon the Lystrians (Acts 14:8-19). They were convinced it was the work of a god and would have sacrificed to Paul and Barnabas, yet soon afterwards these same people stoned Paul and left him for dead. No faith had been awakened in their hearts.

After Philippi, for a period of nearly two years, no mention is made of special miracles wrought by Paul. There is no record of miracles having been wrought at Antioch, Corinth, Thessalonica, Derbe and Berea. This does not prove that no miracles were wrought in these places, but it does prove that the working of miracles was not a sufficiently important factor in their evangelization to be recorded.

Paul puts no emphasis upon the working of miracles, but continually stresses the need for true faith engendered by the Holy Spirit and of hearts cleansed by the Holy Spirit's power. That is, he depended upon the same power that we must depend on today. As we have already pointed out, we believe that it is not in the power of the Gospel to save souls that there is lack in the mission field today, but in the manifestation of the power of the Holy Spirit in converts and churches, and this, certainly, cannot be attributed to the absence of miracles.

We would not depreciate the value of miracles, for there is no doubt they had, and still have, their place in bearing testimony to the power of God and to the authority with which His servants are invested but, at the same time, their usefulness as an aid to evangelization should not be over-estimated. They served a special purpose. There is no doubt that God used special methods in the introduction of the Gospel to the world at that time and those who have had experience in mission fields today can bear abundant testimony to the fact that now also He works in special ways in regions that are being newly opened to the Gospel. Dr. John Warneck refers to this fact:

> The finger of God is more visibly and more frequently seen in the mission fields of heathenism, warning the ignorant that now is the day of salvation, than it is in Christendom... foreign missions today are not neccessarily accompanied by manifest wonders as in the days of the Apostles... but the marks of God's mighty presence are plainly perceptible in mission work today. God sometimes condescends to show the helplessness of their gods, and His own power to the heathen who know Him not. He sometimes condescends to punish blasphemers, to accompany with His blessing remedies given by His messengers in great weakness, to answer the stammering prayers of those who would like to know whether His power is with them, and in marvellous ways to preserve His servants... The reader of missionary news will frequently come across instances of such things, reminding him of the experiences of Old and New Testament messengers of God.[1]

The writing of the Acts of the Apostles is not yet finished. From every part of the modern mission field comes testimony to the miraculous interventions of God. It would seem that He deals in more direct, or at least more evident, ways with converts recently won from heathenism. He suits His methods to the circumstances of the work and He does not treat as adults those who are but children. To the undeveloped spiritual understanding of the new convert, He stoops to 'give a sign' while to those who are further along the way He speaks by the 'still small voice in the secret place of communion. To the 'heathen in his blindness', He is willing to give proof; but to the wilful unbelief of Christian lands He 'answers nothing'.

Organization

The Early Church missionaries did not have the benefit of

---

[1] *The Living Christ and Dying Heathenism,* pp. 175-176.

greater financial support or better Mission Boards. They had no Mission Boards and no human guarantee of support. They went forth in faith, looking to the Lord alone for guidance, for protection, and for the supply of every need.

Comparing the general conditions faced by these first missionaries with those under which we work today, the material advantages would seem to be all in our favour. We surpass them far in number of workers, in funds, equipment and facilities of all kinds. We have the advantages of quicker and more comfortable travel, better means of communication and greater guarantees for life and property.

So far as the people among whom the Apostles worked are concerned, we find they were but normal human beings exactly comparable to those in non-Christian lands today. Were the poorer classes of those days better educated, more intelligent, of stronger character? Had they a higher moral standard? Was the heathen of that day superior to the heathen of today? Were men then more capable of true faith and of becoming Evangelists and preachers and Elders of the Church? Surely it would be absurd to say they were. The basic conditions are all exactly the same now as they were then. The heart of man is just the same as it ever was. Satan's power and methods have not changed. And certainly God's power has not become less. Much of our difficulty in rightly appraising the missionary situation in Apostolic times comes from the tendency to invest that period with a glamour, with no true basis in reality, which would explain the success that was achieved as all due to extraordinarily favourable conditions and an unusual manifestation of God's power. That may serve as an excuse for the present lack of success and power, but it is not true to the facts. Is it not clearly evident that the explanation for our present comparative lack of success must be sought not in the realm of the material but in that of the spiritual?

CHAPTER III

CHRIST'S MISSIONARY METHOD

THE study of New Testament principles and methods of evangelization and church planting must begin, not with the Apostles, but with Christ. It was from Him that the Apostles learned the principles they afterwards used. It was His example that taught them the methods they employed. It was their faithfulness in following His teaching and example, linked with the manifestation of the Holy Spirit's power, that brought success.

For three short years Christ preached the Gospel and taught a small group of fishermen and others the work of evangelism. He worked in a far-off time, it is true, but He was dealing with men — men who were entirely human and representative. He was dealing with eternal values and unchanging principles, with universal human weaknesses and limitations, needs, fears and aspirations. Nothing could be more fruitful to all engaged in Gospel ministry than a careful and prayerful study of the principles underlying His ministry on earth.

General Principles

In the following outline we have endeavoured to indicate, in very brief form, the principles of His work.

1. He identified Himself with the people to whom He came. To find men He became a man. To win the Jew He became a Jew, lived as a Jew and observed Jewish customs, except where principle was involved. He lived their life with them and gave Himself unreservedly for them. He did not stand apart or hold Himself aloof in any way. He identified Himself with the people as a whole, not with any particular class. He did not live a shel-

3

tered life or a life of ease and comfort but faced life with its toil and hardness.

2. He took men as He found them. He gave His message in the common language of the people and in a form understood by all classes and conditions of men. He did not use the language of the philosopher or of the Schools. He did not address His message to the intellect but to the heart with its universal need.

3. Having come to seek men, He went out to find them — into their streets and homes, their cities and villages. He did not build a great Temple and call men to come to hear Him, He tramped the highways and byways up and down the land, giving His message on the hill-side, by the sea-shore, in the humble cottage or at the banquet, in the Temple or in the street, wherever He found men to listen.

4. He obeyed the laws of the land, even recognizing the foreign government in control and paying tribute when it was due. He taught respect and obedience to those in authority.

5. He chose twelve men to continue the work after He was gone. They were to be the founders of the Church that was to be established. He gave them a practical training in the field, preparing them to be Evangelists, or church-planters, not Pastors.

6. He planned for the establishment of a native Church under native leadership from the beginning, entirely self-governing, self-supporting and self-propagating under the direct guidance of the Spirit.

7. So far as finances were concerned, He did not bring gold from Heaven to pay 'native workers' and build temples. Nor had He any human resources but lived a life of faith in every sense. He and His disciples preached the Gospel without charge. They looked to God for the supply of their daily bread and shared in a common fund from which the simple needs of all were met. He did not hold the purse; Judas held it. He and His disciples owned nothing and owed nothing. When the rich young ruler would have joined them, Christ instructed him to sell all he had and give it, not to their common fund, but to the poor, and then to come with them.

8. After three years of ministry, He retired from the field leaving His disciples, who had given much evidence of weakness and lack of understanding, to be the founders and leaders of the Church under the guidance of the Holy Spirit.

9. He made no attempt to reform religion, government, or society, but said that new wine could not be put into old bottles, or a new patch on an old garment. He preached the Gospel that would by its own dynamic power sweep the old away and bring in an entirely new order.

10. He established no institutions to aid in the accomplishment of His purpose. He employed no human means to attract men. He built no Temple to preach in and used no ceremony or ritual. For results He depended entirely on the simple preaching and teaching of the Gospel in the power of the Holy Spirit.

11. He never compromised or temporized. Opposition, danger, flattery, criticism, success or lack of success never caused Him to waver in His adherence to principle or to turn to other methods. He rendered absolute obedience to the Father's Word and will.

Our Lord did not establish a congregation. That could be effected only after His sin-offering had been made and accepted — after His death and resurrection — and when the Holy Spirit had filled the members of His Church and manifested through them the gifts necessary for its ministry. But He revealed to His disciples the foundation upon which it was to be built and the principles of its structure. It was to the pattern that He had given that the Church of the New Testament was built.

He did not leave untrained and spiritually inexperienced disciples to be the instruments in the founding of His Church. He had been preparing them for three years. During that time they had shown much weakness, but before He left them the victory had been won in each of them — in all but one. Thomas' doubting heart had been conquered. The self-love and rejection of the implications of the Cross in Peter's heart had given place to an absolute love that yielded all. Doctrine had been carefully taught. Thorough experience in the preaching of the Gospel and in the life of faith had been given. Self had been faithfully dealt with and the victory won. These truly yielded instruments, filled with the power of the Spirit, were the men Christ left to continue the work. The manner in which He brought them to this place is considered in the following chapter.

CHAPTER IV

THE TRAINING OF THE DISCIPLES

IT is evident that the Lord regarded the teaching of the disciples as of primary importance. He gave particular attention to it during the three years they were with Him. He was the Master-teacher; but His method differed greatly from our modern method.

The Men He Chose

The men He chose were drawn mostly from the respectable working class. The majority of them had received small educational advantages and were not considered as men of culture. The Scribes and Pharisees regarded them, even after Pentecost, as "unlearned and ignorant men" (Acts. 4:13, cf. 1 Cor. 1:27). They would be considered as undisciplined, prejudiced, narrow-minded, provincial, untrained to think or to cooperate with others. Their life had been lived under the influence of a decadent religion and a demoralized age.

Temperamentally, they were a cross-section of mankind. It is, indeed, to a great extent, the variety that existed amongst them in character, natural disposition and genius that makes their experiences so fascinating and instructive to all classes and types of men today.

A Practical Training

It is instructive to note what our Lord did not do. He did not choose men of education, culture, wealth, influence or social standing. The power was to be wholly of God. He did not seek to prepare a large number of disciples: only twelve. He did not establish a formal school for their training, a School of the Prophets, or a seminary. In fact He omitted many things that today would be regarded as essential and did many things that would be considered the wrong thing to do.

The method used by our Lord in the training of the disciples was intensely practical. It combined theory with practice, precept with example. He had said that He would make them fishers of men, so He took them out among men that they might learn to know men and their conditions and needs and thoughts and problems and sin, and discover the secret of the approach to the hearts of men. He took His pupils into the great laboratory of a sin-cursed world: into the street and market-place, the city and the open field, the rich man's palace and the humble cottage of the poor. He brought them face to face daily with men, women and children in real life: with Pharisee and sinner, humble men and hypocrites, scoffers and persecutors, true seekers and seekers for personal gain, the sick and the dying, those who blessed and those who cursed, the ignorant and the learned, officers and servants, rich and poor, rulers and slaves.

He led them into direct contact with all the 'isms of the day and showed them by actual demonstration how to meet the self-righteousness of the Pharisee, the materialism of the Sadducees and the worldliness of the Herodians. They saw how to deal with the Nicodemuses and the Mary Magdalenes. When the rich young ruler chose to keep his riches rather than to join our Lord's disciples, the great Teacher was careful afterwards to make sure that His pupils understood the case and all its implications. The woman at the well of Samaria afforded the object of that great masterpiece of personal dealing, the lessons of which were used for the instruction of His disciples.

To teach them how to work, He took them where the work was done, instructing them as a master-carpenter would initiate his apprentices into the secrets and skills of his trade — by practical demonstration and actual experience.

After they had been with Him for a time, He sent the Twelve forth two by two that they might have experience in carrying on alone the ministry in which they had seen Him engage. They had to go forth in faith taking no funds and only the simplest, most necessary equipment. When they returned, He went apart with them into a desert place to review with them the lessons derived from their practical experience. Later He sent out a larger number — seventy — under the same conditions. It was under these conditions they would have to go forth as church-planters after His departure, therefore this experience was necessary to them.

Study Periods

While practical experience was the basis of the method used, a definite place was given to the study of the lessons learned in the work of the day. Frequently the Teacher took His disciples aside to instruct them more fully regarding the things that had taken place. It is clear that these times of private study with the Master apart from the multitude were essential and of the greatest value to the disciples. However, indispensable as they were, they were secondary to the practical instruction. The practical experience was not considered as an opportunity to put into practice the theories learned in class. On the contrary, the classes were for the purpose of considering the experience obtained in the practical work.

One Text Book

There was only one text book used—the Scriptures. The philosophies of the day were not studied. It was not considered necessary by our Lord that the founders of the Church should have a theoretical knowledge of these philosophies, either to give them culture and polish or to enable them to refute error. Yet they did get a very practical knowledge of them and of how to meet them as they came into contact with them in daily experience.

They had no text-book on psychology, yet they did learn psychology — the greatest psychology the world has ever known. They learned to know men and they learned to know themselves. They came to know what was in man's heart and mind. They received from God the knowledge of what is in man and came to understand men as God understands them.

They had no text book on logic, but they learned the logic of divine wisdom as they met the error of human reasoning. Their Teacher spent no time on subjects that had only a remote bearing upon their work. He led His pupils immediately to foundational truths and principles in their practical application. After all, is practical truth not the only real truth?

Purpose of the Training

The purpose of their training was to prepare them to be Evangelists, or church-planters. Our Lord did not prepare them to be Elders or Pastors of churches. Their work was to be like His work: they were to evangelize. They were trained for aggressive work, for going out to meet the foe and to storm him in his citadels. Such was to be the work of the leaders of the Church. They founded churches, but they never remained as Elders of local churches. As leaders they must lead forward — to conquest and extension. The immediate care of the local churches was to be the responsibility of local men with gifts for local ministry.

Ten Essentials

In the preparation of the disciples our Lord evidently gave particular attention to the following points:

1. He was continually seeking their spiritual development. He made full use of all their experiences to teach eternal values. We have but to think of the occasion when the mother of James and John came seeking the highest places for her two sons, and the manner in which He dealt with the individual difficulties of Peter, Thomas and Philip, to realise how careful and watchful He was regarding the spiritual condition and progress of each one. It was the happenings of every day experience, the temptations and faults and failures of the disciples, that He used as the basis for this instruction. And how wisely and lovingly He did so! Here also theory was learned in the practical school. He brought them to the place where they were willing to deny self and to take up the Cross and truly follow Him. Nothing less than that would have served His purpose.

2. He taught them to evangelize. The practical method which He used to train them to know how to meet men and deal with souls, how to preach and teach, has already been stated.

3. He taught them to know and use the Scriptures. He Himself was continually using them. All His teaching was based upon them; all His reasoning and arguments were derived from them. Here again the same method is employed: they learned to know and use the Scriptures by using them.

4. He taught them to have faith in God directly for the supply of all their material needs. He had left all to live among men and

become the Saviour of the World; they left all to follow Him. He had not where to lay His head; and so it was with them. They left all and went forth with Him, possessing nothing and with no material resources, looking to God alone for the supply of all their needs, sharing together with the Master out of the common fund of God's supply, of which Judas was the Treasurer. This accomplished four important things: it detached them from the world; it made them exercise faith; it obliged them to walk near to God; it caused them to be living witnesses to God's power and faithfulness. These things were necessary to their witness.

5. He taught them to minister in the power of the Spirit alone and not to have recourse to ritual, ceremony, forms of service, programmes, emotionalism, sentimentalism or any other human means to attract or influence. He revealed to them that the power that would draw men was the power of His Cross.

6. He taught them the life and ministry of prayer in the Spirit, though they entered into it only after the Holy Spirit had come to dwell in them.

7. He taught them to live and minister in absolute obedience to the will of God, withholding nothing for self but placing themselves entirely upon the altar.

8. He taught them to exercise unwavering faith, to doubt not but to have absolute trust in God and confidence in His power and faithfulness.

9. He taught them absolute love to God and absolute love to their fellow men — the love that serves, seeking nothing for self and counting it all joy and all gain to give all.

10. He taught them to work together; to cooperate as a group directed by the Spirit of God, none seeking the preeminence and all serving each other.

Intercessory Ministry

The place that the prayer of faith took in the accomplishing of all this is important. That the Lord prayed many times for these men He was teaching, when He went aside to be alone with the Father, is certain. Two examples of His prayer ministry for them are given us. He told Peter that He had prayed for him that his faith fail not (Lk. 22:32). Then in the seventeenth chapter of John's Gospel we have His great intercessory prayer for them, in which we also are included.

Personal Example

Personal example also played a very important part in this teaching. The disciples were called upon to do nothing that they did not see their Teacher doing. They learned to evangelize by following Him, seeing Him do the work, sharing with Him the fatigue of the road, the heat of the day, the unceasing toil, the dangers, the hopes and disappointments, the mocking and the triumphs. It was thus they learned to preach, to seek the lost, to have compassion on the multitude. They watched His walk of absolute obedience to the Father's will. They saw Him forego all material wealth and live a life of faith. They saw as He continually went apart to spend long hours, even whole nights, in prayer. They knew He never took an important step without first having spent much time in prayer to the Father. They saw His patience, His meekness and His humility. They knew the purity of His life. They saw Him as in utter rest of faith He slept in the midst of the storm. They saw Him in Gethsemane as He yielded to God's will and to the Cross, and they saw Him on the Cross. Finally, they saw Him in His resurrection life. By His own example He taught them the spiritual values of truth, humility, patience and love and trained them to be no sluggards and to seek not ease and luxury, but to pray and work, to sow by all waters and to wait patiently for the fruit.

He gave them an example of perfect love. He had taught them that the first and basic commandment was to love God with all the heart, mind and strength and the second to love their neighbour as themselves and He demonstrated to them a life lived in perfect obedience to these commandments. He Himself denied self and took up the Cross. When Peter said to Him "pity Thyself"—think not of sacrificing Thyself — He administered the severest rebuke that He ever gave to a disciple (Matt. 16:23, marg.). Then He used that incident to teach the absolute necessity that every follower and servant of His should accept the full consequences of an absolute denial of self. He loved His disciples with a love that never wavered, no matter how slow of understanding or faithless they might be: "He loved them to the end".

The Development of Character

A great writer has said: "Talent develops itself in solitude, character in the stream of life." This is true, but, like many such sayings, it is not the whole truth, for talent "wrapped in a napkin" and not used will not develop; and there can be no doubt that Moses and Paul gained much in character from the years spent in the desert. God uses a blend of the two in the training of His servants. In our Lord's life and in His teaching of the disciples we can see the two in action. The deserted mountain side during the silent hours of the night for prayer, or during the day for study alone with the disciples had its place as did also the days filled with weary marches and preaching to throngs of needy people.

"It has been commonly thought", says another writer, "that protected ease is the most favourable condition of life, whereas all the noblest and strongest lives prove to the contrary that the endurance of hardship is the making of the man, and the factor that distinguishes between existence and vigorous vitality. Hardship makes character". This is true in the natural realm and it is also deeply true in the spiritual realm.

. The disciples had three years in a hard school — the school of experience. It was experience under the guidance and supervision of the Master Teacher. Surely that Teacher knew the best method of teaching men. Was it not the right kind of school to prepare the disciples for the task that was to face them — evangelization in the power of the Spirit alone?

The Modern Method

We might continue with great profit to study the manner in which the great Teacher taught His disciples, the principles He applied and the things He taught, how by questions He made them continually think for themselves, how He drew vital questions from them, how He prepared them to stand alone when He would be no longer with them; but enough has been said to reveal His method.

It might be said that the method our Lord used was suitable for the training of founders of the Church but that it was not intended that it should be copied in the preparing of the men who were to carry on the Church's ministry. But this argument is invalidated by the fact that every principle of our Lord's method was applied in the training of Paul, Timothy, Titus and all the other Evangelists of the Early Church. Of the manner in which these were trained we shall deal in a later chapter.

The study of Christ's teaching method leads us to ask certain questions. Should His method be followed today? If it were followed, would its results be more satisfactory than those of the method at present in vogue? Would the training of the disciples have been so effective had Christ used our modern method? Would a modern seminary course have fitted them better, or as well, for their ministry as the practical training which they received?

In our modern method the teaching of theory is the basis of the instruction given. A limited amount of practical work is added; limited both in scope and in amount. No real attempt is made to give a comprehensive and thorough course of practical experience. The time available after the book study is taken care of does not permit of it. In our Lord's teaching method practical experience was the basis and theory was taught from the lessons of experience.

Results

When our Lord left His disciples, or when Paul left Titus in Crete, these young Evangelists did not have to begin to learn how to put into practice the theory they had been taught. So complete had been their experience already that no unfamiliar situation could arise. They knew exactly what their work would be, the conditions under which they would have to do it and how to go about doing it. And they had reached the place of personal spiritual victory.

When we send young preachers, trained by our modern method, into their fields of service, they are really not half prepared for their task. Being to a great extent inexperienced and, consequently, with undeveloped Christian character, they find themselves continually faced with new and difficult situations, with little more than theory with which to meet them. Should we blame them too severely if their methods are not always the wisest and best, or if they are often perplexed and disheartened and, in not a few cases, become discouraged and fail?

We shall give this matter further consideration in later chapters.

CHAPTER V

JERUSALEM: THE PLANTING OF THE FIRST

CONGREGATION

THE Church indwelt by the Holy Spirit was born in a prayer meeting in the upper room of a private house in Jerusalem. It was there that the disciples, in obedience to Christ's command, waited to be endued with power from on high and it was there that His promise was fulfilled and the Holy Spirit fell upon all who were gathered together, men and women, yielded in faith and of one accord in prayer.

Christ had taught His disciples that a congregation was two or three gathered together in His Name with Him present in the midst to build. He had told them of the Church's authority as a result of His presence and of how, when those gathered knew His will and asked it in the unanimous prayer of faith, He would do it. Before His ascension He had told them to wait in Jerusalem for the promised Holy Spirit. So they obey His instructions and, right from the beginning, we see in Jerusalem His followers at prayer, asking unanimously according to His revealed will. Then we see the Lord do what they have asked. (Matt. 16:16—18; 18:17—20.)

Even in its inception the Church was guided to proceed strictly in accordance with the principles laid down by Christ. The delay between His ascension and the fulfilment of the promise to send the Holy Spirit was to permit of this. It gave time for this first congregation to pray in faith unanimously for the Holy Spirit's coming so that when He came it was not only in fulfilment of the promise but also in answer to the prayer of the Church. Even in the initial act of establishing the Church no exception was made and no principle set aside.

Out of that faith, obedience and waiting in prayer of a company of humble disciples, in the ancient Capital of God's chosen people — who had just rejected the Christ and crucified Him outside the city wall — God brought into being the Church, against which "the counsels of hell shall not prevail". There, in that prayer-gathering in Jerusalem, the hour of another divine Dispensation struck and men and women filled with the Holy Spirit, and possessing the gifts of the Spirit which Christ had promised, went down into the streets to preach Christ crucified and risen and the day of God's free grace.

It was a group of humble people: fishermen and others. None was great or wealthy or learned. They had done nothing but pray in faith according to God's will. They knew the Church was to begin in Jerusalem and that they were to evangelize the world, but they had made no plans. They had not sought to organize or to form boards or committees. They had been told that when the Holy Spirit came His power and guidance would be their sufficient enabling for all the work, and they thought only of being filled with Him, knowing His will day by day and doing it in His strength.

When that group of humble people were filled with the Spirit, the gifts or manifestations of the Spirit appeared immediately in all. All took part in the public preaching of the Gospel. Those who heard them were amazed and Peter explained the significance of what was taking place. He showed that it was the fulfilment of prophecy and had its roots in the Old Testament Scriptures (Acts 2:16—21). It was the beginning of the Church filled with the Holy Spirit, the Body of Christ, "the fulness of Him who fills all things everywhere with Himself" (Eph. 1:23, Conybeare), in which every member, man or woman, is a priest unto God to offer spiritual sacrifices.

The Church began with every member active in ministry. Twice in the prophecy quoted by Peter it is repeated that both men and women are to take part in this ministry. So it was done on the day of Pentecost and so it was to continue to be done.

A sample of the preaching that day is given. There is nothing extraordinary in Peter's discourse. There is nothing of human wisdom or eloquence. The outstanding feature is his use of the Scriptures, of which, evidently, he had a thorough knowledge. His discourse is little more than a recapitulation of Scriptural statement, presented with clarity and boldness. It was the presence of the Spirit that brought conviction and repentance to the hearers. Such was the preaching on the day of Pentecost.

A clear picture is given of the life and ministry of the new church. All were filled with the Spirit and were exercising gifts of the Spirit. All were preaching the Gospel. The unity of the Spirit and the love of Christ were manifested among them.

The three thousand converts were baptized without delay, and these gathered with the congregation, taking part in the witness. The new converts were filled with the Spirit, but they did not suddenly become possessed of ripe spiritual knowledge and experience. They had to develop spiritually by the normal process.

The congregational life consisted of the teaching of the doctrine which the Apostles had received from the Lord, the communion of the breaking of bread, and prayer (Acts 2:42). The study of the Scriptures occupied an important place. The ministry of the Word in the congregation did not consist of textual sermons but of the study of Apostolic doctrine. The result was that all were thoroughly instructed in that doctrine. The 'breaking of bread', or the Lord's Table, was not an occasional ceremony. It was the central symbol of the spiritual communion of the congregation and was observed frequently. Prayer also was continuous, engaged in by all.

The witness of the congregation consisted of the preaching of the Good News in the streets, in the Temple, in private homes and wherever there was an opening. In this all took part. There was not just one preacher, or twelve, but thousands of preachers. All were 'priests unto God', ministering freely and continually through the gifts of the Spirit. Naturally, the impact of the witness of such a congregation upon the city and surrounding regions was great and the Gospel spread.

The Apostles did not monopolize the ministry of the Word. In the synagogue the Elders presided but any member could expound the Scriptures. So it was in the Church also. The Apostles' ministry was to lay the foundation, pass on the doctrine received from the Lord, oversee the new congregation until local Elders were appointed and take part with all in the preaching of the Gospel. Later the gifts of government and teaching were manifested in others and the Apostles moved elsewhere.

To recapitulate: the life and activity of this congregation consisted of four elements —

1. The teaching of doctrine.
2. The Lord's Table.
3. Prayer.
4. The public preaching of the Gospel by all.

Nothing of human method was added to aid or attract. The equipment was gloriously adequate. The ministry was complete and balanced. There was not mostly the preaching of the Gospel with little teaching, or mostly teaching and little preaching of the Gospel. Our Lord's commands to teach and to preach were both obeyed.

Social contact among the believers was provided by the *agape* or 'love feast'. They gathered in each others' homes to eat together. In this there was no division between rich and poor, for those who had means took extra with them so that there would be ample for those who could bring nothing.[1] This social fellowship was centered in the home, where it should be, not in the church, and the Lord was the centre of it, for even in that gathering they met in His Name and recognized His presence by the breaking of bread.

There were many poor in the Jerusalem congregation and this club feast contributed towards meeting their need. It was not an innovation, for such repasts were common in confraternities.

There is one phase of the church-life of this congregation that is not always understood. It is stated that,

> Those believing were at the same place, and had all things common, and the possessions and the goods they were selling and were parting them to all, according as any one had need. (Acts 2:44,45. Young's Lit. Trans.).

Moffatt translates the passage as follows:

> The believers all kept together; they shared all they had with one another, they would sell their possessions and goods and distribute the proceeds among all, as any might be in need.

This matter is mentioned again in Acts 4:34. In the Greek the words 'sold' and 'parted' in 2:44, 45, and 'were' and 'brought' in 4:34, are in the imperfect tense, expressing continuous action

---

[1] It is this 'love feast' that Paul refers to in I Cor. 11:20-22, but there it had degenerated into something quite different. Instead of sharing together, each ate what he had brought, so that the rich fared sumptuously while the poor lacked.

in the past. That is, at different times, different believers, as there was need and they were moved by the Spirit, sold all or part of their possessions and distributed the proceeds to those who were in need.

Two things are stated: first, that the believers "shared all they had with one another"; second, that possessions and goods were being sold and the money given to the poor.

Commenting on Acts 2:44, Clarke writes:

> At all the public religious feasts in Jerusalem, there was a sort of community of goods. No man at such times hired houses or beds in Jerusalem; all were lent gratis by the owners. The same may be well supposed of their ovens, cauldrons, tables, spits, and other utensils. Also, provisions of water were made for them at the public expense. (Shekalim, cap. 9. See Lightfoot here.) Therefore a sort of community of goods was no strange thing at Jerusalem, at such times as these.[1]

The converts in Jerusalem did not live a communal life. The money received from the sale of property was not put into a common fund from which all received an equal portion. There is no suggestion that those who were supporting themselves gave up their employment or pooled their earnings. Distribution was made only to those in need. Among these were the widows mentioned. (Paul gives the rules for the support of widows in 1 Tim. 5:3—14; they were strict.) Had all the congregation been receiving equally from a common fund, the complaint regarding the distribution to the Helenist widows could hardly have been made.

Those who sold possessions did so voluntarily. It was not required that they do so. When Ananias sold a possession and falsely asserted that he had brought the entire proceeds to give to the Lord, Peter said to him,

> While it remained unsold, was not the land your own? And when sold was it not at your disposal? How is it that you have cherished this design in your heart? It is not to men you have told this lie, but to God. (Acts 5:4, Weymouth.)

The clear inference here is that Ananias had been under no obligation to sell his possession, and when it was sold he was not obliged to give away the proceeds. His sin was in retaining a part when he said he was giving all.

---

[1] *Commentary on the Bible.*

Circumstances peculiar to Jerusalem made the number of poor among the Christians in that city unusually great. This condition continued and the churches that were established later in Gentile lands felt it necessary to send contributions for the poor in the Jerusalem congregation.

The practice of our Lord and His disciples, who went forth possessing nothing of this world's goods and having a common purse as they ministered the Word and lived a life of faith, also throws light upon what took place in Jerusalem. Peter said to the Lord, "Have we not left all to follow thee?" When the rich young ruler had wished to follow Christ as a disciple, our Lord said to him, "Sell everything you possess, and give the money to the poor, and you shall have wealth in Heaven; and then come, follow me" (Luke 18:22, Weymouth). The selling of one's possessions was not necessary to faith in Christ, but this young man wished to join the company of the One Who had become poor that He might make others rich, and to do so he must be willing to dispossess himself of all this world's goods. He found the cost too great, to the sorrow of the Master.

In Jerusalem the Twelve continued this practice. No doubt some of those who sold their possessions and gave the money to the poor had heard the call to go forth as witnesses of the Gospel. Barnabas, the only one named, besides Ananias and Sapphira, of those who sold possessions, most probably was so actuated, for God called him to the ministry of church-planting.

In none of the other churches, subsequently founded, was there a sharing of goods as in Jerusalem. There was no necessity for it, for those in need were not so numerous. Barnabas did not ask that the converts in Antioch should do as he had done in Jerusalem.

The practice that had been followed by our Lord and His disciples was continued among those who went forth to preach the Gospel, "taking nothing of the Gentiles". Paul and the other Evangelists left all and followed the Lord in a life of faith. But that was an entirely different matter to the sharing of goods in the Jerusalem congregation.

What took place in Jerusalem was the natural outcome of the presence of the Spirit of the Lord among His people, the manifestation of the gifts of mercy and giving. The rule for the Church, which is one Body, is that all the members "should have the same care one for another. And whether one member suffer, all the

4

members suffer with it." In Jerusalem this was manifested in a practical way meeting the situation that existed. Even their enemies admired the love that was shown among the Christians. This voluntary manifestation of the love of Christ, and the sacrifices that were gladly made for one another, bore a greater testimony and brought more glory to the Name of the Lord than would have been done by a regimented communism.

Naturally, to understand the manner in which the Holy Spirit led in the forming of the church in Jerusalem, we must view it in the light of the teaching given by our Lord regarding the Church. The principles which He laid down were applied strictly and found gloriously sufficient.[1]

The Church was Christ's and He was to build it. He was to be present personally in every gathering of its members, to make His will known and to work through them by His Spirit in answer to united, unanimous prayer that was according to His will.

All this we see put into effect in the congregation in Jerusalem. It is a congregation that begins and continues in unanimous, Spirit-guided prayer. Christ is present in the midst, building His Church. He guides every action. His will is sought and obeyed. The work is done by His power in answer to the prayer of faith. We see Christ, the Head of the Body, working, not theoretically but actually, through the members yielded in full obedience to do His will.

The Lord had commanded that the preaching should begin at Jerusalem and that command was obeyed. The congregation that came into being in that city was Jewish. It was the first, and in the manner of its beginning it was, in some respects, unique. It was the direct result of the initial experience of Pentecost and was formed around the band of disciples who had been with Christ. And yet its development was entirely normal, for it conformed in all things to the principles laid down by the Lord for the structure of the Church.

Although the Apostles laid the original foundation of the Church in Jerusalem, and that foundation was perfect, the congregation in Jerusalem is not presented as the model congregation. The Holy Spirit evidently purposely avoided presenting any one church as a model for the future. The form of organization

---

[1] Christ's teaching on the Church is dealt with in chapter 12.

of the Jerusalem church is described only partially, and so it is with all the other New Testament churches. But by bringing together all the details given of the different churches we get the complete pattern. And with that pattern before us as we examine the record of any church, we find that the Holy Spirit provides ample evidence to show that all were organized in exactly the same manner.

We might have expected that a detailed account would be provided of the organization given by the Spirit to the first congregation. But it was not God's purpose to do so and we can discern the wisdom of His action. The Church is one and indivisible. Every gathering is equal and none can be set above another. There could be no 'Mother Church'. Not even the church in Jerusalem could be put in a place over others as the model assembly. Any congregation may become unfaithful and depart from the true, spiritual order. Actually, the church in Jerusalem did so. The order established in Jerusalem was the model order but the congregation was not the model congregation. When other churches were founded, they were organized exactly as the Jerusalem church was, but this was done, not because the Jerusalem congregation was so organized, but because it was God's order for the whole Church.

It is instructive to observe the Apostles' ministry as church-planters in Jerusalem for it provided the model followed by all who engaged subsequently in that work. In the company of Apostles ministering in Jerusalem, Peter took the lead as Paul did later in the company of Evangelists that planted the churches in Gentile lands.

While Peter took the lead at this period, his leadership did not involve any spiritual authority over his fellow-Apostles. This is made plain in the answer which our Lord gave him when he enquired regarding John's future. The Lord replied, "If I desire him to remain till I come, what concern is that of yours? You, yourself, must follow me". (John 21:22, Weymouth). John, just as Peter, was under the Lord's direct leadership. The Lord never delegates to another any of His authority over His servants.

The Twelve provided a nucleus around which the converts could gather, and authoritative, experienced leadership for the company of believers, at Pentecost and in the period immediately following, until the infant church became established as the Holy

Spirit completed its structure, giving local men the necessary experience and manifesting in them the gifts of the Spirit for government.

There are two aspects of the Apostles' ministry. As the Twelve Apostles, there was a special ministry entrusted to them, involving a special spiritual authority. They laid the original foundation of the Church delivering to the Church what Christ had taught regarding both doctrine and the Church's structure. (Acts 2:42; Eph. 2:20). In that ministry they had no successors: the foundation they laid was perfect and permanent. But also they did the work of Evangelist, or church-planter. That is one of the basic, continuing ministries in the Church, for the carrying on of which the Holy Spirit raised up an ever increasing number.

The gift of the Spirit for government was, at first, manifested only in the Apostles. They had not possessed it before Pentecost, but the wisdom which the Holy Spirit gave them for the leadership in the congregation in Jerusalem is apparent. It was some time later that others gave evidence of possessing it. This was in accordance with God's order for the Church. An Elder or Deacon is not to be a 'novice', but one who has been proved. Even at Pentecost the Holy Spirit made no exceptions to this rule. Before Elders or Deacons could be appointed, sufficient time had to elapse to enable them to prove themselves and gain the necessary experience. Meanwhile, the Apostles acted as Deacons and Elders of the congregation, presiding and attending to the business matters such as the distribution of funds to the widows.

Our Lord, knowing the order He was to establish in His Church, had anticipated this need and prepared for it by the training and experience which He had given to the Twelve during the previous three years. For the leadership of the first congregation in its beginning men were provided who were not novices.

The Apostles lived by faith. When the lame man at the gate of the Temple called Beautiful asked alms of Peter and John, Peter said to him, "Silver and gold have I none; but such as I have give I thee." Peter was still the man who had left all to follow Christ, possessing none of this world's wealth. So it was also with his fellow-Apostles. The Jerusalem congregation numbered thousands and could have supported its leaders handsomely, but there was no salaried ministry. The Apostles lived 'by faith'.

As a result of the miracle wrought on the lame man, Peter and John were arrested and ordered to cease preaching in the Name of Christ. But they answered that they must obey God rather than man. Christ had commanded them to preach the Gospel to every creature. The prohibition by the authorities clashed with His command, so there could be only one answer.

The miracle was an act of compassion. It was a sign of the presence of divine power. But it did not result in the salvation of many souls; the salvation of souls was the fruit of the preaching of the Gospel in the power of the Spirit.

When the two Apostles returned to the congregation, the matter was immediately taken to God in prayer. The church did not meet to consider what steps should be taken, but to pray. What they asked was not protection but the grace to continue witnessing boldly to the Gospel. They based their prayer upon Scripture. It was answered and they were filled with the Holy Spirit for this witness. The Church in Jerusalem continues to be a church at prayer obeying Christ's command and seeking the power of the Spirit for every step.

It is at this juncture that Barnabas unites with the Church. He was to take part in the evangelization of the Gentiles, but about seven years were to pass before he would be ready to be sent forth. There was no undue haste in the Spirit's work. The instruments must be fully prepared. From the beginning the procedure is normal and the Holy Spirit takes time to do a thorough work.

The first case of discipline has to be dealt with. Ananias and Sapphira were guilty of the sin of hypocrisy: they pretended they had given all to God. The awful punishment which God meted out to the first appearance of this sin in the Church was intended as a warning for all time of His hatred of it and of the need to exclude it utterly. It is the deadly sin within that most endangers the Church and from which the Church, at all costs, must cleanse itself.

The church that tolerates a member with a lie in his heart and life is a church with a lie in its heart and life and it will not experience the manifestation of the presence and power of Christ. All the New Testament Evangelists were faithful in insisting upon the exercise of discipline in the Church.

This judgment was not the act of Peter: it was the act of the Holy Spirit. Peter merely stated what sin had been committed. It was the Holy God who smote the offenders.

After this, the power manifested in the healing of the sick is mentioned. All manner of diseases of the body, and diseases of the mind due to the influence of evil spirits, were healed. As Christ was permitted to direct the congregation and guard its purity, so He was able to manifest through it the fulness of His power.

There is a second outburst of persecution and the Apostles are cast into prison. Once more they are ordered to cease preaching in Christ's Name and again they answer as they had answered before. They are beaten and the command is repeated that they preach not in the Name of Jesus. When released, "they went their way, rejoicing that they had been deemed worthy to suffer disgrace on behalf of the NAME. But they did not desist from teaching every day, in the Temple or in private houses, and telling the Good News about Jesus, the Christ." (Acts 5:41,42, Weymouth.)

About this time, complaints were made in the church regarding the distribution of funds, the Hellenists asserting that their widows were neglected. The flesh was not eradicated. The old antipathy between Hebrew and Hellenist was ready to flare up at any moment and rend the church, producing disaster, but it was not permitted to do so. The Holy Spirit guided and the church went forward unitedly and victoriously. It was triumphant, not because it was free from internal dangers, but because the Holy Spirit was in control and permitted to guard its unity.

The Apostles, led by the Spirit, suggested to the church that the time had come for the appointment of servants, or Deacons, to serve in the distribution of the funds. Certain details are given regarding the procedure followed in the appointment of these Deacons:

> Then the twelve called the multitude of the disciples unto them, and said, It is not reason that we should leave the word of God, and serve tables. Wherefore brethren, look ye out among you seven men of honest report, full of the Holy Ghost and wisdom, whom we may appoint over this business. (Acts 6:2,3.)

Here we find the following facts:

1. The Apostles acted together. Peter did not act alone.

2. The Apostles took the initiative and called the church together, suggesting that Deacons be chosen to meet the need that had arisen for their services.

3. Those chosen were to be:

    (1) Members of that congregation.

    (2) Men of good report.

    (3) Men filled with the Holy Spirit.

    (4) Men of wisdom.

4. The whole congregation makes the choice.

5. The Apostles prayed and laid their hands upon those who were chosen.

It is interesting to note that a majority of those chosen were Hellenists. The importance of this does not lie principally in the fact that the complaint had been made by the Hellenists, but in God's purpose to prepare Greek-speaking men, experienced in ministry, to take the Gospel, a few years later to the Greek-speaking world. The congregation did not know it then, but the Lord was building for the future. He could do so because He was being permitted to build His Church.

This procedure in the appointment of these Deacons followed closely the custom in the Synagogue. There can be no question that they were Deacons. In the Synagogue there were almoners (servants-deacons), chosen by the congregation to distribute the alms to the poor.

The term Deacon is not used in this account. It does not occur in the Acts. But Luke describes the service to be rendered by the seven — service performed by Deacons in the Synagogue, as was well-known to all. It is the service rendered by the Deacons in the Early Church. 'Deacon' in this technical sense is used by Luke's companion in ministry, Paul.

It may be that these were not the first Deacons appointed in Jerusalem. In the Synagogue the Deacons were often called "the young men". It is possible, therefore, that the "young men", referred to by Luke, who carried out the bodies of Ananias and Sapphira for burial were Deacons.

When we compare the procedure followed in the choosing of Deacons in Jerusalem with that practised by Paul and his companions in the appointment of Elders, we find that both were the same. The spiritual requirements of a Deacon stated by the Apostles differ not from those detailed by Paul in his instructions to Timothy.

How the Deacons in Jerusalem were chosen is not described. Luke records that "in all the churches" of the Gentiles Elders were appointed "after prayer and fasting" (Weymouth). There is every reason to believe that the same procedure was followed in the praying church in Jerusalem. The Deacons would not have been elected by a majority vote, but, without doubt, the Spirit made known to the church at prayer those whom God had appointed to that ministry and to whom He had given the necessary gifts. (1 Cor. 12:11, 18, cf. Acts 13:1-4.)

The place that was being given to prayer by the leaders of the church is evident in the statement made by Peter when the appointment of the Deacons was suggested: "And we will give ourselves continually to prayer and the ministry of the Word." Prayer occupied the first place. With them it was as it had been with their Lord when He ministered on earth. Then they had not been men of prayer and had been unable to fellowship with Him in it. But now they are filled with the Spirit and are men of prayer.

The organization and ministry of the Church were simple and entirely spiritual. As Clarke says there were

> ...no expensive ceremonies: no apparatus calculated merely to impress the senses, to produce emotions in the animal system, 'to help' as has been foolishly said, 'the spirit of devotion'... No strange fire can be brought to this altar: for the God of the Christians can be worshipped only in spirit and in truth.

There was activity: ceaseless and fervent activity in which every member, men and women, young and old, took part. But it was not institutional or organizational activity. There were no Societies or Guilds or Boards or choir or human attraction of any kind in this church. There was no organizational machinery; no creaking wheels to keep turning; no round of congregational activities to keep the energies of the members directed inwards. All the time and strength was occupied in obeying the command to teach and preach the Gospel, reaching outward in an ever extending witness — to Judea, Galilee, Samaria and the World.

The activities of this great congregation did not centre in a 'church building'. It had no such building. The houses of its members were its meeting places. The Jewish religion had centred in the Temple. The Temple of Christ is in the hearts of His people. No building made with hands has any significance to the Church. Christ is present in His fulness wherever two or three members are met in His Name.

In this congregation in its early years we have the Church in its original purity as God intended and intends it to be. The congregation was large, the situation in which it was placed bristled with problems and difficulties, but its organization and ministry were entirely adequate. They were a perfect and sufficient vehicle for the Holy Spirit's work and the manifestation of Christ through His Body.

Just when it was that Elders took their place in the congregation in Jerusalem, we do not know, but about seven years after Pentecost, when the church in Antioch came into being, there were Elders in the Jerusalem church. Not long after Barnabas and Paul had begun their ministry at Antioch, when that congregation of new Gentile converts sent an offering to the famine-stricken brethren in Jerusalem, it was "to the Elders", and not to the Apostles, that they sent it (Acts 11:30). Barnabas and Silas, it would seem, had been Elders in Jerusalem before going forth as Evangelists.

By the time the church in Antioch was founded, the Twelve had ceased to occupy the prominent place in the Jerusalem church which it had been necessary for them to take in the beginning. There is every warrant to suppose that two or three years after Pentecost the will of the Lord was made known to the church and to the Apostles as to who were chosen of Him to be the Elders of the congregation and that these were then duly appointed. When this group of Elders took up their ministry of oversight in the congregation, the obligation of the Apostles to preach the Gospel first at Jerusalem was fulfilled. Henceforth it is the task of world evangelism that becomes prominent and to this great undertaking the Apostles dedicate themselves cooperating in it as Evangelists, or missionaries. Their identity as the Twelve is never lost, and never will be throughout eternity, but as the Holy Spirit had now brought into being the permanent structure of the Church, they take their place within that structure.

In Jerusalem, when Paul and Barnabas brought the matter of the Judaising teachers before the church, the Apostles alone did not deal with it. They met together with the Elders of the church (Acts 15:4-29). James, who was not an Apostle, presided. This is the last time that the Apostles as a body are mentioned as taking part in the decisions of any church. From then on they are scattered and it is Evangelists, not Apostles, that are prominent.

The manner in which the Apostle's ministry blended into the structure of the Church, in which there was to be no continuing order of Apostles, is one of the greatest evidences of the presence of the Spirit of Christ and the power of the Holy Ghost in these men. It revealed a humility not natural to man. At the first they had acted as an authoritative, specially privileged and specially commissioned body of leaders, yet, as the Church grew and the Spirit raised up those in whom He manifested the gifts of the

Spirit for the permanent ministries, they never thought of continuing to impose their authority, either individually or as a Council of Twelve. A most striking example of this is seen in Peter's attitude when, at Antioch, Paul successfully withstood him on a point of doctrine. He did not claim any superior Apostolic authority. His judgment was mistaken but his heart was right with the Lord.

The attitude of the Twelve to the Church brought into being by the Holy Spirit, in the founding of which they had been given such a prominent place, surely carries a deep lesson for the church-planter today. They did not stand in the way of the Holy Spirit raising up, guiding and using the men He chose for the carrying on and extension of the Church's work. The Apostles, and all the New Testament missionaries, took the attitude that John the Baptist had taken before them: 'He must increase, but I must decrease'.

CHAPTER VI

ANTIOCH — THE ONE BODY

THE first twelve chapters of the "Acts of the Apostles" deal with the preaching of the Gospel to the Jews and the planting of the Church in Jerusalem, Judea and Samaria. Our Lord had commanded that the Gospel should be preached in these regions first. During that period, the company of twelve Apostles is prominent. Peter takes the lead. The instruments used are chiefly Galileans or Judeans. In the other sixteen chapters it is the preaching of the Gospel to all nations and the planting of the Church throughout the world that is recorded. It is the company of Evangelists that is prominent. First Barnabas and then Paul are the leaders. The instruments used are principally Greek-speaking Jews born in Gentile lands and Gentiles.

It was not until about seven years after Pentecost that a beginning was made in the evangelization of the Gentiles. Why did the Holy Spirit delay so long? The reasons are clear: (1) the Apostolic foundation had first to be fully laid and (2) instruments had to be thoroughly prepared. When the Holy Spirit finally thrust forth His witnesses, the basis had been firmly laid and they were trained and experienced. The delay was worth while, for the result was work well done, a Church well built, and expansion that, when it did take place, was both sound and rapid.

The fact that the Holy Spirit was at liberty to manifest His gifts as He willed through all had made it possible for Him to prepare for the future. The Jerusalem congregation could not have known at the time the full reason for all that He was doing. It was not necessary that they should. All that was necessary was that He have liberty to work, using each one as He would for the present work and preparing them for that which He was to do in the

future. In Jerusalem, and in the churches which He established
later, we can see how He did this.

The persecution that broke out in Jerusalem against the new
and aggressive Church forced many of its members to scatter to
other regions. God had protected the infant Church and kept it
in comparative security until the initial work of planting was
complete and until His people were sufficiently established and
experienced. Those who were scattered were not babes in Christ.

Many of these were Jews who preached the Word "to none but
unto the Jews only". But others who were Greek-speaking men
from the Greek colonies in Cyprus and North Africa, converted
Hellenists and Greek proselytes, went to Antioch in the north of
Syria (the third greatest city in the Roman Empire, surpassed
only by Rome and Alexandria) and there preached the Gospel
to the Greeks.

F. B. Meyer says,

> Antioch will ever be famous in Christian annals, because a num-
> ber of unordained and unnamed disciples, fleeing from Jerusalem in
> the face of Saul's persecution, dared to nreach the Gospel to Greeks
> and to gather the converts into a Church, in entire disregard of the
> initial rite of Judaism.[1]

But the significance of Antioch is greater even than that. It is
there that God's purpose for the Church is fully realized. In
Jerusalem we see the bud opening; in Antioch it bursts into full
flower. The church in Jerusalem was at first purely Jewish. The
door was not opened immediately to the Gentiles. The Twelve
were a purely Jewish company. Through them, in Jerusalem, the
Holy Spirit laid the foundation of the Church firmly upon the
basis of the past Dispensation. The Church 'is built upon the
foundation of the Apostles and Prophets' (Eph. 2:20). It is the
outcome, the realization, of the promises, symbols and hopes that
had gone before.

But now the foundation has been laid. The Spirit, through the
Apostles, has formed the structure according to the pattern revealed by Christ and has delivered to the Church the doctrine
which He taught. The keys have been used, opening the door to
both Gentiles and Jews. So there springs up in Antioch a congregation of the Church in its complete form. This is not a Jewish

---

[1] *Paul, a Servant of Jesus Christ*, p. 80.

congregation. Nor is it entirely Gentile. It is 'the new man' of which Paul writes in Eph. 2:11-22, formed of Jew and Gentile united in one, the enmity and distinction between the two having been abolished in Christ.

The forming of the Antioch congregation is a work of the Spirit using others than the Apostles. Their special mission is now largely fulfilled. The Antioch congregation is built upon the foundation they have laid, but their presence or personal ministry is not now essential. No man or group of men is to continue to be essential. Christ is the Builder and His Spirit is the one who is to lead forward calling and using whom He will, directing every step, empowering every act, accomplishing every work.

Not only was it not the Apostles, it was not even men of Jerusalem or of Judea or Galilee, who were used by the Holy Spirit to take the Gospel to Antioch. In Jerusalem our Lord used men of Galilee and Judea but to take the Gospel to the Greek-speaking people He used Greek-speaking men born in Greek Colonies. (We shall see later that Paul and those God associated with him also hailed from the regions they were to evangelize.)

These were not uninstructed believers, inexperienced in ministry. In the Jerusalem congregation, as we have already seen, the ministry of the Word was the privilege and responsibility of all. All had gifts of the Spirit and exercised them freely. All were experienced in the preaching of the Gospel, so that those who had to flee to other cities were prepared instruments, usable in the hands of the Spirit.

They knew by experience what a church should be, how it should be organized, how it should carry on its work and witness and how it should face persecution. It is stated that those who fled to Antioch had gifts for preaching and teaching. If these believers had gone from a modern congregation in which the ministry of the Word was the responsibility of one man, while the other members did little more than attend the services to be led in worship and instructed, how restricted would have been their usefulness. The scattering of such a congregation would have brought little result. Indeed, something would have had to be done to keep in touch with them to prevent them from being engulfed in the world. But when the Jerusalem congregation was scattered it meant that each one who fled was an active and capable witness sent forth to evangelize.

Antioch was not the second congregation formed. Other congregations, filled with the Spirit, had already been springing up in Judea, Galilee and Samaria (Acts 9:31). Philip, who had been one the Deacons in Jerusalem, but later became an Evangelist, was one of those who took part in the establishing of these congregations. The form of organization in these churches was the same as in Jerusalem. The men who went from Jerusalem to Antioch were not unaccustomed to the existence of new congregations and would introduce no change in the established procedure. The Holy Spirit did not establish a new order in Antioch, so far as the structure of the church is concerned. In the new congregations there was no indecision as to the form which their organization should take, or experimenting; nor was there only a partial introduction of the permanent order. The Holy Spirit filled each church from the beginning and established it firmly and fully in accordance with the divine order. Wherever He fills a church, that order will be the natural medium for its corporate life and witness and it will always be found a sufficient medium for the work of the Holy Spirit.

When the church in Jerusalem heard of the new company of believers gathered out at Antioch, Barnabas was sent to aid them. Evidently he had gifts of the Spirit to contribute in the work of establishing the new congregation, gifts that were necessary and that the preachers and teachers already there did not possess. Naturally he would have, for God had been preparing him to go forth as a church-planter.

He had been for seven years an active member of the congregation in Jerusalem and had become one of its leading men. No doubt he was one of the Elders and, therefore, thoroughly acquainted with its structure and life. Possibly he had been cooperating in the establishing of churches in Judea and Samaria. He was a man who had been proved; he was filled with the Spirit and experienced in ministry. He was a Jew, but not of Palestine. He was Greek-speaking and a native of Cyprus, which formed part of the province of Cilicia, of which Tarsus, Paul's native city, was the capital. Antioch, the capital of Syria, lay not far south of Tarsus and was on the highway between that city and Jerusalem. It is certain that both Barnabas and Paul were already acquainted with Antioch.

The procedure followed by the church in Jerusalem in the

sending out of Barnabas is not stated, but we can take it for granted that he was sent in obedience to the will of the Lord revealed by the Holy Spirit, as when he and Paul went forth from Antioch.

Barnabas, after seeing the work of the Spirit that was in progress at Antioch, continued his journey to Tarsus where Paul was witnessing (Gal. 1:21-23). He knew that Paul had been called to preach the Gospel to the Gentiles, so he sought him to join in the ministry at Antioch. It is recorded that for a year these two carried on a teaching ministry there as 'guests of the church' (Acts 11:26, Weymouth, 5th Ed.).

During this year the Holy Spirit, through the prophecy of Agabus, notified the church of an impending famine, so without delay financial aid was sent to Jerusalem. Barnabas and Paul were chosen as the bearers of the gift which they were to deliver to the Elders. It is significant that financial assistance did not go from Jerusalem to Antioch but from Antioch to Jerusalem. No money was sent to Antioch to help establish the work. It was taken for granted that the new congregation would be self-supporting from the beginning. Nor did either Barnabas or Paul receive support from Jerusalem. They had been earning their living, Barnabas in Jerusalem and Paul in Tarsus, and it seems they continued to do so in Antioch.

Of the church in Antioch, Campbell Morgan says:

How was the Christian Church in Antioch constituted? Certain men of Cyprus and Cyrene had preached in Antioch to these Greek men the Gospel of the Lord Christ; and these men hearing the Gospel of the Lord Christ had believed and been baptized by the Holy Ghost. That company of men and women, in living union with the living Christ by the baptism of the Holy Spirit, constituted the Church. There had been no consecration of a building. There had been no apostolic visitation. The Church was not the result of official action, but of the proclamation of the Lord, and belief in Him and baptism into His life, by the overruling of God... Presently they cooperated with the Church in Jerusalem; but Antioch was independent of Jerusalem; and the Holy Spirit could speak to the Church in Antioch.

In that Church in Antioch were gifts bestowed by the Spirit: 'prophets and teachers'. Whence came these gifts? From the Lord Himself. How? By the bestowment of the Holy Spirit.

Some of the men are named. Barnabas, whom we know well as a man of Cyprus. Simeon was called Niger... It may be he was a Jew... It may be, as some believe, that he was an Ethiopian, a proselyte who had taken a Jewish name. Lucius was of Cyrene. This was a man with a Latin name. Manaen was the foster-brother of the Herod who murdered John. He was in this company gifted either as a prophet or a teacher. And, finally, Saul. What a fine and glorious blend there was in this company. Thus the Spirit bestows gifts upon men![1]

We are given a vivid glimpse into the manner of working of this church in the first four verses of the thirteenth chapter of Acts:

> Now there were in the Church that was in Antioch certain prophets and teachers; as Barnabas, and Simeon that was called Niger, and Lucius of Cyrene, and Manaen, which had been brought up with Herod the Tetrarch, and Saul. As they ministered to (were worshipping — Weymouth and Moffatt) the Lord, and fasted, the Holy Ghost said, 'Separate me Barnabas and Saul for the work whereunto I have called them.' And when they had fasted and prayed, and laid their hands on them, they sent them away (lit.. let them go). So they, being sent forth by the Holy Ghost, departed unto Seleucia, and from thence they sailed to Cyprus.

As it had been in the Jerusalem church, here also faithful ministry in the power of the Spirit was accompanied continually by earnest and humble seeking of His will in prayer (Acts 2:42). While they are thus engaged, the Holy Spirit reveals the will of the Lord, the Head of the Church. When the Spirit had spoken to them through Agabus, they immediately obeyed. Now it concerns Barnabas and Saul: these two must go forth to bear the Gospel message to those still in darkness. While in Antioch, Barnabas and Paul were listed among the 'prophets and teachers', but now they are called to the ministry of Evangelist, or churchplanter.

It was the custom for pious Jews to attend a public gathering twice a week in the Synagogue to worship God and to fast. It is a similar gathering of the church that is referred to here.

Some, reading this passage superficially, have taken it to mean that it was to the five mentioned that the Holy Spirit spoke, not to the congregation, and have based upon it the practice of taking from the congregation the responsibility and privilege of knowing the will of the Lord and doing it, and giving that responsibility and privilege to a group of Elders. This is contrary to the principles laid down by our Lord in His teaching regarding the Church. It is contrary to the equal priesthood of all believers recognized by all the New Testament writers and carefully practised by the New Testament missionaries in all their dealings with the churches. (See "The Church a Theocracy", p. 137;

---

[1] *The Acts of the Apostles.*

pp. 141-144; and pp. 281, 282; 304-305. In the New Testament churches there is no instance of the guidance of the Spirit for a congregation being given to a special group within the congregation. That would substitute an oligarchy for the theocratic government of Christ. Even the Twelve were not given such a position. There can be no intermediaries, be they individuals or groups, between Christ, who is in the midst, and the congregation. No man can have special sacerdotal or ecclesiastical privileges above his fellow members. To do so is to introduce the principle of sacerdotalism — Nicolaitianism, which the Lord hates.

If in this passage it is the group of preachers who receive the guidance, it means the introduction of an entirely new procedure, a new principle, the application of which would have far reaching consequences. Carried to its logical conclusion it would give us the Roman Catholic Church with its priestly intermediaries and hierarchy.

But in the Greek there is no lack of clearness as to the meaning. The word translated "ministered" is a term used of public ministry. Weymouth's translation, "as they were worshipping", quoted above, gives the true meaning.[1]

How did the Holy Spirit speak to the Church? We are not told. The fact that the manner is not specified leaves a certain freedom of method to the Spirit. It might be that while they were at prayer one of the brethren, believing it was the Lord's will, said so, following which all felt the assurance that it was God's will. (That was the procedure in the case of the vision of the man of Macedonia given to Paul and confirmed to his fellow workers.) Or, it might be that Barnabas or Paul stated that he had heard God's call and that then the Church received the confirmation. However it was, the Holy Spirit made his will known clearly to all, not by a majority vote, or even by a unanimous vote, but by a clear inner conviction given to all by the Holy Spirit, a conviction so definite that all knew it to be nothing less than the voice of the Spirit.

What was done was not the fruit of human reasoning or plans. Christ was present in the congregation building His Church. The

---

[1] Campbell Morgan says of this, "These men of Antioch, not the teachers only, were engaged in sacred ministry to the Lord," *The Acts of The Apostles*, p. 310.

time had come for another step forward in His will and He made it known to a congregation that was in prayer before Him, listening to His voice and prepared to obey.

The church obeys without question. They might have reasoned with apparent justice that these two were required in Antioch. 'They are our teachers; their ministry is being blessed here and should we not establish well the work at home before spreading out to other parts?': so they might have spoken; but no, the Holy Spirit had revealed the Lord's will and the wisdom of the Head could not be doubted. After all, the Church's primary duty was to evangelize the world, in obedience to the Lord's command. How great would have been the loss to the Church had· these two stayed in Antioch!

There followed the simple ceremony of the laying on of hands, symbolising the anointing by the Holy Spirit for the work to which He had called and the participation of the whole Church in the call. This act speaks of the unity and inter-relatedness of the Church. The call given to one member affects the whole Body. The ministry Barnabas and Paul were sent to was a part of the Church's ministry. The whole Church shared in the responsibility, and the Elders, by the laying on of hands, acknowledged this, saying in effect, 'As you go, called, sent and equipped by the Holy Spirit, we, the Church, go with you!" Barnabas and Paul acknowledged it by waiting until the confirmation of their call was given to the congregation. This was, of course, in no sense a commision to preach the Gospel; Barnabas and Paul already were preachers of the Gospel. They had received their commission from the Lord, the gift from the Holy Spirit (Gal. 1:11, 12; 1 Cor. 12:11).

The laying on of hands, or the touching of another with the hand, was commonly practiced in the Early Church, as it had been also in Old Testament times. It is just a simple and beautiful expression of spiritual unity between the one who prays and the one for whom prayer is made. The symbol was used on a variety of occasions. Indeed, it could be used any time when one prays for another. The raising of the hand, as in Luke 24:50, has the same significance.

The laying on of hands has no virtue in itself; the power is in the prayer if it is according to God's will. It is not an ordinance as baptism or the Lord's Supper. No command is given concerning it to the Church. It is not enjoined as a testimony. It has nothing to do with spiritual growth or obedience or membership in the Body of Christ. It conveys no power or authority. It is never considered as important in itself. It is nothing more than a symbolic gesture; nevertheless, as such, its meaning is rich and beautiful. It was only as a gesture that our Lord used it. In that sense only it was used in the Early Church. When rightly understood it is spiritually profitable and should be employed in the Church.

Barnabas and Saul went on their way, sent, as it says, by the Holy Spirit. The church did not send them; it 'let them go', or 'released' them — for that is the meaning of the word used.

There are a number of important things to be noted here. Antioch was a predominantly Gentile congregation of recent converts, a newly founded congregation in the 'mission field'. Barnabas had been sent from Jerusalem, so should not the confirmation of his call to go further afield have been given by the Holy Spirit to Jerusalem? Or should not Barnabas have referred the matter back to Jerusalem for consideration? Evidently not; he was not under the direction of the Church but of the Holy Spirit. The Holy Spirit gave the confirmation through the Church, but that could be done through the part of the Church at Antioch just as through the part at Jerusalem. The Church is one, and the gathering in Antioch is as much the Church as the gathering in Jerusalem. The Head of the Church is present in every gathering.

Normally, the confirmation will come through the part of the Church with which God's servant is ministering at the time. So a congregation of new converts with dark skins in a foreign land is equally a part of the Church with the old-established white congregation from which the missionary went forth, and can receive the Holy Spirit's guidance just as directly and has entered into all the privileges and responsibilities of the Church on a full equality with all other assemblies of the Church. It is evident that the Holy Spirit — and Barnabas and Paul — considered the congregation in Antioch to be just as fully a part of the Body of Christ as the congregation in Jerusalem. The Elders in Antioch could act in the laying on of hands as representing the whole Body of Christ just as the Elders in Jerusalem.

The confirmation given to the Church by the voice of the Spirit regarding the call of Barnabas and Paul is highly important.

God's servants waited for it. They did not consider it as ordina-
tion to ministry but merely as confirmation of the fact that they
were called as Evangelists, a fact which they already knew. The
call is made known not only to the individual called but also to
the Church. The Church is one Body, an organism. All its members are interdependent, all its gifts are interrelated, and all its
ministries are related to the whole Body. These matters are given
further consideration in later chapters.

It is noticeable that no organization had been formed to unite
the different congregations that were springing up. There was
complete and effective unity and cooperation, but it was entirely
spiritual, the natural outcome of the fact that Christ was being
permitted to build His Church and that the Holy Spirit had freedom to teach, lead, work His will and coordinate the activities
of the churches. There were not even congregational barriers. It
was just one Church meeting in different places. Believers from
Jerusalem preach the Gospel in Antioch because they happen to
be there. The converts gather with them. Barnabas goes from
Jerusalem and Paul from Tarsus to help them. Agabus and other
preachers from Jerusalem visit Antioch and minister freely there.
The Antioch believers feel responsible to help the poor in the
Jerusalem gathering. It is all just one Body, its members cooperating in full unity under the guidance of the Spirit.

Why did the Holy Spirit initiate the world missionary ministry
of the Church at Antioch and not at Jerusalem? And why did the
Twelve take no part in this first step? The reason is obvious. The
Jerusalem congregation was Jewish. The Twelve were also, in a
very definite sense, Jewish. But the congregation in Antioch was
neither Jewish nor Gentile. It represents, as we have seen, the
complete development of God's purpose for the Church in which
there is "neither Greek nor Jew, circumcision nor uncircumcision,
Barbarian, Scythian, bond nor free, but Christ is all and in all."
The company of Evangelists that had its beginning in Antioch
was formed on this same principle: it was a mixed company,
neither Jewish nor Gentile. Differences of race and nationality
were abolished and all were one in Christ. The Twelve had their
roots deep in Judaism; the company of Evangelists had all its
roots in the Church and is representative of the Church in its
full significance. Later, the Twelve cooperated in the ministry of
world-wide evangelism, but it was not as the Twelve that they

did so. They laboured as Evangelists cooperating with the other Evangelists.

This is a fact of no little importance. Unfortunately it has not been generally understood. Failure to perceive it has obscured to some extent the significance of the ministry both of the Apostles and of the company of Evangelists. It has been thought that the Twelve were slack in fulfilling the command to evangelize the world and stayed too long in Jerusalem. There is no suggestion in Scripture that that was so. On the contrary, it is evident that the different moves at this period were timed by the Holy Spirit in accordance with God's purpose and mark the successive steps in bringing to pass God's full thought for His Church.

It was the Church in its complete development as seen at Antioch — the One Body, indwelt, led and empowered by the Spirit, recognizing no distinctions of race, nationality or social position — that Barnabas and Paul went forth to extend throughout the world. It was congregations after this pattern that they established wherever the Holy Spirit led them. The structure of the Church will be considered in detail in later chapters; meanwhile we shall follow the steps of this new party of Evangelists and note the principles that governed their ministry.

As Saul went forward to the ministry to the Gentiles to which he had been appointed, a significant change takes place. No longer does he use the Jewish name Saul; henceforth he is known by the Gentile name Paul.

CHAPTER VII

THE TRAINING OF THE CHURCH-PLANTER

THREE times in Paul's Epistles it is emphasized that those who would occupy places of responsibility in the Church must first have been proved and have shown themselves called and worthy. This certainly was true of those called of God to the ministry of Evangelist in the Early Church.

One is at first surprised to find that it was not until about seven years after Pentecost that the beginning was made at Antioch in the evangelisation of the Gentiles. God does not hasten as men hasten. Experience can come only through experience, and that takes time — not months, but years.

The time was not being wasted. God had chosen a number of instruments and during those years He was preparing them. Such great and rapid progress was made in New Testament times in the evangelisation of the world that it is easy to overlook the fact that no short-cuts were taken in the preparation of those whom God used in that work. It was due, in no small measure, to the thoroughness of the preparation of the instruments that such results were obtained.

God requires fully prepared men for His work in the building of His Church. When man thinks that something less than that can be made to do because of the apparent need for haste, serious defects are introduced in the laying of the foundations and the structure that is raised is faulty and inadequate. Man's haste blocks the way for the effective working of the Holy Spirit. Second-rate spiritual instruments can bring only second-rate spiritual results.

We shall see also that God has His own way of preparing His instruments — a way which He has always used, whether He was dealing with an Abraham, a Jacob, a Moses, a David, a Peter, a Paul, a Luther, a Knox, a Madam Guyon, a Murray McCheyne, a Muller, or a Hudson Taylor. It is by thorough training in the school of hard experience with much testing and proving — and God commissions none without it. Nor has He ever accepted a substitute for it.

We have already seen that this was the method used by our Lord in the preparation of the Twelve. To be filled with the Spirit is not sufficient. It is essential, but there must also be knowledge and experience. It is sufficient for the preaching of the Gospel and witness, as at Pentecost, but not for ministry that requires the exercise of spiritual authority and leadership.

The great majority of those called to the ministry of Evangelist in the Early Church were men of more or less the same social standing as those whom the Lord chose as His Apostles. They were not ignorant men, but they were neither influential, rich nor learned. God's purpose in this was to 'confound the wisdom of the wise' of this world.

Secular education and culture are good things and serve useful purposes, but they belong to the natural, not to the spiritual sphere. We would not depreciate the value of the mental discipline and the store of information that education gives. God has so made us that mental exercise is necessary to mental development and health just as physical exercise is necessary to physical development and health. Mental development fits us for life. It is our duty to do all possible to fit ourselves for life. But let us not confound the natural with the spiritual. No amount of mental development will confer spiritual wisdom or power. Nor does it add to spiritual power. There is a profound significance in the fact that Christ chose men not possessed of much of this world's learning. It would be foolish to say that the learning and culture of that day were less highly regarded than our modern learning and culture are today. On the contrary, the New Testament record shows that the learned, the rich and the powerful were just as influential then and that they were proud, exclusive and disdainful of the 'ignorant and unlearned' preachers of the Gospel.

Such a criticism did not cause the Apostles to feel the need of more secular learning and culture. Paul did not feel that the young men who accompanied him required it. Their reliance was on a power that was greater than the power of the mightiest of men and on a wisdom compared with which the deepest knowledge of man is so immature and incomplete as to be reckoned 'foolishness'. Had they stooped to grasp at what fhe world counts power and wisdom they would have let go that which is infinitely greater. Instead of triumphing, they would soon have been overwhelmed. It was not until the second century that philosopher-theologians established schools for the giving of such instruction.

The preparation of the Evangelist, like that of the Disciple, was intensely practical. Experience, coupled with a thorough acquaintance with God's Word, gave him an understanding of that Word that was profound and practical. His message was rooted deep in personal experience: he witnessed to that which he knew and had proved.

We shall consider the preparation given to some of the New Testament Evangelists:

Paul

Having been brought up a strict Pharisee, and having studied under Gamaliel, Paul had an extensive knowledge of the Old Testament Scriptures. On the day of his conversion, when about thirty years of age, on the road to Damascus, he offered himself for Christ's service, crying, "What wouldst thou have me to do, Lord?" He was told then what his mission was to be: he was to go to "the Gentiles, unto whom now I send thee to open their eyes and to turn them from darkness to light and from the power of Satan unto God, that they may receive forgiveness of sins and inheritance among them that are sanctified by faith that is in me" (Acts 26:18).

This call was in accord with the new order. Every one who becomes a member of the Body of Christ is at once appointed by God to a ministry in that Body (1 Cor. 12:11, 18). Paul's history from this moment is not the history of the man but of the carrying out of God's purpose through him. His conversion, call and preparation all belong to the Church Dispensation. He had not been in the company of disciples that followed the Lord and were taught by Him prior to Calvary. He had not known Christ in the flesh. His instruction and preparation were the work of the Holy Spirit now acting in Christ's place in the Church.

After his conversion, Paul preached the Gospel boldly in the synagogue in Damascus, being given wisdom to confound those who opposed and to prove from the Old Testament that Christ was indeed the Son of God. It was normal that the gift of preaching should be manifested immediately. Then he withdrew to the Arabian desert. There he remains out of sight for three years until his return to Damascus, where his life is threatened, and his visit to Jerusalem, where Barnabas presents him to the brethren. His sojourn in the desert was a period when he had to go through the discipline of waiting. God had first to prepare him before he could send him forth to his work. The possession of the gift of preaching was not a sufficient preparation. He needed much himself before he could instruct others. What followed later shows how deep were the foundations laid by the Holy Spirit during this time and how intimately Paul had come to know his Lord.

It is a truly marvellous thing that the zealous Pharisee, deeply versed in the theology of his sect, should have had the structure of his religious beliefs so completely changed in so short a time. In his Christian doctrine there is no trace of the Pharisee. What was error has been completely unlearned. The truth revealed in Christ is visioned without a shadow of uncertainty. Grace is based upon law but untainted with legalism. The new pact is the fulfilment of the old but the principles of the two are never confounded. Such a thorough and complete transformation in the thinking of such a man, only the Spirit of God could accomplish. Such is the light that the Holy Spirit will give to every truly born-again child of God.

No doubt while in Arabia Paul had witnessed to the Bedouins, the inhabitants of the desert then as now.[1] Nor would he have been silent when residing in his own city of Tarsus, after his visit to Jerusalem. His own kindred and the wide circle of his acquaintances in that great city of learning and trade would undoubtedly have heard from his lips of the Christ whose service he had entered on the road to Damascus. It was while at Tarsus, evidently, that he had the remarkable vision he speaks of in 2 Cor. 12:1-10, and it was there that Barnabas sought him, desiring his cooperation in the ministry of teaching in the new church at Antioch.

The year which he spent at Antioch with Barnabas was an experience of the utmost value for the future Evangelist. A new congregation was being formed and recent converts were being instructed. He laboured in company with Barnabas, a man of longer experience who had seen the growth of the Jerusalem

---

[1] Cf. Gal. 1:16,17.

church from its early days and who, evidently, had taken a responsible part in its work and oversight. Here Paul learned by actual experience what he required to know about the organization, oversight and ministry of the local congregation. He went with Barnabas to take the church's offering to the Elders of the church in Jerusalem. With the church in Antioch he engaged in the 'ministry before the Lord' and the 'fasting and prayer' and saw how the Holy Spirit spoke to the church, revealing to it the will of the Head. Then, finally, the confirmation of his call was given to the church and he set forth with Barnabas, sent by the Holy Spirit to·the work to which the Head of the Church had appointed him on the road to Damascus.

Paul was not going out from a seminary to learn how to put into practice the theories he had been taught. He had already preached the Gospel, faced persecution, taught new converts and taken part in the founding of a new congregation. He was taught in the Word, experienced and proved and thoroughly acquainted with the work he was being sent to do.

The principles employed by the Holy Spirit in Paul's training did not differ from those used by our Lord in the preparation of the Twelve. In both cases the instruction was based upon practical experience.

As we have seen, Paul received his call on the day of his conversion, but it is only now that he is permitted to go forth. The confirmation of his call had to be given to his brethren. Thus his call was related to the ministry of the Church: he was a minister of the Church and his work was a part of the Church's work. He was not an isolated or independent worker but a member of the Body, performing that part of the Body's work to which he was appointed of God.

Because Paul had 'sat at the feet of Gamaliel' and was an educated man, it has been assumed by some that there is to be found the secret of the success of his ministry. However, no support is to be found in the Acts or in Paul's Epistles for such an assumption. On the contrary, he is at great pains to make it clear that he had determined "not to know anything but Jesus Christ and Him crucified", nor to employ 'enticing words of man's wisdom', but to preach entirely in the power and demonstration of the Holy Spirit. If Paul's declarations in the first and second chapters of 1 Corinthians, in the third chapter of Philippians, in Galatians 2:20 and in many other places, are accepted as sincere and true, then we must acknowledge the fact that his power and authority were the result of his faith in God, his absolute yieldedness to the Holy Spirit and his close communion with his Lord, which permitted the Holy Spirit to manifest His power through him. Paul's success came from something infinitely higher and deeper and mightier than the learning and wisdom and training of men. His power was entirely spiritual and his own testimony is that, to obtain that spiritual power, he, with all his knowledge and pride, had to go down into death as utterly worthless and undone.

Barnabas

Not a great deal is told of Barnabas' preparation. Indeed, it is only of Paul that details are given, for he is the one presented to us by the Holy Spirit as the typical Evangelist of the Church.

Barnabas was a Levite and no doubt was well versed in the Old Testament Scriptures. He had joined himself with the Lord's people shortly after Pentecost and seems to have been one of the Elders in the Jerusalem church. He was, therefore, a man of proved Christian character and of no little experience in the Church's ministry. It is said of him that "he was a good man and full of the Holy Ghost." (Acts 11:24). It was about seven years after his conversion that he was sent to Antioch, so ample time had been given for a thorough preparation. The confidence of the church in Jerusalem in him is expressed in their sending him to Antioch.

Timothy

It was from his mother and grandmother, Godly women, that Timothy received his knowledge of Scripture. He had been taught it from childhood. His conversion probably took place during Paul's first visit to Lystra. He knew how the Jews were stirred to hatred and how Paul had been stoned on that occasion. In spite of the persecution, Timothy had become an active and faithful witness, not only in Lystra but also in Iconium, so that when Paul returned on his second journey, several years later, Timothy was recommended by the brethren in both these places (Acts 16:1-3; 1 Tim. 4:14).

Silas

Like Barnabas, Silas was from the Jerusalem church. He had become one of the chief men in that congregation, gifted as a preacher (Acts 15:32), possibly an Elder, and was chosen to accompany Barnabas and Paul as one of the bearers of the letter in which the Jerusalem brethren repudiated the judaisers who had been disturbing the church in Antioch.

Mark

Mark's case is instructive. He was related to Barnabas who took him on the first missionary journey but he withdrew in Pamphilia. His call was not confirmed to the church by the Spirit. It was because of all this that Paul considered he should not be taken on the second journey. Barnabas insisted on taking him and this caused the separation of the two Evangelists. Years later we find Mark among Paul's companions and Paul states that he was profitable to him.

There is no evidence that Mark, when Barnabas first took him, was a man of experience who had proved himself in ministry in the local church, as was the case with Barnabas and Paul. That he was called of God as an Evangelist, there is no doubt because he later engaged profitably in that ministry. That he became a man filled with the Holy Spirit and a useful instrument in God's hands is very evident, not only from Paul's later commendation of him, but also from the fact that he was used by the Spirit to write the Gospel which bears his name. The reason for his initial failure was his lack of spiritual preparation at that time. He was not yet spiritually equipped. Possibly, big-hearted Barnabas let his sympathy for his young kinsman influence him to go ahead of the Lord, and the inevitable trouble developed. The best will fail before they are adequately prepared by the Holy Spirit. Mark's case makes very clear the need for such a preparation.

Philip

As one of the seven Deacons chosen in the Jerusalem church, Philip was a man "full of faith and of the Holy Ghost". Not very long afterwards he was one of those whom God used in the second step of the preaching of the Gospel — the witness in

Samaria, and we see him there as one truly led and used by the Holy Spirit. About eighteen years later we find him as 'Philip the Evangelist', receiving Paul and his company in his home in Caesarea. Just when he was called to leave his ministry as a Deacon at Jerusalem and become an Evangelist is not stated.

These cases make it evident that a definite method was followed by the Holy Spirit in the preparation of those called to be Evangelists. The men He sent were thoroughly experienced and proved. No exceptions were made by the Spirit and when man did so, failure was the result.

The steps in the Evangelist's preparation may be summarized as follows:

1. He was personally and definitely called of God to that ministry.

2. He had a thorough knowledge of the Scriptures.

3. There was a period of preparation covering several years, during which he proved himself in the ministry of the local church, manifesting the gifts of the Spirit which had been given him and acquiring knowledge and experience.

4. Only when that preparation was complete was he released by the Spirit to go forth.

5. Then the confirmation of his call and his going was given to the brethren among whom he was ministering.

6. There follows the participation of the church in his call through the laying on of hands.

7. He goes forth, sent by the Holy Spirit, in company with other Evangelists, gaining further experience and cooperating in the work as the Holy Spirit leads.

CHAPTER VIII

A COMPANY OF EVANGELISTS

THE basic factor in the ministry of the Evangelist is the fact that
Christ goes with him. Just as in the assembly of the Church all
authority and power come from Christ who is present in the
midst, so also in the Evangelist's ministry all depends upon the
active presence of the Lord with him (Matt. 18:20; 28:19, 20).

His authority is the fact that he goes in Christ's Name, sent by
Him and that Christ Himself goes with him; his power comes
from Christ who speaks and works through him. That this is so
is made very clear in the record of the labours of the New Testament Evangelists. The record of their labours is the record of
the acts of the Lord as He led them and spoke and worked
through them.

Simple Beginnings

The group of Evangelists whose history is given us in the New
Testament as the typical group of church-planters had a small
beginning and a comparatively slow growth. At the first, Barna-
bas was the leader, but he lost that place when he separated from
Paul — and, evidently, from the Lord's purpose — in favour of
Mark. From that time the record of the group continues with
Paul as the leader.

This missionary company began with two members: Barnabas
and Paul. (Mark was with them, but he was taken by Barnabas,
not sent by the Spirit. He abandoned them at Perga.) At the
commencement of the work, for the preaching of the Gospel, the
teaching of the new converts and the establishing of the first
congregations, two was a sufficient number. It provided the necessary fellowship in prayer and ministry.

After the separation between Paul and Barnabas, Paul continued the work accompanied by Silas. But soon a third is added
— Timothy. Then Luke joins the company at Troas; and from
then on, in the course of the years that followed, one after
another were joined to the company as God called them and the
Holy Spirit prepared them. As the work went on and the field of
labour extended and the number of churches multiplied, it became
necessary that the number of Evangelists in the company should
increase, so the Holy Spirit added to their number as there was
need.

As we follow them in their work and in the growth of the company, the principles that governed their fellowship become clear.
In that group we have given to us a typical missionary fellowship. Missionary organization, policy, methods of work, Church
organization and supervision, candidates, leadership, financial
support — all these and every other problem of missionary
endeavour are seen in their practical application to the task as
well as in their relation to the basic principles of the Church.

When the Evangelists went forth from Antioch, those who remained behind did not form themselves into a Missionary Board
or Council, nor did they undertake responsibility for their direction or support. They did not even consider that confirmation
regarding the future movements of these missionaries should be
given through them. The Jerusalem church had not taken that
position towards Barnabas when he went to Antioch.

The Antioch brethren would certainly continue steadfast in
prayer for Barnabas and Paul. Possibly, at times, they contributed
towards their material support though it is evident that there
were long periods when they did not do so.[1] Those who went
forth were sent by the Spirit; they were responsible to God, and
looked directly to Him for the supply of all things and to the
Holy Spirit for guidance. As Dr. Chapell puts it:

The Holy Spirit is the missionary board of the Church, selecting
the pioneers and assigning them their fields of labour, and directing
their journeys, sometimes sending them contrary to the dictates of
human wisdom. (Acts 13:2-4; 14:26,27; 16:6-10.) [2]

They were not a company of missionaries dependent upon a

---

[1] Cf. Phil. 4:15.
[2] *Biblical and Practical Theology*, p. 112.

'Home Base'. They were dependent upon God and established churches that were dependent upon God. They found a sufficient Base in the presence of the Lord with them and in His power and faithfulness to fulfil His Word.

However, we must not conclude that the Evangelists acted independently. Wherever they were they worked in close fellowship with the missionary group, with the congregation in that place and with the Church as a whole. Fellowship and confirmation of guidance came from their fellow-labourers and from the part of the Church with which they happened to be at the moment.

They were church-planters, a ministry that is related to the Church as a whole. In his letters to various local churches, Paul stresses the fact that he was appointed by Christ as a minister of the Church. He was not the minister of a congregation. His ministry was to the Church at large, the whole Church. To him the congregation in Antioch or anywhere else was just a gathering of the one Church — of the members who happened to reside in that locality. He never speaks of himself or of his ministry as being related in any special sense to Damascus, where he was baptized, or to Antioch or to any other church. So it was also with all his fellow-workers. They did not consider that they had a special attachment or responsibility to the congregations with which they had originally fellowshipped. The ministry to which they were appointed was to the whole Church. They planted new congregations and ministered to any congregation, anywhere, that was in need of their ministry.

One important outcome of this was that wherever these missionaries went their association was not with some congregation or group of congregations in a distant, foreign land, but simply with the Church. They were as definitely and closely related to the converts won in a new field as to any other members of the Body of Christ. This influenced profoundly both their own outlook and that of the converts, avoiding the associating of the Gospel they preached with a foreign organization or country.

To understand the structure of the missionary group and its relation to the Church, it is essential to understand that it was not a subsidiary of the Church as is the modern missionary society. It was the most vital, indispensable part of the Church's life. The missionaries were the leaders of the Church, not agents of it. Their ministry was not only to new churches but to the whole Church. The Evangelist was just as responsible to see to the welfare of the 'Home churches' as of those in new fields. This aspect of the Evangelist's ministry is dealt with in later chapters.

International but Not Foreign

The composition of this company of Evangelists is of great interest. Among Paul's companions in ministry the following are named: Barnabas, Mark, Luke, Silas, Timothy, Titus, Epaphras, Tychicus, Trophimus, Aristarchus, Apollos and Demas. Barnabas separated, accompanied by Mark, but later Mark again became one of the company.

Paul, like Barnabas, was a Jew but not of Palestine. He was a native of Tarsus, the capital of Cilicia, and a Roman citizen. He set out from the church in Antioch. Barnabas was a Helenistic Jew from the Island of Cyprus, a part of the Province of Cilicia, and came from the church in Jerusalem. Therefore, Paul and Barnabas were both Cilicians. Luke was a Gentile, possibly a native of Antioch, the capital of Syria. Because he bore a slave name it is considered possible that he was a slave who had obtained his freedom. It was not unusual for a slave to be a physician. Silas, another Helenistic Jew, was a Roman citizen. He was from the church in Jerusalem. Timothy, with a Greek father and a Jewish mother, was from Lystra in Lycaonia, on the bare tableland in the south of the central plateau of Asia Minor. He was one of Paul's converts. Titus, a Greek and uncircumcised was also converted through Paul's ministry. Aristarchus was from Macedonia, Tychicus and Trophimus from the province of Asia in Asia Minor. Several races, countries and languages were represented. All spoke Greek. A number also knew Hebrew. No doubt several were acquainted with other languages used in the regions from which they came. As we have already noted, they were mostly men of humble rank, though, apparently, not without some education.

Here is not a group of foreign missionaries from a 'Homeland' assisted by 'native brethren'. Indeed, we see that God called men who were natives of the regions that were to be evangelized. Although several were Jews, none was born in Jerusalem or Palestine, with the probable exception of Mark. All were natives of Gentile lands, with, possibly, that one exception.

Moreover, the Holy Spirit sent these missionaries first to their native regions. Barnabas and Paul, when they set out from Antioch, were both led first to Barnabas' native Cyprus. From there

6

they journeyed north evangelizing in the cities of Pisidia and Lycaonia, neighbouring territories in Asia Minor on the west and north of Cilicia. They were never more than about 150 miles distant from the frontier of their own Province. To them that whole section of Asia Minor would be familiar, native territory. They were not "foreign missionaries" but missionaries to the world, including the homelands.

On the so-called second and third journeys, Paul, after ministering again in his own native Cilicia, went gradually further afield, to Greece and Macedonia, and later to the other Provinces of Asia Minor, but, as he did so, we find men from these regions being joined to the company: Timothy, from Lycaonia, Titus a Greek, Tychicus and Trophimus from Asia, Aristarchus from Macedonia, etc. Also, it will be noted that when members of the company were sent to visit different churches, those chosen were often men who came from the region to be visited. It is not without deep significance that the Holy Spirit guided in that way. While the company of Evangelists was an international group, it could not appear as a markedly foreign group anywhere because almost everywhere they went there were some of their number from that district and neighbouring regions.

This was of immense advantage to the preachers of the 'new religion'. They were not a group of foreigners from a distant land sent by a foreign organization and supported by foreign money. There were some among them who understood the people, their language, customs and religion and, no doubt, already had personal contacts of one kind or another among them. They did not appear to the people, therefore, as strange and outlandish. The suspicion and prejudice naturally aroused by something purely foreign was largely avoided and a more ready hearing obtained.[1]

It should be noted that, usually, there were not many missionaries together in any place. Occasionally we find a larger num-

---

[1] Typical of the reaction produced in modern mission fields by foreign control and money is the following statement by A. Chakravarty, a prominent Indian pastor:

"It would be no exaggeration to say that far and away the most serious stumbling block to the real progress of the Gospel in this country at the present time is the foreign leadership and domination of the Indian Church. That domination cripples and paralyses the Church and renders it utterly unfit for the task of evangelism. At whatever cost, this evil should forthwith be exorcised from the body

ber gathered together for a brief period, but as a rule, after the group had become more numerous, they were fairly widely scattered. When breaking new ground, two or three always cooperated, but when revisiting established churches, one sometimes went alone, though frequently there were two.

Most of the Evangelists were from towns on caravan routes or busy ports and were accustomed to travelling. Journeying on foot, on horseback, by camel, or sailing ship, was not strange to them. It is interesting that Paul's trade was that of tent making. He wove the hair cloth for tents such as are used to this day by Arab travellers and desert dwellers in those regions. That must have given him wide contacts throughout Asia Minor and Syria, for Tarsus was an important centre of commerce.

Recruits

As the work spread, new recruits for the company of Evangelists were not brought from Jerusalem or Antioch. Several of the first Evangelists were from those churches but the later additions to the company were almost all Gentiles from the new churches in the 'mission fields' of Asia Minor and Europe. These, no matter where they were from, or of what race, were not received as 'native Evangelists' but as regular members of the company. In that company, all were actually, not just theoretically, one in Christ. Gentiles of various races and Jews worked together taking no account of such differences. It had to be so as the Body of Christ is one Body in which "there is neither Jew nor Greek, circumcision nor uncircumcision, Barbarian, Scythian, bond nor free: but Christ is all, and in all" (Col. 3:11). These Evangelists bore practical witness to this truth.

We have seen that the obtaining of recruits for the company was the work of God. He called them and the Holy Spirit pre-

---

of the Indian Church... To Hindu and Moslem eyes, foreign leadership and support of the Indian Church are a standing shame and disgrace to the Indian Christian... Not outstanding administrative ability and learning, but holiness of life, a deep humility and pastoral zeal are the qualities which are indispensable... Such graces are no monopoly of any single race, but God in His mercy vouchsafes them to African and European, Indian and Chinese alike, as He wills." — World Dominion, July-Aug., 1945.

pared them, joined them together and sent them forth. Barnabas desired that Paul should accompany him and the Holy Spirit set His seal upon it confirming it to the church. Paul had already been called. Later, Paul was led to take Silas and Timothy, and the churches concerned signified their assurance that it was God's will. The order is that the call is given to the individual concerned; the Holy Spirit leads those already engaged in the ministry to feel that God would have that one join with them; then this is confirmed by the Spirit to the local church.

There was no propaganda for the recruiting of candidates. The churches were taught that God would call whom He chose to the different ministries and prayer was made that He would thrust forth labourers. Fewer were sent than would be thought necessary today, but those who went were fully equipped and efficient and failures were few. With the methods which they employed, a small number sufficed to establish churches throughout a great region comprising different races, nations and languages.

The Holy Spirit's leadership was recognised and relied upon absolutely and nothing was interposed in any way to hinder His complete freedom of action. He was the worker, using the instruments He had chosen and prepared for the bearing of the testimony. Never were these instruments allowed to look to man for guidance and support. At all times and for all things they were dependent upon God. Moment by moment they had to know His will and everything depended upon their absolute obedience to it.

Spiritual failure on the part of any instrument meant that that one no longer received the Spirit's guidance; the power departed from him and he fell out by the way. So it happened with Demas.

Financial Support

The financial support of this company of Evangelists was entirely a spiritual problem. They went forth in faith. Before the Holy Spirit sent them, their preparation had been such that they feared not to go trusting God directly for all the supply of their temporal needs. The churches from which they went had not undertaken to support them. However, donations were sent to them from different churches and individuals, though, not infrequently, they supported themselves by working at their trades. The contributions which Paul writes of came from Macedonia. It was gifts from there that met his need while he ministered at Thessalonica and at Corinth in Greece (2 Cor. 11:8, 9). Again, when in prison in Rome, he acknowledges gifts from Macedonia, from the church in Philippi (Phil. 4:10-18). There is no doubt, of course, that other churches contributed, but it is interesting that the donations mentioned by Paul were from one of the more recently formed congregations. At one period it was the only church that ministered to his support (Phil. 4:15).

It is evident that new churches as they were formed were taught their responsibility to contribute to the support of the Evangelists. A congregation did not consider that its responsibility was principally towards those who had gone out from among them or from their own nation. In supporting Paul, the Macedonians were supporting a Cilician Jew from a church in Syria labouring in foreign lands.

A definite policy was followed by these Evangelists in regard to the receiving of financial support from the churches. They taught them their responsibilities in financial matters but never made requests for the supply of their own needs. Twice it is recorded that Paul asked the churches to pray for him that he might be enabled for the work, kept faithful and protected from danger, but there is no request for prayer that his financial needs be met.

Had Paul requested financial support of the churches, there is no doubt it would have been given as readily as were the gifts for the brethren in need in Jerusalem, but he would do nothing that could make it appear that he desired any man's silver or gold, or that his trust was in man and not in God. That some churches were not always as faithful as they should have been in this respect seems to be inferred in what he wrote to the Philippians (Phil. 4:15).

When he had occasion to refer to his own financial needs in letters to the churches, he was very careful to make it clear that he was making no appeal. After reminding the Corinthians that he had received nothing from them for preaching the Gospel to them, he states that he would continue to minister to them without charge (2 Cor. 11:9-12). Then, while he gratefully acknowledges the gifts from Philippi, he makes it plain that it is in God he trusts for the supply of his needs not in man. He testifies to God's faithfulness and explains the spiritual benefit he had derived from the times when he was permitted to suffer want.

Then he affirms with all the authority of personal experience that his God would also supply all their need (Phil. 4:19). His testimony was:

> I do not refer to this through fear of privation, for (for my part) I have learned, whatever be my outward experiences, to be content. I know both how to live in humble circumstances and how to live amid abundance. I am fully initiated into all the mysteries both of fulness and of hunger, of abundance and of want. I have strength for anything through Him who gives me power. (Phil. 4:11-13, Weymouth.)

It is very interesting to compare this with the advice he gave to the young missionary, Timothy:

> And godliness is gain, when associated with contentment; for we brought nothing into the world, nor can we carry anything out of it; and if we have food and clothing, with these we will be satisfied. But people who are determined to be rich fall into temptation and a snare, and into many unwise and pernicious ways which sink mankind in destruction and ruin. For from love of money all sorts of evils arise; and some have so hankered after money as to be led astray from the faith and be pierced through with countless sorrows. But you, O man of God, must flee from these things. (1 Tim. 6:6-11, Weymouth.)

These passages throw much light upon the financial principles that governed the lives of these Evangelists. No doubt Paul had in mind the recent case of Judas, the Treasurer of the Lord's company of disciples, whose love of money so corrupted his mind and heart that he betrayed his Lord for silver. Judas is not the only one that love of money has tempted. We can understand why the Lord called upon His disciples to leave all to follow Him and why the Evangelist is required to give a similar testimony.

Not only in the receiving of money for their own support did these early missionaries guard their actions most strictly against any possible misinterpretation, but also in the handling of gifts sent by the churches to Jerusalem. When Paul carried the gift, he had the churches choose men to accompany him as witnesses. He gives his reason for this in 2 Cor. 8:20, 21:

> For I guard myself against all suspicion which might be cast upon me in my administration of this bounty with which I am charged; being 'provident of good report' not only 'in the sight of the Lord', but also 'in the sight of men'. (Conybeare.)

The Gospel is Free

While gifts were accepted from even the most recently formed churches, it was not the practice of the Evangelists to receive financial support from the congregation to which they were ministering. Paul states his position emphatically in this matter in 1 Cor. 9:11-18:

> If I have sown for you the seed of spiritual gifts, would it be much if I were to reap some harvest from your carnal gifts? If others share this right over you, how much more should I? Yet I have not used my right, but forego every claim, lest I should by any means hinder the course of Christ's Glad-tidings. Know ye not that they who perform the service of the temple, live upon the revenues of the temple, and they who minister at the altar share with it in sacrifices? So also the Lord commanded those who publish the Glad-tidings to be maintained thereby. But I have not exercised any of these rights, nor do I write this that it may be practised in my own case. For I had rather die than suffer any man to make void my boasting. For, although I proclaim the Glad-tidings, yet this gives me no ground of boasting; for I am compelled to do so by order of my master. Yea, woe is me if I proclaim it not. For were my service of my own free choice, I might claim wages to reward my labour; but since I serve by compulsion, I am a slave entrusted with a stewardship. What then is my wage? It is to make the Glad-tidings free of cost where I carry it, that I may forego my right as an Evangelist. (Conybeare.)

Two fundamental principles are adduced here: (a) he who labours in the Gospel has a right to receive financial support; (b) the preaching of the Gospel is free. These two principles would seem to be contradictory. Paul is most definite in asserting both and it is clear that he was strictly faithful in practising both. He preached the Gospel without charge, accepting no payment from the congregation to which he was ministering. However, he accepted gifts from other congregations. It was the duty and privilege of other churches to send support to the Evangelists to enable them thus to preach the Gospel without charge to those to whom they went (2 Cor. 11:9). If the other congregations failed to send support, Paul still preached the Gospel without charge, and earned his living by working at his trade. So the two principles were applied without contradiction.

Paul said he would rather die than fail in this testimony and leave himself open to the charge that he sought wages from those to whom he preached. Evidently it is a most important part of the Evangelist's witness before the churches. While he has a right to be supported, the effect of his example makes it necessary to forego this right so far as those to whom he is actually ministering are concerned.

Wages cannot be taken for giving that which is free. Paul considered himself as in the position of a slave whose master had commissioned him to dispense his free bounty. From those to whom he distributed this bounty he could not take wages. Therefore, he and his companions could not do other than they did; nor can any who preach the Glad Tidings of free grace. In acting thus, Paul is but practising principles which he was always careful to teach:

> But beware lest, perchance, this exercise of your rights should become a stumbling-block to the weak... 'all things are lawful', but not all things build up the Church. Let no man seek his own, but every man his neighbour's good; ...not seeking my own good, but the good of all that they may be saved. I beseech you follow my example, as I follow the example of Christ. (1 Cor. 8:9; 10:23,33; 11:1, Conybeare.)

Paul was not alone in this practice. The whole company of Evangelists worked according to the same principles. Barnabas and Paul followed the same rule during the first missionary journey (1 Cor. 9:6). At Ephesus Paul supported himself and his companions with the labour of his hands (Acts 20:35). He asks the Corinthians: "Did Titus make a gain of you? walked we not in the same spirit? walked we not in the same steps?" (2 Cor. 12:18).

In some places, as we have seen, the Evangelists engaged in secular work to support themselves. During the three years at Ephesus those ministering there were supported by the income which Paul obtained working at his trade. At Thessalonica also Paul worked for his living. The reasons for this may be seen in what he wrote to these churches concerning the matter:

> For what is it wherein ye were inferior to other churches, except it be that I myself was not burdensome to you? forgive me this wrong. Behold, the third time I am ready to come to you: and I will not be burdensome to you: for I seek not yours, but you: for the children ought not to lay up for the parents, but the parents for the children. And I will very gladly spend and be spent for you; though the more abundantly I love you, the less I be loved. But be it so, I did not burden you; nevertheless, being crafty, I caught you with guile. Did I make a gain of you by any of them whom I sent unto you? (2 Cor. 12:13-17).
> For neither at any time used we flattering words, as ye know, nor a cloke of covetousness; God is witness: Nor of men sought we glory, neither of you, nor yet of others, when we might have been burdensome, as the apostles of Christ... For ye remember, brethren, our labour and travail; for labouring night and day, because we would not be chargeable unto any of you, we preached unto you the gospel of God. (1 Thess. 2:5,6,9.)
> For you yourselves know that it is your duty to follow our example. There was no disorder in our lives among you, nor did we eat any one's bread without paying for it, but we laboured and

toiled, working hard night and day in order not to be a burden to any of you. This was not because we had not a claim upon you, but it arose from a desire to set you an example—for you to imitate us. For even when we were with you, we laid down this rule for you: 'If a man does not choose to work,. neither shall he eat.' (2 Thess. 3:7-10, Weymouth).

The record shows that Paul worked at his trade to earn his living during a total of six or seven years. During more than twenty-five years, evidently, he was supported entirely by the offerings he received from the churches. Even when he worked for his living, what he earned was not always sufficient, for he wrote to the Corinthians, among whom he had worked at his trade, "And when I was with you, although I was in want, I pressed not upon any of you, for the brethren, when they came from Macedonia, supplied my needs" (2 Cor. 11:9, Conybeare).

Paul's example in this matter teaches us that the missionary may at times be led of God to earn at least part of his living. But that is done only in places where such an example is necessary to the local church. In most places the testimony of living by faith is what is needed. Any secular work engaged in to earn a living must be of a temporary nature that can be left at any moment when the missionary is called to move on. Also it must not encroach upon the time required for the Lord's work. Devoting time to earning a living when that time should be used in teaching or evangelism can never be justified. Missionaries have erred in this, establishing businesses that have made demands upon their time and thought and caused them to settle in one place thus ceasing from their true calling.

By missionary, of course, we mean the church-planter, not one who serves as Aquila and Priscilla did in Ephesus, establishing a business and taking an active part in the work of a local church — a ministry that, while not that of the church planter, is nevertheless truly Scriptural and useful. So-called "self-supporting missionaries" (not a scriptural designation) should be careful to distinguish between these two ministries.[1]

It may be that sometimes the failure of the churches to minister to Paul's need made it necessary for him to earn his living, but this was permitted by God. God could have supplied his need otherwise in these instances but did not do so because the spiritual

---

[1] See p. 428.

need of those to whom Paul was ministering at the time made
it necessary that they see him working with his hands. He was
a preacher not only by word but also by example, and he was
prepared to make any sacrifice to be faithful in both.
Of Paul's ministry in Corinth, Luke writes:

> After this he left Athens and came to Corinth. Here he found a
> Jew, a native of Pontus, of the name of Aquila. He and his wife
> Priscilla had recently come from Italy because of Claudius's edict
> expelling all the Jews from Rome. So Paul paid them a visit; and
> because he was of the same trade —that of tent-maker— he lodged
> with them and worked with them. But, Sabbath after Sabbath, he
> preached in the synagogue and tried to win over both Jews and
> Greeks. (Acts 18:1-4, Weymouth.)

Having proceeded in such a natural way and having given such
a practical example to the churches, he was in a position to speak
as he did to the Ephesian Elders:

> No one's silver or gold or clothing have I coveted. You your-
> selves know that these hands of mine have provided for my own
> necessities and for the people with me. In all things I have set you
> an example, showing you that, by working as I do, you ought to
> help the weak... (Acts 20:33-35, Weymouth.)

Paul, as we have seen, made frequent references to his example
in this respect in his letters to the churches. In many places that
example had been a necessary part of his ministry. It put him in
an unassailable position when he had to deal with the unfaithfulness of many in the Corinthian Church. No one could accuse him
of seeking ought that was of this world, or of being simply a
professional preacher.

Alexander Whyte, commenting on Paul's statement to the
Ephesian elders, remarks [1]:

> We do not at first sight see exactly why Paul should be so sore,
> and so sensitive, and so full of such scrupulosity, about money
> matters. But he had only too good cause to say all he said, and do
> all he did, in that root-of-all-evil matter. It was one of the many
> most abominable slanders that his sordid-hearted enemies circulated
> against Paul, that, all the time, he was feathering his own nest...
> I defy you! he exclaimed, as he stood up in indignation and held
> out his callid hands — I defy you to deny it. I have coveted no
> man's silver, or gold, or apparel. Yes, ye yourselves know that
> these hands — and as he held them up, the assembled elders saw
> a tongue of truth in every seam and scar that covered them —

---

[1] *Bible Characters*, vol. 6, pp. 149, 150.

these hands have ministered to all my own necessities, and to them that were with me. Noble hands of a noble heart!

Had his apostolic stipend been in their power to reduce it or to increase it; had a fund for his old age, or a legacy for his sister and her son been at all in Paul's mind; then, in that case, he might have been tempted to keep back some things in his preaching, and to put some other things forward.

He challenged the false Evangelists who opposed him to give a similar example:

Or is it a sin (which must rob us of the name of apostle) that I proclaimed to you, without fee or reward, the Glad-tidings of God, and abased myself that you might be exalted? Other churches I spoiled, and took their wages to do you service. And when I was with you, though I was in want, I pressed not upon any of you, for the brethren, when they came from Macedonia, supplied my needs; and I kept, and will keep myself altogether from casting a burden upon you. As the truth of Christ is in me, no deed of mine shall rob me of this boasting in the region of Achaia. And Why? Because I love you not? God knows my love. But what I do I will continue to do, that I may cut off all ground from those who wish to find some ground of slander; and let them show the same cause for their boasting as I for mine (2 Cor. 11:7-12, Conybeare.)

In a note on the twelfth verse Conybeare says:

The literal English of this difficult passage is, 'that they, in the ground of their boasting, may be found even as I.' De Wette refers 'wherein they glory' to the Apostolic Office. We take it more generally. A more obvious way would be to take the phrase (with Chrysostom and the older interpreters) to mean their abstaining from receiving maintenance; but we know that the false teachers at Corinth did not do this (compare ver. 20 below), but, on the contrary, boasted of their privilege, and alleged that St. Paul, by not claiming it, showed his consciousness that he was not truly sent by Christ. (See 1 Cor. ix.)

It is true, as Paul himself taught, that 'the labourer is worthy of his hire', but that truth must take its true place in harmony with all the other principles governing the ministry of the servant of God. No church could have paid Paul in money the value of his services. To have accepted less in payment from those to whom he ministered would have valued his ministry at just what they paid. But no, he was God's servant, not theirs, and he retained the full dignity and liberty of his ministry. Had he accepted anything like what his services were worth in silver and gold, his ministry would have lost much of its power as an example and he would have been called what we have heard a Christian business man call a popular modern preacher: 'a highly paid spellbinder'. He would not have suffered want or known what it was to be hungry. He would have avoided the poverty that makes many rich. His ministry would have lacked that which gave it reality and he would have lost his spiritual authority. It is not to be wondered at that the false Evangelists who opposed him were not able to meet his challenge to do as he did: to accept no money from those to whom they preached, trusting only in God, and paying the price of a true spiritual ministry. It is so today. Paul stood upon ground which placed him beyond all challenge.

It is necessary to draw attention to the fact that not all so-called faith is true faith. Paul did not have a group of friends from whom he was sure he would receive support and with whom, for that reason, he was careful to keep in close touch by correspondence. As we have seen, he gave no hints of personal financial need and made no request for prayer that his needs be met. It is, of course, right to keep those who cooperate in prayer informed about the work, but that is another matter.

The ground of Paul's actions in this respect was the fact that he was following Christ's example. Of Christ he said,

> For ye know the grace of our Lord Jesus Christ, that, though he was rich, yet for your sakes he became poor, that ye through his poverty might be rich. (2 Cor. 8:9.)

Using practically the same words he says of his own ministry:

> But in all things approving ourselves as the ministers of God... as poor, yet making many rich. (2 Cor. 6:4,10.)

When Christ sent forth the Twelve, two by two, and later the seventy, to preach and witness as they had seen Him do, He told them to take no supply of money with them and only the clothing that was absolutely essential. They had to go in faith, possessing nothing, and trusting God for the supply of every need as Christ Himself was doing. When they returned He asked them, "Lacked ye anything?" and they answered, "Nothing".

Christ and His disciples had so walked: Paul and his fellow-workers did likewise. Following the One Who had 'emptied Himself', Paul 'counted all things but loss'. It could not be otherwise for one who would follow and represent Christ.

In the second century writing, the "Teaching of the Twelve Apostles", the financial principles applied by Paul and his companions are seen to be still in practice. It says significantly,

If anyone, speaking by the Spirit asks you for money or anything else, heed him not; but if he counsels you to give to the poor judge him not.

Although Paul and the other New Testament Evangelists refused absolutely to accept material support from a congregation to which they were ministering, there was a practice, which was universal in the churches, that they did not reject. When a visiting servant of the Lord departed to continue his journey to another point, it was the custom for the congregation to provide him with the food that he required to take him to his next stopping place. It was an act of hospitality related to the customs and the conditions of travel at the time, but also, amōng the churches it was regarded as an offering of Christian love. Paul refers to it several times and it would seem that he took pleasure in it because of the loving fellowship which it signified. It is spoken of in the following passages:

They also loaded us with honours, and when at last we sailed they put supplies on board for us. (Acts 28:10, Weymouth.)
Help Zenas the lawyer forward on his journey with special care, and Apollos, so that they may have all they require. (Titus 3:13; Weymouth.)
I hope, as soon as ever I extend my travels into Spain to see you on my way and be helped forward by you on my journey... (Rom. 15:24, Weymouth).
Therefore let no one slight him, but all of you should help him forward in peace to join me; for I am waiting for him and others of the brethren. (1 Cor. 16:11, Weymouth.)

There was nothing inconsistent in receiving this offering. It was in no sense payment for their services, but a love gift to speed them with the Gospel to other regions.

There is an interesting reference to this custom in the "Teaching of the Twelve Apostles":

Behold how, according to the precepts of the Gospel you should act towards apostles (missionaries) and prophets (preachers). Receive in the Name of the Lord apostles who visit you, while they remain with you one or two days: he who stays three days is a false prophet. When the apostle leaves, you should provide him with food that he may be able to journey to the city to which he is going: if he asks for money he is a false prophet.

The 'one or two' and 'three' days mentioned here are, of course, symbolical. The meaning is that a true missionary would not impose upon their hospitality.

The Married Evangelist

It would seem that Paul and some at least of his fellow-workers were unmarried, but by no means all the Evangelists were single men. Philip was not, and we are given a glimpse of his home in Caesarea. Four daughters were preachers, and it was to his home, naturally, that Paul and his companions went when they passed through that city (Acts 21 : 8, 9). Paul, writing to the Corinthians, asked, "Do they deny my right to carry a believing wife with me on my journeys, like the rest of the apostles, and the brothers of the Lord, and Cephas?" (1 Cor. 9:5, Conybeare). It is evident from this that not a few Evangelists were accompanied by their wives as they journeyed from place to place.

An interesting and suggestive modern example of this is provided by Dr. and Mrs. Jonathan Goforth. Describing the manner in which they established churches in new districts in North China, Dr. Goforth said:

> Another kind of work, carried on after 1900, was this opening of new centers throughout our field. My wife joined me in this and we took our children along. We would rent a compound and stay at least a month in a center. This had the decided advantage in that it reached the women as well as the men. A man may hear the Word of God and believe, but his heathen wife or mother can make it hot for him at home. In this way we opened many centers of light. Now we have proved it so often that we have the conviction that we could go into any unevangelized center in North China with an earnest band of male and female workers and within a month have the beginning of a Church for Jesus Christ.[1]

Conditions vary greatly in different parts of the world and what is possible in one region may not be possible in another. For gathering together a group of converts that is to continue under the direction of a Pastor, a month may be sufficient, but to lay the foundation for a New Testament congregation, usually a longer period is necessary. Not infrequently, a year, or two years, is required. This makes it possible for a married Evangelist to move his home to the place of his ministry. Particular circumstances, of

---

Foreign Missions Conference Report, Washington, 1925, p. 77.

course, may make it impossible. When the Evangelist is revisiting a church to give further instruction, his stay being not more than a few months, it may be neither necessary nor practicable for him to move his family. If he has children of school age, it would be impossible. This means that both he and his wife must be prepared for the sacrifice entailed by his having to be absent from home for long periods. The fact must be faced that the methods of work of the planter of churches cannot be modified to suit his domestic arrangements; on the contrary, if he is called to the work of an Evangelist, his home life must be subordinated to the obligations of his ministry, though, of course, not to the extent that the fundamental responsibilities towards his home are neglected.

The sacrifice entailed need not be exaggerated. Men in other callings — sailors, soldiers, scientists, commercial travellers and others — make a similar sacrifice to business, duty, or science and consider themselves sufficiently rewarded.

This is not a matter in which specific rules can be laid down to cover all cases in all lands. No details are given regarding it in the New Testament record. The only rule is that the Evangelist must be absolutely faithful to the principles of his ministry, arranging all his private affairs so that they conform to its demands and contribute to its accomplishment.

What has been said above indicates the place taken in the Evangelist's ministry by men, married and single and by married women. Single women appear not to have taken part in the travelling ministry, though there is ample evidence of their efficient cooperation with Evangelists in local work. That single women are called of God to assist Evangelists in their ministry can not be questioned for it is evident that God has done so in many cases. Their ministry, however, would seem to be related particularly to the witness of the local church.

CHAPTER IX

COOPERATION AMONG EVANGELISTS

THE New Testament missionary group, though not under a Director or Home Board was not leaderless. The independent missionary or the leaderless company of missionaries are not in accordance with the pattern given in the New Testament. The New Testament example shows that neither the congregation nor the missionary group was a free-for-all. In both, spiritual leadership is necessary for coordination and supervision.

The relations of the company to their leader and to one another were based upon simple spiritual principles. They had been called to their ministry by God, and the Holy Spirit had brought them together into a company for cooperative work. That there should be a number working together was necessary. The Church is not an aggregation of independent units but a Body composed of members interrelated and mutually dependent one upon another. Even among Evangelists, all having the gifts of the Spirit necessary for their ministry, there are many variations of the same gifts in the different individuals and the Holy Spirit brings together a company having among them not only all the gifts, but all the variations of these gifts, necessary for the doing of the work. No one member of the Body, no matter what ministry he is called to, is sufficiently equipped to make him independent of the cooperation of other members. So we have presented to us in the New Testament this model group of Evangelists with their beautiful fellowship and gloriously effective cooperation under the guidance of the Holy Spirit.

They were held together in a strong bond of unity. Though often separated for long periods with inadequate means of communication, their loyalty to their common ministry and to one another did not waver through the course of many years. This was the work of the Holy Spirit, for they were not pledged to the rules of an order or organization. The Holy Spirit had joined them together and He kept them together.

Affection and confidence are revealed in many of Paul's references to his fellow-workers. There was a perfect understanding amongst them and all stood steadfastly and consistently for the same things. The secret of this unity is undoubtedly the fact that all were guided by the Holy Spirit. No one sought aught for himself, and as all knew the will of the Spirit the unity of the Spirit prevailed amongst them.

Coordination

It is stated that Paul's fellow-workers were sent by him on their various missions. That this sending was not done arbitrarily is made evident by Paul's account of the manner in which he approached them on these occasions:

> So that I have desired Titus (to revisit you), that as he caused you to begin this work, so he might lead you to finish it... But, thanks be to God, by whose gift the heart of Titus has the same zeal as my own on your behalf; for he not only has consented to my desire, but is himself very zealous in the matter, and departs to you on his own accord (2 Cor. 8:6, 16, 17. Conybeare.)
>
> As for our brother Apollos, I have repeatedly urged him to accompany the brethren who are coming to you, but he is quite resolved not to do so at present. He will come, however, when he has a good opportunity (1 Cor. 16:12, Weymouth.)

It was the custom for a believer, when he travelled, to carry a letter of recommendation from the congregation with which he met. Evangelists also went recommended. False missionaries were seeking to introduce wrong doctrine and practice into the churches and the churches were responsible to reject them, so it was right that the true missionaries should go properly recommended. (Rev. 2:2; 2 Cor. 11:13.)

These Evangelists did not go simply as individuals on their own authority; they represented and spoke for the group of Evangelists. When Timothy or Titus showed to the churches the letters they carried from Paul, the leader of the company, they were placed in a strong position. The church that rejected their ministry would know that it was not simply the individual Evangelist who had come to them that they rejected, but the whole company of Evangelists. Paul in his recommendations always identified him-

7

self fully with them: they were his fellow-workers to be received as he himself would be received.

The Evangelists worked together as a company. Each one was led individually and directly by the Holy Spirit. No one was obliged to go anywhere if he felt that it was not God's will that he should go. Paul did not insist that they go where he thought they should go. Yet no one acted independently. The journeys and ministry of all were coordinated through the leader. Thus the needs of the whole field and of all the churches were properly cared for, which would not have been the case had the ministry of the Evangelists not been effectively coordinated.

It does not seem difficult to reconstruct what took place. Paul and his companions were thoroughly acquainted with the different churches and were exercising a continual ministry of prayer for them all. When communications were received revealing difficulties in a congregation, the matter would be prayed over and God's will sought. If it were felt that a certain one should visit that church, Paul would suggest it to him. If that one had assurance that it was God's will and that he went forth 'sent by the Spirit', then he undertook the mission. From what Paul wrote regarding the going of some, it would seem that the thought of their going had originated first with them and that they had proposed it. But it had been confirmed by the Spirit to all that it was God's will. Otherwise Paul would not, and could not, have written commending them and associating himself fully with them in their going.

Not Delegated Authority

These fellow-workers of Paul have been called 'Apostolic Delegates'. That title is not used in Scripture, nor is any that approximates to it. The use of unscriptural terms is always dangerous, often introducing confusion. There is no evidence that apostolic authority was or could be delegated. The title was coined in an attempt to avoid the difficulty that seemed to be presented by the authority exercised in the churches by these Evangelists. To call them 'Apostolic Delegates' segregates them in a special class that could have no successors and divests the example of their labours of any practical meaning to the Evangelist of today.

We believe, however, that there is no real difficulty either in the ministry which they performed or in the authority which they exercised. To any missionary with experience in new fields, where groups of converts and recently formed congregations require to be cared for, the ministry of Timothy in Ephesus, of Titus in Crete, and of the others in the various churches which they visited, was entirely normal and necessary.

Paul does not call his fellow-workers 'Apostolic Delegates'. He calls Titus 'a partner with me', 'my comrade in my labours' and refers to others of his brethren as 'apostles' (2 Cor. 8:23). He speaks of Epaphroditus as 'my brother and comrade' and an 'apostle'. His second letter to the Corinthians, and the Epistles to the Philippians, Philemon and Colossians, he sent as from himself and Timothy. First and Second Thessalonians he wrote as from 'Paul, Silas and Timothy'. He says of Timothy, "he is engaged in the Master's work just as I am" (1 Cor. 16:10, Weymouth).

Luke and Mark were used by the Holy Spirit to provide the Church with authoritative records of the earthly life and ministry of the Lord. Luke was the instrument chosen to write the account of the founding of the Church and the labours of its first Evangelists. These honoured servants of the Lord acted, not as 'Apostolic Delegates', but as ministers of the Church, appointed and authorized directly by Christ and empowered by the Holy Spirit.

Confirmation of Guidance

Through the leader the Holy Spirit coordinated the ministry of the company. But Paul did not exercise an arbitrary leadership, nor was the will of the Spirit revealed to him alone. It is the company that is spoken of as being guided by the Spirit on the journey north through Asia Minor:

> Then Paul and his companions passed through Phrygia and Galatia, having been forbidden by the Holy Spirit to proclaim the Message in the Province of Asia. When they reached the frontier of Mysia, they were about to enter Bithynia, but the Spirit of Jesus would not permit this. (Acts 16:6, 7, Weymouth.)

The account given by Luke of the vision Paul, as leader, received of 'the man of Macedonia' shows the participation of all in the guidance given through that vision. After stating that Paul saw the vision, Luke changes from the singular to the plural, saying,

> And after he had seen the vision, immediately we endeavoured to go into Macedonia, (we) assuredly gathering that the Lord had called us for to preach the gospel unto them. (Acts 16:10.)

Confirmation regarding the will of the Spirit was received by all, although it was to Paul that He had spoken. The principle involved here is the same as when Paul's call was confirmed to the brethren in Antioch. It is one of the important principles governing the receiving of guidance from the Spirit and one of the great safeguards. The Holy Spirit may reveal His will to one, but that one waits until confirmation of the guidance is given to his brethren. The danger of mistaken guidance, or of going ahead of God's time, is greatly lessened by this procedure. No doubt it had much to do in preserving the unity of the Spirit in the company of Evangelists.

An instance that illustrates very clearly the principles involved is Paul's insistence on going to Jerusalem when warned by the Spirit through his brethren not to go. We believe that in this case Paul failed to give heed to the fact that what he thought was the guidance of the Spirit was not confirmed to the church or to his fellow-workers.

It is worth while to follow closely what took place. Paul, with representatives from a number of churches, was carrying the proceeds of a collection to Jerusalem. Passing by Ephesus, he told the Elders of that church that, "now, behold, I go bound in the Spirit unto Jerusalem, not knowing the things that shall befall me there; save that the Holy Ghost witnesseth in every city, saying that bonds and afflictions abide me" (Acts 20:22, 23).

When they reached Tyre, the brethren there warned him "through the Spirit, that he should not go up to Jerusalem" (Acts 21:4). At Caesarea they stayed at the home of Philip, a fellow-Evangelist. Agabus, from the Jerusalem church, met them there. He was well known to Paul as one truly guided by the Spirit. (Acts 11:28). He, in a most dramatic and unmistakable manner, warned Paul of what would befall him if he went to Jerusalem. Agabus claimed that his warning was from the Holy Spirit. Then Paul's companions — Luke and the others who were in the company — together with the brethren at Caesarea, among whom was Philip, "besought him not to go up to Jerusalem" (Acts 21:10-12).

His answer was:

What mean ye to weep and to break mine heart? for I am ready not to be bound only, but also to die at Jerusalem for the name of the Lord Jesus. And when he would not be persuaded, we ceased, saying, The will of the Lord be done (Acts 21:13, 14).

The phrase, 'The will of the Lord be done', does not imply that his fellow-workers and the church were persuaded that what he was doing was God's will, but simply means that, having done all that they could do, they left the matter in God's hands that He should work out His will concerning it.

Paul went on to Jerusalem with his companions. The church there received them gladly; but it advised Paul to demonstrate publicly his faithfulness to the law by accompanying four Jewish Christians who were under a Nazarite vow, paying the expenses connected with their vow. King Agrippa I had done this not very long before to win favour when he ascended the throne.

It was pointed out to Paul that there were many thousands of Jews in the congregation who were "all zealous of the law" and that he was accused of being unfaithful in its observance. He was counselled, therefore, to prove that he "walked orderly and kept the law" (Acts 21:20, 24). He accepted this unspiritual advice, went to the Temple, was recognized, mobbed, nearly lost his life and began an imprisonment that lasted several years.

That Paul's motives were sincere and, in some respects, laudable, in insisting on going to Jerusalem and in accepting the counsel of the church in Jerusalem, is beyond question. He was prepared to be faithful to his ministry even to the facing of death and he desired earnestly to remove any barriers to full fellowship with his brethren in Jerusalem. He had been at great pains to have the collection made among the churches, as may be seen in his references to it in several of his letters, and his great hope had been that this evidence of his interest, and of that of the churches he had founded, in the poor in Jerusalem would be received as a proof of his genuine love towards the brethren in Jerusalem. To have desisted from going personally with the gift to Jerusalem would have frustrated, it would have seemed, the whole plan he had cherished for years and was just about to realize. To give up this plan at the last moment would not be easy. But, evidently, it was not God's plan. Above all other considerations was obedience to the will of God revealed by the Holy Spirit and based upon a clearer sight and higher wisdom than man's.

The counsel given to Paul by the churches and by his fellow-workers on the way to Jerusalem was repeatedly declared to be the voice of the Holy Spirit. These churches and fellow-workers were not walking in disobedience. They were unanimous and there was no reason to doubt that the Holy Spirit was speaking through them. Their counsel did not affect the mission on which the party had been sent, for Paul alone was forbidden to go to Jerusalem.

On the other hand it was well known that the church in Jerusalem was compromising with Judaism. Its members had no right to be "zealous of the law", nor had it any justification for asking Paul to give evidence that he "walked orderly and kept the law". The counsel it gave meant the compromising of principles for which he had consistently contended. It was not claimed that their advice was from the Holy Spirit; there is no suggestion that prayer was made about the matter; and there was definite reason to doubt that they were in a position spiritually to receive guidance from the Holy Spirit. The church in Jerusalem is not now filled with the Spirit, guided by the Spirit and continuing in prayer as it was at the beginning. The Elders think more of what the legalistic members of the congregation will say than of the Lord's will, and instead of taking the matter to the Lord in prayer they judge with human judgment and advise a procedure based upon human wisdom.

The fact was that this advice given to Paul contradicted basic truth that he had taught to the churches.[1] Participation in such a purification ceremony, involving a Jewish sacrifice, was a denial of the completeness of the sacrifice of Christ and the fact that no other sacrifice could avail anything (Heb. 10:1, 2, 9-12).

All this causes us to think of the danger of compromise. It is an easy thing to compromise fundamental truth as given in God's Word when there is any association with a Church that has compromised in any matter. Ministry to such a church in the presenting of God's Word to it can be entirely right. But any conforming to its compromise, association with it or participation in its work is wrong and will give the advantage to Satan and bring defeat.

For a seemingly adequate reason — his desire to bridge the gulf between himself and the brethren in Jerusalem (for he was a man of strong affections) — Paul rejected the truly spiritual counsel given by the churches and his fellow-workers. For the same apparently good reason he accepted the unspiritual compromise recommended in Jerusalem. His reason was based upon

---

[1] Rom. 3:19-28; 4-6; 6:7; 7:1-6; 8:3-4; Gal. 2:15-19; 3:10-25; 4:9-11; 21-31.

what appeared to be sound human judgment and a pure motive, but it was contrary to God's wisdom and will. God knew what the condition of the Jerusalem church was and that failure would be the result.

This experience of God's servant, recorded with such detail, is rich with deep lessons. Though it seems that he was mistaken in the action which he took, his heart was right with the Lord. The Lord did not reject him and the Holy Spirit did not abandon him. Nor did his companions forsake him: the company continued its widespread ministry during the years of difficulty that followed, and God so overruled that His servant was enabled to continue his witness in a number of places and before many people, finally being taken to Rome to minister and, later to be released.

It is instructive to compare this visit to Jerusalem with the previous one when Paul, Barnabas and others went there to denounce the Judaizers from that church who had been disturbing the church in Antioch. On that occasion, the Lord had revealed to Paul that he should go (Gal. 2:2); the church in Antioch confirmed his going, sending representatives with him; he stood uncompromisingly against the Judaizers and his mission was entirely successful, although he had encountered serious opposition, to which he refers in his letter to the Galatians.

There is another aspect of the incident that is significant. It is thought that the success of Paul's ministry was due to the natural mental ability, strength of character and education which he undoubtedly possessed. Here we see him guided by his own reasoning. Here is Paul the man — and a great man, a great mind, an organizer with an iron will and steadfast purpose, fearless and ready to lay down his life for a worthy cause. His plan was excellent and he executed it with courage and resolution; but the outcome was complete failure. The wisdom of the wisest of men is not sufficient for guidance in the Church. The Lord's wisdom alone is sufficient and His guidance must be sought and obeyed always and in everything. It was only the faithful overruling of God during the years that followed that made possible the continuance of Paul's ministry. This appears to have been the only occasion when Paul was guided by his own wisdom and not by the Spirit.

It is with hesitancy that we refer to what appears to be an error on the part of so great and faithful a servant of the Lord, but we have no doubt that he would be the first to desire that we should profit by any mistake he may have made. He was always careful to disclaim any thought that he was personally perfect. It is because of the great spiritual value of this incident that the details are so fully recorded in the Word. In God's Word, His servants are not presented to us as perfect men. The Apostles were not. God gives us examples of men who, though just men and liable to err, triumphed through faith and the power of the Spirit.

The Safeguard

The lessons to be learned from this company of New Testament missionaries are obvious. It may be objected that a full application of the principles which governed the company in a Mission today would not provide the necessary organic stability or material support. Too much would depend upon the apparently intangible — upon the Holy Spirit. There would be nothing material to fall back upon to hold things together if, for any reason, the Holy Spirit's control and guidance failed. All that, of course, is true. God has not provided us with the example of a model human organization, proof against all difficulties and dangers, that will continue to function when faith fails. Indeed, it is the lack of formal organization that is conspicuous (though, of course, a perfect and complete spiritual order is evident). God intended that it should be so. If a missionary company comes to the place where it is unable to continue functioning by spiritual rules, where the Holy Spirit cannot freely guide them and manifest His power through them as the New Testament teaches He will do, where faith fails and the machinery of human organization is needed to hold them together and enable them to continue functioning, then surely the time has come when the spiritual usefulness of that company has ended and it should cease to exist. How many organizations have been perpetuated by human machinery when the power has long since departed from them?

By the exclusion of such human machinery, God has safeguarded His work, ensuring that where faith fails and the Holy Spirit can no longer function, the structure must fall to the ground. By removing this safeguard we may give permanence to forms but we will succeed only in perpetuating a human structure that will bear at the best second-rate fruit, that will be a burden to the Church and an obstacle to the true work of the Holy Spirit

CHAPTER X

PAUL THE CHURCH PLANTER

METHODS are but the practical application of principles. We must, therefore, as we study the methods of evangelism of the Early Church missionaries, endeavour always to discern the underlying spiritual principles.

The founders of the Early Church were true to the example of the Master. He evangelized; so did they. He travelled, ceaselessly, tirelessly, fearlessly, preaching and teaching. He did not wait for circumstances to be favourable. He had come to seek the lost, so He went out to find them and He thought not of Himself, that true Shèpherd of the sheep, but tramped through city and country, over mountain and desert, in cold of winter, in heat of summer, in malaria infested regions, sparing not Himself, considering not comfort, caring not though He had not where to lay His head, giving Himself, a sacrifice, that the lost might be found. The disciples had received His Spirit, so they did likewise. They travelled and preached and sought the lost as their Teacher had done, until they had followed every highway and by-way that was known and established the Church throughout the world.

The nature and scope of the missionary vision of the New Testament Evangelists is expressed in Paul's letter to the Romans, where he tells of his desire to visit them. He was writing from Corinth during his third visit to that city, in A. D. 60, about fifteen years after he first set out from Antioch.

But —to speak simply of my own labours— beginning in Jerusalem and the outlying districts, I have proclaimed without reserve, even as far as Illyricum, the Good News of the Christ; making it my ambition, however, not to tell the Good News where Christ's name was already known, for fear I should be building on another man's foundation... But now, as there is no more unoccupied ground in this part of the world, and I have for years past been eager to pay you a visit, I hope, as soon as ever I extend my travels into Spain, to see you on my way and be helped forward by you on my journey, when I have first enjoyed being with you for a time. But at present I am going to Jerusalem to serve God's people... So after discharging this duty... I shall start for Spain, passing through Rome on my way there; and I know that when I come to you it will be with a vast amount of blessing from Christ" (Rom. 15:18-29, Weymouth).

Writing from Greece to Rome at the end of fifteen years' labour, he could say that he had made the Gospel known from Jerusalem to Illyricum, beyond Macedonia, and that now, as there was nothing left for him to do in those regions, he was going to Spain and would visit Rome on the way. How many missionaries today have spent fifteen years in one place nursing a comparatively small group of believers!

In his writings to the churches, Paul often refers to whole provinces instead of to single cities — Asia, Galatia, Macedonia, Achaia, Spain! The vision of these Evangelists was world-wide and their plans were laid for the evangelization of the world — not of a city, or even of a province. Their purpose was to get local churches established in every region throughout the world as soon as possible so that these congregations, under their Elders, should complete the evangelization of their surrounding territories.

It might be thought that covering such a vast field the work could not be done thoroughly or the churches adequately taught and firmly established, but, actually, the method of evangelism followed produced churches better instructed, more vigorous and more capable of carrying on their own work than does the modern method of concentrating upon a restricted area.

On their so-called first missionary journey, which lasted about three years, Barnabas and Paul did not go very far afield. They began in Barnabas' native Cyprus, travelling from end to end of that island, visiting the principal towns; then they returned to the mainland, passing from town to town in the Provinces bordering Cilicia on the west and north — Pamphilia, Pisidia and Lycaonia.

Their objective in each town which they entered was the establishing of a congregation. The length of their stay varied according to circumstances. Frequently they were forced to leave because of persecution. They were guided by the Holy Spirit from town to town and God kept the door open to them in each place until His purpose through them at that time was accomplished and a congregation of converts was left sufficiently established to carry on the witness.

First of all, the Gospel was preached. The converts were immediately baptized and gathered into a congregation for fellowship, instruction and service. The teaching which was given to them was not superficial or elementary but thorough and complete. God's servants did not shrink from giving them immediately all the counsel of God.

Elders were not appointed until later: these must not be new converts but men who have been proved. But the other gifts of the Spirit such as those of preaching, 'the word of wisdom', 'the word of knowledge', etc., were immediately manifested and the converts continued to meet together for prayer and fellowship, the Holy Spirit being present to teach and guide.

Having gone as far as Derbe, near the Cilician border, the missionaries retraced their steps, revisiting the new congregations. It was during this return journey that, after prayer and fasting to know those whom God had chosen, Elders were appointed in the churches — after a lapse of one or two years.

During the interval, while the Evangelists were absent, the churches had been on their own. It had not been possible for them to rely upon the greater experience of the missionaries who had brought them the Gospel. They were thrown upon the Lord and forced to depend directly upon the Holy Spirit and to seek and exercise the gifts of the Spirit. What they had been taught could not remain as powerless theory: they had to put it into practice, and so they learned that it was not just dogma but truth and power. The effect of this upon the spiritual development of these converts will be readily understood. The direct result was that vigorous spiritual life was evident in the churches from the beginning, and men of experience were ready in a comparatively short time to take their places as Elders and Deacons and even to go forth as Evangelists in Paul's company.

It is evident that the teaching given by the Evangelists on their first visit must have been sufficiently complete to enable the new congregations to know how to proceed. The way of salvation, prayer, the guidance of the Holy Spirit, the gifts of the Spirit, the organization of the Church, giving, and the responsibilities of the members towards one another — all this must have been thoroughly taught.

From the beginning, the churches were all self-supporting. No financial help of any kind was given to them. In all things, both spiritual and material, they were dependent, not upon man, but upon God.

At the end of three years we find Barnabas and Paul back in Antioch where, for the next two years, they take part again in the ministry of that congregation. This was not an interlude in their missionary ministry but a continuation of it.[1] They returned to Antioch this time as Evangelists for further ministry as they did to other new churches. During their three years' absence, this church had continued its witness faithfully. But we soon see why the Holy Spirit had led the two Evangelists back at this time. Judaizers from the church in Jerusalem had appeared, seeking to introduce the bondage of legalism, saying that circumcision was necessary to salvation. Paul and Barnabas successfuly opposed their false teaching. It is part of the Evangelist's duty to rebuke the teachers of false doctrine and protect the churches from them. In doing what they did in Antioch, therefore, these missionaries were fulfilling their ministry.

It was decided that the two Evangelists and certain others from the Antioch church should go to Jerusalem to take up the matter with the church there. Paul had personally received a revelation that he should go (Gal. 2:2). But the decision was not made by the Evangelists alone; they acted in conjunction with the church in Antioch. That congregation confirmed the fact that it was God's will that the journey should be made and sent representatives with the missionaries.

Paul set out on this journey to Jerusalem to defend the Gentile churches against the Pharisee Judaizers. Just fifteen years before that he had travelled part of this same road, from Jerusalem to Damascus, a bigoted Pharisee, persecuting the followers of Christ.

Regarding the so-called Council which Paul, Barnabas, Titus and perhaps others from the Antioch congregation attended in

---

[1] Hatch says: The arrangement of, Paul's active life into 'missionary journeys' is artificial and unsatisfactory... If the latter part of his biography be broken up into chapters at all, it would be much more useful to divide it according to the centres at which he settled from time to time and from which his activity radiated, Corinth, **Ephesus,** Caesarea (probably), and Rome" (*Paul*, Enc. Brit.).

Jerusalem (Acts 15:1-31), Dr. G. Campbell Morgan says:[1]

This has sometimes been called the story of the first council of the Christian Church. To that description of the gathering in Jerusalem, Farrar in his 'Life and Work of St. Paul' objected, for excellent reasons. He showed that the council in Jerusalem was not a convention of delegates, but a meeting of the Church at Jerusalem to receive a deputation from the Church at Antioch, and to consider a subject of grave importance in the matter of missionary enterprise. He pointed out, moreover, that this gathering in Jerusalem was for purposes of consultation, and not for final and dogmatic decision.

Almost all councils subsequent to the first have attempted to fix some habit or ritual, or to give final form to the expression of some great truth. Neither of these things was attempted in the gathering at Jerusalem.

The sending of these brethren from Antioch to Jerusalem is really an instance of cooperation between two congregations in the matter of discipline. Professing Christians from the church in Jerusalem were disturbing the church in Antioch by teaching false doctrine. The Jerusalem congregation met and affirmed its adherence to the truth, thus condemning the false teachers. The decision was put in writing so that the missionaries might carry it with them among the churches as evidence that the Judaizers did not have the support of the congregation in Jerusalem, as they evidently claimed.

Again Campbell Morgan writes:[2]

Luke's picture must be interpreted by Paul's letter to the Galatians. Without suggesting that either account is untrue, it is quite certain that if they be read together we shall catch a different tone. There is a touch in Paul's account of the story, which reveals how keenly he felt certain attitudes taken up toward him, even on the part of the apostolic band. We cannot read Paul's account of the council, and of its findings, without seeing that had they been other than they were, he would not have obeyed them. He was not seeking the authority of the Church at Jerusalem. He was not asking for an expression of truth by James or by Peter, ex cathedra. He was there for purposes of consultation: and had the finding been one that put the Gentiles into bondage, he would have broken with Jerusalem, and all the apostles, in the interests of truth. There are evidences in his account of the story, of the fact that there was a good deal of dissension and difference, and argument, before finality was reached.

The danger that had threatened the church in Antioch having been satisfactorily taken care of, Paul felt the call to go on to

---

[1] *The Acts of the Apostles*, pp. 355, 356.
[2] Ibid., p. 356.

other churches. He said to Barnabas: "Let us go again and visit our brethren in every city where we have preached the word of the Lord, and see how they do" (Acts 15:36). Barnabas was in agreement that God's time had come for them to leave Antioch, so preparations were made for their departure. But now the unity that had prevailed in the missionary company is broken. Barnabas purposes to take his kinsman, John Mark, with them again, but Paul objects on the ground that the young man had abandoned them on the previous journey. As a consequence, Barnabas and Paul separate: Barnabas, with Mark, goes to Cyprus, while Paul, accompanied by Silas, a man of experience in the work of the local church, proceeds north through Cilicia.

It was Paul and Silas that the church in Antioch commended to the Lord and it is the ministry of Paul and of his companions that the Holy Spirit records thereafter. The Antioch congregation would not have commended them to the Lord if it had not received the confirmation of the Spirit regarding their going, nor would the manifest approval of God have followed them as it did had they proceeded contrary to His will. From now on Paul is the leader of the missionary company.

What is generally called Paul's second missionary journey (though, actually, it is just a continuation of uninterrupted ministry) lasted about four years. Stalker speaks of this journey as "perhaps the most momentous recorded in the annals of the human race." First, the new churches in Galatia that had now been carrying on under their own Elders for a couple of years or more were revisited, then the Evangelists, with Timothy added to their number, proceeded north to new territories.

They passed rapidly through the north of Asia Minor, being forbidden by the Holy Spirit to evangelize that region. Much of the way had led through wild and dangerous country. They had to negotiate mountain passes, cross angry torrents, traverse arid, inhospitable regions infested by robbers and malaria. But nothing daunted these ministers of the Lord. It is remarkable, and significant, how little Paul and Luke have to say in their writings of the adventures they met with on their journeys. Paul, in defense of his ministry, catalogues some of them in 2 Cor. 11:23-27. Referring to this passage Stalker says:

Now, of the items of this extraordinary catalogue the book of Acts mentions very few: of the five Jewish scourgings it notices not one, of the three Roman beatings only one; the one stoning it records, but not one of the three shipwrecks, for the shipwreck so fully detailed in the Acts happened later. It was no part of the design of Luke to exaggerate the figure of the hero he was painting; his brief and modest narrative comes far short even of the reality; and, as we pass over the few simple words into which he condenses the story of months or years, our imagination requires to be busy, filling up the outline with toils and pains at least equal to those whose memory he has preserved.[1]

Arriving at Troas on the north-west coast of the Province of Asia, God's will was revealed to them through the vision of 'the man of Macedonia'. Having the assurance that this vision was the voice of God, they crossed immediately to Macedonia, accompanied now by Luke, and spent about eighteen months evangelizing in its principal cities. Then Paul and Luke went south to Athens and Corinth in Greece, while Timothy and Silas stayed behind at Berea for a time to complete the work begun there. Corinth then had half a million inhabitants, 23 temples, numerous theatres, and amphitheatres, one of which could seat 22,000 people. The party remained at least a year and a half in that city, but during this time Timothy returned to Thessalonica for a further period of ministry to the new church there.

From Greece Paul crossed back to Ephesus in the Province of Asia, accompanied by a converted couple, Aquila and Priscilla, with whom he had stayed for a time in Corinth. These two remained in Ephesus, engaging in business and carrying on an active witness while Paul and several companions journeyed south to revisit the churches at Cæsarea, Jerusalem and Antioch (Acts 18:24-26; 1 Cor. 16:19).

It would seem that it was at this time, rather than during his previous visit to Antioch, that the dispute with Peter occurred. Barnabas also was present and he and Peter were influenced by certain brethren from Jerusalem to separate themselves from the Gentile Christians and so compromise their witness. Paul is obliged again to exercise his ministry, denouncing the legalistic error and defending the congregation against the intrusion of false doctrine. It must have been discouraging to him to find two fellow-Evangelists, one an Apostle, so failing in their ministry as to be influenced by the Judaizers, but evidently his faithful protest was successful, because it was backed by the power of the Spirit. Again God had

---

[1] *Life of St. Paul*, p. 74.

led him back to Antioch for the protection of the church from the subtle intrusion of error.

After this, Paul and his companions went on to other regions. The next five years of his ministry, ending with his arrest in Jerusalem, is generally called his third missionary journey. It is really just a continuation of his ministry, involving as heretofore a series of journeys from one strategic centre to another for extended periods of ministry, with shorter visits to a number of places between.

During this period, three years were spent at Ephesus, where Aquila, Priscilla and, later, Apollos had already made a beginning. The Holy Spirit had now given liberty for the evangelization of the Province of Asia. While the work of establishing the church in this city was being carried on, other regions were not neglected. Apollos was sent to Greece; Paul wrote the First Epistle to the divided and carnal Corinthians; Titus visited Corinth; Timothy and Erastus visited Macedonia; messengers and a deputation from the church in Corinth came to consult with Paul and it appears that he made a short visit to that church.

At length Paul departed from Ephesus, proceeding north to Troas, where he waited for Titus; to Macedonia where again he met Titus at Philippi and wrote the Second Epistle to the Corinthians; then west to Illyricum and south to Corinth in Greece.

During the next two years he is slowly retracing his steps: north through Greece; east through Macedonia to Philippi; south to Troas, Asos and Miletus (where he met and counselled the Ephesian Elders), Patara, Tyre, Ptolemais, Cæsarea and Jerusalem. Not having heeded the warning of the Spirit against going to Jerusalem, given through the churches and his fellow-workers who accompanied him, he begins a long imprisonment.

Although this error, as we have already seen, brought as a consequence great difficulties and personal inconvenience, the ministry of Paul and his companions continued unhindered. God so ordered things that His servant was delayed as long as was necessary in places where his ministry was needed. During the two years in Cæsarea, while his trial dragged on, not only was he permitted to witness before Felix, Festus and Agrippa but he and his companions, Luke, Aristarchus and Trophimus, ministered to the church in that city. The enforced three months' stay at Malta gave the opportunity to preach the Gospel to the people of that Island. Three days were spent at Syracuse in Sicily. Then on the

Italian mainland they remained seven days with the church at Puteoli.

During the three years' imprisonment in Rome, Paul had liberty to carry on his ministry in that city. Meanwhile, the Epistles to the Philippians, Colossians, Ephesians and to Philemon were written, delegates came from distant churches, and his fellow-workers were coming and going continuing the work throughout the great and ever-extending field, caring for the churches already established and carrying the Gospel into new regions.

After his release, Paul had several years of freedom which he employed in a ceaseless and widespread ministry. The order of his movements during this period is not so easily followed. We find him visiting a number of places in Asia Minor, some of them, such as Colosse and Laodicea, for the first time. He was also in Macedonia, Greece and Crete. It seems that during this period he made his long-desired visit to distant Spain, spending, probably, two years in that land. As usual, many of his fellow-Evangelists are widely scattered. He wrote the First Epistle to Timothy who was in Ephesus and the Epistle to Titus who had remained in Crete.

The great missionary, after about thirty-five years of incessant labours, is now probably nearing the age of seventy. His health has long been poor and he begins to speak of himself as "Paul the aged". The churches have multiplied greatly and the strength of the Christian faith begins to be fully realized and feared by the authorities. Official opposition is steadily increasing and persecution becomes more violent. Paul is not allowed to continue in freedom any longer, but is arrested and sent a second time to Rome. It seems he is not free to preach as he had done during his first imprisonment, and those who show interest in him put themselves in danger, but he still carries the burden of the work upon his heart and makes his voice heard. He sends Titus to Dalmatia, Tychicus to Ephesus and writes the second Epistle to Timothy.

There is something deeply significant in the final scene. Paul is triumphant to the end. For thirty-five years he had triumphed in life through Christ over every work of Satan; now through Christ he triumphs over Satan in death.

We see him in his last letter to Timothy: a prisoner and terribly alone, yet not alone; old, infirm and in chains, but possessed
8

of unconquerable strength; silenced finally, yet not silenced.
The typical man of faith and servant of the Lord faces the typical man of sin and servant of Satan. Paul is before the judgment seat of Nero and fearlessly witnesses to him of Christ and Him crucified. But the man of sin rejects and slays the messenger of God.

The 'earthen vessel' is broken; but the 'treasure' it contained — 'the light of the glory of God', which had shone forth in Paul — could not be destroyed. Nero's power went down to the grave; Paul continues.

The testimony of Paul's unconquerable faith is given as an imperishable legacy to the Church:

> I have fought the good fight, I have finished my course, I have kept the faith; henceforth there is laid up for me a crown of righteousness which the Lord, the righteous judge, shall give me at that day.

It is the final victory-cry of triumphant, deathless life. And so the testimony of Paul's life was made complete.

The great fight is ended, and Paul receives a martyr's crown; the Lord has triumphed through him gloriously.

As has been seen, the dividing of Paul's ministry into three journeys is artificial and confusing. His ministry must be viewed as a whole, for it is all of one piece, without divisions of interruptions. When the church in Antioch needed help he was led back there, just as he was led to revisit other churches a number of times.

The division of his ministry into the three journeys tends to obscure the plan of action which he followed. Sometimes we see him advancing slowly from place to place, founding new groups of believers. Again, he is revisiting church after church, remaining long enough with each to see that Elders are appointed, to give further instruction, or to combat false doctrine. Frequently we find him settled for periods varying from one to three years, as in Antioch (three visits with a total of about four years), Corinth (several visits with a total of nearly four years), Ephesus (three years), Caesarea (two to three years) and Rome (two to three years). Thus fifteen out of thirty-five years were spent in ministering to five strategic congregations in five different countries. The place at which he settled thus temporarily became the centre for a most active and widespread ministry. Paul and Luke would remain there engaged in a ministry of teaching and preaching, building up the local congregation, while their fellow-workers went out to pay extended visits to other churches in that part of the world.

After a time — never more than three years — all were on the move again, ministering wherever there was need and the Holy Spirit led. Always, the planting of churches in new regions was the ambition of these missionaries but, while they were true to that vision, the care of the churches already founded was a responsibility that was never neglected.

As we have seen, the objective was not the evangelization of a restricted area but of the world. The method which was followed was admirably adapted for accomplishing that purpose, and it was gloriously successful.

Paul stayed long enough in each place to give adequate teaching and lay a solid foundation. He taught the new converts the deepest spiritual truth immediately, relying on the Holy Spirit to give them revelation. He took no financial help to them and had them enter at once into active participation in the work of proclaiming the Gospel. He refused to permit them to lean upon him, but obliged them to depend upon the Holy Spirit directly for His active help. In a comparatively short time he left them, forcing them to take full responsibility for exercising faith and carrying on the local ministry through the gifts of the Spirit. They had known from the beginning that he would do this and were prepared for it.

When he entered a city he did not plan to build slowly; that would have meant lack of faith in the Holy Spirit. He planned to gather a congregation that would be established in the Spirit from the beginning — a congregation like those in Jerusalem and Antioch — and his whole manner of working was calculated to bring this about.

The result was that he left active groups of believers in each place. They had still much to learn and much experience to gain, but he had provided them with a sufficient basis upon which to begin their work. They were experiencing the Holy Spirit's power. They were exercising the gifts of the Spirit for the local witness. United, unanimous prayer was basic among them, as it had been at Pentecost. Satan attacked them fiercely through persecution, teachers of false doctrine and internal dissensions, but any success he had was only temporary and always the final triumph was the Lord's.

Each congregation was a center of divine light and power with an aggressive witness in which all its members took part and which radiated outwards with a missionary vision as unlimited as Paul's. In them was full spiritual life. As the Holy Spirit had been able to speak through the congregations in Jerusalem and Antioch, so He could speak also through these newer churches. We have seen how He warned Paul through the churches in Asia and Syria that he should not go to Jerusalem on his last fateful journey to that city. As the congregations in Jerusalem and Antioch had been churches at prayer, so were these younger congregations (Acts 14:23; 20:36; 21:5; Eph. 6:18-20; Col. 4:2, 3). They were truly spiritual churches, sensitive to the guidance of the Spirit. In each one of them the Lord was in the midst controlling every action, building His Church. They knew how to be guided by Him and were willing to let Him guide. They were not groups of babes dependent upon the spiritual leadership of a Pastor but companies of "priests unto God" each individual responsible and active in the ministry of the Gospel.

Before very long the Holy Spirit calls young men from these new churches for the missionary ministry — Timothy, Tychicus, Trophimus, Aristarchus and others. And so the Church was consolidated, and so it spread, for in it was a living faith that released the living power of the Spirit of God.

Such a Church could not but expand. It was a missionary organization under missionary leadership. It could not be anything else but missionary in its action. The congregations were not organized to live a self-sufficient and self-centered existence; they were organized to fellowship with Christ for the one purpose of evangelizing — of preaching and teaching the Gospel to every creature as He had commanded. It was the organization which God in His infinite wisdom had given to His Church, the pattern which Our Lord had revealed for His continuing Body on earth, in which by His indwelling Spirit He was to carry on His work of seeking the lost. And it was a gloriously adequate organization, perfectly adapted for the forming of a spiritual, aggressive and triumphant Church.

CHAPTER XI

THE CARE OF THE CHURCHES

NOTHING could be further from the truth than to say that congregations of recent converts were abandoned by the New Testament Evangelists and left to sink or swim. The Evangelists were not only the foundation-layers of the Church, they also watched over the welfare of the congregations that were established.

Paul's going forth from Antioch did not end his ministry to that congregation; he returned several times when it was in need to minister again to it — and his return visits were not for a few days, or several weeks, but for a year or two. While he was constantly seeking to carry the Gospel further afield to new places, he was faithful to care for the churches already founded (2 Cor. 11:28). Much time was spent in revisiting them. Whenever a congregation was in need or in danger it was revisited. He kept close touch with every church. How full of instruction and inspiration were the letters he wrote them! How much time, prayer and thought must they have cost him. Congregations and individuals corresponded with him concerning many problems that arose, and he and his companions exercised an unceasing ministry of prayer for them. Yet, although he helped them in their difficulties, he never remained longer with them than was absolutely necessary but obliged them always to carry the full responsibility of the local ministry.

As the area evangelized widened and the number of churches that had to be cared for increased, it became necessary for the company of Evangelists to scatter their forces far and wide. To make this possible the Holy Spirit added an increasing number to their fellowship. The extent to which they were scattered may not be fully realized until we follow the journeyings of the different members. We have already given a sketch of Paul's travels and ministry. The following brief outlines of the ministries of several of his companions will give an idea of their incessant, wide-spread labours and of their faithful and efficient cooperation in the care of the churches as well as in the evangelization of new regions. These outlines, of course, must all be fitted into the record of Paul's ministry, with which they are inseparably linked.

Timothy

This spiritual son and friend of Paul joined the company at Lystra early in the 'second missionary journey'. His first separation from Paul was at Berea in Macedonia where he remained behind for a time with Silas to complete the initial work in the founding of the church in that city. He joined Paul again at Athens and was sent from there to 'establish and strengthen' the Thessalonian church in which serious difficulties had arisen not long after Paul's first, comparatively brief sojourn among them (Acts 17:15; 1 Thess. 3:1). He reported to Paul at Corinth, was with him for a time at Ephesus, then went on ahead to the Corinthian church again (1 Thess. 3:1, 2; Acts 18:1, 5; 1 Cor. 4:17; 16:10). The son of a Greek, much of his ministry at this time was in Greece. During the following winter, he remained with Paul. They were again separated, ministering in different parts, to reunite at Troas (Acts 20:3-5). He was imprisoned with Paul at Rome, both being released probably about the same time (Philemon 1; Col. 1:1; Phil. 1:1; Heb. 13:23). They are together once more at Ephesus, where Timothy remains behind to see that false doctrine is not taught, while Paul goes on to Macedonia and Philippi (1 Tim. 1:3; Phil. 2:19, 23, 24).

Attempts have been made to reconstruct Timothy's character from the counsels which Paul gives in his two letters to him. It has been inferred that Timothy was timid, inclined to neglect the gift that was in him, and even to be tempted by the love of money and youthful lusts. Such inferences are unwarranted. The Lord would hardly have called such an one and the Holy Spirit could not have continued to use him in such a ministry. In the counsels which he gives, Paul is dealing with the natural tendencies of the human heart, not with particular weaknesses of Timothy. He was always mindful of the fact that it was possible that he himself might become a castaway — an instrument set aside. Elsewhere he asks prayer for himself, "That I may open my mouth boldly to make known the mystery of the Gospel...... that I may speak boldly, as I ought to speak." The prayer of the church in Jerusalem was, "That with all boldness we may speak thy Word." There was need for such a prayer and such counsel in those days. Paul was not a timid man, but the courage of the most valiant was not sufficient to face the dangers and persecution that constantly beset these missionaries.

Timothy was a man filled with the Spirit, instructed in the Word, faithful in service and greatly used of God in ministry among the churches. From what Paul writes of him in 1 Thess. 3:2, we may infer that he had the gifts for ministering to the Church as a teacher and comforter.

A clear light is thrown on his character by what Paul wrote to the Philippians when about to send him to them:

> ... for I have no other like-minded with me who would care in earnest for your concerns; for all seek their own, not the things of Jesus Christ. But you know the trials which have proved his worth... (Phil. 2:19-22, Conybeare.)

This is a revealing statement. Timothy, just as Paul, had proved himself through trial and this practical testimony was well known to the churches. His zeal for the churches and his consecration were just as great as Paul's. Paul would not have recommended to the Philippians any one who did not come up to that standard. No second-rate worker would serve for such a ministry among the churches.

Silas

A Helenistic Jew, Silas also ministered largely in Greece and Macedonia. He was scourged and imprisoned with Paul at Philippi. With Timothy he remained behind at Berea to rejoin Paul later at Corinth. Paul mentions his having preached at Corinth (2 Cor. 1:19; 1 Thess. 1:1). While no further details are recorded of his missionary labours, it is evident that he was continually active in that ministry. His zeal as a preacher is mentioned in Acts 15:32.

Titus

Titus was with Paul at Ephesus. From there he was sent to

Corinth, in the year before the second letter to that church was written, to find out how the congregation had reacted to the first letter and to advise regarding the offering for the needy in Jerusalem (2 Cor. 7:6, 7; 8:6; 12:18). Paul reminds the Corinthians that Titus was not a burden to them financially while with them. Titus rejoined Paul in Macedonia, bringing the good news of the repentance and faithfulness of the Corinthian brethren. Then, in company with two others, he returned to Corinth bearing Paul's second letter. Later, he was in Crete with Paul, and remained there after Paul left, to complete the work and see to the appointing of Elders in the churches. While Titus was in Crete, Tychicus, Artemas and Apollos also visited the Island. He was then asked to meet Paul in Macedonia at Nicapolis. Later, he went to Dalmatia. It is probable that he was with Paul in Rome during his final imprisonment (2 Tim. 4:10).

He was a Greek and took an important part in the evangelization of Greece. His spiritual strength and efficiency as an Evangelist are seen in the outcome of the delicate mission on which he went to the divided and carnal church in Corinth after it had received Paul's first letter (2 Cor. 7:13, 15). His zeal for the churches is referred to by Paul in 2 Cor. 8:16: "But thanks be to God, by whose gifts Titus has the same zeal as my own on your behalf" (Conybeare). The tradition that he became Bishop of Crete has, of course, no Scriptural authority; it is contrary to the order which he and his fellow-workers established in the churches and to the meaning of the term 'Bishop' as used by them.

Tychicus

A native of the Province of Asia, Tychicus was much used in ministry to the churches in that region particularly. He became one of the company during the third missionary journey. When Trophimus accompanied Paul to Jerusalem, Tychicus continued in Asia (Act 21:29; 20:4). During Paul's first imprisonment he was with him in Rome (Col. 4:7,8). He went to Asia with the Epistles to the Ephesians and Colossians and to Philemon. As it is most probable that the Ephesian Epistle was a general letter to the churches, its delivery would mean the visiting of a number of churches. He, or Artemas, was sent to Crete while Titus was there (Tit. 3:12). During his second imprisonment in Rome, Paul writes of sending Tychicus again to the church in Ephesus (2 Tim. 4.12; Eph. 6:21, 22).

Luke

Luke, a Gentile, is a remarkable and lovable character. A man of rare ability as a writer, his Gospel is a literary classic. Paul's reference to him as "the beloved physician" shows that he was loved by his fellow-workers and by the churches. He was associated in the ministry with Paul for many years. He joined the missionary company at Troas. At Philippi he remained behind, continuing his ministry in that region for six years until Paul's return. From then on it seems the two did not separate until Paul's death, unless it be, indeed, that Luke is 'the brother... whose praise in publishing the Glad-tidings is spread throughout all the churches', of whom Paul writes in 2 Cor. 8:18 (Conybeare). He continued with Paul in Rome at the last when it was dangerous to do so. He seems to have become to Paul what Paul in the beginning was to Barnabas — a companion in all fellowship and ministry; we might even say, in some ways the second in the leading yoke.

The writer of the Acts of the Apostles and of the Gospel that bears his name tells us little about himself. Under the guidance of the Spirit, he records the ministry of Paul and others but says nothing about his own labours. However, we can be sure that Luke was not inactive during those many years that he and Paul were together. Without doubt he was constantly engaged in untiring ministry — a man deeply taught by the Spirit, with a profound knowledge of the Old Testament Scriptures, intimately acquainted with the history of the founding and development of the Church, of our Lord's teachings and of His purpose for the Church, steadfast, courageous, a faithful fellow-labourer, and ever manifesting the humility of his Lord. The strength of his prayer life[1] and the reality and simplicity of his faith may be inferred from his writings. The key-note of his Gospel is God's free Grace offered to men of every race and nation.

Referring to Luke's Gospel, Farrar says:

It may be regarded as certain that he sets before us that conception of the Life and Work of Christ which was the basis of the teaching of St. Paul ...
We see from St. Luke's own writings, and from authentic notices

---

[1] See p. 411.

of him, that he was a master of a good Greek style; — an accomplished writer, a close observer, an unassuming historian, a well-instructed physician, and a most faithful friend.[1]

Barnabas

Barnabas was the leader of the missionary group during the first five years. He had been truly called and sent by the Spirit. He was filled with the Spirit and there appears to have been much that was noble and lovable in his character. Shortly after Pentecost he had laid all that he had at the Apostles' feet. On Paul's first visit to Jerusalem after his conversion, it was Barnabas who presented him to the Apostles and vouched for him. No doubt Paul owed much to him in the early years of his ministry, for when Barnabas went to Antioch he was already a man of wide experience in the Church's ministry. In their ministry together as church-planters, he and Paul were entirely at one in regard to principle and method and after their separation we find no modification introduced by Paul (1 Cor. 9:6).

Barnabas' weakness seems to have been one of the heart. His insistence on taking his cousin with them a second time although his fellow-worker felt strongly that it was not the will of God, and although, evidently, Mark's call had not been confirmed by the Spirit to the Church, was a serious mistake. It caused him to separate not only from Paul but from the Lord's purpose. For that reason he drops out of the record while Paul, accompanied by one commended to the Lord by the Church, goes on in the will of the Lord as the leader around whom the Holy Spirit gathered the company of Evangelists that was to be so greatly used in the evangelization of the world.

Barnabas' ministry, so far as we know it, was mostly in Antioch, his native Cyprus, and the principal cities in the south of Asia Minor.

Faithful Ministers

There is sufficient evidence, particularly in Paul's references to them, to show that his fellow-workers were men with as definite a call as his and as truly gifted by the Spirit for their ministry.

---

[1] *St. Luke*, pp. 10, 12.

They were as ready to endure any hardness. They worked according to the same principles and bore before the churches and before the world as complete a practical testimony as he did.

Such was the group of missionaries who ministered not only in the propagation of the Gospel but also in the caring for the congregations already established. These churches had the ministry which they required from men filled with the spirit of the Master, men who had made and who continued to make an unconditional sacrifice, following in the steps of the Master, ministering as He did.

Messages Through Messengers

Not only Paul and his companions, but other Evangelists, and the Apostles, doing the work of Evangelists, were engaged in ministering to the churches. A notable example of the sending of messages from the Head of the Church to local congregations that were in need is given in the revelation received by John in Patmos. The Island of Patmos lay off the coast of the Province of Asia, and John, while in prison, would be in touch with the seven congregations on the mainland. The messages which he received from the Lord for these churches were carried to them by 'angels' or 'messengers'.[1] In these messages were counsel, commendation and reproof according to the condition of the church addressed.

The sending of these messages from the Lord by messengers to these churches was in accord with the general practice in the ministry of the Evangelists to the churches. When the Church in Corinth was in spiritual defeat, Paul's letters were sent to them by messengers. Usually, the messengers who bore such messages· were Evangelists.

These 'angel'-messengers, bearers of Heavenly messages, are also called 'stars', reflectors of Heavenly light; instruments held 'in the right hand' of Him who is 'in the midst' of the churches to use in sending a ray of Heavenly light to any church in need of it. The churches are 'golden lampstands', sanctified vessels for the Holy Spirit's fire and light (Rev. 1:12-20). These figures surely are appropriate and revealing of the Evangelist's ministry as the Lord's messengers to the churches.

---

[1] See pp. 241, 476-8.

We have seen that such a ministry was continually being exercised towards the churches.

Whenever a church was in spiritual need of any kind, there were those whom God had provided, ready to minister to them as He directed them, by visits and by written messages. The foundation-layers were also foundation-repairers. If the spiritual welfare of a congregation was seriously threatened — that is, if its foundations were shaken or endangered through backsliding, strife, false doctrine or the unfaithfulness of its Elders — to the extent that the Head of the Church could no longer speak to it directly, He would do so through His foundation-layers. Theirs was a ministry of the greatest importance, indispensable to the welfare of the churches.

This ministry was the Lord's provision for His Church but it fell into disuse when the Church departed from the divinely instituted order. Local and regional officials — presbyters, or priests, and bishops (in the modern sense) — were substituted, and the ministry of the Evangelist disappeared. Consequently, the churches drifted into error and powerlessness. When man changed the order which God in His infinite wisdom had given, the Lord could no longer speak to the churches in need through His messengers.

The value of the ministry exercised by the Evangelists among the churches will be apparent. The intervention of someone from the outside whose call to such a ministry and consequent spiritual authority is generally recognized by the churches is often far more likely to be effective than the appeals of any local voice.

The Evangelist's Authority

The Evangelists were not Bishops or District Superintendents in the modern sense. Their ministry to the churches was governed by different principles. They were not commissioned by the Church but by the Holy Spirit, though their call was confirmed by the Spirit to the Church and recognized by it. Their authority was not ecclesiastical. They had no means of enforcing their judgments. Their authority was purely spiritual. Their message was in accordance with God's Word and, therefore, had the authority of God's Word. It was given to them by the Spirit and accompanied by His power. And their mission had the spiritual backing of their fellow-Evangelists, all of whom were recognized by the Church as called of God to such a ministry. Such authority is actually much more effective and safer than ecclesiastical authority.[1]

When the spirituality of the Corinthian church was low, the Elders failing in their duty, the believers walking carnally and flagrant sin permitted in the congregation, Paul wrote them and Silas visited them. That congregation had been behind none in the manifestation of the gifts of the Spirit but they had become carnal. As Weymouth says: "exuberant verbosity, selfish display, excesses at the Lord's table, unseemly behaviour of women at meetings of worship and also abuse of spiritual gifts, were complicated by heathen influences and the corrupting customs of idolatry".

Paul did not spare them. He was faithful in going to the root of all the trouble. They were carnally-minded and walking carnally. They were not walking and serving in the Spirit. They were not building spiritually by the Spirit upon the true foundation — Christ — and when 'the day' came and their carnal building of wood, hay or stubble was tried by fire it would be burned and they would suffer loss.

However, he did not command upon his own authority nor claim ecclesiastical authority. He boldly affirmed that he in himself was nothing. The fact that he was declaring God's wisdom revealed by the Spirit was his authority. He said:

If any man deems himself to be a prophet or a man with spiritual gifts, let him recognize as the Lord's command all that I am now writing. But if anyone is ignorant (spiritually) let him be ignorant (1 Cor. 14:37, Weymouth).

For, as he had said in 1 Cor. 2:14:

the unspiritual (soulish) man rejects the things of the Spirit of God and cannot attain to a knowledge of them because they are spiritually judged (Weymouth).

Again, in the same letter, he wrote:

But I shall be with you shortly, if the Lord will, and then I shall learn, not the word of these boasters, but their might. For mighty deeds, not simply words, are the tokens of God's kingdom (1 Cor. 4:19, 20, Conybeare).

---

[1] The Scriptural order of the Evangelist's ministry is fully dealt with in later chapters.

His authority was proved by the power of God manifested through him. It was not delegated by any organization or council of men. A man to whom an organization delegates power may or may not be worthy. Even if worthy when commissioned he may become unworthy later. God appoints none who is unworthy and if the one He calls becomes unworthy, God's power immediately ceases to be manifested through him. One with authority from an organization must be obeyed whether he is right or wrong. The counsel of one commissioned by God may be spurned. No church can be forced to accept it, but the probabilities are that it will be accepted if he is truly giving God's message, for his word will be backed by the power of the Spirit. And it is of the greatest importance that the Church should be free to reject whatever is not of God (Cf. Rev. 2:2).

The Corinthian church was certainly a bad case from all aspects but the faith, prayer and faithful ministry of God's servants empowered by the Spirit were triumphant. Let us consider further the manner in which Paul and his Fellow-workers acted.

In dealing with the case of immorality, he did not command but exhorted the church to judge the case, as it was their duty to do, and take the necessary steps to deal with the offender. He did not order the exclusion of the offender from membership on his own responsibility; he simply insisted that the church function as it ought to and do what it already should have done in the circumstances. His complaint was that they were not fulfilling their responsibilities.

They were not ignorant of what they should have done. The principle laid down by our Lord, recorded by Matthew, would certainly have been taught them by Paul. That Paul had Christ's statement in mind when he wrote is evident. In proof of this we have but to note the parallel between what Christ taught and the counsel given by Paul (1 Cor. 5:1-11). In both passages Christ's power and authority, derived through His presence and the revelation of His will, are the only basis of action. The action is taken in the Name of Christ, His will having been made known by the Spirit through the Word and through prayer. What is done is done by Christ speaking and acting through His Body, the Church.

Paul stated his own position in the matter. To be obedient to Christ he could have taken no other position. And he assured them that, as they met to fulfil their duty, he would be with them in Spirit, one with them in their action, and sharing their responsibility — as, indeed, all spiritual men would. His letter roused them to action. They knew it was according to Christ's teaching, and the Holy Spirit bore witness in their hearts to its truth and to their duty. It was not God's servant they obeyed, but the truth with which he faced them. His ministry was to face them with the Word.

The case was judged and the offending member excluded. The moral effect of this action upon the church would be profound. It meant that the church took its stand as a body for that which was right and definitely and voluntarily turned back into the way of obedience to the Lord and sound doctrine and practice.

The moral effect upon the individual who was disciplined would also be great. Had he been able to say that he was put out of the church by Paul, he could have acted much more boldly and arrogantly than under the influence of the judgment and condemnation of the whole congregation of which he was a member.

In this same manner Paul dealt with the divisions in the Corinthian church. He refused to accept the leadership of any party and, far from asserting personal authority, points always and only to Christ as the one Head. He stated that he, Peter and Apollos were nothing but servants; Christ was all (1 Cor. 1:12, 13). He dealt with the Corinthians on spiritual grounds alone, and then left them to do the right thing, because it was right: because it was Christ's will, and not because he, Paul, demanded it. But he knew that behind his words was all the power of the Spirit of the living God, for they were the words of the Spirit, "quick and powerful".

Deliberately and consistently he kept himself in the background, forcing the churches to function, to assume full responsibility and to be faithful to the Gospel on the ground of obedience to Christ and faith in Christ. The weapons of his warfare were not carnal but they were mighty to pull down the enemy's strongholds.

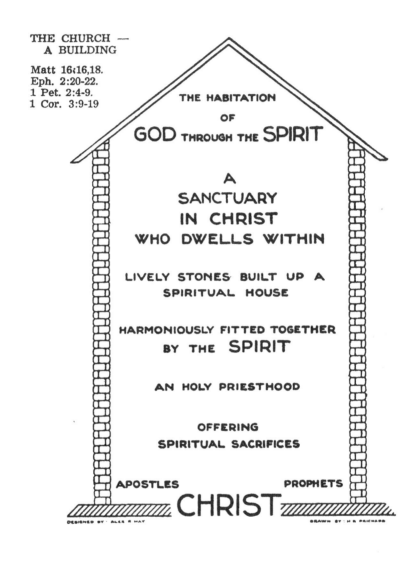

THE CHURCH —
A BUILDING

Matt 16:16,18.
Eph. 2:20-22.
1 Pet. 2:4-9.
1 Cor. 3:9-19

THE HABITATION
OF
GOD THROUGH THE SPIRIT

A
SANCTUARY
IN CHRIST
WHO DWELLS WITHIN

LIVELY STONES BUILT UP A
SPIRITUAL HOUSE

HARMONIOUSLY FITTED TOGETHER
BY THE SPIRIT

AN HOLY PRIESTHOOD

OFFERING
SPIRITUAL SACRIFICES

APOSTLES   PROPHETS

CHRIST

DESIGNED BY ALEX R HAY   DRAWN BY H R PRICHARD

PART II

STRUCTURE OF THE NEW TESTAMENT CHURCH

"Show the house . . .
and let them measure the pattern."

Ezek. 43:10.

TO THE CHURCH

Church of God, the dwelling-place
Of Christ's Heavenly light and grace,
Built in His eternal thought,
Purpose of His wisdom wrought;
Witness of the Throne above
As the channel of His love.
Thee in Christ doth God endue,
Manifold thy wisdom true:
By the Holy Spirit's might,
By His gifts and Heavenly sight
Manifesting Christ in love,
Grace unceasing from above.

Church of God in Heavenly might
Bearer of redeeming light,
Image of the incarnate Word,
Fulness of the risen Lord,
Triumph thou, unconquered yet,
Nor thy heritage forget!
Thy foundations truly laid
To the pattern Heaven made,
Spurn the arm of fleshly might,
Wisdom false and paths of night.
Faithful unto Christ thy Lord
Guard in truth the eternal Word!

Then the living waters deep
In this desert land shall reap
Heavenly fruit to Earth unknown,
Blooms God's loving hand hath sown:
Tears and striving turned to peace,
Hearts alight with lowly grace.
Mighty torrent of God's power
Flowing through thee hour by hour;
As the heart gates open wide
To receive the living tide
Life from death in full release
Springs in joy from love's increase.

CHAPTER XII

THE CHURCH - FUNDAMENTAL PRINCIPLES

THE New Testament church-planters were members of the Church and it was in that relationship that they engaged in their ministry. All their work·was related to the Church: it was a part of the Church's work and conformed always and in every particular to the principles and order of the Church. Therefore, their work, to be understood fully, must be fitted into the background of the organization and procedure of the New Testament Church. To attempt to consider their actions as independent of, or unrelated to, Church order, or to interpret them in the light of modern Church or Mission organization, will only cause confusion of thought and misunderstanding of their methods and principles. When, however, we get a clear view of the order that obtained in the Early Church, then the reason for their actions, the principles that governed their methods, and the consistency of their procedure become clearly apparent.

We present the Church from the missionary point of view. The missionary point of view is the only true one. The Lord founded the Church as a missionary organization. Such was its original structure. It was not an ecclesiastical organization with missionary endeavour as a department of its work. Missionaries were its leaders.[1] Its primary purpose was missionary and all its members engaged in the propagation of the Gospel. Paul's point of view concerning it was missionary. As he and the other New Testament writers wrote of it they were busy planting churches throughout the world. The view-point of the Church that has lost its missionary structure and vision, whose leaders are not missionaries and

---

[1] See pp. 266, 267.

whose objective in ministry has become local, is not the true one; it is false and its conclusions are false.

In a statement that voices the longing which the Spirit of God has put into the hearts of many of the Lord's people to return to God's order as revealed in His Word, and to the place of true spiritual power and unity, two of His servants write:

> In the Scriptures we have a crystal-clear picture of the early biblical church-life...
> If God's Word alone were allowed to become our exclusive guide in church-life, we should find that the diversity, the confusion, and the contradictions so apparent in our contemporary church-life, would largely disappear.[1]

Not only so, but all the fundamental causes of the Church's weakness today would also be removed and the Holy Spirit's power released.

A. T. Pierson, in his account of A. J. Gordon's ministry, describes the Apostolic congregation as (1) an assembly for worship; (2) an organized body for aggressive work for Christ; (3) a school for training disciples; (4) a home for the family of God. Commenting further he says:

> We find not a trace of sacred places, or sacred persons, and scarce a hint of sacred times or seasons. Wherever and whenever God and his worshipping people met, the ground was thereby hallowed and the time sanctified; and all believers seem to have been singularly on a level, preaching the Word, teaching the way of God more perfectly, and even administering sacramental rites... There are no clerical prerogatives, titled officials, choirs or hired singers, no secular trustees, no worldly entertainments, no consecrated buildings, and not a sign of a salaried service of any sort. God seems to be the centre around which the early church crystallized, and the whole organization of believers was free from complicated methods and worldly maxims.
> Work by all, in diverse spheres of activity, according to diversity of gifts, was the law of church life. The Spirit speaks expressly in the Epistle to the Ephesians, that the very purpose of all offices and functions, apostles, prophets, evangelists, pastors, and teachers, was one sublime end: SERVICE. All the gifts and graces bestowed and distributed by the Spirit were for the perfecting of the saints unto the work of serving, unto the building up of the body of Christ, so that there might be the double growth of accession and expansion. The early church had no room for an idle and selfish soul. Every believer was a worker, warrior, witness. He came into the church as soon as he believed and was baptized, to be a member in the body where every member had an office, and must needs

---

[1] *What is the Purpose of the Lord's Supper*, by J. Bolton and C. Stacey Woods, *Our Hope* Mar. 1946.

fulfill his function in order to the health and help of the whole body.[1]

The Divine Pattern

It has been concluded by some that no definite or permanent form of Church organization is given in the New Testament. It is suggested that, at the time of the Apostles, Church organization was still rudimentary in form and only in process of formation and that it was God's purpose that it should be developed and perfected later as the need arose. Such a conclusion, however, is a grave error: it is contrary to the clear teaching of Scripture and throws open the door to whatever organization man may deem necessary.

The fact is that the Apostles, fulfilling the ministry which God gave them, laid a complete and perfect foundation for the Church, both as regards structure and doctrine.[2] A careful and unbiased study of the New Testament will make it abundantly clear that a full and detailed revelation is given regarding the structure of the Church and that all the congregations planted in Apostolic times were organized in accordance with that pattern.

It should be borne in mind that the structure of the local church was based upon that of the Synagogue.[3] The changes introduced are only such as the new spiritual order made necessary. The college of Elders, the 'ministers' (servants-termed Deacons in the Church) and the freedom for any to take part in preaching and teaching, which were the essential features of the Synagogue, were the essential features also of the local church.[4]

In the Christian congregation there was no Chief Ruler or President; that place was occupied by the Lord Who was present in the midst. There was no High Priest or Great Sanhedrin;

---

[1] *How Christ Came to Church*, pp. 108-110.

[2] See comment on Eph. 2:19-22 in chapter XIII.

[3] Prof. Lindsay states, "We may at all events believe that the early Christian organization, if not exactly the same, was modelled upon that of the synagogue, and that the reason why we have so few descriptions and instructions in the New Testament is that the apostles did not require to describe what was so very well known to the Jewish Christians who composed the apostolic Church." — *Christianity, Enc. Brit.*

[4] See chapter XIX.

Christ was the High Priest and His absolute authority was exercised directly through any company met in His Name. Appointments were made and authority conferred, not by a Great Council or Supreme Tribunal but by the Lord Himself. There was no separate priesthood; all were 'living stones', a 'holy priesthood', offering 'spiritual sacrifices' through the gifts of the Spirit manifested through them. In Judaism God dwelt among His people but separate from them. Once a year the High Priest alone could enter the symbolic Holy of Holies. But now Christ has entered the true Holy of Holies, the acceptable sacrifice has been made, the Great High Priest is personally present in every gathering of the members of His Church and His Spirit dwells within each one.

The various statements made by Paul concerning Church order in his Epistles written to different churches at different periods of his ministry, are all wholly consistent with each other and with the basic principles governing the Church which are revealed by our Lord in the sixteenth and eighteenth chapters of Matthew's Gospel. It is clearly evident that Paul and all the other church-planters of that time introduced a complete and uniform order into all the churches.

It is true, of course, that much was changed and much was added in the organization of the Church after the days of the Apostles. A definite tendency to do this had been evident even in their day and had been strongly resisted. To those who would have introduced a different order in Corinth, Paul wrote: "we have no such custom, neither the churches of God" (1 Cor. 11:16). That rebuke in itself proves that there was a definitely established order recognized by all the churches. It clearly implies that the order was uniform in all the churches and that no deviation from it was permitted in any congregation.

Later, however, after Apostolic times, this tendency to modify the divinely revealed order gained ground in the less spiritual churches. Man began to tinker with both the structure and doctrine of the foundation laid by God through the Apostles, and there began the long process of development in the organization of the Church, along the lines of human organization, which reached its height, in the course of several centuries, in the Roman Catholic Church.

To know the doctrines and spiritual truths that God has given us, it is necessary to "search the Scriptures". It is not surprising, surely, that a diligent search of the Word of God is necessary to know the full revelation of the pattern which He has given for His Church.

It is not that the teaching regarding the Church is obscure or difficult to discover. On the contrary, it is clear, ample and detailed. The real difficulty arises when we approach the Word with preconceived ideas. If we have modern Church organization as the basis of our thinking and try to fit Scripture into that mould, we shall find ourselves faced with an impossible task. Not finding what we look for, we may conclude that the revelation is incomplete in that respect. It hardly should be necessary to say that if we desire to know the order and methods practised in the New Testament Church we must seek to approach the Word with an entirely open mind, prepared for any unexpected discovery.

In this outline of the structure and practice of the Church of the New Testament we have sought to bring together in order the teaching of Scripture regarding it. In this order, the different passages of Scripture relating to the matter fit together into a complete and harmonious unity, revealing a structure that is purely spiritual in conception and design and true to every spiritual principle of God's character and dealings with men.

This outline has been tested in practical operation over a period of many years. It is, of course, not presented as an authoritative statement. God's written Word is the only authoritative guide for the believer. Our purpose is to point to that Word and share with God's people the guidance and experience which we believe He has vouchsafed unto us.

In approaching the study of any doctrine or truth in God's Word, it is well to remember that the practice of the Holy Spirit, in the writing of the revelation, has been, generally, to give a key passage in which the basic principles of the doctrine or truth are stated and which will serve as the foundation upon which the whole revelation concerning that matter, found in different passages throughout the Word, may be built up. Usually, there is only one such comprehensive statement.

It is also important to bring together all the passages dealing with a particular truth before forming any conclusions regarding it. To isolate any passage from the whole body of truth revealed on a subject is highly dangerous and has been the cause of much unscriptural procedure and erroneous teaching.

The Key Passages

There are a number of important passages dealing with various aspects of the Church's organization and work, but the passages that are basic, giving the great fundamental principles of the Church's existence, are the statements of our Lord recorded in Matt. 16:16-19; 18:15-22.

In the first passage the fundamental principles of the structure of the Church are revealed. In the second the principles of the local gathering are taught.

Matt. 16:16-19.

Here Christ revealed to His disciples the truth that the Church was to be built, and made known the basic facts concerning it.

1. "I will build my Church." The Church is His and He Himself is to build it. He did not say that man would build it for Him, or that the Church would build itself. This statement is not figurative but literal: Christ is to engage personally, actively, directly in the whole work of building His Church.

2. The Church is to be built upon a rock — upon the fact that Jesus is "the Christ, the Son of the living God". This fact has two related components: (a) Jesus Christ is the Son of God; (b) God is the living God — Who works and manifests His life and power. This rock-fact is not a doctrinal theory but a living, active, omnipotent, omniscient, omnipresent person.

3. Christ used Peter's name (*Petros* — a piece of rock) to illustrate the truth that all who believe what Peter had just affirmed would be pieces of the *petra* (rock) — of Christ Himself. The members of His Church would be those in whom He dwells, partakers of Himself and manifesting Him. It is this same truth that Paul teaches under the figure of the Body, of which Christ is the Head and we the members. That Peter fully understood Christ's meaning at the time seems hardly likely, but that he later grasped its full and glorious significance is evident from what he wrote in 1 Pet. 2:4-9, where he says:

> Come to Him, the living Stone, rejected indeed by men, but in God's esteem chosen and valuable. And yourselves also like living stones be built up into a spiritual house, as a holy priesthood to offer spiritual sacrifices acceptable to God through Jesus Christ (Weymouth).

Quoting Isa. 28:16, Ps. 118:22 and Isa. 8:14, Peter links this fundamental truth with Old Testament prophecy, showing that it had been foretold by the prophets. (Cf. 1 Cor. 3:11.)

4. "The gates (counsels) of Hell shall not prevail against it". The Church cannot be overcome by Satan's wisdom or power — that is, the Church built by and on Christ (not the Church built by man) is unconquerable. The inference is that Satan will attack it; but he will be unable to defeat it. This security is derived from the fact that Satan cannot prevail against Christ, the Son of the Living God, or His work. However, nothing that is of man's building will survive. (Cf. 1 Cor. 3:10-15.)

5. He Spoke of the Keys which were to open the door of the Church to both the Jew and the Gentile. (Acts 2:38-42; 10:34-46.)

6. He stated that what is done by the Church is done in Heaven. This is derived from the fact that what is done is done by Christ as He builds His Church and, therefore, being His work, is done in Heaven as well as on earth. It refers to what is done by the Church which He is building, not the Church which man is building. What is done in the Church by man is not done in Heaven.

Matt. 18:15-22.

In this passage we may discern all the fundamental principles which govern the local church's structure and activity.

(1) Two or more members of the Church, gathered together in the authority and power of the Name of Christ, form an assembly of the Church.

(2) Christ Himself (the Foundation and Builder) is personally present in that gathering. As He is present, His active power, authority and wisdom are present. He is present to build His Church. He is not there as a spectator to watch man build it for Him. "For" at the beginning of this verse (20) indicates that all that has been said previously is dependent upon this fact.

(3) These two or more members of the Church will receive guidance from the Holy Spirit as to what to pray for so that they may unanimously ask the same thing. That unanimous, Spirit-guided petition will be answered (Acts 1:14; 2:1). That is, Christ, who is in the midst, and who is the 'Head of the Body', makes known His will through the Spirit to those who are seeking Him in prayer, and when they ask that from Him He accomplishes it. (Cf. Jn. 14:12-14.)

(4) In this way it is possible for the Church (those members of the Church thus assembled together) to know His will and to be used by Him in the doing of it.

(5) This identical guidance given by the Spirit to all the members is the basis of the unity of the Church.

(6) It is this doing of Christ's will through the Church that gives the Church its authority. It is in this way and on this ground that what is done by the Church on earth is done in Heaven. Actually, it is done by Christ, who is present, through the Church met in His Name and authority and guided by His Spirit to ask what is His will. (1 Jn. 5:14, 15; Rom. 8:26, 27; Acts 13:2-4.)

(7) The mention of two or more in connection with the functioning of the Church (vv. 19, 20) reveals a principle. A single believer cannot function as the Church. One is not an assembly and can never act as an assembly. This principle is of general application in the Church. Each New Testament congregation had more than one Elder and more than one Deacon. The number ministering the Word in the gathering of the church at the Lord's Table is given as 'two or three' (1 Cor. 14:29). Our Lord sent the disciples out 'two by two'. Barnabas sought the fellowship of Paul in the ministry at Antioch. When they separated, each sought another companion. Elders (plural) represent the Church in praying for the sick (Jas. 5:14). Confirmation of Paul's call was given to others of the Church (Acts 13:2).

(8) The responsibility of the church to exercise discipline and to exclude the wilful and unrepentant sinner from its fellowship, and the procedure to be followed in such cases is also stated.

(9) The case was to be taken finally before the church (the local congregation) and the action was to be taken by the church. The responsibility for the action rested upon the whole church, not upon any officials of the Church. The congregation spoken of is one that might not be more than two or three, among whom would be no Elders. In 1 Cor. 4:1-5, Paul writes to the congregation, not to the Elders.

(10) The need for love and patience and forgiveness and the responsibility of the stronger believer, who is in the right, towards an erring brother is made plain.

(11) The disciplinary action is, in reality, taken by Christ, the Builder and Head of the Church. Being present, He makes His will known through His Word and through prayer. The Church then carries out His will, acting in obedience to His guidance.

If it is not His will, the Church acts in vain, for He does not separate Himself from the one it condemns. Likewise, if it fail to act, its laxity does not save the sinning Christian from condemnation, for Christ does not fail to separate Himself from him.

The direct exercise of discipline by Christ in this manner when a church was lax is seen in the message to the Laodicean church (Rev. 3:14-22). The condition of that whole church was such that Christ withdrew Himself from fellowship with it. His promise to be present where two or three were gathered in His Name could not be fulfilled in their case because they were no longer truly gathering in His Name. They met around His Table but He was not present. He did not abandon them utterly: He stood outside the door. He did not cease to speak to them: He continued knocking at the door seeking to be admitted.

The connection between the case of discipline referred to and the teaching regarding the fundamental principles of the Church in this passage is not accidental. In dealing with sinning man, God acts upon the principles that are laid down here to govern the attitude of a Christian to a brother who has sinned against him. When Adam and Eve sinned against God, He sought them out for the purpose of saving them from their sin. Though He has had to separate Himself from sinning man, He takes the initiative to meet man. He did so at the Cross and He does so through the Spirit's pleadings continually. The purpose of the Church — His Body, in which He dwells — is to manifest Him to the sinning world — to seek out those in sin and to bring them to repentance that they may receive forgiveness and eternal life.

(12) It is important to note that all this responsibility rests upon the congregation, not upon the Elders. This principle is carefully observed in the New Testament churches (cf. 1 Cor. 4:1-5; Acts 1:14; 2:1-4; 6:1-6. See p. 294, note 2).

The passages in Matt. 16 and 18, are the only detailed statements made by Christ regarding the Church's structure, but they reveal all the great, basic laws of its construction. These principles laid down by Christ provide for the preservation of the Church's purity, for communication with God, for wisdom, power, fruitbearing, authority, justice, clemency, guidance, unanimity, protection from autocracy and from any abuse of authority (no one man can act alone and unanimity is required) — surely a very complete and adequate equipment. To infringe upon any one of these laws is to weaken seriously the structure and to reduce vitally its efficiency.

It is important to observe that no legislative function is given to the Church. That pertains entirely to the Lord Himself, and His commandments are recorded in the Word, which is the only code of laws and regulations for the Church. No organ is provided in the Church for the legislative function. But there is ample provision of organs for the executive and administrative functions that He would perform through the Church.[1]

It will be borne in mind that the whole doctrine of the Church — its structure, life and ministry — rests upon the foundation of the basic principles of all spiritual life. No one doctrine stands by itself. Each is but an integral part of the whole: one facet, the light of which is but one ray of the same light that comes from all. All doctrines are inextricably interrelated and interdependent. Faith, love, sanctification, prayer, the knowledge of God's will, etc., are all dependent upon each other. And the doctrine of the Church is dependent upon them all.

In our Lord's statements regarding the Church, unanimous prayer is mentioned. The fact that He does not state there the conditions that govern prayer does not mean that the prayer of the Church is not subject to them. It is: it must be "in the Spirit", in faith, according to God's will and offered in the Name of Christ by believers who are walking in obedience to Him.

As we seek to understand the life, ministry and order of the Church, we must remember that it is based upon the foundation of all doctrine — the Cross of Christ on which Christ died, the empty tomb, Christ seated victorious at the right hand of God, and the believer, dead, risen, indwelt by the Spirit and seated with Christ in the Heavenlies. The Church is the assembly of believers who are crucified with Christ, in whom Christ lives and through whom He works and manifests Himself by His Spirit.

This Church is not an organization that functions so long as the organization is complete. It is life: the life of Christ manifested by His Spirit dwelling in the Church; it is power: the power of the Holy Spirit manifesting Christ in and through His Body.

---

[1] The question of the so-called "Council of Jerusalem" is dealt with on p. 108-9. See also p. 252.

The Church a Theocracy

It will be seen that the government of the Church, as Christ taught it, is a pure theocracy. Such a form of government is not acceptable to fallen man. In the first place he has definitely rejected government by God, declaring himself sufficient in himself. In the second place, it is not possible for him to understand or take part in such a government for he is spiritually dead. (1 Cor. 2:14.)

God does not expect the unregenerate man to understand spiritual government but He does require that His children accept it and understand it. The believer who walks in the Spirit will be enabled to do so; the one who is walking carnally will not understand or accept it.

Human Government

Among men there are three main types of government:

(1) Autocracy — an absolute government by one man.

(2) Oligarchy — government by a privileged group.

(3) Democracy — government of the people by the people. "A form of government in which the supreme power is vested in the people collectively, and is administered by them or by officers appointed by them."

The unspiritual believer has introduced all these forms of government into the Church. Today almost the whole Church is organized on one or other of these three systems. The purely theocratic government has been rejected as impractical and human government set up in its place.

The autocratic form of government is found in the Roman Catholic Church, in Denominations with a government in which one man is given supreme control and in congregations where one man assumes a place of priestly privilege in the ministry of the Word. Here men act as intermediaries between Christ and His people. It is no longer Christ in the midst of the congregation, dealing directly with each member, all of them priests, all equal and each one equally responsible to know His will and to permit Christ to carry it out through him by the Spirit. Christ must make His will known to the congregation through specially appointed men and they, if they consider it necessary, will make it known to the Church. Christ must act through them and the Church must seek Christ's will through them. The priestly work being reserved for a few, the others are prevented from fulfilling their responsibility in ministry through the gifts of the Spirit, and the Spirit is not permitted to use them.

The oligarchic form of government is seen in congregations where a group of Elders, in the appointment of whom the congregation has no say, undertake to find the will of the Lord for the congregation. Here again is an intermediary group standing between the Head and the congregation that has met with Him. In many matters the Lord cannot reveal His will directly to those assembled and they are only permitted to know His will through the Elders.

The democratic form of government is found in congregations organized on the congregational system. The responsibility is placed directly upon the entire congregation. Decisions are made by vote and the opinion of the majority rules. It is the majority, not the Lord, that make the decision. It is not the whole congregation waiting before Him in prayer until His will is known and then seeking through the prayer of faith that He carry out His will. And so often strife, division and carnality are the outcome.

In all these systems of government the control is actually placed in man's hands. He may seek to govern in Christ's Name. Christ's presence may be sincerely desired, but belief in His power to actually make His will known and take control is vague and largely theoretic. The result is that, to a large extent, it is man that does the governing and building while the Lord must stand by unheeded.

Where the responsibility is placed upon one man it is hoped that he will know God's will and guide the congregation aright. Where a group of Elders have that place it is expected that they will know His will and the congregation depends upon them. Where the congregation rules it is hoped that the decision of the majority will be Christ's will. The Lord may be able to overrule the existing organization and carry out His purpose in hearts that are truly yielded. But how unsatisfactory it all is; how poor compared to the glorious thing of His purpose.

In the theocratic government of the congregation Christ is present and makes His will known to all through the Word and by His Spirit as His people wait prayerfully before Him. Every member of the congregation is required to know His will. His will is not decided by majority vote, it is revealed by Him directly to each one. It is not decided by the majority because all must know it. It cannot be decided by an intermediary individual or group because each one is responsible to know it and no one can come in between him and his Lord.

The human forms of government produce seriously harmful effects upon the members of the Church. The individual is relieved to a certain extent of personal responsibility. His direct contact with the Lord is restricted and the need for it greatly reduced. The result is that his spiritual experience is restricted and his growth hindered.

The personal, active presence of Christ in every gathering of the Church is a great basic principle that must never be lost sight of. In all Church order and activity the greatest care must be taken that His place is not usurped by man.

We witness the great patience of the Lord as He seeks to build His Church and use His people in the midst of the present circumstances, but how great is His loss and the Church's loss! When the Tabernacle in the wilderness was completed, built according to the pattern that God had given, we are told that the glory of God filled it. When Solomon's Temple was finished, built also to a plan revealed by God, it is recorded again that God's glory filled it. Zerubbabel's Temple was not constructed according to a pattern given by God and God's glory did not fill it. God still continued to be with His people. Many, no doubt, received blessings in the worship in that Temple, but the full glory of His presence was not manifested.

Very similar is the situation that exists in the Church today. The Lord blesses and uses His people when and as He can, but His glory does not fill the Church. But wherever He is given His place the glory of His wisdom, power and absolute victory over all that is of Satan and man will be manifested in that congregation. This is still His order and purpose for His Church and any congregation — even if they be but two or three — that is willing to give Him His place of headship in humble faith and obedience will find that it is so.

The order which Christ gave for His Church is very simple. He is present in every gathering. Every one present is equal. Every one is responsible to know His will. He reveals His will to all. All unitedly and unanimously must ask that that be done. This unanimity is obtained, not by all agreeing to do the same thing but by all knowing Christ's will and yielding to it. Then He does His work through each one by His Spirit. But how is all this to be effected? He said that every one must have taken up his Cross to follow Him. Otherwise they are not worthy of Him. Only the believer that is "crucified with Christ", in whom Christ lives, can be guided by Him in all things. And only the believer in whom the flesh is crucified can have the Holy Spirit's gifts truly manifested through him.

Thus a congregation is a company of those who "take up the Cross daily", living the resurrection life and met with the crucified and risen Christ, who has all power and authority which He manifests through them as they are seated with Him in the Heavenlies (Eph. 1:19; 2:6).

And is not all the human organization in the Church today, and the failure to give Christ His place as Head and the weakness and defeat, the result of the fact that those who meet in His Name are not crucified daily and living the resurrection life through the Spirit?

It was after Peter's confession that Christ was the Son of the living God and Christ's revelation of the fact that He would build His Church and that the gates of hell would not prevail against it, that Satan's war against the Church began. He persuaded Peter to reject the Cross and say to the Lord, "Far be it from thee Lord", or "Pity Thyself". Then our Lord revealed the fundamental requirement for the Church's victory: "If any man would follow me, let him deny himself and take up his cross and follow me" (Matt. 1:13-24).[1] The victorious Church of the crucified Christ must be composed of crucified members.

God's Purpose

It is necessary to see how Christ's teaching regarding the Church accords with God's purpose for this age. Our Lord's prayer, revealing the purpose which He came to fulfil in His own was, "As thou Father, art in me and I in thee, that they may be one in us...... I in them, and thou in me, that they may be made perfect in one" (Jn. 17:21, 23). Paul states that the message he preached to the Church was, "Christ in you, the hope of glory" (Col. 1:27).

---

[1] The significance of this in relation to the Church is considered in the Author's book, *Life in God or The Power and Triumph of Perfect Love,* Chapter 13.

Christ taught that He would build His Church upon Himself, the living Rock, of pieces of living rock — those partaking of His nature through His indwelling presence. Then He taught that when two or three of these were met together as a congregation He, the living Christ, would be personally present in their midst. He made it clear that the whole activity of that congregation was dependent upon His active presence. Paul, in Eph. 4:13-16, explains that the Church is to be the living manifestation of the living Christ: His Body, the fulness of Him that filleth each one with Himself" (Eph. 1:23).

Thus, in the individual believer, in the Church as a whole and in the congregation of believers, the manifestation of the living Christ is the objective, and His active presence the essential of all manifestation of life.

THE CHURCH
—A BODY
Eph. 4:11-16.
I Cor.' 12:12-14.
Rom. 12:4-8.

CHRIST
THE HEAD

HOLY SPIRIT
THE POWER

REVEALS WISDOM AND WILL OF THE HEAD

MANY MEMBERS
BAPTIZED INTO

ONE BODY
AND KNIT TOGETHER BY THE SPIRIT

Each one put in place by God 'Members one of another', 'having the same care one of another'

GIFTS OF THE SPIRIT
FOR
GOVERNMENT
EXPANSION
SERVICE

PURPOSE
1. To make known the Mystery to all men.
2. To make known the manifold wisdom of God to the principalities and powers in the heavenlies.
3. To manifest the fulness of Christ.

FACULTIES

(a) FIVE BASIC MINISTRIES IN ONE OR MORE OF WHICH ALL THE MEMBERS PARTICIPATE

Apostles	Foundation
Prophets	Proclamation
Evangelists	Extension and Preservation
Pastors	Shepherding
Teachers	Instruction

(b) GIFTS OF THE SPIRIT DISTRIBUTED TO ALL THE MEMBERS

Preaching	Proclamation	
Teaching	Instruction	
Faith	Enabling	
Utterance of Wisdom	Revelation	
Utterance of Knowledge	Understanding	
Paraclete Gift	Word of love	Love Gifts
Mercy	Act of love	
Giving	Material service of love	
Discerning of Spirits	Protection	
Ministrations	Material service	
Ruler	Order	
Miracles	Power sign	Sign Gifts
Healing	Love Sign	
Varieties of Tongues	Utterance sign	
Interpretation of Tongues	Knowledge sign	

CHAPTER XIII

THE BODY OF CHRIST

IN the Church teaching given in the Acts and in the Epistles no new principle is added. Our Lord laid a complete foundation and all the Holy Spirit's subsequent revelations concerning the Church are based upon it. They simply reveal the details of the structure: the application of the principles which He laid down.

Next to our Lord's statements we would place the Epistle to the Ephesians. In it we have the revelation concerning the Church as the Body of Christ, and the principles laid down by our Lord are seen in their relation to the life and ministry of the Body. It is essential that we review the teaching of this Epistle if we are to know the Scriptural pattern of the Church.

It is the Body of Christ, the Church as a whole that is dealt with in Ephesians. There is no reference to the local congregation. The practical instructions to believers given in the latter part of the Epistle are all from the standpoint of the life and testimony of the Body of Christ.

It is a clear revelation of Church truth, presenting the 'mystery' of the Body of Christ: the plan which was formed by God "before the foundation of the world", unrevealed hitherto, but now made known unto us in this Dispensation in the time appointed in His purpose. It gives the structure of the Church and states the great spiritual principles that govern this structure, relating the whole to the fundamental purpose of God for man.

It will be readily seen that other passages of Scripture, such as 1st and 2nd Corinthians, that deal with the details of the ministry of the local congregation, should be fitted into the structure of the complete Body revealed in Ephesians.

Anything approaching a complete study of Ephesians as it relates to the Church would require a volume to itself, so it will not be possible to give more than a few very brief indications here, drawing attention to the main features of the spiritual structure that is revealed.

Church Teaching in Ephesians

Theme — The Church, His Body. "In him... to the praise of His glory."
The Object — The manifestation of the fulness of God through the fulness of Christ indwelling the Church.

1:1, 2   Salutation.

1:3-14   Predestined Purpose of God outlined that the position of the Church in relation to it may be understood.

1:3-12   All the spiritual blessings of the heavenly realm have been given us in Christ. It should be noted that at the very beginning of the Epistle, in verse three, it is stated that all the spiritual blessings that are dealt with are possessed only as we occupy our place in Christ in the Heavenlies. The believer or church that is not seated with Christ in the Heavenlies and acting from there with Christ's authority, wisdom and power has nothing. God's ultimate purpose, planned "before the foundation of the world" is —

1. (v. 4) To present us, the redeemed, holy and spotless in His presence in love. The image which God created in His own likeness, but which was ruined by the fall, is thus restored.

2. (vv. 5, 6) That we should enter into the full privileges of spiritual manhood as adult sons. ('Adoption' — cf. Rom. 8:23. See note in Scofield Ed. of Bible.)

3. (vv. 9, 10) To make all things one under the Headship of Christ.

This is God's ultimate three-fold, basic purpose for us in Christ. Later, it is shown that there is a present fulfilment of this purpose, in this Dispensation, attained in the Church in which there is to be revealed the perfect man "unto the stature of the fulness of Christ." (Cf. 3:9-12, 16-21; 4:13-16.) The Church is united as one Body of which Christ is the Head. And we are seated with Him in the heavenlies, possessing 'the fulness of Him that filleth all in all'. (Cf. 1:23; 2:5, 6, 10.)

1:11, 12   Our inheritance.

1:13, 14   The Holy Spirit, promised by Christ, is received by the believer as a seal and earnest of the full inheritance that is to be received. We still dwell in a sin-cursed body, awaiting "the redemption of the body", but the Spirit dwelling within us makes us "partakers of the divine nature". Later, the work and power of the Holy Spirit manifested in the Church and the ministry fulfilled by the gifts of the Spirit are made known. (Cf. 1:17, 18; 2:19, 20; 3:15, 20; 4:4, 7, 11-14; 5:9, 18, 19; 6:10-20.)

1:15-16.   The prayer ministry of God's servant for the Church. We are given an example of the place the prayer of faith must occupy in the ministry of teaching. As Paul, inspired by the Holy Spirit, unfolds the deep truths concerning the Church, he pauses twice to record a prayer to God that the reader might be given by the Spirit the understanding fully and truly to comprehend these truths.

Compare the example of Christ who, after the teaching given to the disciples in the fourteenth to the sixteenth chapters of John, prayed to the Father that it might be accomplished in them (chapter 17).

1:17-23.   Prayer for the Church: that it may have the Spirit of wisdom and insight in the knowledge of Christ and so have the light to know:

1. That to which it is called in Him — all that it possesses in Him.

2. The glory which He has inherited in His people and in the Church which is the Body in which He dwells: all that He possesses in this instrument which He has purchased and made His dwelling-place.

3. The surpassing might of the Holy Spirit given to us, Who dwells in us — the Spirit of resurrection power, through Whom the Church enters into her possessions in Christ and Christ exploits His inheritance in the Church.

1:19, 20-23.   Christ's absolute authority and power as Head of the Church. Cf. His statement: "The gates of hell shall not prevail against it" (Matt. 16:18), and comment in chapter 12.

1:23.   The Church, His Body, 'The fulness of Him'.

In the passages in Matt. 16:16-19 and 18:15-20, it is revealed that Christ is the Builder of the Church and that He is personally present in its gatherings. In Ephesians the Church is shown to us as "the fulness of Him that filleth all in all", through the surpassing greatness of the power of His Spirit Who dwells in the Church.

Conybeare translates verses 22 and 23 thus:

> And 'he put all things under his feet', and gave Him to be sovereign head of the Church, which is His Body; the Fulness of Him who fills all things everywhere with Himself.

In a note on the word 'fulness', Conybeare says:

> We see here again the same allusion to the technical use of the word 'Pleroma' by false teachers, as in Col. 2:9, 10. St. Paul there asserts that, not the angelic hierarchy, but Christ Himself is the true 'fulness of the Godhead'; and here that the Church is the 'fulness of Christ', that is, the full manifestation of His being, because penetrated by His life, and living only in Him. It should be observed that the Church is here spoken of so far forth as it corresponds to its ideal.

2:1-3.   Original condition and position of the members of the Body:

2:4-13.   Present condition and position of the members of the Body:

1. Quickened — 'caused us to share the life of Christ' (Conybeare.)
2. Raised from the dead with Christ.
3. Seated — 'enthroned us with Him, in the heavenly realms as being in Christ Jesus'. (Weymouth.)

Thus the redeemed — the members of His Body — are placed in the position where they participate fully with the Head in His enthronement and consequent absolute power and authority, stated in 1:19-23, and where Christ can manifest His fulness in them. (Cf. 1:3.)

The object of this is (v. 7) "that, in the ages which are coming, He might manifest the surpassing riches of His grace, showing kindness toward us in Christ Jesus"... for (v. 10) "we are His workmanship, created in Christ to do good works which God has prepared that we should walk therein." (Conybeare.)

Taking this in the light of what follows we see that God has thus prepared His instrument, His 'master-work', the Church, for accomplishing the purpose expressed in 3:10-12 and 4:8, 11-13. The 'good works' are not good deeds, but the works wrought through the Church by the gifts of the Spirit as Christ manifests His triumph, power and manifold wisdom through His Body. They are the 'greater works' He spoke of in Jn. 14:12, the testimony which He purposed should be given through the Church.

2:14-18. Jew and Gentile united in the one Body in Christ to form the "new man", the Church. (Cf. 4:13.) The natural enmity existing between Jew and Gentile is destroyed by the Cross and the two are made one. In the Church there can be no difference of race or nationality: all are one in Christ. There can be no Jewish Church or Gentile Church.

2:19-22. The Church, a building compacted by the Holy Spirit and indwelt by God through the Spirit. (Cf. v. 21 with 4:13; cf. 1 Pet. 2:5; 1 Cor. 3:16, 17. Note the exact parallel between the teaching of the two figures: the 'building' and the 'body'.)

This spiritual structure, of which Christ is the chief corner-stone, is "built upon the foundation of the Apostles and Prophets." The Apostles laid the foundation — both structural and doctrinal (cf. Acts 2:42) — as it had been revealed to them by the Lord and the Spirit. Peter, in such passages as his sermon on the day of Pentecost and 1 Pet. 2:4-9, shows that the foundation is based upon the revelation given to the Prophets. Paul traces it further back still, to God's purpose formed "before the foundation of the world".

The foundation laid by the Apostles was perfect

and complete. It was upon that foundation that Paul built. It has become well-nigh buried under the elaborate structures which man has built upon it, but God's purpose concerning it has not changed. For the practice of New Testament methods and principles of church-planting, it is, of course essential that we return to the true Apostolic foundation.

3:1-13.   Paul states the source of his knowledge and describes the mystery to which he, as a servant of the Church, is called.

3:8-12.   To me who am less than the least of all God's people has this work been graciously entrusted — to proclaim to the Gentiles the Good News of the exhaustless wealth of Christ, and to show all men in a clear light what my stewardship is. It is the stewardship of the truth which from all the Ages lay concealed in the mind of God, the Creator of all things — concealed in order that the Church might now be used to display to the powers and authorities in the heavenly realms the innumerable aspects of God's wisdom. Such was the eternal purpose which He had formed in Christ Jesus our Lord, in whom we have this bold and confident access through our faith in Him. (Weymouth.)

The two things which Paul was called to do as a servant of God were: (1) to preach the "good news of the exhaustless wealth of Christ" (which is our inheritance in Him), and (2) to make all men see what is the stewardship of the mystery: the ministry to which all the redeemed are called as partakers of this exhaustless wealth and members of the Church. The result of that two-fold ministry was to be that through the Church the manifold wisdom of God would be made known to the principalities and authorities in heavenly places.

In the churches which Paul established — churches composed of members exercising the gifts of the Spirit — we see the fulfilment of this ministry: we see Christ possessing His inheritance in the Church and the Church possessing its inheritance in Christ.

3:14-19.   For this cause I bend my knees before the Father, whose children all are called in heaven and in earth, beseeching Him, that, in the richness of His glory, He would grant you strength by the entrance of His Spirit into your inner man, that Christ may dwell in your

hearts by faith; that having your root and your foundation in love, you may be enabled, with all the saints,
to comprehend the breadth and length, and depth and
height thereof; and to know the love of Christ which
passeth knowledge, that you may be filled therewith,
even to the measure of the Fulness of God. (Conybeare.)

Paul's responsibility is not ended when he states the
revelation given to him. To the ministry of the Word
he adds again the ministry of prayer. His petition is:
1. That they may be strong in the power of the Holy
   Spirit who is within them.
2. The result of this will be the dwelling of Christ in
   their hearts through faith.
3. And the outcome of this will be the understanding
   of the knowledge-surpassing love of Christ and its
   manifestation. (Cf. 1 Cor. 2:9, 10, 14.)
4. This will mean their being filled to the measure
   of the fulness of God. (Cf. 1:23.)

God is love and love is the basis of God's order for
all things. It is the basis of His order in the Body of
Christ (cf. 1 Cor. 13). Christ manifested the perfect
love of God. He loved the Father with a perfect love
and His neighbour as Himself. As, by the Spirit, He
dwells in our hearts He will manifest through us that
same perfect love.

It will be seen that this prayer goes a step further
than the first one. The first was that they might have
a full comprehension of what we have in Christ, of
what He has in us and of the power of the Spirit. The
second is that they might have full understanding of
His love and be filled with it, which will mean the
true manifestation of the fulness of Christ's life in
them.

The answering of this prayer would mean the accomplishing of the whole purpose of God to which
His servant was called to testify.

In 1:23 it is stated that the Church is to manifest
the *pleroma* of Christ. Here we are shown how the
pleroma of God is to be manifested in the individual
members — by faith through the power of the in-

dwelling Spirit manifesting the perfect love of Christ. Christ is the *pleroma* of God. As Christ is manifested in the believer the *pleroma* of God is manifested. God created man in His image. Through the indwelling Christ that image is again manifested in the redeemed man.

3:20-21.   Now to Him who, in the exercise of His power that is at work within us, is able to do infinitely beyond all our highest prayers or thoughts — to Him be the glory in the Church and in Christ Jesus to all generations world without end! (Weymouth.)

Paul had uttered a bold prayer; he had asked the seemingly impossible — what was, indeed, impossible to the natural man. But now he expresses his praise to God because of his absolute assurance that God was able to answer in a far more glorious manner than we are capable of asking or thinking, through the mighty power of the Holy Spirit Who is within us. The result of this will be that God will be glorified in the Church and in Christ not only now but throughout all eternity.

4:1-6.   You are one body and one spirit, even as you were called to share one common hope; you have one Lord, you have one faith, you have one baptism; you have one God and Father of all, who is over all, and works through all, and dwells in all. (4—6, Conybeare.)

The seven-fold basis of the Church's unity is stated here. The Body of Christ is one and indivisible. The unity is the unity of the Spirit, derived from the presence of the one Spirit who lives in and works through all the members. It is not derived from organization, although the structure given to the Church by God has as one of its chief objects the conserving of its unity. This unity is basic to the whole structure of the Body and of vital importance to its life and testimony (Jn. 17:21-23).

4:7.   But unto every one of us is given grace according to the gift of Christ.

Paul speaks of the work or ministry which the Holy Spirit carries out through the believer as a 'grace' *(charis)*—an undeserved privilege freely granted. Peter also uses the word in the same sense (1 Pet. 4:10). In Rom. 12:6, Paul says, "Having then gifts differing according to the grace (ministry) that is given to us..." (cf. 1 Cor. 3:10).

It is not in the sense of an office that he uses the word, as is evident in other passages:

> ...and His grace which was bestowed upon me was not in vain; but I laboured more abundantly than they all; yet not I but the grace of God which was with me (1 Cor. 15:10).
>
> Whereof I was made a minister, according to the gift of the grace of God given unto me by the effectual working of his power. Unto me, who am less than the least of all saints, is this grace given, that I should preach among the Gentiles the unsearchable riches of Christ (Eph. 3:7, 8).

The grace of God that was with him and that was given him was the working of the Holy Spirit through him accomplishing the work which God purposed to do through him. All the members of the Body of Christ have gifts of the Spirit for the carrying out of ministry: that is, the Holy Spirit manifests His power and wisdom through each one for the accomplishing of the work to which God has appointed.

Grace is something unmerited and given freely. The word is used in several senses. There is God's saving grace manifested towards us in Christ and also there is God's grace manifested through us by Christ's Spirit dwelling in us, using us in witness and testimony. All God's work for us, in us or through us is of the same nature, dependent upon the same principles and effected by the same power. Thus what we possess in Christ and what He does through us is all 'grace': none of it is of us but all of Him; none of it is merited but all is freely bestowed.

Paul also speaks of his work as a 'ministry' — a *diakonia* (the service rendered by a servant). The 'grace' given to him and the 'service' to which he was called was not an ecclesiastical office. It conferred no ecclesiastical power or privilege. His work was simply the part which God privileged him to take in the work of the Body of Christ. He never claimed more than that. The authority and power were not his but the Lord's as he was careful to declare (1 Cor. 3:5). The authority was in the Word of God which he gave; the power was the manifestation of the Spirit through him. The authority and power were real and effective, but they were not of man. Such is all true spiritual ministry.

4:8.   Wherefore he saith, when he ascended up on high, he led captivity captive, and gave gifts unto men.

When our Lord ascended into Heaven triumphant, His redemptive work completed, He fulfilled His promise to send the Holy Spirit. The result of the Holy Spirit's presence is His manifestation in the members of the Church through the gifts of the Spirit (1 Cor. 12:7). Paul quotes Ps. 68:18, showing that the giving of the gifts of the Spirit to men was in accordance with prophecy. The gifts of the Spirit are considered fully in later chapters.

4:9, 10.   Now that word, 'He went up' what saith it but that He first came down to the earth below? Yes, He Who came down is the same Who is gone up, far above all the heavens, that He might fill all things. (Conybeare.)

Here it is shown that 'he who ascended', spoken of by the Psalmist, is none other than Christ. The purpose of Christ's work and of the giving of the gifts of the Spirit is 'that He might fill all things'. The Church has already been described as 'the fulness of him that filleth all in all' (cf. note, Eph. 1:23; 2:17-21); now we are told how this fulness is accomplished and manifested. This reveals the vital importance of the gifts in the accomplishing of Christ's purpose. (Cf. 1 Cor. 12:1.)

4:11, 12.   And gave some, apostles; and some, prophets; and some evangelists; and some pastors and teachers, for the perfecting of the saints, for the work of the ministry, for the edifying of the body of Christ.

Paul has just shown the Church to be one Body but composed of many members. Also he has stated that all the members have graces or ministries and gifts of the Spirit. Now he speaks of the purpose which is to be accomplished in and through the Church and the ministries which the Lord has distributed to all the members for its accomplishment. He states that the Lord has given (appointed) some of the members to be Apostles and some to be Preachers or Evangelists or Pastors or Teachers.

All the members of the Body are called to one or more of these ministries. First, there are the Twelve Apostles. Through them the Holy Spirit laid the foundation of the Church. They have no successors. The other four are continuing ministries. Two of these are for establishing and order and two for witness.

First after the Twelve Apostles are the preachers. Last on the list are the teachers. Our Lord's command to the Church is to preach and teach. Both of these ministries are of wide application. All the members of the Church should proclaim or preach the Gospel (1 Cor. 14:1). There are many forms of preaching and the term used here covers them all as did our Lord's command. At Pentecost the gift of preaching was given to all. Whenever there is a true revival in the Church and the Holy Spirit has freedom to work, the gift of preaching appears generally among the members (cf. 1 Cor. 14:1). Also there are many varieties of the teaching ministry — for the teaching of adults, children, etc. — and not a few members are called to it.

The other two ministries are Evangelist — for the extension of the Church and the planting of congregations throughout the world — and Pastor (Elder) — for the care of the flock.

The Twelve exercised all the other ministries besides that of Apostle. The Evangelists were also preachers, teachers and pastors in a general sense. The preacher might also be a teacher and the teacher a preacher. The pastor (Elder) might also be a preacher or a teacher or both, though some exercised only the one ministry of pastor (1 Tim. 5:17).

Some have interpreted verse eleven as meaning that the men called to these ministries are gifts to the

Church. But this interpretation misses the whole meaning of the passage and is contrary to the principles of the order in the Early Church. It is the result of the unconscious influence of the modern Church order, causing the reader to adjust the Scripture to the prevailing practice. To introduce the principles of the modern Church, with its ecclesiastical offices and its distinction between 'clergy' and 'laity', into the Early Church order, which was based upon the priesthood of all members, is to create confusion. Actually there is no ground whatever for considering the men as gifts. Weymouth substitutes 'appointed' for 'gave' in verse eleven, and this gives the correct sense. Men are called by God and receive from the Holy Spirit the spiritual gifts necessary (1 Cor. 12:11, 18). The men in themselves are not equipped for the work; it is the Holy Spirit who ministers through them. They must depend entirely upon the power of the Spirit, just as those called to other ministries in the Body. They and all others cease to function in any true sense if the Holy Spirit's power is withdrawn or restricted. In 1 Cor. 3:5-10, Paul states that he himself is nothing, but simply an instrument.

Some have thought that 'pastors and teachers' has reference to a double ministry exercised by one person, not two ministries exercised by different persons. But that is incorrect. The two ministries are definitely separate in the lists of gifts given in Romans 12:3-8 and 1 Cor. 12:8-10. There was a separate order of teachers. The Elder was to be 'apt to teach' (1 Tim. 3:2), but not necessarily a teacher in the full meaning of that ministry. It is clearly stated that some were not teachers (1 Tim. 5:17).[1] The list of ministries given here is considered more fully in a later chapter.

The word *katartismos*, rendered 'perfecting' in verse twelve, occurs here only. "It is used by medical writers for the setting of a dislocated limb. The verb from

---

[1] See p. 204.

which it comes is used literally of 'mending' nets (Matt. 4:21), and, figuratively, of 'restoring' sinners (Gal. 6:1)".[1]

The verb *katartizo* — to mend, set in order, adjust — is variously translated:

Matt. 4:21; Mark. 1:19	— mend.
Heb. 10:5	— prepare.
Heb. 11:3.	— frame.
Gal. 6:1	— restore.
Heb. 13:21; 1 Pet. 5:10	— make perfect.
Matt. 21:16; 1 Thess. 3:10	— perfected.
Rom. 9:22	— fit.
Luke 6:40; 2 Cor. 13:11	— (passive) be perfect.
1 Cor. 1:10	— (passive) be perfectly joined together.

Commenting on the meaning of this word in 2 Cor. 13:11, Clarke says the thought is,

Be compact; get into joint again; let unity and harmony be restored.

Regarding *katartisin* in 2 Cor. 13:9, he says:

From kata, intensive, and artizo to fit or adapt... The perfection and rejoicing which the apostle wishes is that which refers to the state of the Church in its fellowship, unity, order, etc.

Beza's comment on this passage is:

The apostle's meaning is that, whereas the members of the Church were all, as it were, dislocated and out of joint, they should be joined together in love.

It will be seen from the above that "perfecting" in Eph. 4:12 does not refer to spiritual perfection but to the perfect fitting together, or setting in order (as in 1 Cor. 1:10) of the members of the Body.

In Eph. 2:21, under the figure of a building, this same unity has already been spoken of: "in union with whom the whole fabric, fitted and closely joined together..." (Weymouth). It is this unity that is pictured in 4:13-16.

Eph. 4:12 may be freely translated as follows:

That the members may be perfectly fitted together in the Body, so that the service of the Body may be rendered, so that the Body may grow.

---

[1] *Century Bible.*

An extension of the same thought is given in 2:21, and 4:16. Thus we see that the five ministries mentioned are given to bring about God's three-fold purpose for the functioning of the Body:

1. The proper coordination and government of the whole Body, to provide for—
2. The orderly and efficient carrying on of all the testimony and ministry of the Body, to bring about—
3. The building up, or growth and extension, of the Body.

4:13. Till we all come in the unity of the faith and of the knowledge of the son of God, unto a perfect man, unto the measure of the stature of the fulness of Christ.

'We all', i. e., the whole Body of Christ. In verses 4-6 the unity of the Body of Christ is emphasized. Verses 7-12 speak of the gifts of the Spirit and the ministries provided for the accomplishing of this unity. In verse 13 the unity to be achieved is described. It is the unity produced by Christ dwelling in His Body, the Church, and manifesting Himself — His "fulness that filleth all in all" — in it and carrying on His work through it by the power of the Spirit. The end to be achieved is the manifesting of "the perfect man", Christ — "unto the measure of the stature of the fulness of Christ". How often Paul emphasized the fact that the Church has and must manifest the plenitude of Christ!

In 1:23 it is stated that the Church is to manifest the *pleroma* of Christ. In 3:13 we are shown how the *pleroma* of God is to be manifested in the members of the Church. Here we see how the *pleroma* of *Christ* is to be manifested in the Church.

4:14. That we henceforth be no more children, tossed to and fro, and carried about by every wind of doctrine, by the sleight of men, and cunning craftiness, whereby they lie in wait to deceive.

Here we have the description of the condition of the Body when the ministries provided for it are not duly exercised.

This is in contrast to the condition described in verse 13. 'Children' are contrasted with 'the perfect man'; 'Tossed to and fro and carried about with every wind of doctrine' ('wind' — which produces disunity), contrasted with 'unity of the faith'; 'sleight of men' and 'wiles of error', contrasted with 'the knowledge of the Son of God'.

Such is the condition of the Church generally today and the reason is that the five ministries are not exercised as God intended them to be.

4:15, 16.   But speaking the truth in love (or, dealing truly in love) may grow up into him in all things, which is the head, even Christ: from whom the whole body fitly joined together and compacted by that which every joint supplieth, according to the effectual working in the measure of every part, maketh increase of the body unto the edifying of itself in love.

Weymouth translates verse 16 as follows:

Dependent on Him, the whole body — its various parts closely fitting and firmly adhering to one another — grows by the aid of every contributory link (connexion of the supply), with power proportioned to the need of each individual part, so as to build itself up in a spirit of love.

These two verses are a picture of the functioning of the Body:

1. As all the members together 'work truth' in love, they grow into Him, and He occupies His place as the Head of the Body.
2. Christ, the Head, controls the whole Body and supplies all its needs.
3. The Body is entirely dependent upon Him.
4. All the parts are firmly joined to Him and to each other.
5. Through the gifts of the Spirit, Christ proportions all the power needed for the ministry of every part.
6. The effectual working together of all the parts empowered and coordinated by the Head brings about the growth of the Body in love.

In verses 1-16 of this chapter we have the heart of the revelation concerning the functioning Church. Here is disclosed the wonderful organism which God, in His infinite wisdom and perfect foreknowledge, planned 'before the foundation of the world', in which the fulness of Christ is now to dwell and through which the manifold wisdom of God is to be displayed. First its sevenfold unity is declared. Then the gifts of the Spirit with which it is endowed for its ministry are mentioned. The five fundamental ministries are revealed. Their purpose is the carrying out of the Lord's commands to 'preach' and 'teach' and to bring about the coordination of the members of the Body so that all may work together efficiently, each one in its place, contributing, through the gifts of the Spirit which all possess, to the building up of the Body through the adding to it of those who are saved.

This is the instrument which God has prepared for the present accomplishment of His purpose for man in Christ, the full realization of which will be consummated when Christ and the Church are united in the Heavenlies.

4:17-6:20.   After describing the structure of the Body, Paul speaks of the testimony of the members, for upon their testimony — upon the manifestation of life within the Body — depends the fruit that is to be borne.

First, in 4:17-5:21, he deals with general principles, then he takes up social relationships, in 5:22-6:9, and finally, in 6:10-20, shows the Church upon its knees, clad in its spiritual armour: the Church engaged in ceaseless prayer, invincible and victorious in Christ.

4:17-5:21.   The personal walk and testimony of the member of the Body of Christ.

5:22-33.   The married life of the member of the Body of Christ and the analogy between it and the relation of Christ to the Church.

Here is seen the importance of the testimony of the

home in the Church's witness. The family is the unit of human society, the fundamental institution in God's order for man. It also occupies a central place in the witness of the Christian community — that is, of the Church. The love of the husband for his wife is to be a testimony to the love of Christ for His Church and the love of the wife for her husband is to be a testimony to the love of the Church for Christ. It is in the home, not in the gathering of the Church, that the practical testimony to the relationship between the Church and Christ begins. That testimony will be given in the Church only to the extent that it is given in the home.

6:1-4.   The home life of members of the Body of Christ.

6:5-9.   The testimony of servants and masters who are members of the Body of Christ.

6:10-20.   The spiritual warfare of the Church. The Church faces the fierce and continual opposition of Satan. Christ said that "the gates (counsels) of Hell" will not prevail against the Church. In this passage of Ephesians we have that statement amplified. Here we have presented the spiritual enemy of the Church and the spiritual armour for equipment and for victorious defensive and offensive warfare. The full employment of this armour ensures the defeat of all the counsels of Satan against the Church.

In this passage we see:

1. The power and the armour by which the members of the Body of Christ, that is, the Church, may withstand the enemy and remain victorious.
2. The purely spiritual nature of the foe.
3. The armour (which is revealed spiritual truth appropriated):
   (1) The belt of truth — the truth revealed by the Holy Spirit in the Word of God. The believer or Church must not be girt about with man's wisdom, methods or strength.
   (2) The breastplate of righteousness — the right-

eousness of Christ imputed to and manifested in the believer. Protection for the heart.

(3) The foot-wear of messengers of the Gospel of peace who witness in obedience to Christ's command. This footwear — active testimony — is an essential armour.

(4) The shield of faith — absolute faith in God and in His Word: Faith is able to bring to naught every work of Satan, because it takes hold of spiritual truth. The Word of God is the sure weapon for defence when it is appropriated by faith.

(5) The helmet of salvation — eternal life through faith in Christ. Protection for the head.

(6) The sword of the Spirit — the Word of God, which the Spirit wields through the believer and the Church. The weapon for offensive warfare wielded by the Spirit through the gifts of the Spirit manifested in the members of the Church.

These are the truths that constitute the indispensable armour of the believer and of the Body of Christ. The neglect of any of these truths means weakness and defeat.

6:18-20.   Prayer ministry of the Body of Christ.

1. Continual prayer 'in the Spirit'. Unceasing prayer, guided by the Spirit, is indispensable to the life and ministry of the Church.

2. Continual watchfulness unto prayer for all members of the Body of Christ. Each member of the Church has a spiritual responsibility for all.

3. Prayer for the missionaries. Every member of the Church participates through prayer in the ministry of the extension of the Church. (Cf. Col. 4:2-4.)

6:21-24.   Conclusion of Epistle.

CHAPTER XIV

A BODY FOR WITNESS

THE Church is presented in the New Testament as an organism — the Body of Christ. He is the Head of the Body, the Holy Spirit is the power in the Body and the redeemed are the members of the Body (1 Cor. 12:13; Eph. 1:10,22,23; 4:15; 5:25-30, 32; Col. 1:24).

The Purpose

The purpose for which God has brought this Body into being is that it might be a channel for the accomplishing of His will for man. From the beginning it has been His will to manifest His image in man. He created man in His own likeness and when man fell in sin and lost that likeness God did not desist from His purpose but pledged its final fulfilment. He will present man faultless before the presence of His glory (Jude 24; Eph. 1:4).

For the carrying out of this purpose Christ came into the World and manifested in a human body the perfect image and glory of God. Then, after His substitutional and sacrificial work, by which He cleansed and justified all who believe in Him, He 'penetrated' the heavens into the presence of God's holiness and glory in that same human body raised from death, the accepted sacrifice and the Forerunner, and sat down at the right hand of God in the place of absolute authority and power. That body, that image and likeness of God, is no longer on earth in visible form, but after it had been received into glory, and as a consequence of that triumph, the Holy Spirit came, sent by Christ in His stead, and another body came into existence: the Body of Christ, the Church, in which Christ continues to dwell through the Spirit and through which He carries on His work of manifesting the image and likeness — the love, holiness, wisdom, power and glory — of God.

God's will for this earthly body is that "all (all its members) should come in the unity of the faith and of the knowledge of the Son of God, unto a perfect man, unto the measure of the stature of the fulness of Christ" (Eph. 4:13). He would manifest through this Body His manifold wisdom and reveal in it the image of His Son (cf. Rom. 8:28, 29).

That this Body is made up of men still dwelling in 'the body of death', the flesh, in which the 'law of sin and death' is still present, only makes the display of God's power and wisdom greater and more glorious. What a triumph: to take these bodies, redeemed, yet still subject to death, justified, yet still capable of sinning, and make them His temple, the dwelling-place of His glory, while yet they live in this world whose prince is Satan! Could anything be more wonderful? Could any work be more Godlike? Could there be a greater demonstration of the transcendent power and wisdom of absolute love, of its limitless resources, and of the utter impotence of Satan's wisdom and might to resist God's purposes?

It is this Body, through the power of the resurrection, in face of all that Satan and man have done and can do, that God would fill 'with all the fulness of God' and fashion as the image of Christ (Eph. 1:23; 3:19; 4:13-16).

Through this continuing Body, Christ would do the 'greater works' of which He spoke. In the midst of this present Satan-conceived and Satan-controlled world system He has a body of witness through which He would manifest the mighty, victorious power of the resurrection, awaiting the day of 'the fulness of times': the day of the complete realization of His purpose (Jn. 14:12; Phil. 2:10, 11).

The Head

Christ is the Head of this Body. All power and authority are derived directly from Him. As the head in the human body is the seat of all intelligence and control, so is Christ in the Church. This is not merely a spiritual figure; Christ is to be given that place actually in all that it implies. He is not the figure-head of the Church. His position is not that of a nominal king, or even of a constitutional monarch, whose government acts in His name but who has no actual say in its decisions and merely signs the decrees presented to him, having, actually, little more than a title of glory. (That is the place given Him today in the organized Church.) Christ governs personally; His government is absolute; His will must be known and done in every detail of the Church's life and activity and the congregation that does not do so lives in rebellion, weakness and defeat.

The structure of the Church is all based upon the fact that Christ is the active Head. No provision is made to ensure that the Body will continue to function if the Head is not given His rightful place. It is of the utmost importance that this be clearly understood, because the natural reaction, when any lack of power appears in a congregation, is to seek to remedy the situation by increased effort or additional organization of one form or another, instead of by seeking to find at what point the Head is not being permitted to function or is not being obeyed, and for what reason the power is withheld.

When two or more members of the Body of Christ are met together in His Name, He, the Head, meets with them. He is personally present in the midst. This presence is not something unsubstantial and unreal; Christ is there in all His glory, authority, wisdom and power. He is there, not as a spectator, but to act, to lead, to reveal His will, to build His Church and to carry on personally His work of witness through it. To the Church at prayer He makes known His will, and in response to the Church's unanimous, believing prayer that is according to His will He speaks and works through it by His Spirit, who is in each member, and brings His purposes to pass.

Apart from Christ, the Church has nothing but the natural power and wisdom of its members. It is as a body that is palsied, sick, incompetent, its members uncoordinated and uncontrolled, acting according to their own individual whims and fancies. A limb or an organ acting independently of the brain is a handicap and a danger to the whole organism. Such was the church in Laodicea. There Christ was outside the door; it was not His image but the image of fleshly man that was manifested: man with his wealth, human wisdom, good works and respectability. That was what they offered as worship to God and as testimony to the world, and they were blind to their poverty and did not realize that the Head was no longer with them.

In Christ and through His presence the Church possesses all

things: all power and authority, all wisdom and grace. As Head of the Church, He is seated at the right hand of God, over 'all principality and might and dominion and every name that is named'. And we, the members of the Church, are seated there with Him.

We must beware of the danger of merely giving intellectual assent to spiritual truth and regarding it as true in theory but failing to actually believe it and act upon it. What is taught in God's Word regarding the Church is not mere theory; it is truth, present as well as eternal, practical as well as spiritual. We are not given visions of theoretical perfection that have no real relation to present, practical experience. The statements concerning the Church are not just beautiful, pious language. The Holy Spirit has not inspired God's servants to write impractical visions. They are true and of tremendous and glorious significance to all who will receive them by faith. And this means that through Christ's actual presence in the Church and the absolute power and authority that are His, through the guidance which He personally gives and the working of His Spirit through each member, we can definitely expect that every congregation that is giving Christ His place as Head in all things will be victorious in life and witness.

The Holy Spirit

1. The Power in the Body. — The power in the Church, the Body of Christ, is the Holy Spirit. The work which He is to perform in the Church was stated by our Lord in the final, basic teaching which He gave to the disciples in the fourteenth to the seventeenth chapters of John's Gospel during the last days before the Cross. There we have the key passages relating to the Holy Spirit and His work (Jn. 14:16-18, 26; 16:7-14). These form part of what is the key teaching regarding the spiritual life and service of the believer in Christ in the Church Age.

Philip's request, "show us the Father and it sufficeth us", was used by our Lord as the starting point for the giving of this teaching. In answer, Christ said that in Him they saw the Father, for He spoke no word that the Father did not speak through Him, and did no work that was not wrought by the Father through Him. The works that He did proved that the Father was in Him and He in the Father (Jn. 14:7-11). Then in the 12th verse He reveals the transcendent truth that, as it was with the Father and Him, so it was to be with Him and those who believe on Him: "Verily, verily, I say unto you, he that believeth on me, the works that I do shall he do also; and greater works than these shall he do; because I go unto my Father." As He was one with the Father, and the Father spoke and worked through Him, so His disciples were to be one with Him and He would speak and work through them. As He states in verse 23, "We (He and the Father) will come unto him and make our abode with him"; and then in 17:23 "I in them and thou in me, that they may be made perfect in one; and that the world may know that thou hast sent me, and hast loved them as thou hast loved me" (cf. vv, 18, 21, 22, 26). In this we see Christ indwelling His Body, the Church, and speaking and working through it.

Then, in the teaching that follows, our Lord revealed the place that prayer, love, obedience, endurance, abiding and fruitbearing were to take and the great mission which the Holy Spirit was to fulfil.

2. His Mission. — In outline, what is stated regarding the Holy Spirit in these chapters is as follows:

(1) Christ gave the disciples the promise that when He left them He would request the Father to send them the Comforter — the other Paraclete, or Advocate ('the One who stands by to Help') who would be with them forever (14:16).

(2) The Paraclete is also the Spirit of Truth, whom the World cannot receive because it cannot perceive or know Him (14:17, cf. 1 Cor. 2:14).

(3) Those who are Christ's would know Him because He was to be in them (14; 17; 1 Cor. 2:12-16).

(4) Christ was not going to leave them orphaned; in the coming of the Spirit to them Christ Himself would come. He would be invisible to the World but seen by them. Because He lives they also would live. Then they would understand what He had just been teaching them: that He is in the Father, and they in Him and He in them (14:18-20; cf. v. 12).

(5) The Paraclete, who is the Holy Spirit, was to be sent by God at Christ's request to teach them all things and bring all that Christ had said to their remembrance (14:26).

(6) The Paraclete, the Spirit of truth, proceeding from God, was to testify of Christ. The disciples would also witness — the two witnessing together. In the following Chapter our Lord

makes it clear that nothing can be done by the believer without Him. All is to be done by His Spirit speaking and working through those in whom He dwells (15:4-8, 26, 27; cf. 14:12).

(7) It was expedient that Christ should leave the disciples so that He could send the Holy Spirit to be in His place. It was necessary to the carrying out of God's purpose in and through the Church. It was better for them that He should be within them forever, speaking and working through them, than present with them in the flesh (16:7).

(8) When the Holy Spirit came He was to do the work of convicting the world of sin, of righteousness and of judgment (16:8-11).

(9) As Teacher, He, the Spirit of truth, would reveal to them all truth concerning Christ and concerning the future (16:12, 13).

(10) He would not speak as from Himself but would speak the words of Christ, glorifying Him and revealing Him. Thus, although for a little while they would not see Him, after a little while they would see Him — when His Spirit had come. Then, because of His continual presence, no man would be able to take their joy from them (16:14-22).

In these chapters our Lord reveals how, through His indwelling Spirit, the believer is identified with Him in life, prayer, word and work. The believer, of himself — of his own power and wisdom — can bear no fruit. "Without Me ye can do nothing". But, as he abides in Christ and Christ manifests Himself by His Spirit through him, he will bear abundant fruit. Then Christ will do His 'greater works' through him. The believer will then know Christ's will and pray according to Christ's will. In answer to that prayer Christ will do that which is asked. All this depends upon the believer's love to Christ which begets obedience and opens the way for the indwelling Spirit to perform that work which He has come to do.

3. His Work. — The manner in which He is to do this work of helping, teaching, witnessing, glorifying Christ and revealing Him is recorded in the New Testament writings. His work is:

(1) To regenerate. Titus 3:5; Jn. 3:3-8; 2 Pet. 1:4; Jn. 1:13.

(2) To baptize into the Body. 1 Cor. 12:13.

(3) To maintain the unity of the Body. Eph. 4:3, 4.

(4) To testify of Christ and glorify Him. Jn. 15:26; 16:8-11, 14; Acts 5:32; Rom. 8:16; Gal. 4:6.

(5) To teach and reveal truth. 1 Cor. 2:9-14; 1 Jn. 2:20, 27; Eph. 5:18, 19; 6:17; Jn. 14:17, 26; 16:12, 13.

(6) To give gifts to the members of the Body according to His will. 1 Cor. 12, etc.

(7) To guide. Acts 13:1—4; 16:6, 8.

(8) To give power. Luke 24:49; Acts 1:2-8; 4:31; Rom. 15: 18, 19; 1 Cor. 2:4; Rom. 8:11; Eph. 6:17; 1 Thess. 1:5.

(9) To give victory. Rom. 5:5; 8:1-16; 15:13; Gal. 5:22-25.

(10) To bear fruit. Gal. 5:22, 23; 1 Cor. 2:1-5; 1 Thess. 1:5; Acts 1:8; 4:31.

(11) To pray through the believer. Rom. 8:26; Eph. 6:18; Jude 20.

4. Pentecost. — Our Lord's final instructions to the disciples after His resurrection were that the Gospel was to be preached and taught in all the world to every creature. But He told them not to commence that work until the Holy Spirit had come and they had been endued with power (dynamic power) from on high (from God).

On the day of Pentecost the 'other Paraclete' came and filled every one of those met together in prayer. In that moment they were baptized into the one Body (1 Cor. 12:13). Then, immediately, the Holy Spirit began to perform His work in the Church, filling its members with power and manifesting gifts of the Spirit for witness in each one. The immediate result was the preaching of the Gospel with power and authority by all the members of the newly formed Church of Christ and the conversion in one day of three thousand souls.

Pentecost is not to be repeated for it is not ended and will not be completed until the Church is caught up from the earth. The Holy Spirit came on that day to remain in the Church. So long as He remains, Pentecost continues for the Church. The Church needs no new Pentecost, but just to enter fully into the Pentecost power she already has: that·is, to be filled with the Spirit Who now dwells within.

Peter explained the significance of what happened on Pentecost, stating that it was the fulfilment of Joel's prophecy:

And it shall come to pass in the last days, saith God, I will pour out of my Spirit upon all flesh: and your sons and your daughters shall prophesy, and your young men shall see visions, and your old men shall dream dreams: and on my servants on my hand-maidens I will pour out in those days of my Spirit; and they shall prophesy (Acts. 2:17, 18).

The Church had come into being: the Church through which the Holy Spirit was to witness, teach, reveal Christ and glorify Him.

The Members

When the step of accepting Christ as Saviour is taken, a twofold work is immediately wrought in the believer by the Holy Spirit: (1) He is 'born from above', 'born of the Spirit', made a 'partaker of the divine nature' (Jn. 3:3-8; Titus 3:5; 2 Pet. 1:4); (2) He is baptized (immersed) into the one Body by the Spirit (1 Cor. 12:13).

Membership in this one Body of Christ also makes all believers 'members one of another' (Eph. 4:25; Rom. 12:5). This is in accordance with our Lord's present purpose for His people as expressed in His prayer to the Father recorded in John 17:

That they may all be one; as thou, Father, art in me, and I in Thee, that they also may be one in Us: That the world may believe that Thou hast sent me... that they may be one even as we are one, I in them and Thou in me that they may be made perfect in one, and that the world may know that Thou hast sent me, and hast loved them as Thou hast loved me... that the love wherewith Thou hast loved me may be in them, and I in them.

It is also in accord with God's eternal purpose for His Son: "To make all things one in Christ as head" (Eph. 1:10, Conybeare).

This oneness in the Body of Christ involves mutual responsibilities and necessitates mutual cooperation. The members of the Church are exhorted not to forsake the assembling of themselves together, to 'have the same care one for another', and to 'consider one another to provoke unto love and to good works' (Heb. 10:24, 25; 1 Cor. 12:25). A member of the Body is not an isolated unit and cannot attain complete development nor function fully except in his place as a member of the Body.

The Unity of the Church

The Body of Christ is one and indivisible:

"There is one body, and one Spirit, even as ye are called in one hope of your calling; one Lord, one faith, one baptism, one God and Father of all, who is above all, and through all, and in you all" (Eph. 4:4-6).
"There should be no schism (division) in the body" (1 Cor. 12:25)

Christ cannot be divided. The Holy Spirit will never lead to division, because it is contrary to God's Word, God's purpose and God's order. He can and will lead to separation from that which is false and sinful, but never to anything that means separation from, or the dividing of, the true Body of Christ, or that will imply in any sense a breaking, or weakening, of the unity of its testimony, ministry and fellowship.

There is no Scriptural justification for the existence of the present divisions of the Church. They are contrary to the explicit teaching of the Word and to the whole intention of God concerning the Church. They violate every principle of the Scriptural teaching regarding the organization, testimony and ministry of the Church. This fact should be kept carefully in mind by the planter of churches. Why should he propagate man's divisions along with the Gospel among new converts?

The unity of the Body of Christ is the "unity of the Spirit" (Eph. 4:3). It comes from the fact that the same Spirit indwells each and every believer. It is not derived from organization. All the unity of the Body in testimony and service as well as in fellowship is derived alone from oneness in the Spirit.

It follows that unity cannot be obtained, or preserved, by organization but only by the Spirit. There will be spiritual unity among all who are truly guided by the one Holy Spirit. He is not the Spirit of confusion but of unity and love (1 Cor. 14:33). It is man's wisdom and man's will that cause division (Jas. 3:14-18). The result of what is a true work of the Holy Spirit in each member will always be the 'harmonious fitting together' of all the members, and the effectve coordinating of their respective spiritual gifts. Disunity prevents Him from doing this. The unity produced by the Spirit must be sought and depended upon in true faith. And He must be permitted to preserve it. The manner in which this unity of the Spirit is obtained by the Church has already been seen in the key passage in Matthew 18.

It will be evident that the uniting of two or more divisions of the Church is not a true step towards restoring the unity of the Body of Christ: it simply creates a larger division. It does not produce a return to the Scriptural order of unity in the Spirit but retains all the marks of sectionalism. Such a union usually means the sacrifice of principle, and no sacrifice of principle can ever produce unity which is the unity of the Holy Spirit.

CHAPTER XV

THE GIFTS OF THE SPIRIT

WE have seen that when Christ ascended up on high, 'leading captivity captive', He 'gave gifts unto men' — gifts resulting from the presence of the 'Spirit of promise' in all the members of the Church and intended for the carrying on of the work of the Body of Christ (Eph. 4:4-16). The Holy Spirit came on the day of Pentecost, the gifts of the Spirit are bestowed and every member of the Church participates in their possession.

Knowing of no work that deals adequately with the subject of the gifts of the Spirit, we have felt it necessary to go into the matter thoroughly, giving the Scriptural teaching regarding them, for it is of the highest importance to the Church and to the individual believer that they be understood.

Let us distinguish between the "fruits" of the Spirit (love, joy, peace etc.) and the "gifts" of the Spirit. The fruits are the manifestations of the Spirit in our daily living. The gifts are the manifestations of the Spirit through us in service.

Types of Gifts

Several lists of gifts of the Spirit and of ministries carried on through the gifts are given in the New Testament writings. One, with the functioning of the local church in mind, is found in 1 Cor. 12:28:

1. Apostles
2. Prophets
3. Teachers
4. The working of miracles
5. The healing of the sick
6. Serviceable ministrations (helps)
7. Government (oversight)
8. Varieties of tongues

In the list given in Romans 12:3-8, Paul writes of gifts provided for different ministries:

1. Prophecy
2. Ministration (material)
3. Teacher
4. Exhorter
5. Giver
6. Ruler (presider)
7. He who shows mercy

The list in 1 Cor. 12:8-10, is of various gifts of the Spirit for the ministry of the Gospel:

1. Utterance of wisdom
2. Utterance of knowledge
3. Faith
4. Healing
5. Miracles
6. Prophecy
7. Discernment of spirits
8. Varieties of tongues
9. Interpretation of tongues

The great importance of understanding the gifts of the Spirit is emphasized by Paul. He says: "Now concerning spiritual gifts, brethren, I would not have you ignorant" (1 Cor. 12:1). Weymouth's translation reads: "It is important, brethren, that you should have clear knowledge on the subject of spiritual gifts". Yet this is one of the subjects least understood by Christian people today It is seldom adequately taught. Unfortunately, the teaching of it is left to groups whose presentation of it is extravagant and unsound. This has confused the thoughts of many regarding it, even causing some to consider it a subject best avoided. Thus Satan has succeeded largely in robbing the Church of its essential equipment for ministry.

In the third verse of 1 Cor. 12, it is stated that "no man can say that Jesus is the Lord but by the Holy Ghost". No one can truly witness even to the lordship of Christ in his own life except by the light and power of the indwelling Holy Spirit. The flesh — the natural or soulish man — is incapable of doing so. If that be so, how can the natural man do the work of God and carry on spiritual ministry? He cannot. Spiritual work can be done only by the 'power and demonstration' of the Spirit.

Commenting on 1 Cor. 12:1, Dr. A. T. Pierson says:

> It is not strange if Paul, writing by the Spirit, says, "I would not have you ignorant concerning such matters" for this is the climax of all revealed truths of practical importance to the child of God. From his first salutation of Jesus as Saviour and Lord, to his very entrance into heaven, everything, in sanctification, growth, and service, depends upon his relations to the Spirit of God. The one great practical question is, "Received ye the Holy Ghost when ye believed"' (Acts 19:2). However little as yet we may know the Spirit, all holy living and holy service depend absolutely upon His working in us. How much may the measure of His power be increased when we do know Him and enjoy conscious union with Him! John Owen declared, in his "Pneumatologia", or Doctrine of the Spirit, that the test of our soundness in the faith, in this dispensation of the Spirit, is our attitude towards Him: and it is not too much to say that our measure of knowledge of the Scriptures and of Christ absolutely depends upon our practical acquaintance with the Holy Spirit.[1]

The Nature and Purpose of the Gifts

The word *charisma* means a gift of grace, a free gift. It does not mean a natural talent, but something bestowed that is neither purchased nor merited. What is referred to is not something we already possessed, but something provided freely by God.

The gifts of the Spirit are also spoken of as *pneumatikon* (spirituals, or spiritual manifestations) and as the 'manifestations of the Spirit' (1 Cor. 12:1, 7). In one instance *charisma pneumatikon* (a grace-gift spiritual manifestation) is used (Rom. 1:11). These terms describe what the grace-gifts actually are. The Holy Spirit dwells in every true believer and a gift of the Spirit is the Holy Spirit manifesting His wisdom and power through the believer in some particular way, unmerited by us, for the carrying out of a part of the work of the Body of Christ.

Unfortunately, the true nature of the gifts or manifestations is often not understood. Some confuse them with natural talents. Others regard them as spiritual powers which the believer comes to possess and which he may employ when and as he wishes. An examination of the Greek terms used makes it clear that neither of these conceptions is correct. A gift of the Spirit is a grace-gift, a spiritual manifestation, a manifestation of the Holy Spirit

---

[1] *The Making of a Sermon*, pp. 62, 63.

through the believer. It is simply the Holy Spirit working through us in a given manner, at the time He, the Spirit, chooses, for the carrying out of the ministry to which we have been appointed of God. It is not something given as a possession but a privilege conferred of having the Holy Spirit use us as an instrument in certain ways and manifest His own power through us.

This does not make the power manifested any less. It is power from on high. But it means that the power is not ours and does not function at our behest nor for our glory. It is manifested only as we walk in full surrender and exercise true faith

The Trinity participates in the witness of the Body of Christ through the gifts of the Spirit. This is stated in 1 Cor. 12:4-6. Conybeare's translation brings out clearly the significance of the passage:

Moreover, there are varieties of Gifts, but the same Spirit gives them all; and (they are given for) various ministrations, but all to serve the same Lord; and the working whereby they are wrought is various, but all are wrought in all by the working of the same God.

The gifts or manifestations of the Spirit are given to each believer for the carrying out of the ministry to which God has called him: "But we have special gifts which differ in accordance with the diversified work entrusted to us" (Rom. 12:6, Weymouth). They are manifested through the individual member, but they are related to the work of the whole Body. Their purpose is the building up of the Body (Eph. 4:12, 13).

"But all these (gifts) worketh that one and the selfsame Spirit, dividing to every man severally as he will" (1 Cor. 12:11; cf. 1 Cor. 7:7). The Holy Spirit distributes them to every believer. There are no exceptions: every believer has a gift or gifts apportioned to him or her. That is, the Holy Spirit would manifest Himself through every believer in the accomplishing of some part of the work. Every believer is responsible to exercise these gifts. If any member is not fulfilling his ministry through the exercise of the gifts of the Spirit, he is disobedient, unfaithful and unfruitful and the Body of Christ is, to that extent, not built up and suffers loss. The gifts are given by the Spirit 'as He will'. As the believer cannot choose the ministry he is to perform, so also he cannot choose the gifts the Holy Spirit will manifest through him. The choice is made by the Spirit, and the believer must accept the Spirit's choice.

12

All the gifts of the Spirit are equally necessary, equally honourable and equally important. They are but different manifestations of the same Spirit and are all essential to the accomplishing of the one purpose: the building up of the Body (1 Cor. 12:20-24).

The Holy Spirit knows what gifts are necessary for the work He would do through each congregation or group of God's servants. If each member is functioning, each one in his or her place in the Body, there will be all the wisdom and power for all the work that God wishes to accomplish through that congregation or group. Thus the Lord who is present in the midst will carry out, by His Spirit, His work and will through every company gathered with Him.

Power from on High

Our Lord spoke of the Spirit who was to come to the Church as "power (*dunamis* — dynamic power) from on high" (Luke 24:49). Again He said, "But ye shall receive power (*dunamis*) after that the Holy Ghost is come upon you; and ye shall be witnesses unto me both in Jerusalem, and in all Judaea, and in Samaria and unto the uttermost part of the earth" (Acts 1:8). The power is the Holy Spirit and the work of witness was to be done through the gifts of the Spirit manifested in the members of the Church. Paul states that his preaching was "not with enticing words of man's wisdom, but in demonstration of the Spirit and of power (*dunamis*)...... not in words which man's wisdom teacheth but which the Holy Spirit teacheth" (1 Cor. 2:4, 13). The Holy Spirit's presence in Paul gave revelation and power. The gifts of preaching, wisdom and faith were being manifested through him. The Holy Spirit guided him as to what to say, gave authority to what was said and wrought conviction in the hearts of the hearers.

No doubt Paul had, to a certain extent at least, the natural ability to express himself in public discourse. But it is perfectly clear that he did not regard any such talent as a gift of the Spirit. He was a man of learning and could have used his knowledge of philosophy and literature to compose eloquent and convincing orations after the manner of his day. But he deliberately did not do so. As he says, "I came not with surpassing skill of speech or wisdom. For no knowledge did I purpose to display among you, but the knowledge of Jesus Christ alone and Him — crucified" (1 Cor. 2:2, Conybeare). The word translated 'purpose' here implies reasoned judgment resulting in a definite resolve. By a free act of his will Paul decided not to employ human wisdom but to depend entirely upon the Holy Spirit.

The Holy Spirit expresses Himself through man's own powers. He uses a man's knowledge of speech and writing. If a man has a natural aptitude along these or any other line, the Holy Spirit may elect to use it. But that natural aptitude is not the gift of the Spirit. We must voluntarily and decidedly determine not to trust in it for fruit or power. It is of the soul, a soul power. A gift or manifestation of the Spirit is of the Spirit, a spiritual power. Any reliance upon the soul power for the production of spiritual fruit, any confidence in it, will be a hindrance to the Holy Spirit and may actually prevent Him entirely from using it (cf. 1 Pet. 4:10, 11).

The fact that one has a natural talent does not always mean that the Holy Spirit will elect to use it. Because one is naturally of ready speech, or even eloquent, it does not follow that he will be given the gift of preaching. Also, the lack of a natural aptitude in a believer does not limit the Holy Spirit in using him as He wills. The Spirit may manifest in him any ability which he did not naturally possess. Frequently believers with no aptitude as speakers have been given the gift of preaching in one form or another and been greatly used by the Spirit. So it is with any other gift. In the giving of the gifts the Holy Spirit is sovereign. The believer must be satisfied to accept the gifts the Holy Spirit elects to manifest through him.

Principles Governing the Gifts

1. Paul said: "I will pray with the Spirit, and I will pray with the understanding also" (1 Cor. 14:15). This statement throws much light on the Holy Spirit's work through the believer. The believer is not passive. Mind, will, emotions and body actively participate in the work. The participation is intelligent and voluntary. The whole man, spirit, soul and body, acts as one. No part may act independently of the others.

2. "Yield... your members (faculties) as instruments (tools) of righteousness unto God" (Rom. 6:13). As Paul definitely and

deliberately determined not to use man's wisdom and eloquence but to rely completely and entirely upon the Holy Spirit's power (1 Cor. 2:2), so the believer must act by the definite exercise of his will and faith and humbly, but resolutely and consistently, put himself into the position in which the Holy Spirit can use him and manifest His gifts through him. In this way the whole man will act as a voluntary instrument of the Holy Spirit.

3. Another important fact is indicated in 1 Cor. 14:32: "the gift of Prophecy does not take from the prophets the control over their own spirits" (Conybeare). In the misuse of the gifts in the church in Corinth, those who indulged in excesses evidently claimed that they acted under the compulsion of the Holy Spirit. They are told, however, that the will of the one using the gift remains sovereign. God never infringes upon the freedom of the will. It follows that the one using a gift continues to be fully responsible for his actions. He cannot excuse an action that is not in accord with the Word by claiming that he was under the control of the Spirit. He can refuse to be led into extravagances by his emotions or by evil spirits just as he can either permit or refuse to permit the Holy Spirit to minister through him.

4. Rebuking the misuse of the gifts, Paul writes: "God is not the author of confusion but of peace" (v. 33). As love is the governing principle in the employment of the gifts, the fruit will always be the manifestation of love to God and to the members of the Body of Christ. Confusion, disorder, dispeace in the congregation, is never the work of the Spirit of God. They will never be produced by any true gift of the Spirit of God. Whatever bears such fruit is a false gift.

5. In the twenty-ninth verse, those who listen to the messages of the preachers are instructed to 'judge'. The possession of a gift of the Spirit does not confer infallibility upon the one who exercises it. What is really from the Spirit will be true, but at any point man's own thought or will may be expressed. Therefore, it is necessary to compare all that is said and done with Scripture to see if it be according to God's Word. The authenticity of the message or work must be confirmed by the written Word and the witness of the Spirit. No confidence is to be put in the man who is the instrument. The final authority is the Word of God. The hearer is not excused for the acceptance of error.

6. The faithful exercise of the gifts brings increased efficiency in ministry. Paul counselled Timothy:

Do not be careless about the gifts with which you are endowed... Habitually practise these duties, and be absorbed in them; so that your growing proficiency in them may be evident to all (1 Tim. 4:14, 15. Weymouth).

The increase of knowledge of God's Word and of experience of the workings of the Spirit that comes in faithful spiritual ministry leads to greater proficiency. It makes it possible for the Spirit to use more fully the one through whom He would work. The one who is used becomes more understanding of the Spirit's will and manner of working, and so more able to enter by faith into intelligent and voluntary cooperation in the Spirit's work.

7. Love is the basic principle upon which all God's order is founded and Paul goes into considerable detail to make clear its importance in the Church's ministry. The thirteenth chapter of First Corinthians, termed the 'Love Chapter', is generally quoted out of its context. It is a part of the teaching regarding the gifts of the Spirit and their exercise. In this chapter it is made clear that faith, hope and love are the basic elements of the Church's spiritual existence. But it is shown that love is the greatest of all as being the source of all. Even faith is valueless — can have no true existence, indeed — without love.

The manner in which love must control the exercise of the gifts is stated:

Love is longsuffering; love is kind; love envies not; love speaks no vaunts; love swells not with vanity; love offends not by rudeness; love seeks not her own; is not easily provoked; bears no malice; rejoices not over iniquity, but rejoices in the victory of truth; foregoes all things, believes all things, hopes all things, endures all things (Conybeare)

Love is perfect and eternal; the gifts are not. The day will come when that which is partial and imperfect will cease and its place be taken by that which is perfect and complete. The gifts shall cease, but love remains for ever. However, meanwhile, let the gifts be exercised in love.

Love as manifested in Christ is the perfect, heavenly psychology. The psychology of that love is Godly, pure, beautiful, and noble. It attracts, influences, wins by the irresistible power of absolute truth, absolute beauty and absolute justice, which are its very essence.

Much has been written about the psychology of religion, pastoral psychology and the psychology of the pulpit. But psychology as man knows it is not based upon love. It teaches to profit from man's weaknesses, his egotism, his love of adulation, position, self-manifestation, power, pleasure, ease. It works largely through man's emotional reactions, manipulating them skilfully to produce the desired results. The psychology of love appeals to the whole man, spirit, mind and heart. Its motive is never ulterior, never selfish or egoistical. It is incapable of appealing to, or taking advantage of, any weakness of man. It would scorn to seek to accomplish good by such means. It has a better way, a perfect way, for the accomplishing of that which is good. It succeeds by producing true love, which is the highest good and the source of all good. It acts upon the principle that only good can produce good, therefore it first creates good that the true fruit may be obtained.

The psychology which the Holy Spirit uses is the psychology of Christ's love. He does not work without it: without it He would be powerless. The gifts of the Spirit are based upon it: indeed, the true gifts are expressions of it; without it they are but 'sounding brass and tinkling cymbal': vain forms in which God is not present.

This love, of course, is something beyond the love of man. It is God's love, pure, selfless, as manifested through Christ and it can work through man only as Christ dwells in him, filling him with His own Spirit, freeing him by the law of the Spirit of life from the law of sin and death that would reign within him.

It is the principle of this psychology of love, as it bears upon the exercise of the 'gifts' or 'manifestations' of the Spirit, that is taught in this chapter. It will be seen that the cost to the one who practices it is commensurate with the results that are gained. Christ had to meet the cost in full Himself. Of Him it demanded utter humility, obedience, self-abnegation and, finally, the absolute sacrifice of the Cross. The cost to any who would have Christ's Spirit manifest a gift of the Spirit through him can never be any less.

8. The gifts of the Spirit are provided for the work of a body: for taking part in a corporate ministry. The Body is composed of many members. These, since they are members of the one Body are members one of another. No member can draw apart from that relationship or separate himself from the responsibility of cooperation with the rest of the Body. A complete ministry cannot be carried out through any one member alone. No member has all the gifts of the Spirit necessary for a complete ministry.

This is why the 'lone wolf' in Christian service fails to accomplish a solid, complete, or abiding work.

In the human body, the functions of the different members, while clearly differentiated, yet are definitely interrelated and interdependent. Each is intended to be but a part in the whole. The coordination of all is necessary for the fulfilling of the full purpose of the body. So it is in the Body of Christ. One member of the Body alone may exercise the gifts of the Spirit given to him and, up to a certain point, be blessed in the using of them, but the full purpose for which they were given will not be accomplished if his ministry is not related by the Holy Spirit to the work of the Body. To realise a complete ministry, other gifts of the Spirit, possessed by other members of the Body must contribute their part.

"From whom the whole body fitly joined together and compacted by that which every joint supplieth, according to the effectual working in the measure of every part, maketh increase of the body unto the edifying of itself in love" (Eph. 4:16).

It is for this reason that several Elders are needed in a congregation. No one Elder has all the varieties of the gifts for Eldership that are needed for a complete ministry. For every part of the ministry of the Body the Holy Spirit brings together several members possessing among them the different varieties of the gifts needed for the doing of that particular work. Then the work of all the different groups must be coordinated by the Spirit. The ministry of the teachers must be coordinated with that of the preachers. The Elders' ministry is necessary to bring order into the gathering of members. The ministry of the love gifts is needed for the well being of the whole Body. Each gift contributes a part, and all the parts fitted together by the Spirit blend in union to manifest the fulness of Christ.

As the work of the whole Body is coordinated by the Spirit, each gift acquires its fullest value and bears its richest fruit. The Body of Christ is built up, one Body in which He is one with the Father and we are one with Him, and there is manifested in the Church "the perfect man... the measure of the stature of the fulness of Christ [1]."

9. It is stated that 'the gifts and calling of God are without repentance' (Rom. 11:29). That is, when God gives gifts of the

---

[1] See comment on Eph. 4:1-16 in chapter 13.

Spirit and the call for the carrying out of a work, He will not be turned aside from His purpose by whatever difficulties may be encountered. Satanic opposition will be met, men will reject God's message and God's messenger, but the gifts, the call and the purpose of God continue unchanged and God's servant must go forward in obedience and faith carrying out the ministry to which he is called. Our Lord said, "No man, having put his hand to the plough, and looking back, is fit for the Kingdom of God" (Lk. 9:62).

This does not mean that one who has been called, say as an Elder, will always be gifted and called as an Elder even though he become unfaithful. Such an one becomes unfit for his calling, the gifts of the Spirit are no longer manifested through him and his call is given to another (Acts 1:20; 2 Tim. 4:10). The gifts are functions wrought by the Spirit. When the functions cease the ministry ceases and the one who was the instrument ceases to be the instrument.

10. We may 'quench' or 'grieve' the Spirit. The gifts of the Spirit cannot be used carnally. They are not a power or a commodity given to us as a possession that may be used rightly or wrongly: they are the wisdom and power contributed by the Spirit, which will not be manifested through an instrument acting carnally. It is possible for a preacher to continue preaching, a teacher teaching, an Elder ruling, even when carnal, but the Holy Spirit's grace-gifts will not be present. Theirs will be spurious ministry, performed in the wisdom and power of man without the light and enabling of the Spirit: without the "demonstration of the Spirit and of power". That is what took place in the Corinthian church. They had not come behind in any grace-gift, but through carnality the Spirit was grieved and quenched and could no longer give understanding or power. They no longer appreciated the Spirit's wisdom and power but sought human eloquence and the "enticing words of man's wisdom".

Every Believer's Responsibility

The Holy Spirit dwells in every born-again believer in Christ (Rom. 8:9). We have already referred to His mission and work in the Church. He has not come to be a passive bystander. Nor is it His purpose to manifest Himself only at special times or through certain individuals. He is life (Rom. 8:2) and He is dynamic power (Luke 24:49). The Holy Spirit is a living power Who is continually active in every member of the Church. The manifestation of His life and power in and through a believer is hindered only if He is resisted, grieved, or tempted (Acts 5:9; 7:51; Eph. 4:30).

Through every believer He would glorify Christ, manifesting Him to the world and convicting the world of 'sin, righteousness and judgment'. To have Him do this the believer does not require to obtain His presence — He is already present — but to walk in full obedience and faith. It is necessary to believe what God's Word says about Him and believe that He will fulfil His work in us (1 Pet. 4:10, 11; 1 Cor. 12:7, 11, 18; Rom. 12:6).

CHAPTER XVI

THE MEANING OF THE GIFTS

IT is important to have a clear understanding of the meaning of the different gifts or manifestations of the Spirit and the purpose for which each is intended. We would classify them as follows:

1. For the proclamation of the divine revelation. — The gift of Prophecy or Preaching is provided for this ministry.

2. For the teaching of the divine revelation. — The gift of Teaching.

3. For enabling. — Through the gift of Faith the believer is enabled to stand upon revealed truth and trust in power that is beyond the sphere of human possibilities.

4. For revelation. — The gift of the Utterance of Wisdom is given for the stating of the deep spiritual truths revealed in the Word regarding God and His thoughts and purposes.

5. For understanding. — The gift of the Utterance of Knowledge is provided for the stating of the practical application of spiritual truth to daily experience.

6. For protection. — The gift of Discernment of Spirits provides protection against Satan's deceptions.

7. For the practical manifestation of the love of Christ in the Church. — There are three gifts: Mercy, the Paraclete gift, and Giving.

8. For maintaining order. — The gift of Government or Presiding.

9. For secular service. — The gift of 'Serviceable Ministrations' or Helps. This is required for all secular service, including the Deacon's ministry.

10. As special signs of the presence of God's power. — There are four sign gifts: Miracles, Healing, Varieties of Tongues, and Interpretation of Tongues.

1. For the Proclamation of the Divine Revelation.

Prophecy, or Preaching. This is one of the basic ministries of the Spirit and is dealt with in the following chapter. It is provided for the carrying out of the Lord's command to preach the Gospel to every creature and should be sought by all (Mark 16:15; 1 Cor. 14:1).

2. For the Teaching of the Divine Revelation.

Teaching. As one of the basic ministries this gift is considered in the following chapter. It is given that the Lord's command to teach all nations may be fulfilled (Matt. 28:19; Eph. 4:11).

3. For Enabling.

Faith. It should be observed that:

(1) The gift of Faith is purely spiritual in nature. It comes from God. It cannot be exercised by the natural power of man alone.

(2) The Holy Spirit gives the faith necessary for every ministry to which any member of the Body of Christ is called.

The gift or manifestation of faith mentioned in the list in 1 Cor. 12:9, is something additional to what we may term saving faith, though it is of the same nature, for all true faith is given by the Spirit. The gift of Faith is a manifestation of the Holy Spirit exercising faith in the believer, to the extent that it is necessary, for the carrying out of any ministry for which it is required. George Müller exercised the gift of Faith. He was called to a ministry that required the exercise of faith for the accomplishing of God's will and the gift of Faith was given him for that purpose. He humbly testifies to this:

It pleased the Lord, I think, to give me in some cases something like the gift... of faith, so that unconditionally I could ask and look for an answer.[1]

The existence of this gift of faith and the need to rely upon it continually should never be lost sight of. Every member of the Church needs it for the carrying out of the ministry to which he or she is called. It is through the lack of its exercise that the

---

[1] A. T. Pierson: *George Müller of Bristol*, p. 438.

ministry of many fails to accomplish that which God purposed for it. Through lack of this faith we descend to the use of our own human powers instead of relying upon the Spirit's power and permitting Him to work through us by His wisdom and gifts.

It is essential in all ministry. No ministry can be carried on in the power of the Spirit without it. We must believe that God can and will accomplish all that is necessary to the carrying out of the ministry to which He has called us. Paul could not have continued his ministry without positive, unwavering and continual faith.

The fact that love is basic in the exercise of true faith is stated in 1 Corinthians 13:2. This is more important than may seem at first sight. It is really impossible to exercise faith fully for a person if love for that person is lacking. Take away love from God and what would be left? Take love from the believer's ministry and nothing is left but an empty shell. It should be realized also that it is impossible to have complete faith in God if He is not loved with all our strength, heart and mind. To the extent that love to Him is lacking, confidence in Him will be lacking. To the extent that there is love for self, the world and riches, there will be confidence, or faith in these. But perfect love for God will bring perfect faith in Him. Only the crucified heart and mind can exercise faith.

4. For Revelation.

The Utterance of Wisdom *(logos sophias)*. In the second chapter of First Corinthians, the difference between the wisdom of God and the wisdom of man is made clear. In that statement, Paul claims to have this 'utterance of wisdom'. It is the teaching or declaring of that which is in God's mind and heart, of God's wisdom and purpose, of something that the natural eye cannot perceive, the natural ear cannot hear and the natural heart cannot imagine — something beyond man's natural powers to discover but revealed in the Word and made known by the Spirit. It is theoretical knowledge of spiritual truth revealed by the Spirit.

A preacher or teacher with this gift will be given revelation and understanding by the Spirit to declare and explain deep spiritual truths and principles.

The first part of Ephesians (1:1—4:16) is an example of the

Word of Wisdom. It deals with God's revealed purpose regarding the Church's life and structure and the great spiritual principles that govern them.

5. For Understanding.

The Utterance of Knowledge *(logos gnoseos)*. Knowledge is information and practical understanding acquired by study or experience. The 'utterance of knowledge' is the practical application of spiritual truth to the life and ministry of the believer. The second part of Ephesians (4:17—6:20) is an example of the Word of Knowledge. It deals with the life and witness of the member of the Church, based upon the spiritual principles that govern the Church.

This practical spiritual understanding is received from the Holy Spirit and is not the fruit of the natural intelligence. It is for the giving of counsel regarding the practical things of the believer's every-day life. The messages of a preacher or teacher with this gift will be practical, applying spiritual principles to life and conduct.

6. For Protection.

Discernment of Spirits. In view of the fact that the members of the Body of Christ face the continual opposition of a host of evil spirit-beings and that these beings may pose as messengers of light and may counterfeit the gifts of the Holy Spirit, it is necessary that there should be a gift of discernment to enable the believer to distinguish between the true and the false.

This gift is provided and is of vital importance. There is no need for the believer ever to be misled or to be in doubt as to whether what he sees or hears, or the thoughts that enter the mind, are the work of the Holy Spirit or of Satan.

The fact that a gift of the Spirit has been given for this purpose makes it clear that the natural intelligence is not capable of such discernment. Scriptures that relate to this gift are: 1 Cor. 12:10; Acts 5:3; 1 Cor. 2:14, 15; 1 Jn. 4:1, 2; Rev. 2:2. Cf. Mk. 8:32, 33.

7. The Love Gifts.

All the gifts of the Spirit are manifestations of love, but the following are particularly for the practical manifestation of Christ's love among the members of His Body.

Love may be manifested by the human heart. It is necessary to understand that these love gifts go beyond what is possible to the human heart. They are for the manifestation, through the believer by the Spirit, of the love of Christ, which is the love of God — the love described in 1 Corinthians 13 (Cf. Eph. 3:17-21).

Human love has limits of endurance and can fail. It is imperfect in its judgment. In the final issue it always reserves the best for self. We become tired and discouraged dealing with a 'weak brother'. We are hurt when no appreciation is shown.

Christ manifested these three practical love gifts. He came to our help freely as the Paraclete and gave His all for us, withholding nothing for self.

(1) **The Showing of Mercy.** Young's literal translation renders this, 'doing kindness'. This gift is for the doing of acts of love. It is for the practical manifestation of compassionate kindness. Conybeare translates it: 'he who shows pity'. This is not just the feeling of pity but the expression of it in acts (cf. Jas. 2:15-17).

The practical manifestation of pity by God is spoken of in Isaiah 63:9:

In their affliction he was afflicted, and the angel of his presence saved them; in his love and in his pity he redeemed them; and he bare them, and carried them all the days of old.

Christ's pity for us was expressed in acts — His whole life on earth was an expression of it. His sacrifice on the Cross was the supreme manifestation of it.

This gift of the Spirit is for the manifestation of practical, compassionate love among the members of the Body of Christ — 'members one of another' — so that they may 'have the same care one for another' (1 Cor. 12:25). It was to this that Christ referred when He spoke of "whosoever shall give you a cup of water in my name because ye belong to Christ..." (Mk. 9:41). We are exhorted to 'bear one another's burdens'.

This is not just kindness springing from man's heart: it is Christ's love manifested by the Holy Spirit through the believer. It is something much deeper and stronger than sympathy aroused through the stirring of the emotions.

It will be readily seen that this gift is of wide application and performs a very gracious, necessary and beautiful ministry. A notable example of it is given by Mme. Guyon's maid-servant, who shared her imprisonment in the Bastille and died there in the year 1700. Although she was deeply taught of the Spirit and unusually gifted, as Thomas C. Upham writes,

> ...she desired to be what God would have her be, and to be nothing more, and nothing less... She had not a doubt that God, who had given remarkable powers to Mme. Guyon, had called her to the great work in which she was employed. But knowing that her beloved mistress could not go alone, but must constantly have some female attendant, she had the conviction, equally distinct, that she was called to be her maid-servant.[1]

This Christ-like gift of practical, compassionate love is manifested often unseen and always with Christ-like humility. It is of the utmost value, greatly needed and richly used of God in the Body of Christ. It may be manifested in the giving of a cup of water, in ministry to the sick and needy, in Dorcas labours, in an orphanage or a hospital. However, we must be careful to distinguish between what is merely human love and what is the true manifestation of the Holy Spirit's gift. What is of the Spirit will originate with Him, will be absolutely under His guidance, will be done in Christ's name, will have as its object the manifesting and glorifying of Christ and will produce spiritual fruit (1 Pet. 4:10, 11).

(2) **The Paraclete Gift.** The Greek word *paraklasis* (inadequately translated 'exhortation' in Rom. 12:8) is interesting. It is the work performed by the *parakletos* (paraclete). It is variously translated: consolation (14), exhortation (8), comfort (6), entreaty (1). *Parakletos* is used as a title of Christ, translated 'Advocate' (1 Jn. 2:1). It means 'one called alongside to help'. Our Lord used it as a title of the Holy Spirit. He said He would give 'another Paraclete (Comforter) that he may abide with you forever' (Jn. 14:16, 26).

The Paraclete gift is one of the most wonderful and gracious of the gifts of the Spirit manifested through the believer. The Paraclete, through the 'other Paraclete' dwelling in us, would use us as His instruments in the carrying out of His paraclete work towards the members of His Body. The Holy Spirit would

---

[1] *Life of Mme. Guyon.*

manifest Himself through us, ministering comfort, consolation, encouragement, exhortation or counsel to one another. Could a more glorious work be ours?

The gift has not to do particularly with public discourse. It enables one believer to go alongside another believer to minister spiritual help in time of need. As the Showing of Mercy is a ministry through acts of love, so the Paraclete gift is a ministry through words of love. It is a love gift for the manifesting of the love of Christ in the Church. Like most of the gifts, it has a wide application. Indeed, it should be manifested through everyone in whom the Paraclete dwells. For the encouraging of young converts, the counselling of any who may be in spiritual need, the comforting of the sick, the strengthening of weak brethren, the Paraclete gift is needed. In our Lord's dealings with Peter and in His prayer of faith for him when Peter was too weak to pray for himself, we see Christ exercising this gift (cf. 1 Thes. 4:1; Heb. 3:13; 1 Pet. 5:1).

The difference between the Paraclete gift and the gift of Showing Mercy may be illustrated simply as follows: A believer visits another who is sick to minister spiritual encouragement. To do this he requires the Paraclete gift of words of love. Or, the visiting believer may go into the kitchen and prepare a meal, or help care for the children. For such ministry the gift of Showing Mercy, or acts of love is needed.

All this, of course, may be simulated by the natural heart, so great care must be exercised that the exhorting, counselling, comforting, etc., come not from our own proud heart but are the true work of the indwelling Paraclete manifesting His perfect love. On one occasion the counsel which Peter gave to the Lord brought the rebuke "Get thee behind me Satan".

(3)· **Giving.** It is enlightening to compare the different passages in which the word *metadidomi* (give, or impart) is used: Rom. 1:11; Luke 3:11; Eph. 4:28; 1 Thess. 2:8. This gift is for the manifesting of the love of Christ among the members of the Body through material ministry.

Giving must be under the direct guidance of the Holy Spirit. It is a gift of the Spirit and should not be controlled by the emotions or sentiments. Much giving to God's work is done in response to appeals to the emotions and is, therefore, not a true manifestation of the gift of giving.

Giving must be on a purely spiritual basis. When it is truly impelled by Christ's love and under the guidance of the Holy Spirit, it is raised from the material plane to the spiritual and is a gift of the Spirit. As such it occupies a definite place in the spiritual ministry of the Church and produces spiritual fruit.[1]

8. For Maintaining Order.

Government or Presiding. Anyone whose ministry involves the exercise of spiritual authority requires this gift. Those who exercise spiritual authority in the Church are the Evangelist and the Elder. The Scriptural teaching regarding their ministries is given in a previous chapter. They deal with the people of God, with members of the Body of Christ, with a priesthood of royal lineage and with spiritual issues, therefore their every act must be guided by the Holy Spirit. It must be the act of Christ, the Head of the Church, otherwise it is without spiritual power or authority.

There are other spiritual ministries that require this gift. For example, George Muller required it for the direction of the Orphanage which God had called him to establish. For the guidance of any work, no matter of what nature it may be — wherever the objective is the producing of spiritual fruit — the gift of the Spirit for governing or presiding is necessary.

We have already noted the fact that the gift of government given to the Church does not include the legislative function.[2] Those who oversee cannot make laws or by-laws; nor can the Church. Christ has given a complete equipment of laws and regulations for the life and work of the Church. All procedure must conform to these.

There is always a subtle temptation to legislate. It is done to protect the Church, to safeguard the believer and to maintain the purity of doctrine. But it always means the introduction of. human principles of government, of human authority, of material safeguards. It has led the Church away from the divine pattern and always will do so.

9. Secular Ministry.

'**Serviceable Ministrations**', or **Helps.** Deacons require this

---

[1] See also Chapter 28.
[2] See p. 140.

13

gift for the carrying on of whatever secular ministry may be required in the Church. This has been dealt with in the previous Chapter.

This gift is necessary also to all engaged in any other secular ministry the object of which is the obtaining of spiritual fruit. For instance, one called to minister through a Gospel Book Store requires it. Those who care for the funds and the book-keeping and editing, etc., in the office of our missionary fellowship must have it.

It must always be borne in mind that spiritual fruit can be produced only by the Spirit; it cannot be produced by work done through natural wisdom alone. No secular ministry can of itself produce spiritual fruit.

10. Sign Gifts.

The sign gifts, or miracle gifts, were given for a special purpose. They bore a special testimony at the beginning of the Dispensation. Their manifestation was a fulfilment of prophecy (Acts 2:17-20). At first they were much in evidence (Acts 2:43), but they became less common after the martyrdom of Stephen. In the later years of the Apostles' ministry they are rarely mentioned.

(1) **Miracles.** This gift of the Spirit has been dealt with already in the section on Miracles in Chapter 2. To say that miracles have ceased, would be incorrect. God continues to do many miraculous things. But the power to work miracles manifested through a person is not usually seen, and when it is, it is not a permanent gift but rather a special, temporary manifestation for a special purpose.

(2) **Healing.** That God still manifests His power in restoring the sick is unquestionable. But when He does so, it is for a special purpose. In the later years of the Apostles' ministry, it is quite evident that not all the sick who sought the Lord in faith were healed. God refused to remove Paul's 'thorn in the flesh', and made known His reason to His servant. Paul accepted the reason as satisfactory. Paul advised Timothy to take a remedy for his stomach's sake (1 Tim. 5:23). He left Trophimus at Miletus sick (2 Tim. 4:20). Did these servants of the Lord lack faith? Why was the gift of healing not employed? We can be certain that God had a sufficient reason for not healing immediately these servants of His on those occasions.

God's primary purpose for His children is the forming of the image of Christ in them (Rom. 8:28, 29). Whether He heals or not will depend upon which will contribute to the accomplishing of that purpose.

The gifts of the Spirit are manifested, not when men desire to use them, but when the Holy Spirit wishes to do something that will be to the furtherance of God's work. If it is not to be to the furtherance of God's purpose, He does not manifest His power.

A gift of healing is manifested in many false cults. Not infrequently believers have been misled into extravagances that have been used of Satan to discredit the truth. In these extravagances, psychic, or soulish, powers, the influence of evil spirits and the glorying of the flesh are to be discerned.

It is necessary to be carefully on guard in this matter. All Scriptures dealing with the subject must be taken together. To isolate certain passages and build a doctrine upon them is to misuse the Word of God and to fall into error. We must be scrupulously careful always to observe the fundamental laws of interpretation.

The gift of healing is still manifested, but it is not given a place of prominence. It is only used at certain times and for certain purposes. The gift of healing claimed by not a few is not a true gift of the Holy Spirit.

James gives the procedure to be followed in the Church in this matter. When a believer is sick he is counselled to call for the Elders of the church. Wherever there is a church established this should be the procedure. Normally, it is through them that the gift of healing will now be manifested. In regions where there is no church and no Elders to call, the gift will, no doubt, be manifested through individual servants of God. Note the fact that it is not one, but several Elders who are to act. The Elders will anoint the sick one with oil and pray for him. The Lord will restore the sick one, if it is in accordance with His will to do so.

The Elders represent the church. Their act is an expression of the unity, the fellowship, and the mutual responsibility existing in the Body of Christ. This practice should be more common in the churches.

(3) **Varieties of Tongues and Interpretation of Tongues.** Explicit instructions were given regarding the use of the gift of tongues and its interpretation in the fourteenth chapter of 1

Corinthians. In quoting from this chapter we shall use Cony-beare's translation.

In verses 2-4 Paul compares the gift of Tongues with the gift of Prophecy or Preaching:

> He who speaks in a Tongue, speaks not to men but to God; for no man understands him, but with his spirit he utters mysteries, but he who prophesies speaks to men, and builds them up, with exhortation and with comfort. He who speaks in a Tongue builds himself up alone; but he who prophesies builds up the Church.

Then, discussing the matter he says,

> (v. 6) Now brethren, if when I came to you I were to speak in Tongues, what should I profit you... (9) So also if you utter un-intelligible words with your tongue, how can your speech be un-derstood? you will be speaking to the air... (11) If, then, I know not the meaning of the language, I shall be as a foreigner to him that speaks it, and he will be accounted a foreigner to me... (18, 19) I offer thanksgiving to God in private speaking in Tongues (to Him) more than you all. Yet in the Congregation I would rather speak five words with my understanding so as to instruct others, than ten thousand words in a Tongue. Brethren be not children in understanding... (27) If there be any who speak in Tongues let not more than two, or at the most three, speak..., and let them speak in turn; and let the same interpreter explain the words of all. But if there be no interpreter let him who speaks in Tongues keep silence in the Congregation, and speak in private to himself alone... (40) And let all things be done decently and in order.

It is quite evident that this was written to correct the abuse of the gift of tongues in the carnal church in Corinth. Paul stresses the very limited scope of its usefulness. It had been given a pro-minence and a place not intended by the Lord. In the congre-gation the gift of preaching is much more profitable and a strict limit should be placed upon the use of the gift of tongues.

The counterfeit of this gift has caused great confusion among believers. The modern 'Tongues Movement' is largely soulish, although there is no doubt that in it there have been definite manifestations of the activity of evil spirits.

The appeal of the movement has been largely due to two reasons. In the first place, the lack of adequate teaching regarding the work of the Holy Spirit and the gifts of the Spirit has left many of God's people in ignorance of the truth and open to deception. Many of those who have been deceived have earn-estly desired a greater knowledge of the truth and have been conscious of the need of a deeper experience of the Holy Spirit's power. Being untaught they did not have discernment to recognize the error. In the second place there is a strong appeal to the flesh. It is a manifestation in which the flesh may readily glory.

The fruit of the counterfeit has given ample evidence of its origin. Confusion is the immediate result. All the rules laid down in the fourteenth chapter of First Corinthians to govern the use of the gift are disregarded. The gift is not made to comply with God's Word, but is regarded as superior to it. That in itself is sufficient evidence to prove that it is not of the Spirit of God, for the Holy Spirit will always act in strict conformity to Scripture. Other fruits that have been much in evidence are false doctrine and sin. Our experience has been that wherever this error has entered among believers on the foreign field a sad situation has soon developed. Sin has become open and rife and the Gospel testimony greatly hindered.

All the evidence proves without any possibility of doubt that the gift of tongues is not manifested today except in comparatively rare instances and for a special purpose, and that it usually occurs in the case of individuals when alone. (Dr. R. A. Torrey's experience is an example of this.) This fully conforms to the advice given by Paul and to his own practice. While he did not forbid the public use of the gift, he makes it clear that he did not use it himself in his public ministry, considering it not intended, or adapted, for that purpose. He had used the gift in his private communion with God and he advises the Corinthian believers to use it in private only unless there is an interpreter present.[1] Paul definitely does not regard it as a necessary or even as a useful part of the ministry in the congregation. In the modern counterfeit of the gift, as in Paul's time, women are prominent, exercising their supposed gift in the gathering of the church, often with hysterical and unseemly excesses, in complete disregard of the fact that it is not permitted that they do so (vv. 23, 34, 40).

It will be noticed that this gift is not mentioned in the lists given in Ephesians and Romans. Evidently, it was not given prominence in churches that were spiritual. There is no record of the gift of Tongues having been used by Christ. All the other gifts were manifested by Him.

----

[1] See Neander's *Planting and Training of the Church*, pp. 136, 137.

The Gifts are Not Withdrawn.

Verses eight to thirteen of the thirteenth chapter of 1 Corinthians are cited by some writers as teaching that the sign gifts were to cease after the apostolic age. We deplore the modern counterfeit of the gift of tongues, but we do not feel that this passage gives any ground for saying that any gift has ceased. In the fourteenth chapter, as we have already seen, it is made clear that the gift of tongues has a very restricted usefulness and that the gift of prophecy is superior to it. In the thirteenth chapter, the gift of tongues is the only sign gift mentioned. But along with it, the gifts of prophecy (in the sense of 14:3) and knowledge are also named as destined to cease. It is not said that these gifts shall cease during the Church Dispensation but "when that which is perfect is come". Paul is distinguishing between the gifts of the Spirit and the three eternally basic principles, faith, hope and love, the greatest of which is love. These principles are perfect and eternal and shall never cease. But the gifts of the Spirit by which man in the flesh ministers in this age will be replaced by something far superior. In the day when we see Him face to face and our knowledge is complete and we have put on incorruption, then the gifts of the Spirit which are God's gracious means of manifesting His Spirit through imperfect man, will cease to be, for then the light shall be perfect and shall never go dim and we shall minister with Him in the fulness of our heritage. Meanwhile, the gifts of the Spirit continue that the glory that shone in Christ may be manifested now in these 'earthen vessels' (2 Cor. 4:6, 7).

Variations of the Gifts

The number of gifts listed is comparatively small. But it must be understood that each gift designated is not of uniform manifestation. Each designation actually represents a class of gifts. In each class there are many variations. It is important to keep this in mind when speaking of a gift of the Spirit.

In a group of preachers there may be as many variations of the gift of preaching as there are preachers. Many different varieties of preaching are needed and God supplies them all. Different varieties of the gift of preaching are needed for preaching to adults, to a large audience, to one individual, to a family circle, to young people, to children of different ages, in the open air, etc. Likewise, different varieties of the gift of teaching are required for teaching adults, children of different ages, etc. So it is with all except the sign gifts.

No one man can carry on a complete ministry along any line. Although he may have the gift of preaching, the range of his gift is limited. Other preachers with other varieties of the gift are needed for a complete ministry of preaching. The Holy Spirit will provide all the variations of all the gifts necessary in a congregation if there is liberty given for the exercise of the gifts by all.

This is in harmony with the constitution of the Church as a Body composed of cooperating, interrelated, interdependent members. For this reason several Elders are needed in a congregation. Each one will have different variations of the gift of oversight to contribute, and if a congregation has all the Elders God intends it to have, all the variations of the Elder's gift that are needed will be present.

The same principle is evident in the group of Apostles. No two were alike in the variations of the gifts possessed, but together they had a complete equipment for their special work. In any sphere of Christian ministry and service this principle applies. The Body is one, composed of many different members and each member is necessary to all the others and no one is sufficient in himself.

It will be realized that, in view of this fact, the greatest care must be taken always to permit the Holy Spirit liberty to manifest His gifts through all and, also, to bring together into cooperation all those He wishes to unite in any particular ministry.

The bringing together by the Spirit of Paul and his fellow-missionaries is an example of this. Man's arrangements, or choice, would have deprived the Holy Spirit of this indispensable liberty of selection; it would have made impossible the functioning of these spiritual laws, and confusion, weakness and loss would have resulted. Naturally, the Holy Spirit can accomplish His work perfectly and fully only where there is true obedience to the principles laid down in God's Word — principles which we must obey and which the Holy Spirit will never disobey. It will be evident that the Spirit can have complete liberty of action only in the form of structure which God has ordained for the Church and revealed in the New Testament.

A Full Provision

A study of all the gifts of the Spirit given by Christ to men when He ascended up on high, reveals the fact that a gloriously complete provision was made for all the needs of the Church. The organization of the Church, its government, extension, instruction, witness and corporate life are all fully cared for. All is to be done by the Holy Spirit manifesting His gifts through the members. There is no part of the work, spiritual or material, for which there is not a gift of the Spirit. No part of the work — not even that of the Deacon, or the performing of acts of love, or the giving of material aid — is left to man's natural judgment or ability. The flesh has been entrusted with no part in it. There is a complete spiritual enablement. It is indeed 'the Church, which is His Body, the fulness of Him that filleth all in all', through which 'the manifold wisdom of God' is manifested.

The fact is that Christ, indwelling the Church by His Spirit, has given it His own spiritual equipment. All His ministry was performed in the power of the Holy Spirit and through the gifts of the Spirit.

> The Holy Spirit's gifts were first revealed
> In all the glory of their Heavenly might
> In Christ the living Word, the Son of man;
> Nor spake He ever word or action wrought
> But by the Spirit of the Living God.
> The great Apostle of our faith is He;
> The Prophet, Priest, the Bishop of our souls;
> The Shepherd true that guards His own sheep-fold;
> The Servant come to minister in love.
> With deeds of love He took my place in death;
> With words of love He healed the broken heart;
> With gifts of love uncounted riches gave;
> In words of wisdom showed the mind of God;
> In words of knowledge taught us how to live.
> He healed the sick, the blind; the dead He raised;
> The lying craft of Satan full revealed.
> These gifts of grace He gave to His redeemed
> When He ascended to His Throne on high.
> They are His work, His wisdom, and His might:
> The power of truth and love; indwelling light
> That fills the Church with Christ, the perfect man.

It is these faculties of the Spirit, through which Christ ministered, speaking the Father's Word and doing the Father's work, that the Holy Spirit brought to the Church. Christ, present in the Church, would build it through the same spiritual power which

He employed when on earth. The power, the method and the objective have not changed.

How incalculable has been the Church's loss as it has neglected its spiritual faculties and as man's wisdom and talents and methods and power have taken the Spirit's place. Man's power, controlled by his own mind and will, have been substituted for the gifts of the Spirit, bringing impotence, defeat and disaster. Why should we not, through obedience and faith, enter again into our heritage and give to the Lord and to the Holy Spirit their rightful place?

Naturally, only spiritual members can carry on the true spiritual order in the Church—members such as were found in the churches in New Testament times. But the members of those churches were spiritual because the order in the churches was spiritual. They had every opportunity and encouragement to be spiritual. They were ministered to by those who had gifts of the Spirit and they were expected to take part in the ministry through the gifts they possessed. The Holy Spirit was given His place and He was faithful to carry out His work.

If the Church's work is to be accomplished today we must return to the place where the power that is greater than man's power — the 'power from on high' — is again manifested; where man is not working alone, but Christ the Lord, through His Spirit dwelling in the members of His Church, is speaking His Word and doing His work through His people by His own mighty power.

It is not that the gifts of the Spirit have ever completely disappeared. At all times since the Church began the Spirit has been ready to work through any believer who would permit Him. Gifts of the Spirit were manifested in some of the Early Church Fathers. The Montanists definitely believed in the gifts and depended upon them. Genuine gifts of the Spirit are seen in such men as Huss, Luther, George Fox, Archbishop Usher and those spoken of in *The Scot's Worthies* — Wishart, Knox, Erskine, Peden and many others. They became especially evident in times of great persecution when God's people were pried loose from all that is of the world and from dependence upon material things and forced into a close walk with Him. Thus we find them appearing among the Scottish Covenanters and the French Huguenots after the repeal of the edict of Nantz.

In times of revival, when the Holy Spirit has been working

with freedom, His gifts have reappeared. Campbell Morgan describes what took place in the Welsh Revival in 1904:

> There were the organs, but silent; the ministers, but among the people, rejoicing and prophesying with the rest, only there was no preaching. Yet the Welsh Revival is the revival of preaching in Wales. Everybody is preaching. No order, yet it moves from day to day, week to week, county to county, with matchless precision, with the order of an attacking force.

Naturally, the gifts of preaching and teaching have always been the most common, and many are the men and women through whom the Holy Spirit has manifested these gifts. In such preachers and teachers as Samuel Rutherford, Whitefield, the Wesleys, Finney, McCheyne, Bonar, Moody, we see God's Spirit at work. The gift of faith is seen in Muller, Hudson Taylor, Sister Abigail, Amy Carmichael and many others. Such spiritual power was not natural to these servants of God; they did not have it in themselves. We have heard Campbell Morgan and R. A. Torrey tell how powerless and ineffective their ministry had been before they came to the place where they were yielded to the Holy Spirit and He was able to make them His instruments, manifesting Himself through them. So it was also with Finney and Moody and with all through whom the Holy Spirit has manifested himself.

We have mentioned only a few names of men and women whose ministry has made them prominent, but there are many others whom God has used in less conspicuous but no less valuable service who have had or who have, true gifts of the Spirit. However, many as these are, their number is very small compared with the multitudes of Christians through whom the Spirit has not been able to accomplish His work, whose service and testimony has been largely, if not wholly, in the power and wisdom of man. In the Church as a whole we see man's wisdom, eloquence, organization, schemes and effort. The Spirit of the living God must stand aside. His gifts are considered too impractical. The result, of course, is blindness, darkness, powerlessness and defeat. Even earnest men and women labour on, looking to God in a measure, but never entering the place of power, never having the Holy Spirit's gifts fully manifested through them, never becoming, as God purposed, full co-workers with Him and channels of His power.

God's people must be brought to understand this. It was understood in the Early Church. The Holy Spirit was known, believed in, given His place; and so His power was manifested, not just through a few, but generally among all the members of the Church. A congregation was a gathering of believers in all of whom the Holy Spirit was manifesting His gifts. All the gifts were manifested and coordinated throughout the Church by the Spirit so that Christ was fully revealed and His work accomplished.

We must permit the Spirit to free our minds and hearts from the materialism and rationalism that are such deadly tools of Satan and walk in living union with the Spirit of the living God, not only declaring our faith in His presence and power but entering into the experience of its reality.

In establishing congregations we must be faithful through faith, teaching, prayer and example, to lay claim to nothing less than the full accomplishing of God's purpose, which means that all the members will enter into that relationship with the Holy Spirit which will enable Him to manifest Himself through them in the building of the Church.

Our Lord did not simply say, "Ye shall be witnesses unto me"; He said, "Ye shall receive power, after that the Holy Spirit is come upon you: and ye shall be witnesses unto me". That statement still stands unaltered. The command has not been withdrawn; nor has the provision of power to carry it out. Paul was not stressing a secondary matter when, by the Spirit, he urged the Church, "Now concerning spiritual gifts, brethren, I would not have you ignorant", nor when he counselled Timothy: "stir up the gift that is in thee".

Counterfeits

We must bear in mind always the fact that for every true gift of the Spirit there are two types of counterfeits. There are similar manifestations produced by evil spirits. Also there are similar manifestations that are purely of soulish origin. There is Satan's counterfeit and man's counterfeit. There are Evangelists and preachers and teachers of false doctrines and false cults that are directly inspired by evil spirits. Also, there are servants of God who depend upon human eloquence, learning, organizing ability, art, etc. In the accompanying chart the different counterfeits are shown.

Also it should be observed that there are two types of the soulish manifestation, the one intellectual, the other emotional.

The mind of man is naturally rationalistic and discounts all that is of the Spirit. It rejects actual dependence upon the Holy Spirit's power. If it accepts the doctrine of the Spirit it does so only theoretically, and for practical purposes substitutes the wisdom of man's mind — eloquence, learning, organization, methods, schemes, etc. It may pay lip service to the Spirit, crediting Him with having a part in the results, but its confidence has been in its own wisdom. It may speak of preaching as a gift of the Spirit but it depends for success upon the human factors. The other type of soulish manifestation is emotional. The doctrine of the Spirit is accepted but emotionalism is confounded with the power of the Spirit.

The employment, consciously or unconsciously, of soulish psychology may produce profound emotional reactions. A religious atmosphere that is purely emotional may be created easily. Emotional singing may intoxicate the senses. A magnetic personality may be used to hypnotize an audience. All this is often mistaken for spiritual power, even in doctrinally sound churches. It is said, 'we felt the power of the Spirit', when what was felt was purely emotional.

Architectural surroundings, ritual, vestured preachers and choirs, sentimental illustrations and singing can produce a feeling of worship that is entirely emotional and only a counterfeit of the true sense of the presence of the Spirit of the living God and of true worship in the Spirit. What is nothing more or less than 'mob psychology' may succeed in arousing fanatical religious fervour. This may be purely soulish and not the direct work of any spirit, but evil spirits immediately take advantage of it. The Holy Spirit would never countenance it or use it (cf. Jn. 4:23, 24; Phil. 3:3; Lev. 10:1-3).

Thus we can see that while there is the true manifestation of the Holy Spirit's working and an equally real manifestation of the working of evil spirits, there is also a middle ground; there is a working that is soulish — that has to do with powers latent in the natural man. It is psychological and emotional. The emotions are not wrong; they are God-given. They may be deeply stirred by the Holy Spirit. The basic emotion is love and the Spirit certainly seeks to stir our love for God. But we must beware of that which is not the true work of the Spirit — not merely of that which openly opposes the Spirit's work but of that which simulates it and counterfeits it and so robs us of what is gloriously real and true and leaves us with an empty husk. The Holy Spirit, while He will profoundly stir the emotions, will never throw them out of balance. On the contrary, He will always bring our whole being, as God has made it, into true balance that we may walk in true union with the Spirit to the glory of God. The power of that which is of an evil spirit, or which is purely of man's own powers, does not effect this true balance; it introduces confusion and prevents true unity and cooperation with the Spirit of God. Thus its ultimate result is the ·accomplishment of Satan's purpose. We need the discernment of the Spirit in all these things.

It will be found that emotional religion and sin are not incompatible. This proves that such emotional religion has nothing to do with the Holy Spirit. Roman Catholicism is largely an emotional religion. It is possible for a devout Catholic to live on a low ethical and moral plane, having no true sense of sin. Pentecostalism is largely emotional religion. It also can be tolerant of sin. Such we have found to be the case in many of the Pentecostal congregations with which we are acquainted in South America. Believers from other churches who are led astray by the movement generally lose their keen sense of sin, frequently to a disastrous extent. In Pentecostal congregations where sin is rife, members, themselves in sin, will be active in the use of "gifts" of tongues, prophecy, healing, and in giving revelations. These gifts, of course, are not true gifts of the Holy Spirit. He could not manifest Himself through such instruments. They are false gifts: deceptive emotional counterfeits of which evil spirits not infrequently take advantage.

Soulish faith and worship is superstition. It has been said that,

The assigning of qualities and properties which can only be predicated of solid substances to mere surfaces, is superstition.

This is a real and very subtle danger. To attribute supernatural virtue to natural phenomena is superstition. To attribute to the Holy Spirit that which is of man is superstition. Such faith and worship is without true substance. "Faith is the substance of things hoped for, the evidence of things not seen" (Heb. 11:1). True faith and worship take hold upon that which, though invisible, has true substance — upon spiritual fact, which has infinitely truer substance than that which is material. True faith and worship are not superstition because God and His Spirit exist and work and manifest themselves. But to say, for instance, that hymn singing is spiritual when it is merely emotional or that the power of the Spirit is in a message that has merely stirred emotion, is superstition. Preaching or singing or any other religious exercise that does not lead us to the true substance, which is God Himself in His real presence and active power is superstition — an empty thing and vain that only deprives us of that which is real.

Sacramentalism is of this nature. It invests symbols and rites with attributes that belong to God; with virtue that pertains to Him alone. Idolatry in all its forms (and sacramentalism is one of them) belongs to this category. It causes men to worship and put confidence in something other than God.

How much of this superstition there is that keeps us from entering into true fellowship with God; into the living power of the life that He gives; into true participation with Him in His work!

Dr. J. H. Jowett points out another danger:

Whatever creates in me a sense of power tends to make me atheistic... How is it? It is thus: When I become conscious of the possession of any power I begin to think of myself as a cause rather than as an effect. I find that I can originate enterprise, I can create enthusiasm, I can stir human hearts, I can win public applause, I can move my fellow-men. Recognizing myself as a power I begin to think of myself as a creator, a cause, and ignoring all the other causes, I lapse into an atheism which leaves out God. I am a king's ambassador, but I come to regard myself as a king...[1]

We must ever be watchful not to lose sight of the fact that when we use the natural powers independently, without true submission to, and reliance upon, the Holy Spirit, we are acting independently of God. We are assuming a position of independence, considering our own powers and wisdom sufficient. That is Satan's attitude to God and when we take that position we lay ourselves open to Satanic influence, deceptions and control. He who does not permit himself to be led by the Spirit of God is in rebellion against God and, therefore, is under Satan's influence. It makes no real difference whether the independent action is intended to bring benefit to ourselves entirely, or is offered to Him as service or worship.

---

[1] Sermon on *Perils of Power.*

One through whom the Holy Spirit manifests Himself is always faced with these dangers. God says that no flesh may glory in His presence (1 Cor. 1:29), but the flesh in every man seeks avidly for glory. Satan is always alert to take advantage of any opening of the door to self and he is a past-master at making use of every such opportunity. However, there is no reason why he should do so. The believer who walks in obedience and faith will be given discernment and enabled to walk and serve in the Spirit and the Lord will be faithful to manifest His triumph through him and fulfil His purpose concerning him.

THE GIFTS OF THE SPIRIT

Spokes of the diagram (clockwise from top):
INTERPRETATION OF TONGUES
VARIETIES OF TONGUES
HEALING
MIRACLES
DISCERNING OF SPIRITS
FAITH
TEACHING
PREACHING
UTTERANCE OF WISDOM
UTTERANCE OF KNOWLEDGE
THE PARACLETE GIFT
MERCY - ACTS OF LOVE
GIVING
SERVICEABLE MINISTRATIONS
OVERSIGHT

OF THE SPIRIT

GIFTS OR MANIFESTATIONS

THE LOCAL CONGREGATION
CHRIST IN THE MIDST

GOD'S PROVISION FOR THE EXTENSION, MINISTRY AND GOVERNMENT OF THE CHURCH

The Holy Spirit, the Paraclete, manifests Himself through the members in the following ways:

For the Establishing and Care of the Church as a Whole—

Evangelists (missionaries, or church-planters) —

> As foundation-layers they lay the foundations of new churches and, where necessary, repair damaged foundations in established churches. They minister in the extension of the Church and exercise a watchful care over the Church as a whole.
>
> They are ministers of the Church as a whole and the whole Church cooperates with them.

Travelling Preachers and Travelling Teachers —

> Providing a special preaching and teaching ministry to the Church in general.

For the Local Church's Life and Testimony—

Preachers — For the proclamation of the Gospel.
Teachers — For the teaching of the Scriptures.

Those with the gifts of the Spirit for other ministries such as those of faith and love, etc. — For manifesting the love, wisdom and power of Christ in His Body, for its well-being and for its testimony.

Elders — For the oversight of the congregation.
Deacons — To care for business matters.

CHAPTER XVII

THE BASIC MINISTRIES

IN Ephesians 4:11 it is revealed that the Lord, at His ascension, provided five basic spiritual ministries or types of service for the carrying on of the Church's work, they are:

1. Apostles.
2. Prophets.
3. Evangelists.
4. Pastors.
5. Teachers.

We would refer the reader back to the comments on Ephesians 4:1—16[1] where it is seen that these ministries were given for the Church as a whole, the Body of Christ. The purpose for which these ministries are given is there explained. It is important to remember that they are not for a chosen few but that every member of the Body should engage in one or more of these ministries. The ministries are to be carried on by the gifts or manifestations of the Spirit. These we shall consider in the next two chapters. Meanwhile we shall observe the five fundamental ministries as they are revealed in Scripture and as they were practised in the New Testament Church.

There is another ministry, a material one, that of Deacon, which we shall also deal with in this chapter.

A ministry is the service which Christ's Spirit carries out through a member of the Church. The place which the believer is to occupy in the Body of Christ, or the ministry he is to perfrom, is decided by God: "But now hath God set the members every one of them in the Body, as it hath pleased Him" (1 Cor. 12:18). No man may choose a place for himself, nor may he be

---

[1] See p. 156-160.

appointed to a ministry by man. Every member is set by God in some place in the Body. There are no exceptions. There is no believer without a definite responsibility towards the work of the Body. None can be isolated from the Body in his ministry.

Paul was appointed to his ministry by the Lord when he was saved. That is the normal procedure. His preparation for that ministry took time. That also is normal. Every born again child of God is immediately appointed to ministry and begins his spiritual preparation for the full carrying out of God's purpose through him. The extent to which this is accomplished depends upon the believer's faithfulness.

Paul is very definite in claiming that he was called of God to the ministry he was performing (Gal. 1:1, 11, 12). The call had been confirmed by the Spirit to the church in Antioch, but it was given by God directly to Paul in the first place.

He frequently speaks of his ministry as a *diakonia* (service). He also calls it the *charis* (grace which God had given to him) (1 Cor. 3:10; Rom. 12:6; 15:15; Gal. 2:9). Peter also uses the word in the same sense (1 Pet. 4:10). *Charis* means free, unmerited favour. Paul's call to ministry was not due to any merit in himself. He stresses this fact in many places (Phil. 3:4—10; 2 Cor. 3:4—6; 1 Cor. 3:4—21). Whatever ministry we are called to, it is purely of grace. Thus both the ministry to which God calls us and the gifts of the Spirit manifested through us for that ministry are gifts of grace — unmerited, but freely given. For the success of our ministry this must be borne in mind continually. Paul did so. What a spiritual ministry actually is has been explained in the comment on Eph. 4:7—12.[1]

I. Spiritual Ministries

The general aspect of the revelation regarding the five ministries provided for the Church as a whole has been dealt with in the comments on the fourth chapter of Ephesians.[2] They are God's provision for the Church to ensure its unity, the efficient coordination of its witness and its spiritual growth and welfare (Eph. 4:11, 12). It is, of course, a perfect provision. In their original form these ministries proved gloriously adequate.

---

[1] p. 155.
[2] Chapter XIII.

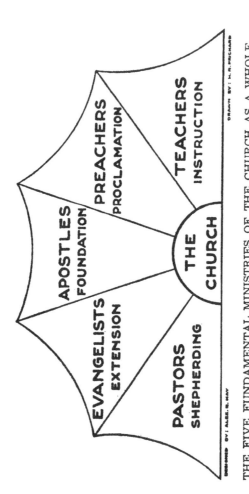

THE FIVE FUNDAMENTAL MINISTRIES OF THE CHURCH AS A WHOLE

In one more or these (with the exception of that of Apostles) all the members take part. (Eph. 4:11-14.)

Four of the ministries are continuing. Two of these — Prophets (preachers), and Teachers — are for the carrying out of our Lord's two commands — to preach and to teach. The other two — Evangelists and Pastors — are for the planting and general care of the congregations and the oversight of the local congregation. It is interesting to compare these four ministries with the four activities of the church in Jerusalem described on pages 47, 48. In each case there are four, the number which speaks of God and man together. The one presents the complete basic equipment for the Church as a whole, the other the complete activity of the local congregation.

Naturally the preservation of the original purity of these ministries was of supreme importance to the welfare of the Church and it was to be expected that Satan would seek to rob them of their true meaning and power. This he accomplished in no small measure through the changes which he succeeded in bringing about in the exercise of the gift of presiding and the ministry for the care of the congregation — the ministry of Pastor or Elder. The outcome was that the foundation laid by the Apostles was set aside, the ministry of the church-planter practically lost,[1] and the ministries of preaching and teaching taken from the congregation and reserved for the Pastor. The ministry of presiding swallowed up the other three ministries. The history of this change is traced in a later chapter.[2]

We shall consider the five basic spiritual ministries in the order given in Ephesians.

1. Apostle:

'Apostle' means an envoy, ambassador, one sent on a special mission. The term was in current use. In the New Testament it is used as follows:

(a) As a title of Christ who is The Apostle (Heb. 3:1).

(b) As the designation of the Twelve Apostles.

(c) Evangelists, whose ministry was the planting of churches, were also called apostles (Acts 14:4, 14; 2 Cor. 8:23; Phil. 2:25; Rev. 2:2; etc.).

An Apostle speaks and acts with the authority of the one who sends him. Christ was sent by the Father. The Father spoke and

---

[1] See pp. 250-2, 262-3, 290.
[2] Chapter 18.

worked through Him. The Twelve were appointed by Christ and spoke with His authority. His Spirit spoke through them. Those who were apostles in the general sense were also sent by Christ. He spoke and worked through them.

The Twelve Apostles.

There are two aspects of the ministry which the Twelve Apostles performed. They had a special position and a special mission. But also they engaged in the regular ministry of the Church as Evangelists or church-planters.

(1) **The Special Position and Mission of the Twelve.** The Church is 'built upon the foundation of the Apostles and Prophets' (Eph. 2:20). Christ is the foundation, not the Apostles and Prophets, but they laid the foundation (1 Cor. 3:11). The part taken by the Prophets in this was stated by Peter at Pentecost and by the New Testament writers generally, who are careful to quote from the Scriptures to show that the foundation laid was in accord with the revelation given to the Prophets. The part taken by the Twelve has three aspects:

(a) The Holy Spirit, through them, laid the doctrinal foundation of the Church, delivering the doctrine which the Lord had taught them. It was 'the doctrine of the Apostles' that was taught in Jerusalem (Acts 2:42).

(b) Through them the Holy Spirit laid the structural foundation of the Church as it had been revealed to them by the Lord. This included the use of the Keys, opening the door to Jews and Gentiles (Matt. 16:16-19; 18:15-20).

(c) They form the link which joins the old Dispensation with the new. Through them the unity and continuity of God's purpose is preserved. Their roots are in the glorious Dispensation that has ended; their ministry is in the more glorious new Dispensation.

As a foundation for this special mission and position, the Twelve were called and appointed by the Lord in the flesh prior to the Cross; they were trained by Him and were His companions during all His ministry on Earth; they were eye-witnesses of His life, crucifixion and resurrection. All were Jews born in Galilee or Judea.

As had been prophesied, Judas fell in sin and lost his place as one of the Twelve (Ps. 69:25; 109:4-8). He was replaced by Matthias. The manner in which Matthias' choice was determined was in accord with accepted practice prior to Pentecost. (Lev. 16:8; Prov. 16:33.) He fulfilled the essential conditions for being one of the Twelve: he had been in the Lord's company as a disciple during the whole of His ministry, from the baptism of John until His ascension, and was a witness of His resurrection (Acts 1:21, 22; cf. Lk. 22:28).

The validity of this appointment has been questioned. Peter gives the Old Testament prophecies as the ground for the action. It is never questioned in the New Testament writings. On the contrary it is evident that Matthias acted subsequently with the other eleven (Acts 2:14; 6:2; 1 Cor. 15:5, where, by inference, Paul recognizes him as one of the Twelve). Evidently the validity of the appointment was never doubted by the Apostles or the apostolic Church.

It has been asked why the Lord Himself, after His resurrection, did not appoint another Apostle. No reason is given. Between His resurrection and ascension He gave counsel to the disciples but took no official action.

The position given to the Twelve is a permanent one, and there are always only twelve. In the Lord's Kingdom they are to sit on thrones judging the twelve tribes of Israel. In the New Jerusalem, the city wall has twelve foundations in which are the names of the twelve Apostles of the Lamb (Lk. 22:28—30; Rev. 21:14; cf. Eph. 3:20).

It is important to observe the limitations of the authority of the Twelve. They had no authority vested in themselves. Christ's Word and the Scriptures was their only authority; the power of the Spirit was their only power. They had no High Priestly authority. They were not a Sanhedrin. In the contention with Paul, Peter made no claim to have the authority to judge in a question of doctrine and practice.

The last time the Apostles were together as a group was when Barnabas and Paul visited the Jerusalem congregation with the complaint against the Judaizers who had gone from Jerusalem to Antioch. On that occasion the Apostles assembled with the Elders of the local church. It was not one of the Apostles, but James, who presided over the gathering. The whole congregation participated in the decision. There we see the practical recognition of the fact that the authority belongs to the Lord, not to any Council of men, and that the responsibility to know and do His will belongs directly to the local assembly of the Church.

After that the Twelve were widely scattered. They did not constitute a Great Council of the Church. It was not necessary that they should do so. The doctrine which had been delivered to the Church constituted the complete revelation of the mind and will of God for man in this age; the order which had been instituted in the Church was the permanent, perfect order. Once these had been delivered to the Church and the Keys used, the responsibility for the extension of the Church — for the propagation of this doctrine and order — fell upon all the Church, including the Twelve, equally. For the carrying out of this work the gifts of the Spirit were given to all and each member was called to a ministry. All were priests unto God. No one, not even the Twelve, had extra priestly authority above that of his fellows.[1]

The unity of the Church and its direction were to be effected by the Holy Spirit. In His prayer to the Father recorded in the seventeenth chapter of John's Gospel, Christ revealed the source of the Church's unity. In verses 21-23 He shows that it is as each member walks in unity with Him and the Father that all the members will be united as one. The spiritual unity of the Church can be effected in no other way and the Lord provided no mechanical means to produce it or conserve it.

Finally, the doctrine and order of the Church was committed to writing through the inspiration of the Holy Spirit, and these writings constitute the permanent authority of the Church in all matters of doctrine and practice. The authority now resides where it has resided from the beginning, in the revelation given through Christ and not in any Council of men. That is the supreme and only authority for the Church. No church or Council of churches may change in any way the doctrine and Church principles taught by Christ and delivered to the Church by the Apostles. Those who do so, no matter what their reasons may be, set aside the

---

[1] Referring to this subject, Neander writes: "As all believers were conscious of an equal relation to Christ as their Redeemer, and of a common participation of communion with God obtained through him; so on this consciousness, an equal relation of believers to one another was grounded, which utterly precluded any relation like that found in other forms of religion, subsisting between a priestly caste and a people of whom they were the mediators and spiritual guides. The Apostles themselves were very far from placing themselves in a relation to believers which bore any resemblance to a mediating priesthood; in this respect they always placed themselves on a footing of equality." *Planting and Training of the Church*, p. 129.

divine revelation, the teaching of Christ, and substitute man's wisdom and order.

It is clear that the nature of the special mission and position of the Twelve precludes any possibility that they should have successors.

(2) **Their Regular Ministry in the Church.** The special ministry of the Twelve in the Church was completed in a comparatively short time. But they also engaged in the regular missionary ministry of the Church. As Evangelists, or church-planters, they continued to minister in company with an increasing number of others called to that ministry.

They were Apostles with a special call, preparation and witness, but they were also missionaries ministering in the regular work of preaching, teaching and founding congregations, as did Barnabas, Paul, Luke, Timothy, Titus, Silas, and others.

On the day of Pentecost the Holy Spirit came upon all — Apostles and other disciples — equally. With His coming the gifts of the Spirit for the ministry and government of the Church immediately appeared. All received the gifts for witness. At first the Apostles alone were given the gift of government but later that gift was manifested in others. At first they were the only ones called to the ministry of church-planting; later, others were called to that ministry.

It is helpful to distinguish between the two aspects of the Apostles' ministry, because they explain the difference between the position which the Twelve occupied at Pentecost and immediately afterwards, and that which they took later. It also enables us to know what part of their ministry is intended to be a permanent example for the Church to follow.

They founded the first congregation — that of Jerusalem. In laying the foundation of that congregation they acted both as the Twelve Apostles and as Evangelists. As Apostles they laid the first, perfect foundation; as Evangelists they established the congregation and ministered as Deacons and Elders until the Holy Spirit prepared and revealed the men who were appointed of God for these local ministries. They presided at the appointment of these men and then, before very long, scattered throughout the world.

After that they no longer kept together as a group of Apostles and are seldom mentioned. Their special mission fulfilled so far as the present was concerned, they merge into the general missionary ministry, establishing congregations on the model that had already been fully revealed. At Antioch and elsewhere the presence of the Twelve, or of one of them, was not necessary.[1] In the first twelve chapters of the Book of Acts the Twelve Apostles are prominent; from then onward it is Paul and the missionary company with him that occupy the scene.

Misconceptions.

Failure to discern the true nature of the special mission of the Twelve and to distinguish between it and their participation in the regular missionary ministry of the Church has caused not a little confusion not only regarding their mission but also regarding the ministry of the missionary or church-planter.

This has been due, in no small measure, to the conception of these ministries that developed with the growth of sacerdotalism. They came to be interpreted in the light of the prevailing system and not according to the order revealed in Scripture. They were vested with ecclesiastical and sacerdotal powers, prerogatives and glory entirely out of keeping with the revealed spiritual order.

The influence of this interpretation persists to the present day, tending to obscure the vision of the original simple and purely spiritual order. The Twelve are credited with priestly powers above their fellows. Paul and sometimes Barnabas are numbered with the Twelve. The ministry of Timothy, Titus, Silas and their companions is accounted for by classing them as 'Apostolic Delegates', an unscriptural term; then finally, and rather inconsistently, they are turned into Diocesan Bishops.

Paul was an apostle — one sent on a mission. He emphatically claims that he was and that he was appointed to that ministry by the Lord. But he does not claim to have been numbered with the Twelve; nor does Barnabas. The ministry to which Paul insisted he was called was that of a planter of churches, not that of an eye-witness and companion of the Lord's ministry from the baptism of John until He was received up into Heaven. For him to have been numbered with the Twelve was impossible. To say that he or Barnabas were Apostles in that sense is to do violence to Scripture. In the first place, they could not have fulfilled the

---

[1] See pp. 60, 68.

essential requirement stated in Acts 1:21, 22 (cf. Lk. 22:28). In the second place, the Lord appointed twelve only and made it clear that in the future there would be but twelve (Lk. 22:28-30; Rev. 21:14).

When the Lord met Paul on the road to Damascus He did not appoint him to be numbered with the Twelve; He called him to the missionary ministry of the Church. When the Spirit sent forth Barnabas and Paul from Antioch He did not send them as numbered with the Twelve; He sent them forth to the missionary ministry — as church-planters.

Paul never acted as one of the Twelve. Their special mission was practically completed before Barnabas and he were sent forth from Antioch. The Holy Spirit waited until the foundation had been fully laid before initiating the permanent ministry of world evangelism or church-planting. Paul recognized the Twelve in the position which they occupied (1 Cor. 15:5). He taught that the Church is built upon their foundation (Eph. 2:20). When he and Barnabas met with the Apostles and the church in Jerusalem, or at other times, there is no suggestion that either of them considered himself as being numbered with the Twelve.

He and Barnabas were church-planters and in that sense they were men sent on a mission — apostles. In that sense Luke calls them apostles shortly after they were sent forth from Antioch (Acts 14:4, 14). In that sense Paul calls himself and his fellow-workers apostles (2 Cor. 8:23; Phil. 2:25). He uses two similies to describe the ministry to which he was called. He spoke of himself as a planter of congregations and as an architect laying the foundations of congregations.

In 1 Cor. 9:1, 2, Paul writes, "Am I not free? Am I not an Apostle. Can it be denied that I have seen Jesus, our Lord? Are you not yourselves my work in the Lord? If to other men I am not an Apostle, yet at any rate I am one to you; for your very existence as a Christian Church is the seal of my Apostleship. That is how I vindicate myself to those who criticise me." This passage is often quoted to prove that Paul claimed to be one the Twelve. But he is making no such claim. He is simply claiming to be a missionary and to have done the work of a missionary in the founding of the Church in Corinth.

As we have seen, the Twelve also performed this missionary ministry; but it was as a regular ministry of the church that they engaged in it, not as their special mission as the Twelve. They took part in it as members of the Church. In that ministry the fact that they were of the Twelve did not make them superior to others whom the Lord had called as church-planters. The attitude of Paul, Luke and the other church-planters makes this clear. The call of all was from the Lord directly. All worked to the same Apostolic pattern. The authority of all was the same — the Word of the Lord — and they were all responsible to the Lord. In this work the Twelve and the other church-planters laboured as one.

This is more important than it may appear to be at first sight. The wrong interpretation places Paul and the other New Testament church-planters in a false position, preventing us from having a true understanding of their ministry and depriving the Church of the practical value of their example. It is, indeed, a triumph of the enemy, relegating Paul and his companions to a position which largely nullifies the purpose for which their example is recorded.

Paul's ministry and that of his companions is recorded in detail because he and they provide the typical example for the exceedingly important permanent ministry of church-planting. Paul belongs entirely to the Church Dispensation. He had not been with the Lord prior to the Cross. His conversion, call and training took place after Pentecost. He is the example of what Christ, indwelling the Church by His Spirit, purposes to do through the Church in this Dispensation. He and his fellow-workers are the typical missionary group. Among them were men of different races and nations. The Jews in the group, with the probable exception of Mark, were all born in Gentile lands. They were all Greek-speaking men. Paul was a Roman citizen. It was not a Jewish company but a Church company: Jews and Gentiles together in the one Body with no distinction between them. They went forth from Antioch, the congregation in which God's purpose for the Church first came fully to fruition — in which Jew and Gentile are seen as one Body in Christ.[1]

The Jerusalem congregation was Jewish. The Twelve were a Jewish company with their roots in Judaism. But Paul and his fellow-church-planters were purely of the Church, composed of men called, prepared, brought together and led by the Spirit, and

---

[1] The significance of the Church in Antioch is considered on pp. 60, 68.

it is to them that first place is given in the record of the extension throughout the world of the Church that was founded by the Twelve. The fact that Paul was not numbered with the Twelve does not detract from the importance of his ministry; on the contrary, it greatly increases its significance to the Church today.

2. Prophet:

The ministry of the Prophet in the Church was defined by Paul as,

...speaking unto men to edification and exhortation (encouragement, and comfort (1 Cor. 14:3, Cf. Eph. 6:19).

Scofield describes the Prophet of the New Testament as "not ordinarily a foreteller, but rather a forth-teller". He is one who speaks for God, giving forth revealed truth.

A Prophet in the Church is a preacher who gives forth the Word of God in the wisdom and power of the Holy Spirit. The active presence of the Holy Spirit, inspiring empowering, controlling and guiding changes what would be merely a discourse uttered by man into a 'gift' or 'manifestation' of the Spirit. Such Spirit-inspired utterance is prophecy. The New Testament Prophet does not necessarily foretell the future, though he might do so as did Agabus. God still often causes us to know His will for the immediate future. But the Church now possesses the complete revelation in the New Testament and no new revelations can be given through the Prophets. However, those who preach require the inspiration of the Holy Spirit to enable them to perceive the truth contained in the Word, and they need His presence to give power to the Word that is preached.

The true preacher gives forth the truth revealed to him by the Spirit from God's Word (1 Pet. 4:10, 11; 1 Cor. 2:1-16). Whatever there may be in his discourse that is of "enticing words of man's wisdom" is not of the Spirit and is not true preaching in the New Testament sense. The preacher exercises the gift of the Spirit only in so far as he is inspired by the Spirit. At other times he is making use of his natural ability.

A preacher's eloquence may be mistaken for the inspiration of the Spirit, and the effect of eloquence, or the influence of personality, may be mistaken for the power of the Spirit.

This was the first gift of the Spirit manifested in the Church. It appeared immediately the Holy Spirit came at Pentecost. On

NEW TESTAMENT PROPHET - PREACHER

Ministry
To tell forth the wisdom of God revealed by the Spirit through the Word.

Some of the many varieties of Gift

$\left\{ \begin{array}{l} \end{array} \right.$

Preaching to the unsaved

   ,,   ,, believers

   ,,   ,, children

   ,,   ,, young people

   ,,   in the open air

   ,,   informally to a few

   ,,   ,,   ,, individuals

A ministry that all may exercise in one form or another.

that day all — Apostles and other believers, men and women — exercised the gift.

In the list of ministries in Ephesians 4:11, as also in the list of gifts in 1 Cor. 12:28, it is given second place, after Apostles. The Apostles were of first importance in the initial founding of the Church. The witness of the Church, the proclamation of the Gospel as commanded by Christ, through the gift of the Spirit for preaching comes next in importance.

This seems to be the gift most widely distributed. It is not necessarily a formal discourse. The modern distinction between the humble talk, or message, and the aristocratic sermon has no place in Scripture; indeed it is contrary to the principles of the manifestation of the gifts of the Spirit in the Church. There are, however, many varieties of the gift. The variety possessed by one may be for the telling forth (preaching) of God's Word to adults; that of another may be for witness to children, or in the open air, or to unbelievers, or to believers, or to a small company of two or three, or to individuals. All are exercising the same gift for the proclamation, or telling forth, of the Gospel. The importance of this gift is apparent. All believers are counselled to seek it (1 Cor. 14:1). Therefore, all should possess it in one form or another.

3. Evangelist:

The terms 'Apostle', in the general sense of the word, and 'Evangelist', were used to denote those called to the ministry of the extension of the Church. Both titles are descriptive: 'Apostle' has reference to their mission as messengers of the Church; 'Evangelist' to their work as propagators of the Evangel.

'Apostle', used to designate missionaries, is found in Acts 14:4, 14; 2 Cor. 8:23 ('messengers': lit. 'apostles'); Phil. 2:25 ('messenger': lit. 'apostle'); 2 Cor. 11:23; Rev. 2:2.

'Evangelist' is the term used in the list of the basic ministries in Eph. 4:11. There the Twelve are designated Apostles. To have used the same term again, in the more general sense, for a different ministry, would have been confusing.

There are two other occurrences of the word Evangelist. Philip is called 'the Evangelist' (Acts 21:8). He is first heard of as one of the seven chosen as Deacons in the church in Jerusalem (Acts 6:5). He did not continue in that service but was later called to

THE EVANGELIST (Missionary)

THE CHURCH PLANTER:
THE FOUNDATION LAYER AND
FOUNDATION REPAIRER
OF THE CHURCH.

Purpose — The Extension of the Church

Ministry {
The preaching of the Gospel
The teaching of converts
The forming of Churches
The care of Churches
A ministry of prayer and faith

the ministry of Evangelist. Such a call-to a wider ministry is of frequent occurrence.

Paul wrote to Timothy: "do the work of an evangelist, accomplish thy ministry in full measure" (2 Tim. 4:5, Conybeare). Weymouth translates this: "do the duty of an evangelist and fully discharge the obligations of your office."

On this passage Conybeare and Howson make the following comment:

> The term Evangelist is applied to those missionaries who, like Philip and Timothy, travelled from place to place, to bear the Glad-tidings of Christ to unbelieving nations or individuals. Hence it follows that the Apostles were all Evangelists, although there were also Evangelists who were not Apostles.

Of interest also is Conybeare's translation of 1 Cor. 9:18:

> It is to make the Glad-tidings free of cost where I carry it, that I may forego my right as an Evangelist.

In a note on that translation he says:

> The passage may be literally rendered: 'It is, that I should, while evangelizing make the Evangel free of cost, that I may not fully use my right as an Evangelist.'

Fausset says:

> The Evangelist founded the church; the teacher built it up in the faith... They (Evangelists) travelled about freely where their services were needed, either to propagate the Gospel or to inspect and strengthen congregations already formed.[1]

In the second century writing, "The Teaching of the Twelve Apostles", the travelling Evangelists are called Apostles.

That the two terms, Apostle (in the general sense) and Evangelist, continued to be regarded as synonymous up to the time of the sub-apostolic Church is seen in Tertullian's question, "Who are false apostles unless spurious evangelists?" — *De Praescr.*, iv.

Writing of the time of Trajan, Eusebius states:

> For, indeed, most of the disciples of that time animated by the divine word with a more ardent love for philisophy[2], had already

---

[1] Bible Cyclopedia. See also Neander's *Planting and Training of the Church*, p. 148.

[2] Following the usage of their time, Eusebius and Chrysostom frequently write of the life of self-abnegation as the "philosophical" life.

15

fulfilled the command of the Saviour, and had distributed their goods to the needy. Then starting out upon long journeys they performed the office of evangelists, being filled with the desire to preach Christ to those who had not yet heard the word of faith, and to deliver to them the divine Gospels. And when they had only laid the foundations of the faith in foreign places, they appointed others as pastors, and entrusted them with the nurture of those that had recently been brought in, while they themselves went on again to other countries and nations, with the grace and the cooperation of God.[1]

The term 'Evangelist' occurs only three times. But the title 'Bishop', designating one who presides in the congregation, also is used in only three passages, the title 'Deacon' in but two and 'Pastors' in only one. However, there is ample evidence both in Scripture and in the history of the Early Church to gives us a clear understanding of the true significance of all four terms.

In modern usage, the term Evangelist denotes one who preaches only to the unsaved. Such an one, however, is, in the Scriptural sense, simply a preacher, exercising the gift of preaching; only, in his case the variety of the gift possessed is for preaching salvation through repentance and faith to unbelievers. As such preaching to the unsaved must be one of the principal activities of every congregation, that variety of the gift should be found, in some form, in most, if not all, believers.

The scarcity of such preachers today is due to the fact that in the modern congregation the gifts of the Spirit are not encouraged, with the result that the gift of preaching is not generally manifested among its members and a preacher from outside has to be called in to give the Gospel to the unsaved in their midst or in their neighbourhood. No doubt some of those termed Evangelists in the modern sense are really called to the full ministry of the Evangelist in the New Testament sense, but are fulfilling only a part of their ministry.

A common misapprehension regarding the meaning of the Evangel, or Gospel, or Good News, has been the cause of some confusion of thought and, to some extent, has been responsible for the misunderstanding of the ministry of the Evangelpropagator, or Evangelist. The Gospel is not just the truth concerning the remission of sins and eternal life through faith in the substitutionary offering of Christ on Calvary; it is the whole rev-

---

[1] *Church History*, III, XXXVII.

elation given to us in the New Testament of the 'mysteries' that were before hid but now are made known to us. Salvation through faith, the resurrection power of the Spirit in the believer, the believer's position as seated with Christ in the heavenlies, the purpose of God to manifest Christ in and through the Church, the pattern given by God for the Church, the gifts of the Spirit for ministry, and the future hope of the believer — all these are the Gospel, the Good News.

Paul in his ministry did not declare just a part of the Gospel, he gave the whole revelation of God in Christ. Thus, when he speaks of himself as a preacher of the Evangel — an Evangelist — he does not mean simply a preacher to the unsaved, but a preacher of the whole Evangel. That is what he means when he counsels Timothy to fulfil his ministry as an Evangelist.

There is no Scriptural ground for considering that the Evangelist's ministry was limited to the preaching of the way of salvation. The New Testament Evangelist was, indeed, a preacher of Christ to the unsaved, but his ministry was not fulfilled until he had gathered the converts together as an assembly of the Body of Christ and delivered to them the whole counsel of God. He was the extension agent, the church-planter, the missionary responsible for establishing the Church in unevangelized regions and the counsellor of the churches established.

The Missionary Epistles

It is unfortunate that the Epistles to Timothy and Titus should be called the Pastoral Epistles. It is difficult to understand why they were ever so called, for neither their object nor their content give any ground for such a designation. They were written by an Evangelist, after a life-time of experience, to Evangelists, or missionaries, not to Pastors, and they deal definitely with the life and ministry of the Evangelist. They might be called a Manual for Evangelists. They give instruction and counsel to the young missionary or church-planter regarding his ministry. Timothy and Titus were not Pastors; they were Evangelists and when Paul wrote to them they were engaged in that ministry.

A thorough and prayerful study of these Epistles is essential to the missionary today. It is for him particularly that they are preserved. They reveal clearly the purpose and scope of the missionary's ministry. The instructions regarding Elders and Deacons and those who walk disorderly and the emphasizing of the need for personal faithfulness in ministry and for being content with having just food and clothing, are directed to missionaries.

Any missionary acquainted with the needs and problems of the mission field will appreciate the wide missionary experience and depth of insight into these needs and problems given by the Holy Spirit to the writer of these Missionary Epistles. In every line we see the old, experienced church-planter, thoroughly acquainted with the difficulties, dangers and temptations of the missionary's life and ministry. It is the veteran missionary giving practical advice to the young missionary. Paul knew the roughness of the road, the hardness of the fight, the subtlety of the enemy, the special dangers and temptations that beset the missionary, and the need for constant vigilance and preparedness.

The Jewish Prototype

The ministry of the Evangelist, or church-planter, was not something entirely new. In the Jewish economy there were men, appointed by the Great Sanhedrin, who travelled wherever there were colonies of Jews, to see to the examination and appointment of rulers or elders of the synagogues.[1] As Edersheim states,

> All the rulers of the synagogue were duly examined as to their knowledge, and ordained to the office. They formed the local Sanhedrin or tribunal. But their election depended on the choice of the congregation; and absence of pride, as also gentleness and humility, are mentioned as special qualifications.[2]

The Evangelists were, in a sense, delegates of the Church. Their ministry was, of course, much wider than that of the delegates of the Sanhedrin. Judaism was not missionary in spirit; Christianity is primarily missionary. The Church's delegate was an Evangelist — an Evangel-propagator. Moreover the authority of the delegates of the Church was not derived from a High Priest on earth, or a Chief Apostle, or a Great Council, but from the Great High Priest, Christ Himself, who was present in every gathering of the Church. They were commissioned directly by Him and equipped by His Spirit. The Lord made His will known to the local gathering of the Church, which acknowledged the

---

[1] *Berach,* 55a, Sanh. 92a, Chag. 5b.
[2] *Life and Times of Jesus the Messiah,* Vol. I, p. 438.

appointment by the laying on of hands (Acts 13:1-4). This call and its acknowledgment by the Church was the authorization of these delegates of the Church.

The principles governing the two ministries — that of the Church's delegate and that of the Sanhedrin's delegate — were of course fundamentally different, the difference arising from the fact of Christ's personal presence in the gathering of the Church and of the presence of the Holy Spirit — the 'other Paraclete' — in every member.

The Evangelist's Ministry

The ministry of the Evangelist has five aspects:

(1) The salvation of souls through the preaching of God's message of salvation;

(2) The teaching of converts;

(3) The gathering into congregations of new groups of believers;

(4) A watchful care over these churches;

(5) A constant ministry of prayer and faith for them.

The following is an outline of the call, preparation and ministry of the Evangelist. The different points are considered more fully in other chapters.

(1) Their call was received direct from the Lord.

(2) It was made known to the Church by the Holy Spirit (Acts 13:2-4; 16:1-3).

(3) Their preparation:
    (a) Under the providential guidance of the Holy Spirit they obtained knowledge and experience participating in the life and work of the local churches.
    (b) They had studied the scriptures.

(4) The Church, having received from the Holy Spirit the confirmation of an Evangelist's call, associated itself with him by the laying on of hands (1 Tim. 4:14; 2 Tim. 1:6; Acts 13:2. 3).

The missionary group which they joined also had confirmation regarding their call. (Acts 11:22-25; 12:25; 15:40; 16:1-3; 20:4; 2 Tim. 2:2; 2 Cor. 8:19.)

(5) Their work and authority:

(a) To preach and teach. 2 Tim. 4:2-5; Titus 2.

(b) To establish churches. Titus 1:5; Acts 14:23.

(c) To oversee churches and Elders. 1 Tim. 1:3; Titus 1:5; 1 Tim. 4:11-13; 5:1, 17, 19, 20; 2 Tim. 4:2-5; Titus 2.

(d) To reprove. 1 Tim. 5:20, 21; Titus 1:13, 14; 2:15.

(e) To reject heretics. This involved the duty of a watchful care in regard to doctrinal soundness and the rejection of any whose walk, teaching or beliefs are not according to sound doctrine. Titus 3:10, 11; Acts 15:1, 2; 1 Tim. 1:3, 4.

(f) To minister through prayer and faith.

(6) The nature of the Evangelists' ministry made it necessary that they should be able also to act at times as Elders and Deacons (1 Pet. 5:1; 2 Jn. 1:1; 3 Jn. 1:1). In the establishing of new churches they had to undertake the functions of these ministries, as the Apostles did in Jerusalem, until Elders and Deacons were appointed. When visiting an established congregation they met with the Elders. They never, however, settled down anywhere to do the work of a local Elder. Had they done so they would have ceased to be Evangelists and would have become simply Elders of a local congregation.

(7) It was not required that an Evangelist should have served first as an Elder before becoming an Evangelist, though many of them did so.

(8) The Evangelist is not vested with ecclesiastical power to enforce his orders. He has no authority to make decrees or to demand obedience on the ground of his office. His power is entirely spiritual; his authority is solely the Word of God. His authority lies in the fact that he has been called of God. His ministry includes the forming of churches, counselling them where there is need and rebuking any who may depart from the Scriptural order or from sound doctrine. In no case can he make a demand upon his own authority, but he can insist upon compliance with what is taught in the Word. His power to enforce compliance with the Word is entirely spiritual. Having received the call and the gift of the Spirit for this work, his actions, when in accord with the teaching of Scripture, will be accompanied by the Spirit's power and the authority of the Spirit's utterance.

He presents to the erring church the Word of the Lord. Their obedience will be to Christ. As Paul said, the Evangelist is only Christ's messenger and nothing in himself.[1] If the Lord's Word is rejected, all His servant can do is to report the case to the other churches, which will deprive the erring assembly of fellowship with the faithful brethren. Even in this, however, he cannot give orders. He can only show the churches their Scriptural duty. Those that are spiritual will comply. But their compliance will be with the Word of God, not with the Evangelist's order. "It is written" is the Evangelist's authority. Those who are spiritual will obey the Word and separate themselves from all who walk disorderly. Thus no spiritual congregation is under obligation to comply with the instructions of an Evangelist when these are not truly based upon Scripture. Any departure from the teaching of God's Word will immediately deprive him of all spiritual power and authority with those who are spiritual.[2]

(9) Evangelists had no arbitrarily fixed spheres of authority or responsibility. Any church, in any country, might be ministered to by any Evangelist, no matter by whom it had been founded. Peter was sent especially to the Jews, Paul to the Gentiles. But Peter could minister to any Gentile church and Paul to any Jewish church. When Apollos visited churches founded by Paul, some made his visit the excuse for seeking to introduce division. Paul, in dealing with the matter, did not question Apollos' right to preach and teach, nor did he lay claim to superior authority or regional jurisdiction; he simply pointed out that neither he nor Apollos were anything but servants and that Christ was Head and must be all and in all. However, the great desire of the Evangelist always was, as Paul expressed it, "to preach the Gospel, not where Christ was named, lest I should build upon another man's foundation" (Rom. 15:20. Cf. I Cor. 4:15; 2 Cor. 10:13, 14, etc.).

(10) Evangelists were all equal in rank. However, in a company or fellowship of Evangelists, one was recognized as leader. The leadership of that one was accepted, not because of superiority of rank, but because of the evidence of God's appointment. Barnabas and Paul are examples of such leadership.

(11) An Evangelist did not carry on his ministry alone. Two or more worked together.[3] Titus was left alone for a time in Crete

---

[1] 1 Cor. 1:12-15; 3:4-7; 2 Cor. 10:3-5.
[2] Cf. Rev. 2:2; 2 Cor. 11:13; Gal. 1:8. See pp. 98, 124.
[3] See p. 138.

and others went alone on special missions to certain places, but this separation from their fellow-workers was only temporary and contact was maintained by correspondence and a continued cooperation in prayer. There were no 'independent' missionaries.

(12) There are several reasons why a group of Evangelists work together:

(a) The strength derived from a united prayer-fellowship is obtained.

(b) No Evangelist possesses all the variations of the gifts necessary for the accomplishment of a complete work. So the Holy Spirit brings together a company of Evangelists possessing among them the different varieties of gift required for the task He wishes performed.

(c) As the number of churches to be cared for increases and the extent of the field grows, it becomes necessary to have a company of Evangelists, cooperating together, to care efficiently for the work.

(13) Other aspects of the Evangelist's ministry, such as his support, guidance, Mission Boards, Mission organization, etc., have been dealt with in previous chapters. His relation to the Elders is considered later.[1]

The modern term 'missionary' is a true equivalent of 'apostle', used in its general sense of one sent on a mission. However, it has become so associated with modern missionary practice that it does not now convey the exact New Testament sense. The New Testament missionary was much more to the Church than one who went to foreign lands to found churches, or than one who preached to down-and-outs or foreigners in the Homeland. He was not only the foundation-layer of the Church; he was also the foundation-repairer. When anything went wrong in any church anywhere — not only on the 'foreign' field but on the 'Home' field also — to the extent that local instruments could not be used to put things right, it was the missionary's ministry to intervene. Paul said that 'the care of all the churches' weighed heavily upon him.

The vital importance of such a ministry to the Church will be realized. It was that ministry that kept the New Testament churches sound and faithful, preventing the Corinthians from becoming engulfed in sin and disorder, the Galatians from falling

---

[1] See also p. 283.

hopelessly into error and Diotrephes from continuing to usurp authority. As time passed, this ministry became lost to the Church to a great extent. The modern Bishop, based upon the principles of human government, was substituted. The loss sustained by the Church through its disappearance has been incalculable. It is one of the basic ministries which Christ gave to the Church when He ascended up on high, essential to its welfare as well as to its work. Its return is urgently needed by the Church.

4. Presbyter (Elder), Pastor, Bishop:

The term 'Presbyter', or Elder, designating those who preside in the congregation, occurs frequently in the New Testament.

The term 'Pastors' designating those who shepherd the congregation, is found only in Eph. 4:11. In Acts 20:17, 28 and 1 Pet. 5:1-4, it is stated that the Elders should perform the work of Pastors (cf. original Greek).

These terms were used in the synagogue. The Elders, of which there were several in each synagogue, were also called Pastors or Shepherds. The meaning of the terms was, therefore, well known.

The term Bishop, applied to those who have the oversight in the congregation, occurs only in 1 Tim. 3:1, 2; Tit. 1:7; Phil. 1:1. That the Elders should serve the congregation as Bishops is stated in Acts 20:17, 28 and 1 Pet. 5:1-4 (cf. original Greek). In Tit. 1:5, 7, both terms are used with reference to the same office.

(1) It is generally admitted that in the Early Church the three titles, presbyter (Elder), Pastor and Bishop, all referred to the ministry of one and the same person. Neander writes:

> The guidance of the communities was therefore most probably entrusted everywhere to a council of elders... Besides the usual name, 'presbuteroi', given to the heads of the Church, there were also many others, denoting their appropriate share of action, as shepherds (pastors) ...That the name 'episcopoi' or bishops was altogether synonymous with that of presbyters, is clearly evident from those passages of Scripture where both titles are used interchangeably (Acts 20; Comp. v. 17 with v. 28; Titus 1:5 with 1:7), and from those where the office of Deacon is named immediately after that of Bishop, so that between these two offices no third one could possibly intervene. This interchange of the two apellations shows that originally they were perfectly identical.[1]

Bishop Lightfoot states:

---
[1] *Neander's Church History*, Vol. 1, pp. 255, 256.

THE ELDERS

Purpose The spiritual oversight of the local congregation.

Ministry Ruling and presiding as Bishops. Watching over the spiritual state of the Congregation — shepherding — as Pastors.
A Ministry of Prayer and Faith.

It is a fact now generally recognized by theologians of all shades of opinion, that in the language of the New Testament the same officer is called indifferently 'bishop' or 'elder' or 'presbyter'.[1]

However, the three terms are not synonymous, although they designate the same person. 'Presbyter' has reference to rank or office, while 'Pastor' and 'Bishop' have reference to the duties performed. Their true significance is made clear in the following passages where all three are used:

In Acts 20:17 the title Elder *(presbuterous)* is used:

And from Miletus he sent to Ephesus and called the Elders of the Church.

Then, in the 28th verse, speaking of the duties of these Elders, Paul says:

Take heed to yourselves and to all the flock among which the Holy Spirit has placed you to take the oversight (**episcopous** — bishops) for Him and act as shepherds (pastors) to the Church of God, which He has bought with His own blood (Weymouth).

Peter in his first Epistle, makes a similar statement. Writing to the Elders *(presbuterous)* he says:

Be shepherds (pastors) of God's flock which is among you. Exercise the oversight (**episcopeo**) not reluctantly but eagerly... and then when the Chief Shepherd (Pastor) appears, you will receive the never-withering wreath of glory. (1 Pet. 5:1-4, Weymouth.)

In a note on the word 'oversight' *(episcopeo)*, Weymouth says:

Lit. 'being bishops', an indication that in the early Church the office of bishop was identical with that of elder or presbyter.

Both Paul and Peter instruct the Elders to minister faithfully as Bishops and Pastors. These passages make it clear that the Presbyter, or Elder, had two functions to perform:

(a) He was a Pastor, shepherding the flock, and

(b) He was a Bishop, presiding over the congregation.

Christ is called 'the Shepherd (Pastor) and Bishop of our souls' (1 Pet. 2:25). That presents Him as The Elder over the whole Church, exercising both phases of the Elder's ministry.

While, for the sake of convenience, we have dealt here with the whole ministry of the Elder, it should be noted that only one phase of that ministry, that of Pastor, is mentioned in the Ephesian list. The reason for the distinction made in that list

---

[1] *The Christian Ministry,* p. 97.

appears to be that presiding as Bishop has an exclusively local significance, pertaining simply to order in the gathering of the local church, while shepherding as Pastor, though performed in a local group, is part of a basic ministry to the whole Church. The Ephesian list, as we have seen, has reference to the Church as a whole and not to the local congregation.

This distinction is important. When changes crept into the organization of the Church and the two phases of the Elder's ministry were separated and given to different individuals, the purely local ministry of Bishop was exalted over that of Pastor and transformed into a ministry to the Church as a whole, displacing that of the Evangelist or missionary, in complete contradiction to the divine order.

(2) The appointment of Elders is considered in Chapter 21.

(3) The qualifications of the Elder are given in 1 Tim. 3:1-7; Titus 1:5-9 and 1 Pet. 5:1-4. He must be:

(a) Above reproach in his marriage.

(b) One who rules his house well, whose children are believers and not disobedient, riotous, worldly, but giving a good testimony. For how could a man who is not able to govern well his own household be capable of governing in the congregation?

(c) One who is given to hospitality.

(d) One who is not overbearing or who likes to have his own way or desires to lord it over God's flock. One not of stubborn self-will.

(e) One who is an example for the flock to imitate.

(f) One of blameless life, of dignified bearing, soberminded, not a man of passionate temper but self-controlled, not given to wine, not selfish or covetous, not given to quarreling, upright and saintly.

(g) One who is just and honest in all his business dealings. One who is not a lover of money. One who would not seek the office for personal gain.

(h) Able to instruct others.

(i) Sound in doctrine.

(j) Not a new convert, for such an one would be liable to become blinded with pride and fall under the same condemnation as the Devil.

It will be observed that, for the most part, these are not special qualifications that the generality of believers will not possess.

Every true believer in Christ who is walking in the Spirit will have most of them. There are, of course, several special qualifications. The Elder must be 'apt to teach': able to give instruction to those who may seek it or require it. Of the Elder, and also of the Deacon, it is required that not only he, but also his wife and family, bear a testimony that is above reproach. This is necessary to those whose ministry requires the exercising of authority in the congregation and whose home is a place in which Christian hospitality is given. For those who do not have to exercise authority — for the preacher, teacher, etc. — it is only required that their personal testimony be true.

Let us note what is not required of the Elder. It is not stated that he must have the gift of preaching. First Timothy 5:17, makes it clear that not all the Elders in the New Testament churches were preachers or teachers.

Of course, the Elder may have these gifts, but they are not a necessary equipment for the Eldership. In the Ephesian list, the Prophet, or Preacher, is second, the Pastor fourth. There the Pastor is not the Preacher.

It will be realized that what is considered today as the most essential equipment of the pastor — the gift of preaching — is not required of him in the Word. This is because that gift is for any and all the members of the congregation, not particularly for its Elders.

It is not stated that the Elder must be gifted by the Spirit as a Teacher, but simply that he be 'apt to teach'.[1] The variety of the gift of teaching which he requires is made clear in the statement in Titus 1:9 — "that he might be well qualified both to encourage others with sound teaching and to reply successfully to opponents" (Weymouth).

Speaking of the Elders in the Early Church, Prof. Lindsay states:

It seems evident that their special function was to rule or to exercise discipline rather than to teach... The gift of preaching or exhortation was looked upon as a gift of the Spirit independent of office; and the earliest office bearers were men who ruled rather than men who taught. Open preaching was continued for a long time in the post-apostolic church, and is distinctly recognized in the so-called Apostolic Constitutions.[2]

---

[1] See pp. 157-8.
[2] *Christianity,* Enc. Brit.

Hatch says:

> It is clear that the presbyters in the primitive Churches did not necessarily teach. They were not debarred from teaching, but if they taught as well as ruled they combined two offices. In the numerous references to presbyters in the sub-apostolic literature, there is not one of their being teachers, even where such a reference might have been expected, as for example in the enumeration of the duties of presbyters which is given by Polycarp in the form of an exhortation to fulfil them.[1]

The requirements which the Holy Spirit has laid down for the Elder are not such as are necessary to priests, or clergy, or pastors in the modern sense. They are those necessary to Elders whose particular ministry is to act as overseers of an assembly of 'priests unto God'. The Elder is not pictured as one who is saintly above the average or gifted by the Spirit above his fellows for the ministry of the Word, but simply as a true believer, sound in the faith, unblamable in his life, who has special gifts of the Spirit to preside in the gathering of the church and to see that all goes well with the flock of God.

It is nowhere stated or implied that the Elder is appointed or specially authorized to administer the 'sacraments'.[2] He has no priestly function above that of the other members of the congregation who are all 'priests unto God'.[3]

(4) The Elders are chosen from among the members of the congregation they are to serve. They are not called from outside (Acts 14:23, etc. Cf. Acts 6:3).

(5) The ministry to which the Elders are called is an important one. Its two parts — Bishop and Pastor — overlap so that it is not always easy to distinguish clearly between them, but the following gives the purpose of each.

(a) As Bishops, the Elders are overseers of the local congregation. In this capacity their responsibilities are:

(i) To preside over the gatherings of the church. They are

---

[1] *The Organization of the Early Christian Churches,* p. 78.

[2] See pp. 271, 272, where the historical evidence is given.

[3] Referring to those who were called of the Lord to the ministries of Evangelist, Elder and Deacon, Bishop Lightfoot says: "The priestly functions and privileges of the Christian people are never regarded as transferred or even delegated to these officers. They are called messengers of God, servants or ministers of the Church and the like; but the sacerdotal title is never once conferred upon them. The only priests under the Gospel, designated as such in the New Testament, are the saints, the members of the Christian brotherhood. As individuals, all Christians are priests alike." *Philippians,* p. 182.

responsible to see that order is maintained in the meetings of the church and that all is done in accordance with Scripture.

(ii) They act as the leaders of the congregation, taking the initiative where necessary in that which concerns its corporate life.

(iii) They act in representation of the congregation in pronouncing its decisions and in the laying on of hands.

(iv) As the ones who preside they must not permit a weak brother to engage in disputing and criticising. They must not allow wrong doctrine to be taught.

(v) They must see that there is full liberty for the exercise of all the gifts of the Spirit by all who possess them, but that no one minister who has not a gift of the Spirit to do so.

(vi) They must see that the Scriptural procedure is followed in the case of any who may fall into sin.

(vii) At times they had to act as judges and arbiters in disputes between brethren, although, evidently, others besides the Elders may perform this service. Christians are forbidden to go to law against each other. Rather than do so they should suffer the loss of their goods. But they may bring their differences before the saints.[1]

(b) As Pastors, the Elders are responsible for the shepherding of the flock. This means a continual watchfulness over the spiritual needs of the congregation and covers every phase of its life and activity. The principal aspects of their ministry as Pastors may be stated as follows:

(i) They must see that new converts are properly cared for,

---

[1] On this matter Hatch states, "Hardly had the organization of the Christian communities begun before St. Paul looked upon it as an intolerable scandal that 'brother goeth to law with brother'. He deprecates litigation of any kind; the Christian rule was a rule not of litigation but of forgiveness... In those early days it may have been the case that the assembly itself, or persons chosen by the assembly, acted as arbitrators: and to this St. Paul's words point: 'If then ye have judgments of things pertaining to this life, set them to judge who are least esteemed in the Church'. But when the organization of the churches was more complete it is clear that the jurisdiction belonged to the council of presbyters. 'Let not those who have disputes', says the clementines, 'go to law before the civil powers, but let them by all means be reconciled by the elders of the Church, and let them readily yield to their decision'." — *The Organization of the Early Christian Churches,* pp. 72, 73.

visited, instructed, baptized, and that they take the places apportioned to them in the congregation by the Lord.

(ii) They should see that all phases of the ministry are taken care of: the instruction of the children, the preaching of the Word to saved and unsaved, the teaching of the Scriptures, the visitation of those who are sick, the care of those who are weak in the faith and the ministry of prayer.

(iii) The responsibility for the actual preaching and teaching of the Word does not fall upon them more than upon any other member of the congregation. Their particular duty is to exercise a watchful care over the spiritual state of the congregation. The ministry of the Word is the responsibility of all the members and the Elders take part in it on an equality with the others.

(iv) They give instruction to any who require it.

(v) They exercise a continual prayer ministry. When called, they pray for the sick (Jas. 5:14).

(6) They are to be obeyed and held in honour. However, as with the Evangelist, an Elder's power is entirely spiritual, derived from the presence of the Holy Spirit enabling him for the ministry to which he is called, and his authority is solely that of the Word of God. The Elders are to be obeyed only when they do and teach what is right (Heb. 13:17; 3 Jn. 9-11).

(7) There is a special reward, 'a crown of glory that fadeth not away', for the Elder who has been faithful in his ministry (1 Pet. 5:4).

(8) In the case of an Elder who falls into sin, the responsibility to intervene falls upon the Evangelists. The procedure to be followed is given in 1 Tim. 5:19, 20; cf. 3 Jn. 9, 10.[1] The passing of judgment is the responsibility of the congregation.

(9) There were several Elders in every congregation. The group of Elders of a congregation was termed the 'presbytery'. We read of "the Elders of the church" in Jerusalem, Ephesus and Philippi. Barnabas and Paul "ordained Elders in every church". The mission of Titus in Crete was to "ordain Elders in every city". Peter addresses "the Elders who are among you". James counsels the sick to call "the Elders of the church". It should be noted that the Epistles of Peter and James were addressed, not to one church

----

[1] See pp. 282, 309.

only, but to many. There is no example of a church ruled by one Elder.

The ruling of the congregation was done by the presbytery, not by any one Elder. There was no Chief Elder. No doubt one would act as chairman or spokesman when occasion required, but it would not always be the same one, and the one who acted would do so only in a representative capacity. See Acts 11:30; 15:2, 6, 22, 23; 20:17, 28; 21:18; Jas. 5:14; 1 Tim. 4:14; Phil. 1:1. In the last reference the Greek word *'presbuterion'* (presbytery) is used.

Seeking something in the New Testament Church to give ground for the modern position of the Pastor, some have suggested that possibly the 'angels' of the seven churches in Asia, mentioned in the first three chapters of Revelation, occupied such a position. However, there is no true ground for such an interpretation. It is based entirely on supposition. It is opposed to all the other evidence, both Scriptural and historical, which is unanimous in showing that each local church was presided over by several Elders. Surely it is impossible to base, or to justify, a practice on ground so inadequate.

A note on 'angels' (Rev. 1:20) in the Scofield edition of the Bible says: "The 'messengers'... figure any who bear God's message to a church". That seems to be the natural and true interpretation. It is in full accord with the practice of the New Testament Evangelists.[1]

(10) It is not required that an Elder should first have exercised the ministry of Deacon before becoming an Elder.

(11) The practical application of the Elder's ministry is considered in chapter XXXIV.[2] See "Structural Changes", p. 248.

5. Teacher:

The commission which Christ gave to His disciples before His ascension was to preach and teach the Gospel (Mk. 16:15; Matt. 28:19, 20; Acts 2:42; 4:29, 31).

Thus, preaching and teaching are the two main channels through which the Church's witness is carried on, and the gifts of the Spirit for these are, naturally, of primary importance (cf. Rom. 12:3-8; 1 Cor. 12:8-10).

To a considerable extent, preaching involves teaching, but there

---

[1] Cf. 'Messages through Messengers', p. 123, and pp. 476-7.
[2] See also chapter XII:12.

16

THE TEACHER

Ministry   To teach the things relating to God and to His will and purpose revealed by the Spirit through the Word.

Some of many Varieties
$\left\{\begin{array}{l}\text{Teaching adults} \\ \text{,,} \quad\quad \text{women} \\ \text{,,} \quad\quad \text{young people} \\ \text{,,} \quad\quad \text{children}\end{array}\right.$

is a definite and distinct gift of teaching exercised by Teachers called to that ministry by the Holy Spirit, and recognized as such by the Church.

As with the gift of preaching, there are variations of the gift of teaching. The gift of one will be for the teaching of the Word to children; of another, for the teaching of young people; of yet another, for the teaching of older people, and so on.

In many cases a teacher's gift is exercised in the local congregation with which he fellowships. But in other cases his ministry is to the Church as a whole. Such 'Doctors', or Teachers travel from church to church exercising their ministry. They are recognized by the whole Church as Teachers.

A congregation in which the ministry is mainly one of preaching will not be well taught in the things of God. A congregation where the ministry of teaching largely predominates, will fail to bear an active witness to the unsaved. The two ministries should be equally balanced. Where the Holy Spirit has full control it will be so. Eph. 4:11; 1 Cor. 12:28; Acts 13:1; Jas. 3:1. (See Chapter 33.)

II. Secular Ministry

The ministry of the Deacon is not listed among the five basic spiritual ministries. It may be classed as the one secular ministry in the Church.

Deacon:

In the New Testament, *diaconos* (the current word for servant) and *diaconia* (service) are frequently used in a general sense. They are also rendered 'minister' and 'ministry'. In the general sense they were applied to any member of the Church and to any service for the Lord. Paul speaks of Epaphras as a 'faithful *diaconos* (servant) of Christ' (Col. 1:7). The term is applied to our Lord (Rom. 15:8). As Hatch says, "All work which the members of the community did for one another, including that which was done by the apostle himself, was a 'ministry' (diaconia)".[1] However, as with the term Elder (presbuteros), the current word for an elderly man, 'deacon' also was used to designate a particular ministry.

---

[1] *Enc. Brit.*

1. The Deacon, in the technical sense, is one who serves: a ministering servant. He is responsible for the temporal affairs of a congregation (1 Tim. 3:8-13; Acts 6:1-6; Phil. 1:1). He should have the gift of 'helps' or 'serviceable ministrations' (1 Cor. 12:28; Rom. 12:7).[1]

2. He is to be chosen from among the members of the congregation he is to serve (Acts 6:3).

3. The character and qualifications of a Deacon are given in 1 Tim. 3:8-13 and Acts 6:1-6:

    (1) He must be a man of serious demeanour, trustworthy, honest, not given to wine, not greedy of base gain.

    (2) He must be sound in the faith.

    (3) He should not be a new convert but one who has been proved.

    (4) He is to be a man of honest report.

    (5) He must be full of the Holy Spirit.

    (6) His wife must be a believer with a good testimony and his home well governed.

4. There were several Deacons in each congregation (Acts 6:3).

5. They attended to the business affairs of the congregation, such as the care of the funds and the distribution of the money intended for the poor of the congregation.[2]

6. Their service as Deacons did not include any spiritual ministry. At the appointment of the Deacons in the Jerusalem church the Apostles said:

> It is not reason that we should leave the word of God and serve tables... we will give ourselves continually to prayer and the ministry of the Word.

Here a clear distinction is made between the material ministry of the Deacon and the ministry of the Word. The duty of these Deacons was to attend to a business matter. However, they may also have gifts of the Spirit for other ministries, such as preaching or teaching, in common with all the other members.

7. While the ministry of the Deacons is secular and to do with material things, it must not be thought that natural talent is to be wholly or chiefly relied upon for its accomplishment. The seven in

---

[1] See pp. 53, 54.

[2] The writings of Origin and Cyprian (49th letter) show that as late as the third century it was the duty of Deacons to care for the church funds.

the Jerusalem church, whose work was the distribution of money to the poor, had to be men "filled with the Holy Spirit". The wisdom and guidance of the Holy Spirit and the manifestation of His power causing spiritual fruit to be borne is just as necessary in the Deacons' work as in any of the other ministries. No matter what the ministry or gift be, it is the Holy Spirit who is to administer it.

There is deep wisdom in the fact that it is the Deacons and not the Elders who handle the funds of the congregation. Those who have the responsibility for the spiritual oversight of the church do not touch the funds. This protects them from possible criticisms and also from the temptation to use the control of the money for political ends. (History bears striking testimony to this.)[1] Those who care for the funds have no spiritual authority in the church, and that to them likewise is a protection from criticism and temptation.

There is no clear evidence that women were appointed to the ministry of Deacon. In the general sense, the word *diaconos* was applied to women just as to men and *diaconia* was used of any ministry performed by women. In that sense Phoebe was a servant of the Church. There were women, such as the widows spoken of by Paul in 1 Tim. 5:3-16, who dedicated themselves to ministry connected with the Church. These were servants or ministers of the Church, but not deaconesses in the technical sense.

The appointment of Deacons is considered in chapter XXI and on pp. 53, 54.

---

[1] See pp. 249-50. Cf. 86.

CHAPTER XVIII

HISTORY'S EVIDENCE

CHURCH historians, in their investigations of Early Church practice, have too often approached the matter from a rationalistic standpoint. Harnack's viewpoint is entirely rationalistic. Hatch's viewpoint is fundamentally so. Even Neander, influenced by Schleirmacher, was not entirely free from the rationalistic conception. Nevertheless, though the viewpoint of such writers has led them to wrong deductions, the historical facts which they have brought to light are of the greatest value.

The only true approach to the study of Early Church procedure is the one which accepts God's Word as authoritative and sufficient and interprets subsequent historical facts in the light of the Scriptural record and revelation. The rationalistic approach builds upon the findings of historical research, attributing but secondary importance to the Scriptural record, setting aside the revelation of God's purpose and plan for the Church, and ignoring the spiritual factors. Upon their findings they build their conclusion, which is, of course, that the changes that gradually took place were the natural result of man's developing intelligence and of changing conditions and were necessary and good. This purely rationalistic conclusion is accepted generally today, even by sincere Christians who believe God's Word to be the only rule of faith and practice.

Our position is that God has given us in Scripture a complete revelation of the structure which He purposed for the Church, of the testimony which the Church is to bear, and of the means by which that testimony is to be borne, and that the New Testament record provides a sufficient practical example of the functioning Church for our guidance. This position is, we believe, the only one a Bible Christian may take.

Viewing the subsequent history of the Church from this stand-point, it is not difficult to trace and understand the trends that led away from the divine order, to discern the corruptions that were introduced and the causes that led to them. It is entirely a spiritual problem. The Church as established at Pentecost was a spiritual organism dependent upon spiritual wisdom and power. But man's mind is rationalistic: it rejects the unseen, spiritual factor; it would substitute that which is tangible — that which it sees and understands. Moreover, man's heart, by which his mind is largely controlled, is proud, self-confident and unyielded to God; it seeks to glorify itself and would offer to Him sacrifices of its own works.

Our Lord said, "Blessed are they that have not seen and yet have believed." Paul wrote to the carnal Corinthians, "no flesh shall glory in His presence... he that glorieth let him glory in the Lord... For the wisdom of the World is foolishness with God" (1 Cor. 1:29, 31; 3:19). These statements go to the root of the matter.

God's Word, we are told,

"is sharper than any two-edged sword, piercing even to the dividing asunder of soul and spirit, yea, to the inmost parts thereof, and judging the thoughts and imaginations of the heart". (Heb. 4:12, Conybeare.)

The sharp sword of God's Word separates between that which is of the soul (of the natural man) and that which is of His Spirit. It judges and condemns that which is of the natural heart — the thoughts and judgments and schemes of man. In God's Word concerning the Church this separating is demanded — and here is where the battle is joined. To God, man's wisdom is foolishness; to man, spiritual wisdom is foolishness. Paul says,

These are the things whereof we speak, in words not taught by man's wisdom, but by the Spirit; explaining spiritual things to spiritual men. But the natural man rejects the teaching of God's Spirit, for to him it is folly; and he cannot comprehend it, because it is spiritually discerned. But the spiritual man judges all things truly, yet cannot himself be truly judged by others. (1 Cor. 2:13-15, Conybeare.)

It is only to be expected that in the history of the Church we should witness a conflict between the wisdom of man and the wisdom of God; between the natural man and the Spirit. A Church which is "the fulness of Christ" Who is present in the midst, Who reveals His will to His people, Who manifests Himself through the gifts of the Spirit, carrying on His work through the members of His Body, could not be accepted by the natural mind as intelligible and practicable, therefore a substitute must be formed, constructed according to man's wisdom and served by man's works. Christ said that God is a Spirit and must be worshipped in Spirit and in truth. Man sought a way to offer human worship — through ritual, good works, human ability, buildings, music and art — the worship that Cain offered.

Structural Changes

There is much evidence in the early writings of the Church that reveals the gradual changes that took place in its order. The original foundation — structural and doctrinal — was laid, according to God's purpose, by the Apostles. This foundation was perfect and complete.[1] That it continued to be maintained for a time is evident. This is seen in the "Teaching of the Twelve Apostles" an ancient writing composed in the early part of the second century, in which there is much that is of interest. It shows the local church under the leadership of Bishops (Elders) and Deacons. 'Apostles', who were travelling Evangelists, were supported by the freewill offerings of the churches but took no money from those they were actually ministering to. Prophets and teachers were also sometimes itinerant. This shows the general structure of the Church still unchanged. But there is evidence that important changes were already creeping in. As Taylor says:

> The worship, the services, the ministers, were losing the simplicity of earlier days, and assuming that ritualistic and priestly character which we find not indeed fully developed, yet unmistakably present, in the pages of Justin Martyr, of Irenaeus and of Tertullian.[2]

We can refer here, of course, only briefly to the main features of the changes that took place and the causes underlying them. The writings of the Fathers of the Church of the first and second centuries bear unanimous testimony to the fact that a plurality of Elders presided in each church in their time. They

---

1 See comment on Eph. 2:19-22, p. 151; also pp. 214-6.
2 Preface to 2nd Ed. *Early Church History*, by Backhouse and Taylor.

refer to no case where one Elder ruled over a church. Polycarp, writing to the Philippians about a hundred years after that church was founded, counsels them "to submit themselves to their Elders and Deacons". Tertullian, speaking of public worship in the church about the year 200 A. D., says, "certain approved Elders preside".[1]

During the second century it seems to have become common for the Elders in a congregation to choose one of their number to preside over them, and to apply to him the designation of Bishop. Even then he was not considered as of higher rank, but simply as *primus inter pares*.[2] Eusebius (300 A. D.), writing of the time of the Apostles, uses the terms Bishop and Presbyter interchangeably.[3] This is common in the writings of the early Fathers.[4]

The testimony of Scripture and of history, both equally clear, leave no room for question that originally each congregation was presided over by several Elders, all equal in rank and authority.

For several centuries it continued to be the general practice for Elders to earn their living in secular employment. Cyprian, in the middle of the third century, objects to the long absences of some of the Elders on matters of business. It was much later that the clergy were forbidden to engage in trade. During the fourth century, the idea that they should separate themselves from secular life gained ground. It was the result of the growing distinction between clergy and laity. Gradually, the priesthood of all believers was replaced by a priestly order that was regarded as representing the visible Church and as the channel through which Christ worked and the Holy Spirit spoke.

The manner in which the power of the Elders grew and finally became vested in one man is not difficult to discern. Hatch attributes great importance to the influence of the power which belonged to the Elders as administrators of the Church funds. There is no doubt that this was an important factor. It was not God's purpose that the Elder should administer the Church's bounty.

---

[1] Apol. 39. See also Clement. Epist. Clem. ad Jacob c. 7.
[2] See Neander: *Planting and Training of the Church*, book 3, Ch. 5.
[3] *Church History*, III, XXIII.
[4] See pp. 233-4, 284, 318-9.
An enlightening discussion of this whole matter will be found in Hatch's "The Organization of the Early Christian Churches". We do not, of course, agree with Hatch's general argument and conclusions, which are in the main rationalistic, but he gives a precise statement of historical facts.

That was to be the work of the Deacons. The final responsibility for the administration of the funds of the congregation belongs to the congregation. The Elders, representing the congregation, have a general responsibility to see that the funds are distributed according to the will of the congregation, but nothing more. The wisdom of God in not placing the Church funds in the hands of the Elders has already been noted.[1] But Elders and Bishops early assumed this authority, which, naturally, increased their importance and was at least one of the contributing causes of the growth of their power.

Originally, the final spiritual authority in all things resided in the congregation, but the increasing lack of spiritual power as Christ's presence came to be regarded more as theoretical than as actual, and dependence was placed upon human factors instead of upon the Holy Spirit's gifts, made it inevitable that men with a certain natural ability should be depended upon and therefore become prominent. Under these conditions the oversight of the congregation by a group of Elders, all of them equal, who took no more part in the ministry of the Word than the other members, became impracticable and it was unavoidable that authority would come to be vested in one person and that the authority of that one should steadily increase. This development was aided by the example of the system of government in vogue in city, state and the heathen religious systems. Once started upon this road, it was only a matter of time for a complete human system of government to be developed.

Another structural change of great importance and far-reaching consequences which gradually took place was the disappearance of the Evangelist's, or church-planter's, ministry and the final substitution of the authority of the Diocesan Bishop. This was an inevitable consequence of the growth of the Elder's power. The authority which the Chief-elder assumed clashed with that of the Evangelist. As did Diotrephes, he would spurn the missionary's counsel.

The eclipse of this ministry — one of the five basic ministries

---

[1] See pp. 244-5. The care which Paul took in the handling of Church funds is mentioned on pp. 86.

in the Church[1] — was an irreparable loss. No longer were there foundation layers and repairers for the extension of the Church and to minister to congregations that fell into difficulties. The Pauls and Lukes and Timothies and Tituses — who went to the aid of the Church in Corinth when it became carnal, who defended the church in Antioch against heresy, who saw to the appointing of Elders in the congregations in Crete, who exercised a purely spiritual ministry with only spiritual authority and bore a full spiritual testimony in their own lives before the churches — were replaced by the Cyprians. Many congregations were in serious spiritual difficulties but the ministry which God had provided for such had disappeared. Bishops, with regional authority and ever increasing ecclesiastical power, replaced the Evangelists. These Bishops, by such authority, might create and conserve organizational unity but they could not impart or conserve spiritual life.

Many of those who should have been ministering as Evangelists and living by faith, as Paul and his companions had done, settled down permanently in the larger cities. Such men took the lead over the Elders of the local congregation, thus contributing to the rise of the Chief-elder and the Bishop.

A strong impulse towards the development of the episcopate was given by Cyprian about the middle of the third century. A comparison between Cyprian and Paul will reveal the great change that had taken place in the Church. Cyprian, before his conversion, had been a teacher of rhetoric. He came of a patrician family, was highly educated, brilliant and wealthy. After his conversion he threw himself with enthusiasm into the work of the Church and distributed his wealth among the poor. He was made an Elder shortly after his conversion, while still what Paul would term 'a novice'. His popularity grew until the church in Carthage clamoured for him to become their Bishop, surrounding his house to plead with him until he gave his consent. There was no prayer and fasting by the church, or voice of the Spirit revealing the will of the Lord regarding the appointment, as had been the order in Paul's time. That belonged already to a time that was gone.

It is not surprising that Cyprian knew not the use of the spiritual weapons that Paul had employed so effectively in dealing with problems in the churches. Paul did not stoop to use carnal

---

[1] See pp. 250-2.

weapons. He appealed to an authority that was higher than man's. To him the power of the Spirit of the living God Who was with him was sufficient to raze to the ground the strongest fortress that the enemy might build within the Church or outside of it. Cyprian appealed to the authority of councils and sought to protect the doctrine and unity of the Church by increasing the power of the Bishops.

He and Paul worked on different planes, guided by different principles. Both were men of learning, zeal, ability and courage. Both sought earnestly to establish the Church on earth and both met a martyr's death. Cyprian has been described as 'arrogant', 'confident of his own powers'. Paul was filled with the Spirit of Pentecost; in him was the strength and humility of the Lord. Cyprian was the product of the political and human tendencies of the Church of his day. The one built with purely spiritual materials — 'gold, silver, precious stones' — the other perceived not that he was introducing 'hay, wood and stubble'.

Another important development, which was natural and which has exerted a profound influence in many ways, was the introduction of the Church convention or council. Of this Mosheim says:

> These councils, of which no vestige appears before the middle of this (the second) century,[1] changed nearly the whole form of the Church. For, in the first place the ancient rights and privileges of the people were very much abridged by them; and on the other hand, the influence and authority of the bishops were not a little augmented.[2]

Doctrines and practices have been fixed by these Councils, by no means always in accordance with God's Word, and the definite tendency always has been to give to the decisions of Councils a greater authority than to the Word of God. Councils, great and small, have, in great part, substituted the wisdom of man for the guidance of the Spirit.

Doctrinal Changes

These radical structural changes would not have taken place had the way not been prepared for them. Running parallel with the changes in organization were spiritual and doctrinal changes

---

[1] Cf. pp. 108-9.
[2] *Ecclesiastical History*, p. 63.

CHART OF THE GIFTS OF THE SPIRIT AND THEIR COUNTERFEITS

Gifts or Manifestations of the Spirit	TRUE MANIFESTATION OF THE GIFTS	SOULISH COUNTERFEIT	SATANIC COUNTERFEIT
	In the exercise of these the natural powers function freely but are voluntarily submitted to the Holy Spirit.	Here the natural powers function independently, not directed by Holy Spirit. In this state they are under influence of Satan, being in attitude of independence to God. Much of present activity of Church is carried on by means of these counterfeits.	The natural powers, consciously or unconsciously, are under the direct influence or control of evil spirits. Satan-inspired religious cults and political systems are carried on, partially at least, by means of these counterfeits.
Preaching	Preaching revealed truth in power and demonstration of the Spirit.	Preaching with enticing words of human wisdom, depending upon oratory, emotionalism, sentimentalism, etc. 1 Cor. 2:1,4.	The preaching of doctrines that are false and untrue to God's Word, under the direct inspiration of evil spirits. 1 Tim. 4:1.
Teaching	Teaching the things of the Spirit with wisdom and light given by the Spirit, depending upon Him to give understanding to the hearer. Eph. 1:16-19.	Teaching in man's wisdom, depending upon man's ability to give understanding. Col. 2:18; Rev. 2:20.	Teaching of false or unsound doctrine under inspiration of an evil spirit. 1 Tim. 4:1; 2 Cor. 11:14, 15.
Faith	Holy Spirit-given faith in what is in accordance with God's Word and will.	An effort to believe that depends entirely upon will power and emotional attitudes.	Faith, inspired by evil spirits, in occult power of any kind or in false doctrine or satanically inspired political systems. 1 Cor. 10:20.
Utterance of Wisdom	Holy Spirit-given clarity in the stating of revealed spiritual truth.	Spiritual truth stated with reliance upon natural ability to give understanding.	Revelations supposed to be from the spirit world received from evil spirits.
Utterance of Knowledge	Application of spiritual truth to practical experiences of life under inspiration of the Spirit.	Human wisdom's attempt to adjust spiritual truth to the practical things of life. Acts 26:9; Rom. 10:2.	Satan-inspired systems, based upon satanic principles, for the betterment of conditions among men and nations.
Paraclete Gift	Holy Spirit-inspired counsel, consolation, etc. manifesting the pure love and wisdom of Christ.	Effort to help and counsel based upon human wisdom.	Counsel inspired by Satan and based upon his principles, as Peter's advice to Christ. Matt. 16:22, 23.
Mercy Acts of love	Holy Spirit-inspired acts of love manifesting the love of Christ.	Acts of love inspired solely by human kindness. Limited by the limits of human love.	Manifestations of interest in human welfare that are inspired by Satan. Gen. 3:1, 4, 5.

Giving	Giving that is under the direction of the Holy Spirit.	Giving for merit or merely as a duty or in response to emotional or sentimental appeals.	Giving inspired by Satan that supports that which carries out his purpose. False systems do not lack for money.
Discernment of Spirits	Given by the Spirit to distinguish between what is from Him and what is a deception wrought by Satan.	Human wisdom's attempt to judge between what is of God and what is of Satan. Cf. Heb. 4:12.	Evil spirits immediately discern what is of Christ and may impart that knowledge to one under their control. Mk. 1:23, 24; 5:7; Acts 19:15; Jas. 2:19.
Serviceable Ministrations	Material service rendered under the guidance and with the wisdom of the Holy Spirit. Ex. 35:30-35.	Material service done in the wisdom and power of man and offered to God.	Ability and cunning given by Satan to those he is using enabling them for the carrying out of enterprises inspired by him.
Ruler	Ruling under the guidance and with the wisdom of the Spirit.	Dependence upon human ability, such as the psychology of leadership, for ruling and leading.	Ability to rule, displayed through wisdom and personality, given by evil spirits.
Miracles	Direct intervention of Divine power in response to faith given by the Holy Spirit.	Natural phenomena or coincidences attributed to God's intervention by emotional religious enthusiasm.	Miracles wrought through the power of Satan. Cf. Pharaoh's magicians.
Healing	Healing wrought by God's power in response to faith given by the Holy Spirit.	Healing, real or imagined, resulting from the employment of psychic means, such as suggestion, and attributed to Divine intervention.	Healing wrought by the power of Satan as seen in certain false cults.
Varieties of Tongues	Utterance produced on certain occasions by the presence of the Holy Spirit.	Ecstatic utterance produced by bringing certain soul powers into a state of unnatural excitement, or by feigning such utterance. Confusion and the glorifying of the flesh are the result.	Utterance of an evil spirit through a person under its control. Such utterances may feign piety, but are unsound and often vile. Confusion and unscriptural doctrine and practice are the result.
Interpretation of Tongues	Revelation given by the Spirit of the spiritual meaning of an utterance given,	An interpretation that is feigned, or that is imagined as a result of religious excitement that is purely emotional.	Interpretation suggested to the mind by evil spirits. May feign piety but is unsound and often unholy.

that were just as radical. The basis of the Church's faith became undermined to a more serious extent than is generally realized. There is no doubt that much of the blame rests upon such apologists and teachers as Justin, Tatian, Athanagoras, Clement and Origin, who were able men and sincere converts to Christianity but who sought to reconcile the doctrines of Christianity with the philosophies of Greece. They fell into the error against which Paul had so earnestly warned and so resolutely stood, and they had recourse to the wisdom of men. They built up a new theology that embraced much of the philosophy of Plato. They sincerely sought to defend the Christian faith against the attacks of heathen philosophers but endeavoured to meet their opponents on their ground and to present Christianity on a reasonable, philosophical basis. In doing so they moved the foundation of their building from the eternal, spiritual Rock to the shifting sand of man's wisdom.

Justin, Tatian, Athanagoras and Clement had been students of Greek philosophy before their conversion and they did not, as Paul did, determine to know nothing but Christ and Him crucified, nor divest themselves entirely of what he termed "philosophy and vain deceit after the tradition of men, after the rudiments of the world, and not after Christ."

Origin studied under Clement in the catechetical school in Alexandria, the second city in the Roman Empire and the meeting place of the East and the West. This school was established in the second century and was the first in which Christian youth was taught a blend of philosophy and Christianity.

Clement was a learned man, a philosopher and professedly an Eclectic. He taught a metaphysical theology. Origin became a great scholar and deeply versed in the writings of the Greek philosophers. He was also a great theologian. In his system of theology he reconciled Christianity with Plato's philosophy and laid the basis of the theology that has prevailed since then in the organized Church. He succeeded Clement in the Alexandria school. Later, when he was forced to leave Alexandria, he founded a school in Caesarea. Many eager students from different parts of the world were attracted to his classes and so the influence of his teaching spread widely throughout the Church.

Writing of this period Mosheim says: —

Those who were initiated into the mysteries of philosophy wished that many, and especially such as aspired to the office of pastors and teachers, might apply themselves to the study of human wisdom so that they might confute the enemies of truth with more effect and teach and instruct others with more success.[1]

At first this, the 'modernism' of its day, was opposed by the majority of Christians, but, through these schools, it gained ground steadily until its triumph was complete. How often, since then, has history repeated itself!

Christian doctrine as taught by these philosopher-theologians was no longer the purely spiritual wisdom which the Holy Spirit had taught through the founders of the Church. The Holy Spirit was not given His true place, either as the life within or as the power for ministry.

Christian doctrine, in its true sense, is revealed spiritual truth, its light spiritual, its power spiritual. It is Spirit and it is Life. Its reception requires spiritual enlightenment. It is not mere dogma to which intellectual assent is given but God's life and light in the inner man. The philosopher-theologians sought to make it intelligible to the natural mind. To do so they humanized it and materialized it and reduced it to theoretical dogma. The Spirit was excluded, the life was lost and only the dead letter remained. That which is spiritual became theoretical and man was left to his own resources. The power from on high was gone; doctrine became but a code to be subscribed to: an empty shell. The Holy Spirit was still in the Church to manifest His life in any who would receive the truth in simple faith, and some did so, but the great majority lived and served by lifeless dogma.

Thus Christianity became a religion, founded upon revealed truth, but fitted into the mould of human thought, its theology not the pure, divine revelation, but a human interpretation and adaptation of it; its power no longer the active presence of the Spirit of the living God but the ability of man to do God's work for Him. The spiritual factor, for practical purposes, was largely excluded. God became a God afar off. In dogma He was still the Creator of the universe, omnipotent and all-wise, but that He manifests His omnipotence among men was not credited. Christ indwelt His Body only in a theoretic sense. Faith in the presence of the Spirit lost its reality and the manifestation of His gifts became steadily less. The Church no longer experienced the limitless resources of the Christ in the midst but limited itself, through

---

[1] *Ecclesiastical History,* p. 62.

human reasoning, to the limits of man's mind. It had given ear to
"Philosophers, who darken and put out
Eternal truth by everlasting doubt."[1]
The prophetic parable of the leaven which the woman took and
hid in three measures of meal — the philosophy of Satan and
fallen man mixed with the spiritual equipment provided by the
presence of the Spirit of the Triune God — that spread its influence until it had permeated the whole mass, was already fast
being fulfilled.

As we review the evolution that took place within the Church
during the first three centuries, we find three distinct stages. The
first is characterized by life. The unity of the Church in the
beginning was based upon the indwelling life of the one Spirit
and was spontaneous. Unity in doctrine and order was demanded,
but these were merely the true fruit of life. In the second stage,
life is waning and unity is sought through the unity of doctrine.
It is not now the pure doctrine that is the fruit of life but the
theology of the schools. There is no limit to the variations of man-
made dogma, so disunity increased. In the third stage, the unity
of the Church is sought through organization. A mechanical unity
is devised, based upon ecclesiastical organization and authority.

As the Living Christ was prevented from manifesting Himself
in His Church, and the unity of the Spirit — the unity that comes
from living unity with Christ[2] — ceased to exist, spiritual doctrine
gave place to theology and spiritual order to organization. Finally,
the whole structure came to depend entirely upon organization,
life being but nominal and theology important only as it affected
the unity of the organization. The Christian faith became a
religion; the Church, the Body of Christ, became an organization.

Through the doctrinal and structural changes that had been
introduced during the second and third centuries the way was
prepared for what was to follow. By the time the great influx of
pseudo-converts occured under Constantine, the Church did not
find it impossible to receive them, nor did they feel so out of
place as they would have in the Church of the first century.

Paul had written: —

But I fear, lest by any means, as the serpent beguiled Eve
through his subtlety, so your minds should be corrupted from the
simplicity that is in Christ. (2 Cor. 11:3.)

---

[1] Cowper.
[2] Jn. 17:21-23.

His fear had not been unfounded.

The Fourth Century Onwards

The conversion of the Roman Emperor Constantine early in the fourth century is the great turning-point in the history of the Church. Before that time changes had crept in comparatively slowly and there had not been lacking a strong opposition on the part of the more spiritual minority, already considered schismatics by the "Church", but after Constantine's conversion the process became rapid and thorough, embracing every phase of the Church's life and ministry. The foundation having been altered it was comparatively to easy reconstruct the building.

Of Constantine's conversion, Fisher writes:

> That there mingled in this decision, as in most of the steps of his career, political ambition, is highly probable. But he sincerely believed in the God whom the Christians worshipped, and in the help which, through His providence, He could lend to His servants. Constantine showed afterwards in various ways that the old superstitions yet lingered to some extent in his mind. He was never fully weaned from the cultus of Apollo. There were occasions when he ordered pagan soothsayers to be consulted. That he did not receive baptism until the day before his death was not due, however, to a lack of faith, but to the current belief, in which he shared, that the holy laver washed out the guilt of all previous sins... Constantine himself did not attempt to put down heathen worship by coercive means... But in many ways he used his personal influence, by persuasion and by distributing offices and other rewards, to gain converts to the Christian side. He even delivered discourses to applauding auditors in his palace. He called himself, the historian Eusebius tells us, in relation to the Church, "bishop in externals". This was said in a tone of pleasantry, but it expressed the view which he actually took of his ecclesiastical function... It was inevitable that under such a monarch there should be large reinforcements of the Church from the ranks of the heathen. It was unavoidable, too, that a considerable proportion of these new adherents should be actuated by interested motives. Imperial favour, in the room of imperial hostility, was now to be the source of the peril of the Church.[1]

All this is eloquent of the condition that already prevailed in the Church. It was in no state spiritually to face the dangers of the situation that confronted it. Great numbers of heathen were permitted to enter merely by a change of name, bringing with them heathen ideas, superstitions and idolatrous customs. Augustine excuses what was done; he says:

---

[1] *History of the Christian Church*, pp. 87-89.

When peace was made (between the State and the Church) the crowd of Gentiles who were anxious to embrace Christianity were deterred by this, that whereas they had been accustomed to pass the holidays in drunkenness and feasting before their idols they could not easily consent to forego these most pernicious yet ancient pleasures. It seemed good then to our leaders to favour this part of their weakness, and for those festivals which they had relinquished, to substitute others in honour of the holy martyrs, which they might celebrate with similar luxury, though not with the same impiety.[1]

It was at this time that monasticism, a reaction against the prevailing worldliness, became popular. A holy life came to be considered as only for the few and possible only for those who withdrew from contact with the world.

The hierarchical organization, patterned after the government of the Empire and the heathen religious systems of the day, was rapidly perfected. This culminated later in the establishing of the Papacy. The substitution of a human form of government for the divine order and of a soulish system of worship for that which was purely spiritual, became complete. As Lord Macauly says: —

In the fifth century, Christianity had conquered Paganism, and Paganism had infected Christianity. The Church was now victorious and corrupt. The rites of the Pantheon had passed into her worship — the subtleties of the Academy into her creed.[2]

During all this time, the Lord was never without witnesses to the true order and there were churches and groups, generally called Montanists in the early centuries, that sought to remain faithful to the doctrines and practices of the Apostles, to guard themselves from all compromise with the world and to walk and serve in the wisdom and power of the Spirit. These, however, were a decreasing minority and the Church as a whole, composed of all types, including untaught Christians, worldly Christians, ambitious leaders and multitudes of nominal Christians, many of whom had entered the Church without conversion, continued to drift further and further from the God-given order.

Of the Montanists, the spiritual remnant of those days, and the conditions against which they protested, Hatch says:

The gift of ruling, like Aaron's rod, seemed to swallow up the other gifts. Then came a profound reaction. Against the growing tendency towards that state of things which afterwards firmly established itself, and which ever since has been the normal state

---
[1] Ep. p. 29.
[2] *Essay on Lord Bacon.*

17

of almost all Christian Churches, some communities, first of Asia Minor, then of Africa, then of Italy raised a vigorous and, for a time, a successful protest. They reasserted the place of spiritual gifts as contrasted with official rule. They maintained that the revelation of Christ through the Spirit was not a temporary phenomenon of Apostolic days, but a constant fact of Christian life. They combined with this the preaching of a higher morality than that which was tending to become current. They were supported in what they did by the greatest theologian of his time, and it is to the writing of that theologian (Tertullian) rather than to the vituperative statements of later writers that we must look for a true idea of their purpose... It was a beating of the wings of pietism against the iron bars of organization. It was the first, though not the last, rebellion of the religious sentiment against official religion.[1]

The importance which the Montanists placed upon the gifts of the Spirit and their free exercise by all members of the Church is significant. The new organization which was growing up in the Church, with its ritualism and sacerdotalism, necessarily meant the end of the free exercise of the gifts of the Spirit. It was as it gained the field that the gifts of the Spirit disappeared, the Holy Spirit's freedom to manifest Himself and to use whom He would was taken away, the Church became dependent upon the natural talents and material wealth of men and its spiritual power was lost.

It was thus that Satan succeeded in robbing the Church of a great part of its spiritual heritage. Since then the general manifestation of the gifts of the Spirit among the members of the Church has been regarded as something peculiar to the Early Church.

Harnack, a Rationalist, while seeking to justify, on the ground of expediency, the changes that were introduced into the structure of the Church, admits the sources from which they sprang. His judgment of what took place is characteristic of the attitude of those who view the matter solely in the light of human possibilities and power and regard the presence, power and active intervention of the Holy Spirit largely as matters of theoretical dogma, scarcely intelligible, except to a few, and of no practical application.

He pictures the Church before Constantine's time as simply "a few small congregations scattered over the Roman empire", inadequately organized, exclusive, and incapable of evangelizing the world. To accomplish her world-wide mission, he says,

---

[1] *The Organization of the Early Christian Churches*, pp. 112-125.

She had to renounce her original peculiarities and exclusiveness; or, retaining these peculiarities and clinging to the old modes of life, she must remain a small, insignificant sect, barely intelligible to one man in a thousand and utterly incapable of saving and educating nations.

Describing the transformation that was effected in the Church, he says:

She marched through the open door into the Roman state along all its thoroughfares by imparting to it the word of the Gospel, but at the same time leaving it everything except its gods. On the other hand she furnished herself with everything of value that could be taken over from the world without straining the elastic structure of the organization which she now adopted. With the aid of its philosophy she created her new Christian theology; its polity furnished her with the most exact constitutional forms; its jurisprudence, its trade and commerce, its art and industry, were all taken into her service; she contrived to borrow some hints even from its religious worship.[1]

Then he sketches the history of "those believers of the old school (the Montanists) who protested in the name of the gospel against this secular church, and who wished to gather together a people prepared for God regardless alike of numbers and circumstances."

A truer comment on what took place is made by Dr. Arnold. He speaks of,

...the pretended conversion of the kingdoms of the world, to the kingdom of Christ in the fourth and fifth centuries, which I look upon as one of the great **tours d'adresse** that Satan ever played, except his invention of Popery. I mean that by inducing kings and nations to conform nominally to Christianity, and thus to get into their hands the direction of Christian society, he has in great measure succeeded in keeping out the peculiar principles of that society from any extended sphere of operation, and in ensuring the ascendancy of his own.[2]

Regarding the greater intelligibility so confidently claimed for the rationalized Church, we may quote the Philosopher against the Rationalist. Coleridge speaks of the time when

in Council and Synod the Divine Humanities of the Gospel gave way to speculative Systems, and Religion became a Science of Shadows under the name of Theology, or at best a bare Skeleton of Truth, without life or interest, alike inaccessible and unintelligible to the majority of Christians. For these, therefore, there remained only rites and ceremonies and spectacles, shows and semblances. Thus among the learned the substance of things hoped for (Heb. xi:1) passed off into **Notions**; and for the Unlearned the

---

[1] *Montanism*, Enc. Brit.
[2] *Life of Dr. Arnold*, by Dean Stanley, p. 48.

Surface of Things became Substance. The Christian world was for centuries divided into the Many that did not think at all, and the Few who did nothing but **think** — both alike **unreflecting,** the one from defect of the **Act,** the other from the absence of an **Object.**[1]

The religious Rationalist's difficulty resides in the fact that he knows not by experience the power of the Spirit of God; therefore it is excluded as a practical possibility from all his thinking. The basis of his thinking being thus seriously incomplete his conclusions necessarily are false.

To describe the Church of the second century as nothing more than a few small, scattered congregations, completely lacking the organization and power necessary for the evangelization of the world, may be convenient to Harnack's argument, but it is a gross mis-statement. It is entirely contrary to fact. It ignores the power of the Spirit manifested so gloriously through Paul and the other Early Church Evangelists, and the effective, spiritual organization that enabled the Church to spread rapidly throughout the world, to resist successfully the fiercest storms of persecution, and to bear an effective testimony for Christ to all classes and races of men. It was at the end of the second century that Tertullian wrote, "We are of yesterday, and we fill the world".

The history of the reorganized Church during the centuries that followed surely speaks for itself. It marched in to take possession in the Roman State, consolidated its position until its dominion was well nigh absolute, and led the world into the corruption and ignorance of the dark ages, when much even of the light of the culture that had flourished in the heathen nations of Greece and Rome was eclipsed. It availed itself of every art and artifice that man had devised and developed the strongest human organization ever known. It created titles and conferred authority: it added ceremonies ever more solemn and gorgeous. It built Cathedrals and filled them with pomp and art. But it never conquered the world; it was conquered by it. It intrigued and plotted and persecuted, but it did not make the world Christian in anything save the name. On the contrary, it filled the world with superstition and idolatry.

It is amazing that a man of intelligence with an open Bible could fail to perceive the true difference between the purely spiritual, conquering Church established by the Apostles and the proud human structure which was subsituted for it. But the spir-

---

[1] *Aids to Reflection,* p. 134.

itual structure is unintelligible to the mind of man because it depends upon the presence and power of the unseen Spirit of God. The human structure is understandable and seems indispensable. The fact that the spiritual structure was efficient and successful is set aside. Its success cannot be explained in terms of human organization, wisdom and works, therefore, to depend upon it is regarded as out of the question.

Even the evident weakness and failure of the human structure does not convince man's mind. He will mourn over it and seek to, improve it, but he fears to discard it altogether and to return to the simplicity of the purely spiritual structure. To do so requires faith.

As Harnack states, the reorganized Church borrowed hints from the heathen religions. This went much further than is generally realized. Not only in the matter of images, candles, feast days, sacramentalism (adapted from the Mysteries), ceremonies, and processions did the Church copy from the heathen, but also in organization. Sacerdotalism — the clergy, the hierarchy, the centralized, autocratic government, the division between clergy and laity — followed the pagan pattern, not the Hebrew. The new structure which the Church adopted differed in many vital points from that of the Jewish system. On the other hand, the structure of the Church as established by the Apostles was true in every detail to the principles of the Hebrew pattern. The High Priesthood of Christ and the priesthood of all believers is exactly foreshadowed by the Tabernacle priesthood. The model for the Christian congregation was the Jewish Synagogue. The teaching, the types, the hopes of the Jewish religion are all fulfilled in the New Testament Church.

Steps in Departure

Summarizing the evolution that took place in the structure of the Church, we find that:

1. The Presbytery, composed of several Elders, all equal in position and authority, gradually becomes a Presbytery with a President, who takes the title of Bishop.

2. The authority of this President of the Elders increases until he becomes the chief authority in the congregation.

3. The result of this is that the plurality of Elders is gradually eliminated, one Elder, or Bishop, alone ruling the congregation.

4. Meanwhile another development is taking place. The Bishop of a congregation in an important town assumes authority over those of congregations in the smaller towns and villages in the surrounding districts. So the Bishop of a diocese comes into existence.

5. The Bishop of a diocese, with regional, ecclesiastical authority, replaces the Evangelist — the church-planter and foundation-layer with purely spiritual authority to found churches and generally guard their foundations.

6. All this is done with the intention of providing more efficient organization for the Church. The root cause is the increasing lack of the Holy Spirit's power in the Church, which grows with the increasing departure from the spiritual order. Thus a vicious circle is established — lack of spiritual power leads to departure from God's order and departure from God's order produces still greater lack of spiritual power.

7. Other consequences develop. The growing ecclesiastical authority of Elder and Bishop, the general spiritual declension resulting in the non-manifestation of the gifts of the Spirit and lack of desire to take part in spiritual ministry, all paved the way for the ministry of the Gospel to become professional and for those who ministered in the Gospel to become a separate class.

8. The general lack of spiritual equipment made it seem necessary to have specially trained men for the ministry of the Gospel. So a formal theological course became a requisite — finally the chief requisite — for spiritual ministry. This was done with a desire to increase the effectiveness of the ministry.

9. Then those who were not specially prepared and authorized to preach the Gospel were discouraged from doing so, and, ultimately, forbidden. Thus the priesthood of all believers was superseded by a priestly class and the ordinary Church member became a layman, largely inarticulate so far as ministry is concerned.

The Church that emerges, structurally and spiritually, has few points of similarity to the Church founded by the Apostles. The principles of spiritual government and service have been replaced by the principles of human government and service.

It is interesting to note what happened to the five basic spiritual ministries which the Lord gave to the Church for its coordination and witness — the ministries of Apostle, Prophet or

Preacher, Evangelist, Pastor, Teacher.[1] The Apostolic foundation became buried under a human structure. The ministry of the Evangelist, or church-planter, in its full sense, was lost. The Pastoral ministry absorbed the ministries of Preacher and Teacher and all the other priestly functions. The Pastors became clergy and the other members of the Church laymen. Thus the ministries of preaching and teaching, given to the whole Church for the carrying out, by every member, of the Lord's commands to preach and teach, became prerogatives of the clergy. The rest of the Church, deprived of its priestly privilege, was largely silenced.

It is a sad history. Instead of returning to the place of surrender and faith when it found itself weak, to give free course to the Spirit's power, the Church sought strength and protection by adding human organization and conferring power upon human leaders.

Paul and the other New Testament Evangelists had used spiritual weapons to overthrow the strongholds of human reasonings that the enemy of the Church was ever seeking to build up through carnality and false doctrine. But these spiritual weapons were laid aside by their successors. To use them, Paul and his fellow Evangelists had to pay the cost of sacrifice, dying daily to all that was of the flesh, 'filling up what is lacking in the suffering of Christ for His Church's sake'. But the price was no longer paid and the human weapon of ecclesiastical authority was grasped.

The servants of Him Who had not where to lay His head, Who was poor and meek and lowly, Who refused the glory of the Kingdoms of this earth, Who yielded His body a sacrifice, no longer followed in His footsteps filled with His Spirit. The doctrines of the Nicolaitans (priestly assumption) and of Baalam (compromise with the world), against which the New Testament Evangelists had warned and successfully contended, gained the day. The glory of the Church became riches and forms, its leaders great men in the earth, its power the authority of men, enforced, if need be, by the sword.

But the imposing organization that was formed, with all the might of its authority, found itself still powerless to exercise spiritual control over the hearts of men, to unite them in true worship and to guard the soundness of the faith. What the New Testament Evangelists had accomplished in their material poverty

---

[1] See comments on Eph. 2:19-22; 4:11-16, chapter 13.

and defencelessness through the weapons of faith, prayer and the Word of God, the humanly organized church with its wealth and power was impotent to do. The grasping of the weapon of human power made it necessary increasingly to use that weapon even to the extreme of ruthlessness and cruelty, in complete contradiction of the Spirit of Christ. The placing of dependence upon human wisdom excluded more and more of the Spirit-revealed wisdom of God, bringing increasing darkness. The rejection of the reproach and suffering of the Cross of Christ and of the humble, self-denying walk of Christ, gave place to the world and the flesh until spiritual light was only a struggling ray and those whose life was in the Spirit seemed but a voice crying in the wilderness.

This change which took place in the Church, which Renan describes as "the most profound transformation in history" was not something entirely new in the history of men. It was just a manifestation of the tendency that has been natural to the human heart since the Fall. Man's wisdom has always led away further and further from the purity of the revelations that God has given him. Our Lord said of the Pharisees, "Full well ye reject the commandment of God, that ye may keep your own tradition" (Mk. 7:9). In our own contact with Indian tribes we have been struck with the evidence that exists that their present animism is the corruption of a faith that had once been pure, acknowledging one holy God, the Creator of the Universe, but had degenerated, passing through the various stages of organized religion, priestcraft and idolatry until it reached its present primitive state.

Dr. A. P. Martin writes,

A wide survey of civilized nations shows that... man was not left to construct his own creed, but that his blundering logic has always been active in its attempts to corrupt and obscure a divine original... China, India, Egypt and Greece all agree in the mono-theistic type of their early religion. The Orphic hymns long before the advent of the popular divinities celebrated the **Phantheos,** the Universal God. The odes compiled by Confucius testify to the earlier worship of **Shangte,** the Supreme Ruler. The Vedas speak of "one unknown true Being, all-present, all-powerful; the Creator, Preserver and Destroyer of the universe".[1]

But all these religions have wandered far from God. In the organized Church we see the same process at work. Human organization, rationalized theology, priestcraft, idolatry, superstition, all have been welcomed by the wisdom of man. Were it not for

---

[1] *The Chinese,* p. 163.

the continued presence of the Holy Spirit dwelling in those who are truly the Lord's and ever seeking to lead back to the purity of the original revelation, the night would have closed in upon the whole Church many centuries ago and not a glimmer of light would remain today.

The Reformation

In the 16th century came the great spiritual awakening of the Reformation. Much that had been lost was regained. The glorious light of the Gospel shone forth once more. However, there was not a complete return to the simplicity of the Early Church order and practice. The restoration of Apostolic doctrine was not sufficiently complete to exclude entirely the theology of the schools. The Holy Spirit was not given His full place. His power and wisdom were not relied upon entirely; therefore His gifts were manifested only partially. The right of all believers to take part in ministry through the gifts of the Spirit was not fully regained. The distinction between clergy and laity was retained, although in a modified form. The unity of the Church was not restored, and the communions that were organized continued to depend, partially at least, upon human forms of government. The Protestant clergy replaced the Roman Catholic priesthood, and the churches that emerged, so far as the principles of their structure were concerned, were reformed Roman Catholic churches rather than New Testament churches. Some of the Reformers saw the New Testament pattern but judged that it was impossible or inconvenient to return to it.

Lord Macaulay, in a discerning comment on the reasons why the Reformation did not continue to gain ground after its initial, sweeping victories, and why the reformed bodies that came into existence were ineffective in the further extension of the Church, says:

In truth, Protestantism, for aggressive purposes, had no organization at all. The Reformed Churches were mere national Churches. The Church of England existed for England alone. It was an institution as purely local as the Court of Common Pleas, and was utterly without any machinery for foreign operations. The Church of Scotland, in the same manner, existed for Scotland alone. The operations of the Catholic Church, on the other hand, took in the whole world. Nobody at Lambeth or at Edinburgh troubled himself about what was doing in Poland or Bavaria. But at Rome, Cracow and Munich were objects of as much interest as the purlieus of St. John Lateran. Our island, the head of the Protestant interest, did not send out a single missionary or a single instructor of youth to the scene of the great spiritual war. Not a single seminary was established here for the purpose of furnishing a supply of such persons to foreign countries. On the other hand, Germany, Hungary and Poland were filled with able and active Catholic emissaries of Spanish or Italian birth; and colleges for the instruction of the northern youth were founded at Rome. The spiritual force of Protestantism was a mere local militia, which might be useful in case of an invasion, but could not be sent abroad and could therefore make no conquests.[1]

The reformed Church had lost the unity which the Church of Rome's superb human organization provided, and it failed to regain the true spiritual unity of the New Testament Church. The unity of the Church of Rome was derived from its centralized, autocratic, totalitarian organization with the Pope at the head. The reformed Church cut off the head of this organization, together with some of its limbs, thus losing the power of common volition and action. The great artificial nerve centre that united the whole in one having been removed, the fragment of the organization that was retained was adequate only for local and sectional activities. So organized, the reformed Church was not equipped for conquest and able to do little more than defend itself.

Had not only the head but the whole body of the Roman Catholic organization been discarded and the full New Testament order re-established, the Church would have become again the Church militant, unified and united for conquest. The New Testament organization was especially designed for world conquest. It knew no frontiers, national or racial. It could know no sections, or divisions, or regional jurisdictions. None of the leaders of the New Testament Church were men of local or regional interests: they were missionaries: men with the world as their parish. The Church looked not to national or regional leaders but to world leaders whose ministry and vision were world-wide. As was the vision of its leaders, so was that of the Church — world-wide. The passion of every leader of the Church was to plant churches throughout the world. The ambition of every church that was founded was to send on the Gospel witness to the regions beyond. The Church was entirely apart from national loyalties. The whole Church was one Church through the one God, one Lord, one Spirit, one hope, one faith, one baptism, and it all existed for the one great purpose — the immediate evangelization of the whole world. The ministry of the Word was the responsibility of every

---

[1] *Essay on Ranke's History of the Popes.*

member. The Church was one great, undivided company led by Christ with every member mobilized for conquest.

The extent to which the Reformation failed to regain the spirit of the Church as it was after Pentecost is seen in the fact that, as Dr. Bready points out:

> ...neither the Reformation in the sixteenth, nor Puritanism in the seventeenth century, was possessed of any foreign missionary zeal... Luther and Zwingli, Calvin and Melanchton, Knox and Cranmer, Latimer and Ridley, were too absorbed by the problems at their door, to see far afield... A study of the lives of Milton and Bunyan, of Baxter and Fox, of Hampden and. Marvell will reveal no urge to foreign missionary effort.[1]

Had the Church of the Reformation returned to the New Testament order, its subsequent history would have been very different: it would have been one of united, aggressive action under the direction and in the power of the Spirit, and of glorious conquest. We do not mean to say that the Church would then have been entirely free from false teachers, or from those who would have sought to introduce division; the New Testament Church was not free from such. But, like the New Testament Church, it would have been sound at heart, the great body of believers united in purpose, faithful in witness and true in doctrine, and it would have triumphed over every work of the enemy.

The reformed Church feared to depend entirely upon God, upon the leadership of the Lord and the power of the Spirit. Each sectional group retained what to it seemed indispensable in the human organization of the Roman Church. And it is that human strength, that arm of flesh, that has been its undoing, causing weakness, disunity and failure in the centuries that have followed. It has hampered the Church's movement, restricted its vision, introduced divisions, dissension and bitterness, closed the mouths of multitudes of witnesses and made it weak and vulnerable in the face of its foes.

In Modern Times

There have been various attempts in modern times to return to the New Testament order and there are to be found not a few congregations that bear a humble and true witness, seeking to follow the revealed, spiritual pattern in all things. As is to be

---

[1] *This Freedom — Whence?*, pp. 253, 254.

expected, these movements have had to face the most persistent efforts of Satan to destroy them and bring them into disrepute. It is right that they should be attacked. The true New Testament Church is equipped with wisdom and power through the Spirit to resist every attack of Satan and to vanquish him in his strongholds, and the Lord allows it to be tested to prove it and permit it to witness to its victorious strength. If it does not possess that strength it is not truly New Testament and it is well that its weakness be revealed. It is the Church's triumphing over Satan's attacks through the power of the Spirit that glorifies Christ.

To those who desire to see a true and full return to the New Testament order and power, the reasons why these movements have failed to accomplish more than they have are of the greatest interest. They reveal the pitfalls that beset the true Church and the strategy that Satan uses to bring it into defeat.

The apparent causes have usually been the internal dissensions and divisions that developed. These, together with the opposition, and even persecution, that have had to be endured, tended to create a party spirit and exclusiveness. Such a reaction was natural from the human standpoint, but it led back to the very conditions against which these movements had set out to bear a witness. Often Satan has succeeded, in a comparatively short time, in creating an internal condition in these movements that has caused the Scriptural order which they advocated to become associated, in the minds of people generally, with the very opposite of what it really is. Such an outcome is a strategical triumph for Satan for it causes the true order to be misrepresented, misjudged and misunderstood.

The apparent causes of weakness in these movements, however, were not the real causes: they were only symptoms. The reasons for spiritual defeat of any kind are always fundamentally the same. They are deep-seated in the human heart. There is failure in the basic principle of the believer's and Church's life and service — the manifestation of God's love as required in 1 Cor. 13. There is failure to manifest the 'perfect man' — Christ — through a life lived in the power of the Holy Spirit. There is a walking in the flesh instead of in the Spirit. There is the overlooking, or setting aside, of spiritual principles, with the result that unspiritual principles are put into operation, giving the control to the heart and mind of man and preventing Christ from manifesting the fulness of His love, wisdom and victorious power.

These are the fundamental causes of failure in the witness of the Church from its first days. Purity of doctrine and correctness of form do not give exemption from them because the fleshly heart of man is always present and can be subjected only by the power of the Spirit; by the daily application of the Cross; by the continual operation of the 'two-edged sword' separating the soulish from the spiritual. Scriptural doctrine and Church order are essential, but they are only vehicles for the manifestation of the Spirit of God and only avail as the life of the Spirit flows through them. In the hands of the flesh they become a travesty.

In some of these movements, the Holy Spirit's work of distributing the gifts of the Spirit to all the members of the Body was recognized, but He was not given His place fully as the power imparting spiritual life and giving victory over the flesh to the believer. There has often been a fear and avoidance of anything beyond the most elementary teaching regarding His work and power. Reacting against false and extravagant teaching, some have taught that, since His work is to glorify Christ, we should be occupied with Christ and not with Him. Thus Satan has succeeded in introducing the opposite extreme. The resulting lack of knowledge of the believer's walk in the Spirit, and of the need for the daily crucifying of the flesh that such a walk might be possible, has left a gap in the spiritual armour that could not fail to have serious consequences. It has prevented a full understanding of the need for the application of the Cross in the believer's life and of the triumph that is possible in his personal experience through the victorious life of Christ within.

Moreover, the Holy Spirit was not given His full place as the power, teacher, and guide of the Church. The result was that — since the Holy Spirit is Christ's Spirit in the Church — Christ, the Head of the Church, Who is present in the gathering of the Church, was not given His full place. His will was not sought in continued prayer by the Church until it was made known by the Holy Spirit. To the extent that this was lacking, Christ could not build His Church. The work of building, therefore, was done, partly at least, by man, and so we find persisting the same fundamental cause of weakness that brings spiritual powerlessness to all communions.

So often there has been failure at some vital point to adopt the true spiritual structure for the Church. Nearly always intermediaries of some kind are placed between Christ and the congregation, the spiritual authority and responsibility being placed to some extent at least in the hands of a pastor or a group of Elders, depriving the Lord and the congregation of their true relationship to each other. There is failure to understand and give full place to the theocratic government of Christ in the gathering of His people.[1]

On the mission field their work has not, in general, spread as would be expected in the light of the results obtained from the New Testament order in Early Church times. This has been due, not only to the fundamental causes of weakness already mentioned, but also the failure, in many cases, to put their principles of church organization into actual practice. Missionaries have feared to leave the work in the hands of national Elders and have remained indefinitely with the congregations they founded, virtually acting as their pastors during many years. The cause of this attitude is, undoubtedly, the lack of a full appreciation of the Holy Spirit's work in the Church and of His power to manifest Christ's resurrection life and the gifts of the Spirit in the converts and to give them guidance and wisdom. Another evident cause of weakness is the lack of the full ministry of the Evangelist, in the New Testament sense, as well as of God-appointed leadership for the coordination of the missionary ministry such as is found in the New Testment missionary company. A leaderless group of missionaries is not in accordance with the New Testament pattern.

An interesting outcome of the great revival in Wales at the beginning of the present century was the establishment of many congregations that instinctively adopted the New Testament form. In the established churches at the time it was considered presumption to claim assurance of salvation. Those who were converted in the revival had unshakable assurance of salvation and, also, they were filled with the Spirit and the gifts of the Spirit for public testimony were manifested through them. Not being permitted to exercise their gifts in the existing churches, they built halls where they could meet and have freedom to pray, preach and testify. They did not intend to withdraw from their churches, but soon found that they were no longer welcome in them, so they formed themselves into congregations, each presided over by several Elders. A notable feature is the lack of any

---

[1] See p. 141.

sectarian spirit. They welcome fellowship with all who are truly the Lord's people, and accept the ministry of any one from any church so long as he is true in doctrine.

Some of these congregations have finally associated themselves with existing groups of churches, adopting the order practised by these and settling down to a more or less formal church existence. But there are still a number of independent congregations with a vigorous spiritual life. They seek to give the Holy Spirit His place in both the individual believer and the church. But there is weakness through failure to seek the direction of the Head of the Church in all matters through prayer and on account of the lack of Evangelists in the New Testament sense.

During the last twenty years, owing to the increased rationalistic and materialistic tendencies in the Denominations, many hundreds of congregations have severed their connections with these bodies and declared themselves independent. In the majority of cases, the objective has been freedom from unscriptural organizational restraint and doctrinal error. There has not been any marked concern regarding a return to the New Testament order in organization, except in a few cases.

Viewing what has taken place during these two decades among the increasing number of independent churches, the general trend is already clear. Many of them are grouping themselves together again into associations, seeking unity and strength. Some of these groups at first adopt a loose form of organization in an endeavour to preserve the independence of the individual congregation but, little by little, more organization is added, the authority of conventions and councils is increased, and new Denominations come into existence which, inevitably, through time, will develop along the same lines as the older organizations, with the same results. Thus history continues to repeat itself for, wherever man takes a work of the Spirit and adds human organization to secure its life, he plants the seed that will grow and spread until it chokes the true life of the Spirit.

A more decided seeking of the way back to the full New Testament order is evident today among missionaries especially and among individuals and small groups in Christian lands. It is sufficiently widespread and numerous to be recognized as a definite movement of the Spirit. It is a deeply spiritual movement, calling to complete personal consecration as well as to a return to the God given pattern for the Church and laying stress upon the necessity for giving Christ His place of leadership in the Church and for ministering in the true power of the Spirit. It has been slow of growth but increases steadily and God's full purpose concerning it is not yet revealed, but it is evident that it is a response to the never-ceasing call of the Spirit of the Lord to return to the way of obedience and power. But even in this movement signs of danger are not lacking as individuals or groups tend to place an undue emphasis upon some form or doctrine, thus disturbing the balance of the true spiritual order.

Down through the centuries of increasing darkness, from the time when the light of the Early Church began to wane until the present day, God has never been without witnesses to the true walk in the Spirit and to the New Testament order of the Church. There has always been a remnant, a company of faithful men and women — the true witnessing Church — that has refused to bow the knee to that which was unspiritual and false. Montanists, Priscillianists, Paulicians, Cathars, Bogomils, Waldenses, Albigenses, Hussites, some Baptists, Mennonites, Covenanters, Stundists, Brethren, Independents, to mention only a number of the larger and better known groups, appear as light bearers amidst the darkness. Not all of these rid themselves entirely of the influences of their times. Some were inclined to overstress some particular phase of truth. The purest testimonies were sometimes borne by smaller groups that have remained nameless. But in all there was a sincere desire to return to the life-giving doctrines of Scripture and the spiritual power of God's order, which they did in great part, bearing a witness which God blessed.

As each one of these groups in turn tended through time to lose its first love and purity, to live in the glory of its past and not in the power of the Spirit, to add organization and to depend upon dead formulas instead of on the living Word, other testimonies were raised up to carry on the witness. And this the Spirit will continue to do so long as the Church remains on Earth. For that reason, our faithfulness must ever be to the true Church and not to any Denomination or group.

The 'Great Whore

Never has the New Testament way become popular, and it never will. Always its testimony has been sealed with the blood of the martyrs. In every age many thousands have had to pay for their faithfulness with their lives.

The history of the Church makes one thing absolutely clear: the unity, doctrinal soundness, Scriptural order and power of the Church can be preserved only by the power of the Spirit. Equally evident is the fact that the Holy Spirit can do this only as there is absolute surrender to the Lord and obedience to His Word. The introduction of man's wisdom and power at any point inevitably brings loss of spiritual power, authority and communion and leads to division, stagnation and defeat until an effective witness ceases.

The Apostle John, who saw the tendencies already manifested in the seven churches of Asia — tendencies that, although seemingly insignificant then, revealed the presence of principles completely alien to the spirit of the true Church — was given the vision of their future development and of the monstrous thing they would produce, which he described as "The Great Whore that sitteth upon many waters" (Rev. 17:1). It is thus that the Spirit describes the Church that is adulterated with the ways and thoughts of man; that, because of lack of faith and consecration, has failed to rely entirely upon the spiritual equipment which God has provided, but has created a system of its own, adding whatever man's wisdom judged to be necessary.

The 'Great Whore' will be not only the Church of Rome, but the whole humanly organized Church. It is the unfaithful helpmeet, trafficking with the things of the flesh: the Church that has put the hand of flesh upon the work of the Spirit, substituting the headship of the mind of man for the headship of Christ, the gifts of man for the gifts of the Spirit, a man-made organization for the spiritual order given by the Lord, offering sacrifices of man's works.

Let us recognize the fact that it is not in the final development of this evil thing that the greatest danger lies to the believer, but in its first subtle and apparently innocent beginnings. It starts as a very little thing, appearing to be harmless and helpful, but it spreads as a leprosy. It is an evil that, once it is permitted to enter, tends ever to increase. Its introduction produces weakness that makes necessary the constant adding of more organization and newer methods.

When a congregation sets out upon the quest for power in the realm of the natural — in organization, ritual, forms of service,

18

oratory, psychology, music, architecture, art, learning, culture, emotionalism, sentimentalism — it follows a will-of-the-wisp that will lure it on deeper and deeper into the death-dealing bog of human works. The end is inevitable and ever the same. It leads to that which is the opposite of what God purposed: to a work of man instead of a work of God, based upon man's wisdom instead of God's wisdom, responding to the heart of man and not to the heart of God, equipped with the energy of man instead of the power of the Holy Spirit, adulterated and corrupt; a negation instead of a testimony, the measure of the stature of the fulness of man instead of "the measure of the stature of the fulness of Christ": the "Great Whore which did corrupt the earth with her fornication" (Rev. 19:2) instead of the "glorious bride, without spot or wrinkle or any other defect, but to be holy and unblemished" (Eph. 5:27. Weymouth).

Dean Alford, in his commentary on Matt. 12:43-45, after applying the passage to "the Jewish Church", says:

Strikingly parallel with this runs the history of the Christian Church. Not long after the Apostolic times, the golden calves of idolatry were set up by the Church of Rome. What the effect of the captivity was to the Jews, that of the Reformation has been to Christendom. The first evil spirit has been cast out. But by the growth of hypocrisy, secularity, and rationalism, the house has become empty, swept, and garnished: swept and garnished by the decencies of civilization and discoveries of secular knowledge, but empty of living and earnest faith. And he must read prophecy but ill, who does not see under all these seeming improvements the preparation for the final development of the man of sin, the great repossession, when idolatry and the seven (more wicked spirits) shall bring the outward frame of so-called Christendom to a fearful end.

We do not expect that there will be a general return on the part of the organized Church to the true spiritual pattern and unity of the New Testament Church. God's Word gives us no ground to expect that there will be such a return. But Christ's plan and purpose for His true Church has never been altered and His promises to it have not been withdrawn. He will meet with it as its Head wherever it gathers truly in His Name, and, as it permits Him, He will build it, manifesting Himself in the fulness of His life and power through the gifts of His Spirit in all the members. To the extent that any congregation, be it composed of but two or three, will walk in the Spirit in full obedience to His Word, fleeing everything that is of man's method and wisdom, He will fulfil to the letter His declared purpose, in it and through it, and the gates of hell shall not prevail against it.

PART III

NEW TESTAMENT CHURCH ORDER

"And the Lord said unto me, son of man, mark well (marg. — set thine heart) and behold with thine eyes and hear with thine ears all that I say unto thee concerning all the ordinances of the house of the Lord, and all the laws thereof; and mark well the entering in of the house, and every going forth of the sanctuary."

Ezek. 44:5.

FAITH AND DOUBT.

Doubt said, 'That man failed me
Fell in time of test.
One so weak and faithless never can
  Be led into God's best.'

Faith said, 'God is able'.
Doubt said, 'Yes, of course;
But this case much harder is than most
  And quite beyond recourse.'

Faith said, 'This recorded,
All is possible
(When in truth it is the will of God)
  To faith unshakable.'

Doubt said, 'God is able,
That unquestioned be,
But full many a reason why this thing
  He cannot do I see.'

Faith said, 'God hath spoken
And He surely will
Vanquish all impossibilities
  And every word fulfil.'

Doubt said, 'Think a moment,
If we fail, why! then
Will the cause of God be brought to shame
  Before the eyes of men.'

Love said; 'Peter failed me
Even at the Cross,
But in loving faith I prayed for him
  Lest he should suffer loss'.

Faith said; 'As love joined me.
Sorrow's darkest days
Changed to triumph, and we Peter saw
  A pattern in faith's ways.'

Love said, 'There is one power
O'er all other might;
Such God's Throne, the power of love-born faith
  Is Victor o'er the night.'

RADIATING WITNESS OF
THE CONGREGATION
THROUGH THE GIFTS
OF THE SPIRIT

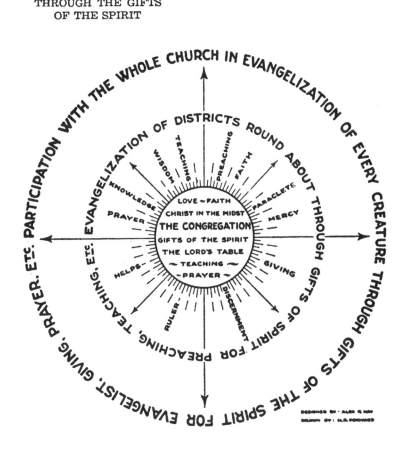

CHAPTER XIX

THE CONGREGATION

A CONGREGATION, or a local gathering of the Church, is a company of believers in Christ met together with Him in His Name. As we have seen, two or three is a sufficient number to constitute a gathering of the Church.

The principles laid down by our Lord regarding the gathering of believers (the local church) have been considered in chapter XII and we would refer the reader back to that chapter for the ground-work for this chapter.

A congregation is a company of 'priests unto God':

> Come to Him the living stone... And be yourselves like living stones that are being built up into a spiritual house, to become a holy priesthood to offer spiritual sacrifices acceptable to God through Jesus Christ. For it is contained in Scripture, 'See, I am placing on Mount Zion a Cornerstone, chosen, and held in honour...' To you believers, therefore, that honour belongs; ...you are a chosen race, a priesthood of kingly lineage, a holy nation, a people belonging specially to God that you may make known the perfections of Him who called you out of darkness into His marvellous light. (1 Pet. 2:4-9, Weymouth.)
> To Him who loves us and has freed us from our sins with His own blood, and has formed us into a Kingdom, to be priests to God, His Father... (Rev. 1:6, Weymouth.)

Peter pictures the Church as a building constructed of living stones, all like unto the Living Stone, or Chief Cornerstone, which is Christ, and as a company of priests of royal lineage, with Christ as the great King High Priest. A congregation is a local gathering of these 'priests unto God', with Christ, the High Priest, present in the midst.

In the Tabernacle, the priesthood of believers was foreshadowed. The priests assisted the High Priest: they did not have High Priestly authority, being just assistants. Their main duties were:

1. They could come nigh the vessels of the sanctuary and the altar.

2. (a) In the 'holy place': to clean, trim and light the lamps; to burn incense on the golden altar; to put shewbread on the table. Ex. 27:21; 30:7; Lev. 24:5-8.

(b) In the Court: to see that the fire on the altar never went out; to remove the ashes from the altar; to offer the sacrifices morning and evening; to blow the silver trumpets and the jubilee horn.

3. They inspected persons declared to be unclean and declared them clean or unclean.

4. They taught the law.

5. They acted as judges. Deut. 17:8; 19:17; 21:5.

It is not difficult to see in the above the foreshadowing of the ministry of the believer in Christ as a "priest unto God" under Christ, the eternal High Priest. In the study of the Tabernacle priesthood there are rich lessons to be learned regarding the priesthood of believers, its privileges, limitations, duties, temptations and dangers.

In the Synagogue also there was much that foreshadowed the more glorious, spiritual order that was to be in the Church when the Lord Himself was present. There were several Elders, or Pastors (not priests) in each synagogue for the general oversight of the congregation and the ordering of the services, and other officers — ministers (Deacons) — for special purposes such as the distributing of alms and the teaching of children. The presence of a priest was not required. No officials were appointed for preaching, the reading of the Scriptures or prayer. At the time of our Lord these acts of worship and spiritual service were freely performed in turn by any member of the Synagogue. Visitors from other synagogues also were at liberty to read and expound the sacred books. It was this liberty that gave our Lord and the Early Church Evangelists the opportunity to preach the Gospel so freely in the synagogues. For the holding of a service there had to be at least ten present. The rulers of the synagogues were chosen by the congregations they served, but were examined by delegates from the Great Sanhedrin.

In the local gathering of the Church, we have a company of 'two or more', all of whom are 'priests unto God', who minister freely through the different gifts of the Holy Spirit distributed to all. The fundamental difference between the synagogue and the local church is that in the church, as a result of the work accomplished on the Cross, Christ is present in the midst and His Spirit dwells in each member, manifesting Himself through each one by the gifts of the Spirit.

The local church has Elders and Deacons appointed by God and equipped by the Holy Spirit. The Deacons (servants) attend to the funds of the congregation and whatever other material ministry may be necessary. The Elders form a group with authority to ensure the orderly functioning of the gathering of 'priests unto God' each one of whom has authority and gifts of the Spirit to minister before God.

The ministry of these Elders is to shepherd and oversee. As Elders they are under-shepherds and under-bishops of the great 'Shepherd and Bishop of our souls', not priests under the great High Priest — that is the privilege of all believers. They are, of course, priests, but only in the sense that all are priests. They have no additional priestly privileges beyond those possessed by all believers. In the synagogue the Elders did not act as priests.

A gathering of believers met in Christ's name is a church whether there have been Elders appointed or not. The term 'church' simply means an assembly and does not necessarily imply the existence of organization. In the assembly, whether it be composed of only two or of many, Christ, the great High Priest, Shepherd and Bishop, is present in the midst, and as they seek Him in prayer and through the Word He gives guidance, wisdom, power and authority. The importance of Christ's presence in the gathering is dealt with elsewhere.[1]

The congregation our Lord spoke of was composed of 'two or three', without Elders or Deacons, yet its equipment, authority and responsibility were complete. It is evident, therefore, that all these belong to the congregation, not to a pastor or group of Elders (Matt. 18:15-20.)[1]

Many of the groups of believers gathered together by Paul and his fellow-workers continued for a time to meet together and carry on ministry without Elders and without the presence of an Evangelist. The members of these congregations exercised freely the gifts of the Spirit that are manifested immediately on conversion — preaching, faith, the love gifts, etc. The preachers would

---

[1] See chapter XII.

preside at the gatherings. They did not do so in any sense as Elders but simply as preachers leading a meeting.

The New Testament Evangelists exercised a direct responsibility towards new congregations even when not present, so that the fact that these churches did not yet have Elders did not mean that there was no one with authority to intervene if necessary and render whatever aid might be required at any time.

A very small congregation may not require Elders but the lack of properly constituted local authority in a larger group would be a source of weakness and Elders and Deacons should be appointed as soon as it becomes clear who the Lord has chosen for these ministries.

There can be no such thing as branch churches. If a number of believers find it more convenient to meet together in their own district instead of with a, perhaps, larger gathering at a distance, they may do so with the full status of a gathering of the Church. If there is sufficient justification for them meeting apart there is no reason why they should not do so.

A gathering of the Church has definite responsibilities whether it has Elders or not. It should exercise discipline. It is the duty of all believers to separate themselves from those who continue in sin or teach wrong doctrine. Because there are no Elders, it does not follow that a congregation must suffer the presence of some one who is in sin, or listen to the teaching of error.

A congregation is responsible to judge all who come to it claiming to be Evangelists or Teachers and to reject any who are not sound in their teaching. If an Evangelist or Teacher who has been a true servant of the Lord depart from the way of obedience and sound doctrine, he will not be received by a spiritual congregation. Paul speaks of the false apostles (missionaries) who were seeking to introduce error into the churches, and the Lord commends the church in Ephesus for rejecting them (2 Cor. 11:13; Rev. 2:2; Gal. 1:8. Cf. 1 Jn. 4:1).

The final responsibility for all the testimony falls upon the whole congregation and is shared equally by every member, man and woman, young and old. The ministry of the Word through the gifts of the Spirit is the responsibility of every member. In the appointment of Elders and Deacons, the congregation must know God's will as to who are chosen of Him. In a case of discipline it is the congregation that must judge the matter and act. For the ministry of prayer, the whole congregation is responsible. It must find out God's will through prayer and take its stand in the prayer of faith for the success of the testimony and the defeat of Satan's work.

If the Elders of a congregation fall into sin, act arbitrarily, or fail in their duty, it is not helpless. Any member may write to the Evangelists acquainting them with the facts. John corresponded with the 'elect lady' regarding such a matter. The Evangelists are warned, however, not to judge an Elder on the testimony of one person (1 Tim. 5:19). If a congregation as a whole fails in its duty, any spiritual member may appeal the matter to the Evangelists. Spiritual members of churches wrote to Paul and other Evangelists about divisions, sin and false doctrine in their congregations and their appeals were responded to immediately.

While the local congregation has inalienable privileges and responsibilities, it possesses these only because it is part of the Church as a whole. It cannot in any sense stand apart from the whole Church. If it does so, it introduces division. Its individual existence is due entirely to the limitations imposed by distance. It is simply the gathering of those members of the Church who happen to live near enough to each other to be able to meet together.

By the Church, of course, we do not refer to any organized group of churches, but to the whole true Body of Christ, the one and only Church. The believer's membership is in that Church (1 Cor. 12:13). He meets with the local congregation because he is a member of the Body of Christ. Scripture does not speak of members of a local church. It speaks only of 'members of His Body' and 'members one of another'. It is incorrect to regard a believer's membership as being in a local congregation. It is in the Church, and as a member of the Church he meets with the local gathering of members of the Church. At the same time, his participation in the fellowship and ministry of the Church is partly through the local gathering with which he meets, and he has definite responsibilities towards that gathering. The local congregation has its particular form of spiritual organization provided by the Lord so that its local testimony and witness may be effectively coordinated and guarded, and all who meet together have a definite responsibility towards it. Each one must be faithful in the ministry to which God has called, in the place where God has put him.

Letters of recommendation are spoken of in the New Testament. When a believer travelled to regions where he was unknown he sometimes carried such a letter from those who knew him. These letters were considered as helpful in some circumstances but were never regarded as essential. But there was no such thing as a letter transferrring the membership of a believer from one local church to another. A member of the Body of Christ is a member of the whole Body. He has the right to meet with the members of the Body anywhere. His membership cannot be transferred from one part of the Body to another because it is not in a part of the Body but in the whole Body.

The question arises as to whether a believer should continue to meet with a gathering which is not a true meeting of the Church, or in which he cannot exercise fully the ministry to which he is called of God and the gifts of the Spirit with which he is provided. A true church will be composed of born-again believers in Christ. Unsaved people are not members of the Church and a gathering of such people, no matter by what name they may call themselves, is not a church. A believer has no Scriptural right to be in any other gathering than a true church. Also, God has placed each one in the Church for ministry, and if that ministry is hindered by unscriptural order in a congregation, it is very probable that the believer is not where God intends him to be.

It will be understood that it is of the greatest importance that every congregation fully understand the responsibilities that fall upon it, and that every member realise his or her personal responsibility as a 'living stone' like unto the Living Stone, fitted into a living 'habitation of God through the Spirit'. It is the Evangelist's duty to make sure, through the prayer of faith and the teaching of the "whole counsel of God", that all have this knowledge.

In the chapter on "Cooperation between Congregations" there is a further discussion of the principles governing the local gathering of the Church.

CHAPTER XX

ELDERS AND CONGREGATION

THE Elder's place in the structure of the Church and the ministry to which he is called have already been considered. We would
take up here his relationship to the congregation in which he
ministers. As we have seen, the tendency from the beginning has
been that the gift of presiding should swallow up all the other
gifts and with them the priestly privileges that belong to all
believers. Neander goes to the root of the matter:

> The monarchical form of government was in no ways suited to
> the Christian community of spirit. The preeminence of a single
> individual at the head of the whole was too likely to operate as a
> check on the free development of the life of the Church and the
> free action of the different organs, in whom it was necessary to
> keep alive a consciousness of mutual independence. The individual
> on whom everything would in such a constitution be made to
> depend, might acquire too great an importance for the rest, and,
> consequently, become the centre around which all would gather,
> in such a manner as to obscure the sense of their common relation
> to that One Who ought to be the centre of all.[1]

This states clearly one of the greatest dangers that face the
Church: the possibility of a man assuming a place that belongs to
Christ and a function that is the responsibility of the Holy Spirit.
It is the danger of Nicolaitanism — 'priestly assumption', as
Scofield terms it — which made its first appearance in the church
in Pergamos.

Dr. Chapell, late Dean of Dr. A. J. Gordon's Missionary Training School, writes with reference to this subject:

> We are very apt to copy from our past and from our surround-
> ings, thinking that what is customary is right. But our past and
> our present are sadly shadowed by the centuries of the apostasy.

---

[1] Neander's Church History, pp. 253, 254.

in which the god of this age has so largely ruled. In these centuries the clergy have been elevated and the laity depressed; the Bible has been forbidden, and the cup of the communion withheld; and thus the idea has largely prevailed that the mass of the membership have nothing to do except to passively receive salvation. Although Protestants may have abjured most of these things theoretically, yet the practical influence of them remains, so that nine-tenths of the membership of many churches have no proper idea of their privileges and duties as members of the Body of Christ. A resolute return, therefore, to the Scriptural ideal of the Church is necessary. Every member should be expected to be fully consecrated, filled with the Holy Ghost, and constantly bearing witness to the wonderful privileges and powers of spiritual life in Christ. Any member not decidedly active and aggressive in Christian work and testimony, should be made to feel decidedly out of place and in need of immediate repentance. If all the gifts of the Church are to be utilized, surely the gifts of every member of the Church must be brought into service.[1]

Andrew Murray says:

When the Reformation came, there was a great change both in life and doctrine. And yet how far the Reformation was from being a return to Pentecost... throughout the Church as a whole, how far the life was from being after the New Testament model.[2]

A comment by Dr. A. T. Pierson is:

We unconsciously learn to tolerate evils which, if suddenly confronted in a purer society, would shock and overwhelm us. If from a primitive apostolic church life a man like Stephen had been, in a moment, transported into the modern corrupted church atmosphere, he would have been stifled.[3]

As early as the beginning of the third century Tertullian found it necessary to say, "Custom without truth is error grown old". There is not a little in our modern Church order and practice that has no Scriptural warrant. Yet, because it has long been the custom, it is accepted without question as an essential part of the divine order. Customary procedure, Denominational Manuals and Disciplines, rites, ceremonies, methods and forms of organization, come to have a more real authority than the Word of God. The authority credited to these is practical; the authority credited to God's Word is relative and theoretic.

The Scriptural pattern for the Church places equal responsibility for witness upon all and gives a ministry, and corresponding gifts of the Spirit, to every member. The natural tendency has

---

[1] Chapell: *Biblical and Practical Theology*, pp. 219, 220.
[2] Murray: *Back to Pentecost*, p. 62.
[3] *Making of a Sermon*, p. 50.

always been to turn to man's own talents for the doing of the work instead of depending upon the gifts of the Spirit. The reasons for this are:

1. To give liberty to the Spirit to work, the believer must be walking in full obedience. The life of Christ is manifested only as the flesh is brought into death. The cost of this is not agreeable to the natural heart, and the temptation is to avoid it and to seek an easier and more agreeable way.

2. To rely upon the gifts of the Spirit requires faith — faith in God; in the unseen: in a power that seems intangible and appears impractical to the natural mind. It is much easier to profess faith in the power of the Spirit theoretically, but to proceed with the doing of the work on the natural plane, using man's natural abilities.

Nicolaitanism — the spiritual predominance of a priestly or ministerial order — was the direct outcome of this. The men who appeared to possess the greatest natural aptitude became prominent and dependence was placed upon them instead of upon the Lord and upon the Spirit. To require that these men be specially trained and to consider that the 'laity', lacking this training, were not capable of engaging in spiritual ministry, was only a step farther.

Francis Wayland, speaking on this subject, is reported as follows:

> He declared that a refusal to employ every labourer was equivalent to abandoning the effort to evangelize the world. He objected to giving to education a place not authorized by Jesus Christ, thus establishing a ministerial caste. He declared that if it were true that a Baptist is not to preach the Gospel without years of heathen learning, or if he does that he is a backwoodsman of whom everyone ought to be ashamed, we are dead and plucked up by the roots.[1]

Warnings such as that of Wayland have not prevented the Church from moving steadily away from the New Testament order.

The earliest confessions of faith of the Baptists — those of 1643 and 1689 — recognise the plurality of Elders. A comparatively small section of the Baptists still hold that a plurality of Elders, or Pastors, is necessary in every congregation.[2] Baptist congregations

---

[1] Gordon: *A. J. Gordon, A Biography*, p. 266
[2] *Enc. Brit.*

were organized in this manner in Scotland, the north of Ireland and the north of England. In their original form, those Baptist churches followed the New Testament order to a remarkable extent.

Harvey,[1] presenting the position generally taken by the Baptists today, states that now the plurality of Elders is generally considered as something peculiar to the Apostolic age, necessitated by the absence of men specially prepared for the pastoral office, and by the circumstances of that period of persecution when believers met in small groups and their Elders were often imprisoned. The reduction of the number of Pastors to one in each congregation is regarded, he says, not only as legitimate, but as better suited to the circumstances of our present times.

There is, of course, no Scriptural ground for such a position. Surely the fact that the Scriptural order proved its strength when the Church was weak numerically and in every other respect, except spiritually, and during two centuries of persecution, should be accepted as evidence of its effectiveness and of God's wisdom in ordaining it for His Church. What authority have we for substituting a class of specially trained men for those chosen by God and empowered by the Holy Spirit and where do we derive the wisdom which enables us to judge our order preferable to God's order in this modern age?

There can be no question, from the human standpoint, as to the reasonableness of the arguments adduced in favour of departure from the Scriptural order. The reduction of the number of Elders to one in each church conforms to modern Denominational practice. It is the most practical form of human government. It facilitates Denominational organization. It is necessary and logical where a ministerial order exists. It is convenient for the believer or nominal member who wishes to limit his spiritual activity to worship and to put the responsibility for ministry upon a Pastor. But do these reasons justify the setting aside of the revealed pattern which divine wisdom devised?

We have referred to the strength of the Scriptural order in the early centuries of the Church, but its effectiveness is just as evident today. A report on the condition of the evangelical churches in Spain after several years of severe persecution under the Franco regime, states:

---

[1] Harvey: *The Church*, chapter 7.

One striking fact emerges from the reports so far to hand. It seems clear that progress has been most marked in the churches that have sought to develop a lay ministry. Those churches that had learned to depend entirely on one man for all the work of the Church have suffered grievously when the Pastor has been torn violently from their midst; some of them have scarcely recovered.[1]

Weakness of the Modern Pastorate

While affirming the fact that the modern idea of the pastorate differs from the order practised in the New Testament Church, we do not call in question the call or consecration of the faithful, self-sacrificing Pastor whose motive is neither gain nor fame but only the glory of his Lord. All honour to the men who bear aloft the torch of the true Gospel witness amidst the present darkness. There are, of course, all types of Pastors in the churches today. There is the modernist (or, more correctly, the modern Rationalist) denying the fundamental doctrines of the faith; the unconverted man, incapable of bearing spiritual fruit; the ambitious man, eager for personal success; the man who is not filled with the Spirit, but depends upon human power and wisdom. But there are also those who are men of God, seeking earnestly to serve Him and truly called by Him to preach or teach. If the dependence of some is upon human methods and power, their teaching lacking in spiritual depth, and their witness restricted within conventional limits, the fault lies rather with the systems of which they are the products than with themselves. They work as they were trained to work and teach that which they were taught, endeavouring to be faithful to their Denominations and to God. But there are some who rise above the limitations of their connections and, obeying the impulse of God's Spirit, permit Him to manifest freely through them the gifts He has granted to them. We know Pastors in the Homelands who are sacrificing as much and enduring joyfully as great hardship as the pioneer missionary. They are true servants of the Lord, men with whom it is a privilege to fellowship.

Such men are called to ministry and there can be no thought of curtailing their ministry. The only question there can be is as to the spiritual order of the ministry. To conform our ministry to the divine order revealed in Scripture is, of course, our duty, and it is in doing so that the richest fruit will be reaped.

---

[1] Article on *Prospects in Spain*, in *World Dominion*, Nov.-Dec., 1945.

No one realizes more keenly than the Godly Pastor the unsatisfactory conditions that exist today, the powerlessness of the Church as a whole and the need for a fresh vision that the Holy Spirit's power may be released anew in its glorious fulness.

These are days when, in the words of Dr. Max I. Reich, "every green thing is eaten up by orthodoxy, rationalism and philosophy"; when, even in the evangelical witness, emotionalism, sentimentalism and the 'psychology of the pulpit' pass for the power of the Holy Spirit; when humility is discounted, man's abilities replace the Spirit's gifts, the honour is given to the herald instead of to his Lord and the egotism of man's heart intrudes into the most sacred things.

We must go back to the Cross. There we must be consecrated anew, our hearts cleansed and lit with the fire of that Offering, filled with that all-sacrificing love; our spirits renewed with the quickening power of the resurrected Life and established in that triumph which has seated us with Him in the ·heavenlies 'far above all principality and power and might and dominion'.

And we must go back to the way of the Spirit, to the simplicity of that order which strips man of all that in which he would confide or boast and permits the Lord to build His Church and to manifest His power by the Spirit.

The question that arises is, do we really accept God's Word as our only rule of faith and practice or do we permit the natural rationalism of the mind to cut out the parts that it considers impracticable or inadvisable? The Church's power is spiritual and the more we rule out of the spiritual basis the more power is lost. Of course there also is the danger of a spurious spirituality that is mere emotionalism, or that is definitely Satanic, but the greatest cause of the Church's loss of power through the ages has been the unwillingness of man's mind to believe in the actual power of the Holy Spirit.

Another difficulty in following the New Testament way comes from the heart. There may be lack of humility. The cost of taking the way our Lord trod, the way the Apostles and Paul and his companions followed, may seem too great. If the heart hankers after position, the praise of men, comfort or gain, then that way will be an offence to us. "Blessed is he", said our Lord, "whosoever shall not be offended in me." But there are not a few who are not deterred by any of these things and are quite prepared

19

for any sacrifice that the glory of the Lord may fill His Church. Considering the Godly Pastors of today — the men who are truly called of God — in the light of New Testament Church order, what should be their true place and ministry? Some of them quite evidently have the gifts of the New Testament Elder or Pastor. Others, probably, are called rather to the ministry of teaching. But there is no doubt that not a few are called to the work of the New Testament Evangelist, or church-planter, whose ministry should be the establishing of congregation after congregation, leaving each one a complete and fully functioning unit in which all the necessary ministries and gifts are manifested.[1] How much greater would be the scope and productiveness of such a ministry, and how much more satisfying to the hearts of those whose call it really is!

These church-planters would not necessarily need to go beyond the frontiers of their own lands to have ample scope for the exercise of their ministry. The spiritual need in the so-called Christian lands is appalling. There are still many millions of unsaved in these lands and room for as many truly New Testament congregations as there would be groups of converts to form them. America, for instance, with its 70,000,000 churchless, is actually one of the greatest mission fields. This church-planting ministry has been practically lost to the Church in what are termed Christian lands. Those whom God has called and the Holy Spirit gifted for the extension of the Church are side-tracked in the modern pastorate with incalculable loss to the Church. It is largely for this reason that there are still so many millions of heathen in every so-called Christian land. The situation can be met only by a return of this basic ministry.

Let us seek to discern, in the light of the New Testament order, what are the weaknesses of our modern system. To take some typical examples will be, perhaps, most helpful.

Here is an apparently highly successful Pastor. His message is sound, his teaching is strong, and his preaching is used to the salvation of souls. It is quite evident that he has gifts of the Spirit, that he is exercising them and that the power of the Holy Spirit is manifested through him. A large congregation gathers week after week to worship and to be instructed. He is their spiritual father, their Spirit-taught teacher. In the congregation are hun-

---

[1] See pp. 149-50, 213, 262-3.

dreds of intelligent, sincere Christian men and women. Some are Sunday School teachers and it is hoped that young people will volunteer for the foreign mission field. But the great majority confine their spiritual activity to worship and, perhaps, a little personal witness. They have little or no knowledge regarding the gifts of the Spirit. They feel no personal responsibility to take part in the ministry of the Word in the congregation, and if they did feel such an urge there would be no opportunity to take part. Spiritually they are dependent upon their Pastor. They look to him for food, leadership and for the bringing of the unsaved to Christ. The situation is like that in a certain team of horses, of which the driver said, "Yes, they're all willin'. The leader is willin' to work and the others are willin' to let him'."

This Pastor is called away and the great congregation is left practically helpless, and, unless another equally capable leader takes charge, it is likely to dwindle and disintegrate. We know churches that once were large and flourishing and decidedly orthodox and evangelical that, a number of years later, after a succession of Pastors, are now content to tolerate the preaching of men whose theology is more than doubtful. These congregations are like helpless children.[1] They never grow up to manhood — 'to the measure of the stature of the fulness of Christ'.

Why had these congregations not sufficient spiritual vitality and knowledge to continue the witness for which they once seemed to stand? The reason is that they had never really taken part in that witness. It had been carried on for them by one man. They had given him moral support and enjoyed his ministry. Now they give that support to another. True, a few with more evidence of possessing life in themselves had withdrawn, unable to endure unsound doctrine, but the great majority remained, including many converts of the Godly Pastor's ministry.

But why, after sound teaching so ably given, were they not strong enough and instructed enough to discern, refute and refuse the subtle, false doctrine so pleasingly presented? The answer is that the knowledge of the majority was never much more than head knowledge. For most of them it was really the Pastor's knowledge, not their own. It had little or no opportunity to translate itself into experience and to become truly a part of themselves. It was still only a theory; a right one, of course, but nothing more. It was all the fruit of another man's study and

[1] See comment on Eph. 4:14, ch. 13.

experience. The church member felt that he was untrained and incapable of discovering for himself such deep spiritual truths in the Word. He got no experience of seeking in the Word, through the Holy Spirit's illumination, the revelation needed for himself, or for others in ministry in which he was responsible to take part.

His knowledge being little more than theory, it was comparatively easy to let it lie in abeyance, or to replace it by another theory that could be made to appear attractive and plausible. His conviction was not clear enough or of sufficient depth to make impossible the toleration of that which was contrary to it.

The ministry of that Godly Pastor had seemed highly successful — and up to a point it was successful: there was fruit; but his congregation remained as a dependent child, spiritually immature. Dr. A. T. Pierson describes such a congregation as "only a sheaf, of which the pastor was the bond, and which, when the bond is removed, falls apart". Is it not by the quality and permanence of the fruit that the real success of a ministry is to be judged?

The result was not due to any lack of spiritual gifts or faithfulness on the part of the Pastor but to the church order which deprived the members of their privilege of engaging fully in ministry and of exercising the gifts of the Spirit given to them.

The same result would follow inevitably such a procedure in any sphere of life. One who does not have to undertake responsibility in life will not develop mentally or morally. His character will remain undisciplined and his intelligence fallow. Similarly, the exercise of responsibility in spiritual ministry is necessary to the development of spiritual character and intelligence. These cannot be acquired by listening to sermons. As Carlyle aptly says, "To sit as a passive bucket and be pumped into, can be exhilerating to no creature, how eloquent soever be the flood of utterance that is descending". Teaching alone will not produce Christians fully developed in understanding and efficient in service. Theory without practice and experience would never make a physician or an engineer or a farmer. Theory will never produce the physical power necessary to the athlete. It will never create a public speaker or an administrator or a leader of men. The instructor may be a brilliant and conscientious man, but the pupil must always learn to apply the instruction by practice. It is in the practice that he really learns. In no sphere is experience so necessary as it is in the spiritual.

Would we have such a Pastor curtail his ministry or cease to exercise freely the gifts which the Spirit has apportioned to him? No, by no means. He is called of God to ministry. But had he done what Paul would have done with the congregation, giving it adequate teaching and leading its members into the full exercise of the gifts of the Spirit, how different would have been the situation when he left them! He would have left a congregation like those that Paul left behind him.

The New Testament order would not curtail the ministry of such a man; it would widen its scope. The loss that is sustained through the modern order is not just that the development of the gifts of the Spirit in the local congregation is prevented but that men such as these are hindered from giving to the Church at large and to the unsaved world a ministry that is so greatly needed.

How different was the effect of the New Testament order upon a congregation. Each church was a hive of activity — not institutional activity, but spiritual activity — through the exercise of the gifts of the Spirit by all the members; an activity that radiated outwards, extending in an ever widening circle, reaching farther and farther afield as new converts increased the membership and the numbers seeking scope for ministry multiplied. And in the congregations there was the evidence of developing manhood: of growth in knowledge and experience. It could not have been otherwise. A congregation that participated fully in the responsibility of the ministry of the Word and that faced the adversary together with united faith and prayer must needs grow in spiritual stature and strength.

When present in modern congregations, whether of a hundred or a thosuand members, we have often thought of the power in their midst that is so effectively bottled up. Let us suppose there is one with a membership of several thousand, all of whom are saved people, sound in the faith. It will have many congregational activities: Bible studies, prayer meetings, women's and young people's Societies: a great organization, the 'running of which requires much thought and unstinted service on the part of many. It is a community of Christians led and taught by its Pastor, enjoying his ministry and the various community activities provided for it. To a great extent it is a community living within itself and for itself.

Around it, no doubt, are many thousands of people, a great

proportion of whom are as benighted as the heathen in any mission land. The impact of this great congregation of Christians upon its neighbourhood is exceedingly small. It has existed for many years and, as things are, can go on indefinitely, living its own pleasant life apart from the coarse and unhappy world that surrounds it. It preaches the Gospel — at least its Pastor does every Sunday night in their comfortable building. Any may hear who care to come. A few come, and of these some are saved and the great congregation proudly rejoices in these results.

Besides this, the congregation, perhaps, pays a 'missionary' to carry on a 'Mission' in another section of the city, and he is helped by two or three earnest volunteer 'workers'. There may be an open-air meeting held by a few unassuming brethren who are willing to go into the streets to proclaim Christ. A number of young people have gone out to foreign fields as missionaries and every year there is a carefully organized drive to raise money for their support. Therefore, this congregation is considered to be a 'great missionary church'.

This great congregation is carrying on most of its witness by proxy. It pays a Pastor to preach for it, a 'Home Missionary' to witness to the 'down and outs' in the slums, and supports some missionaries evangelising in foreign fields. But what are the great majority of the members doing? They are all saved people, members of the Body of Christ and, therefore, all provided with gifts of the Spirit for ministry, yet they actually do little more than attend the services, enjoy the Pastor's teaching and rejoice when souls are saved through his preaching. As some one has written,

> "Around us lies the harvest field; we do not gather grain
> By going to our meeting and returning home again."

What a great stream of power is dammed up in that congregation. When the Holy Spirit fell upon the company of believers at Pentecost, manifesting the gifts of the Spirit in them, all went out into the streets witnessing in the power of the Spirit and thousands were saved. And they all continued preaching, refusing to stop, even in the face of persecution. The Holy Spirit of Pentecost has not been withdrawn from the Church. His power has not become less. The Lord's command to preach the Gospel to every creature still stands and obedience to that command continues to be the primary and urgent duty of every one who has been born of the Spirit; a duty which cannot be delegated to some one else.

What would happen in the great modern city congregation if it were really to become New Testament in structure and power; if every member were to engage in the ministry through the gifts of the Spirit? How mighty then would be its impact upon its Godless neighbourhood and upon its city. No longer would it be a community living largely within itself and for itself. No longer would it minister by proxy through a few. No longer would the scores of thousands of unsaved around it have to come into its beautiful building to hear the Gospel preached. Nor would there be either time or inclination for the trifling, formal activities of the modern congregation. No, Christ's command would be obeyed as it was in the Jerusalem church and there would be two or three thousand Christian men and women, young and old, filled with the Spirit of the Master, pressing out into the streets and homes and markets as He did, seeking the lost wherever they are to be found, thinking not of themselves, willing to suffer and to be considered the offscouring of the earth and rejoicing in the reproach of the Cross.

This is no mere idealistic picture: it is simply what God has purposed for His Church. Such was the New Testament Church. But the 'improvements' which man has introduced for 'efficiency' for his comfort and for material stability, have given us a Church that scarcely resembles the Church of the New Testament. Now most of its members keep their talents comfortably wrapped in a napkin, for many specious reasons. But all the reasons that may be given can never outweigh the commands of the Master nor excuse for the neglect to use the spiritual equipment provided, nor release from the responsibility to witness to the perishing souls around us; nor will they save us from the blood-guilt for those whom we never warned, nor from the terrible condemnation of the Christ when we meet Him as Lord and He declares us to be 'unfaithful servants'. We shall not be able to say to Him, 'We paid a Pastor to do it'.

The Underlying Causes

Comparing the order followed in a modern, formal church with that of a New Testament congregation, it is not difficult to discern the underlying causes of our weakness. There lacks in the church of today — in its structure, its services and its ministry — the practical recognition of the priesthood of all believers. The participation of all the members in the ministry through the gifts of the Spirit is not permitted.

Of course, there are congregational activities in which members are urged to take part. A few may have a true ministry in the teaching of Sunday School classes. Then there are committees, Boards, Societies, guilds, clubs — wheels, and wheels within wheels, each one revolving around its own centre, laboriously and with many a creak, and getting nowhere. To a great extent, these activities are mere substitutes for the true activity of the Spirit. They are largely human works carried on in man's wisdom and strength. They had no place in the churches founded by the Apostles. They give a sense of religious activity, but, spiritually, they are, to a great extent, sterile for they do not attain the objective of all true ministry — the increase of the Body through the salvation of souls.

The true New Testament church is a centre of light and power, its energy radiating not inwards but outwards. Its power is the Holy Spirit's dynamic power, exercised in and through each member for the accomplishment of Christ's command that His message of salvation be taken to the ends of the earth and to every creature.

The existing state of affairs has its roots deep in the human heart. It releases the church member from having to pay the cost of obeying the Lord's command to preach and teach the Gospel. He does not personally have to engage in public, personal witness. He avoids the offence of the Cross in the humbling of the flesh that is entailed in open and aggressive preaching of the Gospel in the streets and homes of his city. He finds an apparently satisfactory reason for occupying himself almost entirely with the cares and pleasures of this life while he retains some one else to witness for him. If he is a member of some committee or an usher, he can feel that he is fulfilling his duty to serve. In his adequate church meeting-place, eloquent Pastor and formal church services he finds the practice of religion agreeable, respectable and comfortable. Deep spiritual experience and knowledge of the Word are essential only to the Pastor. The members can feel that they have not the training or time to know God intimately through His Word or to engage in any spiritual ministry. It is excusable for them to live on a lower plane.

The congregation is practically helpless. If the Pastor is absent for a Sunday, it must hire another preacher from outside to minister to it while it sits and listens. Nor would it be willing to listen to the preaching of a local brother seeking to practise the gift of the Spirit given to him. Human standards of eloquence, refinement, dignity and order have risen up as an irresistible barrier to the divine order and to the liberty of the Spirit to use whom He would. Peter and John would not be acceptable because they were 'ignorant and unlettered' men, Paul because of his old-fashioned doctrine and his sermons that were lacking in 'enticing words of human wisdom'.

The congregation has no practical knowledge — and little theoretical knowledge — regarding the gifts of the Spirit for ministry. It may be that even the public worship of many is largely a matter of the emotions rather than of the Spirit. Intellectual and emotional enjoyment is derived from the eloquent sermon, the religious music, the hymns, the order of service, the architectural surroundings and the concourse of people.

Unsatisfactory situations can exist also in congregations that are organized on the New Testament order. The visible forms of the order are without power in themselves; in fact they are such that they cannot stand alone. It is the presence of Christ in the gathering of the Church, the guidance of the Spirit through the prayer of the Church and the gifts of the Spirit manifested through the members of the Church, that provide all the wisdom and power and produce all the fruit.

A certain appearance of the true order may exist where man is in control and spiritual death reigns. In such a case it will be discovered that at some vital point the true order is not being followed. A congregation may have its Elders, but if one dominates and imposes his will, or if they have become an oligarchy, arrogating to themselves privileges that belong to all, monopolising ministry, discouraging young believers from exercising their gifts, forgetting that they are but chairmen of a gathering of 'priests', ruling harshly and not by prayer, faith and love, or failing to submit all their actions to the guidance of the Head through prayer, then, of course, the true spiritual order no longer exists.

The first point of departure from the true order is usually in the ministry of prayer. So long as the direction of the Head of the Body is being obtained faithfully through prayer, the Church will not depart far from His will. Immediately man's wisdom and will begin to assert themselves and take control, the prayer ministry slackens, with the best of excuses. As soon as that takes place, the connection with 'Headquarters' is broken: the ship has lost its Captain and is in the hands of usurpers.

The Holy Spirit may have more liberty to manifest Himself and there may be greater blessing in a congregation that is not organized on the New Testament pattern but in which the Lord is loved and His Word obeyed as far as it is known than in one in which the order is seemingly correct but the heart not right. A congregation bearing a Denominational label may be less sectarian at heart than one claiming to be undenominational.

This does not prove that the Scriptural order is unimportant; it simply demonstrates that the letter without the Spirit is dead. Given two congregations in which the conditions otherwise are equal, the one that is true to the Scriptural order will give the Holy Spirit greater freedom, will see a much fuller accomplishment of God's purpose, will experience a more abundant life, will have a deeper knowledge of God's Word and reap riper fruit than the one that is not. Its members will be all Spirit-taught, active, experienced ministers of the Gospel, not dependent children as will be the members of the other congregation, no matter how spiritual and sound in doctrine it may be .

The Lord does not abandon a congregation that is not wholly faithful. He never abandons His people. When a congregation of believers in Christ loses its first love and departs from the way of the Spirit, He does not forsake them. His Spirit is in them and continues to seek to lead them and manifest His power through them. In so far as a witness is given, He will use it to the salvation of souls. If they have 'a little strength', as the church in Philadelphia, the Lord will still seek to keep the door of witness open to them. Even if they sink to the level of the church in Laodicea, where He can no longer meet together with them, He does not leave them utterly: He stands at the door and knocks .

So long as a congregation witnesses to the Gospel, souls will be saved, but the growth and obedience of these converts depends upon the faithfulness and obedience of the congregation. If the Holy Spirit's work in the believers is restricted, they will remain more or less babes in Christ. If the Spirit is untrammelled and fills the church, He will lead them on into the fulness of experience, manifesting His gifts through them and accomplishing the ministry to which God has appointed them. The tragedy of the

Church today is the poverty of that which it has to offer the convert and the spiritual immaturity of the members even of the more spiritual congregations.

We have spoken frankly — we trust not too frankly, for we have no desire to wound. Naturally, we have generalized; there are exceptions. But does not every spiritual believer, every one who loves the Lord, grieve deeply at the general powerlessness and ineffectiveness of the Church today? Is it not most urgently necessary that we turn to God and His Word and seek the reason in absolute faithfulness? Victory is not to be gained by temporizing or compromising, or by seeking to patch up that which is of man's wisdom or to inject spiritual power into man's work, but by obedience and returning to God's way that the power of the Holy Spirit may be released.

Full Time Preachers and Teachers

In the Early Church there seem to have been travelling Teachers and Preachers who devoted their whole time to the ministry of the Gospel. It is to be expected that there will be such today, and they should have full opportunity to exercise their ministries. There will be ample scope for their ministry. Such preachers and teachers must never monopolize permanently the ministry in any congregation. It is easy to reason, "I have the gift of preaching (or teaching) and I am only exercising my gift and engaging in a preaching (or teaching) ministry", and consider that to be a sufficient justification for setting aside the normal order. God calls to such ministries, not that the opportunity for ministry of others should be curtailed, but that the witness of the Church should be extended.

There is no clear indication that any Elders gave their whole time to preaching or teaching. Paul in 1 Tim. 5:17 merely states that some Elders engaged in preaching and teaching and infers that others did not do so. He definitely counselled the Ephesian Elders to support themselves, and that, evidently, was the general practice.

The Elders' Ministry

It is necessary to understand clearly the Scriptural limits of the Elders' particular ministry and not confound it with other ministries that are the privilege of all. The Elders' ministry has to do with the maintaining of the true order in the congregation. As Paul said to the Ephesian Elders,

Take heed to yourselves and to all the flock among which the Holy Spirit has placed you to take the oversight for Him and act as shepherds to the Church of God, which he has bought with His own Blood. (Acts 20:28, Weymouth.)

To oversee and shepherd, as they must do, is a ministry that requires no small portion of wisdom, patience and faith. They must see that freedom is given to all for the exercise of the gifts of the Spirit. At the same time, they must be faithful to prevent any misuse of this privilege. It depends upon the Elders whether there is order or disorder in the gatherings. Theirs is an exacting, a many-sided and a glorious ministry. The fact that they take only a share, on an equality with all the others, in the ministry of the Word in the congregation does not mean that their work is any less important.

The whole testimony and ministry of the congregation comes under their direct supervision. The analogy of the shepherd fits their case admirably. The shepherd does not actually feed his sheep; they feed themselves; but he sees that they have good pasturage and that none strays into danger. He assists the weak, carries the lambs and protects the flock against dangerous intruders.

The Elders form the first guard against the teaching of wrong doctrine (the Evangelists being the second guard). They should not permit anyone to minister the Word who does not teach the truth or who has not the gift of the Spirit for such a ministry. They should see that all the rules regarding discipline are observed by the congregation, that those who need visitation are cared for, that the young people are encouraged to minister according to their gifts, that candidates for baptism are cared for as is necessary and that all the spiritual activity of the church is carried on as it should be.

As shepherds they have as their example the ministry of the Good Shepherd who 'gave His life for the sheep'. When one of the flock was missing from the fold He sacrificed all and endured all to find it and carry it tenderly back to the fold. Such must be the Christ-like, glorious ministry of the Elders as shepherds of the congregation serving under the 'Chief Shepherd'.

As Bishops they preside over an assembly of priests of royal lineage. The ministry of the Word is the privilege and responsibility of all and the Elders simply see that it is carried on as it should be by all according to God's Word. They are not priests ministering to laity, but leaders of equals; not professors teaching a class that never graduates, but leaders of a team. Their leadership and presiding should be inconspicuous. When all goes well they have no need to intervene.

There is a special prayer ministry that is the responsibility of the Elders. There are matters for prayer that cannot be brought before the whole Church. Their duty as shepherds makes it necessary for them to pray not only for the congregation as a whole but for individual members. New converts, believers in special need, the sick and 'weak brethren', must be prayed for definitely and continually. Members who are slow to grasp spiritual truth, who are not growing in grace or manifesting the gifts of the Spirit as they should, or showing signs of coldness or carelessness, must be upheld in faith. The Elders, through prayer, will wage many a contest with Satan and win many a victory unknown to any but themselves and the Chief Shepherd. This prayer ministry of the Elders is as essential and vital to the spiritual well-being of the congregation and the continued power and success of its witness as is the prayer ministry of the congregation. Behind all the Elders' work, bringing guidance for every decision, every action, and bearing all that is done through to a victorious conclusion, must be this continual and believing prayer ministry.

The Presbytery

The Elders act as a group. There is no Chief Elder. No one can act independently of the others. Every decision must be the Lord's will discovered through the Word and united prayer. It is necessary that they have their regular prayer meetings, giving time to waiting upon the Lord to know His will. They must be careful not to assume responsibilities that pertain to the whole congregation.

In the synagogue the Elder's duty was to see that order was maintained. No one might minister the Word without their consent.[1] For arranging for those to minister at meetings of the church other than the Lord's Table, the Elders should seek the

---

[1] Where there are no Elders, see p. 324.

Lord's will sufficiently in advance to give the necessary time to the preachers for preparation. Those desiring to minister should advise the Elders and obtain their consent — except in meetings such as the one around the Lord's Table. At those meetings the Elders have the authority to silence any one who is not ministering in the Spirit. That of course, will be done only in extreme cases. Usually it is sufficient to speak privately with an offender after the meeting.

CHAPTER XXI

THE APPOINTMENT OF ELDERS AND DEACONS

IT is expressly stated that Elders and Deacons should not be unproved, new converts. In the Jerusalem church, Deacons and Elders were not appointed until sufficient time had elapsed to make possible the acquiring of the necessary experience. On the outward part of the 'first missionary journey' of Paul and his companions, groups of believers were gathered out in a number of places. On the return journey, a year or more later, these groups of believers were revisited and it was then that Elders were appointed. It was to do a similar work of completing the organization of groups already gathered out that Titus remained behind for a time in Crete (Titus 1:5). This, evidently, was the regular practice.

The principles governing the appointment of Elders and Deacons are the same. The manner in which Elders were chosen is described in Acts 14:23:

> And when they had ordained them elders in every Church, and had prayed with fasting, they commended them to the Lord, on whom they believed.

Weymouth's translation reads:

> And in every Church, after prayer and fasting, they selected Elders...

The prayer preceded the appointment of the Elders. It is stated that the same procedure was followed "in every church". In the choosing of Deacons recorded in Acts 6:1-6,[1] and in the appointment of Elders described here, the procedure is identical:

1. The Evangelists take the initiative.
2. The Evangelists present act together.

[1] See pp. 54-5.

3. Those chosen are members of the congregation in which they will minister.

4. The responsibility for the choice rests upon the whole congregation, with which the Evangelists unite in prayer to know the will of God.

5. The appointment is made after prayer and fasting to know God's will.

6. When God's will is known as to who are appointed by Him, the Evangelists publicly pray for those who are chosen and lay their hands upon them.

The Elders were not appointed by the missionaries[1]; nor were they elected by vote, although the word in the orginal ($\gamma \varepsilon \rho \iota \tau o$-$\nu \varepsilon \omega$), translated 'selected', implies general consent.[2] God's will was discovered by each church through "fasting and prayer". General consent was obtained through all having come to a knowledge of God's will. The fact that there was fasting connected with the praying shows that it was more than the offering of one or two prayers. They continued in prayer for a considerable period until God's will became known. When, through prayer, they had certain knowledge as to the ones whom God had placed as Elders in a congregation and to whom the Holy Spirit had given the gifts for oversight, expression was given to the conviction by the laying on of the hands of the Evangelists.

It is of interest to compare with this the order followed in the appointment of the Evangelist, for it also is based upon the same principles, although, necessarily, there are certain differences in detail (Acts 13:2-4). Paul reminds the Ephesian Elders that the Holy Spirit had placed them in that ministry (Acts 20:27). As the Evangelists were appointed by the Spirit, so were the Elders. In both cases, the appointment is made, not by the church, nor by man, but by the Holy Spirit, the revelation of His will being obtained through prayer.

At the appointment of Elders in a church, the Evangelists took the initiative and presided. The instructions regarding the qualifications of Elders are given not to the churches but to Evangelists — to Timothy and Titus. As we have seen, an important part

---

[1] See pp. 137-44.
[2] Note also that 'ordain' (kathistemi) in Tit. 1:5 should be 'place'. Titus was to see to the placing of Elders, presiding while the congregations did the choos-ingas in Jerusalem (Acts 6:1-6).

of Titus' work in Crete was seeing to the appointment of Elders in the congregations. He was responsible to see that the complete Scriptural order was established in each congregation.

In the Jewish economy, the elders of the synagogue, while chosen by the congregation, were examined by delegates of the Great Sanhedrin to see if they met the requirements for Elders in the synagogue, which were very similar to those which Paul states as necessary for the Elder in the church. The practice in the Church followed closely the Jewish pattern, with, of course, important differences, which have been already noted.[1] That some one outside the congregation should come to preside at the appointment of Elders is quite evidently a wise provision. It definitely tends to ensure a truer and more unbiased selection.

The participation of Evangelists together with the congregation in the appointment of Elders and Deacons continued during the first two centuries. The writings of Cyprian in the third century show that by that time the unanimous consent of the Elders of the region and of the congregation was considered sufficient.[2] Finally — much later — both Elders and congregation lost the privilege. of expressing their opinions and the appointment was made by the Diocesan Bishop.

God's Word makes it clear that it is He who places each member in the Body 'as He wills' and that the Holy Spirit distributes the gifts of the Spirit as He wills (1 Cor. 12:11, 18). It is, therefore, presumption for man to do the choosing. A majority vote cannot decide as to who have been chosen by God as Evangelists, Elders, Deacons, etc. To say that one so chosen is God's choice is to confound and confuse terms and values in a manner that would not be permitted in law, business or any other sphere.

The confirmation of the call of Barnabas and Paul given by the Holy Spirit to the church in Antioch is usually cited as evidence that the call of an individual must be confirmed by the vote of the church. Yet the plain fact is that the church in Antioch did not vote on the matter. In human procedure, the nearest thing to what they did is, doubtless, a vote of the congregation. But they did not follow human procedure. The Holy Spirit made His will known to all those who were before God in prayer and

---

[1] See pp. 133, 228.
[2] Ep. LXVII; LIV, 5.

they acted in obedience to His guidance. That procedure and an action decided by majority vote are entirely different things.

It is certainly taught here that the call of an individual should be confirmed to the church, but the confirmation is given by the Spirit to those in prayer. Since each one is put in his place by God, the only thing the church can do in the matter is to find out what God's choice is and acknowledge it. That is what happened at Antioch. The record of what took place there emphasizes the fact that the church did nothing more than this. The action was taken by the Holy Spirit. The church obeyed His guidance. Not only did He take the initiative, but He was in command personally and directly in the whole matter from beginning to end.

Qualifications

The ministry and qualifications of Elders and Deacons have already been considered.

It should be borne in mind that Elders do not all have exactly the same type of gift. This is recognized in 1 Tim. 5:17:

Let the Presbyters who perform their office well be counted worthy of a twofold honour, especially those who labour in speaking and teaching. (Conybeare.)

The Lord may call a man to the Eldership who does not have the gifts for public preaching and teaching. This does not mean that he will have no gifts for proclaiming or teaching the Word. We have in one of our congregations the type of Elder that seems to be referred to. He takes no part in public preaching or teaching, but he has decided gifts of the Spirit for presiding at the gatherings of the church, for counselling individuals and for personal evangelism. He is wise in counsel, strong in prayer and has the confidence and respect of the congregation. He is a good overseer and pastor.

One of the principal reasons why the testimony of the Elder's home, as well as his own, must be above reproach, is that his ministry makes it necessary that he be "given to hospitality". His home is required as a background to a very important phase of his work. It is a Christian home to which those who are in need of counsel or friendship may be invited and where the young people of the congregation may be gathered for inspiration and fellowship. The ministry that may be exercised through the

Elder's home is of great scope and importance. It is very necessary to the congregation and will bear rich fruit. In view of this, we can understand why God requires the testimony of the Elder's wife and children to be such as will aid and not hinder his ministry.

The great temptation that faces the missionary and the church in the appointment of Elders and Deacons is to be swayed by various considerations, such as the apparent ability of some man, or a desire for haste, to consider men who do not come fully up to the Scriptural standard. Paul had this danger in mind when he wrote such explicit instructions to Timothy and Titus. Of course, if missionary and church will wait before God in prayer until His will is known, there will be no danger of making mistakes. Certainly, the Holy Spirit will never give liberty to set aside God's Word and appoint a man who does not fulfil its requirements. We have never seen any good result from the appointment of one whose own testimony, or that of his wife or family, was not entirely above reproach, or who had not the required gifts of the Spirit.

To have a man act as Elder or Deacon in any sense, partially, or temporarily, whose appointment has not been duly confirmed to the church by the Holy Spirit, is not in accordance with the Scriptural order. We may not appoint a man to act temporarily in the church until the Lord makes the appointment. There can never be any Scriptural reason for it. It is harmful to the man concerned and to the church and usually ends by creating difficulties that are very hard to overcome later. In new congregations where Elders have not yet been appointed, preachers may preside at meetings without any thought that they are acting as Elders.

It is not right to appoint men as Elders who do not have a clear understanding of what their duties are to be and how they should proceed in carrying them out. They cannot have that knowledge unless they have actually seen a congregation led as they must lead it. That means that the missionary must stay long enough to give the example. As we have seen, it is made very clear in the Word that only men of experience can be appointed as Elders and Deacons. Much difficulty has resulted in many places because those appointed had not been given an adequate example before appointment. A few studies on the subject are not an adequate preparation. The Evangelist must do a thorough, careful work, teaching by example as well as by precept.

If the church of which the new Elder is a member knows, as it should, how to pray in the Spirit, he will be accustomed to seeking the direction of the Lord through prayer in all things. It is essential that the Elders meet at least once a week for prayer that all their acts be guided by the Head of the Church. They should understand clearly that nothing whatever should be done by them unless it has been received from the Lord in united prayer.

It would, of course, be impossible for a man to fulfil the ministries of Elder or Deacon who could not or did not attend the prayer gatherings of the congregation. He would not know the Holy Spirit's guidance to the church.

It is necessary also that the Elders understand clearly that no Elder can act alone. One may be the spokesman on an occasion, but he must speak in the name of the Presbytery. The principle of the two or more acting in all matters concerning the Church must be observed.[1]

It has been objected that the laying on of hands for Evangelists, Elders and Deacons is fraught with danger because those whose call has thus been recognized by the church may be tempted to arrogate to themselves privileges and authority that rightly belong to no man. For that reason some have set aside this symbolic act, so rich in spiritual significance.

But do we have the right to judge what God has ordained for His Church and omit what we consider inadvisable? Dare we presume to change God's order for the Church any more than Moses would have dared to alter the slightest detail of the divine pattern for the Tabernacle? Had Moses introduced any modification in the plan for the Tabernacle, God would not have dwelt in it, for the touch of the hand of flesh, the imprint of man's proud wisdom and the guilt of man's rebellious heart would have been upon it, and Moses would have had the whole burden of it to carry henceforth upon his own shoulders. Are we not carrying many a burden for that reason?

When the true meaning of the laying on of hands is understood we have not found that there is any danger involved. The danger comes only when an unscriptural significance is attached to it and it is made the symbol of the investiture of a priestly or ministerial caste.[2] We can omit nothing from God's order, just as we can

---

[1] See Chapter 12; 6 (7).
[2] See p. 66.

add nothing to it, without paying the price for our presumption and disobedience. The pattern which God has given us for the Church is perfect, complete and glorious.

Those Who Fail

The procedure to be followed in the case of an Elder who falls into sin has already been mentioned.[1] The Church is not required to continue to accept as an Elder one who has fallen into sin or become unspiritual or who no longer manifests the true gifts of the Spirit nor fulfills his spiritual calling.

When an Elder or Deacon is unfaithful, the Evangelist, or church-planter, should intervene.. Paul instructed Timothy,

Against an elder receive not an accusation, but before two or three witnesses. Them that sin rebuke before all, that others also may fear. I charge thee before God, and the Lord Jesus Christ, and the elect angels, that thou observe these things without preferring one before another, doing nothing by partiality.

In dealing with such a matter the Evangelist must not act arbitrarily. In the first place, there must be more than one witness, and the charges must be clearly proved. Then, it is evident·that the Evangelist must act in conjunction with the congregation, the revelation of God's will by the Spirit given to all through the Word and through prayer being the basis of the action.

In the sub-apostolic Church this practice was continued. The deep wisdom of God's order in requiring that one from outside the congregation should come in to preside when such a matter has to be dealt with will be readily discerned. It would be difficult, and in some instances impossible, for a congregation to deal with such cases alone.

---

[1] See p. 240.

CHAPTER XXII

BAPTISM AND THE LORD'S TABLE

THE spiritual communion of the Church, the Body of Christ, centres around the symbolic ordinances of Baptism and the Lord's Supper, the observance of which are commanded by our Lord.

1. Baptism.

Baptism testifies through its symbolism to all that has been accomplished in the believer through the death and resurrection of our Lord Jesus Christ. The water of baptism is the symbolic tomb into which the whole being is submerged to rise again 'in newness of life' (Rom. 6:3-5). The testimony given through baptism is that:

(1) The believer has been baptized into the one body of Christ by the Holy Spirit. 1 Cor. 12:13; Gal. 3:27; Rom. 12:5; Col. 3:15.

(2) The believer has been united with Christ in His death. In this union with Christ, the flesh, "the body of sin" — the entire fallen, sin-ruined being with its intelligence, will and desires — is judged and crucified. By faith, the believer reckons himself "dead unto sin". Rom. 6:3-14.

(3) The believer has been united with Christ in His resurrection, justified, regenerated, and has become a new creature in Christ, raised by the power of the Holy Spirit and walking in the Spirit in newness of life. Through union with Christ in His death and resurrection, he is dead to the law, dead to the world and to his past life of sin. The life which he now lives, he lives in Christ, by faith, and in Him he participates in the reproach of the Cross and in the victory of the Cross over all the power of Satan. He has been translated from the dominion of Satan into the Kingdom of Christ. Matt. 28:19; Acts 9:18; 10:47, 48; 16:33; Rom. 6:3-5; Col. 2:12; Acts 2:38.

The true meaning of baptism has been obscured by the influence of centuries of clericism and ritualism that have intervened since apostolic times. We must be careful not to invest it with a significance that is founded upon ritualism and custom and not upon Scripture. It is nothing more than a symbolic act that testifies to what has already taken place by faith. To speak of it as the door by which the Church is entered is incorrect. The Church has already been entered through the baptism of the Spirit on conversion. Baptism is merely the believer's public testimony, exceedingly important as such but nothing more. It is right that a convert should not be received at the Lord's Table before baptism, not because baptism confers necessary grace, but simply because there can hardly be certainty regarding the genuineness of the conversion of one who is not willing to take the first step of obedience and make public confession of his faith. For baptism the Early Church did not demand spiritual maturity but only clear evidence of conversion.

The Baptism of Converts

It is a common practice in the modern mission field to require converts to pass through a period of probation before baptism. This was not done in the Early Church; on the contrary, it is recorded that converts were baptized immediately.[1] Some, no doubt, turned out unsatisfactorily. Simon, the sorcerer, had to be denounced sternly by Peter shortly after his baptism. Such cases occurred, but they were dealt with at once by discipline.

The true meaning of Matt. 28:18-20 should be noted. The Revised Version and other versions give the correct translation which indicates that the teaching comes after the baptism.

Three centuries after Paul's time, the baptism of whole communities filled the Church with paganism. It would be incorrect, however to attribute that procedure and its results to New Testament practice. Paul and his fellow-evangelists would not have

---

[1] Mosheim says: "At the first promulgation of the Gospel all who professed firmly to believe that Jesus was the only redeemer of mankind, and who promised to lead a holy life conformably to the religion He taught, were received immediately among the disciples of Christ; nor did a more full instruction in the principles of Christianity precede their baptism, but followed it." — *Ecclesiastical History*, p. 40.

accepted those pseudo-converts for baptism. Moreover, had any been admitted unawares, the New Testament Church discipline would have been enforced and they would have been excluded.

When the Ethiopian Eunuch had come to the place where he could sincerely say, "I believe", he asked the question which most genuine converts ask: "What doth hinder me to be baptized?" Philip's answer was: "If thou believest with all thine heart, thou mayest". Baptism was simply the outward symbol of conversion and it followed immediately upon acceptance of Christ. However, it was not done precipitately or carelessly. Examining the Eunuch's case, we find that:

1. Philip was led by the Spirit to him.

2. The Eunuch had been reading the Scriptures and the Spirit had been dealing with him before Philip met him. There had been previous preparation by the Spirit through the Word.

3. Philip sat down with the Eunuch and instructed him in the Scriptures. He made sure the Eunuch understood the Gospel message.

4. The Eunuch asked for baptism. The desire for baptism came from the witness of the Spirit within, not from the urging of God's servant.

5. Philip questioned him as to the reality of his faith. He had to be satisfied that the Eunuch was truly a believer.

6. Immediately Philip was satisfied that the Eunuch was a true convert, he baptized him.

In this case, Philip had a sufficient basis for an assurance that the conversion was genuine. There was full recognition given to the work of the Holy Spirit, definite instruction was provided and, finally, the candidate was questioned as to his faith. We do not know how long this process took, but it was all accomplished in a comparatively short time. This does not mean, of course, that all cases will be as rapid. It may not be so easy to determine with certainty that there has been a true work of the Spirit. While there is no Scriptural foundation for the practice of making genuine converts wait a prescribed period before baptism, there is also no warrant for the immediate baptism of doubtful converts. Discernment is given through the Spirit to the servant of the Lord and we can confidently expect that guidance will be received concerning every candidate if we are faithful to seek it.

Each candidate should be questioned very carefully. If it is found that there is lack of understanding on any fundamental point, it should be corrected. If there is sin in the life or something that should be put right, it must be faithfully dealt with. We definitely consider that a lack of willingness on the part of a professing convert to put things right and walk in obedience to God's Word is sufficient ground for doubting the genuineness of his conversion and refusing baptism until such time as the fruits of regeneration appear.

While Scriptiure makes it perfectly clear that instruction should come after baptism, that does not mean that we are prohibited from explaining what the Christian life means to a convert before he is baptized. We have seen great harm done through carelessness in this matter. Persons who are not born again by the Spirit have been baptized and accepted at the Lord's Table although there were no fruits meet for repentance. Naturally, there was not the necessary reformation in these lives afterwards. The spiritual testimony of the congregation, as a result, was very low and the power of the Spirit lacking.

When a true convert asks for baptism, our experience has been that their attitude is one of faith and surrender and that they truly desire to obey the Lord. They are glad to have the Christian walk explained to them and ready to put right anything that may not be pleasing to the Lord. But when the Lord's servant is not faithful to give them the whole counsel of God, there is a tendency that they continue in disobedience and become hardened therein.

The practice we have followed in the examination of candidates for baptism is as follows:

1. The Lord's guidance is sought in prayer.

2. The candidates are brought in one by one and questioned. The questions are grouped under four heads:

(1) Conversion. It is sought to make absolutely certain that the candidate has really accepted Christ in faith as Saviour and understands clearly the scriptural ground of his salvation.

(2) Evidence of Regeneration. Matters such as gambling, drinking, dancing, smoking, card playing, debts, dress, make-up, etc. are dealt with. Those who are single are warned that a believer may not marry an unbeliever. Those who are married are questioned to make sure that there are no irregularities in their marriage. Among primitive people matters such as witchcraft and tribal customs that are sinful are mentioned.

3) The Meaning of Baptism. The candidate should understand

that baptism is merely a testimony and act of obedience and know its symbolic meaning as given in Rom. 6:4-11.

(4) The Responsibility of the Member of the Body of Christ. We make sure that the candidate understands his responsibility to take part in the ministry of the congregation through the gifts of the Spirit given to him and united prayer.

3.   The candidate is then asked to retire, while his case is put before the Lord in prayer to see if there is assurance or not that he should be baptized. He is then advised as to the clothes he will need, etc., for the baptism, or, if he is not accepted, the reasons are explained to him.

A thorough examination of this nature takes time, of course, but it is necessary.

The practice of having the congregation vote upon the acceptance of the candidate is not according to Scripture. There was no such custom in the New Testament Church. It is an individual matter not a congregational matter.

We have personally had experience of both the New Testament and modern methods. For thirteen years we required a probation of one year before baptism. For a longer period we have baptized without delay all of whose conversion we were certain, as soon as they desired it. Reviewing the results of our own experience, and that of our fellow-missionaries and of the congregations, we can say without hesitation that the Apostolic method is altogether superior. There have been mistakes, of course, but they have been much fewer. A smaller proportion have proved unfaithful. The believers thus baptized have taken their places much more readily and satisfactorily in the spiritual witness of the congregation and their spiritual growth has been quicker and stronger.

The fact that there was no delay in baptizing converts made it possible to gather them together into functioning congregations without delay, with all the advantages that gives. It avoided the deadening influence which a period of probation almost always has upon a new convert filled with zeal, who is prevented from exercising the gifts of the Spirit until he has passed the prescribed period and been baptized. By the time he is baptized, his first love has passed and he has become accustomed to being an idle Christian, simply attending 'worship' and listening to sermons, instead of taking his full part in the witness of the congregation.

In the symbolism of the Lord's Table there is the continuation of the testimony given through baptism. Baptism symbolizes the transcendent work and victory of the Cross, which brought the believer into living union with Christ; the Lord's Supper commemorates this work and union and symbolizes the continuance of all that it signified. The believer is now abiding in Christ, as the branch in the vine. He is in Christ, dead, justified, risen and living in continued union with Him. Life, and the continuance of life, is in and through Christ. The believer lives as Christ lives in him and he lives in Christ.

The Lord's Supper points to the future, bridging the space of time between the believer's union with Christ by faith and the visible consummation of that union, when the whole Body will be united and all the redeemed, in bodies glorified, incorruptible, and like unto His, shall gather with Him at His coming and shall be forever with the Lord. Matt. 26:28-30; Luke 22:14-20; 1 Cor. 11:20-34.

The Lord's Supper also symbolizes the oneness of the Body of Christ, the Church—the oneness of the members of the Body with Christ and their consequent oneness with each other. It is the meeting of the Church as the Body of Christ. 1 Cor. 10:16, 17.

The central place which this meeting occupies in the fellowship and spiritual edification of the Church must be realized. It is regarding this meeting particularly that Paul writes in 1 Corinthians, chapters 10-14. It is in this gathering of the Church as the Body that the Holy Spirit ministers to the spiritual needs of the Body through the members, through whom He manifests the necessary gifts.

It is a symbolical feast and an actual feast. Symbolically, the Body feasts upon Christ, and through the Spirit of Christ present in the midst, a spiritual feast is provided of food from the Word for the nourishment and upbuilding of the Body. That the Church met thus every Lord's Day is clearly inferred in Acts 2:42, 46; 20:7.[1]

It is important to distinguish between this gathering together of the Church and other gatherings such as those for the teaching of the Word and the preaching of the Gospel. These were not meetings of the Church in the same sense. In them there might

---

[1] That this was still the custom in the sub-apostolic Church is seen in the *Teaching of the Twelve Apostles,* which says, "On every Lord's day assemble together and break bread." Ch. XIV.

be only one or two members of the Church present and many unbelievers.

At The Lord's Table

It should not be difficult to imagine ourselves in a gathering of a New Testament congregation established by Paul and his fellow-workers. The accounts that are given of these gatherings and the instructions laid down concerning them, enable us to know exactly how they were conducted. The meeting we attend will be held, most likely, in the home of one of their number. As we enter on the first day of the week and take our place we find that most of those around us are of the 'common' people. There may be a few Jews amongst them, but the great majority will be Gentiles. Possibly many are slaves. But we sense an attitude of love and a spirit of unity—all are one in Christ. Reverence, dignity, simplicity and a joyful spirit of worship and spiritual communion characterise the little gathering.

They are met together on this day as the Church, the Body of Christ, for the breaking of bread. The several Elders of the congregation are there and also those who minister as Deacons. They are men of grave and dignified bearing. One of the Elders presides. His duty is to see that the Scriptural order is followed. All who have the gifts of the Spirit and are led of the Spirit to do so, are free to take part. There are those present with the gifts of preaching, teaching, "the word of knowledge", and "the word of wisdom". Different ones will ask for psalms or hymns to be sung, or read and perhaps explain passages of Scripture, or engage in prayer. Two or three will address the gathering. It is understood that the message of none should be so lengthy that it will not leave time for others to take part (1 Cor. 14:29, 30). The Elders would not permit any one to take part who does not evidence the necessary gift of the Spirit to do so, nor would they allow any 'weak brethren' to engage in 'doubtful disputations'. No one living in sin or conforming to the world could take part and a teacher of wrong doctrine would be silenced immediately.

We will partake with them of the bread and the wine commemorating the Lord's death and symbolizing the unity of the Body. Those who have an offering to give will, as they enter or on retiring, deposit it in the offertory placed, no doubt, inconspicuously, somewhere near the door. But there is no appeal for money. All give, as they are able to do so, unto the Lord.

Such was the gathering together of the Church on the Lord's Day, when it met as the Body of Christ. Disorders and abuses sometimes manifested themselves, as in the Corinthian church, but these were exceptions and were speedily and sternly rebuked by the Evangelists. Generally, the conduct was orderly, the testimony consistent and the power of the Spirit manifested in mighty power. This gathering of the Church was not centered around a sermon but around Christ. The essential element was the liberty of the Spirit to lead the gathering and to glorify Christ using whoever He chose. There was a full recognition of the priesthood of all believers. It was the centre of the congregation's life and fellowship. It was *the* gathering of the Church when, in a special way, it met together with its Lord, members of His Body and members one of another. As the Holy Spirit led, there was worship, communion and ministry.

The importance of this gathering and the rich blessing which it brings to the congregation become evident when it is given its true place, its simplicity restored and the Holy Spirit permitted to control. On the practical side, we have found it of great value in the spiritual life and development of the believers individually and of the congregation as a whole. The fact that every one, from the youngest to the oldest, is responsible for the ministry in the meeting produces a different attitude. If there is lack of liberty and power, none can say, 'The pastor was not at his best today'. It is realized that the fault is in the congregation and the matter will be taken to the Lord in prayer in the following prayer meeting.

Usually, the whole service is of a piece, all the prayers, readings, hymns and messages fitting together in one clear message from the Lord in a way that makes it evident that the Holy Spirit is in control. But there are occasions when it is not so. This meeting is a true barometer of the congregation's spiritual state. The spiritual life cannot wane without it being evident in this gathering. Thus the Lord can deal with His people.

It is in this meeting that the preachers may exercise their gift of speaking to the edification of the Lord's people and it is blessed to see them develop. We have seen newly baptized converts greatly blessed as they have had some passage to read or word to give in the first communion service in which they participated. They have found that from the very beginning the way was open for them to enter into their responsibilities as members of the Body of Christ called to take part in its ministry.

There is no definite statement in the New Testament as to whether the churches celebrated the Lord's Supper when neither Elders or Evangelists were present. But there seem to be clear indications that they did. At the Jewish Passover it was not necessary for a priest to be present. The head of the house presided. It seems reasonable to expect that if an Elder or Evangelist had to be present for the celebration of the Lord's Supper it would be stated. Is is evident that their presence was not necessary. It would seem that at the "agape", at which there was the "breaking of bread", it was usual for the head of the house in which it was held to act as master of ceremonies. It was not necessary that an Elder be present. Nowhere is any ground given for the thought that the Elder is invested with special authority to dispense the 'Sacraments'. That is an idea that comes from the Church of Rome; from the unscriptural distinction between clergy and laymen.

The historical evidence as to the practice of the Early Church in these matters is conclusive, as Hatch demonstrates. Referring to Tertullian, he says:

> The view which he took of the nature of office in the Church was that it does not as such, confer any powers upon its holders which are not possessed by the other members of the community... As an ordinary rule, 'it is only', he says, 'from the hands of the president that we receive the Eucharist': but if there be an emergency, a layman may celebrate as well as a bishop. 'That which has constituted the difference between the governing body and the ordinary members is the authority of the Church': but 'where three Christians are, though they be laymen, there is a Church'.[1]

While Tertullian's writings show plainly the influence of the steadily growing ritualism, they make it clear that even in his day it was recognized that the ordinary member could preside at the Lord's Table and that it was the advanced ritualistic party that sought to reserve the privilege for the officers. In regard to the administration of baptism, the situation is shown to have been exactly the same. Again we quote from Hatch:

> By one of those slow and silent revolutions which the lapse of many centuries brings about in political as well as religious communities, the ancient conception of the office (of Elder) as essentially disciplinary and collegiate has been superseded by a conception of it in which not only is a single presbyter competent to discharge all a presbyter's functions, but in which also those func-

---

[1] *The Organisation of the Early Churches*, p. 124.

tions are primarily not those of discipline, but 'the ministration of the Word and Sacraments'.[1]

When there are Elders or Evangelists present, one of these, naturally, will preside at the gathering around the Lord's Table, not because they are specially ordained to dispense Communion, which they are not, but simply because it is their ministry generally to preside in the congregation, for which they have the gift of the Spirit.

The one who leads, be he Elder or not, simply presides at the gathering to maintain order. He should do so as inconspicuously as possible. After anouncing a hymn or offering a prayer to open the meeting he should make no further attempt to lead until the time for partaking of the elements, after which the singing of a hymn closes the meeting.

If possible, the seating should be arranged around the table and the plate and cup pass from hand to hand to avoid the impression of it being given by the one who presides. It is the Lord who gives the symbols of His body and blood to all.

The question arises as to whether a congregation of a few believers in an isolated place may not abuse this privilege and partake of the Lord's Supper unworthily. That is possible, but it need not happen, for they should be properly instructed, and, if need be, the Evangelist may intervene and advise the congregation to walk in obedience to God's Word and to exercise discipline, excluding from the Table any one who is in sin, as Paul did with the Church in Corinth.

As is to be expected, Satan has spared no effort to rob the Lord's Table of its place, its meaning and its power. Sacramentalism, ceremonies of various types, even crude superstition, have all tended to transform it into a ritual. Clericism has taken away the liberty of the Spirit to lead and to speak through whom He would. Even where the simplicity of the gathering has been retained, man has often usurped the Spirit's place. The younger brethren may be discouraged from taking part. The freedom of the Spirit may be hindered by rules that the messages should be restricted to certain subjects: for instance, that only the death of our Lord should be dealt with; or that there be only what is termed "worship" — worship understood in a very restricted sense. Such limitations are based upon surmise and reasonings and are without

---

[1] Ibid, p. 77.

any true Scriptural warrant. Man in his wisdom is always tempted to put forth his hand to steady the ark.

There is no support in the New Testament record for the thought that no man should lead the gathering at the Lord's Table because in that meeting the Lord Himself presides. He must preside in all gatherings of His people. But He has given the gift of presiding because it was His purpose to have instruments to use in presiding over the meetings of His people. It is He who does all the work in the congregation but He does it by His Spirit through the members of His Body.

Nor is there any example of a gathering at the Lord's Table where one passes the bread, another the cup and so on. At the Passover and in the example given by our Lord, one presided. Evidently at the agape the master of the house presided. It is never good to introduce a practice based upon reasoning, no matter how spiritual it may seem, and not upon the New Testament example.

Where there are no Elders, any man may preside if he is spiritually fit to do so and has the necessary gifts of the Spirit. It may be done by different ones in turn. It should not be left just for any one who "feels led" to do it. That has no Scriptural support and makes it easy for the forward and the unspiritual (and often the unspiritual are forward) to usurp the lead. Following the practice in the synagogue, while all had the privilege of ministering when led by the Spirit to do so and when possessed of the necessary gifts of the Spirit, yet the Elders of the congregation were responsible to see that only those took part who should do so. Where there are no Elders, this responsibility falls directly upon the congregation. It is the duty of the congregation, in such a case, to decide who may or may not preside or preach. In a very small congregation this presents no serious difficulty. (See p. 323-325).

The breaking of the loaf and pronouncing of the words "This is my body broken for you" is unscriptural. It is carefully stated that His body was not broken. It was given. In the best original manuscripts the word "broken" does not appear.

The attacks of Satan and the difficulties created by man are no reason for abandoning God's order. We dare not do so; the loss is too great. All who will gather sincerely and humbly in obedience to the divine order will find that, while the enemy will continually seek to make a breach that he may enter in to spoil, the Lord is present to lead on in continual triumph. The Lord is abundantly able to guard His Church if we but permit Him, and we have seen Him do so gloriously in many places. The deep desire of many of God's people today to return to the simplicity and power of God's order is expressed by two of His servants:

> It would seem that neglect of the Lord's Supper, the failure practically to recognize its central place in the life and worship of the Church, the forms and ceremonies currently employed, and the situation which prohibits the people from functioning as priests by participating whole heartedly in worship, are reasons for the powerlessness of the evangelical church today. The time may not be far distant when an increasing apostasy and a complete decline in spirituality may in many cases force true believers again to the simplicity of the "church in the house" as in the days of the apostles. Without pomp or earthly glamour or form, Christians will again gather around the symbol of the Saviour's death and so worship Him in simplicity and in truth. The leadership of these meetings will not be relegated to a presiding clergy, but the Holy Spirit will lead through the Christians present.[1]

---

[1] *What is the Purpose of the Lord's Supper?* by J. Bolton, a business man, and C. Stacey Woods, Director of the Inter-Varsity Christian Fellowship. "Our Hope", March, 1946.

Chapter XXIII

GATHERINGS FOR MINISTRY

For the Preaching of The Gospel

The proclamation of the Gospel message in the form of preaching to groups of people, large or small, and to individuals, occupies the central place in the work both of the Master and of His disciples. The gift of preaching is the greatest of the Spirit's gifts for evangelism. The Lord and His disciples had a message to give to the whole world, so the first thing to be done was to deliver it. The method was direct. There was no preparation of the soil other than that which God in His providence had already accomplished. The place where the preaching was done mattered little—it could be in the Temple, the private residence, the street, the market place, the mountain side, the sea-side, the desert, the palace, the judgment hall, the prison—it only mattered that people be there to hear.

When preaching in the Temple, the message would naturally enter is as part of the Temple service. With the Scriptures open the Evangelist would reason from them, declaring Christ. In the same way he preached the Gospel in any other place, showing Christ as revealed in the Scriptures. The preaching was not accompanied by any ritual of any kind. It was not part of a formal service of worship. The preacher simply rose with the Scriptures in his hand and reasoned from them.

A meeting for the preaching of the Gospel is not a gathering of the Church. The preacher may be the only member of the Church present. It should be remembered that unbelievers cannot take any true part in worship. Of course, public prayer asking the blessing of God, and the proclamation of the Gospel message in song, are quite in keeping in such a meeting, but they are not a necessary accompaniment of the preaching of the Gospel.

Careful note should be taken of what was not done in these gatherings. The preachers depended entirely upon the power of the Holy Spirit for power to create interest and to produce results. They never had recourse to any of the aids that lack of faith suggest. They had no beautiful buildings, costly organs, trained singers, vestured choirs, orchestras or impressive forms of service. There were no catchy tunes and sentimental choruses or hymn tunes played on saws. They did not advertise themselves with lauditory adjectives as super-preachers, famous teachers and world travellers. No, there were none of these things that seem so essential where the flesh intrudes and the power of the Holy Spirit is lacking. Oratory, psychology, architecture, art, music, learning, culture, organization were not used as substitutes for spiritual power. There was nothing soulish, no jokes interspersed to jog the flagging interest, no playing upon the emotions, no tricks of oratory. Their belief in the Holy Spirit was not just theoretical: they really depended upon Him and upon Him alone.

The preaching was definite and urgent. The Gospel was proclaimed with no uncertain sound. The preachers went directly to the point, stating clearly and boldly the issues involved: there was no compromising or temporising or attempt to make the Gospel more palatable to the audience. Paul's anxiety ever to be a faithful preacher of the pure Gospel appears in his request to the Ephesian church that they pray for him, "that I may fearlessly proclaim its message as I am in duty bound to utter it" (Eph. 6:20, Way's Translation).

It is also evident that there was both the intention and expectation of getting immediate results. These preachers were not sowing with the vague hope of reaping perhaps months or years afterwards. They proclaimed a simple and full Gospel and urged men to immediate acceptance. There was urgency in their message—the urgency born of a passionate love for Christ—the fruit of the Spirit—which translated itself into a similar love—the fruit of the same Spirit—for those whom Christ loved and for whom He died. Thus Paul could write truly and with passionate emphasis to the Corinthians, "We pray you in Christ's stead, be ye reconciled to God".

The practice in the New Testament Church was that at the Lord's Table several with gifts of the Spirit took part as they were led. But there is no example of such a procedure at any other gathering. When Paul or others taught, or preached to the unsaved, one presided and preached, as did our Lord also.

Where there are Elders, they will see that there are speakers and leaders for the different meetings.[1] Such was the duty of the Elders in the synagogue. Where there are no Elders, the responsibility falls directly upon the congregation. This responsibility belongs to the whole congregation, men and women, not just to the men. To reason that those who act in such a matter are acting as Elders is wrong, because when Elders act in the matter they are acting for the congregation. The final responsibility in all things belongs to the congregation.

Beyond this there is no New Testament example. It is not stated how the congregation in this matter exercised control regarding those who preside and speak. Where there is no such example, the procedure must be based upon general spiritual principles. And care must be taken not to introduce customs that seem spiritual yet run counter to these principles.

Reasoning that leads to practices that appear to be "more spiritual" than the simple order given in Scripture is not inspired by the Holy Spirit. It leads to a false superior spirituality in which the flesh finds glory. And that, of course, will produce death, not life.

There is the practice of waiting until the last moment before a gathering for teaching or preaching, and then asking, "who feels he has the Word for this meeting?" There is, of course, no suggestion of such a procedure in the New Testament Church.

Why wait until the last moment to know the Lord's choice? It is important, whenever possible, to give the teacher and preacher time for preparation through prayer and study of the Word. For that reason the normal procedure should be to find out the Lord's will regarding those who should minister in plenty of time to permit of a thorough spiritual preparation. To do otherwise is not more spiritual; it has its roots in self-confidence.

Moreover, it opens the door to the carnal believer. In a small group of believers without Elders, a member who had been active in preaching was excluded from fellowship because of sin. This congregation had the practice of letting any one lead and preach at any meeting who might feel he was led to do so. The result was that, when the missionary came on a visit this disciplined member

----

[1] See pp. 323-5.

did not attend, but, when the missionary was not there, he presided and preached and the congregation, though it felt he should not do so, was helpless to prevent it. Had this congregation sought the Lord's will at their prayer meeting during the week as to who should minister in the following week's services, they would have exercised their authority and fulfilled their responsibility in a way that was in accordance with Scriptural principles and the difficulty would have been avoided.

For the Teaching of the Word

In the Gospels we have graphic pictures of two types of meetings for the teaching of the Word. In the one we see Christ teaching the multitudes, and in the other we listen with the disciples as He teaches them alone, apart from the throng, preparing them to be His witnesses. The Evangelists were continually exercising a teaching ministry among the churches. Such meetings were not open meetings, as was the gathering at the Lord's Table. One with the gift of teaching exercised his ministry, it might be in one gathering, or in an extended series of meetings as when Paul preached and taught daily for two years in the school of Tyrannus.

The Sunday School

No such thing as a Sunday School is spoken of in the New Testament. The question, therefore, arises as to whether it should form part of the Church's ministry. It should. There is no doubt that the Holy Spirit gives to some gifts for preaching and teaching of a type especially suited for the evangelization and instruction of children. That these gifts should be excercised and that those who possess them may gather children together to hear the Gospel or for systematic instruction surely is beyond question.

There are, however, some aspects of the matter that require consideration:

1. We must never lose sight of the fact that in both the Old and New Testaments the responsibility for the spiritual instruction of children is placed by God upon the parents, not upon the priesthood or upon the Church. The Church certainly has a ministry towards children as towards all people, but it cannot relieve parents of the responsibility that God has placed upon them. No matter how efficient the teaching given in Sunday School may be, it can-

not take the place of the instruction in God's Word that should be given in the home by the parents. Any failure to appreciate this truth produces weakness both in the home and in the church.

2. It must be remembered also that those who are given the gift for government in the congregation are the Elders. God has placed them in the church for its oversight and they are responsible directly for the supervision of all the spiritual activities of the congregation. While those with gifts of the Spirit for ministry to children should be given full freedom to exercise their gifts, it is not Scriptural to form a separate Sunday School organization. The congregation cannot be divided into a number of semi-independent, or even dependent, organizations. No gifts of the Spirit or officers are provided for the running of such organizations.

3. In ministry to children, just as to adults, dependence must be entirely and directly upon the Holy Spirit. The teachers must be called of God to this ministry. They must receive their messages from the Spirit directly through the Word, and these must be given "in power and demonstration of the Spirit". The Bible alone should be used in the classes. Sunday School magazines, etc., may be helpful in the preparation of the lesson, but they should not be introduced into the class.

Where the Holy Spirit is present as He should be, there will be no need for psychological and emotional aids such as prizes, hand-work, gifts, yearly entertainments, picnics, etc. To secure the attention and interest of the children, and to get them to memorize Scripture, the teacher should not turn to soulish aids but seek the inspiration and power of the Holy Spirit.

After conducting Sunday Schools organized according to the latest modern methods, we excluded everything that would in any way take the place of direct dependence upon the Holy Spirit. Prizes, picnics, Christmas entertainments[1], contests, hand-work, etc., were all abandoned. The results have fully justified the step. The teachers have had to depend directly upon the Holy Spirit, and that has brought blessing to them and to the children. They found a power that was more real and effectual. The spiritual results have been decidedly superior. Different motives, attitudes and loyalties have been produced that are of far-reaching conse-

---

[1] It should be remembered that the observance of religious feast-days is not permitted to the New Testament Christian. (Col. 2:16-23; Gal. 4:9-10.)

quences, leading to a true appreciation of spiritual values, giving Christ the central place, and bringing a direct dependence upon the Holy Spirit. The children memorize Scripture just as readily, but they do so, not for a prize, but to know God's Word. The Scripture learned from that motive means much more to them. They try to get other children to come to Sunday School, not to gain points in an aeroplane race, but because they want their companions to know Christ and to learn of Him. Here, too, the motive is of no small importance. There has been no difficulty in holding attention and interest. The atmosphere of the Sunday School is certainly more healthy spiritually. There is a deeper spiritual tone and a greater sense of the presence of the Spirit and of the Lord.

Women's Meetings

There is no place in the structure of the Church of the New Testament for women's organizations of any kind.

There can be no question that women may be gathered together to hear the preaching of the Gospel or to study God's Word; and women who have the gifts of the Spirit to do so should have liberty to minister to them. But the details of all such ministry should be directly under the supervision of the Elders. Women are members of the congregation on the same basis as men and the ministry they engage in is under the direct supervision of the Elders just as is that of men. There is no need for a Women's Committee to oversee women's meetings. All women with the gifts of the Spirit will be given full freedom for the exercise of their gifts. Any special decisions in regard to time, place and speakers for women's meetings are the responsibility of the Elders just as are such questions regarding any other meetings in connection with the testimony of the congregation.

Choirs

The song of praise is acceptable unto God when it comes as an expression of praise and adoration inspired by the Holy Spirit. But singing in itself is not worship, no matter how beautiful the words or accomplished the singer (Jn. 4:23, 24).

Singing can be spiritual or it can be wholly a matter of the emotions. It is only the Holy Spirit's inspiration in the heart of the singer that gives the song its spiritual value. If the inspiration comes but from the fleshly heart, if the objective is simply the creating of a religious atmosphere or the beautifying of a service, if it is an offering of man's work presented to God, then it is not worship and it is not acceptable to God—it is of the same nature as Cain's offering.

It is no secret that, so far as modern church activities are concerned, it is in the choir, the quartette and the soloist that the vanity and pride of the human heart find their most productive soil.

There were no choirs or orchestras in the churches founded by the Apostles. Neither the New Testament Evangelists nor the churches needed them. There is nothing that they will do to draw souls to the meetings and to stir the heart that the Holy Spirit will not do without them, and do better, if He is really present in power. If he is not, no choir can take His place or do His work. When it seems that the drawing power of a choir, or quartette, or music, or a better organ, is necessary to attract people to hear the preaching of the Gospel, let us seek rather to discover why our preaching has lost the drawing power of the Gospel given forth in 'power and demonstration of the Spirit'. Such things cannot give spiritual power, nor can they make our worship "a sweet-smelling savour" to the Lord.

This does not mean that the singing of the Gospel message will never be used by the Holy Spirit. When a singer is truly ministering in the Spirit with a humble heart and a consecrated walk, his ministry may certainly be used of God. Souls have been saved through the singing of the message of salvation. But the regular church choir has no place in the spiritual order of the Church. As has been truly said:

> The praise of the sanctuary should not be turned into an entertainment by a few trained performers. We cannot praise the Lord by proxy, and the church should not attempt to compete with the play-house.[1]

As to permitting unconverted persons or unconsecrated Christians to take any part in ministry through singing, we shall quote the solemn words of A. J. Gordon:

> We are believers by the cleansing of the blood and the indwelling of the Spirit; have been constituted 'a spiritual house, an holy priesthood to offer up spiritual sacrifices'; but instead of using our

---

[1] J. H. Snowden: *The Psychology of Religion*, p. 246.

ministry in humble dependence on the Holy Ghost, we have brought up minstrels from Egypt, that 'music with its voluptuous swell' may take the place of that chastened, self-denying, holy song which no man can learn but they that have been redeemed... When I can consent to have the communion table moved out into the court of the Gentiles, and call upon the thoughtless and unconverted to receive the sacred elements lying thereon, then I may see the propriety of bringing a choir of unregenerated musical artists into the Holy of Holies of the church, and of committing to their direction the service of song.[2]

---

[2] *How Christ Came to Church*, pp. 48. 49.

CHAPTER XXIV

THE YOUNG PEOPLE

In the New Testament churches there were no young people's organizations of any kind, either auxiliary to, or separate from, the congregation. However, young people took an important part in the ministry of the Gospel as preachers and Evangelists and, no doubt, in many other ways. Timothy, Titus, Mark and others were evidently quite young men when they began their ministry. The ministry of these and of all the other young converts was carried on within the normal order in the Church.

The same principles apply to young people's organizations as to the Sunday School. The order of the New Testament congregation does not permit of auxiliary organizations within its structure and no gifts of the Spirit are provided for their Presidents, Secretaries, Treasurers, etc. The Church is one Body: there can be no divisions within it and no segregation of particular groups. Men and women, old and young, work together as one through the various gifts and coordinating direction of the Spirit.

It is not healthy to create an exaggerated youth consciousness among young believers. It is natural and right that youth should seek the companionship of youth but it is not natural or right for them to withdraw from normal cooperation with older believers in the Church's witness. When they do so, both lose much that is of great value and an element is introduced into the congregation that is contrary to its nature.

To state these facts, however, does not solve the problem of the young people in the modern Church. Young people's Societies have come into being to meet a need, and they have seemed to be the only way of meeting that need. The organized Church is no longer New Testament in form; the prevailing order in the ministry of the Word gives little or no opportunity for the young people to take an active part, and, very often, no aggressive Gospel ministry is carried on.

The only way to make possible an active testimony in which the young people could take part, and to provide the necessary coordination of their witness, seemed to be to form independent, or semi-independent, associations. These Societies have made possible active, cooperative witness and have provided young people with experience, which they could not have obtained within the existing order in their churches. Nevertheless, we must face the fact that young people's Societies are not in God's original plan for the Church, and if the Church were where it should be they would not need to exist.

The spiritual activities carried on by some of these Societies are Scriptural and excellent. Those who founded them and many who carry on their work are men and women whom God has called to a ministry among young people and to whom the Holy Spirit has given gifts for such work. As far as has been possible, the Holy Spirit has used these instruments and blessed their ministry. But what is the ultimate objective which the Lord and the Holy Spirit have purposed to attain through the gifts which He gives for ministry among young people? It is the building of the Church. It is not just the conversion and spiritual good of the young people, but the leading of these young people immediately into the place which they should occupy in the Church as members of the Body of Christ. A young people's society, no matter how active and thriving it may be, does not attain that objective. Its organization stands in the way. It substitutes an artificial order that bars the young people from normal participation in the activities of the congregation. The result is that, beyond a certain point, their spiritual development is restricted, for, while much of their activity is good and useful, they are not led into the full purpose of God for them in the spiritual structure of the Church. Then, when youth passes and they no longer qualify for the young people's organization, they find themselves with no adequate sphere of active service, instead of being able to continue on in normal cooperative ministry with all ages as the New Testament order made possible.

Of course, not all organizations do this to the same extent. Some, particularly those that are engaged primarily in soul-winning, have comparatively little in the way of organization. But even in these cases, exceedingly valuable as is their work, great would be the gain if God's full pupose were kept in view and their ministry made to conform fully to the principles of the spiritual structure of the Church.

Because of the existing Church order it is not possible, in many cases, to attain fully to the true Scriptural order. That does not mean that nothing should be attempted for the young people in such places; most certainly everything possible should be done; but what is done should not depart from the principles of the Scriptural order. We may not be permitted to introduce the full spiritual order, but at least we should introduce nothing that will perpetuate an unscriptural order.

It will be understood that the objection to organization is only to that which substitutes for, or interferes in any way with, God's order for the Church, or hinders the liberty of the Spirit in the carrying on of His work. For example, it may be quite legitimate and helpful for a group of soul-winners or Bible teachers to fellowship together in their ministry and to make the necessary arrangements to do so, but if they organize themselves or their converts for fellowship and service in a manner contrary to that which God has ordained, they make a serious mistake. Even where the organization does not affect the order of the Church, care must be exercised. For instance, it is necessary that a Summer camp for young people be efficiently organized, but the greatest care must be taken that regulations and programmes do not deprive the Holy Spirit of liberty, or substitute for His guidance and power.

The structure of the New Testament congregation was adequate to care for the needs of young and old in the early years of the Church, and if it is put fully into practice it will be found just as adequate today. The Lord did not forget the needs of the young people when He formed the plan for His Church. They are provided for by divine wisdom in the way that is best for them and best for the Church. Any additions or modifications in the structure He has ordained necessarily bear within them inherent weakness that must inevitably bear its own fruit..

Making Concessions

Work among young people must always be true to the principles of the spiritual ministry. To do otherwise is to open the door to forces that will nullify the true work of the Spirit. It may seem advisable and even necessary to make concessions to 'the spirit of modern youth': that is, to the youthful human heart. Young people will desire them and, perhaps, demand them. For a time, such concessions will bring an appearance of success, because they will have the support of those who are not definitely spiritual, but their fruit, in the long run, is always found to be unsound.

All depends upon what we are seeking to obtain: whether it is faith and obedience without compromise, or a more or less formal religious profession. If it is the former, we must remember that spiritual life without compromise can never be obtained by compromise. We must be prepared for the fact that what we offer will not be popular, for it cannot be attractive to the flesh. It will be resisted and to maintain it will mean constant watchfulness and conflict.

We must be prepared also for the fact that some will reject it. But those who do will do so because they deliberately choose compromise, and no concessions would prevent them doing so.

If we compromise to meet them half way to hold them, we lower the spiritual standard of the whole congregation's life and witness to that extent. Henceforth that is our standard. Our purpose may have been to hold the young folk until they could be raised later to a higher plane but what we do actually is to lower permanently our own plane.

It is this that has gradually brought the downfall of many a spiritual church. A new congregation is formed of truly converted, spiritual people. The highest standard is set in its testimony and seems to be established permanently. As the years pass, the believers' children grow up. Among them are all types: some are spiritual; others are attracted by the world. In an endeavour to hold the latter, concessions are made. It seems better to do so than to lose them. One concession leads to another. The result is that the young people as a whole are brought down to the lowered standard and the congregation comes to have two distinct groups: the original, older members who are spiritual, and the younger group that is indefinite in its testimony and compromises with the world. Finally, the more spiritual element gives in or is crowded out and the congregation becomes a modern, formally religious church.

If there had been a refusal to lower the standard and permit any compromise, some young people would probably have been lost to the membership—though much fewer than was feared—but the congregation would have retained the purity of its spiritual life and the power of its witness. By the compromise nothing worthwhile was gained and everything was lost.

How to Meet the Need

But what is to be done to solve the problem of how to meet the need of the young people and hold them? This is a matter of primary importance, but we cannot do more here than indicate some general principles.

There are two extremes that must be avoided, for both of them bring death. Compromise is fatal, but so also is a joyless rigidity that is sometimes mistaken for true spirituality. Young people may be frozen out by older Christians whose spirituality has become more a code of prohibitions than a manifestation of the virile holiness of the Spirit of God.

Older Christians who, very properly, have the leadership in a congregation, must not be forgetful of the needs of the young people. There should be a true appreciation of the characteristics of the adolescent age, which is the most critical from every point of view. Up to that age, children have been content to accept passively what they are taught. They trust their teachers implicitly and their activity consists of imaginative play. In the adolescent a profound change takes place. Independence asserts itself. He begins to think for himself and is impelled to express himself independently in action. He wants to do things and to do them on his own. He wants to experience life personally and practically. He is not unwilling to receive instruction and counsel but he resents being led by the hands as a child or being considered as incapable of attempting anything real.

He is no longer satisfied with make-believe; he wants the real thing. This must be clearly understood by the leaders of the congregation. If there is nothing real for him to do in the congregation he will seek something real to do outside. He may find that the older people of the church think he is far too young to engage in any real spiritual activity—nothing beyond some petty organizational task in Sunday School—but he sees that the world does not consider him too young to experience any of the things which it offers. It will invite him to drink, play cards, smoke, dance, swear and everything else that it does. That door to experience is wide open to him, and it is attractive, not only because of what is sinful in it but also because it has the appearance of being real, mature life.

Theoretical dogma that has little expression in practical activity repells the adolescent because it has no appeal to him. The adult may fool himself with it; the youth scorns it. On the other hand, a faith that dares to be practical, holiness that has the courage to be real, a love for Christ that produces action in practical service— these have a mighty appeal to him. He does not understand truth that seems purely theoretical, but he seeks and readily understands truth that is practical.

Youth is not an abnormal state, nor is it purposeless or fruitless. Each period of life has its particular characteristics. God has ordered that it should be so and there is a wise purpose in each one. All are necessary to normal development. In the Church all the members, young and old, have a place. The Holy Spirit's gifts are given to every one, no matter of what age, as soon as he is saved. The Holy Spirit will use the child and the youth, manifesting Himself through them in a manner suitable to their age and experience.

The Elders of the congregation must recognize this and prepare for it. There are gifts of the Spirit provided for ministry to young people and it is very important that some in the congregation manifest them. It need not be the Elders who do so. Possibly it will be someone younger than they, but they are responsible to see that this ministry is adequately carried on. If there is no one with such a gift of the Spirit, prayer should be made until some one is provided. It is God's will that there should be someone, for it is a necessary ministry, therefore, it may be confidently asked that the provision be made.

In Sunday School, the teaching given to adolescents should have a definitely practical aspect with regard both to life and service. They should study God's Word, not just to know it, but to know how to use it. They should be led into the practice of faith and prayer as practical things, not simply for their own lives, but to influence men and situations, to find out God's will and to bring it to pass.

Converted young people should be made to understand that they are just as responsible as the older believers to take part in the active ministry of the congregation through the gifts of the Spirit given to them. In a congregation that is truly New Testament there will be abundant spiritual activity—united prayer, preaching, teaching, open-air work, cottage meetings, house-to-house witnessing, tract distribution, personal work. According to their gifts, the young believers should be expected and urged to participate in all these activities.

It is here that someone gifted by the Spirit is needed, to see that the young people are given suitable opportunities to take part and to properly encourage them to do so. They will rally round one who will lead them with sympathy and understanding and counsel them wisely. And they greatly need such an one, for while they crave for action they lack experience and balance—two things which they instinctively know only practical work will give them.

There is wide scope for young peoples activities within the true order of the Church. There is much that can be done to encourage the young people and to provide activities and fellowship suitable to their needs that is quite legitimate and not contrary to the principles of the spiritual order.

It is impossible to go into detail here regarding such activities; we shall but mention one or two examples. There is no reason why young people should not be gathered together for ministry suitable to their age in special meetings. Summer camps can provide excellent opportunity for intimate spiritual ministry. Excursions to some district, in city or country, may make possible both fellowship and service. We have found that a good plan for an excursion is, first of all to meet together for prayer at some convenient point, then to separate into twos for house-to-house visitation, tract distribution, personal work and to invite the people to an open-air or cottage meeting to be held in the evening. After that, all may gather together to have something to eat, putting together whatever they have brought. Finally a meeting is held, led by one of the young people and open for brief messages or testimonies by all who wish to take part.

It is required that an Elder should be 'given to hospitality'. The young people certainly need homes open to them where they may gather together in a home atmosphere that is both spiritual and sympathetic. In every congregation there should be this provision.

In this way the young people's needs will be met by the means which God has provided. It does not guarantee that all young people will be converted, or that all those who are will walk in full yieldedness to the Lord, but it is by far the most fruitful way. And it is the only way that will produce fruit that is sound and fully mature. Moreover, it is the only way that will preserve to the congregation the New Testament standard of spiritual life and power.

A demand on the part of the young people of a congregation to have a separate organization of their own should not be taken by the Elders as the inevitable signal that the time has come when concessions will have to be made to youth, but as evidence that there has been a serious decline in the spiritual activity of the congregation. In a church where there is true New Testament activity, the young, in common with all the other members are so busy that they feel no need, and would have no time, for a separate organization.

Young people of one of our congregations were asked by members of a young people's Society why they did not organize themselves. The others told them of their organization, election of officers, business meetings, committees, etc. Our young people replied "But we would have no time for all that". They were so busy attending Bible Studies and prayer meeting, preaching the Gospel in the open air and in indoor meetings and engaging in tract distribution from door to door, that they would have had to neglect some of that vital work to find time to keep the wheels of an organization running. They were taking part in real ministry in full cooperation with the whole congregation. They needed nothing more and could have nothing better. They had what God purposed they should have in the Church, their ministry was counting as He intended it should, and they were satisfied.

CHAPTER XXV

THE MINISTRY OF WOMEN

We shall not attempt to settle all the difficulties of Scriptural interpretation in the matter of women's ministry. However, there are some fundamental principles that seem to be clear and that are vital to the witness of the Church.

The key passage of Scripture regarding the exercise of the gift of preaching is that which describes its initial manifestation in the church at Pentecost—Acts 2:1-21. On that day, all, both men and women, were together in prayer, all received the Holy Spirit and the gift of the Spirit for the public proclamation of the Gospel was manifested through all in the streets of Jerusalem to the salvation of many souls. This had been foretold explicitly in Joel's prophecy, cited by Peter. It was in accord with the Lord's command to all to preach the Gospel.

The manner in which the Church began is the manner in which it is to continue. Every member has the Holy Spirit and every member has gifts of the Spirit for publicly witnessing to the Gospel. And the record shows that the Early Church did continue as it had begun.

The Holy Spirit did not make a mistake or an exception on that day when He used women as well as men in public preaching. It was the fulfilment of prophecy. It is the order God instituted in the Church at the beginning and all the subsequent teaching regarding women's ministry should be fitted into it — and it will be found that it does fit in.

That women as well as men took part in prayer and preaching in the congregation is clearly indicated in 1 Cor. 11:4, 5. It is stated that the four daughters of Philip, the Evangelist, were preachers. However, the number of women preachers mentioned in the New Testament is smaller than that of men. This accords with the fact that in the previous Dispensation the number of Prophetesses was comparatively small.

It is evident that women assisted in many ways the work of Paul and his companions. He speaks of "Phoebe our sister, who is a ministering servant of the church at Cenchrea", of "Priscilla and Aquila, my fellow-labourers in the work of Jesus Christ", of "Mary who laboured much with me", and of "Tryphena and Tryphosa, the faithful labourers in the Lord's service" (Rom. 16:1, 3, 6, 12, Conybeare). Phoebe was the bearer of his letter to the church in Rome. Priscilla, along with her husband, was used by the Lord to lead Apollos into a clearer knowledge of the truth. Paul refers to the faithfulness of Eunice and Lois in instructing Timothy in the Scriptures. He acknowledged with deep gratitude temporal ministry received from women (Acts 16:14, 15; 18:26; Rom. 16.2).

It appears that the widows supported by the church, spoken of in Paul's letter to Timothy (1 Tim. 5:4-13), occupied their time with various kinds of ministry. We have seen widows thus occupied. They gave incalculable service in prayer, visitation work, personal witness and the preaching of the Gospel. They did this, not because we told them to do it but because they felt it was the work for which the Lord had called them and given them the gifts of the Spirit. No doubt it was such ministry that the widows and other women mentioned by Paul performed.

Some of the New Testament Evangelists were accompanied by their wives. But it does not seem that any single women participated in their travelling ministry. The sphere of the ministry of unmarried women and widows appears to have been the local church, mostly, at least.

There is a special teaching ministry to younger women that older women of ripe spiritual experience are called upon to undertake (Tit. 2:3-5). It is a ministry that is very necessary and fruitful, and one that would be difficult for a man to perform. Paul did not advise Timothy, the missionary, to do it but to have the older women undertake it.

Scriptures that May be Misunderstood

Paul wrote to Timothy, "I permit not a woman to teach, nor to claim authority over a man" (1 Tim. 2:12, Conybeare). Here, of course, he is stating a general principle and not speaking particularly of women in the Church. But we find the same principle applied in the Church. No women were called to the ministries which involved the exercise of spiritual authority, such as those of Apostle, Evangelist, Elder, Deacon, Teacher. Yet Paul evidently did not intend to prohibit such a teaching ministry as Priscilla exercised towards Apollos. Therefore he does not mean that in no circumstances may a woman teach the Gospel to a man. What he prohibits is the taking of the position or attitude of an authoritative Teacher of men.

That a gift of teaching is given by the Holy Spirit to many women is an evident fact. But only to men is given that variety of the gift of teaching which causes the one who has received it to be recognized by the Church as a Teacher and who, in that capacity, will minister to the Church as a whole.

The passage in 1 Cor. 14:34, 35 presents difficulties which must be recognized and taken into consideration as far as we are able to do so. We dare not build a practice upon one verse to the exclusion of other passages that also bear upon the subject. The fundamental rules of interpretation must always be scrupulously observed. The passage in question should be considered in the light of 1 Cor. 11:5, the second chapter of Acts and all the other references to the participation of women in ministry. Doing so does not remove all the difficulties presented by this passage—probably it increases them—but it will prevent us from making wrong deductions.

Regarding the passage itself, we must consider, first of all, the context, which shows Paul to be correcting abuses in the Corinthian church, particularly in the gathering at the Lord's Table. We must note the fact that the word translated 'woman' is usually translated 'married women' (Matt. 5:31, 32; 14:3, etc.) and is so rendered in this passage in Weymouth's version (3rd. Edit.), the Twentieth Century New Testament, the Welsh Bible, etc. The reference to their husbands in verse 35 shows that this rendering is correct. Does this mean that a distinction is made between married and unmarried women in the matter of speaking in public? There is no ground given in Scripture to believe so. Nowhere is such a distinction made.

Paul says, "as also saith the law'. The Old Testament law says that the woman must be in subjection to the man, but it does not say that women cannot prophesy in public nor that they cannot prophesy in the presence of men. On the contrary, the law permitted Prophetesses. Two of these were married women. Nowhere in the New Testament is it said that a woman may not preach, or that she may not preach in the presence of men. No example is recorded of women preaching only to women. But the fact is stated that women preached, and the inference is that men were present. It is interesting, in this connection, to note Conybeare's rendering of 1 Cor. 11:11:

Nevertheless in their fellowship with the Lord man and woman may not be separated the one from the other.

Even if Paul had said that women may not preach in the church, it must be remembered that the term 'church' is never used of a building, but always of the assembly of God's redeemed. Paul was writing of the official gathering together of the Church, which is the gathering around the Lord's Table. A woman who is preaching the Gospel to a gathering of unbelievers, men and women, indoors or outdoors, would not be "in the church"; indeed, she might be the only member of the Church present.

The suggestion that the speaking referred to here by Paul was simply chattering does not seem to meet the case. That there was chattering on the part of some is not improbable, but the reference to the need for subjection and the advice that if information is required it should be asked of their own husbands, indicates that more than irresponsible chattering was involved. But also, if their speaking had been preaching, the counsel to ask their husbands would not be intelligible and it could hardly have been said that their preaching was a "shame". To have drawn forth such a sharp rebuke from one who had not been slow to express appreciation of ministry rendered by women, there must have been, not just chattering, or the asking of some simple and sincere questions, however out of place, or a spiritual word quietly given, but a serious breach of order involving a fundamental principle. The principle concerned is evidently that spoken of in 1 Tim. 2:12—that women were not to assume the place of teachers or rulers of men. Possibly one or two women in the congregation, of a type not unknown in modern congregations, had taken advantage of the existing, undisciplined condition of the church (for which, in the first place, the men in the position of authority were responsible) and were urging their questions and insisting upon the acceptance of their judgment. No doubt the wives of some of the men were acting in an unseemly way trying to dominate in the church. Perhaps the trouble also had some connection with the misuse of the gift of tongues.

As we have seen, Paul is writing of the meeting of the church around the Lord's Table as the Body of Christ when the Holy Spirit ministers spiritual food through several preachers. It is stated in the twenty-eighth verse that one with the gift of tongues must 'keep silence', if there is no interpreter present. Then, in verse thirty, it is said, "If any thing be revealed to another that sitteth by, let the first hold his peace (lit. 'be silent')". In both these cases it is not absolute silence that is enjoined. Those referred to are not commanded to take no part in prayer, singing, the reading of the Word, etc., but simply not to speak in the circumstances stated.

Inferences have been drawn from this passage, and that in 1 Tim, 2:8-15, that have, in some cases, deprived women of the right of uttering a word in prayer or hymn in a meeting in which a man is present. This has only inference for support, and there is nothing more dangerous than to build doctrine or practice upon such ground.

The passage in 1 Tim. 2:8-15 is sometimes quoted as teaching that men should pray everywhere but that women should be silent. Competent Greek scholars throw much light upon this passage. The Greek word here translated 'silence' is not the same one so rendered in 1 Cor. 14:34. Is is *hesuchia*, meaning 'quietness', 'tranquility', 'stillness'. In v. 2 it is rendered 'quiet' and in 2 Thes. 3 : 12 'quietness'. The literal translation given in the 'Englishmen's Greek New Testament" of 1 Tim. 2:11, 12 is as follows:

Let a woman learn in quietness in all subjection; but I do not allow a woman to teach nor to exercise authority over man, but to be in quietness.

This rendering agrees with that of the Revised Version. In these verses it is the husband and wife that are referred to. Young's Literal Translation reads:

Let a woman in quietness learn in all subjection, and a woman I do not suffer to teach, nor to rule a husband but to be in quietness.

If in verses 8, 11 and 12, it is taught that women may not pray in public, then it is in contradiction to 1 Cor. 11:5. The fact is, however, that both these passages teach the same thing: women may pray in public but should be attired in a modest and seemly fashion. Prof. Ramsay says:

The necessary sense of the word "likewise" (in 1 Tim. 2:9) is that women are affected by what is said about men. Paul wishes that women too should pray everywhere.

Conybeare in a note on this verse writes:

After "women" we must supply "pray" (as Chrysostom does), or something equivalent (to take part in worship, etc.) from the preceding context.

An ingenious translation of these passages relating to women's ministry has been advocated by some women teachers. It turns Paul's statements into questions asked of him by the church in Corinth and makes him answer championing the liberty of women to occupy any position of authority in the congregation. The account of the Fall in Genesis 3 is also made to read so as virtually to reverse the position of the woman. However, no support is given by the chief Greek and Hebrew authorities to these new renderings, and, furthermore, the new version of the account of the Fall has led those who advance the theory (who, otherwise, were sound in the faith) into other statements that are contrary to sound doctrine.

How Women Have Been Used

We believe that much help will be obtained in coming to an understanding of God's purpose in regard to women's spiritual ministry by considering the manner in which He has used women in the Church from Apostolic days until now. The facts accord with what appears to us to be the teaching of Scripture. We know that the Holy Spirit does not play fast and loose with God's Word. He never acts contrary to it, so that what we see to be truly His work should aid us in understanding the meaning of the Word.

Women have always been greatly used in the public preaching of the Gospel to the salvation of both men and women. There are some notable examples of this and it cannot be denied that these women ministered in the power of the Holy Spirit and with the blessing of God. There are many men today who have been saved through the preaching of women. We cannot refuse to acknowledge those whom God uses and through whom the Holy Spirit manifests his gifts. We cannot question God's knowledge of His own will or the Holy Spirit's understanding of the Word.

Since the time of Priscilla, women have been used of God in teaching the Word. Spiritual understanding and knowledge is given to women just as to men and God would have them impart the knowledge they have received and has never forbidden them to do so.

We have in mind the example of one woman who was greatly used of God in leading men and women into a deeper knowledge of spiritual things. For years she conducted a Home for fallen girls, the work being supported by God in answer to the prayer of faith. She came to have a deep experience with the Lord and knowledge of spiritual truth and was led out into a ministry of witness to what He had revealed to her. She travelled far, visiting many churches that invited her to witness to them. She refused always to stand in a pulpit, wishing it to be understood that she took no place of authority nor regarded herself as a Teacher of the Church. God used her and the Holy Spirit was with her and many of God's people were blessed. It is true, of course, that there are comparatively few such cases.

Some women who have begun in this way with blessing, have later assumed a place of authority as Teachers of the Church, and it seems that, as they have done so, there has been a withdrawing of the Holy Spirit's revelation and protection; emotion has clouded judgment, sentiment has obscured truth, and human wisdom has led into exaggeration and error.

Considering the Church as a whole as we see it at present, we find a great divergence in practice in the matter of women's ministry. On the one side is the extreme of restricting them from engaging in any spiritual ministry in the presence of men. On the other is the opposite extreme of opening to them all the ministries which involve the exercise of authority in the Church. At the one extreme, where there is complete prohibition, we find that there is an atmosphere of bondage and a tendency to a legalistic and harsh spirit. It is not usual to find there that the Spirit is working with liberty and power or that the joy of the Lord is in the hearts of His people. The rivers of living water are not flowing freely and the land is parched and thirsty. At the other extreme, there is evidence of a lack of spiritual depth. There is shallowness and superficiality. There may be much emotional activity and soulish effort, but there is lacking the true and abiding fruit of a deep, solid work of the Holy Spirit.

God's blessing is not upon either extreme. Where then is there the evidence of His presence and favour? We believe it is half way between the two, where women freely manifest all the gifts of the Spirit for ministry, with the exception of those for the exercise of authority or the administration of the affairs of the Church. It seems that there the Lord is pleased to give the greatest blessing; there is where the Holy Spirit works with greatest freedom, where the most and the truest fruit is borne.

Our experience in missionary service has been that God has

certainly called women to be preachers and to witness to the truth that the Lord has revealed to them; that the Holy Spirit has given them the gifts of the Spirit for such ministry and that much true fruit has been borne through their testimony. We have not found that God has given a woman the gifts of the Spirit necessary for laying the foundation of a new church, for administering the affairs of a congregation, or for ministering authoritatively as Teachers of the Church. We have found that in a congregation where women take a prominent place in the ministry of the Word at the Lord's Table or in the direction of the church the men remain inactive and continue to be immature spiritually.

However, though women are not church-planters, they have gifts of the Spirit which make them indispensible helpers in the work of church-planting as also in the carrying on of the ministry of a congregation.

In the work of evangelism, the ministry of women is of great importance. In the first place, they have an entrance among women and children, and gifts for such ministry, that men do not have. Usually, a woman can visit more freely in the homes of the people than a man can, which means that, since women and children form the greater part of the population, the woman worker has by far the largest field and greatest opportunity for ministry through personal contacts. In the homes of unbelievers, this minstry will aim at the conversion of all, irrespective of sex or age, with whom contact is made; in the homes of believers, its object will be to instruct in spiritual truth and lead all, men and women, into a full knowledge of what is possessed in Christ. Here, certainly, there is no limitation to her ministry.

A ministry of great value to the churches, especially to smaller groups of believers in more isolated places, may be carried on by a couple of lady workers. They may go to a place where there is a nucleus of believers and minister for a few weeks or months, particularly among the women and children. The object is not just to give teaching to women and children but to prepare the women to be able to carry on their own meetings and to conduct a Sunday School for the children. Thus something permanent is left behind that is of great importance to the life, growth and ministry of the local church. This is a ministry that contributes directly to church-planting.

In the Home

We have been very conscious of weakness in many churches due to a lack of understanding of the great principle that underlies women's ministry in the Church. Their responsibility in regard to the witness of the family life is often not realized. It is thought that the gifts of the Spirit for ministry through the home and to the home are inferior to other gifts such as public preaching and teaching.

To understand the true place and importance of women's ministry in the Church it is necessary to realize the central place given to the family in God's order. The family is the unit of Christian society. It is the basic human institution in God's order. Its unity and the interdependence of its members are fundamental. This is as marked in the New Testament as in the Old. A man cannot serve as an Elder or Deacon of the church, no matter what his personal fitness may be, if his wife and children do not give a faithful testimony. His fitness for responsibility in the assembly is judged by the testimony of his whole family.

The vital center of the witness of the community of believers is the family. If the spiritual life and testimony in the families is weak, the church will be proportionately weak. If the power of the Gospel is manifested in Godly homes, the testimony and power of the assembly is assured, not only for the present but also for the future.

It is at this vital point that woman has her special work. It is for this service that she has been endowed with special qualities. In the Church as in the home, man is responsible for the maintenance and government of the household, while woman's work has to do with the family life within. It is the mother, to a great extent, that gives the home its atmosphere. The testimony of the Christian home can hardly be above that of the mother. On the woman, therefore, to a great extent, depends the testimony of the Christian community, the spirituality and power of its corporate witness.

In and through the home, woman builds both for the present and for the future. The faithfulness and spiritual knowledge of the next generation of believers depends to no small extent upon the believing women of this generation.

As we have seen, woman's sphere in the family opens to her a wide field for evangelism and teaching. She has an entrance among the women and children of both believing and unbelieving households that a man cannot have. She has a ministry to them, because of her special qualities, that is impossible to a man. How great and urgent is the need for her ministry in this sphere!

God has placed both man and woman in the home. Both are equally necessary. He has placed men and women in the Church and there also both are equally necessary. Woman is not inferior to man either in the home or in the Church. Both are equal before God, but both do not have the same work to perform. The one is the complement of the other. Each has been endowed by God for a special work and responsibility. Without the man's ministry an assembly would be poor. Without the woman's ministry it would be equally poor.

God's order is perfect. All the spiritual gifts and qualities of both men and women are necessary to complete the Body and to bear the witness to the grace of God manifested in Christ for the salvation of men.

We realize that in the discussion of this matter we have left difficulties of interpretation only partly solved. We would acknowledge the difficulties involved. We feel that to do so is the only safe course to follow. To ignore any of them, for the sake of any theory built upon isolated texts, or upon an uncertain interpretation of some word or passage, is unsafe. We can endeavour to steer, what, from the teaching of Scripture as a whole and the evidence of the Spirit's work, appears to be the right course. If we do so in sincerity we are not likely to go far wrong.

One thing is beyond question: the ministry of women is of the most vital importance to the Church. There is need for care, in seeking to comprehend the full purpose of God, that we avoid anything that would limit in any way the freedom of the Holy Spirit to use fully every instrument in accordance with the divine purpose. Let us remember that Satan's purpose is to close the mouths of as many witnesses as possible. The Revised Version rendering of Psa. 68 : 11 is significant: "The Lord giveth the Word: the women that publish the tidings are a great host."

CHAPTER XXVI

COOPERATION BETWEEN CONGREGATIONS

In the New Testament Church there was no human organization to bind the different congregations together. There were no hierarchies or Synods or Councils or Conventions. There was no attempt even to give organized unity to the congregations of a country or district. It was not necessary. They were not disunited. A congregation did not think of itself as separate or independent. The whole Church was one. Though the forms of human organization were lacking, the Church possessed a structure that ensured unity—a unity more perfect than that which human organization can achieve, that made it indivisibly and powerfully one and yet that did not infringe upon spiritual liberty. It was only when this spiritual structure began to be set aside, when the true unity was lost sight of as spiritual light and life waned and a sense of separation and division arose, that a remedy was sought in human organization.

Since Babel, man's idea has always been to seek strength by multiplying his own strength: that is, by association and confederation. God's objective is unity. In the spiritual sphere unity is primary (Jn. 17:11, 21; 1 Cor. 12:25). It is necessary to full strength and a complete witness. Lack of unity is contrary to God's order. It is produced by lack of obedience and faith. It is sin and brings weakness. But the unity which God has given to the Church is not the unity of organization and confederation; it is the unity of the one Body, the unity of the Spirit.

The burden of the Lord's prayer for His disciples, recorded in the seventeenth chapter of John's Gospel, is that there might be unity. He said,

That they all may be one; as thou, Father, art in me, and I in thee, that they also may be one in us; that the world may believe that thou hast sent me. And the glory which thou gavest me I have given them; that they may be one, even as we are one! I in them, and thou in me, that they may be made perfect in one; and that the world may know that thou hast sent me, and hast loved them, as thou hast loved me.

Here is revealed the source of the Church's unity and the importance of this unity to the Church's witness. We are united one with another as we are all in union with Christ and God. The more perfectly we are united-with Christ and with God through the Spirit in their life, purpose and will, the more truly shall we be united together as members of Christ's Body. And the manifestation of this unity is essential to the witness to Christ and to God's love. Without it the Church's witness to the world will be unconvincing.

As we are one with Christ by the Spirit in His will, then we shall all walk according to His will, Christ manifesting Himself and working through us. This is the unity which God has given to the Church and there is no other. If the Church fails to enter into this unity it will seek in vain for unity. Unity. cannot be produced by organization or creed. It is the manifestation of the life of Christ filling His Body, and its cost is the cost of full surrender and obedience to Him.

Man recognizes the value of unity and feels the lack of it, but he seeks it in his own way, not in God's way; he seeks it in himself, not in God. In the Church he has sought to multiply his own strength to produce spiritual power and fruit. He has produced the artificial unity and strength of human organization, but in doing so he has trangressed the laws of spiritual unity and has fettered the Spirit. He has violated the basic principle of the Church's being and disrupted the true order of its life. This, of course, could not be done without causing serious damage to the organism resulting in disorganization and loss of strength.

The desire to create unity among congregations by organization and confederation arises in part from a misunderstanding of the true nature of the congregation. Although the purity of the Gospel message may have been retained, the Scriptural structure of the Church is obscured by the accustomed modern order. The true unity of the Body being no longer fully discerned and the means for the expression of that unity set aside, the congregation finds itself isolated and thinks of itself as practically a separate unit. Faced with the opposition of the world as time goes on, it comes to realize its weakness and loneliness and endeavours to find strength and fellowship through confederation with other congregations.

The three main systems that have evolved as a result are the episcopal, presbyterian and congregational. In each óf these may be recognized a fundamental principle of the original order, although it has been modified to conform to human organization. The episcopacy has sought to retain the strength of the New Testament Evangelist's ministry. Cyprian claimed that the Bishops were the successors of the Apostles. But it has substituted ecclesiastical authority for spiritual authority and eliminated the congregational presbytery. Presbyterianism has retained the congregational presbytery but has divided the Elders into ordained Elders and lay Elders, and it lacks the coordinating ministry of the New Testament Evangelist. Congregationalism lays stress upon the spiritual rights of the local congregation, but it has, in general, the same defects as presbyterianism. All have divided the Church into clergy and laymen, releasing the laymen from the responsibility of the ministry of the Word. Each system has the strength and the weakness derived from its order.

We do not have to go beyond the present day to see the process of organization-building among groups of congregations. The generally divided condition of the Church, the inroads of Rationalism and the infringing of the spiritual liberty of the congregation by Denominational organization have caused not a few of the more spiritual congregations to become 'independent'. These congregations, swinging to an opposite extreme, consider themselves, for all practical purposes, as entirely independent and self-sufficient. The result is that each one virtually becomes a separate division in itself. Before very long, however, it becomes conscious of its insufficiency and need for fellowship. Not knowing the spiritual structure of the Body, it turns again to association and confederation. It does so cautiously, because it senses its danger, and it endeavours to safeguard what is considers its rights; but it has set out again on the old path of man's order.

The New Testament congregation, as we have seen, is merely a gathering of local members of the one Church. These derive their membership, not from their association with the local gathering but from their baptism by the one Spirit into the one Body, a Body which is organically one and indivisible (1 Cor. 12:13; Eph. 4:2-16).

The Church is not a loosely formed composite of many small,

independent local bodies. The local gathering acquires its rights, not from its local position, but from the fact that it is an integral part of the one Body. Wherever and whenever any members of that one Body meet together in the Name of Christ, be they two or more, the one Christ, the Head of the Body, the One to whom the Church belongs, the Builder of the Church, is present in their midst. He is there to carry on His work of building His Church—the one Body. The ministry which He carries on through those members of His Body is just a part of the ministry of the Body. The authority and power derived from His presence is but the authority and power of the one Church.

The local gathering can act with the full authority of the Church as Christ acts through it. But that does not make it self-sufficient or independent. Its unity with the rest of the Body is not just a matter of spiritual affinity and theory. It is a practical reality and essential to the manifestation of full life. Without it, the life and ministry of a congregation must remain incomplete.

This becomes clearly evident when we consider the order that prevailed in the New Testament Church. While, naturally, the local company of members of the Church was responsible for the carrying on of the local witness and was fully equipped with gifts of the Spirit for such ministry, there were important functions that were performed by the Church as a whole. The ministry of the Evangelists—world evangelism and church-planting—was related to the Church and not to any individual congregation. They were ministers of the Church. The local church came into existence through their ministry and its continued spiritual security depended upon it. When a church fell into spiritual declension, as did that of Corinth, or into doctrinal error, as with the Galatians, or if Elders abused their office, as did Diotrophes, it was the Evangelists, ministers of the Church as a whole, who intervened that the spiritual order and sound doctrine might be restored. In the appointment of Elders and Deacons in the local churches also it was Evangelists who took the initiative and presided.

The evangelization of the world and the establishing of new churches was the work of the Church as a whole. The command is to every individual believer—to the Church. When a young man went forth from a congregation to minister as an Evangelist—as Timothy from Lystra and Silas from Jerusalem—he did not go as representing that congregation. He did not have any particular responsibility to it nor did it to him. He had become a minister of the Church. There is no record as to which congregation some of the New Testament Evangelists came from. Barnabas and Paul were not originally from Antioch and had been ministering there but a year. Paul was careful to make it clear that he was a minister of Christ, a minister of the Church, and not subject to the jurisdiction of any particular congregation, not even to that of the church in Jerusalem. (Cf. 2 Cor. 8:19).

The whole Church was responsible for the support of the Evangelist. Paul's support came largely from the newer churches such as that in Philippi. He appealed to all the churches for prayer. The Church as a whole was responsible to support the Evangelists in prayer (Eph. 6:18-20; Col. 4:2-4).

The Evangelists worked together in groups irrespective of the congregations or countries from which they had come; and any Evangelist could visit and minister to any congregation anywhere. The great importance of the Evangelist's ministry in linking the whole Church together as well as in its extension will be observed. In no small degree the Church's unity found its practical manifestation in the Evangelists. Inevitably, the loss of this phase of the Evangelist's ministry coincided with the loss of effective spiritual unity in the Church.

There were also travelling Teachers and preachers who served the Church as a whole. When a believer who travelled where he was unknown carried a letter proving that he fellowshipped with a gathering of the Church, he was received by any congregation (2 Cor. 3:1; Acts 18:27). He was a member of the Body of Christ, therefore he had a right to meet with the members of the Body anywhere. When believers in one region were suffering from famine, other congregations sent them financial aid (Acts 11:29; 2 Cor. 8:1-4, 19; 9:1-13). The congregations sending these gifts combined in choosing the messengers who were to take them to their destination.

Any action taken by any congregation was considered as an action of the Church. Christ was in the midst. It was He who acted through the members of His Body gathered together, and what was done by that gathering on earth was done in Heaven. The disciplining of a believer in sin or the laying on of hands upon one sent forth by the Spirit as an Evangelist were acts of the Church. Even the laying on of hands upon the sick by the local Elders was an act of the Church. It is not the church of Corinth or the church of Jerusalem that is spoken of but 'the Church in Corinth', 'the Church in Jerusalem'. Of course, if the action were not taken under the guidance of Christ, it was not valid and was not an act of the Church.

All this unity of action was the natural outcome of the fact that the whole Church was one indivisible Body with one Spirit and one Lord. It was not the product of organization. Any congregation that stood apart from this unity in life and ministry would have been poor indeed and greatly restricted in its ministry. The lack of organization left every congregation free to participate in this unity and all spiritual congregations naturally did so.

The Church today is split by many deep-rooted divisions. Differences of both doctrine and order separate the members of the Body. Not every so-called church is a true church. In some not only is there little life but many of those who gather are not born again of the Spirit. Such a gathering, though it call itself a church, is not a church. The leaven of which our Lord spoke has been working for nigh two thousand years. Many 'birds of the air' have lodged and hatched their broods in the branches of the 'mustard tree'.

To effect the unity of the Church in the situation that exists is not a simple matter. A recognition of the true Church is possible and a unity of fellowship with all that is of the Spirit is also possible. But full unity in spiritual fellowship and ministry depend upon unity in doctrine and practice.

It should not be difficult to know to what extent we may fellowship with brethren with whom we do not see eye to eye in everything. In the first place, we must bear in mind the fact that all the members of the Body of Christ are 'members one of another' and that all must have 'the same care one for another'. Every member has a definite and direct responsibility for every other member. All must minister one to another through prayer and through the gifts of the Spirit given for ministry and for the manifestation of the love of Christ in His Body.

Our fellowship with other members of the Body should never be less than that which the Lord has with them. How dare we refuse to have fellowship with those with whom the Lord has fellowship? To withdraw ourselves from them when He has not done so is wrong: it is of human wisdom; it is of the proud, unloving, fleshly heart. An attitude of spiritual superiority or of sectarianism can have no justification.

23

The principles that should guide us in our fellowshipping with brethren who may be 'weak' or uninstructed are clearly set forth in the fourteenth chapter of the Epistle to the Romans. There we see that lack of full light is no reason for refusing fellowship to a brother in Christ. However, a restriction is imposed upon the weak brother: he is not to be permitted to enter into discussions in the congregation about things that are unprofitable. The weak brother's weakness must not be permitted to intrude into the ministry of the congregation. A restriction is imposed also upon those with fuller light: they must be careful to do nothing that would be a cause of stumbling to a weaker brother. All is to be done according to the rule of love.

We cannot, however, under any circumstances permit fellowship to go to the extent of compromising principle or participating in any practice that is unscriptural. Spiritual fellowship will always be possible to some extent where there is not deliberate sin, but fellowship in ministry becomes impossible when there is a serious difference in doctrine or practice. To a spiritual believer or congregation, cooperation with those who are definitely and deliberately compromising with worldliness or with unscriptural doctrine or practice is deadly. The spiritual believer or congregation that does so is compromising. There is a false idea of the duty of fellowship that leads into danger. It is sentimental and not spiritual. It is not true fellowship for it is not of the Spirit or in the Spirit. It does not raise those on a lower spiritual level to a higher level; on the contrary, the unity which it brings is at the cost of compromise and lowers the spiritual standard of the stronger to that of the weaker.

While this is true and needs to be stated clearly, we must also recognize the danger, always present, that the fleshly heart and mind will erect barriers to full fellowship that are not placed by God, and condemn, or insist upon, things that do not affect the spiritual principles clearly laid down in God's Word and are, therefore, non-essential. The two basic truths that govern this matter are the unity of the Church and the command to reject false teaching and practice. Either of these can be stressed to the extent that the other is infringed and this we must always be careful not to do, for serious loss is the result in either case. The truly spiritual believer will find ample guidance in the Word to enable him to know to what extent fellowship in service should go, if, by God's grace, he holds to the simplicity of the Word and is on guard against the reasonings of the human mind and the spiritual pride of the fleshly heart that are ever ready to lead us away, if not to one side, then to the other, from the true path of God's order.

Let us never forget that the love of the members of the Body of Christ one for another must never be affected. There must always be spiritual fellowship between those in whose hearts Christ dwells and we are never released from spiritual responsibility towards all the members of the Body of Christ. This truth is not affected by the fact that full cooperation in ministry may not be possible. The spirit that would cause members of the Body of Christ to stand entirely aloof from other members of the Body of Christ is not the Holy Spirit. Even for the member in sin and excluded from fellowship, the spiritual believer has an inescapable responsibility. He must pray for him in true love and faith.

When establishing a new congregation, we should be careful to see that there is clear understanding regarding its true position in the Body of Christ. Anything that savours of a Denominational or party spirit is wrong: it is the spirit of division. On the other hand, it would be just as wrong to fail to warn against the dangers of unscriptural doctrine and practice. The new believers must know that the leaven has been at work as our Lord said it would be and that at all costs it must be excluded from their midst. They must know that sound doctrine and the Scriptural order in the congregation are not matters of minor importance. Paul was careful to see that the churches were thoroughly warned and instructed regarding such dangers.

Not seldom have we seen believers who had been insufficiently warned and instructed regarding error led away when they came into contact with teachers of wrong doctrine or with the fleshly appeal of the organization and methods of modern churches. They had been taught that the Church was one but had not been warned sufficiently about the leaven. When they found differences in other congregations they regarded them as just local differences of custom and were ensnared. This danger is perhaps greatest on the foreign mission field for, it is sad to say, there are those who are ready to take advantage of believers and churches that are not sufficiently warned, that they might capture them for their own Denominational groups.

When groups of New Testament congregations are formed these should know each other and the unity in fellowship and ministry that ought to exist amongst them should fostered. It is essential to their full spiritual life and ministry. The privilege and duty of all to participate together in the evangelization of the world through prayer and material ministry to the Evangelists should be understood and practised from the beginning. Since it is in this ministry that the unity of the Body finds its primary practical expression, the lack of it will mean serious spiritual loss. The members of a congregation will not develop full spiritual life without it nor enter into a true understanding of the unity of the one Body.

There can be no thought of restricting the fellowship among congregations to those established by a particular missionary company. That would mean the introduction of an abitrary division in the Body. There should be full fellowship among all congregations anywhere that are true to New Testament doctrine and practice. Wherever the Word of God is obeyed and the Holy Spirit has liberty, there the fellowship will be full. It would be wrong to ask a congregation to 'join' a group of churches. There can be no other joining than that already accomplished by the Spirit. It would not be wrong to ask a congregation to fellowship with others that are like-minded. It ought to do so.

It would be wrong to call a group of churches "The New Testament Church". The New Testament Church is the whole true Church. But it is not wrong to say that a congregation is a New Testament church, if that is a statement of fact and not a Denominational designation. It is what the congregation ought to be. It is not necessarily wrong to distinguish those that are New Testament in doctrine and practice from those that are not. It may be necessary to do so. Of course, a congregation may say it is New Testament when it is not. It is the fact, not the claim, that makes full fellowship possible.

The Church is one Body. All the members of that Body are members one of another and no member can escape his responsibility towards all the other members. To a certain extent fellowship must be with all. With some it will be full; with others it will be limited. Our Lord withdrew from fellowship with the church in Laodicea, and stood without. However, He did not cease ministering to it: He continued knocking. In the church in Sardis He still sought 'to strengthen the things that remained'. With churches that walked in obedience and faith, His fellowship was full: He 'supped with them' and they with Him. So it is with Him today and so it must be with the members of His Body.

CHAPTER XXVII

DISCIPLINE IN THE CHURCH

The unity of the Body of Christ is the outcome of the fact that the one Spirit dwells in every member. The spiritual communion of the members with Christ and with one another comes from the indwelling presence of the one Lord. It is dependent upon obedience to Him, the Head of the Body. Where sin exists the communion is broken.

Moreover, the testimony of the Church is its walk in the Spirit. The Holy Spirit manifests Christ in each member and acts through each one to carry on the work of Christ through His Body. The presence of sin makes it impossible for the Spirit to do this.

Our Lord Himself stated the Church's duty to exercise discipline, excluding from its fellowship any member who persisted in sin and disobedience. To exercise such discipline is as definitely a commandment of Christ to the Church as is baptism or the partaking of the symbols of His death (Matt. 18:15-20). It is unquestionably a matter of primary and vital importance to the spiritual wellbeing of the Church.

The teaching of Christ regarding discipline was carried out in the Early Church. Abundant evidence of this is provided in the Epistles. The leaders of the New Testament churches insisted that there should be no compromise with sin. To countenance the intrusion of sin in any form into the churches would have been fatal. Sin and worldliness would soon have swallowed up the churches, as can be readily seen in the case of the Corinthian church.

That the power to discipline may be abused is no proof that it can be dispensed with. The Apostles were not unfamiliar with the difficulties that might arise. John, gentle and loving as was his nature, had to deal sternly with Diotrephes, who had caused members to be cast out of the church for no legitimate reason but simply to satisfy his own pride of heart.

The disciplining of sinning members of the Church is necessary for the spiritual health and strength of the Body. In the building up of truly Christian, spiritual, victorious congregations, it is indispensable. The church which surrenders this privilege and shirks this responsibility through weakness or fear, sells her birthright and faces defeat, for sin and the world will creep in and rob that church of all its power. Life and joy will fade; the Holy Spirit will be grieved and quenched; the Lord, the Head of the Church, will be offered the lip service and gold of wilful and proud sinners spurning His commandments. There can be only spiritual death in such a congregation.

In the bringing of a case for discipline before the church, the Elders take the initiative. When they fail in this duty, the Evangelist is responsible to exhort the congregation to act in obedience to Scripture, as Paul did in his first letter to the Corinthians (5:1-9).

Where there are no Elders, those who are spiritual should take the initiative in seeing that discipline is exercised. In every case it is the congregation's responsibility.

The only discipline which the Church can impose is the exclusion of the sinning member from the Lord's Table and from the fellowship of believers (1 Cor. 5:11). This is not exclusion from the Body of Christ.

A member of the Church who falls into sin or who teaches false doctrine should be dealt with according to the principle and procedure given in Matt. 18:15-17; 1 Cor. 5:1-6, 11, 13; Titus 3:10; 1 Tim. 1:20; 5:19, 20.

1. There must be witnesses.

2. Before bringing the matter before the church, two attempts should have been made privately to bring about the repentance of the sinning member.

3. If the difficulty is between two brethren, the one who is in the right must act according to Matt. 18:15.

4. If private attempts fail, the matter must be brought before the Church, represented by the local congregation.

5. If bringing the case before the church does not lead to repentance, the believer who thus persists in sin and rebellion is to be 'delivered unto Satan for the destruction of the flesh that the spirit may be saved in the day of the Lord Jesus'.

6. The place of prayer in the action taken by the church is stated in Matt. 18:18-20.

The delivering of the sinning member 'to Satan for the destruction of the flesh' has as its object the bringing of that one to repentance. He has deliberately chosen to serve Satan instead of Christ and has refused to repent. The Church then takes the position that it can only accept his choice and leave him to bear the consequences. The case of the Prodigal Son illustrates the consequences of backsliding. The son—for he was a son, not an unbeliever, and continued to be a son—leaves his Father's house and goes into the far country to live riotously and waste his substance. For a time all is pleasant, but the day of famine comes and the flesh begins to suffer. It is the suffering of the flesh, the result of sin, that works repentance and brings the sinner to the place where he 'comes to himself', listens to the inner voice of the Spirit, and resolves to return to the Father's house. It is still his Father's house and he is still a son, though an unfaithful one. Thus Satan is used as an instrument for the final accomplishing of God's purpose in the sinning believer. So Hymenaeus and Alexander were delivered over to Satan that they might 'learn not to blaspheme' (1 Tim. 1:20).

The Father does not prevent the son from going. He cannot, for the son's will is free. The son must make his choice, for which he alone will be responsible. The Father did not disown him: he desired, waited, believed and watched for his return. When the Church delivers the sinning believer over to Satan, it does not give him to Satan; it acknowledges the fact that the sinner has deliberately left home and gone into the far country. It has done everything possible to bring him to repentance but has failed. It is forced, therefore, to leave him to Satan. But he is delivered to Satan only for the destruction of the flesh—"that the spirit may be saved in the day of the Lord Jesus". He has gone to the world for the gratification of the flesh, and the Church, while it acknowledges his going, claims for him, in an act of faith, the destruction or death, of the flesh. It does not decree his ruin but claims his reformation and restoration. It acts, not for his undoing but for his good. Its action springs from true love and the faith with which the Lord prayed for Peter.

The discipline imposed by the Corinthian church had the desired effect. The one who had sinned was brought to repentance and restored to the fellowship of the Church.

The fact that a believer in sin has been excluded from fellow ship does not release the Church from its duty to pray for him and to continue steadfast in faith and love for him until he is restored. An attitude of harshness must not be shown. Exclusion from the Lord's Table excludes also from all participation in ministry. But it does not debar from attendance at meetings.

Whenever such an one gives evidence of true repentance he is to be restored and treated with love and humility.

In the elder brother of the Prodigal Son may be seen the attitude of the self-righteous, pharisaic member of the Church towards the repentant sinner who is received back into fellowship. A true repentance has brought the sinning one back into the place of fellowship with the Lord, and his joy and the Father's joy is evident. This is offensive to the self-righteous member. He is not in surrender to the Lord himself and does not experience the joy of the Lord in his own heart. The harshness and lack of love in his heart reveal the fact that he himself is in sin, although it is not open sin that brings exclusion from the Lord's Table. "All that I have is yours", the Father reminded him, but, although he was living in the house and all it contained was his, he was getting little or no joy out of it for he was not possessing his possessions. Actually, he was walking in the flesh, not in the Spirit.

The attitude that should be adopted towards the restored member is stated in 2 Cor. 2:6-8.

The Father of the Prodigal did not wait inside the house to receive the returning sinner. He had been faithfully watching for signs of his return and saw him coming when he "was yet a great way off", and ran to meet him in the way and welcome him. Such is God's attitude to the sinning believer who is returning and such must be the attitude of the Church. The Church must go out to meet him on the road and welcome him.

The Church has no authority to chastise or punish. Only God can do that. The member who falls into sin but truly repents when dealt with before judgment is passed by the Church, has been forgiven and cleansed by God. There is no Scriptural ground for excluding such an one from the Lord's Table for a stated period as a punishment for his sin. The Church cannot impose penance. Sin cannot be atoned for in such a way. Only true repentance can bring cleansing and where that cleansing has been obtained the Church can do nothing but acknowledge it. When God has forgiven, the Church cannot delay forgiveness.

When fellowship is restored between the repentant sinner and Christ, the Church cannot refuse fellowship.

The Scriptures dealing with the various cases requiring discipline by the Church may be listed as follows:

1. In disputes between brethren. Matt. 18:15-17.
2. The believer who sins. 1 Tim. 1:19; 2 Cor. 13:2; 1 Cor. 5:4, 5, 11; 2 Cor. 2:6-11.
3. He who teaches false doctrine. 2 Jn. 10, 11; Rom. 16:17; Gal. 5:10, 12; 2 Thess. 3:6; 1 Tim. 6:3-5; Tit. 1:10, 11, 13; 3:10.
4. He who is rebellious. 2 Thess. 3:6, 14, 15; 1 Tim. 6:1-5.
5. The weak brother. Rom. 14:1-23; 15-1; Gal. 6:1.
6. The Elder who sins. 1 Tim. 5:19, 20.
7. The Believer and the World. A believer should not marry an unbeliever nor enter into business partnership with unbelievers. 2 Cor. 6:14, 15; 1 Cor. 7:39.

In the application of discipline for wrong doctrine, care must be exercised not to go beyond the intention of Scripture. There must be no compromise with doctrine that is false. But the doctrine spoken of as false in the New Testament is not doctrine that is wrong because the one concerned is not fully instructed or misapprehends the meaning of Scripture. It is doctrine that is heretical, Satanic in origin, and accompanied by wrong practices; it is doctrine that separates from fellowship with the Lord. An examination of the passages of Scripture dealing with the matter will make this clear. There are two dangerous extremes: laxness in enforcing the exclusion of false doctrine and practice will corrupt the Church, while harshness towards lack of knowledge will divide the true Body of Christ. It must be remembered that true life can be present where there is not yet full light. We cannot separate from us one with whom the Lord, the Head of the Body, is fellowshipping. This does not mean that one without full light should be permitted to teach incorrect doctrine in the congregation. The attitude that should be adopted toward such is dealt with fully in the fourteenth chapter of Romans. It is helpful to read this passage in other translations, such as those of Conybeare and Weymouth.

One writer, dealing with this matter, says truly:

The long exercise of love and patience will be very good for the assembly, and particularly for the elders; the investigation and exposition required will conduce to general confirmation in the faith; and the risk of friction and disruption will be greatly reduced.

But these measures require much spiritual vigour for their successful application whereas excommunication is too often but the resort to force by those who are officially powerful but morally impotent, and this not by any means in the Church of Rome alone.[1]

The gathering together of a congregation to pass judgment upon a member who has fallen into sin and has persisted in his refusal to repent is spoken of in Matt. 18:25-20, and 1 Cor. 5:1-7. This is a most solemn, though sad meeting. Naturally, where there are Elders these will deal with such a matter first and it is only brought before the congregation after two attempts have been made to bring the sinning member to repentance. The facts will have been thoroughly sifted by the Elders with much patience and prayer. When the congregation is called together to pass judgment, the accused and the witnesses also having been summoned, the Elders, as those who preside, should see that the matter is put clearly before the congregation. Great circumspection should be exercised in the stating of the case. The recounting of details of sinful conduct, beyond what is absolutely necessary, should be carefully avoided.

As the congregation, in passing jugdment, is to act for Christ, the Head of the Church, it should be in a prayerful attitude, seeking to know His will. After the case has been presented, as much time as is necessary should be given to prayer until there is assurance regarding God's will. If the congregation is assured that the accused is guilty and unrepentant, then that one must be pronounced as handed over to Satan for 'the destruction of the flesh', the meaning of that phrase being made clear.

Regarding the restoring of such an one to fellowship after repentance, the only instructions given are in 2 Cor. 2:6-8. It is not stated that the church should gather together for this purpose. All that is required is the assurance, received through prayer, that the repentance is genuine.

There is no Scriptural ground for requiring that the one who is to be restored should make a detailed and public confession of sin before the congregation. Evidently no such demand was made of the one who had been disciplined in the Corinthian Church. Detailed public confessions of sin are morally and spiritually hurtful to all concerned.

---

[1] G. H. Lang: *Affiliation*, p. 16.

CHAPTER XXVIII

THE MINISTRY OF GIVING

Giving is listed among the gifts of the Spirit. It is a spiritual ministry and should be exercised under the inspiration of the Spirit, not of the emotions. This ministry is possible to the believer only because of· his position in Christ. The flesh has no right to serve God in any way or give anything to God.

General Principles

For whosoever shall give you a cup of water to drink in my name, because ye belong to Christ, verily I say unto you, he shall not lose his reward.

The principles that were to govern giving in the new Dispensation of Grace were laid down by our Lord in the statement recorded in Mark 9:41:

Analyzing this statement we find the following facts:

1. The gift was only a cup of water. The insignificance of its value shows two things:

(1) That the material value of the gift is of no importance, so far as the giver's act is concerned, and

(2) that the object and motive give the act all its value before God.

2. The conditions of the gift:

(1) It is given to one who is in Christ.

(2) It is given to him because he is Christ's.

(3) It is given to him in Christ's name.

3. That gift will not go unrewarded by God.

It is clear that no reward is promised here for any gift, no matter how great its material value, that does not fulfil all the three conditions· stated.

The gift must be given in the Name of Christ. We hardly need to say that this does not mean the mere use of a phrase. Christ said that where two or three are gathered in His Name, He is there in the midst of them, yet He was not present in the Laodicean church although it was professedly gathered in His Name. They were not truly gathered in His Name, for there was sin within. Anything done in His Name, in the true sense, must be done by one who is walking in obedience and fellowship with Him, for only such can be guided by Christ to act according to His will.

It follows from this that no one who is not a believer in Christ can participate in the ministry of giving. It is not right, nor is it fair to unbelievers that they be allowed to think that they can partake of this privilege. God does not require nor desire the unbeliever's money. The unbeliever cannot offer good works to God. His sacrifices are an abomination to God. It is wrong to give him any ground to think that he can gain merit by giving to God or even that God will accept his unsanctified gift. The believer can give because his gift is sanctified in Christ in Whose Name it is given (cf. 3 Jn. 6, 7; Isa. 1:10-16; Prov. 15:8; 21:27; 28:9; Jer. 6:20; Amos 5:21-24; Gen. 4:3-5; Jn. 4:24; 2 Cor. 6:14).

In another passage our Lord stresses the importance of the motive of giving and states the principle that must govern the manner of giving.

> But beware of doing your good actions in the sight of men, in order to attract their gaze; if you do, there is no reward for you with your Father who is in Heaven.
> When you give in charity, never blow a trumpet before you as the hypocrites do in the synagogues and streets in order that their praises may be sung by men. I solemnly tell you that they already have their reward. But when you are giving in charity, let not your left hand perceive what your right hand is doing, that your charities may be in secret; and then our Father — He who sees in secret — will recompense you. (Matt. 6:1-4, Weymouth.)

Giving must not be done publicly but in secret. No one, not even the Elders of the church, should see or know what any one gives. Our duty is to God alone. To Him we give and He alone should know what we give. Making known the names of givers and the amounts they give is unscriptural. Secrecy in giving is not attractive to the natural heart, but God's will is that the natural heart should have no part in it. He wishes it to be a truly spiritual act, free from any touch of the flesh and we must be faithful to make it so. If the flesh has a part in it, it is not the work of the Spirit and it is not accepted by God.

Teaching the Churches

The teaching which Paul gave to the Churches regarding giving will be found in the following passages: 2 Cor. 8:1-4, 9, 12-15; 9:6-12; 1 Cor. 16:2; Rom. 12:8; Heb. 13:16; 1 Tim. 6:17-19; 1 Cor. 6:19-20.

In these passages we see that

1. All that we are and have belongs to Christ.
2. Giving should be done in the Name of Christ.
3. The motive should be purely spiritual, not fleshly.
4. He who gives should give with liberality.
5. Our giving is judged by the willingness of the giver, not by the amount given.
6. Giving should be in proportion to what a man has—as God has prospered him.
7. The offering should be given regularly each first day of the week.
8. It should be given in secret.

The Poor

It should be carefully noted that the Church is made responsible only for the poor of the Church (though the individual believer is not exempted from a moral duty to other poor) and that its gifts to them must be governed by definite rules. The rules are given in 1 Tim. 5:4-13. They are:

1. The recipient must be a faithful believer who has given and is giving a good testimony.
2. Assistance should be given only to such poor as have no relatives whose duty it is to care for them and whose advanced age or physical condition is such that they are unable to support themselves.

These rules governing the giving of financial aid to widows are strict and wise. They must govern all similar cases. The poor are not to be pauperized but to be taught to have faith directly in God. It will be seen that much giving to the poor, based upon sentiment or the emotions or done as a good work, is contrary to the rules laid down in Scripture. It does not create or strengthen faith but weakens it. It is not the true fruit of divine love. (See also, Acts 6:1; Gal. 2:10; Jas. 2:15; 1 Jn. 3:17; Luke 11:41).

The Support of the Worker

The Church's financial responsibility towards those who labour in the Gospel may be summarized as follows:
1. Those who labour in the Gospel have a right to live by the Gospel. 1 Cor. 9:7-14; 2 Cor. 12:13; Gal. 6:6; 1 Tim. 5:17, 18.
2. Evangelists received financial support from the churches. 2 Cor. 11:8, 9; Phil. 4:10-18.
3. At times Evangelists supported themselves. Paul always gave his services without charge, sometimes supporting himself, but more often being supported by gifts sent by churches already established. Acts 20:33, 34; 2 Cor. 11:7-9; 12:13-17; 1 Thess. 2:5, 6, 9; 2 Thess. 3:7-9; 1 Cor. 9:1-23.
4. Paul advised the Ephesian Elders to support themselves as he had done when amongst them. Acts 20:34, 35 (cf. Weymouth's Translation).

The Offering

What the believer gives is given to the Lord because it is His and out of love for Him. It is a transaction between the giver and Christ, which takes that which is purely material into the realm that is purely spiritual. The gain which comes to the giver is entirely spiritual.

The offering given each first day of the week should be made in such a manner that all the principles governing giving are observed. It would seem that the most satifactory way to provide for this is by having a box placed in a not too conspicuous place near the door. This makes it possible for the giving to be secret. It should be done only at the gathering of the church at the Lord's Table, so that only believers may contribute. It should be taught that the believer's responsibility is toward the Lord only, not toward the church or the Elders. What he gives is given to his Lord as his Lord instructs him; if he does not give, it is to his Lord that he does not give. The believer is much less ready to fail the Lord than to fail the church. He may find reasons for not giving as he should to the church; he can find none for not fulfilling his duty towards his Lord. He may feel little incentive to give to the church; he finds a deep satisfaction in giving to his Lord.

Specially designated gifts can be taken care of by enclosing them in an envelope, or suitable receptacle, with the object stated but the name of the donor not given.

Regular offerings should not be received at any other gathering. Collections should not be taken in Sunday School or at young people's meetings, women's meetings, etc. Children or young people who are not saved cannot give to the Lord and should be so taught. Those who are the Lord's are members of the Church and should be taught to take their place as such and to give their offering at the gathering of the Church in the Scriptural way.

Practices such as having members of the Sunday School come to the front on their birthdays and give a penny for each year they have lived are completely unscriptural. That practice is contrary to Scripture on the following points:

(1) It makes the giver do his giving publicly.

(2) It obliges him to give whether he desires to do so or not.

(3) It decides the amount he should give.

(4) It sets aside the fact that giving is a gift of the Spirit and must be done under the guidance of the Spirit.

(5) It causes a child to give what is not his and costs him nothing. (If he has nothing to give God asks nothing of him.)

(6) It causes unbelievers to give thinking their gift is accepted by God.

Many other practices, if taken to God's Word, would be found equally unscriptural. How often there is failure to consult God's Word regarding what is done in His Church in His Name!

There can be no question that a true adherence to the Scriptural principles of giving excludes all manner of drives for raising funds, solicitations or appeals for donations and pledges, bazaars, etc. Even the yearly money efforts of 'Missionary Week', with their emotional stimulants such as raising thermometers, the breaking of records, and such like, are out of harmony with the principles of spiritual giving.

We have found that in every case where there is a true understanding of the believer's responsibility toward God in this matter there is no lack of faithfulness in giving or of funds for the work of the Lord.

The gift of Giving is dealt with in chapter 17.

CHAPTER XXIX

THE GUIDANCE OF THE SPIRIT IN THE CHURCH

Christ is the Head of the Body. He is personally present in every true gathering of members of His Body. It is His Church and He is present to build it. He governs and His will must be known and done.

Christ does His work through the Church and the Church participates voluntarily and intelligently in that work, but it is never authorized to make decisions in His Name or to carry out in His Name a programme of its own making. It must find out what His will is and act in obedience to it. By His Spirit He reveals His will to those who are gathered in His Name, enabling them to go unanimously to Him in the prayer of faith that is according to His will and that, therefore, is assured of an answer. All this, as we have seen, is clearly revealed in our Lord's teaching concerning the Church given in the sixteenth and eighteenth chapters of Matthew and in what is taught in the Acts and in the Epistles. The practice of the New Testament Church conformed to it.

The principles of guidance are as follows:

1. God reveals His will; in the first place, through His Word. Therefore, a thorough knowledge and searching of God's Word is necessary. Part of the Holy Spirit's ministry is to bring to our minds what the Lord has said.

2. While God's will is made known clearly in His Word, there are details of time and place that must be revealed from day to day by the Holy Spirit. For instance, God's Word states that it is His purpose that there be Elders in a church, but the church must wait upon God in prayer until the Holy Spirit reveals who have been chosen by God to engage in that ministry among them. Paul and his fellow-workers, as they went forward in obedience to God's

command to preach the Gospel to every creature, were guided by the Spirit as to where to go and when.

3. The Holy Spirit will never give guidance that is contrary to, or differs from, the guidance given in God's Word. He will never lead to the doing of anything that will mean adding to, or taking away from, that which is required in God's Word. Any leading that results in modifying the order given in the Word for the Church's structure and ministry does not come from the Holy Spirit. His guidance is always for the carrying out of God's Word.

The only way in which the Church can find out Christ's will is by waiting upon God that the Holy Spirit may reveal it through God's Word and through prayer.[1] There is no substitute provided for this. God has not provided an alternative and easier procedure for the Church when it is not in the condition spiritually to be able to get the revelation of His will from the Holy Spirit. The only way open to such a church is, through repentance and faith, back to the place of revelation.

There is no evidence of any such gathering in the New Testament Church as the modern church business meeting. Anything that had to be decided was made a matter of continued prayer until God's will regarding it was known. Nor were matters decided by majority vote. The true business meeting of the congregation is the prayer meeting. Only those who take a part in the ministry of prayer can know God's will for the congregation in any matter and no one else has any right to express an opinion.

The modern business meeting and the vote are substitutes introduced into the Church by man. They are human institutions based upon the principles of human government and, though they are necessary for the regulation of human affairs in the present condition of the world, they have no place in spiritual government. Spiritual government does not depend upon man's wisdom or the opinion of the majority. God's government is absolute. His will must be known and His will must be done. Christ is the Head of the Body and all the members of the Body must be entirely submitted to His guidance. The acceptance of this fact doctrinally and the direct contravention of it in the practically prayerless discussions and majority votes of a church business meeting, is one of the amazing anomalies in the life of the Church today.

The church business meeting, or the Committee or Council

---

[1] See pp. 375-80, 451, 456, 459-60.

24

Meeting, opened, probably, by a prayer asking for God's guidance, then proceeds to a discussion of the matters to be considered. Those who take part in the discussion will be sincere, no doubt, so far as their knowledge and ability go. It has been our experience that the most spiritual members are not usually those who are most ready to take part, particularly when fleshly feelings are roused. As the matter has been referred to human judgment, there will probably be a number of different opinions. The discussion may become heated and may degenerate into a struggle of wills and end in a "church fight". At the best, a 'satisfactory' compromise is sought that may be accepted by all. When the matter is put to the vote, the majority decides the issue. Then the meeting is closed in prayer asking God to bless what has been decided by the church.

How will God answer that prayer? Was what was decided His will? Some of those who took part might say they thought it was His will. Others might be sure it was not His will. Most would probably not care to say that they had any assurance of God's will one way or the other, but would feel they voted for what they judged best under the circumstances. What place had the Head of the Body in the decision that was made? And what place was given to the Holy Spirit in the proceedings?

The fact that an action is according to the will of the majority gives us no right to consider it to be God's will and to expect Him to accept it and bless it. The business meeting and the vote reveal man's judgment, not God's will. When applied to the government of the Church they introduce all the weakness that is inherent in man's lack of spiritual wisdom and give the opportunity to the human, fleshly mind to presume to take the direction of the things of God. They appear to be an easier and quicker substitute for the spiritual way. They are more reasonable to the natural mind. They can be used by the believer who does not wish to give the time to continued prayer, who does not know how to obtain a knowledge of God's will or who is not in a position spiritually to know it.

If it is not possible for us to be guided by the Holy Spirit into a definite knowledge of God's will; if the clear teachings of Scripture regarding the guidance given by the Holy Spirit is not to be taken seriously but to be regarded as merely spiritual figures of speech, or some such thing, then we must have the business meeting and the majority vote and do God's work for Him as best we can. But if God's Word is true and the Holy Spirit does do what the Scriptures teach He will do, then we do not need that type of a business meeting.

God's purpose is that there should be unity in the Church. It is the 'unity of the Spirit' that is to be manifested. The Holy Spirit's purpose is to bring about that unity, revealing the will of the Head to all the members of the Body. If Christ's will is known by all, there will be unity. In no other way can true spiritual unity be obtained. It is only natural that men's opinions and judgments should differ and clash. But when all are subjected to the will of the Head revealed by the Spirit, there is no clash but a unity that glorifies Him and makes it possible for the Spirit to carry out His will.

This is not just theoretic perfection that is 'too good to be true'. It is God's will for the Church, taught in His Word and, therefore, entirely and always possible to all who will take it by faith.

The knowing of the will of the Head revealed by the Spirit is essential to the life and work of the Church. A congregation that has not learned so to walk will never be victorious. It will continue to be weak and immature spiritually and will always need the direction of a human leader. The missionary who lacks faith to lead a congregation into this experience will never establish churches that can be left to be guided by the Holy Spirit.

Problems

Various questions will arise regarding the practical outworking of this matter.

1. What about members who are 'weak brethren' and do not get to know God's will?

The fact that 'weak brethren' are to be received but not to 'doubtful disputations', makes it clear that such are not to be permitted to disturb the true spiritual life of the Church. In a congregation that has been fully taught and that is walking in obedience to the Lord, the great majority of the members will know how to find God's will through prayer. Among these there should be unanimity, and when there is there seems to be no reason for delaying the doing of God's will because of a 'weak brother' who evidently does not know it. Moreover, as the prayer meeting is the business meeting, those who do not take a definite part in the prayer of the church can have no say as to what is God's will for the church, for they do not know the guidance the Spirit has given and can only express their personal judgment, which is of no spiritual value.

2. Should the congregation wait until there is unanimity as to God's will?

Yes, because it is required that the Church's prayer be unanimous (Matt. 18:19).[1]

As is stated above, ignorance of God's will on the part of one or two spiritually 'weak brethren' does not affect the position of the congregation. But until all who are walking in obedience and humility before God come to have assurance about God's will, no step should be taken. No matter how much it may seem that a matter is urgent—or no matter how apparently unimportant—the congregation must wait until the will of the Head is definitely known. God's Word does not say that His will must be known, except in very urgent or in unimportant cases. The Head knows exactly what the situation is and if He delays it is for a good reason. We have never seen good come from haste, but we have often marvelled at God's wisdom when He has restrained from action when apparently it was folly to wait. He had seen factors invisible to human sight. In this, as in all things, the Head wants absolute confidence and obedience.

3. What of the brother who becomes convinced that he knows God's will and would insist upon his opinion?

If the Elders of the congregation are fulfilling their duty to govern and to see that all things are done according to Scripture, "decently and in order", such a brother will be counselled and, if necessary, silenced and not permitted to disturb the congregation. It would be pointed out to him immediately that he is unscriptural and out of order, for all, and not just one, must know God's will, and that, for that reason, it is probable that he is mistaken.

4. A question may arise regarding the casting of lots to determine who was to replace Judas Iscariot and complete the number of the Twelve. Is that not New Testament practice? It is clear that that procedure has no place in New Testament Church order. It is pre-Pentecost and pre-Church, both as to time and order. It belongs to the old order. It occurred before the coming of the Holy Spirit as the guide, teacher and power of the Church. It is natural, therefore, that it should be based upon a different principle. After Pentecost no such procedure was ever followed. In the Church, when God appoints a man to a ministry, the Holy Spirit makes it known to the congregation as when Barnabas and Paul were sent forth from Antioch. (See p. 182.)

---

[1] See pp. 138, 376.

CHAPTER XXX

PRAYER'S PLACE IN THE CHURCH

Prayer is not listed among the gifts of the Spirit. Yet the fact that it must be "in the Spirit" is definitely stated. Paul said he prayed with the Spirit and with the understanding (1 Cor. 14:15). Then in Ephesians 6:18 he counsels the Church to be "Praying always... in the Spirit". In Jude 20 we read, "building up yourselves in your most holy faith, praying in the Holy Ghost". Romans 8:26, 27 states the matter clearly "... so the Spirit gives help to our weakness; for we know not what we should pray for as we ought; but the Spirit itself maketh intercession for us, with groans which words cannot utter. But He Who searches our hearts knows what is the desire of the Spirit, because He intercedes for the saints according to the will of God" (Conybeare). James says: "The inwardly prompted (by the Holy Spirit) supplication of a righteous man exerts a mighty influence" (Jas. 5:16, Weymouth, note).

All true prayer is guided by the Holy Spirit. We pray with the understanding but the heart and mind must be in yieldedness to the Holy Spirit that He may be permitted to reveal God's will, directing us as to what to pray.

Christ's Teaching on Prayer

Our Lord, in His final teaching to the disciples prior to the Cross (Jn. chapters 14-17), revealed the place that prayer was to take in the work to be done. After explaining (in 14:8-14) that all that He had said and done was the work of the Father manifesting Himself through Him, He told His disciples that they would participate in a similar way in the great work which He was to do after His ascension. As He was in them and they were in Him,

He would work His work through them. And this was to be done in answer to prayer that is according to His will. Verses 12 to 14 read:

> Verily, verily, I say to you, he who is believing in me, the works that I do — that one also shall do, and greater than these shall he do, because I go on to my Father; and whatever ye may ask in my name, I will do, that the Father may be glorified in the Son; if ye ask anything in my name I will do it (Young's lit. trans.).

This is in accord with what Christ had already taught regarding prayer in the Church (Matt. 18:15-21).

In the fifteenth chapter of John, speaking of the vine and the branches, our Lord states that our right to ask what we will is dependent upon our abiding in Him and that the resulting abundant fruitbearing in answer to prayer will glorify God:

> If ye abide in me and my words abide in you, ye shall ask what ye will and it shall be done unto you. Herein is my Father glorified, that ye bear much fruit; so shall ye be my disciples (15:7, 8.)

Later, in the same chapter, He says:

> Ye did not choose out me, but I chose out you, and did appoint you, that ye might go away, and might bear fruit, and your fruit might remain, that whatever ye may ask of the Father in my name He may give you (15:16, Young.)

The fact that He has sent us gives us authority to ask for fruit. When He calls us to a work, we have a right to pray for that work, and when we ask according to His will He has promised to answer. Such fruit will remain—it will not be consumed in the fire of testing: it is eternal.

Then, in the sixteenth chapter, speaking of the joy that was to be theirs after the resurrection, He counsels them,

> ...verily, verily, I say to you, as many things as ye may ask of the Father in my name, He will give it you; till now ye did ask nothing in my name; ask and ye shall receive, that your joy may be full (16:23,24. Young.)

Fulness of joy is to be the result of fruitbearing through answered prayer.

When we compare the teaching on prayer given in these chapters of John with that in the key passage on the Church in Matthew 18:15-20, it will be seen that what is taught in John is complementary to the statement in Matthew. In Matthew the order is dealt with; in John the spiritual principles underlying the order and their application are revealed.

The implications of this teaching are far-reaching and vital. That this was understood by the Early Church is obvious in the New Testament record. The power and fruitfulness and success of the Church in those first years was due to its obedience and faithfulness in giving prayer the place it is intended to take.

The purely spiritual nature of the Church's order and power has been seen. Absolutely essential to this order is a continual knowledge of God's will. The guidance of the Holy Spirit must be received for everything that is done. The principal medium of communication between the Church and God is prayer, and as that communication must be continuous, prayer must be unceasing.

It is through Holy Spirit-guided prayer that is according to God's will that the Church asks that God's will be done. There can be no substitute for this procedure. God's will must be known definitely by the Church and then its accomplishment must be asked of Him in believing prayer. In answer to that prayer He carries out His will.

The Prayer of the Church

The prayer of the Church cannot be offered by one member alone. There must be at least two (Matt. 18:19). One member is just an individual believer; two can act as a corporate body. Just as two or more met together in the Name of Christ form a gathering of the Church, so these two or more may go to God in prayer as a gathering of the Church with all the privileges and responsibilities of that position.

Our Lord stated categorically that the prayer of the Church would be answered. We know that the receiving of an answer to the prayer of the individual believer is subject to certain clearly stated conditions:

1. The believer must be abiding in Christ (Jn. 15:7).
2. He must be walking according to God's Word (1 Jn. 3:22).
3. His prayer must be according to God's will (1 Jn. 5:14, 15).
4. His prayer must be 'in the Spirit' (Eph. 6:18; Jude 20; Rom. 8:26, 27).
5. He must pray in faith (Jas. 1:6, 7).

It is obvious that the prayer of the Church, if it is to be answered, is subject to the same conditions. However, another condition is added:

6. Those praying must be of one mind, asking the same thing (Matt. 18:19).

This is logical and right; it could not be otherwise. Those who are met together in the Name of Christ are met together with Him, the Head of the Body. If they are each one abiding in Him and walking in obedience to His Word, they will be guided by Him to know His will. If all know His will, they will be of one mind—in agreement with His mind—and will ask the same thing. In that case they have the absolute certainty, guaranteed by Christ's own word, that their prayer is answered.

All prayer must be according to God's will. His will is revealed in His Word and by the Holy Spirit. In the first place, therefore, the petition, whether of the Church or of the individual, must have a definite Scriptural basis. For instance, it is in accordance with Scripture to ask God to 'thrust forth labourers into His harvest'. We need no special or further revelation from the Spirit to make that petition. He has already revealed to us in the Word that we should do so and we are lacking in obedience and faithfulness if we do not do so. There are details, however, regarding the thrusting forth of labourers, that are not directly revealed in the Word. The Holy Spirit must reveal to us directly who should go and when, and where. When we know these details, we ask God in faith to accomplish His will regarding them. This prayer is as definitely based upon God's Word as the petition to thrust forth labourers. A petition that has not a true Scriptural basis cannot be according to God's will.

All prayer must be in the Spirit. That does not mean any extraordinary sensation or attitude. Paul said to the Corinthians: "I will pray with the Spirit and I will pray with the understanding also" (1 Cor. 14:15). We lift our hearts to God, willing that His Spirit reveal His will to us and direct our prayer, and in simple faith we expect He will do this. We seek humbly to have no plan or desire of our own but to be utterly yielded, so that even if He leads us to feel that His will is the very thing we least desire, or if He bids us wait and do nothing when we think action urgent and necessary, we shall be ready to obey Him immediately and implicitly. It does not mean having our mind a blank. We have full control of our mental faculties, but our own intelligence and knowledge are not sufficient to enable us to know God's will; therefore we require revelation from the Holy Spirit. We have full control of our wills and remain fully responsible for what we think or decide, but we voluntarily and intelligently determine to be absolutely willing for His will.

When we go to God in such an attitude of faith and obedience, He fulfils His Word, and the Holy Spirit gives us, as we pray, a sense of assurance or lack of assurance, of liberty or lack of liberty, which, as a 'still small voice', is sufficiently clear to enable us to know whether that about which we are enquiring is God's will or not; whether we should go forward or wait. It is not a thing that has to be practised and learned gradually. The youngest convert, the moment he seeks God in prayer in the right way, becomes conscious of such guidance. The difficulty is not to pray in the Spirit, but to be watchful that we pray always in the Spirit and not in the flesh presenting our own plans and desires to God, and to be faithful in waiting for guidance and obeying the guidance that is given.

Writing of the united prayer of the Dohnavur Fellowship. Miss Amy Carmichael says:

We grew into a kind of prayer that is, for us at least, very helpful. We ask to be led by the Holy Spirit from point to point, each prayer leading on from the preceding prayer till the particular subject laid on our hearts has been dealt with, and we have the assurance that the Lord will complete all, as Kay translates Ps. CXXXVIII, 8.

This way of prayer is just the opposite to the kaleidoscope kind, which darts hither and thither all over the earth or over a number of scattered interests (often within the limits of a single long prayer) leaving the mind which has tried to follow perhaps dazzled, perhaps tired. It is a much simpler thing. Such prayer is often brief; it is often silent, or it may take the form of song, and we are lifted up as with wings to our Lord's feet. It is possible only when all who are praying together do thoroughly understand one another, are, indeed, as one instrument under the control of the Spirit of God who moves on each severally as He will, or unites all in silence or in song. Such prayer asks for something not easily defined. Darby's translation of Ex. XXIII, 21, "Be careful in His Presence", comes to mind as a word that expresses its quietness and awe, and the jubilant psalms show its joy.[1]

Our own experience in united prayer has been very similar. The Lord has continually led us on progressively from one thing to another. We might feel that a certain matter should be asked in prayer, but when we sought to do so the leading was to pray for something else. We would realise then (or, perhaps, find later) that it was something that had to be taken care of before the Holy Spirit could give us liberty to ask what we knew was His will.

---

[1] *Gold Gord*, pp. 77, 78.

Through such prayer the Lord continually deals with us, showing us our lack of faith, or faithfulness, or power, and causing us to put right things that are wrong. It keeps all walking close to Him, for as soon as any coldness creeps over the believer he finds that the Holy Spirit no longer leads—and then the only prayer that is possible is a more or less formal repetition of beautiful sentences and vague petitions.

After united prayer, we usually give an opportunity for a very brief expression on the part of each one of what they feel the Lord's word was while they prayed—whether there was a sense of liberty or check; the assurance that the matter was settled, or the urge to continue in prayer; the evidence of a blocking on the part of the enemy, or the certainty of victory. This is often rich and revealing and enables us to know what the Lord is saying to all and to what extent He is giving unanimity as to His will.

(The manner in which a congregation may pray together and come to know the Lord's will is described on pp. 451—6, 458—9).

It is interesting to see sometimes (by no means always) when a new one joins the prayer group, how at first he may not perceive the Spirit's guidance and his comments be quite out of harmony with the rest, but how, before very long, he too will get a vision beyond the range of natural sight and know what the Holy Spirit is seeking to reveal.

It is through such prayer in the Spirit that the Church communicates with Christ, its Head, Who is present in the midst, and it is through such prayer that He is enabled to make known His will to the Church and to guide it in all its acts.

In prayer that is guided by the Holy Spirit and made in faith there is no uncertainty, there is nothing haphazard, there are no vain repetitions or merely formal prayers, or long prayers to be heard of men, or petitions that are contrary to God's will or that simply have no relation to that which God wishes to do. More than that, there is complete agreement among the members of the Church met together, not because they have agreed to agree, but because all have been guided in prayer by the Holy Spirit into a knowledge of God's will. What great possibilities of power, of victorious action and of testimony to the glory of the Lord are open to the congregation that faithfully engages in such prayer!

There is another principle that should be applied in the prayer

gathering of the church. The Elder who presides is responsible to
see that the ministry of united prayer is exercised in accordance
with the teaching of the Word. Just as no one should be permitted
to preach if it is evident that he is not doing so under the guidance
of the Spirit and is just giving forth human wisdom, so also no
one should be allowed to engage in prayer that is not 'in the
Spirit'. Of course, the greatest care must be exercised not to restrict
liberty in prayer or to cause a sense of restraint, but there are
intrusions of the flesh in prayer gatherings that hinder the unity
of the Spirit and the receiving of guidance.

There may be the one or two who think it necessary to make
long prayers. This may be due to lack of knowledge regarding
true prayer, or to a desire for prominence. Some have the habit
of preaching and exhorting in their prayer. Such prayer is not
in the Spirit, for He will not preach through the one who is praying to God: He will pray through him. It must be understood
clearly that in prayer we are speaking to God and not to man.
When we preach in prayer, or seek to use beautiful phrases and
well chosen words, our thoughts are upon the effect of our prayer
upon the hearers and we are not speaking to God with mind and
heart directed to Him alone. When the Holy Spirit is really in
control of a prayer meeting such things disappear.

The power of a prayer does not depend upon its length or the
number of petitions made. Let us keep in mind the example of the
Lord's recorded prayers. In Gethsemane His prayer was brief.
Not an unnecessary word was added. It was not couched in what
we might call formal prayer language. He said to God in simple
language what had to be said and nothing more. So it was in His
prayer at the tomb of Lazarus. In the 'Lord's Prayer' also we
find nothing but definite statements and petitions, stated clearly
and briefly.

Regarding preachers in the assembly of the Church, in gatherings
where there is liberty for all to take part who have the gift of
the Spirit to do so, it is said, "if anything is revealed to some.
one else who is seated there, let the first be silent" (1 Cor. 14:30,
Weymouth). This simply means that no one has the right to
monopolize the time, but must limit his message so as to permit
others to take part who are led to do so. The same principle holds
good in the prayer meeting. It is not the place for long prayers.
It must be remembered that all, or many, who are present wish to
take part. The prayer that is in the Spirit on such an occasion will

be to the point, stating briefly what the Spirit gives liberty to say and not a word more.

As a rule, all public prayers should be brief, as were our Lord's. They usually will be brief if we are really praying to God. What is not really prayer to God should be excluded. It has no more place on the platform than in the prayer meeting. As we speak to God shall we give Him a comment on the message that has been spoken, a sermonette, or an exhortation? Should we in prayer seek to urge sinners to repentance and faith and believers to consecration? To do so is a misuse of prayer. As we do it we are not speaking to God but to the audience. In many a public prayer a great part is directed to the audience and only one or two petitions to God.

When we are called upon to pray, do we not think of the effect upon the audience and feel that we must make a prayer that will be sufficiently eloquent and adequate to the occasion, instead of truly seeking God, guided by His Spirit to ask that which is His will that we may know He will hear and answer? To carefully exclude all but true prayer in meetings brings great blessing. It means that true contact is made with the living God, true prayer is offered that He will answer and the door is opened for Him to work in power.

We remember the impression made upon us in our youth by the prayers of C. M. Alexander in great evangelistic meetings. They were very simple and very brief. He asked God to use the message and the hymns and to save souls; nothing more. And God answered. We had been accustomed to earnest but formal and rather long prayers that were intended to take their place in a form of service. Alexander's prayers had no polish but they took us straight to God and they had power.

The Early Church at Prayer

The occasion for the teaching in Matthew 18:19 on Church prayer was our Lord's statement regarding the procedure to be followed in a case of contention between two believers. Met together in the Name of Christ and in His presence, the Church is guided by the Holy Spirit, through the Word and through prayer, to ask unanimously that which is God's will. This prayer of the Church will be answered and what is done by the Church on earth in accordance with God's will is done in Heaven. What is done is God's act, wrought by Him through the Church. The medium of this action is the prayer of the Church inspired by the Holy Spirit.

The principles guiding the Church's procedure in this case of discipline apply to all decisions that the Church must make. There is unity through the knowledge of God's will by all and the prayer of faith is answered as God, in response to that prayer, carries out His will through the Church.

God's will originates always in His mind and heart. It does not originate in us, either in the individual believer or in the Church. That will God reveals to us as we abide in Christ and walk in obedience to His Word and seek Him through prayer.

There is much evidence in the New Testament of the carrying out of this procedure. The Church as the Body of Christ came into existence in the gathering for prayer that culminated in Pentecost. The delay between the ascension of Christ and the coming of the Holy Spirit was, we believe, partly at least, that the fulfilment of the promise might be linked with the prayer of the Church. Our Lord had taught that all the work of His Church was to be done by Him in answer to prayer that was according to His revealed will, so right from the beginning this was the procedure followed. The disciples met to pray for the fulfilment of the promise and the Lord carried out His will in response to their prayer of faith.

All the conditions for prevailing Church-prayer were met in that prayer meeting. It was a gathering of true believers in Christ. All were of one accord. They were met in obedience to His instructions, asking and waiting for that which He had told them He would do. They were praying according to His will and they were praying in faith doubting nothing. They continued in prayer, not just for one hour, but for days. They continued, as they had been instructed to do, until they received the answer. The outcome of that prayer gathering, was the birth of the Church, the Body of Christ, indwelt by the Spirit of Christ—the Church that from that day marched on triumphantly, irresistibly, gloriously.

That little group of disciples had not gathered to form plans for the planting of the Church in Jerusalem, for its organization, or for the evangelization of the city. They did none of the things that man would have considered so necessary—yea, so pressing that there would have been no time for prayer.

That little company of un-worldly-wise instruments of the great Builder of the Church, hidden away from the world in an upper room and engaged in obediently, unitedly and trustingly waiting for Him, were only praying. They were nothing to the world: weak, few in number, poor. No man's eyes were upon them; only God's. But out of that room, in answer to prayer, faith and obedience, there came forth something that no power of man or Hell could destroy; that not only mightily moved Jerusalem, but shook the Roman Empire to its foundations and conquered and spread until it had filled the then known world.

It is recorded that thereafter "they continued steadfastly in the Apostles' doctrine and fellowship, and in the breaking of bread and in prayers" (Acts 2:42). While the Church was faithful in fellowship and witness, it continued always to be a Church at prayer, and there is the secret of its glorious accomplishment.

Not long afterwards, persecution broke out and Peter and John were called before the Council and forbidden to preach in the Name of Jesus. They stood firm and declared their intention to obey God and not man. Then they returned to their own company and reported. Immediately the church went to God in prayer. This is an incident of great importance revealing much regarding the place of prayer in the Church. Significant details are given of the prayer-gathering that culminated at Pentecost. Here again the Holy Spirit furnishes us with details. The prayer that was prayed by the church on this occasion is recorded:

And they, upon hearing the story, all lifted up their voices to God and said, 'O Sovereign Lord, it is Thou who didst make Heaven and earth and sea, and all that is in them, and didst say through the Holy Spirit by the lips of our forefather David, Thy servant, "Why have the nations stamped and raged, and the peoples formed futile plans? The kings of the earth came near, and the rulers assembled together against the Lord and against His Anointed." They did indeed assemble in this city in hostility to Thy holy Servant Jesus whom Thou hadst anointed — Herod and Pontius Pilate with the Gentiles and also the tribes of Israel — to do all that Thy power and Thy will had predetermined should be done. And now, Lord, listen to their threats, and enable Thy servants to proclaim Thy Message with fearless courage, whilst Thou stretchest out Thine arm to cure men, and to give signs and marvels through the name of Thy holy Servant Jesus.
When they had prayed, the place in which they were assembled shook, and they were, one and all, filled with the Holy Spirit, and proceeded to tell God's Message with boldness. (Acts 4:24-31, Weymouth.)

It should be noted that:

1.   In the face of this crisis the church did not meet together to discuss was and means; it went to prayer.

2.   The petition was made on the ground of Scripture (Ps. 2:1, 2; cf. v. 4).

3. They did not ask for deliverance. They asked for strength to preach the Gospel fearlessly to obey Christ's command.

4. God answered by filling them with the Holy Spirit. They had already been baptized by the Spirit at Pentecost. He was in them. But for every new crisis and for every endeavour the church required the filling of the Spirit for that particular occasion and ministry.

5. Being filled anew with the Holy Spirit they continued boldly witnessing to the Gospel. The 'gates of hell' did not prevail against that church.

With the above we should link Paul's request to the Church, recorded in Eph. 6:18-20:

Continue to pray at every season with all earnestness of supplication in the Spirit; and to this end be watchful with all perseverance in prayer for all the saints; and for me, that utterance may be given me, to open my mouth and make known with boldness the mystery of the Glad-tidings, for which I am an ambassador in fetters. Pray that I may declare it boldly, as I ought to speak (Conybeare).

Not only do we find the Church praying for boldness in its own ministry, but it is asked to pray that same prayer for the servant of the Lord engaged in planting new churches where Christ had not before been named.

Later on, in Jerusalem, we are given another glimpse of this praying church. Peter is arrested and thrown into prison. The church gathers together and continues upon its knees in "long and fervent prayer" (Weymouth), until Peter, after his great deliverance, knocks on the door to join them in glorious praise.

A new congregation comes into being at Antioch composed of recent converts. Will that also be a church at prayer? Yes, there again prayer is the element in which it lives and works. It is while they wait before the Lord in fasting and prayer that the Holy Spirit speaks to them revealing God's will regarding the going forth of Barnabas and Paul (Acts 13:1-4). Christ is able to continue carrying out His will through His Body. Barnabas and Paul set forth "sent by the Holy Spirit". They were not chosen or sent by the will or counsel of men. They knew, and the church in Antioch knew, that they were chosen and sent by God.

So in Antioch it is still the praying church, met together in the Name of Christ, recognizing His absolute headship, waiting upon Him continually in prayer to know His will in everything and to ask its fulfilment and acting only and always in obedience to His guidance.

Paul and Barnabas go forth evangelizing, converts are won and congregations established. In these new churches do we continue to see the Church at prayer? Yes, the curtain is lifted again and we witness the Evangelists presiding at the appointment of the Elders in the new churches. The appointments are made "after prayer and fasting" (Weymouth). It should be noted that the prayer preceded the appointing of the Elders. It was through prayer that the churches received guidance as to who were appointed by God to be Elders. The record states that this was done "in every church" (Acts 14:23). All the New Testament churches were churches at prayer. As Paul and Barnabas had been called and sent by the Holy Spirit, the will of the Spirit being made known to the Church at prayer, so in the churches they founded the same order is followed. It was the normal procedure, practised by the whole Church.

Later, we are given two delightful examples of fellowship in prayer.

Having thus spoken, Paul knelt down and prayed with them all; and with loud lamentation they threw their arms round his neck, and kissed him lovingly, grieved above all things at his having told them that after that day they were no longer to see his face. (Acts 20:36-38, Weymouth.)

When, however, our time was up, we left and went on our way, all the disciples and their wives and children coming to see us off. Then, after kneeling down on the beach and praying, we took leave one of another. (Acts 21:5, Weymouth.)

Their mutual love as believers found its deepest expression and satisfaction in going unitedly into the presence of the Lord in a communion of prayer with the Head of the Body. Those New Testament congregations did not think of offering Paul a farewell supper with laudatory speeches and a presentation. Both they and he had a means of fellowship infinitely more adequate.

Finally, we have the prayer fellowship of the Church, represented by the local Elders, with those who are sick. Any sick believer has the privilege of availing himself of this fellowship, thus having the Church stand with him in the prayer of faith.

A summary of the record given in the New Testament of the Church's prayer activity reveals both the scope and importance of that ministry:

(a1) The initial prayer gathering in which the Church was born is described in Acts 1:13, 14; 2:1-4.

(b) The fact that the Church continued to be a Church at prayer is stated in Acts 2:42.

Then we are given several other typical examples of the Church at prayer, one of each, making seven in all:

(a2) Acts 4:24-31. Faced with persecution and danger, the Church seeks renewed power for a fearless witness.

(a3) Acts 12:1-17. With one of its number (Peter) in prison and in danger of death, it continues in prayer until he is released.

(a4) Acts 13:1-4. It is to the Church at prayer in Antioch that the Holy Spirit gives confirmation regarding the call of the two Evangelists or Missionaries, Barnabas and Paul.

(a5) Acts 14:23. It is through waiting upon God in prayer that Evangelists and churches discovered who had been appointed by God as Elders.

(a6) Acts 20:36: 21:5. Here we see churches fellowshipping in prayer with a fellow-believer and servant of the Lord.

(a7) Jas. 5:14. Through its Elders, the Church stands in faith before God for a member who is ill.

The Holy Spirit has not recorded every occasion on which the New Testament Church prayed. That was neither possible nor necessary, but He has given us examples that open the door for us that we may have a clear vision of its ministry of prayer.

Pray Without Ceasing

In the Epistles to the churches, the Church is continually urged to pray without ceasing. In Ephesians, which is the revelation of the Church as the Body of Christ, we see it, armed with its spiritual armour and with the sword of the Spirit, kneeling before God as it prays, "always with all prayer and supplication in the Spirit, and watching thereunto with all perseverance and supplication for all saints" (Eph. 6:18).

Much is recorded also regarding the prayer ministry of Apostles and Evangelists. When the seven were appointed as Deacons of the church in Jerusalem, the Apostles said, "we will devote ourselves to prayer and to the delivery of the message" (Acts 6:4, Weymouth). It was when "Peter went up upon the housetop to pray" that he received the vision which opened the door of the Gospel to the Gentiles (Acts 10:9). The prayer ministry of the Evangelist is dealt with in a later chapter.

25

It is not just in the Early Church that we see the power of the prayer of the Church. Always, during the centuries that have followed, when the Church has sought God in true, Holy Spirit guided prayer, the mighty power of God has been manifested in blessing, revival and victory. Without such waiting before God in intercession no great blessing has been given.

A modern instance is recorded by Dr. Jonathan Goforth.[1] Twenty missionaries in Korea decided to pray every noon hour until blessing came:

> After we had prayed about a month, a brother proposed that we stop the prayer meeting, saying 'We have prayed about a month and nothing unusual has come of it. We are spending a lot of time. I do not think we are justified. Let us go on with our work as usual, and each pray at home as we find it convenient'. The proposal seemed plausible. However, the majority decided to continue the prayer-meeting.
>
> They decided to give more time to prayer instead of less. With that in view they changed the hour from twelve to four o'clock; then they were free to pray until supper time if they wished. There was little else than prayer. If any one had an encouraging item to relate, it was given as they continued in prayer. They prayed for about four months...

Then the power of the Holy Spirit was manifested. One Sunday evening in a gathering of about fifteen hundred people, an atmosphere that had been hard and unpromising was suddenly changed as an Elder, the leading man in the congregation, stood up and said, 'I am an Achan. God can't bless because of me'. Then he confessed a hidden sin.

> Instantly it was realized that the barriers had fallen and that God the Holy One had come. Conviction of sin swept the audience. The service commenced at seven o'clock Sunday evening and did not end until two o'clock Monday morning, yet during all the time dozens were standing weeping, awaiting their turn to confess. Day after day the people assembled now and it was manifest that the Refiner was in His temple.
>
> It paid well to have spent the several months in prayer for when God the Holy Spirit came He accomplished more in half a day than we missionaries could have accomplished in half a year. In less than two months, more than two thousand heathen were converted. It is always so as soon as God gets first place; but as a rule the Church, which professes to be Christ's, will not cease her busy round of activities and give God a chance by waiting on Him in prayer.

At how great a cost does the modern church fail to give the necessary time to prayer! The price it is paying year after year, decade after decade is its poverty in power and fruit and its ineffectiveness as the witness of the Lord in this world.

---

[1] *The Victorious Life,* pp. 184-188.

The Church of the New Testament was mighty through the Spirit and triumphant in its life and witness. This was because Christ's Headship was recognized and He was able to do His will and carry on His work in and through His Body. It was not because of any special dispensation of blessing upon the Church at that time, but because it was in continual communication with Him through prayer and obedient always to His will. When any congregation, such as that at Corinth, departed from the spiritual way to be guided by human wisdom and counsel, the unity of the Spirit disappeared, the power and blessing were lost, and all the marks of defeat and disintegration became evident immediately, just as in any modern congregation.

Satan Would Prevent a True Ministry of Prayer

If there is one thing above another that Christian people will admit to be necessary and important and yet fail to practise, it is prayer. It is not difficult to see why this should be. It is quite understandable that Satan should do everything in his power to prevent true prayer being made. We all know how plausible and how insistent are the arguments that come into our minds to justify the neglect of prayer. Satan opposes our being active in witness but not nearly so determinedly as our constancy in prayer. If it is a choice between the two he considers activity in witness the lesser danger. He will even present to us the duty and urgency of activity in witness until it would almost seem to be wrong to take the necessary time for prayer! The fact is that he does not fear activity that is not the fruit of prayer.

The modern congregation considers that its duty is to worship, while the spiritual ministry is the responsibility of the Pastor. How many such churches would think it possible or necessary to devote the time to prayer that was given by the New Testament congregations? Even among active evangelical and evangelistic churches, how many would consider it practicable to give the time required for congregational prayer of that nature? A hundred and one reasons will immediately come to mind why it would not be possible to do so. But are any of the reasons really valid in the light of the teaching of Scripture and the practice of the New Testament Church? Can we tell God that we are too busy in our advanced day and generation to obey His Word completely and to conduct the Church just as He told us to and wait to know His will, but that we expect Him to bless us just the same?

Andrew Murray stated the matter clearly:

The more one thinks and seeks and prays, the more we are compelled to the conclusion: the Church lacks the power of the Holy Spirit that has been promised to fit her for her work. When we further ask, what can be the reason of such a lack of the Spirit who has been so definitely promised, and who yearns in love to take possession of God's children and to fit them for their work, the question has but one answer: "Ye have not, because ye ask not." And when the further question comes: What can be the reason that there is, comparatively speaking, so little prayer, while the promise is so rich and sure and blessed — then there is no answer but the confession, with shame — God grant, with deep sorrow and penitence — that we are too slothful, and too worldly to pray in power the prayer that availeth much.[1]

In fairness to the modern congregation, we must admit that it is not surprising that it does not see the practical importance of engaging in such a prayer ministry. The reason for its participation has been partly taken away. The ordinary member has been relieved of the responsibility for the ministry of the Word. This takes from his prayer both objective and incentive. He naturally feels that the main responsibility for prayer falls upon the Pastor, who is responsible for the ministry. All he has to do is to back the Pastor. But when his personal responsibility for ministry as well as for worship is restored, then he feels both the need and the responsibility to enter fully into the prayer activity of the church. When he has little personal responsibility, his prayer must be, to a certain extent, vague and indefinite. He meets to pray for something in which he takes little part. But if he is fully active in the church's testimony and witness, knowing that he is as responsible for it as any other member and that the issue depends upon him personally and directly, then he can be expected to be personally and vitally interested to pray, and to pray through, that guidance and victory may be obtained.

It will be said that for a congregation to be able to wait before the Lord in prayer in this way, the individual members will need to have spiritual knowledge and experience. That is true; but, on the other hand, if the congregation does not so meet for prayer, will the members ever gain such experience? Is it not true that much of the spiritual inactivity and weakness of many Church members results from the fact that they are not required to participate in the responsibility of a vital prayer life in the congregation? There is no doubt that the lack of this responsibility brings

---

[1] *Back to Pentecost*, p. 66.

great loss into the experience even of the spiritual members.

Understanding regarding prayer is not given by man but by the Holy Spirit and we must exercise faith and believe that if we obey God's Word and act according to it the Holy Spirit will give understanding. We never have the right to accept a lower standard than that set in God's Word just because we do not believe it is possible for God to bring His Word to pass. That is pure unbelief and inexcusable.

To engage in such a prayer activity, a congregation will have to meet for prayer. It is hardly necessary to say that the usual midweek church service, commonly called the prayer meeting, which consists of a short sermon or Bible study and a few prayers, is not in the New Testament sense a gathering of the congregation for prayer. This means, of course, as we must sadly admit, that very many churches have no prayer gathering and continue their ministry from year to year without any true congregational prayer activity.

In some cases, a compromise of one kind or another is attempted. It may be sought to organize the prayer of a congregation, by 'sentence prayers' or lists of petitions, into a brief period of fifteen or twenty minutes a week. Let us not be deceived; God never accepts compromises or substitutes.

In other places a faithful and more or less discouraged few meet for prayer in an attempt to carry the dead weight of an otherwise prayerless congregation. We would not minimize the possibilities and value of the prayers of a few, if they are truly guided by the Holy Spirit, but the gathering of a few for prayer does not take the place of the Pentecost or Antioch prayer ministry of a congregation. If those few are used of God in effective prayer to bring the congregation into a realization of its prayer responsibility, then their meeting together will be gloriously worth while, but if they simply continue gathering year after year for a virtually fruitless exercise, they accomplish nothing real and are wasting precious time.

It will be understood that a prayer meeting, no matter how much time is given to it or how many take part, where the prayers are merely the formal expression of many more or less unrelated and indefinite petitions, covering as wide a range as possible and presented without any clear assurance of the Holy Spirit's guidance or definite faith in an answer, is not a Pentecost or Antioch prayer gathering. It must be prayer that is definitely guided by the Holy

Spirit and that leads into a knowledge of God's will so that there can be the united and unanimous asking for the carrying out of that revealed will with the assurance that the prayer will be answered.

The enemy will seek to persuade us that such a praying church is ideal but too spiritual to be practical and too good to be true—and, of course, quite impossible today. He will remind us of all the difficulties and dangers and the believers' weaknesses and lack of knowledge, etc. It will not be difficult for him to present a convincing argument for he has an abundance of material to draw from. But to obey God's Word is not nearly so difficult as Satan and the natural man would make it appear to be.

If we believe that God will fulfil His Word and if we go forward in faith, we shall find that He will undertake. He has never asked us to do what is really impossible. That does not mean that there will be no difficulties. Because we go forward in faith, it does not follow that Satan will cease to attack; rather does he redouble his efforts. Our faith will be continually tested, but God will lead us on step by step, causing us to triumph over difficulties and bringing us to the fulfilment of His purpose. It depends upon our faith and obedience, not upon our ability or upon what is seemingly possible or impossible. It is never impossible for God to fulfil His purpose. It is impossible for Him to fulfil it through us only if we lack faith and are disobedient. The way of full blessing and power according to His promises is open to us if we wil take it and walk therein patiently and obediently by faith.

We have taken part in the founding of congregations that have practised prayer in the New Testament way and we have fellow-shipped with them for many years. We can testify to the fact that it is possible for congregations today to walk in this way giving prayer its true place and being guided by the Lord to know His will and to minister victoriously in face of all the power of the enemy. And the fellowship in such congregations is truly satisfying and glorious.

PART IV

APPLICATION OF NEW TESTAMENT MISSIONARY PRINCIPLES

"As Moses was admonished of God when he was about to build the tabernacle: for, See, saith he, that thou make all things according to the pattern showed to thee in the mount."

Hebrews 8:5.

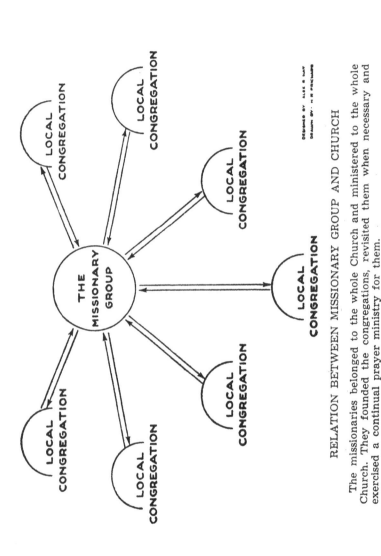

RELATION BETWEEN MISSIONARY GROUP AND CHURCH

The missionaries belonged to the whole Church and ministered to the whole Church. They founded the congregations, revisited them when necessary and exercised a continual prayer ministry for them.

From the congregations young men were called to join the missionary group. The congregations ministered to the missionary group through prayer and giving.

'AND LO, I AM WITH YOU'

He sent us forth to plant the precious seed,
  To water it and care for it
That it might bear to Him an hundred-fold
  In glorious yield of ripened fruit.

He said He sent us not alone to plant;
  But as we go, no matter where,
To sow and tend and reap, there goeth One
  Who cannot fail: my Lord is there.

He has not changed, the Lord who by me stands;
  As He was then, so wise and true,
So gentle and so strong, so is He now
  My steps to guide, my strength renew.

He has not lost the cunning of His hand
  To touch blind eyes and make them see;
The wisdom of His Word is mighty still
  To sinner and to Pharisee.

The love triumphant of His Cross,
  Where all the power of Satan's might
Was foiled and vanquished for eternity,
  Is victor still, though dark the night.

CHAPTER XXXI

METHODS IN CONTRAST

From the time that Paul joined Barnabas at Antioch until the
day of his martyrdom, his plan of campaign never changed; his
methods of work were always the same; the principles that guided
his actions never altered. He had not followed a method that might
be modified by changing circumstances or improved with increasing experience. He carried on the ministry of an Evangelist, or
missionary of the Church, the scope, duties, methods and objectives
of which had been definitely revealed to the Church by the Holy
Spirit. All of his companions, and all others engaged in that
ministry, worked in the same manner. The principles and order of
the Evangelists' ministry were not subject to change any more
than were those of the Elders' ministry. They were according to
God's plan for His Church and, therefore, perfect. No liberty is
given to modify the details of the pattern for the order and
ministry of the Church just as none was given to alter the details
of God's plan for the Tabernacle.

That there is a wide difference between the method of church
planting followed by Paul and his companions and that applied
in modern missionary endeavour, hardly needs to be said. The
brief sketch of Paul's ministry already given is sufficient to make
clear what was his conception of missionary evangelism. As we
have seen, his objective was the establishing of congregations
throughout the whole known world, not the evangelization of a
particular region. He did not organize a 'Macedonia Mission', or
even a 'Mission to Europe'. There could be no geographical
bounds placed to his ministry or to that of his fellow-workers.

He did not open Stations, placing missionaries in them to found
churches and nurse them during many years. He and His companions were an evangelistic party, never establishing themselves

permanently anywhere. Yet his methods were thorough. The manner in which he cared for the churches was efficient.

First of all, congregations were established in the cities to which he was led. He never stayed more than two or three years with a congregation. His longest visits were to large and important centres strategically placed. He did not usually wait for a congregation to be thoroughly established with Elders appointed, but left it as soon as it could carry on its witness through the gifts of the Spirit given to its members. After a year or two, he would revisit it, staying again a few months, or one or two years, as might be necessary, seeing that Elders were appointed and giving whatever further instruction was necessary.

It will be noted that while these Evangelists never settled permanently anywhere, neither was it their practice to make flying visits to preach the Gospel once or twice in a town and then hurry on to the next. Their evangelistic journeys were not trips of a few days, or even of a few weeks, covering as much territory and preaching in as many places as possible in that time. When they entered a town it was to establish a church there and they remained until a sufficient beginning had been made. But where there was no response they did not stay. Their method may at first appear to be slow, but in the end it proved to be by far the most speedy. They obtained definite and permanent results wherever they went.

A cursory reading of the record of Paul's journeys may give the impression that he was continually on the move, travelling from place to place and seldom staying long anywhere. It must be remembered that these journeyings were spread over a period of probably thirty-five years. Nearly half of this time was spent in laying the foundations of five congregations strategically placed in five different countries.

This misconception has led to a common and serious mistake in modern missionary practice—the attempt to establish churches, or to strengthen their foundations, through brief, occasional visits made from a base station. A missionary, after a three weeks' tour, may think he has been following Paul's travelling method, but, probably, he has visited a larger number of places than Paul did in a journey of several years. Paul did not engage in what the modern missionary calls itineration work. Such work does not establish well-laid, strong foundations. Year after year the groups of believers continue to be dependent upon repeated visits. Leaving them thus indefinitely in a dependent position accustoms them to that condition and makes it more difficult to lead them into vigorous spiritual life. Paul left foundations solidly laid because he remained long enough in each place to do a thorough and lasting work.

Small and scattered groups of believers require a ministry of teaching, but that was carried on by preachers and teachers from the stronger congregations who sometimes travelled ministering to the laying of a solid and complete foundation for the church himself, instead of teaching that others should receive the necessary gifts of the Spirit to carry it on, he will be tied down indefinitely to a district.

Paul did not seek to accomplish the thorough evangelization of each region to which he went. The record makes no mention of any endeavour on his part to do so. All his energies were directed to the laying of a solid and complete foundation for the church in the city to which he had been led. When that was sufficiently accomplished he went on to another strategic centre.

The evangelization of the surrounding territory was to be the work of the church that was established. Preachers and teachers from the local church spread the witness, ministering by the gifts, and through the power, of the Spirit.

It was not necessary to pay such preachers and teachers. The missionaries who had brought the light to them had come living by faith, trusting in God for the supply of their material needs or earning their living by the work of their hands, so the local preachers and teachers did not think of doing otherwise.

The Elders of the churches were not paid. They earned their living. Thus their support was no problem. This made easy the establishing of any number of churches even in the poorest communities.

The missionaries were not markedly foreign, nor were they attached to, or supported by, a foreign organization. The converts, therefore, never thought in terms of foreign money or foreign organizations. The Gospel and the Church were, from the very beginning, God's gifts directly to them, in no sense foreign or related to foreigners or to foreign lands, so it was only natural to consider that the propagation of the Gospel in their land would be carried on by local men dependent directly upon God using local resources.

A year or two after a church is founded we find that from among the local preachers and teachers some are called of the Lord as missionaries, and these join themselves to the missionary company with no fear of going forth looking to God for the supply of their needs. So it was not necessary to bring more missionaries from other lands. Nor was it necessary to bring funds from other lands. On the contrary, every newly evangelized field was soon sending the light on to the regions beyond.

The New Testament method was admirably adapted for the establishing of independent congregations. It insisted upon making the local church directly dependent upon the Holy Spirit. That produced, in the shortest possible time, experienced leadership. It set every convert to work immediately using the gifts of the Spirit given to him for service. Responsibility was thrust upon the churches and they were forced to function. They were revisited when necessary to give them encouragement and instruction but, so long as all went well, the Evangelist took no responsibility for their direction or work. If anything went wrong, effective aid was given at once, and the spiritual order restored, but never did an Evangelist consent to remain permanently with a church.

This method required a very real and active faith on the part of the Evangelists. They had to believe that the Holy Spirit could and would do His work in and through the converts. To a great extent our modern method is the outcome of lack of faith; we fear that the Holy Spirit will not be able to do His part until we have made the way easy for Him. The New Testament Evangelists had their eyes upon God and upon His power and faithfulness; what looms large to us is rather the unpromising nature of the material to be used. We find it hard to believe that God can do for them what He did for similar converts in New Testament times, and what He has done even for us. We must come to realize the truth that, as in the natural realm so in the spiritual,

> He who can open the bud does it so simply,
> He gives it a glance, and the life-sap stirs
>   through its veins.
> At His breath the flower spreads its wings
>   and flutters in the wind.
> Colours flush out like heart longings, the
>   perfume betrays a sweet secret.
> He who can open the bud does it so simply.[1]

Writing to the Thessalonians, with whom he had spent but a short time on his first visit, Paul says: "We have confidence in the Lord concerning you". Dr. James Denny comments on this:

---

[1] Rabindranath Tagore.

And side by side with this confidence in God stood his confidence touching the Thessalonians themselves. He was sure in the Lord that they were doing, and would continue to do, the things which he commanded them — in other words, that they would lead a worthy and becoming Christian life. The point of this sentence lies in the words 'in the Lord'. Apart from the Lord, Paul could have had no such confidence as he here expresses. The standard of the Christian life is lofty and severe, its purity, its unworldliness, its brotherly love, its burning hope, were new things then in the world. What assurance could there be that this standard would be maintained, when the small congregation of working people in Thessalonica was cast upon its own resources in the midst of a pagan community? None at all, apart from Christ. If He had left them alone with the Apostle, no one could have risked much upon their fidelity to the Christian calling. It marks the beginning of a new era when the Apostle writes, 'We have confidence **in the Lord** touching you'.

In the Lord, you may depend upon those who **in themselves** are weak, unstable, wilful, foolish. In the Lord, you may depend on them to stand fast, to fight their temptations, to overcome the world and the wicked one. This kind of assurance, and the actual presence and help of Christ which justified it, are very characteristic of the New Testament. They explain the joyous, open, hopeful spirit of the early Church — they are the cause, as well as the effect, of that vigorous moral health which, in the decay of ancient civilization gave the Church the inheritance of the future. And still we may have confidence in the Lord that all whom He has called by His Gospel will be able by His spiritual presence with them to walk worthy of that calling, and to confute alike the fears of the good and the contempt of the wicked. For the Lord is faithful, who will stablish them, and preserve them from the evil one.[1]

Again, referring to Paul's benediction at the close of the second letter to the Thessalonians, Denny writes:

The Thessalonians, a few months ago, had been heathens — they had known nothing of God and His Son — they were living still in the midst of a heathen population, under the pressure of heathen influences both on thought and conduct, beset by numberless temptations and, if they were mindful of the country from which they had come forth, not without opportunity to return. Paul would willingly have stayed with them to be their pastor and teacher, their guide and their defender, but his missionary calling made this impossible. After the merest introduction to the Gospel, and to the new life to which it called those who received it, they had to be left to themselves. Who should keep them from falling? Who should open their eyes to understand the ideal which the Christian is summoned to work out in his life? Amid their many enemies, where could they look for a sufficient and ever-present ally? The Apostle answers these questions when he writes, 'The grace of our Lord Jesus Christ be with you all'. Although he has left them, they are not really alone. The free love of God, which visited them at first uncalled, will be with them still, to perfect the work it has begun. It will beset them behind and before — it will be a sun and a shield to them, a light

---

[1] *The Epistle to the Thessalonians,* pp. 367-369.

and a defence. In their moral perplexities, in all their despondencies, it will be sufficient for them.[1]

There is one point in this statement of Dr. Denny's with which we disagree. Paul and his fellow-workers had been but a short time with the Thessalonians, it is true, but they had given them more than 'the merest introduction to the Gospel'. They had seen to it that through teaching and prayer the young converts had come into a personal experience of victory and power through the Holy Spirit. These converts had been put in vital personal touch with the source of all spiritual knowledge and power. They knew how to go direct to God and get guidance and wisdom from the Holy Spirit, and Paul's letters to them bear abundant witness to the thoroughness of the teaching that had been given to them during his first visits to them.

Paul reminded the Corinthians that his witness to them had "depended upon truths which the Spirit taught and mightily carried home, so that your trust might rest, not on the wisdom of men, but on the power of God" (1 Cor. 2:5, Weymouth). Every care was taken that a truly spiritual foundation should be laid by the Holy Spirit, from the very beginning. For that reason they could be left and it was possible to have 'confidence in the Lord' concerning them.

The Modern Plan of Campaign

In our modern method, when a new field is opened, the procedure is for the missionary to establish a 'Mission Station'. A hall is rented and preaching services begun. Then, if possible, a day-school and college and hospital are established. In some cases, the Institutions will precede the Gospel preaching.

The missionaries are, probably, an entirely foreign group, foreign in language, customs and outlook, regarding themselves as superior to the 'natives', living according to a standard unattainable, possibly, to them, and holding themselves, to a great extent, socially aloof from them. They are evidently well supplied with funds from their own country. The practical value of the example of their lives to those among whom they live is, therefore, greatly reduced. Instead of it being a most effective contribution to the spread of the Gospel, to the instruction of the converts, the strengthening of their faith and the establishment of independent congregations, as

---

[1] Ibid.

was the example of Paul and his fellow-workers, it is, in some respects, a hindrance, being incomplete and so unrelated to the local conditions of life as to seem unreal and impracticable. The plan of campaign is to build up a strong 'Central Station' that will serve as a foundation for the work as it spreads and command the respect and attention of the educated and ruling classes. This is, of course, an expensive programme.

After a while, when a number of converts have been gathered together, some promising young men are chosen from among them to train for the pastorate. The training given is as nearly as possible a copy of the seminary training the missionary-instructor received in his own country.

A 'native' pastor is ordained and placed in charge of a congregation. He must be supported, so the missionary requests the necessary grant from the Home Board.

Meanwhile, there will be an effort to establish congregations in the smaller towns and villages around. Itineration trips are made, first to sow the seed and then to care for any converts that may be won. This work is undertaken by the missionaries, who consider themselves responsible for the evangelization of the region.

"Native evangelists" are employed to assist in the work of evangelization. They too are paid. They expect to be paid, for such is the example that the missionaries have given them.

As time goes on and the work grows, other pastors are trained and given the care of churches. Perhaps buildings are erected for them, paid for by Mission funds. There are hundreds, maybe thousands, of towns and villages in the region and it will be necessary ultimately to provide pastors for all of these.

The funds from the Homeland are limited and the missionary comes to realize that his Mission will not be able to support such a large force, so he begins to urge the congregations to do something to support their own Pastors. The idea is a new one to the national churches for, so far, the foreign Mission has paid the salaries of their pastors. They are quite satisfied to have it done by the rich foreigner, who seems to have an unlimited supply of money which he gets for the asking from the fabulously rich country from which he comes. So they are not inclined to make any whole-hearted effort.

Moreover, it is probable that the missionary is really imposing too heavy a financial burden upon them. The churches are small and poor and it is difficult for them to undertake the financial obligations entailed in the upkeep of a building and the support of a Pastor—a burden which, as we have seen, the New Testament method did not place on the churches founded by the Apostles. Before long, the situation becomes acute. The limit of the financial giving of the 'Home' church is reached. More 'native workers' cannot be employed because there is no money to support them. Then comes a year of shortage when less money comes from the Homeland and the number of 'native workers' must be reduced. The work then practically ceases to expand. New districts cannot be entered or new groups of converts cared for. The whole work is halted by the financial problem. If, however, the congregations had been organized according to the New Testament pattern, such a situation could never have arisen, for there would not have been any financial problem.

On such a mission station the missionaries must remain indefinitely. The time when the local church will be sufficiently established to leave it to carry on the witness in the power of the Spirit never seems to come. After fifteen, twenty, thirty years, the missionaries will be still there. Second generation missionaries may follow their fathers on the same stations. The believers remain immature, the churches weak and dependent.

Under the New Testament system of church organization the financial problem did not exist. In most cases the congregations met in private houses or in rented halls. There was no Pastor to be supported. The congregations were taught to give and they evidently gave liberally, but, as the local expenses were small, the greater proportion of what was given, instead of being consumed by the local organizations, was available for the spread of the Gospel.

The ministry in the congregations was not dependent upon seminary-trained Pastors, but upon the gifts of the Holy Spirit given to all. The churches never became dependent upon missionaries or missionary Societies. Thus the ministry of a church was conducted, not by one man, but by all its members. A congregation was not a company of more or less inactive and permanently immature converts that must always be nursed, but a hive of workers growing in experience and spiritual power.

The missionaries were not tied down to Institutions and dependent churches. They were always free to press on to new fields to fulfil their ministry. Nothing could slow up the progress or spread of the work except unfaithfulness on the part of the individual and

26

the consequent lack of spiritual power. Of that there was evidence, of course, but the Holy Spirit fulfilled His work, the Lord built His Church and Satan did not prevail against it.

CHAPTER XXXII

SPIRITUAL PREPARATION OF THE MISSIONARY

The ministry of the Evangelist is to preach the Gospel, instruct converts, establish congregations and watch over their spiritual welfare. He must lay complete and solid foundations and give a full witness, delivering the whole counsel of God. It will be readily seen that for such an important work special spiritual preparation and gifts are essential. The Evangelist cannot give what he does not have. He cannot effectively teach truths he has not experienced himself. The congregations established will reflect exactly the spiritual condition and knowledge of the one who established them.

As we have already seen, the preparation of the worker is a matter in which God permits of no compromise: the instrument He would use must first be fully prepared and must be willing to pay the price of death to all that is of himself that the true life of the Spirit may be seen in him. In the record of the ministry of the New Testament missionaries, God's dealings with them personally and their spiritual experiences are an essential part of the story.

Why are there so many failures among new missionaries? It is estimated that between thirty and forty percent of new missionaries return home within the first five years. After many years of receiving new missionaries on the field we know the fundamental reason. Those who failed lacked spiritual experience. They did not have the experimental knowledge of the truths they believed. Their beliefs were largely theoretical. They were graduates of schools. They had studied God's Word and could preach it, but it had not become life in them. Prayer guided by the Holy Spirit, the seeking and finding of God's will, the exercise of true faith, dependence upon God alone for the supply of material needs, the death of Christ manifested in the daily life producing life, the resisting of

Satan through the prayer of faith—of these things they had little or no actual experience.

When we changed our policy regarding the acceptance of candidates and demanded, not more scholastic attainment, but the necessary personal experience, the loss dropped to almost nothing.

Personal Surrender

The work accomplished by Christ on Calvary includes a full provision of enabling, victorious, resurrection power for the life and service of both the individual believer and the Church. Through the complete triumph of the Cross we are raised together with Christ, quickened together with Him, seated together with Him in heavenly places, and made possessors of all spiritual blessings in Him in the heavenlies. It is our privilege in Christ, as we are seated with Him in His triumph, to live a life of victory through His Spirit.

A full witness to all this must be given and to do so the messenger must have entered into the experience of it himself. If the experience of full personal surrender and victory should be the normal condition of every believer in Christ, how essential must it be in the missionary! Let us remember what our Lord required of His disciples. Before He left them, He had seen all save one come to the place of full surrender. The outstanding example is Peter. He loved Christ—up to a point. Love of self was still strong and it clouded his vision and finally led him into defeat. Shortly after he had acknowledged Christ as the Son of the living God, a truth which he had received by revelation of God, Satan spoke through him. When our Lord revealed to His disciples the death that awaited Him and the resurrection that was to follow, Peter was scandalized and rebuked Him, saying, "Pity thyself".[1] After a stern rebuke, Christ explained to His disciples that whoever would follow Him must take the same road that He was taking, voluntarily yielding all of self, loving not his own life but loving God with all his heart and mind and strength and his neighbour as himself.

But still Peter did not yield. When our Lord went to the Cross, Peter denied Him. Like many a Christian, he believed in Him but rejected the claims of the Cross upon his own life, and the inevitable result was spiritual defeat. After the resurrection, our Lord faced him with the question, "Peter, lovest thou Me?"; and He pressed

---

[1] Marginal reading.

that question home until He was satisfied that Peter's whole heart was truly yielded to Him—that he had denied self and all that is of this world and accepted the Cross; Then and only then was He satisfied to leave him and entrust to him the ministry of feeding His sheep.

That is the standard that our Lord set for His servants and it has never been lowered. To minister with Him we must meet it.

Paul and those who accompanied him lived in the daily experience of personal victory. They had entered into it before they were sent forth by the Spirit as witnesses of the Gospel. If they had failed at any point to make a complete surrender and to enter into the fulness of Christ through faith, the Holy Spirit would not have considered them prepared for service and would not have sent them.

That the Evangelist have such an experience is absolutely essential. Without it, power for service will be lacking and the testimony of his life will fall short. One who does not live in the experience of the fulness of the power of the Spirit in his life will certainly not experience it in his service. Nor will he be able to give the witness and teaching that those who are saved require. Victorious churches are composed of victorious members; and such churches and members are the fruit only of the worker who through a victorious walk can minister in the Spirit through victorious prayer and witness.

He who would minister in the Spirit must know what it is to be filled with the Spirit. The Spirit is in every one who is born of the Spirit but He can fill us only as we are truly and fully surrendered to Him. It is a matter simply of entering by faith and surrender into the fulness of that which is already ours. We just accept as true what God's Word states. There may be a struggle to surrender fully and let the flesh be crucified but there will be no struggle to receive the Spirit for He is already in us waiting only for freedom, through our surrender and simple faith, to use us fully and fulfil all God's will through us. One who has not permitted Him to do this—or who is not permitting Him to do it—is not prepared for the Lord's work in any sphere; through him there will not be manifested the 'power and demonstration of the Spirit'.

Paul's Example

Paul was able at all times to point to the testimony of his own life, and he did so continually. He had proved God's power and faithfulness fully. He could say, "Christ liveth in me", and again, "God forbid that I should glory in anything except in the Cross of our Lord Jesus Christ, by which the world is crucified to me and I to the world" (Gal. 2:20; 6:14, Weymouth). That being so, he could insist, in his teaching, and stand in faith before God in prayer, that those converted through his ministry should enter into a like experience. He lived a life of faith as his Lord had done. He knew what it was to suffer want, hardness and persecution and demonstrated how to live victoriously by faith in the midst of such circumstances.

He wrote to Timothy:

Make thyself a pattern of the faithful, in word, in life, in love, in faith, in purity. (1 Tim. 4:12, Conybeare.)

Of himself he was in a position to say:

I beseech you follow my example, as I follow the example of Christ. (1 Cor. 11:1, Conybeare.)

It was not enthusiasm or asceticism that led him to live such a life of faith and abnegation. His procedure was based upon definite and sound spiritual principles. He gives us the reason:

For I take heed to give no cause of stumbling, lest blame should be cast on the ministration wherein I serve; but in all things I commend myself as one who ministers to God's service; in stedfast endurance, in afflictions, in necessities, in straitness of distress, in stripes, in imprisonments, in tumults, in labours, in sleepless watchings, in hunger and thirst; in purity, in knowledge, in long-suffering, in kindness, in (the gifts of) the Holy Spirit, in love unfeigned; speaking the word of truth, working with the power of God, fighting with the weapons of righteousness, both for attack and for defence; through good report and evil, through honour and through infamy; counted as a deceiver, yet being true; as unknown (by men), yet acknowledged (by God); as ever dying, yet behold I live; as chastened by suffering, yet not destroyed; as sorrowful, yet ever filled with joy; as poor, yet making many rich; as having nothing, yet possessing all things. (2 Cor. 6:3-10, Conybeare.)

I fill up what yet is lacking of the sufferings of Christ in my flesh, on behalf of His body, which is the Church; whereof I was made a servant, to minister in the stewardship which God gave me for you (Gentiles), that I might fulfil it by declaring the Word of God, the mystery... which is Christ in you the hope of glory. (Col. 1:24-27, Conybeare.)

Christ, through the things which He suffered on earth, in His human body, bore a testimony and left an example that are indispensable to us. Without them His ministry would not have been complete. In Him we see not only the truth and the power of God, but the demonstration of a life lived in that truth and power: 'And the Word... dwelt among us and we beheld His glory'. We cannot say that He does not understand our sufferings and temptations: 'He was tempted in all points as we are'. He does not say to us, 'Do as I said', but 'Do as I did'. He faced the utmost of poverty, rejection, despisal, suffering and death, and it was all part of the ministry in which He was engaged for His Church. He did it all through the wisdom and power of the indwelling Spirit, showing how to live justly and victoriously in the midst of this evil world.

The servant of Christ also must bear such a testimony. The mystery of the indwelling Christ must be manifested in him fully through a practical testimony. The trials and sufferings and temptations and poverty of Paul were an essential part of his ministry. The Church must see him face the world and conquer it through the wisdom and power that he preached. He, also, must be able to say, not, 'Do as I say', but, 'Do as I do, for I do as Christ did'. His converts could not say of him, 'He does not understand the hardness of our lives or the temptations we face; he is well provided for and shielded from anxiety and suffering'.

The testimony of victory over the world borne by Christ through suffering must be continued in His servants. They also must face this world in the power of the Spirit and faith alone and fill up that which is still lacking of this testimony—that practical, self-sacrificing, all-enduring, all-conquering witness which the Church on earth will always need in its ministers. They must minister in their stewardship as patterns in everything to the Church that it also may be led, by such an example, into the fulness of experience as overcomers seated with Christ on His Throne.

The New Testament Evangelists were all willing to minister thus as living examples of the truth they preached: 'as poor yet making many rich', as 'ever dying' yet ever living the abundant, victorious life of Christ. It was when their successors began to consider the cost of such a witness too great and sought to give to the Church a partial witness, in word only and not in example, that their power ebbed away. Then the churches became like them, for there was none to demonstrate the life of the great Shepherd of the sheep and to call them back to such a life. It will always stand as a basic fact in the ministry of the Gospel that a minister of the Lord will not be able to lead the Church into a higher experience than that which he himself demonstrates.

It will be understood, of course, that the afflictions which the servant of the Lord must face are not self-inflicted or sought for but such as inevitably come to one who through faith takes the way of the Cross and challenges the power of Satan. In no other is there any true testimony.

Thus it is that, while Paul's life was one of continual triumph, it was equally one of incessant conflict and testing. In him the converts saw a life of glorious victory in Christ lived in the face of the utmost efforts of Satan to bring defeat. Writing to the Philippians he declared, "I can do all things through Christ which strengthened me" (Phil. 4:13) His Lord had said: "All things are possible to him that believeth". He had demonstrated that truth in His own life. Paul, the servant of the Lord, who taught that same truth must also demonstrate it in his life.

Paul's Experience

When Paul said that he could do all things through Christ he spoke from experience. If it had not been so his testimony would have carried little weight with the Philippians and would bring little conviction to us.

Actually, this declaration of Paul's is the climax to a testimony of the way in which he had proved God in the utmost extremity and had always found Him faithful to fulfil His Word, meeting his need and giving grace in every circumstance. He had just written:

> Not that I speak as if I were in want; for I have learnt, in whatsoever state I am, to be content. I can bear either abasement or abundance. In all things, and amongst all men, I have been taught the secret, to be full or to be hungry, to want or to abound. (Phil. 4:11, 12, Conybeare.)

Therefore he is able to say with all assurance, "I can do all things in Him who strengthens me". And, from his own experience, he could assure the Phillippians:

> And your own needs shall be all supplied by my God, in the fulness of His glorious riches in Christ Jesus. (Phil. 4:19, Conybeare.)

Those who read Paul's words knew that he stated only what he had proved a thousand times to be true. How rich was the fruit of the testimony he gave to these believers of the manner in which God intervened directly in his life, caring for him by His own loving and mighty hand! It strengthened their faith. It made God real to them as nothing else could.

In our childhood, when our Father and Mother were in the early years of their work, establishing a Mission to send the Gospel to the interior of South America, we received our first practical lessons in faith. Our parents were then living by faith and several times Mother showed us a penny, the last in her purse, telling us that she did not know where more would come from but that she knew the Lord would be faithful to provide. And then we would see the provision come. One winter in Scotland she asked the Lord for a Shetland shawl. Some time later a lady called at the house with a bundle under her arm. She was unknown to any of us but told us she was a domestic servant and one of God's children, and that the Lord had put it on her heart very definitely to knit a shawl for our Mother. When she opened the bundle, there was a lovely hand-knitted Shetland shawl. How that humble handmaiden of the Lord rejoiced when she found that, all unknown to her, she had been used to answer our Mother's request to God.

We tell this because of the effect it had upon our own life. It was an experience of priceless value that made an impression that could never be lost and that has borne its inevitable fruit. Such things lift the veil and show us God's hand directly at work. We have seen just that same blessing given to many converts by the testimony we have to give of God's power and loving care in providing for our needs. We have found it an invaluable part of our witness.

While it was necessary to those to whom he ministered that Paul should live by faith and endure hardness, it was necessary also for his own spiritual knowledge and welfare. He says, "Everywhere and in all things I am instructed". Or, as it is rendered in the translation quoted above: "In all things... I have been taught the secret..." Would it not have been better for that servant of the Lord if he had been relieved of all concern regarding the supply of his daily needs? Would he not have been able then to dedicate himself with a more easy mind to the ministry of the Gospel and have done more efficient work?

In the first place, was Paul anxious concerning the supply of his needs? If he had been anxious he would not have been adequately prepared spiritually for his ministry. He emphatically says that he was not anxious. He had been taught the secret of the rest of faith.

He had learned to trust confidently in God's wisdom and faithfulness and to be instructed thereby. Every experience and test of faith contributed to making him and keeping him a man of faith. It was thus, indeed, that he got his deep and intimate knowledge of God's ways and wisdom and power and faithfulness. He could not have gained such knowledge in any other way. How rich he was spiritually! But had he been deprived of those experiences, how poor spiritually he would have been!

Another way might have been easier for Paul; better it would not have been. What incalculable loss would have been sustained by the converts and churches to which he ministered! And would we not be impoverished if we had not that rich and glorious testimony of faith triumphant over every circumstance?

We have known prospective missionary candidates to be advised, "Choose a missionary organization that will be able to support you adequately." From a business point of view this advice is sound: but it was not the policy followed by our Lord or by Paul, and how thankful the Church should be that it was not.

The truth is that it requires a Calvary ministry to establish and build up the Church of the Christ of Calvary. The servant is no greater than his Lord. As the Master walked and ministered in the Way of the Cross, so must we. To engage in that ministry and walk in that Way, there is a price to pay—the price He paid. He who is unwilling to pay it in full will not reap the full harvest. He himself will be poor and those to whom he ministers will be equally poor.

The Spiritual Warfare

The conflict in which the servant of the Lord is engaged is a spiritual one. It is not against man or material things, but against Satan and his hosts that he strives. The weapons of our warfare are not carnal; they are not plans and methods and organization and training and intellectual brilliance. The worker must know the uselessness of all that is soulish: all that is of the natural man. He must himself have faced the Cross in its fullest significance and passed through death so far as all that is of himself is concerned, the flesh being on the Cross by faith, crucified and reckoned dead, that in his whole life and service his walk may be truly in the Spirit. It is only as he ceases to live, that Christ's life can be manifested in him. It is only as his whole being, his whole life.

is filled and controlled by the Spirit, that the fulness of the Spirit's power can be released in him. It is only then that there can be brought into action through the Spirit those spiritual weapons which are mighty to the pulling down of the strongholds of the enemy in spiritual spheres.

The worker who does not know the spiritual warfare or the spiritual weapons, who does not know how to face Satan at the Cross, in Christ—"Who spoiled principalities and powers and made a show of them openly, triumphing over them in the Cross"—is not equipped for the fight.

In all these things the New Testament worker had been fully prepared by the Spirit before he was permitted to go forth. Paul's letters to the newly formed churches abound with evidence of how complete had been his witness to them regarding all spiritual truth.

The level of spiritual knowledge and experience today is generally far below that of the New Testament Church. Can we expect the Church to produce labourers above its own spiritual level? How many churches today are in the place spiritually where a young man will be able to receive a full spiritual preparation in their fellowship? How many congregations would be spiritually capable of knowing the mind of the Spirit regarding the going forth of one who is called, as was the church in Antioch?

Paul did not have to write at the beginning of his missionary ministry as did a missionary quoted by Amy Carmichael:

I realise that I have scarcely begun. I do not think I would dare to call myself a missionary yet. I have stood, as it were, on the edge of His sea of suffering, and have hastily diverted myself with something else, lest He should call me to enter that sea with Him. And yet there is nothing I long more to do. To me there is no more tragic sight than the average missionary. A Hindu bowing down to his idol leaves me ummoved beside it. We have given so much, yet not the one thing that counts; we aspire so high, and fall so low; we suffer so much, but so seldom with Christ; we have done so much, and so little will remain; we have known Christ in part, and have so effectively barricaded our hearts against His mighty love, which surely He must yearn to give His disciples above all people.[1]

How many of us have had just such an experience at the beginning of our ministry! We had been called, but not sufficiently prepared. The Lord met us in His faithfulness, but how many mistakes, how much needless disappointment and suffering and

---

[1] *Gold Cord,* p. 10.

poorly wrought work would have been avoided had we been prepared as God intended we should.

It is not to be expected that a young worker, starting out on his mission, will have the spiritual knowledge and experience of Paul at the end of his career. But the spiritual foundations should be as fully laid as were his when he was first sent forth. All the necessary spiritual gifts should be manifested, and the essential, fundamental experience in the walk of faith, in obedience, in guidance by the Spirit, in absolute surrender, in holiness and in the warfare against our spiritual foe, should not be lacking.

Is it possible to find candidates today who are fully prepared in the New Testament sense? We have found that it is. They may not be in large numbers, but it is not numbers that is wanted.

It is significant that we are not instructed to seek candidates or to send them out. We are told to pray "the Lord of the Harvest, that He will send forth labourers into His harvest". The calling, the preparation and the sending of the candidates is the work of the Holy Spirit. Our part is only to recognize the call He has given. The New Testament way may mean fewer workers, but it will mean fully equipped workers and a greater and more satisfactory harvest, for those who are not truly called by the Spirit are a hindrance and a danger in the work and those who go forth before they are fully prepared by the Spirit are a weakness. They can only produce fruit like unto themselves.

CHAPTER **XXXIII**

THE EVANGELIST'S TEACHING MINISTRY

Those who are sent forth to evangelize have to perform a double ministry: they must preach and teach. Equal emphasis should be placed upon each of these parts of our ministry. When the Holy Spirit leads a group of workers to establish a work in a town, we should expect that, if the group is chosen by Him, there will be among them all the spiritual gifts required for the doing of a complete work. It was undoubtedly for this reason that it was two or three workers, rather than one, who were led to do such work in New Testament times.

Our Lord's ministry was one of preaching and teaching. He travelled continually, preaching the Word to all men everywhere. At the same time, how definite and continuous was His ministry of teaching. In the Gospels, He is presented to us as the Master Teacher, ever engaged in teaching the things of the Kingdom to His disciples and to the multitude. So great a place did teaching occupy in His ministry that, while He was often teaching and not preaching, it can hardly be said that He was ever preaching and not at the same time teaching

He taught the multitude and, particularly, He taught His disciples, laying a foundation of spiritual knowledge, of experience, and of practical understanding of spiritual method and principle, upon which the Church would be built.

As our Lord had done, so did the Apostles and Evangelists. Teaching had a large place in their ministry at all times. During the year that Barnabas and Paul were in Antioch they 'taught' the church. Paul's Epistles to the churches reveal the spiritual depth of the teaching he had given them. Writing to the Thessalonians of the 'mystery of iniquity' at work in the world, the future revealing of the 'man of sin' and the coming of the 'day of Christ', he says:

"Do you not remember that while I was still with you I used to tell you all this?" (2 Thess. 2:5, Weymouth). The churches had been thoroughly instructed not only in what might be called the simple rudiments of the faith but also concerning the deepest truths of revelation.

Sermons that Do Not Build

It is evident that Paul and the other Evangelists of the Early Church did not spend their time preaching sermons on sundry texts. Every message he gave was definitely related to the work in hand—the preparation of those who believed for that which they would have to know and do as members of the church.

Much of the textual sermonizing that is done today accomplishes little that is permanent. Its effect is transient; it is but a momentary stimulant. Congregations that have sat under such preaching for ten and twenty years are today still spiritual babes, both in knowledge and experience. That type of preaching will never prepare a group of converts to be left to carry on their own work. Whatever may be said about it, it is not the kind of preaching that the missionary is called to do, and, for him at least, it means loss of precious time.

What Only the Spirit Can Do

Christ had depended upon the Holy Spirit to reveal spiritual truth to His disciples and to give them spiritual understanding. So also did the New Testament Evangelists. Paul wrote to the Ephesians:

> On bended knee I beseech the Father to grant to you — in accordance with the wealth of His glorious perfections — to be strengthened by His Spirit with power penetrating to your inmost being. I pray that Christ may make His home in your hearts through your faith; so that having your roots deep and your foundations strong, in love, you may become mighty to grasp the idea, as it is grasped by all the saints, of the breadth and length, the height and depth—yes, to attain to a knowledge of the knowledge-surpassing love of Christ, so that you may be filled unto all the fulness of God. (Eph. 3:14-19. Weymouth.)

What depths of spiritual truth and experience are sounded here! Yet Paul believed that the Holy Spirit would cause those to whom he wrote to enter into the understanding of these things that were beyond the human intelligence to grasp.

Let us remember that Paul's letters to the churches were not articles written for the perusal of theologians. They were sent to churches on the 'mission field' whose membership was composed of common people, many of them slaves, recently converted from heathenism. His letters were deeper than the articles in any modern Theological Review, yet he expected his readers to understand them. And they did understand them. His prayers for the churches reveal the secret. Twice in the Epistle to the Ephesians he pauses to record a prayer that the Lord, by His Spirit, would give them the knowledge and revelation to understand, and he had no doubt that his prayer would be answered, for after the second prayer he declared that God can do more than we ask or think by the power of His Spirit within us.

How often have we heard missionaries say, "These people have the mentality of children; all we can do is to give them something very simple for they are incapable of understanding deep spiritual truth." We reap according to our faith, nothing more. Spiritual sight does not depend upon intellectual ability. The missionary must have the faith Paul had in this matter, and remember that Paul's God is his God and that God's arm has not been shortened. If we are relying upon our ability to teach or if we are doubtful as to whether the Holy Spirit will give the understanding to those we are teaching, then, certainly, the fruit will be scarce and its quality poor. But if our teaching is really in the power of the Spirit and we doubt not that He will give understanding, then He will do it—or God's Word is not true.

There is a danger that we must guard against: what is taught may be understood but not appropriated. We have in mind a congregation that had received much doctrinal teaching over a period of many years. Yet the people continued to be spiritually weak and dependent. There was no active spiritual life. Not one among them was capable of preaching or teaching. When the suggestion was made that they think of carrying on their own work, they were aghast—and not without reason.

What was the trouble? Just this: they had been taught many spiritual truths, but these truths had never become practical experience in their lives. We must differentiate between teaching that results in facts being memorized and teaching that leads to the practical appropriation of truth. Spiritual truth, to have any power, must become personal experience. Spiritual truth is not theory, it is life. We may know that Salvation is by faith in Christ, but until that becomes a personal experience it is without power towards us. We may know of the power of the Spirit, of the gifts of the Holy Spirit, of the victorious walk and warfare that should be ours in Christ, but if we do not enter into the experience of these things personally, the knowledge of them can produce no life or fruit.

In this matter there is one thing that the teacher must fully realise: Paul may sow and Apollos water, but only God can create the fruit. This is true in all spiritual work. We may preach the Gospel message of salvation but we cannot accomplish the work of salvation in a single soul. That is the work of the Holy Spirit using the Word that we have preached. We can preach and teach, but we can do no more, except through prayer and faith. The Spirit then deals directly and personally with the individual, applying the truth to him. We cannot produce a true understanding of spiritual things, an experience of the Spirit's power, or the manifestation of a spiritual gift in any one of our hearers, no matter how earnestly we may wish to do so. Only the Holy Spirit, dealing directly and personally with the individual, can do so. Every step in the acquiring of spiritual knowledge and experience must be a personal matter, the outcome of direct dealing with the Spirit.

This was one of the first and most fundamental lessons we had to learn in our work. It threw us upon the Lord in utter dependence, causing us to combine our teaching always with a definite ministry of believing prayer, emphasising continually to the people that they must each one seek the Holy Spirit's illumination and deal directly with Him.

In the congregation we have referred to, the situation was completely changed in a few months' time. The people were earnest believers, really desirous of experiencing more of the Spirit's power in their lives, but they had never fully realized that they should go directly to God, and be dealt with personally by Him, and that it was their own individual responsibility. They had never truly grasped the fact that the spiritual truths they were learning were not just dogma to be believed theoretically, but power to be appropriated personally. Also, in the back of their minds, there had been more or less the thought that only the missionary was capable of the deepest spiritual experience and that it was his job somehow to produce spiritual life in them by his preaching. The missionary had been to blame. For instance, he had taught them about seeking the Lord's will and exercising faith but instead of obliging them to do it he had sought to do it for them.

When they began to see their personal privilege and responsibility, they sought the Lord individually in prayer concerning the matter. Then the Holy Spirit commenced to deal with them individually and the whole situation changed. The evidences of spiritual life became manifest in one after another. Sin was confessed, lives were surrendered to the Lord, true spiritual understanding was received, truths that had been difficult to comprehend, or to accept because of their cost to the flesh, were received with joy, the gifts of the Holy Spirit for service appeared and fruit was borne. All this resulted because of direct, personal dealing between the Holy Spirit and the believer. Thus the teaching ministry of the Evangelist bore fruit and thus also the believers learned to go to the Holy Spirit for light and understanding. Thenceforth they were not dependent upon man.

Theory and Practice

There is another important phase of this matter. In all teaching we should keep in mind our Lord's teaching method. He always combined theory with practical experience. He used experience as the basis upon which to build a knowledge of spiritual truth.

We should note also that while He gave the profoundest teaching regarding such matters as prayer, faith, witness, the work of the Holy Spirit, giving, etc., yet, at the same time, He gave such simple and clear instructions regarding their practice, that the disciples could enter into the experience of them immediately.

When instructing new converts or untaught believers, the teacher needs to be on his guard against obscuring simple, basic truths by burying them in an accumulation of details. In five minutes new converts can be instructed how to pray in the Spirit. All the essential facts can be made known to them in that time and then we can have them kneel with us and pray. One of the main things they have to learn about praying in the Spirit is that they do not have to learn to do it, but to do it—that it is more a matter of faith than of knowledge: that if they go into God's presence in faith, absolutely willing for His will, the Holy Spirit is in them to do His part, and just waiting for them to give Him the opportunity to do it..

A detailed study of prayer is not necessary to the initial experience of prayer. A deep knowledge of the teaching of Scripture regarding faith is not essential to the initial exercise of faith. So
27

it is also with the exercise of the gifts of the Spirit for witness and with the life of victory in Christ.

What we want to do, in the first place, is to get the new convert to take the steps of faith into the experience of these spiritual truths. Never let him feel that they are such profound and complicated things that it will take him a long time to understand them sufficiently to be able to enter into an experience of them.

To teach someone to drive a car, we seat him in the driver's seat, tell him the simple essentials of what to do, and have him start off. We are there to intervene only if a mistake is made. Afterwards, to become a fully efficient driver, he will have to study his car and master the details of its mechanism. And his growing experience in driving will help him to acquire that knowledge.

Let us not think that the new convert needs to know as much as we do now about spiritual truth before he can begin to practise it. Let us not confuse him with profound dissertations on simple facts that the Holy Spirit would reveal immediately to him.

This does not mean that we delay giving thorough teaching, or that a deep knowledge of the Word is of minor importance. It is of the highest importance and the Holy Spirit waits to lead every believer into it without delay. But it should not delay experience; rather it should be founded upon experience. The believer who has experienced what it is to pray in the Spirit will much more readily understand the deep and glorious truths revealed in the Word regarding prayer. To one who does not have such an experience, the truths concerning it will continue to be vague and unreal.

In all spiritual truth, experience is necessary to growth in knowledge. It is, therefore, of the greatest importance that the teacher fail not to take this into account. To one who has no foundation of experience, the doctrine he is taught will be little more than theory. But where there is the foundation of experience, the doctrine will be fitted into its place by the Holy Spirit and will be received as practical truth leading to deeper experience and fuller ministry.

In view of this it will be understood that a teacher who simply teaches theory, no matter how deep and true his teaching may be, and who does not make his first aim, as the Master did, the bringing of the believers into an immediate experience of the truth he would have them learn, will obtain little practical result. He can continue indefinitely giving such teaching without laying any foundation for a church.

It will be understood why, so often, a missionary's brief visit to a church to give a series of Bible studies accomplishes little. He has not taken time to see that what he taught became related to experience. The excellent teaching he had given, therefore, was probably little more than vaguely understood theory to his hearers. It was not so that our Lord taught His disciples or that Paul taught the churches.

A True Balance

We should be careful to see that in a congregation equal emphasis is put on the preaching of the Gospel and the teaching of the Word. We have found that there is a great danger that one may be stressed and the other neglected. A congregation that faithfully engages in evangelism but is not constantly digging deep for the treasures of the Word will be spiritually immature and weak. On the other hand, one in which there may be the deepest teaching, but little effort to take the Word of life to the lost will be self-satisfied and fruitless. The importance of giving teaching to a church cannot be exaggerated, but teaching that omits to stress the church's duty to be ever proclaiming the Gospel is incomplete: it is not properly balanced and not entirely faithful. For full spiritual growth and power, a church must be both instructed in the Word and active in seeking the salvation of souls. Place must be given for the exercise of all the gifts of the Spirit, and for the participation in the ministry, according to their spiritual gifts, of all the members of the congregation. The enemy of souls and of the Church has many effective ways of leading us into defeat and we must be ever watchful against his devices.

CHAPTER XXXIV

THE EVANGELIST'S PRAYER MINISTRY

Our Lord spent much time in prayer. It is recorded that He 'was wont' to go to the place of prayer. He spent whole nights alone in prayer-communion with the Father. A brief prayer occasionally, or even regularly, was not sufficient for Him. The pressing claims of His work, the need and eagerness of the multitudes that followed Him, were not allowed to interfere with the time He spent alone in prayer. He would retire to the solitude of the hills or of the garden of Gethsemane where He might not be disturbed.

Little is told us about what Christ prayed for when He was alone. What He prayed in Gethsemane is revealed to us; also we are given two examples of His intercessory ministry for His disciples—when He told Peter, 'I have prayed for thee that thy faith fail not', and in the seventeenth chapter of John's Gospel. These two instances are sufficient to make known to us the fact that He ministered continually to the disciples through the prayer of faith. They provide an example and reveal a principle. In the first place, we see the responsibility of the one who ministers to others to exercise a ministry of intercession on their behalf. In the second place, we see the fruit of such intercession. Peter was in a condition spiritually in which he was unable to pray the prayer of faith for himself, so Christ, the Paraclete, stood with him, praying the prayer of faith for him.

It is not surprising that, after the example Christ had given, we find the Early Church a praying Church. The Apostles seem not to have been men of prayer before Pentecost: that was their weakness in Gethsemane; but after Pentecost they were men of unceasing prayer. When other work would have encroached upon their time in the Jerusalem church, they refused to become entangled with it, saying, "we shall give ourselves to prayer and the ministry of the Word." They put prayer before preaching.

The place that prayer, particularly intercessory prayer, occupied in the ministry of the first missionaries is carefully recorded in the New Testament writings. Of Epaphras, Paul testifies: "always labouring fervently for you in prayer, that ye may stand perfect and complete in all the will of God" (Col. 4:12). That prayer occupied an important place in Luke's ministry is certain, although he tells us nothing about himself. It is in his Gospel that the place that prayer occupied in the life and ministry of our Lord is most fully revealed. There we see that Christ spent many hours in prayer before every important step that he took. And in the Acts of the Apostles, which he wrote, we see the central place that prayer took at Pentecost and in all the churches that were formed thereafter.[1] There can be no doubt that in the ministry of every member of Paul's missionary company prayer was given the first place.

Even in Paul's letters to the churches he recorded prayers for them. These prayers are not simply evidence of the fact that he engaged in a ministry of prayer; they reveal the character of that ministry.

The two prayers recorded in Ephesians (1:15-23; 3:14-21) are commented on in chapter 27. The contents of the other prayers are as follows:

1. For the Philippians (Phil. 1:9-11) he sought:
   Abounding love;
   Clear spiritual knowledge and perception so as to be able to judge between good and evil;
   A pure and blameless walk;
   That they might be filled with the fruits of righteousness through Christ, bringing glory to God.

2. For the Colossians (Col. 1:9-12) he sought:
   That they should have full and clear knowledge of His will;
   All spiritual wisdom and discernment;
   A walk worthy of the Lord and pleasing to Him;
   Fruitfulness in every good work;
   Growth in the knowledge of God;
   That they might be strengthened by His glorious power;

---

[1] See pp. 380-93.

That they might bear "to the uttermost" every suffering
with patience and joy;
A spirit of thankfulness to God for making us fit to
participate in the heritage He has given His people.

3. For the Thessalonians (1 Thes. 3:10-13; 5:23) his prayer
was:
That God would perfect what was lacking in their faith;
That they would increase and abound in love;
That their hearts would be established in holiness;
That spirit, soul and body would be preserved blameless
unto the coming of Christ.

The fundamental nature and importance of these petitions will
be recognized. Paul was asking God that the churches should be
brought into the place of spiritual knowledge and experience where
they would be fully equipped for all spiritual life, service and
warfare. He was dealing with the deep issues of spiritual life.
These prayers were not concerned with individual difficulties and
local problems, of which, no doubt, there were many. They go
to the root of the matter. The answering of these petitions would
mean the overcoming of every difficulty, the solving of every
problem.

Paul did not hesitate to make such petitions. He believed that
God could and would answer them. As Christ prayed and believed
for Peter, so Paul, exercising the Paraclete gift, prayed and
believed for the churches.

Paul did not pray occasionally for the churches; he prayed
continually. His ministry was not one of preaching and teaching
with some prayer added when time could be spared. With him the
order was that followed by Christ and by the Apostles: "prayer—
and the ministry of the Word."

The prayer of faith is essential to the carrying out of God's will.
God reveals His will to us; we go to God in faith and ask Him to
accomplish it; then He does it in answer to the prayer of faith.

Paul did not make vague appeals to God to bless the churches;
he made specific requests that were in accordance with God's will.
He knew what God's purpose was for the believer and for the
Church, so he asked in faith that it be fulfilled. His two prayers
for the Church, given in Ephesians, ask God for the accomplishment of the fundamental work necessary in the members that it
may be actually 'the fulness of Christ.'

He knew that that was God's purpose for the Church and he asked nothing less. Had he not asked for that he would not have obtained it. "He that asketh receiveth, and to him that knocketh it shall be opened." Had he not had real faith to believe that God would do it, he would not have received it: 'for let not that man think that he shall receive anything of the Lord."

The Evangelist must know what God's purpose is for the Church, then he must have faith to ask God to fulfil His Word and carry out His purpose. And he must realise the fact that he is not authorized to ask for a partial fulfilment. In the Word God has clearly stated what His purpose is for the Church. It is so glorious that the human mind immediately puts a question mark against it and begins to modify it. Then we pray that God will fulfil our modification of His purpose. That prayer is not according to His will and it will not be answered: "we have not because we ask amiss."

The converts that are won through the Evangelist's preaching need to be taught of the Spirit to know the deep foundational spiritual principles of the faith. God will do this in answer to the Evangelist's prayer of faith. Paul had faith to ask that new converts just won from heathenism should be given an understanding of the deepest spiritual truth. He did not pray hesitantly that they might be led on little by little, hoping that perhaps some day, in the distant future, they, or their children after them, might come to spiritual maturity.

The Evangelist who permits the enemy to persuade him to doubt God's power to answer prayer, or the Holy Spirit's power to give understanding to the converts, commits a vital error and stands in the way of the full accomplishment of God's purpose. The results are, in very truth, according to his faith. A most solemn responsibility rests upon him in this matter.

In the congregations, Elders and Deacons must be prepared by the Holy Spirit that they may meet the standard required for such in Scripture. This standard is high and it will seem impossible that any should come up to it for many years. But it is according to God's Word and to His will that they should be prepared to take their place in a year or two, so the Evangelist must continue in the prayer of faith, nothing doubting, until they are made ready.

Difficulties will arise in the churches. The enemy will 'come in like a flood'. Elders and congregations may fall into defeat to the extent that they will not be able to pray the prayer of faith for themselves, as happened in the church in Corinth. Then it is the responsibility of the Evangelist to pray the prayer of faith for them.

The power of the prayer of faith is the greatest power which the Evangelist possesses. It is more potent than his preaching and teaching. While these are necessary and important, they will not be productive of mature and sound spiritual fruit unless they are based upon a faithful ministry of prevailing prayer. We all know the continual temptation to give public ministry first place. How often have we seen God's servants who really believe in prayer allow their prayer time to be the first to suffer when time did not seem sufficient for all the demands of the work. The opportunities for public ministry seemed so important and worthwhile. Then, as the years passed, they wondered why the converts did not enter into a full understanding of spiritual things, why they did not become filled with the Spirit, manifesting the necessary gifts of the Spirit.

These things are the fruit of the travail of the missionary's prayer of faith: precious fruit, sound and ripe that can be obtained in no other way. The servant of the Lord must stand by individuals and congregations in the prayer of faith until there is the full accomplishing of God's Word in them, and of God's purpose for them.

This ministry of prayer must be continuous, constantly watchful and covering every detail of the missionary's ministry. There must be the continual attitude of prayer—the prayer 'without ceasing', that is ever seeking the knowledge of God's will, the guidance of the Spirit, interceding for those who need it and claiming with unwavering faith the full carrying out of God's full purpose according to His Word. The Evangelist's ministry of intercession is an essential part of the equipment the Lord has given to the Church for its spiritual welfare.

The prayer experience of believers and churches will hardly rise above that of the Evangelist. He may teach the place that prayer should have and they may come to have as clear a knowledge of it as he has but if it is largely theoretic with him it will be so with them also. It is the testimony of the Evangelist's example that makes his teaching practical. As we are faithful before the Lord in prayer we can be certain that the Holy Spirit will lead the converts and churches into a true experience of prayer.

CHAPTER XXXV

THE EVANGELIST'S FAITH MINISTRY

Without faith we cannot serve God. What He can accomplish through us is in direct relation to our faith in Him.

In the doing of His will we have an active part to take. We must serve faithfully, fulfilling the responsibility which He has placed upon us. What we do must be done in His wisdom, according to His will and the leading of the Holy Spirit. It must be done in His strength, and in His time, with the full realisation that He alone can "give the increase". But also there must be the clear, unwavering assurance of faith that God can and will "give the increase". God will not be able to do through us anything that we really do not believe He can do, or will do.

The Basis of Faith

True faith is dependent upon a knowledge of God's will. To exercise faith for the carrying out of His purpose we must know what that purpose is. It has been seen that true prayer must be in accordance with God's will. So it is also with faith. This is not realised as generally as it should be. Nowhere in God's Word are we given authority to exercise faith for something that is simply our own plan or desire.

A believer or church has no right to decide what is to be done and then to have 'faith' that it will be done. Faith is believing God, believing that His Word is true and trusting absolutely that He will fulfil it. It is in no sense a species of occult power possesed by the believer which can be used to cause God to do things. It is not an Aladdin's lamp. Faith is 'not staggering at the promise of God'; it is 'being fully persuaded that, what He has promised, He is able also to perform' (Rom. 4:20, 21).

When we know what God's will is, we can have faith that He will accomplish it. It is essential that believers and congregations have a true understanding of this matter so that they may be able to exercise true faith and not presume to usurp the place of Christ as Head of the Church, or of the Holy Spirit as the revealer of Christ's will.

God's Word is full of examples of faith. In both the Old and New Testaments God required it of His servants. Our Lord sought it in those who came to Him: "If thou canst believe," He said, "all things are possible to him that believeth". When the disciples asked Him, "Why could we not cast him out?" He answered them: "Because of your unbelief" (Matt. 17:19, 20). The fasting and prayer were wanting. The disciples thought the power was in themselves and trusted in the authority of their own word.

Paul Exercises Faith

In all ministry in the Church this faith is essential. A deeply revealing example of its application is given by the Apostle Paul in his dealing with the congregation in Corinth. He was faced with a situation fraught with extreme difficulty. The responsibility for dealing with the matter fell upon him. But his right to do so was questioned: "For his letters", it was said, "are weighty and powerful; but his bodily presence is weak and his speech contemptible" (2 Cor. 10:10).

Grave abuses had crept into the church. Many of the members were walking so carnally that their sense of holiness was dulled to the extent that gross sin was tolerated in their midst. Spiritual discernment had been lost and human wisdom had taken the place of the wisdom revealed by the Spirit of God. Their eyes had been taken off the Lord and placed upon men and things. They were carried away with wrong doctrine and divided into factions, each of which acclaimed a human leader. Even many of those who claimed to follow Paul did so, probably, from a carnal rather than a spiritual motive.

Paul had no ecclesiastical authority vested in him by any Council or Association of churches. He could not cause any Denominational pressure, spiritual or material, to be brought to bear upon the congregation. The church in Corinth was not bound through organization to the Church in other places. There were, of course, powerful links, but these were entirely spiritual.

Paul had to depend solely upon the authority derived from God, Who had called him to the ministry he was fulfilling, and upon the power of the Holy Spirit to make God's Word effective. He claimed no other authority or power; yet he acted with absolute confidence. As the servant of Christ, authorized by his call to do so, he put God's Word before them, insisting upon its absolute authority and upon Christ's absolute claims upon them. Then he confidently expected the Holy Spirit to give the authority and power to God's Word and cause that it should be accepted and obeyed.

Paul's Weapons

In his second letter to the Corinthians he states the nature of the power upon which he relied:

For though we walk in the flesh, we do not war after the flesh. (For the weapons of our warfare are not carnal but mighty through God to the pulling down of strongholds.) Casting down imaginations (margin: reasonings) and every high thing that exalteth itself against the knowledge of God, and bringing into captivity every thought to the obedience of Christ. (2 Cor. 10:3-5.)

In this remarkable statement, Paul not only confidently claims the support of divine power, but also states the nature of the opposition which this power is mighty to overcome. The arrogant reasonings of man's wisdom, inspired by Satan, had set themselves up in the congregation in Corinth against the revealed wisdom of God. Man's wisdom and pride were reaching up to occupy the throne which belonged to God alone. As a result, the unity of the Spirit was lost. The wisdom of the Spirit was despised and God's servant was criticised for the lack of human wisdom and eloquence in his preaching. They desired sermons "adorned with persuasive words of human wisdom." The most sacred things were degraded to a grossly material level. The Lord's Table became the scene of feasting and drunkenness and of a selfish display of wealth by those who had means.

The situation was well defined in Paul's stern rebuke: "And you, instead of mourning and removing from among you the man who has done this deed of shame, are filled with self-complacency!" (1 Cor. 5:2, Weymouth).

Paul did not deal only with the outward manifestations of corruption in the church. He begins by stating the basic principles of all spiritual life and ministry. He unsheathes the sword of the Spirit—God's Word. In the first three chapters of his first letter to the Corinthians he goes to the root of the matter and presents the Cross—Jesus Christ and Him crucified, "the power of God and the wisdom of God". To the Greek, confident in his human wisdom, it was foolishness and to the religiously proud Jew it was a stumbling block. But it was the power and wisdom of God to those who believe. It was the one thing that Paul preached, the one foundation which he laid—the only foundation upon which to build that which is spiritual and which will survive the fire of God's judgment and endure through eternity. With spiritual wisdom revealed by the Holy Spirit he contrasts the utter futility of all that has been and is of man's wisdom.

Then, as he goes on to deal with each abuse, he points back always to these spiritual principles. He makes no compromise, accepts no partial obedience, but teaches, citing his own experience and example, that all that is of the human heart, of human wisdom and pride, must go down into death at the Cross so that Christ may manifest His life and wisdom and power fully in each member of His Body.

As we come to realise the condition of the church in Corinth at the time and the absolute character of the demands that Paul made of them, we see the reality, the simplicity and the boldness of the faith of this servant of God. How could he expect a congregation in such a carnal condition even to understand these deep spiritual truths which he gave as the ground of his action and which, he said, can be revealed only by the Holy Spirit and cannot be received or comprehended by the natural man? (1 Cor. 2).

Real Faith

Paul's faith as manifested in his ministry is intensely real and practical. He really believed that God's Word was true and that it would be fulfilled to him and through him as he ministered under the guidance and in the power of the Holy Spirit.

He had recourse to no human weapon of any kind. His faith was not mixed with unbelief. He did not present God's Word with a struggling hope that it might be obeyed. He did not fear that in this case the difficulties might be too great. He did not compromise with unbelief, arguing that it would be necessary to proceed cautiously and slowly, teaching a little at a time, seeking to deal with some of the worst abuses first, hoping that, perhaps later, he might be able to go a little further.

The action which he took was not based upon the possibility of the natural mind comprehending spiritual things, or the likelihood of the natural heart being willing to obey God's Word. Had he been guided by such considerations, he might well have despaired. His action was based solely upon absolute faith in God's Word and in the power of the Holy Spirit to accomplish God's will.

Partial faith is not faith: "For he that wavereth is like a wave of the sea driven with the wind and tossed. For let not that man think that he shall receive anything of the Lord " (Jas. 1:6, 7).

Partial faith is too full of doubtings to be true faith. It has its eyes upon the material difficulties and human impossibilities and has no certainty regarding God's power to overcome them. No matter what lip service it may pay to God's power to fulfil His Word, it has a heart full of doubt. The doubt may be based on solid arguments, providing good reasons why God should not be expected to fully fulfil His Word—but is there not also present a silent but persistent witness, borne by the Holy Spirit in the inner man, that these reasonings are naught but excuses for lack of faith and that if God's Word is true He must be able to fulfil it fully?

The Corinthian believers were not in a condition to have faith for themselves. Evidently there was none among them who could use the weapons of prayer and faith and stand against the work of Satan in their midst. God's servant had to employ these weapons in their behalf and exercise faith for them. This is a solemn responsibility that often falls upon God's servants. Upon their faith, at times, depends the defeat of Satan's work and the liberating of those he has succeeded in deluding.

Only faith could see Peter, the weak denier of his Lord, as the strengthener of the brethren. But faith accomplished it. How often does our faith fail as we look with the human eye upon individuals or situations? And how often, perhaps, does our love fail as the flesh is hurt and patience is tried beyond measure, and so faith is hindered or becomes impossible. Christ's love for Peter failed not, therefore His faith failed not.

Authority in Faith

It is of the most vital importance that the servant of the Lord have a clear understanding of the authority which the believer possesses in Christ. Our Lord is absolute victor over Satan. Animistic tribes believe that there is a supreme being who is good and who wishes them well. But they consider him as much less active than the evil spirits that abound in the world and passive in the face of their activities. These heathens therefore direct their efforts to propitiating the evil spirits and protecting themselves from them. There is much of this heathen attitude in many a believer's mind. Though we assent to the doctrine of God's omnipotence, we are apt to feel helpless when we see the evidences of Satan's power. That attitude is unbelief and inevitably bears the fruit of unbelief. Actually, we may have a more real faith in Satan's power than in God's power.

God permits Satan to test us for our good, but it is not His will that we settle down to accept as inevitable a condition of partial defeat. Patience and longsuffering are true Christian virtues, possible only through the indwelling grace of the Lord, but to bow our heads meekly to endure the triumph of Satan, through unbelief or spiritual inertia, is not Christian patience and longsuffering. Paul showed much patience and longsuffering in the face of Satan's fierce and continual efforts to prevent God's purpose from being carried out through him, but he never for one moment accepted defeat. God's purpose was finally carried out through him always and in everything (2 Cor. 2:14).

We are seated with Christ, the Head of the Church, in the heavenlies (Eph. 1:19-23; 2:6). He is absolute Victor. Satan can do no more than Christ permits him to do—or than we permit him to do. When we know what God's will is it is certain that Satan will challenge us to the utmost of his power. He will seek to discourage us, to turn us from God's purpose by every kind of argument, to frighten us, that our faith may fail, for he knows that the issue depends upon our faith. He knows that if he can raise a covert doubt of God in our hearts, God's purpose can not be carried out fully through us.

When our Lord faced Satan, He challenged him directly with God's Word. There was no compromise. And Satan was vanquished. There are occasions—and they are very many—when we must directly challenge Satan with God's Word and accept no compromise. We have the right to avail ourselves of Christ's power and authority over Satan. When Satan attacks we have the right to take our stand upon God's Word, claiming by faith that it shall be fulfilled and Satan's work completely overthrown. We have seen many a seemingly hopeless situation entirely changed when we have taken such a stand. Until we did so Satan pressed his attacks with confidence, but immediately we challenged him openly and definitely in the Name of Christ, the Victor of Calvary, his defeat and powerlessness were evident.

God permits Satan to oppose and attack us that we may have the opportunity of exercising faith and demonstrating the triumphant power of our Lord. The result depends upon the extent to which we actually believe in God's power and Christ's victory and avail ourselves of them by faith.

But how greatly are we hindered, and how greatly is the Lord hindered in us, by our doubtings—"the sin that doth so easily beset us!" How much blessing fails to be passed on through us to others because we are found wanting in this vital matter? And how much ground is Satan permitted to gain and retain that should have been claimed by faith in the Name of the Lord?

The church in Corinth is generally looked upon as a discouraging example of failure. But rather we consider it as one of the most outstanding and encouraging examples of the power of the spiritual weapons which God has given us to deal' with such a situation. It is recorded for our encouragement as well as for instruction and warning. The Corinthian church had certainly fallen into a desperate state, but God's servant exercised his ministry, dealing with the situation with not a doubt as to God's power, and faith conquered. The victory was gained, every thought was brought 'into captivity to the obedience of Christ', and that church became again a testimony and a power. If the victory could be won in Corinth, surely we have no reason to fear defeat in any situation that we may have to deal with.

Difficulties will be met. Satan will gain local victories and his triumph at times may seem complete. But God has placed in the Church those who have the responsibility and the authority to use the spiritual weapons of our warfare, and if we are faithful in our ministry the final victory over every work of Satan is assured.

CHAPTER XXXVI

THE EVANGELIST'S ATTITUDE TO THE WORLD

Governments

The attitude of the New Testament Evangelists towards Governments and those in authority is clearly defined in their writings. They taught respect of local laws and obedience to authority. Although the existing Government was pagan, they emphasized the divine institution of government. It was only when the demands of those in authority clashed with duty to God that obedience could be refused, and then torture and death should not prevent the Christian from obeying God first. These missionaries never indulged in criticism or ridicule either of a Government or of any in authority. When brought before princes and judges, even when these were corrupt and profligate, their manner, though never weak or servile but always dignified and fearless, was not lacking in the deference due to rank or authority.

The Heathen

"Come ye out from among them and be ye separate", as Paul wrote to the Corinthians, was the keynote in the attitude towards the heathen, so far as their idolatry and sin was concerned. There was no compromise. No point, however insignificant, could be yielded to gain their goodwill. At the same time, there was evidently an avoidance of anything that would give offence. In the sermons preached in heathen cities, as recorded in the Acts of the Apostles, and in the Epistles to the churches, there is no evidence of ridicule or of aggressive attack against heathen practices. The Evangelists were out to win the heathen for Christ. To offend them by attacking their religion while they were still in their blindness had no place in their plan. The preachers confined themselves to the preaching of the Gospel, placing all their confidence in its power and looking to it to accomplish all the reforming necessary.

Social Evils

The attitude towards social evils, such as slavery, bribery, extortion, etc., was similar to that taken towards heathenism. They did not consider themselves responsible for the customs of heathen society. The attitude to slavery is very significant. Nothing was ever said in its favour but it was not resisted and both slaves and masters were counselled to obey the law of the land and above all to manifest the Spirit of the meek and lowly Christ. Yet the Spirit of the Gospel which they preached was the very antithesis of the spirit of slavery and the ultimate extinction of slavery was inevitable. The New Testament Evangelists were not social reformers nor crusaders against social evils. They were preachers of the Gospel and they believed that Christ was the only and all-sufficient remedy for sin in all its manifestations.

A missionary stated a sound principle when he said:

Morality is merely the product of the inner life, and missionaries do not go to heathen lands to try to amend behaviours... I had rather plant one seed of the life of Christ under the crust of heathen life, than cover that whole crust over with the veneer of our social habits, or the vesture of Western civilization.

Local Customs

There appears to have been no opposition to local customs, in so far as these were not sinful. Rather does there seem to have been a general conformity to custom wherever that was possible. Paul certainly made no attempt to introduce Jewish customs along with the Gospel; on the contrary, he insisted upon a Gospel entirely free from Jewish influence, although he himself was a Jew. As a missionary to the Gentiles he divested himself of all that was purely Jewish and presented to them a spiritual Gospel free from foreignness in method and concept. The Gospel he preached was foreign only in that it was Heavenly.

Rich and Poor

These Evangelists insisted that all believers are one in Christ. Within the Church no distinction between rich or poor could be tolerated. There was no effort to appeal to any special class. The Gospel was preached to all classes without distinction. Christ had

28

taught emphatically that with God there is no respect of persons and by His example He had removed all such barriers among his followers.

Any appearance of class distinction within the churches was condemned immediately (1 Cor. 11:20, 21; Jas. 2:1-4). To the Evangelists a soul was a soul irrespective of material circumstances, and they were neither particularly elated over the conversion of the rich nor disappointed if the majority of the members of their churches were poor.

The Race Problem

In Athens Paul declared: "He hath made of one blood all nations of men", and writing to the church in Galatia, he said: "For there is neither Jew nor Greek, there is neither bond nor free, there is neither male nor female, for ye are all one in Christ Jesus", while to the Colossians he wrote: "Ye have... put on the new man... where there is neither Greek nor Jew, circumcision nor uncircumcision, Barbarian, Scythian, bond nor free: but Christ is all, and in all." In these words we have the attitude of these Evangelists to the race problem.

As there was no distinction of class, so there was no distinction of race. An attitude of superiority was never taken to the less cultured or the subject races. Nor was any change of methods deemed necessary in dealing with them. The appeal of the Gospel was considered to be universal and its power sufficient to meet the need of all classes and peoples. The New Testament missionaries never wrote of the 'native believers' or even of 'native brethren'. In the churches there were neither race problems nor nationalist problems, for all believers were brethren and all were one in Christ.

CHAPTER XXXVII

THE EVANGELIST AND MATERIAL MINISTRIES

The New Testament Evangelists did not found schools, hospitals, orphanages, or philanthropic institutions of any kind. Christ had not done so before them. Yet Christ and these first missionaries taught doctrines that made the growth of such institutions inevitable.

One of the gifts of the Spirit which Christ gave to the Church —that of 'pity' or 'acts of Love'—would undoubtedly lead to the carrying out of such material ministries to those in need. It is in Christian communities that philanthropic institutions have flourished.

There can be no question as to the worthiness and usefulness of such material ministries, nor as to whether glory may be brought to the Name of Christ through them when the Holy Spirit is in full control. We have but to think of the institutions established by George Müller, Sister Abigail and Amy Carmichael to realize their spiritual value. The question which we have to consider here, however, is, what place do they have in the ministry of the Evangelist or church-planter?

It is evident that our Lord and the early missionaries of the Church did not use material ministries of any kind as an aid to evangelism. They depended entirely upon the gifts of the Spirit for preaching and teaching, and upon the power of the Gospel to save 'to the uttermost'. The church which they established was a purely spiritual thing, the product of a purely spiritual witness borne in the power of the Holy Spirit.

Actually, the Evangelist, or missionary, is called to a ministry which makes it impossible for him to settle long enough in one place to engage in institutional work. If he does, he ceases to follow his calling. A travelling salesman who settles down to be a storekeeper ceases to be a travelling salesman. The Evangelist is both a foundation-layer and foundation-repairer. For both these sides of his ministry it is essential that he be mobile: able to procede at any time to any place where his ministry is required and free to remain there as long as may be necessary.

,Paul was a tent maker and sometimes supported himself by plying his trade. There is no reason why a physician or school teacher should not do likewise. It may be as definitely God's will that they should do so as it was for Paul. Paul's doing so bore a needed testimony to the churches in some places. But tent-making did not tie him down anywhere one day longer than it was God's will he should be there. He was an Evangelist first and always and the moment his ministry made it necessary for him to move, on he went.

Self-supporting Teachers and Preachers

The ministry of the church-planter should not be confused with that of those who are called to carry on a ministry such as was performed by Aquila and Priscilla at Ephesus.[1] The Ephesian church was nurtured in their home and they engaged in a useful ministry of teaching (1 Cor. 16:19; Acts. 18:24-26). Barnabas and Paul, during their first visit to Antioch, engaged in a somewhat similar ministry. They were there as preachers and teachers associated with the other spiritual leaders of the church. Neither they nor Aquila and Priscilla took a position superior to the local Elders of the church. The local church could develop fully and naturally around them. The valuable ministry in which they engaged was carried on within the normal structure of the local church and contributed effectively to its development.

Not a few business men, teachers and physicians have gone to unevangelized regions to live and earn their living with the object of witnessing for Christ, and in many cases there has been much blessing upon their work. However, although permanently resident in a place, they have, in many cases, considered themselves as Evangelists or church-planters, not simply as preachers and teachers, and have continued indefinitely directing a local congregation and standing in the way of the development of local leadership. Had they understood more fully the true principles of their type of ministry and been prepared to cooperate on an equality with those whom the Holy Spirit would raise up for the

---

[1] See pp. 88, 112, 436.

local ministry, genuine New Testament congregations could have been established. The ministry of such men and women when properly understood, is clearly in accord with the New Testament order and can be used greatly in the extension of the Church.

Medical Work

The spiritual ministry of the physician or nurse who engages permanently in Hospital or Dispensary work will be that of preacher, teacher and soul-winner, not that of church-planter.

Luke might have been called of God to settle permanently at Corinth, or some other place, and support himself by the practice of medicine. He might have established a Hospital and served as an Elder in the church. As a Christian physician he would have been faithful, in cooperation with all the members of the church, in obeying Christ's command to preach the Gospel and he would have had always as his main objective the salvation of souls, making all his professional contacts contribute to that purpose. Had that been God's will for him, his ministry would have been just as honourable, necessary, and blessed of God. He would not have carried on the ministry of church-planting, but would have taken just as essential a part in the testimony of the Church.

Medical work in itself is not a spiritual ministry. It is a material ministry. Spiritual fruit depends entirely upon the faithfulness of the doctor or nurse in proclaiming Christ. Dr. Whitfield Guinness of Honan has stated well the principles that must govern the doctor's ministry:

What can medical science 'per se' do for a heathen or any individual who is out of Christ? It can give ease of body, and to some extent peace of mind, in so far as it banishes pain and annuls the fear of immediate death or of physical incapacity. This is alright as far as it goes, but it does not go very far. The benefit of mind and body, which are both mortal, can only be temporary, while the soul of the individual, which is the man himself, remains 'in statu quo'. After all, a whole sinner is not in much, if any, better plight than a sick sinner. No, the medical missionary who is true to his Divine commission cannot for one moment rest content with the mere patching up of bodies and cheering up of minds.

The commision is, 'make disciples'. Heal if you like; teach if you can; plant trees and plough fields if that be your bent; preach if you are so impelled; but by any means and all means achieve the same end, viz. make disciples; save men and women, boys and girls, from spiritual death, which in horror, hatefulness, and pathos far exceeds the mere corruption of flesh and blood. The command is plain, but it is appallingly easy to put time and brains and strength into the medico-scientific side of one's work to such an extent that the command is all but forgotten. This is, at any rate, the experience of the writer, and may possibly be true in the experience of others also...

> We will arise at midnight to grapple with an acute abdominal case, spending and being spent to save life. We may save it. But if recovery means merely a return to the old habits of living, and ultimate loss of soul, what shall it profit that man or woman? It is, of course, far easier to spend oneself in the operating-room or in the office than in the quest for souls. While the former must not be left undone, the latter must be on no account shelved or relegated to the second place.[1]

Dr. Guinness was faithful in putting these principles into practice:

> But the medical work grew so fast that more important things were in danger of being crowded out, and the doctors had to call a halt. From the first, they saw plainly that unless the spiritual side was carefully guarded it would be swamped by the material.
> They reduced the number of days in the week on which they would see patients, and when still they were overwhelmed with work they had to limit the number of cases to be seen on any given day. First things had to be kept first; and they were of one mind in giving the supremacy to the spiritual.[2]

There are many cases where the Christian doctor has obtained an entrance, through his medical knowledge, into regions that were closed to the Gospel. There is no doubt that through medical work doors have been opened and souls reached where otherwise the Gospel would not have had an entrance. At the same time we must be careful not to give this material ministry, noble as it is, a place which it is not intended to occupy, or exaggerate its importance as a means for bringing souls to Christ.

Our own experience has been that while medical work has often opened doors to the missionary's medicine and medical skill, it has actually not always opened hearts to the Gospel. This is the experience of many missionaries. The loaves and fishes with which the Lord in His compassion fed the needy multitude did not bring true faith in Him. Physical and material benefits do not predispose the natural heart to repentance and faith. On the contrary, we have found that medical work and material assistance have often tended to engender an interested motive in the recipient, as with those who followed the Lord 'for the loaves and fishes'. Such is the heart of the unregenerate man.

It is significant that there is no reference to Luke's medical work, except the title of 'the beloved physician' given to him by Paul. No doubt Paul and many others had reason to be grateful for his medical skill, but, whatever medical work he may have

---

[1] *Guinness of Honan,* pp. 242, 243.
[2] *Guinness of Honan,* p. 177.

done, there is no record of it. Evidently it was not considered to have a direct bearing upon the Evangelist's ministry. No matter by what means contacts were made, whether through Paul's tent making or Luke's medical work, the fruit was all solely the product of the Holy Spirit's wisdom and power.

It will, of course, be realized that the gift of healing, so much in evidence in the first years of the Church Dispensation, is something quite distinct from the science of healing and is intended for a special purpose.[1] It is interesting that while Luke makes no mention of any work of healing he may have done as a physician, he records more of our Lord's miracles of healing than do any of the other writers of the Gospels.

Orphanages

The principles that must govern medical work must also control the work of the school-teacher, orphanage worker, etc.

George Müller was called of God to found and conduct an Orphanage. Through the Orphanage many souls were saved and many lives blessed. The testimony borne by that institution has been greatly used of God to His people everywhere. But what has brought this blessing is not the philanthropical work done but the evidence provided of God's power and faithfulness to provide in answer to the prayer of faith. While engaged in that ministry George Müller also served as an Elder in a local assembly.

Miss Amy Carmichael's work in India is, also, an example of institutional work that contributes definitely to the Church's testimony in a heathen land by making it possible to win souls to Christ who could not otherwise be reached. The strong spiritual testimony borne by that institution is due, not to the value of the material ministry rendered, but to the high spiritual standard of the faith witness carried on through it.

There are worthy secular institutions that have carried on as great, and greater, material ministries, but the worthiness of their work and the benefits they bring give no spiritual witness. Only the wisdom and power of the Holy Spirit can bear spiritual witness and produce spiritual fruit.

Educational Work

In an entirely illiterate community it is important that converts learn to read that they may have direct access to God's Word, for

[1] Cf. chapter 2, *Miracles*.

that is vital to spiritual growth and permanence. But local people can soon be trained sufficiently to undertake that task.

It is necessary that at least some of the converts know how to read. Beyond that, education is not essential to the establishing of a church. We have not found educational work to be very fruitful as an aid to the church-planter's ministry. Even with teachers whose aim was to lead the children to Christ, the spiritual results have been comparatively small. An equal amount of time and strength spent in direct evangelism among children would have produced very much greater results. Speaking generally, the value of the Day School is educational, not spiritual and, therefore, it does not have a place in the work of church-planting. However, where there is a special need for schools in a Christian community, God may lead others, who are not called to the ministry of church-planting, to conduct them and to witness through them to the pupils and their parents.

There are Hospitals, Orphanages and Schools that have been founded in the will of God and that are bearing a valuable spiritual testimony. But, unfortunately, there are many institutions in the mission field that contribute very little and, in some cases, nothing whatever, to the Church's witness. In not a few cases, doctors, nurses and teachers are actually discouraged from witnessing for Christ to patients and pupils. Material ministry is the objective of these institutions, not the salvation of souls, and they have no place in the testimony of the Church. The primary objective of all ministry—the preaching of the Gospel, in season and out of season, to every creature—has been lost sight of. The urge of the Spirit to proclaim Christ and to win souls for Him has disappeared.

These material ministries are no longer a manifestation of the Holy Spirit's gift of Pity. They have become simply man's good works. The Holy Spirit's part has been restrained and it is man's work that is offered to man and to God. All the Holy Spirit's gifts are for the manifestation of Christ; not just of His compassion, but of the whole Christ: Redeemer, Lord and Life. Whatever does not present Him in His fulness is not of His Spirit. The physician, nurse, teacher, tent-maker, whose whole life and every act does not have as its only objective the bringing of all who are lost into living union with Christ has lost his vision and forsaken his Heavenly calling. He is not engaged in spiritual work that will bear eternal fruit but in material work whose fruit is temporal.

In some parts of the mission field a large proportion of the so-called missionary force is concentrated in base stations, engaged in running schools, industrial institutions, Hospitals, and in similar tasks. In great part they are offering the benefits of the Gospel instead of the Gospel itself, ministering to the mind and body, instead of to the soul.

We must not put the cart before the horse. If we want a vineyard we do not hang up bunches of grapes in the field; we plant grape-vines and if the planting and pruning are well done the grapes will be borne in due season.

To offer the material benefits of the Gospel instead of the soul-regenerating power of the Gospel will produce no spiritual fruit. Institutions run by foreigners and supported by foreign money will not create a spiritual, independent, self-sufficient, vigorous church. Nothing but the Holy Spirit's power manifested directly in the salvation and regeneration of souls can do that.

The reason for the putting of stress upon institutional work is unspiritual. The unspiritual man considers such work as of a higher order than the preaching of the Gospel. The education of the mind and the healing of the body is thought to be a more praiseworthy and effective service than the saving of the soul. The establishing of a school brings greater credit than the founding of a church. It is actually considered that the man who gives himself to preaching does so because he has not the training necessary for a higher service!

We have dealt here with material ministries from the point of view of the New Testament church-planter, one who cannot be tied down indefinitely to one particular place. It will be understood that, while the church-planter cannot engage in such material ministry, others may, and those who do, if they are truly called of God and their work is carried on upon purely spiritual principles and in the power of the Spirit, will be used of God to bear an effective testimony.

Some, recognizing the fact that material benefits cannot produce spiritual life and that the church-planter cannot engage in institu-tional work and at the same time carry on the ministry to which he is called, have concluded that all institutional work is wrong in itself. Others, impressed by the material needs of non-Christian communities, have permitted institutional work to turn the Church-planter aside from his ministry—a thing which the New Testament Evangelists never did, although the material needs of many of the peoples to whom they took the Gospel were as great as in any mission field today.

The New Testament Evangelists were not indifferent to the need of the poor. Luke mentions with approval the good works which Dorcas did for the poor in Joppa. He, although he was a physician, did not settle anywhere to carry on a ministry of healing among the needy. This was not because he did not appreciate their need, or minimized the worth of such a ministry, but because it was not the ministry to which God had called him: he was an Evangelist. And he knew that the fulfilling of his ministry would produce Dorcases and all the acts of Christian love in every place in which he established a church. And so it was—and so it will be today.

In the work of the body of Christ all spiritual ministries are equally honourable and necessary. What is important is to know to what ministry we are called, what, exactly, is the purpose of that ministry, and how God has intended that it should be correlated to the general ministry of the Body and to the witness of the local church. When we know these things, our ministry, whatever it is, will bear its richest fruit.

CHAPTER XXXVIII

OPENING A 'NEW STATION'

For the title of this chapter we have used modern missionary
terminology. Paul and his companions would not have spoken of
opening a new mission station but of establishing a new congregation. There is a sense in which the term 'mission station' is quite
legitimate, but, naturally, it is so intimately associated with modern
missionary procedure that it is liable to cause confusion. We
may have quite a clear understanding of New Testament missionary
methods, yet, when we come to open our 'station' we may be
influenced unconsciously by the generally accepted meaning of
that word and led into procedures that are not New Testament.
Having a 'station', we feel we must have a hall, so we rent one;
and having a hall we must have benches and a pulpit, so we
purchase or make them. Until we have these we hardly feel that
we are real missionaries or have a real 'station'. Then we invite
the people to come to our ready-made hall to attend services which
we conduct in the customary way. When converts are won and
baptized they continue to gather in our hall to hear us preach and
teach. We consider them as babes in Christ that will grow probably
very slowly and that will be dependent upon us for years to come.
The term 'mission station' conveys the idea of permanence, and,
though we say our object is the establishing of a New Testament
church we actually proceed on the assumption that we shall be
many years resident on our 'station'.
If we propose to work in accordance with New Testament
methods we must study these methods carefully and apply them
faithfully and fearlessly. When we open our 'station' we are at
once faced with facts. Before that it has been easy to accept New
Testament principles in theory, but now we find that to put them
into practice requires an intimate knowledge of New Testament

missionary procedure and faith that is very real and practical. It is here that many stumble. Through lack of knowledge, or fear to depend entirely upon the Spirit's work, a wrong start is made and things are done that introduce contrary principles right at the beginning and that retard spiritual development.

When Paul took the Gospel to a city he did not open a 'mission station' in the modern sense of the term. He avoided everything that would have tended to make his continued presence necessary. His procedure was all calculated to accomplish in as short a time as possible the establishing of a congregation that would remain as a permanent witness while he went on, very soon, to found other churches elsewhere.

He evidently did not rent a hall or provide benches and a pulpit. Sometimes he preached in the Synagogues; once we find him teaching in the School of Tyrannus; usually, it seems, he met with his converts in the home of a believer. He did not regard his converts as mere spiritual babes whose growth would be uncertain and slow, but as men and women in whom the Spirit of the Lord had taken up His abode and who, through Him, would be guided and taught and enabled for all spiritual living and ministry.

When a married missionary enters a town with the purpose of establishing a church he, naturally, rents a home for his family. Often a room in his house is used for the meetings. It does not seem, in principle, that there can be any objection to doing so for the church may gather in his home just as in that of any other believer. And yet, in practice, it has proved a snare. It is much preferable not to have the meetings in the missionary's home. Having them in his home tends to emphasize the feeling that the carrying on of the work depends upon him, his home and his continued presence and to cause the missionary to have a possessive attitude regarding the work.

When the meetings are started in the home of a convert there is nothing provided except the chairs or other seating accommodation that the family happens to possess. As more seating accommodation is needed it is natural to expect that, not the family, but the group of believers will purchase or make additional chairs or benches. These then become the property of the congregation. This is probably the first experience that the group of believers has in meeting their own needs and it is valuable to them for it sets a precedent and indicates the normal way to be followed in the future. When it becomes necessary to have a larger room for their meetings they will not think it unnatural that the congregation should bear the expense of the rent or building.

If the meetings are first held in a room in the missionary's home it is necessary to be watchful not to slip back into non-New Testament methods. Nothing should be provided that would not be found in any other private home. It is best not to provide Bibles and hymn books. The people who attend should purchase their own and bring them to the meetings. When benches are needed these should be purchased or made by the group of believers. The temptation may be strong to provide at the start the seating accommodation we hope will be necessary, and plausible arguments will not be lacking, but let us keep clearly before us the fact that Paul and his companions did not do so. They gave no material aid to the new churches. Their churches were self-supporting from the day they began and never thought of receiving financial help from missionary or Mission.

If meetings are begun in a room in the missionary's home, it should be made clear that it is only a very temporary arrangement and that some other meeting place should be found as soon as possible, provided by the congregation with no assistance from the missionary. Frequently a missionary finds it difficult to absent himself from his station because the meetings are held in his home and it is not easy to make suitable arrangements for the care of his house during his absence. If the meetings had been held somewhere else he would have been freer in his movements.

Let us not be afraid of the small beginning. It is not absolutely necessary to have a hall when we start work in a town. To begin evangelizing through personal contacts and from house to house and wait until the Lord provides a meeting-place may seem harder, but it produces natural growth and sound fruit. We must guard against letting the difficulties and impossibilities of a situation impress us too greatly and be willing to exercise faith, abide God's time, and trust the Holy Spirit to bring into being in His own way that for which He has brought us to our 'station'.

The work on many a 'mission station' has suffered almost permanent injury from a wrong start. We may easily be persuaded that circumstances demand some deviation from the New Testament procedure. We may purpose that this deviation will be only temporary and will be corrected later, but any compromise, no matter how insignificant and necessary it may have appeared to be, is never easy to correct afterwards. It establishes precedents. Though the course we set be out but a few degrees, in the end we shall find ourselves at a foreign port.

Those to whom we minister learn the spiritual walk as they see us walk in the Spirit and they will continue to do what they have seen us do. We cannot begin the work in one way and then tell them they have to carry it on in a different manner. If our adherence to New Testament principles of church-planting has been in part theoretical, the obedience of the church we establish to the New Testament pattern will also be in part theoretical. Let us never forget that our every action is an example and a precedent. Our responsibility is great, for the influence of what we do will continue in the church in the years to come, leading either to obedience or to compromise.

The manner in which the Holy Spirit led the New Testament Evangelists to act in the founding of a church definitely avoided all that would have made them the centre around which everything must revolve. Their whole procedure indicated the fact that their stay was temporary and that the congregation must fully assume its responsibilities from the very beginning.

First among these responsibilities comes witness. The new converts must be urged from the very beginning to exercise whatever gifts of witness they may have been given. The spiritual growth of many a congregation has been retarded because the missionary has stood in the way of the development of the converts. The missionary will feel that they cannot preach as well as he, and, perhaps, he fears to lower the standard of his meetings. It may seem that there is so great a need for the teaching of the converts that time can hardly be spared in the services to let beginners practice their gifts. If we take these reasonings to the Word of God we shall find that they are false. The converts need teaching, it is true, but experience in the exercise of the gifts of the Spirit must accompany the theoretical study of doctrine if true spiritual progress is to be made in their lives. The converts that are not led into active witness will remain spiritually weak and dependent. If a missionary waits until the converts become mature before permitting them the free exercise of the gifts of the Spirit, he will wait long and in the end will have a church on his hands of immature believers that are dependent upon his continued ministry.

It is not possible to deal with the matter of the starting of the work on a new 'station' by giving a list of 'do's' and 'don'ts'. God has not done so in the Word; but He has laid down principles and given examples that provide ample guidance.

Possibly it would be helpful to avoid the term 'mission station' and speak of a missionary's 'present location'. No matter what terms are used, the fact must ever be borne clearly in mind that he is not establishing a 'station' in the modern sense, but planting a church. Whether his stay be for a few months or for two or three years it must be understood by him and by the church that his ministry is transitory and that he must soon be released to plant another church in another unevangelized town.

CHAPTER XXXIX

PLANTING A NEW CHURCH

We shall now endeavour to give our experience in the actual work of establishing churches on the New Testament model. In the first place we would record a failure. Our first attempt to apply New Testament methods was in a great river region where the people were a mixture of Indian and Latin. There we spent two years. There was great blessing, many souls were saved and the work spread rapidly. The increased power that was the result of the application of the New Testament methods was clearly evident. But we sought to retain much of the modern church organization with its pastorate. The deficiencies of this organization we tried to correct by forming the believers into bands responsible for carrying on a definite work of evangelism, endeavouring in this way to reproduce the spiritual activity of the New Testament congregation. The result, however, was not satisfactory, for the tendency to settle down placidly to let the pastor do the work was always present and finally triumphed.

the New Testament method brought release to the power of the

That experience taught us many things. It proved to us that Spirit, but it also revealed the fact that there could be no combining of man's way with God's way; no putting of a new patch on an old garment; no partial obedience.

Our second experience was in a small interior town where there had been a church established for fifteen years. This congregation was entirely dependent upon the missionary. None of the gifts of the Spirit was being manifested amongst them and, indeed, they knew practically nothing about them. The rent of their hall was paid by the Mission and very little was given in the offering. There was a good proportion of men amongst them but none was able to take a service. They had no sense of responsibility for the work, their attitude being, "It is the duty of the pastor or missionary to preach the Gospel, teach us, visit us and care for us; they are paid to do it; we have not the time, training or knowledge for such work". Their spiritual condition was, of course, correspondingly low.

Two of us ministered to this congregation for six months. At the beginning the situation was hard. In the first meeting it seemed as if an evil spirit was present dominating the atmosphere. The message was on Christ's absolute victory over Satan through the Cross and it appeared that Satan was present to challenge. We felt that the words we spoke hardly reached the people. It was not the first time we had been conscious of such opposition when dealing with that subject. On the following day, the two of us met for prayer, taking our stand by faith on the ground of Christ's victory on Calvary and claiming the exclusion of any influence of the Evil One. Thereafter, there was great liberty of the Spirit in the meetings.

We began by giving spiritual instruction, emphasizing the believer's privileges in Christ and the need for complete separation from all that is of the flesh and full consecration to the Lord.

For a time, prayer meetings were held daily. We sought continually to stress the fact that while we might teach the things of the Spirit we had no power to make these things real in the life of any one. Spiritual experience could be acquired only by each individual dealing directly with the Lord, and the Holy Spirit dealing directly with each individual. We ourselves continued in a definite ministry of prayer for the people that they might be fully equipped in spiritual knowledge and in the power of the Spirit.

After a time, there began to be evidence that a number of believers were passing through hard experiences and we realized that God was answering prayer and dealing with them. Then the break came and hidden sin was confessed by many who sought the Lord in true repentance and yieldedness.

Not until then did we attempt to teach about the gifts of the Spirit and God's order for the Church. Their spiritual significance would not have been understood. When there was true surrender to God, then the Holy Spirit had liberty to reveal spiritual truth and to make that truth active in their lives.

After that it was easier. The Scriptural, spiritual order for the Church seemed to be understood at once. The gift of preaching

29

began to be manifested and it was not long before most of the men were taking part in the preaching of the Gospel in different parts of the town.

Six months later, when we left this town, three Elders and three Deacons had been appointed. The church was paying the rent and all other expenses. Many of the men were taking part in preaching. Cottage meetings were being held in several districts and souls were being saved.

But we had made a mistake. We had taught the congregation regarding prayer, but had not been sufficiently careful to see that they put into practice what they were taught and learned by experience to do nothing until they knew God's will through prayer, and that opened the door to serious difficulties that developed later.

A number of years ago, work was opened in Temperley, a suburban town near Buenos Aires, the Capital of Argentina. This was done in obedience to what we believed to be a definite call from God. For months before, the matter had been made the subject of much prayer in company with fellow-workers. We waited until there was definite assurance on the part of all that it was God's time for us to go forward. As we continued in prayer, others heard the call, and when, finally, the way was opened, there was a company of four—one married couple, a single man and a single woman—who went forth in obedience to the Spirit's leading. We realized later how perfect had been God's choice of our group. Amongst us were the different gifts of the Spirit needed for the work that had to be done.

In Temperley we met almost daily for prayer as a group, waiting on the Lord for guidance. We sought to take no step without first getting definite assurance through prayer that it was God's will and God's time.

A room in a private home was put at our disposal for meetings and a little group of people gathered together for the preaching and teaching of the Word. During the first months, progress seemed slow, but individuals were brought to saving faith in Christ and these were baptized as soon as there was definite evidence of conversion.

Several of the Lord's people living in the district joined with us and we began to meet together as a congregation every Lord's Day to partake of the Lord's Supper. From the beginning, this meeting was conducted according to the instructions given by Paul. As there were yet no Elders appointed, we acted as Elders. We had, of course, taught regarding the gifts of the Spirit and their use. A goodly proportion of those who gathered together were young people and they soon began to take part in the testimony. Twice a week, on week nights, we taught the Word, seeking to lay a foundation of spiritual knowledge, emphasizing at all times the need for complete separation from all that is of the world and of the flesh, and a full personal surrender on the part of every individual, that the Holy Spirit might have complete freedom to teach, guide and use every member of the Body.

As we wished to teach the believers that the congregation must walk by prayer, directed by the Holy Spirit in everything, we began immediately to have a weekly prayer gathering. We explained to them simply what prayer in the Spirit is and how Christ, Who is present in the gathering of the Church, will direct the Church by His Spirit in all its actions. When anything had to be resolved —if an open-air meeting should be started; if the hour of a meeting should be changed, or any other matter decided—we alone did not make the decision but had every believer bear a share of the responsibility of finding out God's will in prayer. Until all could say that they had assurance in prayer that it was God's will, no action was taken.

In the establishing of a congregation there is nothing more important than leading them immediately into the practice of prayer and teaching them how to find the will of God. To neglect this is fatal, for, without it, a congregation will lack spiritual guidance. It will be realized that we could not have done this merely by the teaching of theory. To theory, we had to add example and lead them into the practice. So it must be in all our instruction of a new church: we must teach them the application of truth by personally accompanying them in the practice of it. This is one of the great secrets of the successful ministry of Paul and his companions: a secret they learned from the Master's example.

The Prayer Meeting was for prayer only. There were no hymns and no Bible study—nothing to encroach upon the time for prayer. Without any preliminaries, a brief period (which must be kept brief) was given for the stating of prayer requests, then all the time necessary was devoted to prayer. After all had prayed, the opportunity was given to state briefly what guidance, if any, they felt they had received in prayer. Care must be taken that this period does not degenerate into discussion and the expression of personal opinions. It was explained that they should not tell what they might have been feeling before prayer, but what the Lord had said to them through giving a sense of liberty or lack of liberty while they had sought to mention the various matters in prayer. It was then that we found out whether or not the Lord was giving liberty regarding the matters about which we were enquiring; otherwise, all would have gone from the meeting not knowing what guidance had been received by the others and much of its value would have been lost. When there was not practical unanimity regarding God's will in any matter, a decision was postponed to give time for further prayer.

We sought to make it clear that the power of a prayer is not in its length, or in the beauty of its expression, but in what is according to God's will revealed by the Holy Spirit and comes from a heart fully surrendered and truly seeking God's glory, and that it is necessary to be ever on guard against the tendency of the soul not in vital touch with the Spirit to introduce the verbiage that is offered by man's mind and emotions and not by the Spirit.

No attempt was made to organize the prayer in any way, asking for 'sentence prayers', or assigning petitions to different persons to avoid repetition. We explained that such devices are necessary only when the Holy Spirit is not in control; that they are but substitutes for Spirit-guided prayer and actually restrain the liberty of the Spirit. We must flee all substitutes and take by faith the true and full purpose of God. When the Holy Spirit is not in control, the only thing to do is to get back into the place where He is in control.

The congregation had no "Business Meeting". The prayer meeting was their business meeting. Anything that had to be decided about was made a matter of prayer there and nothing was done until all came to feel it was the Lord's will. That meant that any one who wanted to take part in decisions regarding church matters had to attend the prayer meeting regularly. Matters for prayer and decision were not argued about. Any necessary explanations were given and then all waited to know the Lord's will. It was His will and not man's judgment that had to be known. This required waiting on the Lord and patience but the result has been that this congregation has never had any serious difference of opinion.

When the group of believers began to meet at the Lord's Table, the teaching of Scripture regarding giving was put before them. It was shown that the believer's responsibility was not to the church or to the Elders of the church, but to the Lord. A box was placed in an inconspicuous place near the door, at that gathering only, on the first day of the week, that those who wished to give might do so, as they entered or retired. No appeals for money were ever made. The offering was never announced. Periodically, a statement of income and expenditure was pinned up in a convenient place. No one knows what another is giving. The only time money is mentioned is when the disposal of funds has to be made a matter of prayer to know God's will.

At first the church had no expenses except the purchase of the communion symbols and tracts, but later the rent of a hall had to be paid. Usually there were no other expenses and the balance —generally more than twice as much as the expenses—was given to missionary work. From the amount received in the offering it is evident that most of the members of the congregation must be giving at least a tenth of their income.

Occasionally, financial help was given to some member by the congregation, but great care was taken in this matter. They knew that we lived by faith, looking to the Lord for the supply of our need and this example had a strong influence upon them. When in need they also would look to the Lord in faith and many were the experiences of direct deliverance that they received, which, naturally, were a great blessing and strength to them.

Three persons who had been accustomed to begging professed conversion. The Elders would not permit any material help of any kind to be given to them but told them to ask the Lord in prayer to give them the means to earn what they needed. Two did so and the Lord answered them. Spiritually and morally the results were, of course, excellent. One of these two today owns a house and a horse and cart. The third had come for what he could get and, after attending one or two meetings and showing no true evidence of conversion, disappeared.

A desire to extend the testimony manisfested itself from the first. Open-air meetings were started in the public square. Cottage meetings were begun in other districts and nearby towns. We kept away from some of the meetings, such as that in the open-air, so that the members of the congregation could not rely upon us but had to take full responsibility themselves. The lady-workers did not attend the women's meeting, except occasionally to give some teaching, thus obliging the women of the congregation to carry on their testimony. These two meetings soon proved to be the most fruitful in the salvation of souls.

Within a year and a half, two of the congregation were led to go out as missionaries. The church received the assurance that their call was from the Lord, because there was definite liberty in prayer concerning them, and because the necessary gifts of the Spirit were being manifested in them. Before they left, we laid our hands upon them, offering prayer for them, in recognition of the oneness of the Church with them in their call.

It was a year and a half before it become evident who the brethren were that the Holy Spirit had chosen to act as Elders of the congregation. About that time many of the congregation began to feel that there should be prayer regarding the appointing of Elders. That being so, special gatherings were held for prayer on every available night, the majority of the congregation attending. On Saturdays we met at 6 p.m. and continued in prayer until about 11 p.m.

These prayer gatherings were continued for several weeks, but it became evident that there was a definite lack of liberty in prayer so far as Elders were concerned. In view of this it was felt by all that the Lord would have us wait still longer, so the prayer gatherings were suspended.

Several months later there seemed to be a general feeling that the Lord would have us take the matter up again in prayer. The special prayer gatherings were resumed, and, this time, there was liberty and assurance in prayer.

We had instructed them not to discuss with each other the matter of the Elders, nor to make known to any but us which ones the Lord caused them to feel in prayer had been chosen by Him for that ministry. Thus there could be no lobbying and no one could be influenced by another's thoughts. Of course, no names had been proposed. Each one had to discover God's will himself or herself through prayer. It was a practical test of the reality of guidance through prayer.

Incidentally, this enabled us to help one or two to understand what real guidance of the Spirit in prayer is. For instance, one came to us and gave the name of a man whose wife and children did not give a good testimony. We had the one who gave this name read over the qualifications necessary for an Elder stated by

Paul, then we asked if the person proposed had all of these qualifications. "No", was the answer, "but while I was praying I thought of that name." We then asked, 'Will the Spirit of God ever suggest that we do something that is not in accord with God's Word?" It was realized that He would not do so, and this believer came to see the need of watchfulness and of discernment to distinguish between the voice of the Holy Spirit, the suggestions of our own mind and the promptings of the Evil One. After further prayer he came to know the Lord's choice.

During all this time the Lord was dealing personally with the individual members. While previously there had been no liberty to pray regarding Elders, the leading had been definitely to plead for a deeper work of the Spirit, for a more effective spiritual unity and for the manifestation of the gifts of the Spirit in each member. During that time, many came into a deeper experience of yieldedness and obedience. A few had joined with us who had a background of formal church organization. It took time for things to be unlearned and the purely spiritual outlook of the New Testament Church obtained. Before the Holy Spirit could give freedom for the appointment of Elders, He had a work to do in the congregation, making it a truly united, spiritual body.

These months of waiting on the Lord in prayer for clear guidance, were a rich experience for the church. Great spiritual lessons were learned that have meant much to it since then.

Finally, definite liberty came. We, the missionaries, had for some time known whom the Lord had chosen as Elders. In our own times of united prayer we had been caused to know His will and had been continually praying for these men. Four of the older brethren were showing evidence of the gifts of the Spirit for that ministry. However, we told none of our conviction, waiting until the members of the congregation should individually get through in prayer to a knowledge of God's will. We could see afterwards that the Lord had not kept us waiting a day longer than was absolutely necessary.

Believing that election by majority vote is not the New Testament way we waited until by private conversation with individuals, we knew that God's will had been made plain to all. The four men in question had signified their conviction that God had called them. It was remarkable that each one of them had given only three names. A day was appointed, the congregation called together, and the four names put before them. We reminded them that it had been revealed to all in prayer that these four were the ones chosen by God as the Elders of the congregation. Then, that there might be no possibility of future criticism, we gave the opportunity for any one who might disagree to say so, urging that if any one had felt a check in prayer about any of the four it was a solemn duty to make it known. However, all were agreed in the matter. We drew attention to the fact that these men were not elected by man but chosen by God. They were asked to come forward and we laid our hands upon them, committing them to the Lord. After that we sat down in the audience and the Elders closed the meeting. From that hour the responsibility of the oversight of the congregation was theirs. We, as Evangelists, withdrew from all direct responsibility, feeling that we were now free to devote our attention to other work.

Before continuing the story of the Temperley congregation, we would note the experience of one of our Fellowship, Erland Carlson, in the setting apart of Elders in a congregation in a country district in Paraguay, among a people of simple life and few educational advantages.

We have spent two and a half weeks with the believers in the country district of Colonia Independencia. Thirty to forty met together every afternoon from two to five o'clock to seek the will of God. A week of prayer had been announced, but the Lord led us to continue until there was a clear knowledge of His will. Some learned for the first time in practice what it is to be led by the Holy Spirit in prayer, and to find out God's will. The main burden in prayer was to know God's chosen ones among them as Elders. I had warned them not to converse among themselves or in their homes about the matter, but to seek to know the mind of the Lord only.

By the last day all had unanimously heard the voice of the Spirit, 'Separate unto me Manuel Menelike and José León Garáy as Elders.' We had the unspeakable joy of obeying the voice of the Spirit in setting apart these two brethren with the laying on of hands.

During those days of prayer one felt the presence and power of God in a very real way. It was a time of searching before the Lord. We had the joy of seeing immediate fruit as three believers obeyed the Lord in the waters of baptism and one who had been disciplined last year came back into fellowship. These joined us on Sunday around the Lord's Table. The Gospel services on Sunday nights were richly blessed in the salvation of three souls, and the return of three prodigals who had made a profession of faith last year. Several of the men who had never preached before in public gave messages. Four or five of the brethren gave short Gospel messages in each service. Thus the Lord has raised up men in the congregation who will be used in the extension of the testimony of the Gospel. Some of these have the advantage of speaking the Guarani.

May we say that it was a big sacrifice for these believers to meet for prayer for such a prolonged time. They all are farmers and could only work half days. Some had to work hard from early morning on the farm and to walk one to five miles to attend the time of prayer in the afternoon. The Lord showed them that they had to 'seek first the kingdom of God and His righteousness.' They were richly rewarded and only eternity will reveal that which was accomplished.

Shortly after the Elders of the Temperley congregation were appointed, one of them felt called to the ministry of Evangelist and he and his family moved to another town to establish a congregation there.

The witness had continued to spread. Nearly all of the men take some part in preaching and they do so with spiritual knowledge and power. Usually it is not long after a convert is baptized before he or she begins to take part in the work. In young and old it is expected that the gifts of the Spirit will be manifested. At one time, because of the rapid extension of the congregation's witness, there was a pressing need for more preachers. At the suggestion of the Elders, the church began to pray that God would manifest the gift of preaching in others and save more souls to provide more preachers. It was not long before they had more preachers. They did not pray that God would send more missionaries.

All this had not been done—and it does not continue—without spiritual conflict. The opposition of Satan is felt at every step Often the Lord had to deal with the church and with individual members. Two members have had to be excluded from fellowship because they fell into sin and continued in it. But there is victory and steady progress, not because all difficulty has been avoided, but because the church is in the place where it has the spiritual resources for meeting every difficulty, no matter of what nature, and triumphing over it. We are not promised a victorious Church without conflict, but a Church victorious in ceaseless conflict.

Every now and again the congregation awakens to the fact that things are beginning to slide; but then the matter is dealt with in prayer and the power and victory are regained. Recently they felt there was less power in the open-air meetings. No souls were being saved. It was taken up definitely in prayer by the congregation and the blessing returned. A difficult situation arose in the congregation that was clearly the work of the enemy. It threatened serious harm to the testimony. In prayer the church took its stand on the victory ground of Calvary, withstanding Satan there in Christ's Name and claiming by faith our Lord's own triumph and glory. The Lord's power was manifested and He was glorified.

Trouble arose between two women who were active in witness. Each felt that she should take the lead in a women's meeting in which they were cooperating. The flesh got the upper hand in both to the extent that it became evident in the meetings and a bad testimony was borne before unbelievers. The Elders took the matter to the Head of the Church in prayer. They have their own weekly prayer meeting and never take action, not even asking anyone to speak at a meeting, until all of them have liberty about it in prayer together.

On this occasion, they were puzzled. They felt it necessary to speak to the two women without delay, but in prayer there was no liberty to do so. This went on for several weeks. At the time, one of the Elders, telling us about it, said, "We do not understand it, but there must be a reason and we dare not do anything while this check in prayer continues". A couple of weeks later we heard that the difficulty had disappeared. The Elders had taken no action apart from believing prayer, but both women had become convicted and had confessed to each other, humbled before the Lord.

Of course, this does not imply that the Elders should never intervene in such a case; it simply means that in this particular case God wished to deal with the matter directly. The result of the Elders' obedience was that a true work of repentance was wrought and no hard feelings remained.

A request was made by a professing believer in a nearby town that meetings be held in her house. It seemed a good opportunity for giving a witness in a needy place. The Elders stated the case at the prayer meeting of the church and prayer was made to know if it was the will of the Head. There was a lack of liberty in prayer so the matter was left for further prayer. For several weeks it was mentioned in prayer, but always with the same result. Finally, the Lord definitely closed the door. Then it was discovered that this professing believer had been living in sin and that the neighbourhood knew it. Had meetings been held in that house, the testimony would have been compromised before the people.

Several years ago, we made an extended visit to the 'Homelands'. For a year before our going, our fellow-workers had been in prayer with us about the matter. As we were in Temperley, we asked the local church also to pray. When we, the missionary group, felt the time had come for the journey, the church also had received assurance about it. We remarked to the Elders that we hoped we might be back in about nine months. "No", they said, "in prayer we have felt that it will be much longer than that". It was eighteen months before we returned.

The manner in which they seek confirmation regarding the call of any who believe they are called to the missionary ministry is described in the chapter on the 'Training of the Worker'.

For several years they had been thinking of building and gradually funds had been accumulating, though much less was in hand than would be required. On different occasions the matter had been mentioned at the prayer meeting, but there had never been a unanimous feeling that it was the time to seek the Lord's will about it.

Finally, however, there was a clear conviction that the time had come to make it a matter of definite prayer and it began to take a prominent place in the prayers of all. When the opportunity was given after prayer for all to state what guidance they felt they had received about it in prayer, most said they felt it was clear that the building should be begun. There were some, however, who said they felt no definite guidance about it, so it was left for further prayer. It was several weeks before all felt certain about it. Then, of course, there was nothing to do but to obey God's will.

Someone raised the question as to whether all who could do so were attending the prayer meeting to pray about it. Stock was taken and it was found that when allowance was made for one or two who were sick, several aged people who could not come out in cold winter nights, those whose hours of work made it impossible for them to attend, and several women whose unconverted husbands put obstacles in their way, there were, actually, very few who were absent through lack of desire.

The fact that the money on hand was not nearly sufficient was mentioned, but all said that they should proceed with the building until the money gave out, but that they were sure that it would not give out since God would be faithful to supply for what He had revealed to be His will. They said it would be lack of faith to fear regarding the supply of the needed funds.

Then the question was asked, "When shall we start building?" The Elders replied that the guidance in prayer had been simply that they should build, not as to when they should begin and that, therefore, they would have to continue in prayer to know His time. It took three weeks more before all had liberty to say after prayer that now was the time.

The next question was as to what builder should be asked to give an estimate. That was prayed about at the following prayer meeting and it was found that all had liberty about a certain man. So the work was entrusted to him.

They told him that they were going forward with the building in faith, that they would not go into debt, and that if there was no money at any time the work would have to be suspended. The manner in which the money came in was remarkable. The need was never mentioned. Of course, there was no solicitation of any kind and no scheme to raise money. It was rarely mentioned in prayer in the prayer meeting. There was a quiet confidence that the Lord would supply.

Week by week the money came in. It seemed impossible that so much could be given. The people are ordinary working folk and building costs in war time were high. What came in was just enough to keep the work going. When a large sum was required —for instance, to purchase timber for roofing—a larger amount would come in. There came a time when there was not sufficient in hand to go forward, so the work was suspended. Some one suggested to them that a sermon should be preached to the congregation on Christian stewardship. The Elders smiled when they told about the suggestion. "No", they said, "we shall just tell the Lord about it." The Lord answered and the work went on.

In the congregation there is no organization beyond that given in the New Testament. There are no Societies or Guilds or Associations. There is no choir. There are no Women's, Young People's, or missionary organizations. These are not necessary in a congregation organized on the New Testament pattern. All are so busy in the work that they would not have time to attend the business meetings of such Societies.

The women are active in visitation and soul winning. They have several afternoon meetings a week in different places, their purpose being to reach women who cannot easily attend evening meetings. They are not organized. Their work, as all the other work of the congregation, is under the direction of the Elders.

The young people are active in the work. Most of the young men, as well as the older men, preach and they are kept so busy with preaching and Bible study that their time is fully occupied. The whole field is before them and no restriction is put upon them. Often young people are asked to take the preaching services. If they are beginners they are asked to give testimonies or short messages. The congregation is considered as a training ground in which all must learn to use the gifts of the Spirit that have been given to them.

For the leadership of the Sunday School and for the spiritual instruction of the children, it is sought to find those who have the call and gift of the Spirit for that ministry. The Bible is the only textbook used. The work is on an entirely spiritual basis. No attractions or incentives are provided. No gifts or prizes or picnics are given. There is no Christmas entertainment. Those responsible exercise a continual prayer ministry for this work, looking to the Lord in faith to accomplish through the Word and the power of the Holy Spirit that which it is His purpose to do. The Sunday School does not have a separate organization. The Elders are the final authority. One person with the gift to do so acts as leader. Different young people are asked to lead the Sunday School to give them practice. In the classes the young people are encouraged to prepare the study or a part of it and give it.

The Elders do not take part in preaching more than do the others. One of them is not a preacher. In the Lord's day gathering of the church at the Lord's Table, they take turns in being responsible for the direction of the meeting. The one who leads may or may not take part in speaking. The young men are as free to speak as the older men.

Occasionally, there is a gathering on the order of the *agape* or love-feast. The congregation meets at some believer's home, each one taking something to eat. What is brought is put together and the believers fellowship together in an informal meal. After that there is an open meeting when brief testimonies to God's faithfulness are given. These gatherings are always held in private homes, never in the hall.

Behind all the visible effort in the establishing of this church was a ministry of prayer carried on by the missionaries. We took everything first to God in prayer seeking to be watchful to do nothing until we had found that there was no check regarding it in prayer. Often this prevented us from doing things that we discovered afterwards were inspired only by our own enthusiasm. Also, we prayed for the believers individually. We took the position that what we were seeking to accomplish in them and in the church was God's will according to His Word. We believed that, according to His Word, it was this He had sent us to accomplish, and nothing less than this, and that, therefore, we had a right and responsibility to claim from Him that it should be done, and to accept nothing less. If less were accomplished, it would be due to our lack of faith or faithfulness.

Our faith was tested many a time. A year before the church knew who were chosen of God to be the Elders, we knew. However, one of them, particularly, did not seem promising. He was of ready speech, self-confident, and inclined to be self-assertive. Yet when we prayed about him we always felt he was one God had chosen. We therefore held on in faith for him that God would bring the flesh in him to the Cross and give him true spiritual insight and grace. For more than a year we prayed for him. Sometimes it seemed that our prayers were being answered and that there was evidence of spiritual power, and then he would do something so definitely of the flesh that we were tempted to be discouraged and to wonder if we were mistaken. But God answered prayer and honoured faith and that man became a truly spiritual and success- ful Elder. He is just the same man with the same temptations, but he is really surrendered. He knows now how to get the victory for himself and how to pray the prayer of faith for others.

We exercised a similar ministry of prayer for all the believers, first of all that they should be brought to the place of full yielded- ness and true spiritual knowledge, and then that the gifts of the Spirit necessary for the local church should all be manifested. We have no hesitancy in saying that had we not been faithful in this ministry of prayer and faith, what was done would not have been accomplished and the believers would not have learned to understand the full meaning of prayer and faith.

The danger in giving an example of the establishing of a New Testament Church is that it may be thought that every case will be exactly the same. As a matter of fact every case is different. Some take longer than others. Difficulties manifest themselves in some that are absent in others. We never know in what manner the opposition of the forces of evil will show itself. But the principles governing the task are always the same and we need never fear defeat.

Warning is needed on one point. We find that there is always a strong tendency to doubt that new converts are capable of being taught by the Spirit immediately the basic vital truths of spiritual experience. This is a fatal error. We must not doubt the power of the Holy Spirit or think that intellectual brilliancy is required for the understanding of deep spiritual truth. To leave a new convert with only very elementary spiritual knowledge is to put him in the place where he will learn to be content to live on a low spiritual plane.

Let us take, for example, the prayer ministry of the congregation. The missionary must not wait until he thinks they have become capable of praying in the Spirit before gathering them together for prayer and forcing them to undertake the responsibility of seeking God's will. If he does, he will probably wait a long time, and in the end will find that they have become quite satisfied to let him do it for them. He must insist from the beginning that there is only one way to proceed in God's order, and commence at once to lead them in that way. Then, he must exercise faith before God that He will fulfil His will in them. Great patience will be required, but God will honour faith and in most cases the lesson will be learned much quicker than seemed possible. The one thing that can retard success is lack of faith on our part.

We have found that it is in the matter of the congregation's prayer ministry that the greatest care has to be exercised, both in the founding of a church and afterwards, for it is here that Satan exerts his greatest efforts to prevent the true order being followed. The missionary as well as the congregation is continually tempted to be rushed and careless and to make exceptions. It is the most vital point in the practice of the spiritual order. Here is where the congregation and its Head confer. Here is where wisdom is received and victory won. And it is from this communing with God that the congregation derives the authority for its actions and its right to have faith in God that what it does will be done by the Spirit and accompanied by the blessing of God. It is here that Christ's presence in the congregation becomes effective. Therefore, we need not be surprised at the persistence of Satan's opposition in this matter; but let us be watchful that we be not unfaithful in our ministry.

The Temperley congregation has continued succesfully now for twelve years. What of the future? We have this assurance, that while the congregation continues to walk faithfully according to God's order He will lead it on and give it victory over every assault of Satan. This assurance is based upon God's Word. But from God's Word we know also that if compromise is permitted to enter, no matter in what form, the fellowship with the Lord will be hindered, the Spirit will be bound and defeat will be the result. Even the church founded by Paul in Corinth could fall into utter defeat.

This congregation has functioned from the beginning according to the New Testament pattern. Much greater difficulties have been encountered in congregations that had previously been accustomed to lean upon a missionary or pastor. We do not wish to give the impression that everything will go like clock-work as soon as we seek to establish the New Testament order. We have had to face the same difficulties that manifested themselves in the churches in New Testament times. Elders may fail and carelessness creep into a congregation. We are all just sinners saved by grace and requiring to walk moment by moment near to the Lord. The Evangelist is kept constantly on the alert, obliged to exercise fully his ministries of faith and prayer.

Sometimes mistakes have been made. The missionaries have had to learn by experience for the New Testament order is a new way to all. Some of the congregations, those particularly that for many years had been accustomed to the modern order, are still far from the place where they should be. It is not their fault that they had been taught ways that were not New Testament and we must be patient with them as the Lord was and is with us. But great things have been accomplished by the Spirit of the Lord. Each year sees definite progress. Congregations that had been dependent and powerless are now learning to walk and serve in the power of the Spirit of the Lord. We praise God for what He has done and testify to His faithfulness and power to fulfil His Word to all who will take it by faith.

CHAPTER XL

REORGANIZING A CONGREGATION

To reorganize a church that has long been accustomed to the modern system, and bring it into true conformity with the New Testament order, is much more difficult than to plant a church composed of new believers. It is when one attempts such a task that one comes to realize how fundamentally opposed the one system is to the other and how different are their fruits in the spiritual life of the believer.

One has to deal, not with new converts eager to be led on into spiritual life and experience, but with a congregation of spiritual babes. Indeed, they are worse than babes, for babes are growing, whereas these have had their growth arrested. They are more like a grove of trees that have become stunted and twisted out of shape. The problem is how to renew their growth and give back to them the strength and beauty that God intended them to have. It is comparatively easy to train a young and vigorous sapling, but a tree that has been long deformed and barely has life to subsist presents a much greater problem.

One finds a congregation that, while sound, perhaps, in doctrine, has in its practice much of the Roman Catholic idea of works and little true inner spiritual life. The one who would minister to them and lead them into full spiritual experience should take careful stock of the situation so that he may know exactly where their weakness lies and what their needs are. He should know this, so that, in the first place, his ministry of faith and prayer may be intelligent, and that, in the second place, he may have the necessary sympathy for, and understanding of, those to whom he is ministering.

The difference between them and new converts is that they have become the products of a system which has deeply affected their outlook and actions. To an extent far greater than they realize, they have come to hold spiritual truth as theoretical and not practicable; and this touches every phase of their Christian living and service. It is not that they have no knowledge, or faith, or prayer life, or spiritual experience, but that all of these have been restricted within clearly defined, narrow limits. Within these limits their whole spiritual life is lived; beyond them spiritual truth and experience are purely theoretical.

For that reason, a whole system of organization and works has been developed as a substitute for what is regarded as theoretical, and it is in this organization and works, that, to a large extent, faith is really placed, not in the spiritual factors. Thus it is that, while holding in theory that the preacher must minister in the power of the Spirit, reliance is really placed upon his eloquence, knowledge, personality and training. Faith, to them, is something with little real substance: it is, in fact, little more than a struggling hope that God may in some way give some assistance. Their knowledge of prayer is elementary. At their prayer-meeting—if they have one—they will go over the same vague petitions, repeating the same stock phrases, taking the opportunity to sermonize a little, and covering the world as widely as possible. They know nothing of praying as a church, guided by the Spirit to pray unanimously according to God's will; nor have they as a church ever experienced what it is to wait upon God in prayer until His will has been revealed to all. Theoretically, they believe they should seek His guidance and at their church business meeting a prayer is offered asking for it, but they would consider it impracticable to proceed then to prayer to seek a knowledge of His will. Instead, they discuss their problems, amicably or otherwise, and act according to the opinion of the majority, obtained by vote, thinking that that must be God's will and hoping in a vague way that He will bless it.

In addition to this, there is the situation created by the fact that they have never known the full extent of their privileges and responsibilities as members of the congregation. They have believed that their pastor was responsible for the ministries of preaching and teaching and that whatever ministry they might engage in would be merely supplementary and of an inferior order. They have understood that their duty was to be faithful in attendance at the services, to witness to their friends and neighbours and to invite people to the meetings. They have probably been accustomed to this order for many years, have no sense of personal responsibility for the ministry of the Word in the congregation, and, very probably, are averse to assuming it, being quite satisfied to be free from it.

Also, they are accustomed to all the superstructure that has been erected to aid the Spirit or substitute for His power—Committees, Guilds, Associations, Circles, Societies, etc.—which they have come to regard as part of the sacred order of the Church. Moreover, their spiritual immaturity and lack of experience is such that the thought of dispensing with that superstructure and depending upon the Holy Spirit directly would create panic, their belief in His power not being sufficiently real for any such practical application. Thus we find that, while in theory their dependence is upon God, in practice it is on themselves and their human resources—their own ability, effort and organization.

They have gone far from the place of simple faith where they started when they first accepted Christ as Saviour. Much that is not of faith, much that is carnal and of man's wisdom, has been learned, and it all must be unlearned. This work can be accomplished only by the Holy Spirit bringing the will into subjection, illuminating the mind with spiritual truth, and giving faith. Only He can free them from the accretions of 'man's traditions' that make of none effect the Word of God.

There is a danger which the missionary may easily fall into. Such a congregation, being accustomed to accept the teaching given by their pastor and, perhaps, having confidence in the missionary, may readily give theoretical assent to the New Testament order which he presents. We have seen this happen. The believers saw that what they were being told was certainly in the Bible and, therefore, they did not question it. But their acceptance of it was of the same nature as their previous acceptance of other spiritual truths—largely theoretical. They were willing to make the structural changes necessary, and it was thought that a congregation on the New Testament order had been established. But they did not exercise faith; they had no more life or power afterwards than they had before.

The great essentials to be borne in mind when dealing with such a congregation are not difficult to discern. They are, we believe, as follows:

1. There must be the awakening of true faith and spiritual understanding. This can be accomplished by the Spirit only in those who are truly surrendered to the Lord. Therefore the mis-

sionary's ministry must first seek the fulfilment of this condition. This cannot be done without faith and prayer on the part of the missionary. We have never seen it accomplished without a prayer battle against the enemy's forces. The issue depends upon the reality of the missionary's faith. He must not yield to the temptation to accept anything less than a complete victory, for this matter is fundamental and unless the foundation is truly laid there will be no strength in the superstructure.

2. Only now can teaching be given regarding the Church, for only now can the Spirit cause that there be a true spiritual under- standing and reception of it.

3. True faith must be given. Unless the believers really believe that God can and will do all His Word says He will do, they will be unable to venture in faith; and the New Testament Church order cannot be followed without real faith.

4. Nor can the Scriptural Church order be practised without prayer in the Spirit. It is at this point that many fail. To teach a congregation that it must pray in the Spirit, find out God's will in all things through prayer and engage in the conflict against Satan through prayer, will probably only add to their store of inert theoretical knowledge, unless the missionary is faithful to take time to demonstrate it to them by praying with them until they have learned by experience. This cannot be done by a visit of a few days, or even of a few weeks. The time necessary to accomplish it must be faithfully given. And what shall we say of the missionary who is so hurried during a visit to a congregation that he does not have time to wait with them upon God in prayer regarding what- ever may have to be decided, but makes the decisions himself, although he has just urged them to faithfulness in the observance of the Scriptural order? By this example he has contradicted his teaching and confirmed them in their thought that, after all, it is but theory and that it is really not necessary or possible to practise it.

We cannot say how long it may take to bring a congregation to the place where it has really entered into the practice of prayer. In some cases it will take longer than in others. There may be a quick response from a majority of a congregation or, to begin with, only a few may show willingness and understanding, but the work cannot be considered accomplished until the congregation as a whole, that is, a considerable majority, have entered into true spiritual life and experience.

Until a congregation has actually learned to pray and to make no decision whatsoever until it has discovered God's will through prayer, it cannot begin to function in the New Testament order. No congregation can be considered as able to function spiritually, and the missionary cannot regard his initial responsibility towards it fulfilled, until it has come to that place. Without this, it cannot have its ministry directed by the Head of the Body. It has not learned the first essential of service and of victorious warfare against Satan.

When a congregation has been brought to this point, the spiritual foundation has been laid. What remains to be built will be easy compared with what has gone before. The church has come to the place where it can begin to live and walk and serve in the Spirit and is ready to go forward as the Holy Spirit may lead it. For the rest of the teaching that should be given we would refer the reader to the chapters dealing with the teaching and organization of the Church.

CHAPTER XLI

REVISITING THE CHURCHES

When the foundations of a church are endangered, the foundation-layers must intervene. Their ministry is to lay the foundations and to see that these foundations remain intact.

The New Testament Evangelist did not return to a church to give it a few encouraging sermons or some good advice as to what should be done, but to cooperate with it until matters were put right.

The situation with which the Evangelist will be faced in such a case is probably as follows:

1. A coldness has crept over the congregation. It has become discouraged and powerless. Hidden sin, even open sin, may be present.

2. Probably no fruit is being borne. If there is any, it will be weak and struggling.

3. The prayer ministry of the church will be neglected. Few will be meeting for prayer and their prayers will have no real definiteness, faith or power. Prayer in the Spirit will be replaced by prayer in the wisdom of man.

4. The preaching and teaching ministry will be lacking in the power and revelation of the Holy Spirit. The work of the church will not be carried on with the true gifts of the Holy Spirit and, to a greater or lesser extent, man's wisdom, effort, eloquence and methods will have been substituted.

5. The individual believers will be in a like condition spiritually—out of living touch with their Lord and disheartened. A carelessness and worldliness will be creeping in among the young people. There will be a decreasing concern for the salvation of souls.

The longer the congregation is left in this condition, the more likely is it to drift into the state of the Laodicean church where it will be spiritually dead. But this need not be, and will not be if the Evangelist is faithful in his ministry. It is to meet just such a need that God has called him as an Evangelist and he has the duty and authority to intervene and to lay claim to complete victory.

Now let us consider the principles that must govern his intervention:

1. The congregation that is in need of his ministry has, no doubt, preachers, teachers, Elders, Deacons, etc., responsible for the ministry of the Word and for government. The Evangelist must recognize every one in the position in which God has placed him in the congregation. None should be ignored or set aside unless there has been serious unfaithfulness in testimony or in ministry. Due recognition must be given to the Elders particularly. They are God's appointed instruments and the Evangelist cannot go over their heads unless they persist in a fault which invalidates them for their ministry and makes it necessary that they be set aside.

2. The Evangelist must ever remember, as Paul did, that he has no power or authority in himself (1 Cor. 1:12-15; 3:4-7). The Church has not delegated authority to him; it has simply recognized his appointment by God to his ministry. He, therefore, has no ecclesiastical authority. In his approach to the congregation his reliance must be truly and solely upon the power of the Holy Spirit and the authority of God's Word. He presents God's Word and exercises faith that the Holy Spirit will give conviction and bring the congregation into obedience to its Lord (2 Cor. 10:3-5).

3. This means that the success of the Evangelist's ministry will depend largely upon his faithfulness in prayer and the reality of his faith. Although he has no authority or power in himself, he does have power that is absolute, irresistible and invincible. He must have faith to know that it actually is so. When he goes to the churches, it is, in truth, Christ, the Head of the Body, Who goes through him. Christ, engaged in the building of His Church, is using him as one of His foundation-layers. In Christ's Name he speaks and acts as the Holy Spirit leads him, and he can have the absolute certainty that Christ does not go with him in vain, but will accomplish His work and build His Church so that the gates of hell shall not prevail against it. But let him not think that he is there in Christ's stead. He must remember that Christ is present in the midst in that congregation and that he, the missionary, as

well as every other member of the Body present, is but an instrument. He must be watchful that none of his own wisdom enter
into his ministry: that he touch not the work with the hand of
flesh, but that all be done by the direction and in the power of
the Holy Spirit. He is never authorized to act on his own initiative
or to accept any compromise. God's Word is his manual of faith,
of procedure, of Church order, and he must obey it implicitly in
all things.

We have had many experiences of God's gracious working in
congregations that were in need of an Evangelist's ministry. In
one case a congregation that was still but a few years old had
become discouraged. The reason was evident: the Elders seldom
met for prayer to seek direction of the Lord. Seemingly unavoidable difficulties made it impossible for them to get together.
The prayer-gathering of the congregation was attended by very
few, and these few were crying to God in despair rather than in
faith. Under these circumstances Christ was not building that
church and there was neither power nor joy.

We felt definitely our responsibility to go to their help. First
of all, we laid claim in faith to the accomplishment of God's will.
Our prayer was based on God's Word. It is clearly stated that His
purpose for the Church is that Christ's fulness shall fill it, that
the power of the Spirit shall be manifested in it through His
wisdom and gifts, and that there shall be victory over all Satan's
work against it. This is God's will, and nothing less than this can
be His will. Our ministry as Evangelists made it our right and our
duty to ask God to fulfil His Word. We, therefore, did so, knowing
that He would be faithful to answer.

We contacted the Elders, and told them of our purpose to
cooperate with them in bringing the church back to the place of
power and effectiveness. They received us gladly for they were
conscious of their need. We had prayer with them, claiming
together that God would undertake in the difficulties that had
prevented them gathering regularly for prayer. He answered and
thereafter they were enabled to attend regularly. We met with
them and in faith sought together the carrying out of God's full
purpose for the congregation.

As they had seldom been meeting for prayer, their ministry in
the congregation had not been guided by the Spirit. Actions were
taken, speakers arranged, plans made, without first seeking a

knowledge of God's will. Now all this was changed: nothing was done until God's will was known by all through united prayer. The prayers of the Elders were now Spirit-guided prayers and, therefore, of the kind that 'availeth much'.

After three months it was evident that things were beginning to change. The prayer meeting of the church had continued to be poorly attended. We had been taking part in some of their meetings but not monopolizing the ministry or interrupting the normal life of the congregation. We dealt definitely with the need for the church to get back into living communication with Christ through prayer and to exercise faith for the fulfilment of God's Word concerning the power and triumph of the Church.

Once a week we engaged in a ministry of teaching, dealing with the foundation principles of the Church. As the attendance was poor, only a portion of the congregation—the more spiritual—was reached in this way. Our reliance was chiefly upon prayer. Along with the Elders we were aiming to get the congregation to stand with us in the prayer of faith. Teaching would accomplish nothing practical until it was put into practice.

Then, one Sunday evening when we had been asked by the Elders to minister the Word, there was a particularly small attendance. But those present were the people who had been showing a true response to the spiritual message. We felt that the small audience was of the Lord's ordering and told them so. We reviewed briefly the place that prayer had occupied in the New Testament Church and then asked them if they did not feel that the Lord had provided us now with an opportunity to go before Him in united, believing prayer. There was an eager response. All present knelt down and everyone took part in prayer. There was a definite laying claim to the carrying out of Christ's will and the manifestation of the victorious power of the Holy Spirit.

At the following regular prayer-meeting the attendance trebled and the Elders reported that the praying had been in the Spirit. We had not attended, wishing to leave the Elders to lead the congregation back into the prayer experience that had been restored to themselves. Other evidences of God's presence followed. Unconverted people began to attend the meetings and there were conversions. Power, hope and courage began to return and gradually the attendance at the meetings increased.

The ministry of teaching had to be continued for some months more. The enemy endeavoured in different ways to hinder, but his efforts served only to provide opportunities for the church to learn again to resist him through the prayer of faith on the ground of the Cross.

This was a more or less simple case, but it is a sufficiently typical one to serve as an example and illustrate the principles involved. Every case has its own peculiar characteristics and problems.

In the case described, we did not attend all the meetings of the church. The Elders soon came into the place where they could help to assume spiritual responsibility. In some cases, however, the church, or a portion of it, may be in a better spiritual condition than the Elders. It is impossible to give a procedure that will suit all cases, but there is ample light in the New Testament regarding the principles to be applied and the Holy Spirit gives the necessary guidance as to the details.

Different complications may be present. A not uncommon one is when an Elder, possibly one who had much to do with the beginning of the Gospel witness in that place, becomes unspiritual, and carnally seeks to occupy a dominant position. Sometimes such a case does not yield immediately to prayer. In one instance—the most difficult of this kind we ever experienced—we found it necessary to act according to 1 Tim. 5:20, and rebuke an Elder openly before the congregation because he was in sin and would not repent. But he refused to recognize the discipline, imposed by the congregation, continuing to preach and to baptize. He had started the witness in that locality, most of the believers had been converted through his ministry, and the meetings were held in his house.

There was, of course, nothing else we could do in his case except to leave him to God. God dealt with him in faithfulness. In the course of the next few years he lost his business and his home and had to move away from the district. Several years later he asked to be restored to fellowship in the congregation in the town to which he had gone, and thereafter he proved to be a humble and faithful witness to the Lord. The prayer of faith was answered though the answer had to be delayed for a time.

In one case, where a church was in a poor condition spiritually because it was not seeking the Lord's will through prayer, a missionary attended their prayer meeting for a time, encouraging them to find out God's will for everything. That proved sufficient to bring the congregation back into victory.

No matter what difficulties we encounter, the weapons we must use are the same and the spiritual principles that govern our procedure never vary. Our faith must not waver, we must never compromise and we must never lay the hand of flesh upon the work but meet Satan always through prayer and the Word of God.

Dangers to be Faced

It is well to have in mind the dangers that face us in the work of revisiting churches that are in need of our ministry. The reasons for failure may be summarized as follows:

1. We have found that the chief cause of failure is lack of faith. The temptation is to be swayed by our human judgment and by the difficulties that are always so evident. We find reasons for saying that 'this individual is impossible and we cannot expect God to be able to have full victory in him', or 'that situation is exceptionally hard and it will take a long time to accomplish anything there', or, 'these difficulties are unusually great and it will not be possible to follow New Testament methods strictly in this case'. The fact is that we have authority to claim the fulfilment of God's Word and God is waiting to fulfil it if we have faith to believe. We will get what we have faith to claim, nothing less and nothing more (Jas. 1:7).

2. Another subtle danger is the readiness of the human mind and heart to compromise. Apparently good reasons are never wanting for accepting 'temporarily' something that is not wholly according to God's Word or will. The moment we accept such a situation we are defeated. We will often have to wait patiently until God puts right things that are wrong, but we must never compromise by accepting them, even temporarily. An Elder who in his walk or service it not all that he ought to be; a member who is carnal, disorderly or in sin; practices and methods that are not in true accord with the spiritual order for the Church— any such thing in a congregation is a breach in the wall through which the enemy will continue to introduce his forces until he has brought that church into defeat.

3. A not infrequent cause of failure is the temptation to take things into our own hands to bring to pass in our own way, or by force, what we know or think to be God's will, instead of going forward step by step under the guidance of the Holy Spirit, giving Him place and time to accomplish the work in His way and by His power. When faced with a situation which requires the putting

right of something that is wrong, the Evangelist needs to be watchful unto prayer regarding himself. He may be tempted to act in his own strength, brusquely or precipitately, to put matters right. Patience and faithfulness, love and firmness, will always blend in the work of the Spirit of Christ, and we must be ever on the alert that we take not the work out of the Spirit's hands. The flesh is harsh, hard and legalistic. The Spirit of the Lord is humble, gentle, patient, forgiving, loving.

New Testament Examples

In the record of the work of Paul and his companions we have many examples of this ministry that are varied in detail and rich in instruction. The typical example is that of the church in Corinth. The Holy Spirit has given us in great detail the history of Paul's intervention in that case. Its lessons are intended particularly for the guidance of Evangelists engaged in such ministry. Paul's two letters to the Corinthians are full of vital matter concerning the missionary and the Church and should be studied prayerfully and thoroughly.

His other letters to the churches, John's letter regarding Diotrephes and Peter's counsel to Elders, also throw much light on the subject. The danger caused by teachers of false doctrine as well as other difficulties made it necessary for Paul and his companions to revisit many churches. These servants of God exercised an unceasing vigilance over the churches and were always faithful to go to their aid when their presence was needed.

The messages which were revealed by the Lord to John and given by 'angels', or messengers, to the seven churches in the province of Asia are a rich mine of information and instruction. Their prophetic importance has overshadowed their great value in other respects. They reveal the conditions prevailing in seven different, typical congregations and the manner in which these conditions were dealt with, and the missionary, in his work of revisiting churches today, has much to learn from them.

The following outline of these messages is by no means exhaustive but will serve to indicate their importance in this respect.

Ephesus — Commended:
1. For their work and patient bearing of trial and suffering.
2. For testing and rejecting teachers of false doctrine who claimed to be missionaries.

3. For hating Nicolaitanism (priestly assumption).
Condemned for having lost their first love.

Warned—'Repent at once and act as you did at first, or else
I will surely come and remove your lampstand out of its place—
unless you repent (Weymouth). The way they were taking
would lead finally to the complete extinguishing of their testimony.

Smyrna — To this church there are only words of commendation
and encouragement. They were poor people, true to the Word
and giving a faithful testimony. They are counselled to continue
steadfast in the trials that await them.

Pergamos — Commended for a faithful witness in a wicked and
worldly city and amidst persecution.
Condemned because the doctrines of Baalam and of the Nico-
laitanes (compromise with the world and priestly assumption)
were tolerated among them.
The message is sent from 'Him who has the sharp, two-edged
sword' (the Word of God which divides between the soul, or
the natural, fleshly man, and the Spirit. Heb. 4:12). If they
do. not repent, He says, 'I will come to you quickly and will
make war against them with the sword which is in my mouth'
(the Word of God). (Weymouth).

Thyatira — Commended for love, faith, service, patient-endurance
and increasing ministry.
Condemned for tolerating a false woman preacher whose
teaching led to compromise with the world.

Sardis — There was nothing in this church's witness that could
be commended.
Condemned because, while there was a certain appearance of
life, the church was in reality spiritually dead. They are counselled to strengthen the things that remain and rouse themselves
from sleep.

Philadelphia — This church had only a little power but it had
been faithful to guard God's Word in spite of suffering. They
are counselled to hold fast that which they have lest they lose
their crown of victory. They were on the road to complete
defeat.

Laodicea — Condemned for being lukewarm. For that reason the Lord would vomit them out of His mouth. They were entirely self-satisfied, trusting in their own possessions and powers and blind to their true state. Such was their condition that the Lord no longer met with them. He stood outside the door seeking to be admitted and offering pure gold to those who would pay the price for it—the price of the fire of testing that would burn away the dross—and the feasting of communion with Himself to those who would repent and open unto Him.

The New Testament congregations were not exempt from difficulties and dangers. They were not specially protected. Satan did his utmost to bring the infant Church into defeat and ruin. False teachers, false apostles, strife, divisions, carnality—all these beset the newly formed congregations, and the missionaries of that day had to be continually on the alert, waging an incessant warfare against the forces of darkness. We should not expect anything different today.

Let us not think for a moment that the attacks of Satan against a church that would walk in the Spirit are evidence of weakness: they are evidence of life. A living body must battle to live. A formal, modern church may give an appearance of peace and tranquillity. Its peace is the sleep of death. Its tranquillity is false, for beneath the surface calm the ferment of corruption and distintegration proceeds apace.

A congregation, all the members of which are actively exercising their privilege as priests unto God, presents much greater opportunities for Satanic attack than one whose members take no responsibility in ministry and merely gather together to hear their Pastor's sermon. But the price that is paid for this freedom from danger means the sacrifice of the church's true life and power. Church members who remain ever as children, subject, irresponsible and immature, may be easier to lead and to discipline than a company of 'priests unto God'. A community of serfs will be more tractable and freer from the danger of factions and the manifestation of independence than a community of responsible citizens with equal rights and responsibilities. But who would give up the fruit of freedom and responsibility for the false and pernicious tranquillity of serfdom?

Had the Lord desired to do so—had He, in His all-seeing wisdom, judged that it would have made His Church stronger, more secure, more efficient, more glorious, more truly His Body and the instrument of His Spirit—He could have divided it into clergy and laity, placing the spiritual authority and the responsibility for the ministry of the Word in the hands of a specially prepared priestly class. But He did not do so. We know that He did not fail to foresee the dangers to which the structure which He gave the Church was open. But He gave it that which was best for it—that which would enable it to grow, to be strong and to triumph.

When the Apostles encountered the problems and difficulties that immediately arose in the Early Church, they did not think of changing its order; nor did the Holy Spirit lead them to do so. No, they met the difficulties undismayed with the weapons of the Spirit, and they triumphed; and the Church triumphed and witnessed and grew and was mighty in the Spirit.

Let us not be discouraged by the problems and difficulties that will assuredly arise. We must view them in their true light and meet them with the invincible spiritual weapons of our warfare. The ministry of the Evangelist is a glorious one. He wages a continual warfare. He finds no respite, but he need never see defeat. He strives against a powerful and a subtle foe, but his Captain is mightier and wiser still. He is endued with strength that is invincible and his victories are the victories of the Lord, rich in eternal spoil.

CHAPTER XLII

THE TRAINING OF THE WORKER

The method of teaching which our Lord employed in the training of the disciples and which was used by the Holy Spirit in the preparation of the missionary in the Early Church has already been considered. Christ demonstrated to us the perfect method of teaching As W. A. Squires rightly says:

> Jesus has been called the incomparable teacher of all the Ages. That He is such is evident to an informed and candid mind. The presentation of evidence concerning the matchless power of Jesus as teacher is hardly necessary to convince... that He is the greatest teacher the world has ever known. Many truths which we passively accept, however, are not dynamic in our lives. There are many truths which we accept and at the same time fail to comprehend.
>
> If Jesus is indeed the perfect teacher of religion, the Master workman in the most sublime task ever entrusted to man, the fact has tremendous significance... for every Christian. It is to the whole body of His followers that Jesus says: "Go and make disciples of all nations, teaching them to observe all things whatsoever I have commanded you."
>
> Christians have long believed in the faultless personality of Jesus. They have likewise insisted upon the faultless character of His teachings. If He was perfect in personality, and if He taught a perfect system of truth, it is only logical to assume that He was perfect in the method of teaching which He employed.[1]

Christ's method, as we have already seen, was to teach the theoretical through the practical. He took the disciples out to the work and used their experiences in the work to reveal to them the spiritual principles that must govern their procedure. He made clinical experience the basis of His teaching. Besides this, He insisted that they leave all and, possessing nothing, follow Him in a walk of faith. They lived together, worked together and trusted God together for the supply of every need.

---

[1] *The Pedagogy of Jesus in the Twilight of Today*, Ch. 2.

In the preparation of those who are to engage in the work of the Gospel we should seek to have clearly in mind the governing principles that are laid down in God's Word. Both the method of teaching that should be employed and the objectives to be attained are clearly indicated. There are two fundamental factors that must first be taken into consideration:

1. The basic equipment for all types of spiritual ministry is the same: it is the call of God and the possession of the corresponding gifts of the Spirit. And this equipment is available to all members of the Church.

2. 'Every member of the Church is called of God to a definite, spiritual witness—a ministry. There can be no dividing of believers into those who are called to ministry and those who are not: into 'ministers' and 'ordinary members', 'clergy' and 'laymen'. The modern Church system does this; the New Testament Church does not. All are 'priests' unto God.

This then is the foundation upon which we have to build, and let us see to it that our building is set squarely upon it. If those who are to be instructed do not possess the basic equipment, we teach in vain. If those who are called to ministry fail to recognize the importance of relying upon this equipment, their work will lack power and fruit.

However, the call of God and the possession of the necessary gifts of the Spirit are not sufficient to produce an efficient worker. To become efficient in the exercise of the gifts of the Spirit four things are necessary:

1. A thorough knowledge of God's Word.
2. Personal spiritual experience.
3. Practical experience in the exercise of the gifts.
4. Above all, a faithful walk in the Spirit, because if the Spirit is 'grieved' or 'quenched' no amount of knowledge or experience will give spiritual power

Paul wrote to Timothy:

Make thyself a pattern to the faithful, in word, in life, in purity... Apply thyself to public reading, exhortation, and teaching. Neglect not the gift that is in thee... Let these things be thy care; give thyself wholly to them; that thy improvement (or, as Weymouth translates it, 'your growing proficiency') may be manifest to all men (1 Tim. 4:12-15, Conybeare.)

31

As there is increase in knowledge and experience through the faithful exercise of the gifts of the Spirit there should be a 'growing proficiency' in ministry.

In the New Testament Church there are many different ministries. There are preachers and teachers of different kinds, some ministering to believers, others to unbelievers, some working among children and young people, others among adults. There are those with the gifts for personal work and visitation work. Some are called to be Elders and Deacons, others to go forth as Evangelists to found new churches. All require specialized knowledge and experience that will be obtained in actual ministry. For this the New Testament congregation provided an adequate field. It was the natural and ideal training ground for ministry.

The Church Planter's Preparation

There is one ministry, however, that requires an experience wider than that offered by one congregation: it is that of the Evangelist, or missionary, or church-planter. He must have experience in the planting of new churches.

We have already considered the manner in which the New Testament church-planters were called and prepared. It has been seen that the basis of the practical preparation of Paul, Barnabas, Timothy, Titus, Silas and the others was laid in the local congregation. They had years of experience in active, responsible ministry in the local congregation first of all. There, under normal conditions of service, they learned to minister with the gifts of the Spirit, to pray and to seek the guidance of the Spirit. Taking their place in the functioning church, they became acquainted with its structure, difficulties, problems and dangers, and learned how to deal with them. Ministering the Word to saved and unsaved, they became familiar with men and with the way to reach men. Through it all they were learning, not just doctrine, but spiritual truth in operation; it was all workable, applicable to the facts of real life and capable of accomplishing what was claimed for it. Then, when that preparation was complete and their call to the ministry of Evangelist was made clear, they went forth in company with experienced Evangelists and so gained the further practical knowledge that they required.

The equipment required by the missionary may be summarized as follows:

(1) A thorough knowledge of God's Word.

2) Experience in the ministry of the Word both to unbelievers and believers. This must be more than elementary. He needs to know how to care for and teach new believers.

(3) A thorough, practical acquaintance with the organization, spiritual equipment, procedure, ministry and problems of the local congregation. He must have the knowledge necessary to be able to establish fully functioning new churches, and to instruct and advise the Elders and Deacons of these churches.

(4) Personal experience of prayer "in the Spirit'.

(5) Personal experience of being guided by the Holy Spirit.

(6) Faith to go forth trusting God directly for the supply of every need, both temporal and spiritual.

(7) He must be fully equipped with a personal experience of the walk in the Spirit, victory over the flesh, conflict with the power of Satan and triumph by faith, so that his own life will provide a complete and practical example to the converts and churches of the spiritual truths which he teaches.

Defects of the Modern Method

Having noted the principles and objectives of our task, we may consider the problems of its accomplishment under the conditions that face us today. One great difficulty that confronts us, which did not exist in New Testament times, is the fact that the Church as a whole has departed from the New Testament pattern and does not now provide an adequate field for the practical training of the worker. Nor do modern theological or Bible schools adequately provide this training.

The history of theological schools begins about the middle of the second century. Philosopher-theologians of the Early Church, such as Clement and Origin, believing that they had reconciled Christianity and philosophy, established schools, first at Alexandria and later at Caesarea and other places, to teach their systems to the youth of that day. Students from these schools carried this teaching throughout the Church and paved the way for the great departure from the doctrinal and structural foundation laid by the Apostles that was to take place in the next two centuries.

The original purpose of seminaries and Bible Schools was, in most cases, the teaching of sound doctrine and practice. However, in the modern theological school also there has always been the tendency, seemingly irresistible to the natural mind, to bring the

natural intelligence to bear upon revealed spiritual truth, inter-
preting it according to human standards and the fashions of
thought of the day, and reducing it to what is considered reasonable: turning it, in fact, into an acceptable religious philosophical
system.

These facts, to which both history and present day experience
bear witness, should be given careful consideration. At all costs we
must avoid that which has led to such spiritual loss. No matter
how worth while the immediate benefits that are offered may
seem to be, the ultimate cost is too great.

There are other factors that also need to be taken into consideration. From a practical standpoint the training given has not
always produced satisfactory results. Those who have had experience in giving the usual type of training in seminaries or Bible
Colleges on the foreign mission field have, perhaps, been most
conscious of the deficiencies of the method. That many of the
students, on graduation, are not satisfactorily prepared, either in
spiritual experience or in the knowledge of their task, is admitted
by many. Indeed, it is one of the greatest of missionary problems.
They have little knowledge of men. They have scarcely even learned to know themselves. Their knowledge of the practical problems
to be faced in evangelism and in the Church is far from adequate.
They are not sufficiently experienced and mature spiritually. Often
the graduate has become proud, considering himself superior to his
own people, and ambitious, not to evangelize new fields, but to
settle down in a comfortable pastorate with an assured income.
In far too many cases, when sent out to the work they become
discouraged and fail, or, at best, render mediocre service.

Many a missionary and pastor also, when launched into his
ministry, has been keenly conscious of a serious lack in his preparation. Those sent out from our modern schools are by no
means fully prepared for their task. They may have studied God's
Word, but both personal spiritual experience and practical knowledge are insufficient. Their outlook on their calling may be mistaken and unscriptural. They may think of it rather as a profession,
a career, than a ministry in the New Testament sense, and their
hope may be to succeed in it by their ability as preachers, teachers
and organizers and to win recognition and a good church and
income.

All this reveals defects that are serious and that were avoided
by the New Testament method. We feel that the whole problem of

the training of the worker needs to be carefully reconsidered in the light of New Testament practice that we may return to the method which God purposed and reap in full the fruit He intended that our teaching ministry should bear.

We have mentioned some of the deficiencies of our modern method. It is only right, at the same time, to pay tribute to that which has been and is being accomplished by not a few schools. In many respects, God's blessing is upon their work. In some of them the spiritual standard is high and the teaching given excellent. They are making the study of God's Word available to thousands of young people who otherwise would not be able to obtain it.

Teaching is one of the fundamental ministries in the Church, and of primary importance. It certainly is God's will that those with the gift of the Spirit for teaching should exercise their ministry, and there can be no question that it is right and profitable for God's people to gather together for a period, long or short, for uninterrupted and consecutive study of God's Word. We have already seen that a thorough knowledge of the Bible is necessary to all who minister the Word in any way. Therefore, when a Bible School offers a ministry of teaching its position is sound scripturally.

It is in God's order that a ministry of teaching be offered. Where then is the weakness of our modern schools to be found? It seems to us that it is due to four principal reasons:

1. The teaching we give may not be adequate. We may give thorough courses on doctrine and on the general contents of the Bible, but only a brief sketch of such vital subjects as New Testament Church order, the gifts of the Spirit, faith, prayer and the guidance of the Holy Spirit.

2. The claims which we make for our teaching ministry may be too great. To consider that a course of Bible study, however extensive, is an adequate preparation for ministry is a serious error. The teaching ministry provides an essential part of the preparation of the worker, but equally important are personal spiritual equipment and practical experience. This was definitely recognized by our Lord in the method He employed in the preparation of His disciples.

3. We separate the student from normal contact with the Church's life and work and with the world, depriving him thus of essential practical knowledge and experience. The result is that the knowledge he acquires is largely theoretical. The local church

was the training ground of the New Testament worker.

4.   We fail to attach sufficient importance to growth in personal spiritual experience and to see that provision is made for it. Through being separated to a great extent from the Church's life and from the world the student is removed from the best position for acquiring personal spiritual experience. It is vitally important that he come to know the practical use of faith and prayer both in personal and in corporate ministry, learning how problems should be prayed through, how the guidance of the Spirit is sought and the victory over Satan's work obtained. Actually, the student is taught to consider such prayer and guidance as glorious spiritual truths that have little practical application. They see the School largely run without them. Our Lord not only taught the theory of prayer, faith and the guidance and power of the Spirit to His disciples, He led them into the practice of these truths.

Experience Essential

What is the true objective of the ministry of teaching? It will be accepted that the mere imparting of knowledge is not the objective. If that only is accomplished the purpose has not been attained. The objective can be nothing less than the full manifestation of the life of Christ in the inner man resulting in spiritual fruit borne to His glory. Christianity is life primarily. Knowledge is important, but no matter how great it may be, unless it mean life it is dead. It was life that Christ sought and obtained in the teaching of the disciples and what the Holy Spirit sought and obtained in the preparation of Paul and his fellow-workers. God has never considered knowledge a sufficient preparation for His servants; He always demanded proof of the presence of life.

The objective, therefore, is knowledge translated into experience and fruit. To obtain this, teaching and practice must go together. That is why practical experience was the basis of the preparation of the disciples and of Paul and his companions. Along with the practical experience was given the teaching. The theory was applied, and, to a great extent, it was learned through the application.

The benefits that result from the fellowship and discipline of a well-conducted, residential Bible School must be acknowledged. Such a school provides convenient conditions for study and fellowship. If the objective is just teaching, then these conditions may be adequate. But if the purpose is to give a complete training for ministry, there are serious drawbacks. Our Lord's objective in the teaching of the disciples was not simply to give an opportunity for uninterrupted Bible study but to train for active ministry. To accomplish this He did not use the institutional method. He did place the disciples where they had to learn to live together and work together, but it was in a practical school, living and working under the actual conditions of active service. His purpose was not to train them to live and work together as a community of students, but to fellowship together in ministry and to go forth with one or two companions, or alone if necessary, and to be able to stand alone and to depend upon God directly in every circumstance. To do this He had them join Him in His ministry and in a life of faith. When they went forth alone they were not plunged from the fellowship and protection of a school into the problems, dangers, privations and hardness of the ministry to which they were called.

The cloister method takes the student apart from the practical world of men and facts. It does not develop initiative or teach men to endure hardness and to serve at the battle front at grips with sin, indifference and Satanic opposition. It does not develop the character necessary to men of spiritual action. The effect of a long period of cloister life is not good. We have had occasion to observe it in teaching ex-Roman Catholic priests who had spent many years in monasteries. It tends to unfit men for meeting the conditions of normal life. It leaves certain sides of the character undeveloped and, while it may make students, it is apt to create dependence, a desire for ease and a detached, self-centred outlook.

Our Lord trained His disciples in a hard school. They trod with Him the dusty roads and shared His life of self-abnegation and toil. Paul and his fellow-Evangelists were prepared by the same method. That training produced the men required for the work of evangelism—men strong in practical faith, willing to have not where to lay their heads and to go to the ends of the earth alone with their Lord, to endure want, danger, persecution, despisal and death that souls might be saved and the Church planted throughout the world; men of deep spiritual knowledge and wide experience, who knew men; not soft men, fearful of hardship, disdainful of poverty and desiring comfort and security; not untried and inexperienced men who had yet to learn how the work was done and who would be likely to flounder and perhaps fail when sent forth to the work.

Let us remember that only Calvary experience can prepare for a Calvary ministry. Only men willing for a Calvary experience will be truly willing for a Calvary ministry. Such men are as greatly needed today as they were in the Early Church.

To separate those who are to be trained for ministry from normal church life and activity and from the conditions in which their ministry is to be carried on is a serious mistake. One preparing for the ministry of evangelism and church planting needs the church and the evangelistic field just as the medical student needs the Hospital and the clinic. To send out a young man to practise medicine who had little more than theoretical knowledge, who had little practical experience and never even seen a major operation performed, would not be justifiable. It would be hard on both the young physician and his patients!

We would not suggest that there should be fewer centres where a ministry of Bible teaching is offered. But we do feel that adequate training for ministry should be made available. And it should be made very clear to those who take a course of Bible study that, essential as it is, it is far from being a complete preparation for ministry.

Need it be said that we shall not accomplish our purpose by raising scholastic standards, and introducing cap and gown, degrees and titles. These things are of value in their own sphere but the spiritual realm is not their sphere; they are not equipment for ministry; they cannot confer spiritual power or bear spiritual fruit. Our Lord did not use them to accomplish His purpose and neither should we.

To Provide the Equipment

The problem that faces us is how to unite at the present day all the conditions necessary to provide a complete preparation. The manner in which we, in our own work, have sought to solve this problem may be helpful. Certainly, we have been obtaining very much more satisfactory results than when we had a Bible College run on conventional lines.

We have felt that what is required is, in the first place, a teaching ministry, as thorough and comprehensive as that of a Bible College, fitted into the setting of a congregation fully functioning in strict accord with the New Testament order so as to provide an adequate and normal field in which to acquire the necessary experience. Then, in the second place, those called to be church-planters should be given the opportunity to gain the additional experience they need in the actual ministry of establishing new congregations.

The congregation that has served as the background for our teaching ministry has been described in Chapter XX. Those who are studying, fellowship with this church, taking a normal, active part in its life and ministry. They are not given a privileged position, but are on the same footing as any other members. They take part in the various activities of the church, not because they are students, but because they are members of the Church and have gifts of the Holy Spirit. They are not considered as students but simply as members of the Church called to different ministries, who are studying the Word as all members should. To treat them otherwise would interfere with the Holy Spirit's direction of the church. It would teach the students that this can be done if considered necessary—that, if we judge it convenient, we can ignore God's order and introduce modifications, and that, actually, while obedience to the divinely given pattern must be absolute in theory, it need be only relative in practice. Thus, at the very outset, we would have sown the old weed of fleshly wisdom that soon would have taken control of the whole field and choked the true spiritual growth.

The Bible study classes are held as a normal part of the congregation's ministry. We do not speak of a Bible College, but simply of classes for the study of the Bible. The whole congregation is urged to attend. They are taught that every member is called of God to participate in the ministry of the congregation in one way or another, according to the gifts of the Spirit possessed, and that, for that reason, all, without exception, need a thorough knowledge of God's Word.

It is not considered that the object of the studies is primarily to prepare Evangelists, but to provide the knowledge of the Word necessary for whatever ministry any one may be called to, whether it be that of preacher, teacher, Deacon, Elder, Evangelist or any other.

When young people desire to study God's Word to prepare themselves better for His service, who live where such a teaching ministry it not available, and where, perhaps, there is no such church in whose ministry they could participate, we encourage them to come to us. We receive no one on the understanding that we will train him to be an Evangelist. If a young man tells us he is called to that ministry, we say to him: "That may be so; if it is, God will give confirmation concerning it. Paul had been called several years before he went forth, but when the time came in God's purpose for him to go, the Holy Spirit confirmed his call to the church where he was ministering. So you tell the Elders of the church what you believe God's call to you is, and the church will keep looking to the Lord about it in prayer. If He has called you to be an Evangelist, He will confirm it to the church when it is His time to do so. Meanwhile, minister in whatever way He enables you, study His Word, and become thoroughly acquainted with the order and functioning of the local congregation so that you will be ready for whatever He shows to be His will."

That puts him into the right relation to the Holy Spirit and to the church and gives him the true spiritual and scriptural attitude towards his study and ministry.

We make it clear to all that we cannot prepare them for any ministry. We explain to them that God places each one in his place in the church, that the Holy Spirit gives the gifts necessary for that ministry, and that all we can do is to help them, through our ministry, to obtain the experience and knowledge they need.

The Bible study and the practical experience obtainable in the congregation provide a sufficient preparation for all ministries except that of the missionary. However, as we have already seen, the future missionary must first study the Word and acquire the intimate practical knowledge of the structure and work of the local church that constitutes the basis of his preparation.

We therefore work on the principle that, at the beginning, all, without exception, need the same preparation. As the studies proceed, we, together with the students, seek to know to what ministry each one is called. The call will be evidenced by the possession of the corresponding gifts of the Spirit, a definite assurance as to the call on the part of the individual, and the confirmation regarding it given to the congregation. We feel we should not be hurried in deciding regarding anyone's call. First appearances may be deceptive, either for or against.

For whatever ministry a student is called, the necessary gifts of the Spirit will, sooner or later, manifest themselves, and there should be full freedom for exercising them as soon as they appear. Just as the preacher or the personal worker will be led by the Spirit into the experience required, so will the future missionary.

Some Examples

When there is clear confirmation that a young man in called to the ministry of church planting, we take him into our company as Paul did Timothy. The best way to illustrate our procedure is, perhaps, to give one or two typical examples.

1. A young business man began to attend the Bible study classes soon after his conversion and baptism. After several years, he told us that he believed God had called him to join our group of missionaries. We advised him to tell the Elders of the church about it, which he did. He had been taking an active part in the work of the congregation, speaking at indoor and open-air meetings, etc.

After the church had prayed about the matter for some time, they told him that what they felt in prayer was that he possibly was called but that there was no assurance that it was God's time yet. He continued looking to the Lord and waiting. Meanwhile, we could see spiritual development and increasing evidence of the gifts of the Spirit necessary for the ministry of Evangelist. He was led to take part in ministering to some new groups of converts in nearby towns, which gave him wider experience. About a year later the church was able to say that the Lord had confirmed to them in prayer his call to the ministry of Evangelist. We, the company of missionaries, also were assured that his call was of God. So, after the laying on of hands by Elders and Evangelists he "went forth, sent by the Holy Spirit."

2. A young man was sent to us for preparation. It was believed by the Mission that sent him that he was called to be a church-planter, and this conviction proved to be true. He was an educated man, but only a young convert with little knowledge of the Bible, insufficient spiritual experience and but a vague understanding of the structure and ministry of the congregation. Therefore, he settled down to study and to participate in the ministry of the congregation. He came looking to the Lord in faith for the supply of his needs, so he was able to devote most of his time to study and ministry. He took care of most of his own cooking, washing, etc., a thing he had not been accustomed to do.

From the first he showed the gifts needed by the missionary. They were undeveloped, of course, but he steadily gained proficiency. After a time, when we were convinced of his call, we had him cooperate with us in our missionary activities. A congregation got into spiritual difficulties and it was necessary for us to visit it and minister to it for several months. He took part with us in this ministry, saw how the Elders came back to a true prayer ministry, which brought the congregation again to the place of prayer and power, and he helped in the ministry of teaching. We prayed matters through together and sought God's will together.

A new group of believers was being gathered together at another point. He accompanied us in this work, facing with us all the problems of dealing with the new converts. Later, another congregation needed the ministry of a missionary for a time because of difficulties that had arisen. He went alone to minister to them. The Lord used him and he had a rich and profitable experience although he had to face unexpected problems of a serious nature. From that experience he returned for a further period of Bible study. Then, finally, he made an extended journey, visiting several churches, each with a different problem. On his return he remained with us just long enough to review the lessons learned on his journey and then went forth to join in ministry with those who had sent him to us.

Frequently he attended special classes, additional to the regular Bible studies, in which we considered the experiences he and others were having in such work and sought to make clear the Scriptural procedure and the spiritual principles involved. All his travelling, which covered many hundreds of miles, was done in faith. When he set out he usually had little more than sufficient to take him to his first stopping-place. And he found that the Lord never failed to supply his needs.

3. A young woman came from another congregation to take advantage of the teaching ministry. She was called to devote herself to preaching and teaching, especially in the homes of the people and among women and children. She obtained half-day employment and followed the whole course of study. She took part in the soul-winning activities of the congregation, in visitation work, Sunday School and women's work. She also accompanied experienced lady workers in carrying on such work where a new company of believers was being established. Then she was called upon to undertake alone the leading of a group of women believers to the place where they would take full responsibility for their own meetings, doing all the preaching, teaching and dealing with souls themselves. She stayed in a home where she had to face a trying situation which taught her many lessons.

There have been disappointments. A married couple came with

great enthusiasm that, within but a few months, proved to be more emotional than spiritual. Their hearts sought position, financial security and material comfort. When they realized the cost of following in the footsteps of the Lord in His service, they were offended and withdrew. We were sorry that they failed to get through to victory but glad that their weakness was discovered.

A young man came saying he was called of God. He was so unsatisfactory during the first year that we told him that unless there was a definite change he could not return. He wrote stating his desire to return. The congregation made it a matter of prayer for several weeks and finally all who met for prayer felt it was God's will for him to return. And so it proved, for he became a truly spiritual man.

Our Lord had His disciples with Him three years. All the New Testament Evangelists had several years of practical training before being sent forth by the Spirit. On the ground of this example, and also in view of our own experience in the matter, we consider that the period of preparation should not be less than three years. However, we do not feel that we can definitely set time limits. No one can be considered ready to go forth until the Holy Spirit confirms it to all, and when He does confirm it, no one may impose delay.

Some of those who come to study look to the Lord in faith for the supply of their material needs and give all their time to ministry and study. If they are called to be Evangelists, we feel that the experience of living by faith contributes much to their preparation.

Others take half-day employment. Still others can only give the evenings to study and ministry. We have some day classes, but as far as possible the studies are given in the evening for the convenience of those who are working for their living.

We have arranged the studies so that a comprehensive course can be covered in three years. The subjects studied are, Doctrine, Synthetic Study of the Bible, the Purposes of God as Revealed in the Old and New Testaments, Church History, the Organization and Ministry of the Church, False Cults, Personal Work, Homiletics, the Child and the Sunday School, a detailed study of certain books of the Bible, New Testament Greek, etc. No diploma is given. A young man may say he studied with us but not that we prepared him for ministry. If the church receives the confirmation that his call is of the Lord, that is his authority; otherwise he has none.

Spiritual Experience

There are regular prayer gatherings in connection with the studies. A few minutes are given first for the stating of any special matters for prayer. Then all take part in prayer as they may be led. After prayer, the question is asked as to what guidance may have been received while praying—what answer it is felt the Lord has given to the questions asked of Him or the petitions made, or what was the burden of prayer that He gave. Each one is free to state what he felt was the Lord's word to him. Their practical work is not assigned to them. Each one has to seek the Lord's will about it and then get confirmation from the others in the prayer meeting. Then together they take the problems of their work to the Lord. Every detail of the work and plans is dealt with in prayer in this way and no decision is made or anything done until all feel that, while praying, there is no sense of a check about it but liberty to go ahead. In this way further experience is gained in united, Spirit-guided prayer. They learn the value of seeking confirmation from others regarding God's will and of cooperating together in prayer ministry. Of course, those who are studying also take part in the prayer meeting of the church, which is conducted in the same manner. Thus the fundamentals of prayer and guidance are learned in actual practice and the essential equipment obtained, without which all ministry is as a ship without power and without a compass.

In the teaching that is given, emphasis is placed upon the equipment of personal spiritual experience needed for true spiritual service. By prayer, as well as by teaching, it is sought to bring each one to the place of full consecration and intimate communion with Christ in the fellowship of His sufferings and in the victory of His Cross, that they may know the power of His presence, be truly filled with the Spirit and "in all things approve themselves as the ministers of God." What we seek to keep before ourselves as our main objective is the laying of a true and complete foundation of spiritual experience and knowledge of God's Word in each one. We know that unless a student enters personally into the place of spiritual power his ministry will not be in the power of the Spirit and the fruit which he bears will be like unto himself.

Our Lord's principal objective in the training of His disciples was to bring them to the place where they had denied self and taken up the Cross. By patient teaching and by prayer He sought this continually, dealing with each disciple individually to lead him to true faith and surrender; and He did not commission them finally until He had brought them to that place. Had He not done so they would not have been the faithful ministers of the Gospel, entirely yielded to the Spirit, that they were afterwards. All their knowledge of Scripture and of procedure would have been sterile spiritually without it.

This must be our main objective and our first care today in the teaching of those who are to be planters of churches. The most accomplished student, the most able speaker, will be poor and weak indeed without it; but with it, ordinary men, as were the Lord's disciples, are mighty with true wisdom and power. Until this objective has been realized in a student, nothing has really been accomplished. It is easier to get other results; this requires travail in the teacher; it did so in our Lord. We must be willing to face the cost of being faithful in our ministry of teaching.

We have now in our missionary company several workers who were trained in this way, and the results are altogether superior to those of the old method. Of course, those who go forth still have much experience to gain, but the foundation has been laid: they know how to be led by the Holy Spirit, how to prevail in prayer, how to minister the Word and how to establish a New Testament congregation. They have not become proud. They do not fear to go in faith depending upon God to supply all their need; they do not desire to settle in a comfortable pastorate, but to push on with the Gospel, founding new churches.

Surely, such results are highly satisfactory. It is not possible to 'turn out' large numbers of formally trained workers in this way, but it was never sought to do so in the Early Church, or by our Lord. Now, as then, what Christ wants for the extension of His Church are those whom He has called and whom the Holy Spirit has trained: those who will say with Paul, "For though I preach the Gospel, I have nothing to glory of: for necessity is laid upon me; yea, woe is unto me, if I preach not the Gospel!" These He will be with in power, working mightily through them, building His Church.

But let us not forget that, as in all activities of the Church, while the method of preparing workers is of great importance, it does not of itself produce spiritual results. The power is not in the method but in the Holy Spirit to whom it gives freedom of action. Behind all our ministry of teaching, there has been an unceasing prayer ministry exercised by the teachers. Each student has been made the object of intercession. We have continued to stand before God in prayer and in faith for each one, that He would bring them into the place of full yieldedness, spiritual understanding and fruitfulness and that there should be the accomplishment of all His purpose in their lives. We have seen great changes effected. Every success has been a victory of answered prayer. The students could not have done without this ministry of intercession and we would not have been faithful to them or to our Lord had we not exercised it on their behalf. It took time, and other things had to be set aside to give time for it, but it is to this ministry of prayer and faith, above all, so far as our efforts are concerned, that we must attribute the results that have been obtained.

CHAPTER XLIII

MISSION ORGANIZATION

The New Testament missionary group, or Mission, was a company
of Evangelists. We have already considered the principles that
governed their fellowship and cooperation together. The organization of the company was simple and practical, giving full place
to the authority and work of the Holy Spirit. The group worked
together under the coordinating leadership of one of their number
whose authority was purely spiritual. They had no 'Home Council'
to direct their work or undertake their support. They did not
even have a 'Home End'.

This was based upon definite spiritual principles. The Evangelist
is called by the Lord to a particular ministry—one of the basic
ministries of the Church—and is given special gifts of the Spirit
for the carrying out of that ministry. No one who has not the call
and spiritual equipment of the Evangelist can do the Evangelist's
work or direct it. It would be contrary to the spiritual order of
the Church for a council of men who are not Evangelists to direct
the work of a group of Evangelists. It would not be spiritually
practicable, because, in the first place, they lack the necessary
call and gifts of the Spirit and, in the second place, they lack the
Evangelist's specialized knowledge and experience. In the third
place being called to other ministries, they are unable to devote to
the task the time that is necessary. It would be just as impracticable spiritually for the Elders of a church to be directed and supported through a distant council composed of men who had not
the call, gifts of the Spirit, experience or knowledge required for
the Eldership, however earnest and Godly these men might be.
Those who are spiritually capable of undertaking the missionary
ministry are spiritually capable of undertaking its administration

under the direction of the Spirit. They have the gifts of the Spirit to do so.

The New Testament Evangelists were not independent workers. They cooperated in a company under a leader and, also, their ministry was always definitely coordinated with that of the local churches and of the Church as a whole. The guidance they received from the Spirit was confirmed by Him to their fellow-workers and to the Church.

The modern Missionary Society is of very recent development. There was nothing comparable to it in the early centuries of the Church. Actually, in the New Testament order, the Church was a missionary society and the missionaries were its leaders. In the modern, organized Church the Missionary Society is merely an adjunct and the missionary an agent.

In the Missionary Society, in most cases, the 'Home Council' or 'Board of Directors' is the controlling body, representing 'the donors'. It sends out the missionaries, undertakes their support and assumes responsibility before 'the public'. In the Denominational Society the members of the Board are elected or appointed according to the procedure of their particular Denomination. The members of a Faith Mission Board are usually appointed, in the first place, by the Founder of the Mission. They are generally chosen for their standing and influence. The Board is not representative and, after it is first formed, is virtually self-perpetuating. The missionaries have no voice in its decisions but are regarded as its agents, employed by it, dependent upon it and responsible to it.

From the standpoint of the principles governing the New Testament order, this puts the missionary in a false position and makes it impossible for him to practise fully these principles. The New Testament missionary was not an agent or employee of a Society. He had no connection with any organization or authority in a 'Homeland'—which would be a foreign land to those among whom he ministered. His ministry was related particularly and unreservedly to the part of the Church that existed, or was brought into existence, there. Any confirmation of guidance required from the Church came from that part, and it was there he found his fellowship.

The New Testament missionary group was not dependent upon a Home Base. In modern missionary strategy a strong Home Base is considered a first essential for world evangelism. New Testament missionary endeavour was based upon entirely different principles.

It was not dependent upon man or organization. The missionaries carried their Home Base with them—the presence of the Lord and the Word of God with its promises and power. And upon that alone they established the churches wherever they went. They were sent by God not by man. Their faith was in God, not in man. They depended upon God, not upon man. Through this practical testimony of faith they were able to establish churches that also depended fully upon God.

The modern missionary, because of his organizational connections with a 'Homeland' always considers himself, and is considered by the 'native' church, as really belonging to another part of the Church, another people. His responsibilities, loyalties and sympathies converge at a point thousands of miles away from his sphere of service and radiate back from there, and those to whom he ministers are conscious of that fact and never feel that he is wholly one with them in their part of the Church. No matter how deep may be his sense of responsibility to them and love for them, he can never be altogether one of them and fully share their lot while he is with them as the New Testament missionary did. This affects his ministry profoundly, producing attitudes and effects, in himself and in the converts, that the New Testament order was calculated to avoid.

The congregations which Paul established did not look upon him, and his companions as belonging to some other congregation or to an organization in some other country. They looked upon them as belonging to the Church as a whole. That meant that these missionaries belonged to them as much as to any other part of the Church, and that they were their missionaries for whom they were responsible just as were any other congregations.

There was no distinction between "The Mission" and "the Church" or the "foreign missionary" and the "native church", Some sought to make a distinction between Jews and Greeks but Paul taught the churches emphatically that there was neither Jew nor Greek in the Church but that all were one in Christ. There could be no national, racial or organizational distinctions either in the Church or in the missionary company. They are contrary to the basic principle of the unity of the Body of Christ. There is neither African nor European, yellow nor white, Anglo-Saxon, Latin nor Asiatic. The failure to recognize this is one of the cardinal errors in modern missionary practice. It introduces the principle of division which bears its inevitable fruit.

The responsibilities and authority which the modern 'Mission Board' assumes are reasonable from the point of view of the principles of human organization, but the spiritual order which God has given is based upon the active, not theoretical, presence of the Holy Spirit, and certain powers and responsibilities pertain exclusively to Him and cannot be assumed by a human organization. The Lord alone must do the sending. The true servant of God must be guided at all times and in all things by the Holy Spirit.[1] He must look directly to God for the supply of every need and he is responsible to Him directly. No human organization may act as intermediary in any of these matters.

There is no doubt as to the answer that would have been given by Paul, Barnabas, Luke, Timothy, or any of the other New Testament missionaries, if those who contributed to their support, or any Council that might claim to represent them, had taken the position that, since they provided the money, they had a right to direct those who used it.

Barnabas did not seek authorization from Jerusalem when he was called to go forth with Paul from Antioch. The confirmation of his call was given to the newly established local church—a congregation of new converts in the mission field.

We can hardly conceive of Paul, Luke and Timothy, having to write back to a 'Mission Board' in Jerusalem to ask permission to follow the leading of the Spirit to go over into Macedonia, or enquiring if any funds could be apportioned for that purpose. It is impossible to imagine such a thing because we realize that it would have been completely contrary to the spiritual principles that governed their ministry. Nor could we think of them having a 'Home Council' to accept and send out new missionaries. That would have thrown into confusion the Holy Spirit's whole plan of action and introduced an entirely foreign element. Undoubtedly, Paul would have had some young men sent to him from Jerusalem who were 'zealous for the law', and the missionary company would have become a mixture of legalists and non-legalists, just as today we find mixtures of all kinds. But no, the New Testament missionary group was truly one spiritually because it was the Holy Spirit who called them, joined them together, guided them and kept them together.[2]

It is considered that the modern system makes it easier for the

---

[1] See comment on Jn. 21:22, p. 51.
[2] See p. 199.

missionary, freeing him from concern regarding material needs. That may be true, but there can be only one outcome to any attempt to make easier the spiritual way in which God has intended that His work should be done. If we remove the need for faith where God in His wisdom has ordained that it should be exercised, faith will be stunted; or it may die. Not only does the one who is truly called of the Spirit suffer under such conditions, his spiritual experience and growth being hindered, but it is made easy for many to go to the foreign field who are not truly called or sent by the Holy Spirit, and whose motives in going are based on sentimental, romantic or humanitarian considerations. In the New Testament order we find that the Holy Spirit did not lead to the creation of organizations that would make it easy for large numbers to go out as missionaries. On the contrary, the way was left bristling with difficulties, and comparatively few were chosen and sent; but those few were instruments specially called and carefully prepared by the Holy Spirit.

It is certain that if the way were not made easy, modernist missionaries would not go to the field, for, as was the case in Paul's day, they would lack the true faith to go looking directly to God for the supply of their needs. On the other hand, those prepared and sent by the Holy Spirit would not fear to go and would be all the stronger for going forth in the New Testament way.[1]

The New Testament order does not necessarily exclude a definite cooperation on the part of individuals or groups of the Lord's people with missionaries who have gone forth. Without contravening the spiritual principles that govern the missionary's ministry, individuals and groups may cooperate in the receiving, receipting for and forwarding of funds and caring for other business details, "providing for honest things, not only in the sight of the Lord but also in the sight of men" (2 Cor. 8:21). Such ministry can be of great assistance to the missionaries. Those who perform it will exercise the gift of the Spirit of 'helps' or 'serviceable ministrations'.[2] They will not exercise any authority over the missionary or direct him in his ministry or undertake his support or in any way stand between him and the Holy Spirit or between him and the Church. But they will fellowship with him closely through prayer, faith and service, not as an Executive Council or Board of Directors but simply as helpers in the work of the Gospel.

---

[1] See pp. 87-93.
[2] See p. 193.

In some cases, it was such service as this that Mission Councils at first had in view, but, being organized as Councils, it was natural that gradually they should assume the responsibilities and prerogatives that generally pertain to Councils. During the last two decades, Faith Missions, recognizing the prevailing lack of power, have tended to seek it in 'more efficient organization', a stronger Home Base and 'better business methods'. Home Councils have become Boards of Directors and new policies have been framed. But the power of the Early Church missionary has not returned.

The reason underlying all the organizational aids that we add is, of course, the sneaking fear that the Holy Spirit will not be able to fulfil His part. A contributory reason is the fact that, because the full spiritual order is not being followed, serious difficulties do exist. However, to seek to overcome these difficulties by departing still further from the Scriptural order will only lead us to still greater difficulties. The true solution is to be found in a complete return to God's order. That will not remove all difficulties for we continue to face a powerful foe, but it will release the power of the Spirit and enable Him to lead us in triumph through all difficulties.

Another reason, undoubtedly, is the general lack of understanding, and, in some cases, the misunderstanding, of the Scriptural principles of Mission organization. To not a few, the mention of the Scriptural order brings up visions of impractical, visionary, 'lone-wolf' missionaries; of uncoordinated and inefficient missionary endeavour. How far must we have departed from God's order for the Scriptural pattern to become so dimmed to our eyes! Surely there was nothing impractical, uncoordinated or inefficient about the work of the New Testament missionaries!

A Fellowship

It may be helpful if we describe the form of fellowship which we believe we have been led of God to adopt. We wish it to be understood clearly, however, that we do not presume to present it as the perfect order. The true pattern is in the New Testament, and we can only say that we have sought to follow the principles of that pattern as far as we have been enabled to see them.

It was not long before we found that the full application of the New Testament principles governing the missionary's ministry was not possible if the organization of the missionary group did not accord with the Scriptural model. It was necessary to have our own house in order if we were to be able to teach the new churches that no compromise should be permitted. We could not ask them to do anything we did not do ourselves. But when we could say that we ourselves were practising all that we were teaching them, then, naturally, we found them much more ready to believe and comply.

What we have sought to do is to follow the principles that governed the fellowship of Paul and his fellow-workers. Their missionary group is the model given to us in the Word, and, as we have seen in previous chapters, it provides a complete example of mission organization as well as of missionary practice. As far as we have understood the principles of that fellowship we have endeavoured to apply them. In the first place, it has given us a close and most satisfying fellowship. There has been a strong sense of spiritual unity produced by the Holy Spirit. The spiritual effect of the testimony upon the churches has also been marked, contributing most effectively to their spiritual upbuilding.

We consider ourselves as a fellowship of Evangelists (in the New Testament sense) brought together by the Holy Spirit for the ministry of planting churches wherever He may lead us to go. We may be called a "Mission" in the sense that we are a group of "persons sent on a mission · an embassy". We are not a Missionary Society—an organization in the 'Homeland' sending and supporting missionaries. The group of missionaries are the Mission.

It will be asked how we deal with the judging and acceptance of a candidate at a distance of whom we have no personal knowledge, since that is not undertaken by a 'Home Board'. First of all, we correspond with him seeking to make clear to him the principles for which our Fellowship stands. After that if he still believes it is God's will that he apply, and if we have liberty in prayer to do so, a set of questions is sent him. He is questioned to discover not only his knowledge of Scripture and his doctrinal beliefs but also what experience he has had in ministry, prayer in the Spirit, guidance by the Spirit, victory over the flesh, and the power of God to provide for material need in answer to prayer alone. We ask for references to whom we may write. These may or may not be helpful. If possible, if the candidate is in one of the 'Homelands', we have him meet any missionaries who may happen to be there at the time, or some of those who represent us and stand with us in prayer and who have an understanding of the spiritual equipment required. If he comes from a local church that knows how to get the mind of the Lord through prayer, we ask him to get confirmation regarding his call from the church, as Barnabas and Paul did in Antioch; however, unfortunately, such churches are few. Finally, the application is considered by a group of older missionaries, each of whom receives a copy of the application papers and makes the case a matter of prayer until he feels he knows God's will in the matter. No candidate is accepted unless all have liberty in prayer to do so.

When accepted—that is, when he, we and the local church with which he has been connected (if that be possible) are assured of his call—the candidate, if he is at a distance, must look to God in faith for the supply of his travelling expenses, letting no man know of his need. When he joins the missionary group on the field it will be necessary for him to study New Testament methods and principles of missionary work if he does not already have a practical knowledge of them.

Under the old system, when 'Boards' accepted and sent out our new missionaries, there was a large percentage of mistakes and failures. Our present method has been in practice now for fourteen years and many new workers have joined us. In some cases we have only had their application papers to guide us, but we have found that the Lord has always been faithful to direct us as we took each case to Him in prayer. By His grace, mistakes on our part have been very few. So far, not one who has come out to us from the 'Homelands' has been a failure. In many cases it has been wonderful to find how the Lord had been so evidently preparing them through the years for the work for which He had chosen them.

When a group of new missionaries came to the field we used to wonder, "How many of these will be still on the field five years from now?" That question has been replaced by the assurance that those who come are called by the Lord and will be enabled and kept faithful by Him. We have not sought to persuade young folk to come to us. Our prayer to the Lord has been that He would join to us all those whom He requires for the doing of the work to which He has called us. At the same time we have continually besought Him to prevent the coming of any who where not called, for their sake and for His work's sake. What can be more satisfying than to see those whom He has called going on to the fulfilment of His gracious purpose in their lives? But what is sadder than to witness the struggle and defeat, the disappointment, and sometimes the disaster, of those who have erred as to God's will? There is no need that there be such.

Our desire is only that the Lord build up a fellowship according to His will, that His purpose be accomplished and His Name alone glorified.

We recognize no distinction between 'foreign' and 'native' workers. No one, no matter of what nationality or race he may be, is received into our missionary fellowship unless there is clear evidence that he is called of God to the ministry of church planting and has ·the gifts of the Spirit necessary. If he has these qualifications he is received unreservedly as one whom God has joined to our fellowship, whether he is white, black or yellow, and no matter what language he speaks. All share together with equal responsibility in all spiritual and financial matters. The group of church-planters is one as Paul and his fellow-workers—a company representing several races and countries—were one.

The Elders of the churches earn their own living. The missionaries do not settle in any place as pastors.

We believe that, according to the example given in the Word, after a sufficient beginning has been made in any region, it should not be necessary to bring increasing numbers of foreign missionaries into it, because there should be an increasing number of workers raised up from among the congregations established.

Following the Scriptural example, our missionary company has a leader. This makes possible the coordination of the whole work. He does not exercise arbitrary authority. No action is taken without the prayer confirmation of his fellow-workers. As we have seen, when Paul and his companions went to Macedonia, he received the vision which revealed God's will, but all had the assurance that it was God's call.

We act upon the principle that God will usually reveal His will first to the one principally concerned but that He will give confirmation of it to the group. If it is a matter that concerns only the missionary and a local church, the confirmation will be given through that church. If it concerns only the company of missionaries, confirmation will be given through them. If it affects both the Church and the missionary group the confirmation will be given to both. When Paul went to Jerusalem against the guidance of the Spirit, both the churches and his fellow-workers were conscious of the lack of confirmation regarding his action and made known the fact.

This is in accord with the basic principle governing guidance in the Church laid down by our Lord. As we have seen in a previous chapter, in all matters concerning the Church, Christ, Who is present in the midst, reveals His will to more than one, and it is to the two or more, so far as Church prayer is concerned, that the promise of an answer is given.

Our missionaries are scattered widely through several countries. Some of them are thousands of miles apart. Therefore it is impossible for all, or even many, to come together to find God's will in prayer. For that reason a small group of older missionaries together with the leader, meet very frequently to seek guidance in all detail matters concerning the Fellowship. No missionary is included in this prayer group unless all his fellow-workers feel that he should be. It is from this prayer group that the leader seeks confirmation in all actions that have to be taken. Of course anything affecting the policy of the Fellowship has to be made a matter of prayer by the whole group.

To illustrate the procedure followed, we will describe what is done in the case of the placing of a new worker. When he arrives on the field he is guided in the study of New Testament methods and the language. He is advised to be looking to the Lord meantime to know where he is called to minister. When he feels he has guidance on the matter, he makes it known to the leader who puts it before the prayer group. These, together with the leader, pray until all feel in prayer that confirmation is either given or withheld. If there are other missionaries in the region to which the new worker feels called, the leader communicates with them. They make it a matter of prayer and no move is made until they also believe it to be God's will. This does not leave much room for mistaken guidance. When we apply the safeguards that God has provided for us, we can be fairly certain of our guidance.

Another group of the Lord's servants, the Dohnavur Fellowship, has been led to apply the same spiritual principles. Miss Amy Carmichael writes:

Committees are usually responsible for the guidance of their missionaries. But, without knowing it or meaning it, we soon passed the place where we could look to any for counsel except the One who was near enough to tell us what to do from hour to hour. It was His word which had caused the work to begin, and only He (we write reverently) knew what we should do. And then, too, we always had the feeling that there was more in each apparently small decision than we could understand. We dared not move in anything without a sure direction. Our friends at home were very kind. Sometimes they inquired through their Secretary on the field what our plans were, and how much bigger we proposed to grow, and what our financial liabilities would be. But we could not tell them, for we ourselves did not know. We could only assure them that those 'financial liabilities' would never be theirs to meet, for that responsibility belonged (again we write with reverence) to our Lord and Master, our Unseen Leader.

So we went on looking to Him to tell us clearly what we were to do. I do not mean by that anything mystical, but something as practical as possible. We did not live in the clouds — we have never lived there: our way is in the dust of the ordinary road. But it is not presumption to count upon a promise being fulfilled. It is not 'sooming' [presuming] to lay hold on such words as these: 'If any of you lack wisdom, let him ask of God, who giveth to all men liberally and upbraideth not; and it shall be given him'. 'What man is he that feareth the Lord, him shall He teach in the way that He shall choose'. 'O Lord, I know that the way of man is not in himself; it is not in man that walketh to direct his steps'. London was too far away to direct our steps, but our Lord Jesus was 'very easy to find', so we came to learn that the greatest aid we could ask from our friends was not advice, but the much more effective help of prayer.[1]

George Müller bears a similar testimony:

I further had a conscientious objection against being led and directed by men in my missionary labours. As a servant of Christ, it appeared to me I ought to be guided by the Spirit, and not by men, as to time and place; and this I would say, with all deference to others, who may be much more taught and much more spiritually minded than myself. A servant of Christ has but one Master.

Again, Miss Carmichal says:

We have found it possible to be directed as a company so that we can move together in a harmony of spirit that is restful and very sure. A company has to wait longer than one or two might have to do, but if all be set on doing their Lord's will and be truly one in loyalty and the New Testament kind of affection that makes each one feel safe with each other one, if all flow together to the goodness of the Lord, unanimity is certain. It is not difficult for our Father to make His children to be of one mind in an house, like the city of His purpose, 'that is at unity in itself' — 'Jerusalem that hath been builded a true city, all joined together in one'. And we have always found that before the ultimate word must be spoken, divergent thoughts have vanished, as by some peaceful magic. The interval is sure to be perplexed by a temptation to the futile fuss of talk. Recognise this for what it is, the influence of the adversary (for hurry of spirit confuses), and before long the same quiet word will come to all. If the inmost law of such a company be holy peace, it must be so.

And of one thing we are certain: if prayer be hindered, and we

---

[1] *Gold Cord*, pp. 177, 178.

go on insensitive (he wist not that the Lord was departed from him) or in cowardice we shrink from whatever it must cost to recover loyal unity, then this Fellowship will perish. For a while, but only for a while, it may continue to seem to be. But to the clear eyes of the spiritual watchers, from that first hour of insincerity it will appear as a vanished thing and its Lord will say of it, 'How is the gold become dim. How is the most fine gold changed.'[1]

At the beginning it was thought that a careful review of the teaching of Scripture regarding missionary procedure and church organization would be sufficient for new workers whose call had been clearly indicated, but it was found that this was a mistake and that a period of thorough practical experience was also essential. Although one may be sincerely desirous of following the Scriptural method it is not easy to divest oneself of the influence of the old methods to which one has been accustomed. It is possible to adopt new designations and forms and yet, to a great extent, still be applying principles that are contrary to the New Testament order. The principles governing the two methods are so entirely different and the difference is so fundamental that even apparently unimportant details of procedure are affected. It is not easy at first to realize to how great an extent this is true. It takes time to discover how much we are guided by the principles of the modern order and how often we transgress the principles of the spiritual order. It is only through actual, practical experience that we can come to realize that ways of doing things to which we have been long accustomed and that we follow without thinking belong not to God's way but to man's.

In financial matters, our practice is to teach the new churches their Scriptural duty regarding giving but never to make any mention of our own material needs except to God in prayer. Gifts for support are accepted from any church to which the missionary is not at the time ministering. As was evidently the practice in the company of disciples and in the missionary group of which Paul was the leader, we consider ourselves responsible one for another in material matters. As a group united by the Holy Spirit in ministry, we cannot escape this responsibility; none can live to himself without equal regard to the other's need. Therefore we pool all support funds and share equally in what the Lord has provided. Out of these funds all debts to the world, such as rents, taxes, etc., are first met. Recognizing that individual missionaries

---

[1] Ibid. pp. 183, 184.

may at times have special needs, special gifts to a missionary, so designated, that are not intended for his regular, personal support, are not pooled.

Much of our support comes from several 'Homelands', therefore, where we have no missionaries resident, we have representatives who receive, receipt for, and forward to the field the funds that are given. They also advise and assist new workers going out in regard to passports and passages. As this service is given voluntarily, actual Home End expenses are very small. No propaganda is carried on for the raising of funds.

No distinction is made in the New Testament between 'Home Lands' and the 'Mission Field'. So, when in his homeland, a missionary considers himself as simply in another part of the field, as Paul did when he returned to his own Province of Cicilia, or Barnabas when in Cyprus, and they minister as the Lord may direct them. For their expenses in travelling, they look to God in faith through prayer alone for special gifts to supply this need. For many years our missionaries have travelled widely and have never lacked for anything.

Hudson Taylor said, "Depend upon it, God's work done in God's way will never lack God's supplies". During many years we have proved that this is so. Sometimes we have desired to do things that God did not provide for. In such cases we have always found later that there was a good reason for the withholding of the supply. Our desire had not been God's will. Occasionally we have received gifts designated for some purpose that never proved to be His will. Those who made the designations were evidently mistaken as to God's will. Other gifts have been sent designated for objects that proved later to be in His will. The donors had been led to act according to His will before it had been revealed to us.

Our only guarantee for today and for tomorrow is God's faithfulness to fulfil His Word, but we do not fear for the future. He Who has been faithful hitherto will certainly not fail us in the days to come. He Who hangeth the earth upon nothing, to Whom belongs the silver and the gold and the cattle upon a thousand hills, can He not give us abundantly all things that we need?

We have been proved very often, but we can testify that, during all the years, He has dealt with us in faithfulness and we have not lacked anything that was according to His will. Paul and his companions also were tested. They knew what it was to lack and their faithfulness under testing not only wrought blessing to them but also to those to whom they ministered. The testings that we have been called upon to bear have brought rich fruit. In our weakness His strength has been made perfect and the testimony it has given to the churches has brought spiritual understanding and strength to them that they could hardly have received otherwise. And if we are called as the Master's witnesses, why should we not willingly, yea gladly, spend and be spent that our witness may be full?

There are many intercessors in the 'Homelands' who pray for us. In not a few places groups of these meet regularly to pray together. As our whole work is based upon prayer, these definitely serve with us in an essential and effective ministry of prayer and faith. Such cooperation is necessary to us and is richly blessed. Our fellowship is with all those who truly love the Lord.

Our missionary fellowship is not held together by rules and regulations. All believe that they have been brought together by the Holy Spirit and accept God's Word as the complete text-book of missionary procedure and church organization and this produces a faithfulness to principle, a loyalty to each other and a fellowship together that the finest human organization could not produce. There is a positive spiritual unity that comes from the fact that all stand for the same principles and seek the unity of the Spirit in all their actions. And all this we have continued to experience during many years in spite of the fact that we are just men and women of flesh and blood, prone to every human weakness and requiring to pray much for each other.

And what of the future? We believe that is in God's hands and that He alone can know what it contains and how to meet it when it comes. Our duty is to walk faithfully according to His Word in the present. When another leader is needed by the company of missionaries, God will reveal His choice to all. In prayer His guidance will be sought and only when that is known to all will the selection be made. If the time ever comes when the group of missionaries is not able to discover His will through prayer and to be led in all things by the Holy Spirit, then the time will have come to cease to serve as a fellowship, for the power will have departed and the light gone out.

CHAPTER XLIV

DANGERS BY THE WAY

Mistaken Methods

The greatest harm to a cause is occasioned usually not by its opponents but by those who claim to be its exponents but who misunderstand and misrepresent its true character. This has been so with New Testament methods of missionary work. Some claiming to be following Paul's method have pictured him as a practically independent worker with no definite plan, moving continually from place to place as he felt the urge of the Spirit, preaching a few times in each place and then leaving the converts uncared for. As we have seen, such a conception of New Testament missionary methods has not the remotest relation to the facts as recorded in the New Testament.

Earnest workers, thinking they were following Paul's methods, have failed to realize the care which he took of the new churches, the years which he spent with not a few of them, the thorough instruction which he gave them and the frequency with which he and his fellow-workers revisited them. They have not understood the spiritual principles that united him in close cooperation with his fellow-workers and with the Church in all matters both of ministry and guidance. In consequence, they have acted independently as they personally thought they were led. They have considered that all they had to do was to gather a few converts together and then leave them. The result of such work is, of course, unsatisfactory. It does not lay solid foundations or establish true New Testament congregations.

Enthusiasm, a realization of the great need that exists and emotional appeals may lead young people with insufficient spiritual preparation and experience to go forth before the Holy Spirit has sent them. We have known well-meaning young workers to distribute tracts through a town, preach the Gospel a number of times, hear one or two people make some sort of profession of conversion, and then consider that the town was evangelized, when, in truth, practically nothing had been accomplished. Actually, the reaction following such a visitation makes that town a harder field than it was before.

Such mistaken methods hinder the spread of the Gospel and bring New Testament methods into disrepute. It behoves us all to seek prayerfully to be guided by the Spirit to a clear understanding of God's order and to be protected from any kind of extravagance, from fleshly zeal and human wisdom, that our ministry be truly according to the Word and in the Spirit.

Paternalism

Our experience has been that, in the planting of a church, the greatest difficulty lies, not in the converts, but in the church-planter. It is not easy for him, be he national or foreign, to keep himself out of the way of the spiritual development of the converts. One of the greatest temptations is to indulge in paternalism, treating the converts as children and not as brethren in Christ. It is natural to enjoy taking a paternalistic attitude, being the central figure and controlling every detail of a congregation's activities. He is loved as the one who has brought the Gospel to them and finds it easy to allow himself to be regarded as a spiritual father, so far advanced in spiritual knowledge and wisdom that no convert could be equally taught and led by the Spirit—and he may come to believe this himself.

A missionary who stood for New Testament Church organization in theory but who had been virtual director of a congregation for many years, said to us, "I tell my people that it will be a long time yet before they will be able to do without the aid of a spiritual brother to lead them"—which meant that it would be a long time before any of them could come to the place where they would have the spiritual understanding he had or be led of the Spirit as he was. It is such missionaries that provoked the statement made at a Missionary Conference in Havana by a Latin American delegate, who said that they did not want the missionary of the type that considers himself as "a fourth member of the Holy Trinity". Missionaries will understand what he meant.

Year in and year out, the Evangelist and his wife superintend every detail of the church's life and work, even to the arranging of the flowers on the pulpit. Nothing can be done until they are consulted. They pay the rent, the lighting and the communion wine, and do nearly all the preaching themselves. All this they do with self-sacrificing zeal, wearing themselves out, it may be, to the detriment of their health.

We have seen such situations continue for many years. The believers were not taught regarding the gifts of the Spirit. They were urged to testify that souls might be won, but nothing more. They knew little of the teaching of Scripture regarding the Church and regarding their privileges and responsibilities as members.

Can we be surprised that such congregations never develop spiritually, that the believers never grow to manhood but remain weak and in need of constant nursing and that no spiritual leadership is developed? The church-planter, without realizing it, or desiring to do so, has stood in the way of the Holy Spirit. He will feel that such a congregation is incapable of managing its own affairs and carrying on the work of witness. He is right. If left alone, they might struggle on for a while but ultimately they would probably go down in defeat; at best they would be weak and fruitless.

Pride of Race

Pride of race, nationalism and lack of adaptability to different customs are serious dangers. Whether manifested in the foreigner or the national, they endanger the unity of the Church. The superiority-complex of the foreign worker in his attitude toward the 'native' believers, due to racial and spiritual pride, may be hard to overcome. He may find it difficult to sacrifice completely his desire to have everything done in the way he has been accustomed to and to give the people the freedom they need to do things in their own way, according to their own customs and taste. When the believers have been in the habit of coming to him for direction in everything and he has been accustomed to have his suggestions and instructions obeyed, it may be hard for him to refrain from directing and giving advice, that they may be thrown upon the Holy Spirit and forced to solve their own problems through prayer and faith. When he has so long seemed indispensable, it may not be easy for him to withdraw and leave the people to work under the guidance of the Spirit, gaining experience and wisdom from the mistakes they will undoubtedly make. As one missionary remarked: "It requires a lot of faith, patience and humility to practise Apostolic missionary methods".

Writing of Mr. D. E. Hoste, late General Director of the China Inland Mission, Bishop F. Houghton says,

> But if Hudson Taylor selected Mr. Hoste as his successor mainly on the ground of his intimate relationship with God, I think he was also influenced by his knowledge that Mr. Hoste had learned the secret of a right relationship with the Chinese. In his early years in China Mr. Hoste had the enriching experience of close friendship with that very remarkable man of God, Pastor Hsi. He learned that a young missionary must be prepared to receive as well as to impart, to respect and defer to his Chinese fellow-worker rather than to look for respect and deference from him! It was not alway easy to live with, or to work with, a man of such vivid and dominating personality as Pastor Hsi. But he and Mr. Hoste loved one another, and the Englishman recognized the fitness of Chinese leadership in a church in China. Moreover (as he himself has told me) he found that some points in Pastor Hsi's character which he was at first inclined to condemn as un-Christian were merely un-British. Doubtless Pastor Hsi made similar discoveries, and, in consequence, similar allowances, concerning Mr. Hoste. (Alas, we are still far from appreciating how much there is in the British or American character which tries the patience of our Chinese friends, and makes some of them despair of the possibility of cooperation!)

A young man with the equivalent of a University education, one who was truly called of the Lord and gifted by the Spirit, said to us sadly as he spoke of the ministry for which he was eagerly preparing, "But the foreign missionaries will never believe that we can be taught of the Spirit as they are. They will always feel themselves superior to us".[1]

A conference of Brazilian Pastors that met in Rio de Janeiro to consider the problems of the evangelization of Brazil, put the following statement on record, referring to certain sections of the country where the work of the Gospel is more advanced:

> Since in every case in which the National Church is capable of handling the situation it can do so better alone and unhampered

---

[1] A C.I.M. Report contains the following, "I sat talking, in the city of Chungking, with a university student, and our conversation turned to the days after the war. 'Do you think there will be a place for us out here then?' I asked. 'Yes, I think so', he replied, 'but on one condition — in the past many of you have come out with a superiority complex, and unless you can come here free from racial prejudice, then you come in vain". — *According to Plan*, p. 21.

by missionary outlandishness, it is clear that this invitation to self-denial on the part of certain missionaries is very strong... In the autonomous National Church, the foreigner has no place as Evangelist or Pastor or overseer (episcopos), save as he can sink his foreignness, which none in Brazil has succeeded in doing.

Here the national manifests the same spirit that he rightly condemns in the foreigner. But in the first place the church-planter had failed to teach effectively, by example and precept, the fact that in the Body of Christ there can be neither national nor racial differences.

Such a charge could never have been brought against Paul and his companions. Although he had been proud of his Jewish heritage (and who is prouder of such things than a Jew?) we find nothing that is Jewish intruding into his outlook or manners. All these things he counted but loss: they had died at the Cross. He was willing to be all things to all men, caring only that he might bring souls to Christ. This is a principle of conduct that our Lord taught us by His own example. He laid aside infinite glory to live as a man, a servant—even as a poor man without a place to lay His head—and He adopted man's speech and customs and obeyed man's laws.

The missionary, when in a foreign land, must do all in his power to divest himself of his foreignness. It is not impossible, by God's grace, if he is willing to do it. In the first place, he should be satisfied with nothing less than the mastery of the language or languages in which he has to work. Then, he should refrain from the use of his own language in the presence of the people. One who is not willing to do so fails to demonstrate the spirit of the Master. The flesh still claims a place. We have known a foreign missionary when leading a meeting to change to English always if he had any comment to make about the music to his wife who was at the organ. In a mixed gathering of national and foreign workers the foreign missionaries would sometimes change to English when speaking to each other. Such conduct is, of course, discourteous and unworthy of an ambassador of Christ. We have only to think of the effect it would have upon us if foreign missionaries conducted themselves in such a manner in our country, showing that they considered their language and customs superior to ours. Would we tolerate it? Would it commend their message to us?

The Home

As far as possible, the foreign missionary should adopt the etiquette and customs of the country in which he is working and have his house arranged in the local style so that visitors may feel no sense of awkwardness or strangeness.

He should be "given to hospitality". A most effective part of his witness will be exercised through his home. But this may be hindered by foreignness in his manners or the way in which his house is furnished. If his manners or the style or arrangement of his furniture are strange to his visitors they will not feel at ease. If he tries to make his house "a little bit of home away from home" the people among whom he lives will not feel at home in it.

In work in the great modern cosmopolitan city of Buenos Aires we found it satisfactory to have our home on the standard of the middle class—a home that would not seem extravagant to the poor nor shoddy to the well-to-do.

In interior regions where the standard of civilization was lower we followed the same principle. While working among a primitive Indian tribe our home was built of adobe brick with thatched roof. The windows had wooden shutters and no glass. It was spacious, cool and comfortable. The furniture was hand made from hand-sawn lumber. All was constructed of materials obtainable in the region, requiring only labour and simple tools. It was something the Indians could copy if they wanted to—and they did, for in two or three years they had a number of houses of similar construction.

Dr. A. J. Kinnear of the Dohnavur Fellowship, South India, mentions in a letter the favourable effect produced by conforming to the customs and dress of the country:

A week or so ago I did a tour of about 150 miles visiting a number of ex-patients and others who are interested. No such tours have been possible throughout the war years owing to great pressure of the work here, and this was an absolute revelation of what God has been doing. I should perhaps explain that we live very largely in Indian style, and that when we are out we always eat Indian food and wear Indian dress, a topee being almost the only distinguishing feature! This gives a very ready access to even the higher caste houses and the more orthodox Hindu homes...

A sad, though often thoughtless, disregard of these primary rules of what is scarcely more than courteous conduct has prejudiced many a missionary's witness and wrought great harm. Such an attitude, be it due to racial pride or mere thoughtlessness, finally reproduces itself in the converts, creating barriers, undermining confidence and giving rise to nationalistic feeling.

Equipment

When our Lord sent the Twelve and, later, the seventy out two by two to preach the Gospel, He not only instructed them to go in faith, trusting God for the supply of material needs, but He also told them to take no equipment with them except what was absolutely essential.

Our Lord was not just giving an arbitrary command. All His teaching and actions were based upon vital principles and manifested perfect wisdom. He Himself was doing what He told His disciples to do.

Today there is a growing tendency for missionaries to take great quantities of equipment of all kinds to the field. This is harmful to the missionary and to those to whom he goes to minister. His heart is upon things, not entirely upon his Lord. His trust will be in material equipment, not in the power of the Spirit. His freedom of movement may be hampered by his store of equipment Those to whom he preaches will consider him a rich agent of a rich foreign Mission. He is placed in what seems to be a privileged position—and this may not be entirely distasteful to him. The converts do not get the example they need, being shown how to depend upon the Holy Spirit's power and not upon material equipment. They learn to depend on foreign gadgets, expensive and almost impossible for them to obtain. National workers become jealous because they cannot have all that the foreign missionary has. Our Lord, or Paul, created no such problems.

We have known of missionaries asking for Flannelgraph equipment, saying that a number of young women were trained and ready to go out to the surrounding villages to preach the Gospel, but could not do so because they had no Flannelgraphs. However did Paul and his companions manage to preach the Gospel without Flannelgraphs or other such material aids? We have seen missionaries living in large, beautiful houses with a couple of cars, a couple of servants, expensive furniture and the latest electrical equipment. They were preaching the Gospel to people who could have no such things. Their excuse was that the climate and the protection of their health made it necessary for them to live as they did. Strange followers of the Lord and Paul!

This does not exclude equipment that is really necessary but it would rule out much that is considered essential today. The following questions might be asked regarding any equipment:

1. Will it cause you to depend upon the means instead of upon the Holy Spirit?

2. Will it cause those who see your example to think that the Holy Spirit cannot give enablement for the work without such means?

3. Will it cause those among whom you are witnessing to think of you as rich and better off than they are?

4. Will it create the impression that you are an agent of a wealthy foreign organizaton?

5. You wish to establish churches that are self-supporting; will what you are using contribute to, or hinder, that objective? Will the national workers or the national churches be able to obtain it without financial aid?

6. If it is something that has to be imported from abroad, will it contribute to giving a foreign flavour to the church or the national worker's witness?

Fellowship

When there are a number of missionaries together, permanently or temporarily, they have, as is natural, good fellowship together.

If they are of the same race and language and sojourners in a foreign land, strong natural reasons are added to spiritual reasons for their enjoyment of one another's company. There is a tendency for the missionary group to live in a fellowship of its own apart from their fellow-believers. This we must acknowledge, no matter how enjoyable it may be, to be selfish. To the extent that we indulge in it, we deprive those to whom we have been sent to minister of our fellowship, which they greatly need and which would be very profitable to them. It can be a temptation and a snare and productive of harm and loss to both missionary and converts.

It has already been observed that the New Testament missionaries, as a rule, were widely scattered. It was not often that more than two or three were together in one place. They did not even gather together periodically for fellowship. It is evident that, so far as Christian fellowship is concerned, they found it among the believers to whom they were ministering.

A prayer fellowship among missionaries is essential and must be continuous, but we should not reserve for the prayer of the missionary group matters that are really the responsibility of the local church. We can make the mistake of depending upon the missionary group to pray a church through to victory when we ought to be leading the church itself to pray through. A victory gained through their own prayers will mean much more to them. We are convinced that here is to be found the reason why sometimes the prayer of missionaries for the churches goes unanswered. There is a prayer ministry that we must continually exercise for the churches, but there is also a prayer ministry that they must be taught to exercise for themselves.

The missionary must not hold himself aloof from the church. He is not superior spiritually to the believers to whom he is ministering. Their prayer and faith are as potent as his. He should minister among them as a brother among brethren.

Love One Another

A danger that is faced by missionaries, in common with all Christian workers, is that of criticism. Miss Amy Carmichael refers to this:

> It often appears to us that there is nothing except our private walk with God which is more detested and assaulted by the devil than just this beautiful happy thing, the loyalty that is the basic quality of vital unity[1]. As to others, we made one careful rule: the absent must be safe with us. Criticism, therefore, was taboo. I could not forget the first time when, as a missionary (not expecting to meet it), this snake crossed my path. It was by the sea, on a grey morning after storm, while the waves were still sullen and fell on the shore with a heavy thud, without life and without resilience. Just so these words fell upon me that day. Many years later, a week or two after the little book called 'But' went out from the Dohnavur Fellowship, 'Blackwood's Magazine' brought us this (Farmer is writing about Dr Johnson): "I can excuse his Dogmatism and his Prejudices; but he throws about rather too much of what some Frenchmen call 'The Essence of But'. In plain English, he seems to have something to except in every man's character". And a recent 'Punch': "Do you know that girl?" "Only to talk about". The Essence of 'But' is distilled death: it carries the chill of death.

---

[1] The words 'vital unity' are from Westcott's note on St. John xvii. 22. This unity, he says, is something far more than a mere moral unity of purpose, feeling, affection; it is in some mysterious mode which we cannot distinctly apprehend, a vital unity.

I remember, that day by the sea-shore, wondering if, in the New Testament sense, love, fervent, stretched out, 'growing and glowing', was to be found anywhere on earth. And yet what other way of life could satisfy the heart that was set on living in the ungrieved presence of its Lord? The very thought of Him shames unkindness. It cannot abide before His clear countenance. He held His friends to the highest. Love that does this is love indeed. Lord, evermore give us this love[1].

Not only must our absent fellow-worker be safe with us but also every fellow-member of His Body—and this includes the converts. 'I mention this just that you may pray for him', is often an excuse for passing on something that should have been told to the Lord alone. We found, many years ago, that we had to make it a rule, and hold to it, that we should never discuss the spiritual condition of the members of the congregation at table or at any other time when missionaries gathered together. It always degenerated into pious gossip and Spirit-grieving criticism that was pleasant to the flesh but deadly to the love of Christ that should fill our hearts. Soon the members of the congregation were not the only ones whose every weakness was a cause for judgment and even amusement, but absent fellow-workers also did not escape.

Satan ever seeks to break the unity of the Spirit amongst us. Love is the very essence of the life of the Spirit of God and for that reason Satan would rob us of that love for one another which the Holy Spirit seeks to manifest through us towards all the members of the Body of Christ. Love is the basis upon which the Church of Christ is built: it is the unity that binds it together as one. Above all, therefore, love must prevail in all our dealings one with another.

Giving

The disregard of the Scriptural rules for the giving of material assistance to those in need has been the cause of much harm. Paul said he was not unmindful of his duty to give to the poor, but we can be sure he did not set aside the principles which he was inspired to lay down. Any missionary who has had to take up work on a station where his predecessor, out of the kindness of his heart, had made a practice of giving or loaning money to converts who asked it, will have a keen appreciation of the difficulties created. He finds these believers weakened morally and spiritually. When

---

[1] *Gold Cord*, p. 50, 51.

the dole stops, the foundation of their faith is found to be very
,weak.

It is always pleasant to be able to give money or clothes or food
to those who have little. Our motive may or may not be wholly
good. It can be gratifying to the ego to be the superior white man
distributing to the less fortunate. In any case, it is not the Scriptural giving where the left hand does not know what the right
hand is doing. Certainly the results are not good, for spiritual
growth is hindered. It tends to pauperize and create a spirit of
dependence and, therefore, does serious damage to character. It
causes the convert to seek material and not spiritual benefit. It
places the missionary in a false position and makes it impossible
for him to be, in his own life, a true, practical example of how
they should live.

In our own experience we have found it necessary to be extremely
careful in the matter of giving material help to converts. In fact,
we believe it is necessary to make it a general rule not to give or
loan money when it is asked. There are, of course, occasions when
we are led to minister to those in need but then we should do so
in such a way that it is not known who the giver is. We counsel
those in need to pray to God and trust in Him, as they know we
have to do, and many and great have been the answers we have
seen them get from Him. We have never known Him to fail them,
even as we have testified to them that He has never failed us. This
has brought much blessing and strengthening to them and has
helped to enable them to know their God.

No believer should require to seek help from men; he should in
faith go directly to his Heavenly Father. God then may reveal to
me my brother's need and lead me to minister to him. In that
case the one who receives the help has his faith strengthened; he
thanks God. He knows that God has answered his prayer and met
his need. God had met the need through man, but it is evident to
the receiver that the man was but an instrument in the faithful
hand of God. Such help does not tend to pauperize the receiver,
it strengthens him spiritually and is a blessing to him and others,

The Station System

On some mission fields a paternalistic system has been established. All the 'natives' living at a station are more or less dependent
upon the missionary. He is the Great Chief of the establishment,

and while, on the one hand, he may enjoy his role, on the other, he has endless difficulties in keeping everybody satisfied with what they receive.

A description of this system as practised in one part of Africa is given by a missionary:

> The station system was practically the same in most of the Missions in the region. The natives were gathered together into the mission compound. Everything was provided for them and in this safe place they were not subject to the persecution and heathen customs which would have tried their faith and thus they were freed from the need to live for Christ among their own people.
>
> Their houses were built by the mission boys who received mission money. Each week the hundreds of natives on the station received salt and money with which to buy their food. Periodically all received a loin-cloth. The "teacher's class" received better pay and a shirt as well as a loin-cloth.
>
> The children of the "out-schools" in the villages also received the periodical loin-cloth, and, with each visit of the missionary, some salt. The village chief, where there was a teacher placed, received some gun-powder and a loin-cloth of better material every six months. Thus when a chief came asking for a teacher to be sent to his village it did not necessarily mean that he was desiring the Gospel; sometimes it was for the "loaves and fishes"!
>
> On a station there was morning worship to which all were expected to go. Those who persisted in non-attendance would be punished by being given extra work, etc. The attendance at all services was compulsory for those living on the station.
>
> Offenders against mission station rules were dealt with in different ways on different stations. Corporal punishment was used as was the general custom among the whites, until the Government put a stop to it. The reason given was that the natives are like children and must be so treated to keep them in order.
>
> Since many of the missionaries had the superiority complex in their attitude towards the native, whom they considered as inferior, it was natural that the favoured "teachers" and "pastors" should become coloured with the same attitude when they became full-time workers, or even before. Some of the stations have been in existence for many years having third generation Christians among the natives.

It will be realized that the spiritual understanding, character, growth and experience necessary in converts who are to form New Testament congregations cannot be obtained under such conditions. The whole basis of such a system is wrong. Even if considered merely from the standpoint of character building it cannot be defended. Spiritually it is seriously detrimental. Both missionary and convert suffer harm and the Church is made weak and dependent. In work among primitive people we have found it possible to apply fully New Testament principles and have proved that the

Holy Spirit is just as able to give spiritual wisdom and understanding to the primitive man as to the semi-civilized or civilized
man. The impossibilities are all in our own doubting heart and
human thinking.

This station system involves the missionary in civil administration, which is a serious mistake. As a church-planter his ministry
is a purely spiritual one and he must leave to others all matters
of civil administration. A wise Indian chief, a capable man who
governed well, preached the Gospel and took an active part in an
Indian congregation, had the suggestion made to him by some in
the congregation that he might be an Elder. He rejected the
suggestion and explained to us that he considered that it would be
unwise for him, who exercised the civil power in the tribe, to
occupy an administrative position in the congregation. The two
offices, he said, are of such a nature that they should be performed by different persons. He was a man of true discernment.

· The missionary, consciously or unconsciously, is often misled
by the popular idea that primitive people are mentally inferior to
civilized people; that they are like children intellectually and therefore must be treated as such. This is plausible and gratifying to
the natural heart. It gives an apparent reason for taking a position
of racial and spiritual superiority over the 'native'. It gives an
excuse for considering that the Holy Spirit cannot accomplish in
the 'native' what He can in the civilized white man.

This idea, however, is false. It is contrary to Scripture and to
the principles of spiritual life. Scientific investigations have proved
it contrary to fact. There are untrained and undeveloped minds;
there are minds bound by the influence of custom and erroneous
teaching and belief (2 Cor. 3:14: 4:4; 11:3); but there is no such
thing as an inferior, 'native mind'. Brinton (in direct contradiction
of the evolutionary theory upon which he bases his study) states:

> The question has often been considered whether the mental pow-
> ers of the savage are distinctly inferior. This has been answered
> by taking the children of savages when quite young and bringing
> them up in civilised surroundings. The verdict is unanimous that
> they display as much aptitude for the acquisition of knowledge,
> and as much respect for the precepts of morality, as the average
> English or German boy or girl; but with less originality or
> 'initiative'.
> I have been in close relations to several full-blood American In-
> dians, who had been removed from an aboriginal environment and
> instructed in this manner; and I could not perceive that they were
> either in intellect or sympathies inferior to the usual type of the

American gentleman. One of them notably had a refined sense of humour, as well as uncommon acuteness of observation[1].

Another interesting statement is made by Robert E. Park:

> The difference between a savage and a civilized man is not due to any fundamental differences in their brain cells but to the connections and mutual stimulations which are established by experience and education between those cells. In the savage those possibilities are not absent but latent.

Peter Nielson writes:

> I have lived amongst the Bantu for nearly thirty years and have studied them closely, and I have come to the conclusion that there is no native mind distinct from the common human mind. The mind of the native is the mind of all mankind; it is not separate or different from the mind of the European or the Asiatic any more than the mind of the English is different from that of the Scotch or Irish people.[2]

Our own experience among the South American Indians fully bears out these statements. Christ can manifest the fullness of His life through the black, the yellow and the red just as He can through the white.

We must expect that there will be difficulties. There were difficulties in the churches established by Paul. The New Testament order does not produce perfection in man; whether he be primitive or cultured he is a very imperfect instrument. But God, who knows man thoroughly, has given us in the New Testament order the system best adapted to his need. If we permit human wisdom to modify God's order for His work and for His Church, we shall not eliminate difficulties but multiply them; we shall not restrain the weakness of the human heart but increase its scope for bringing spiritual defeat.

Faith and Prayer

A great source of weakness among missionaries, as among all God's servants, is unfaithfulness in the ministries of faith and prayer. These have been discussed in other chapters and we shall not do more than refer to them here. These ministries require unwavering constancy. The continual encroachment of other things upon the time required for prayer must be resolutely refused. We have always found that whenever there has been a slackening in

---

[1] *Religions of Primitive Peoples*, p. 15.
[2] *The Black Man's Place in South Africa*, p. 75.

these ministries the spiritual level of the work has declined immediately and the enemy has begun to advance. For a time the machine might keep going on its own momentum—and with what pushing we were able to do—but it soon became evident that the true source of power had been cut off.

Paul urged Timothy to be faithful and diligent in ministry. It is easy to let many things encroach upon the time that should be devoted to the service to which God had called. We may become busy with things that are unproductive. Surely we should be as careful with the Lord's time as with the time of an earthly master. Personal correspondence, social calls and recreation are legitimate things—if kept strictly in their place. It is good for a husband to help his wife in the work of the house—but not to the neglect of his ministry. The missionary is not a man of leisure; nor is he his own boss.

Lack of patience, which is lack of faith, is also deadly. It is hard not to help the glorious butterfly emerge from the chrysalis. It is not easy to wait God's time and keep our hands off. We would hurry on before He has completed His work. We would have Elders appointed whose lives or families are not quite up to the New Testament standard. We would be satisfied with a congregation that has not yet learned to find God's will through prayer.

Or, we may mistake our enthusiasm for faith, building upon a fleshly appearance instead of a true spiritual foundation. We may be tempted to spoil new converts. This is a very common error. How many promising lives have been injured in this way. We push them forward, making much of them, until they become self-confident, proud and useless. And so our hand is stretched out, in self-assurance, to hasten God's work, to steady the ark, or to strike the rock and, later, when we see the weakness of our work, we think, perhaps, that God has failed us.

Paul's Counsel.

Paul, in his letters to the missionaries, Timothy and Titus, refers to many matters that require watchfulness on the part of the missionary. He exhorts that "first of all supplications, prayers, intercessions and giving of thanks be made for all men" (1 Tim. 2:1-8). He emphasises to both Timothy and Titus that those who are appointed as Elders and Deacons, and also their wives and families, must be irreproachable in their testimony.

He reminds them that they themselves must be "an example to

the believers, in word, in conduct, in love, in spirit, in faith, in purity" (1 Tim. 4:12). "Give your attention to (public) reading, exhortation and teaching. Do not be careless about the gifts with which you have been endowed... Habitually practise these duties and be absorbed in them so that your growing proficiency in them may be evident to all. Be on your guard as to yourself and your teaching" (1 Tim. 4:13-16, Weymouth). Also, he warns them against the love of money and of not being satisfied with having just food and clothing (1 Tim. 6:6-11).

His advice is very practical:

Earnestly seek to commend yourself to God as a servant who, because of his straightforward dealing with the word of truth, has no reason to feel any shame. But from irreligious and frivolous talk, hold aloof, for those who indulge in it will proceed from bad to worse in impiety, and their teaching will spread like a running sore. (2 Tim. 2:15,16, Weymouth.)

Avoid foolish discussions with ignorant men... a bondservant of the Lord must not quarrel, but must be inoffensive to all men, a skilful teacher, and patient under wrongs. He must speak in a gentle tone... (2 Tim. 2:23-25, Weymouth.)

The charge he gives to the missionary is exceedingly solemn:

I charge you —as in the presence of God who gives life to all creatures, and of Christ Jesus who at the bar of Pontius Pilate made a noble profession of faith that you keep God's commandments stainlessly and without reproach till the appearing of our Lord Jesus Christ (1 Tim. 6:13, 14, Weymouth.)

CHAPTER XLV

THE WAY AND THE COST OF UNITY

True unity in the Church cannot be produced by organization: it is the product of the 'unity of the Spirit', and can be obtained in no other way. It has been vainly sought by other means ever since it was lost through departure from the way of the Spirit. It is the desire of all in whose hearts the Holy Spirit witnesses, and it is possible to all those who will obey the commandments of the Lord.

Unity in the New Testament Church came from obedience to the divine revelation regarding both doctrine and order. On that basis it is to be found today. The New Testament missionaries worked as one because they all worked to the same pattern. Among missionaries today the same oneness is possible on the same ground.

With this possibility in view it is interesting to consider some aspects of the work of 'Faith Missons'. These Missions are usually interdenominational, depending for their support upon the Church in general. Their missionaries are usually spiritual men and women, sound in doctrine, and their witness is used of God to the salvation of souls. However, the results of the work of 'Faith Missions' reveal a weakness that has not been taken sufficiently into consideration. They have not been so successful as Denominational Missions in establishing strong, unified groups of churches.

There are definite reasons for this, arising from the fact that 'Faith Missions' are interdenominational. On that account, there is a lack of unity of conviction and purpose among their missionaries with regard to Church order.

From the point of view of organization, the Denominational

Mission has a distinct advantage. Its missionaries all have as their objective the establishing of a particular type of Church order, with which they are thoroughly conversant and to which they are loyal. It is a more or less workable organization, capable, according to human standards, of providing a mechanical unity and permanence for the community of believers. Thus a unified group of churches is established possessing the kind of strength derived from Denominational unity and loyalty.

The churches of 'Faith Missions' usually have the advantage spiritually. As a rule, their members are all saved people and neither worldly nor unsound in doctrine. But the missionaries who have founded them come from different Denominations. Consequently there is lacking a definite sense of unity and loyalty so far as church organization and policy are concerned, and that, necessarily, is communicated to the churches founded. For that reason there is often no strong bond of fellowship binding together in one the group of churches established by a 'Faith Mission'. In many cases, the unity that exists is little more than the fact that they all depend upon the same Mission—a foreign organization.

There is, possibly, in the same group, a lack of uniformity in the organization of different churches, which operates against a full sense of unity. The organization may be indefinite and insufficient because no definite pattern has been followed and each missionary has introduced whatever organization he thought best or that seemed necessary at the time.

'Faith Missions' generally have been averse to the thought of forming new Denominations. The result is that the uniting of their churches together by organization has been avoided until circumstances have made it absolutely necessary. These Missions have been faced with the alternatives of organizing their groups of churches or having them unite with a Denominational group. The latter course is usually impossible on account of compromise in doctrine and worldliness.

Under these circumstances, 'Faith Missions', in many cases, have finally organized their churches virtually as Denominations. But these organizations have, in general, not been very convincing, either to the missionaries or to the congregations. The missionaries feel no deep personal loyalty to them because they do not really belong to them. All are members of some other Denomination. They are, to a certain extent, outsiders building a new Denomination to which they do not fully belong. It is psychologically and spiritually impossible for them to create in the churches a loyalty and oneness which they do not wholly share themselves.

All this contributes to create a situation that is most unsatisfactory and that has caused much concern among 'Faith Missions'. It is necessary that missionaries labouring together have a common purpose covering the whole of the ministry they are to perform. There must be a common conviction and a common loyalty to principle and order that comes from the heart and that can be passed on to converts and churches.

This is an essential element in missionary ministry that was possessed in full measure by the first missionaries of the Church. Holy Spirit-given conviction regarding the true Scriptural and spiritual order, and loyalty to the Lord's Word, are much more powerful elements and produce more effective results than any form of Denominational loyalty. They unite the missionary group together in a complete oneness of conviction and purpose and they unite the converts and churches in a common bond with them. No human form or organization, no matter how perfect, which we may give to a church or to a group of churches can so effectively accomplish God's purpose for the Church and unite it in a true and fruitful witness. God's order gives freedom to the Holy Spirit to bind all together as one in Christ in absolute loyalty and obedience to Him.

This would not only give true unity among the churches of a 'Mission': it would make one the churches established by all missionary groups working in accordance with the New Testament order. Thus, to that extent, there would be brought about a return to the purpose of God that would restore to us the glorious fellowship and testimony of the early years of missionary endeavour. There can be no question that it would bring glory to the Lord and power to the Church's witness. Of course, such unity will come only where there is a true and full return to the Biblical pattern, for it is not organizational unity but the unity of the Spirit.

This is possible to all who are willing to pay the cost. The personal cost of obedience in this matter may be great, but the cost of not taking God's way is much greater, for it means loss not only to the missionary but to all those to whom he ministers and to the churches that are established—accumulative loss that will increase through the years to come as the standard which he has set is perpetuated in a growing Christian community.

The Personal Cost

It will have been realized that the practice of New Testament missionary methods demands much of the missionary. He must have faced the Cross in the fulness of its significance. He must be prepared to pay the cost to be filled with the Spirit of Christ so that he may manifest Christ.

> Always, wherever we go, carrying with us in our bodies the putting to death of Jesus, so that in our bodies it may also be clearly shown that Jesus lives. For we, alive though we are, are continually surrendering ourselves to death for the sake of Jesus, so that in this mortal nature of ours it may also be clearly shown that Jesus lives. (2 Cor. 4:10, 11, Weymouth).

It will have been observed that what was accomplished by the founders and first missionaries of the Early Church was done through the normal working of the Holy Spirit. It is often thought that Barnabas, Paul, Luke, Timothy, Titus, Silas and the other New Testament Evangelists just suddenly and miraculously found themselves possessed of the necessary knowledge and experience for the ministry they were called to, that the churches sprang up miraculously, that Elders were found ready immediately and that a special dispensation of the Spirit's power was manifested at that time in both Evangelists and converts.

That may seem a plausible excuse for the comparative powerlessness evident today, but there is no ground for it in Scripture. We have seen that Paul and his companions had to go through years of preparation in the school of hard experience, becoming thoroughly acquainted with the principles of spiritual life and ministry and with the structure of the local church, before the Holy Spirit sent them forth to the work. It was seven years after Pentecost before the Lord led out to the evangelization of the Gentile world, because Greek-speaking men must first have years of experience to fit them for the work. Those who ministered did so at as great a cost as is required of us today. In the churches, Elders and Deacons were not appointed until ample time had been given for them to be proved. Even in the church in Jerusalem this was so. And the enemy was just as active in just the same way, spreading false doctrine, causing divisions and using every weakness of the human heart.

No, it was not easier in those early days; the work was done then just as it has to be done today. It was done victoriously because it was done in God's way, in the power of the Spirit, through utter yieldedness, obedience, prayer and faith. Those who are willing to walk in the same way today will reap the same fruit. The whole difficulty is the cost of this walk. It means taking the way of sacrifice that our Lord and the early Evangelists of the Church did not shrink from taking. It means continual death to the flesh with its desires, wisdom and pride. That there are those who are willing for this, there is no doubt. There has always been such a company and there always will be so long as the Spirit of Christ remains among men. The number may not be great, because few will be willing to pay the cost, but the Lord will be with those who do and their labour and testimony will bear eternal fruit.

FINISHED—
And yet just begun:
'Tis the story of the Church
Onward marching, ever such
As at Pentecost was born,
Pressing onward to the morn,
Victor through the darkening night,
Ever in unconquered might
Strengthened,
'Til its course is run.

INDEX

Missionary - see Finance.
Poor, to the - 365, 520.
Theaching concerning given
to churches - 365.
See Gifts of the Spirit.
Goforth, Jonathan - 94, 386.
Gordon, A. J. - 132, 328.
Gossip - 519-20.
Government - see Gifts of the
Spirit.
Governments - Attitude to -
432.
Grace - 154-5, 169, 176, 211.
Greece - 260, 264.
Guidance - 64-5, 99, 108, 111,
137-8, 368, 450-1, 454-60, 494,
506, 511.
Principles of - 368.
Guinness Dr. Whitfield - 437.
Guyon, Mme. - 70, 191.

Hampden, John - 267.
Harnack, Adolf von - 258-61.
Harvey, H. - 287.
Hatch, E. - 108, 238, 239, 246,
249, 257, 318.
Healing - See Gifts of the Spi-
rit.
Heathen -
Attitude to - 432.
In Apostolic Times - 24-6.
Hellenists - 54, 60, 61, 81.
High Priest - 133, 277.
History's Evidence - 246.
Holy Spirit - 35, 44, 72, 148,
168, 250, 254-5.
Guidance - see Guidance;
Church - Guidance of by
the Spirit.
Mission of - 169.
Work of - 170.
Home - see Family.
Homeland - 15, 17, 81, 489, 497,
499.
Hospitals - 399, 437.
Hospitality - see Family.
Hoste, D. E. - 514.
Houghton, Bishop F. - 514.
Huguenots - 201.
Huss, John - 201.
Hussites - 272.

Idolatry - 257, 260, 265.
Independent Congregations -
271, 350.
Independents - 272.
India - 79, 264, 516.
Indians - 523.
Institutional Activity - 293,
296, 324, 337, 459, 460, 467.
Instutions - 35, 432.
Irenaeus - 248.
Itineration work - 395-6, 400.

Jerusalem - 25.
Church in - 44, 79, 100, 295,
338, 383.
Council at - 109.
Paul's visits to - see Paul.
Jews, In Apostolic times - 23-29.
John - 282, 357.
Messages to the churches -
123, 476.
Jowett, J. H. - 206.
Judaism - 23-29, 101-2, 109. -
See Sanhedrin, Synagogue.
Judaizers - 76, 109, 111.
Justin Martyr - 248, 253.

Knox, John - 70, 201, 267.
Korea - 386.

Laudicean church - 113, 139,
167, 298, 356, 471, 478.
Latimer - 267.
Laying on of hands - 64, 66,
77, 304, 308, 456.
Leadership - 51, 78, 84, 96, 231,
270, 505, 510.
Learning, Secular - 71, 74. -
See Wisdom.
Legislative function - 140, 193.
Letters of Recommendation -
97.
Lightfoot, Bishop - 233, 238.
Lindsay, Prof. J. M. - 133, 237.
Litigation - 239.
Loans - 521.
Lord's Table - 46, 139, 300, 311,
315, 316, 340, 358, 366.
Lots, casting of - 214-15, 372.
Love - 138, 161, 181, 189, 268,
519.

Made in the USA
Coppell, TX
14 August 2024

35968222R00302